Computer Engineering and Information Technology

Computer Engineering and Information Technology

Edited by **Fiona Hobbs**

WILLFORD PRESS

New York

Published by Willford Press,
118-35 Queens Blvd., Suite 400,
Forest Hills, NY 11375, USA
www.willfordpress.com

Computer Engineering and Information Technology
Edited by Fiona Hobbs

© 2016 Willford Press

International Standard Book Number: 978-1-68285-246-0 (Hardback)

Printed in the United States of America.

Contents

Preface

This book provides comprehensive insights into the field of computer engineering and information technology. Some of the diverse topics covered in this book are data processing, data analysis techniques, software engineering, multimedia, etc. Those with an interest in the field of computer engineering and information technology would find this book helpful as it contains contributions by internationally renowned scientists and experts that bring forth new frontiers for further research.

The information shared in this book is based on empirical researches made by veterans in this field of study. The elaborative information provided in this book will help the readers further their scope of knowledge leading to advancements in this field.

Finally, I would like to thank my fellow researchers who gave constructive feedback and my family members who supported me at every step of my research.

Editor

Development of a Forward/Backward Power Flow Algorithm in Distribution Systems Based on Probabilistic Technique Using Normal Distribution

Shahrokh SHOJAEIAN[1], Ehsan SALLEALA-NAEENI[1], Ehsan TASLIMI RENANI[2]

[1]Department of Electrical Engineerng, Faculty of Engineering, Khomeinishahr Branch, Islamic Azad University, No 159, 7th Boostan Street, Isfahan 84181-48499, Iran
[2]Department of Electrical Engineering, Faculty of Engineering, University of Malaya, Lingkungan Budi, Kuala Lumpur 50603, Malaysia

shojaeian@iaukhsh.ac.ir, ehsan.salleala@iaukhsh.ac.ir, taslimi.ehsan@siswa.um.edu.my

Abstract. *There are always some uncertainties in prediction and estimation of distribution systems loads. These uncertainties impose some undesirable impacts and deviations on power flow of the system which may cause reduction in accuracy of the results obtained by system analysis. Thus, probabilistic analysis of distribution system is very important. This paper proposes a new probabilistic load flow technique in presence of a 24 hours load changing regime in all seasons, by applying a normal probabilistic distribution in seven standard deviations for the loads and using this distribution function on Forward/backward algorithm. The losses and voltage of IEEE 33-bus test distribution network is investigated by our new algorithm and the results are compared with the conventional algorithm i.e., based on deterministic methods.*

Keywords

Distribution network, forward/backward power flow, normal distribution function, power losses, probabilistic power flow.

1. Introduction

Most of suggested methods to solve power flow in power systems consider deterministic in nature in which loads power have been taken into account constant (e.g., analysis is done in the worst system condition). In those methods, small change in the network requires resolving the power flow.

In addition, the system reliability may decline when the system designers utilize previous deterministic data. Nowadays uncertainties of the power systems are also their effects on the system operation are not undeniable and it is necessary to investigate the performance of the network over these uncertainties.

In previous studies output variation and system performance evaluation is determined by analyzing the input parameters based on probabilistic methods.

The classical deterministic load flow techniques are not able to cope with uncertainties and can only be used within constant power system parameters [1].

Probabilistic power flow was proposed in 1974 [2]. In [2], Borkowska used DC model of network and considered both substations load of different feeders and output information in form of density function. In [3], Dopazo used covariance matrix method however, these methods were developed in [4], [5]. In [6], Zhang and Lee combined the concept of Cumulants and Gram-Charlier expansion theory to obtain probabilistic distribution functions of transmission line flows. It has significantly reduced the computational time whit a high degree of accuracy. In [7], [8], Cumulants and Von Mises function and Monte Calro method have been used to solve probabilistic power flow.

Therefore, evaluating the system and addressing these uncertainties different methods such as probabilistic methods, fuzzy sets and interval analysis have been introduced [12]. PLF could be divided into numerical and analytical methods. Numerical method refers to Monte Carlo's simulation method [11], which is an alternative to the huge number of random variables for determination of PLF in numerical methods.

Due to the fact that implementation of this method could be very time consuming, this method cannot be used in some applications. On the other hand, implementation of the analytical method is faster however, there are many difficulties in implementing this method. The most significant methods in analytical method are Convolution [9] and cumulants methods [10]. Convolution method is based on probabilistic distribution of random variables.

The main contribution of this paper is introducing a simple and practical expansion approach for the well-known forward/backward power flow method. This approach can be used for modern distribution systems which may including several variable loads and renewable energy sources which in turn have non-deterministic power generation level.

After this introduction, in the second chapter using normal distribution function, a probabilistic model of load is presented. The third chapter is began with a review on the forward/backward power flow approach and is continued with introducing a probabilistic version of this approach. To simulate the proposed method, in the fourth chapter IEEE 33-bus test network is considered and results of probabilistic power flow of it is shown in the fifth chapter. The paper conclusion is stated in the sixth chapter.

2.   Probabilistic Model of Load

It is well known fact that electrical loads in power systems are probabilistic in nature. There are two prime parameters in power flow which lead to load change in network, time (daily, weekly, seasonal and annual profiles) and climate conditions. It should be noted that in deterministic power flow these two parameters are ignored and typical sample of consumers' parameters can be obtained from stochastic analyzing.

Load during hour, week, month and season of the year is considered as a percentage of the peak value. Then load profile is created base on this information. A typical load profile is presented in [11]. This paper uses combination of daily load profile for each season and normal distribution function. Figure 1 presents daily load profile for total consumption four different seasons [13].

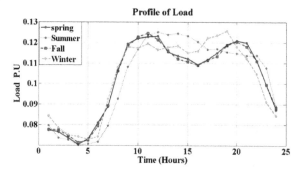

Fig. 1: Average daily load profile in different seasons.

If μ_{PLj} and μ_{QLj} are considered as the average active and reactive power of the jth load and m is a stochastic sample of time, average active and reactive power defined as follows:

$$\mu_{PLj} = \frac{1}{m} \sum_{\forall m} P_{Lj,m}, \tag{1}$$

$$\mu_{QLj} = \frac{1}{m} \sum_{\forall m} Q_{Lj,m}. \tag{2}$$

Also the active and reactive power's variance is calculated as follows:

$$\sigma^2_{PLj} = \frac{1}{m} \sum_{\forall m} (P_{Lj,m} - \mu_{PLj})^2, \tag{3}$$

$$\sigma^2_{QLj} = \frac{1}{m} \sum_{\forall m} (Q_{Lj,m} - \mu_{QLj})^2. \tag{4}$$

Considering the nature of the system loads, normal distribution function can be applied which is defined as:

$$f(x) = \frac{e^{-\frac{1}{2}(\frac{x-\mu}{\sigma})^2}}{\sigma\sqrt{2\pi}} \quad -\infty < x < +\infty. \tag{5}$$

Figure 2 illustrates load profile of the 10th bus of summer season with four-hour interval (6, 12, 18 and 24) using distribution function.

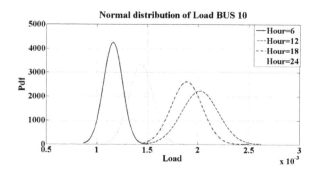

Fig. 2: Load profile of 10th bus of summer season using normal distribution.

3.   Power Flow in Distribution Networks

3.1.   Deterministic Power Flow

In this paper Forward/backward method is used to solve power flow in distribution network. It is assumed that $V_s = 1 < 0$ is the source voltage, $S_{Lj} = P_{Lj} + jQ_{Lj} = V_j I_j*$ is the apparent power of the jth load, S_j is the apparent output power of the jth bus, and I_j is the current flowing through the jth bus. In Forward/backward method, firstly the voltage of the last bus is assumed to be $1<0$ then having the load powers and using sections impedances the following formula can be calculated [14]. A typical single line diagram of a distribution network is shown in Fig. 3.

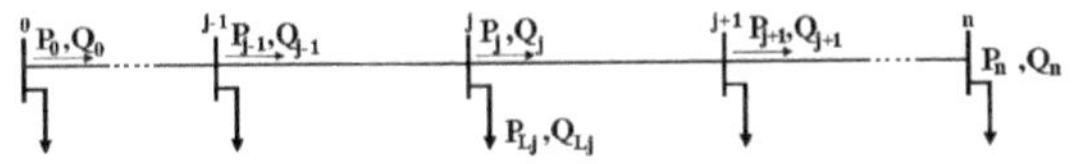

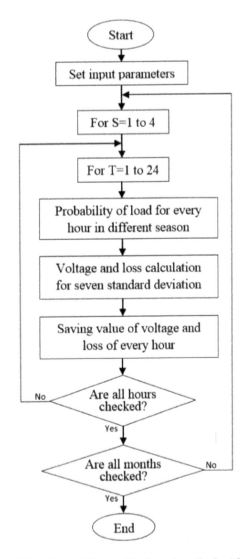

Fig. 3: Single line diagram of a distribution system.

$$P_{j-1} = P_j + r_j \frac{P'^2_j + Q'^2_j}{V_j^2} + P_{Lj}, \qquad (6)$$

$$Q_{j-1} = Q_j + x_j \frac{P'^2_j + Q'^2_j}{V_j^2} + Q_{Lj}, \qquad (7)$$

$$V^2_{j-1} = V_j^2 + 2(r_j P'_j + x_j Q'_j) + (r_j^2 + x_j^2) \frac{P'^2_j + Q'^2_j}{V_j^2}, \quad (8)$$

where: $P'_j = P_j + P_{Lj}$, $Q'_j = Q_j + Q_{Lj}$.

Obtained power in backward path can be used to calculate the first bus output powers. For forward path, the following voltage equation can be used:

$$V^2_{j+1} = V_j^2 - 2(r_j P_j + x_j Q_j) + (r_j^2 + x_j^2) \frac{P_j^2 + Q_j^2}{V_j^2}. \quad (9)$$

Forward/backward operation should be repeated to achieve convergence so that:

$$|V_j^{(k)} - V_j^{(k-1)}| < \varepsilon_v \ , \ |P_{loss}^{(k)} - P_{loss}^{(k-1)}| < \varepsilon_p. \quad (10)$$

Here ε_v and ε_p are the acceptable errors for bus voltages and the system power loss respectively and k is the number of the kth iteration. In this paper, there is assumption that: $\varepsilon_v = \varepsilon_p = 10^{-6}$ pu. Following formula demonstrates how losses are calculated:

$$P_{Loss} = \sum_{j=0}^{n-1} r_j \left(\frac{P_j^2 + Q_j^2}{V_j^2} \right). \qquad (11)$$

3.2. Probabilistic Power Flow

As mentioned in the previous section, in deterministic power flow, if there is an assumption that active and reactive powers of loads are probabilistic, by applying

small changes in Eq. (6) and Eq. (7) and also using normal distribution function, PLF can be defined as follows:

$$P_{j-1} = P_j + r_j \frac{P'^2_j + Q'^2_j}{V_j^2} \qquad (12)$$
$$+ P_{Lj} \sim N(\mu_{PLj}, \sigma_{PLj}),$$

$$Q_{j-1} = Q_j + x_j \frac{P'^2_j + Q'^2_j}{V_j^2} \qquad (13)$$
$$+ Q_{Lj} \sim N(\mu_{QLj}, \sigma_{QLj}).$$

Flow chart of mentioned method is illustrated in Fig. 4, where S and T stand for season and hour respectively.

Fig. 4: Flow chart of Forward/backward method with probabilistic technique.

4. The Studied System

All information about the IEEE 33-bus test network is given in Fig. 5 [14], [15]. Base voltage and apparent power of the system are 12.66 kV and 10 MVA.

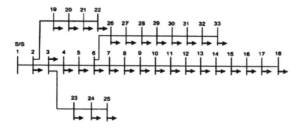

Fig. 5: IEEE 33-bus test system.

5. Result and Simulation

Change of the network loads in different hours of day affects the network losses, capacity of line, voltage and other parameters of network. By dividing normal distribution function to seven parts for every hours of different days in different seasons, the parameters of μ_{PLj}, μ_{QLj}, σ_{PLj}, σ_{QLj} are determined and the probabilistic power flow is solved. Figure 6 shows standard deviations of normal distribution which is assumed to be in the vicinity of the deterministic loads values.

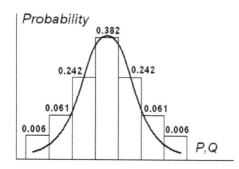

Fig. 6: Change of normal distribution to seven-deviation standard.

5.1. Probabilistic Losses of Network

Table 1 demonstrates P_{loss} in 24-hour and for each standard deviation. Table 2 presents both probabilistic and deterministic total power losses for a few sample hours in each season. Table 2 shows that the power losses obtained are remarkably different which testifies the values of errors in the deterministic method.

Figure 7 to Fig. 10 denotes power losses in all seasons, all standard deviations and 24-hour.

The experiments were carried out on a PC with a Intel Core i5, 2.66 GHz CPU, and 4 GB RAM with the

Microsoft Windows XP operating system. The CPU time for deterministic and probabilistic load flow are 0.110696 and 2.957022 seconds respectively.

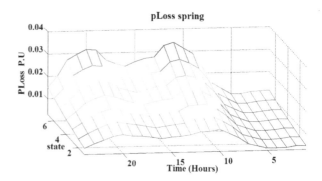

Fig. 7: Losses in spring.

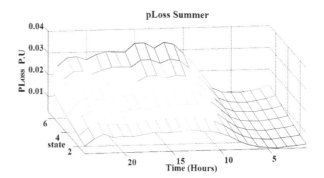

Fig. 8: Losses in summer.

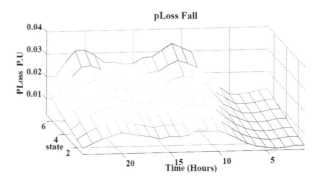

Fig. 9: Losses in fall.

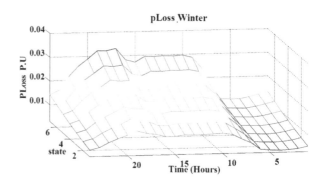

Fig. 10: Losses in winter.

Tab. 1: System loss at each hour for every season for seven standard deviation of normal distribution.

Sample hours	Season	State1	State2	State3	State4	State5	State6	State7
1	Spring	$4.586 \cdot 10^{-3}$	$5.552 \cdot 10^{-3}$	$6.621 \cdot 10^{-3}$	$7.795 \cdot 10^{-3}$	$9.076 \cdot 10^{-3}$	$1.046 \cdot 10^{-2}$	$1.197 \cdot 10^{-2}$
	Summer	$4.776 \cdot 10^{-3}$	$5.815 \cdot 10^{-3}$	$6.968 \cdot 10^{-3}$	$8.239 \cdot 10^{-3}$	$9.630 \cdot 10^{-3}$	$1.114 \cdot 10^{-2}$	$1.278 \cdot 10^{-2}$
	Fall	$4.592 \cdot 10^{-3}$	$5.572 \cdot 10^{-3}$	$6.659 \cdot 10^{-3}$	$7.854 \cdot 10^{-3}$	$9.160 \cdot 10^{-3}$	$1.058 \cdot 10^{-2}$	$1.211 \cdot 10^{-2}$
	Winter	$5.510 \cdot 10^{-3}$	$6.626 \cdot 10^{-3}$	$7.858 \cdot 10^{-3}$	$9.208 \cdot 10^{-3}$	$1.068 \cdot 10^{-2}$	$1.227 \cdot 10^{-2}$	$1.400 \cdot 10^{-2}$
2	Spring	$4.351 \cdot 10^{-3}$	$5.317 \cdot 10^{-3}$	$6.394 \cdot 10^{-3}$	$7.583 \cdot 10^{-3}$	$8.888 \cdot 10^{-3}$	$1.031 \cdot 10^{-2}$	$1.185 \cdot 10^{-2}$
	Summer	$4.319 \cdot 10^{-3}$	$5.149 \cdot 10^{-3}$	$6.058 \cdot 10^{-3}$	$7.050 \cdot 10^{-3}$	$8.125 \cdot 10^{-3}$	$9.285 \cdot 10^{-3}$	$1.053 \cdot 10^{-2}$
	Fall	$4.520 \cdot 10^{-3}$	$5.482 \cdot 10^{-3}$	$6.548 \cdot 10^{-3}$	$7.722 \cdot 10^{-3}$	$9.006 \cdot 10^{-3}$	$1.040 \cdot 10^{-2}$	$1.191 \cdot 10^{-2}$
	Winter	$4.890 \cdot 10^{-3}$	$5.814 \cdot 10^{-3}$	$6.826 \cdot 10^{-3}$	$7.928 \cdot 10^{-3}$	$9.122 \cdot 10^{-3}$	$1.041 \cdot 10^{-2}$	$1.179 \cdot 10^{-2}$
7	Spring	$6.027 \cdot 10^{-3}$	$7.322 \cdot 10^{-3}$	$8.762 \cdot 10^{-3}$	$1.034 \cdot 10^{-2}$	$1.209 \cdot 10^{-2}$	$1.398 \cdot 10^{-2}$	$1.604 \cdot 10^{-2}$
	Summer	$4.895 \cdot 10^{-3}$	$5.892 \cdot 10^{-3}$	$6.993 \cdot 10^{-3}$	$8.200 \cdot 10^{-3}$	$9.516 \cdot 10^{-3}$	$1.094 \cdot 10^{-2}$	$1.248 \cdot 10^{-2}$
	Fall	$6.222 \cdot 10^{-3}$	$7.502 \cdot 10^{-3}$	$8.916 \cdot 10^{-3}$	$1.046 \cdot 10^{-2}$	$1.216 \cdot 10^{-2}$	$1.400 \cdot 10^{-2}$	$1.599 \cdot 10^{-2}$
	Winter	$6.795 \cdot 10^{-3}$	$8.119 \cdot 10^{-3}$	$9.575 \cdot 10^{-3}$	$1.116 \cdot 10^{-2}$	$1.290 \cdot 10^{-2}$	$1.478 \cdot 10^{-2}$	$1.680 \cdot 10^{-2}$
8	Spring	$8.863 \cdot 10^{-3}$	$1.073 \cdot 10^{-2}$	$1.281 \cdot 10^{-2}$	$1.511 \cdot 10^{-2}$	$1.764 \cdot 10^{-2}$	$2.040 \cdot 10^{-2}$	$2.341 \cdot 10^{-2}$
	Summer	$6.849 \cdot 10^{-3}$	$8.243 \cdot 10^{-3}$	$9.786 \cdot 10^{-3}$	$1.148 \cdot 10^{-2}$	$1.333 \cdot 10^{-2}$	$1.534 \cdot 10^{-2}$	$1.751 \cdot 10^{-2}$
	Fall	$8.938 \cdot 10^{-3}$	$1.077 \cdot 10^{-2}$	$1.281 \cdot 10^{-2}$	$1.505 \cdot 10^{-2}$	$1.751 \cdot 10^{-2}$	$2.018 \cdot 10^{-2}$	$2.309 \cdot 10^{-2}$
	Winter	$8.973 \cdot 10^{-3}$	$1.095 \cdot 10^{-2}$	$1.317 \cdot 10^{-3}$	$1.563 \cdot 10^{-2}$	$1.834 \cdot 10^{-2}$	$2.130 \cdot 10^{-2}$	$2.453 \cdot 10^{-2}$
15	Spring	$9.850 \cdot 10^{-3}$	$1.197 \cdot 10^{-2}$	$1.433 \cdot 10^{-2}$	$1.695 \cdot 10^{-2}$	$1.983 \cdot 10^{-2}$	$2.298 \cdot 10^{-2}$	$2.641 \cdot 10^{-2}$
	Summer	$1.212 \cdot 10^{-2}$	$1.473 \cdot 10^{-2}$	$1.765 \cdot 10^{-2}$	$2.088 \cdot 10^{-2}$	$2.445 \cdot 10^{-2}$	$2.836 \cdot 10^{-2}$	$3.263 \cdot 10^{-2}$
	Fall	$9.381 \cdot 10^{-3}$	$1.153 \cdot 10^{-2}$	$1.395 \cdot 10^{-2}$	$1.663 \cdot 10^{-2}$	$1.960 \cdot 10^{-2}$	$2.286 \cdot 10^{-2}$	$2.643 \cdot 10^{-2}$
	Winter	$1.067 \cdot 10^{-2}$	$1.287 \cdot 10^{-2}$	$1.531 \cdot 10^{-3}$	$1.799 \cdot 10^{-2}$	$2.093 \cdot 10^{-2}$	$2.414 \cdot 10^{-2}$	$2.762 \cdot 10^{-2}$
16	Spring	$9.233 \cdot 10^{-3}$	$1.124 \cdot 10^{-2}$	$1.349 \cdot 10^{-2}$	$1.597 \cdot 10^{-2}$	$1.871 \cdot 10^{-2}$	$2.171 \cdot 10^{-2}$	$2.498 \cdot 10^{-2}$
	Summer	$1.149 \cdot 10^{-2}$	$1.392 \cdot 10^{-2}$	$1.662 \cdot 10^{-2}$	$1.960 \cdot 10^{-2}$	$2.288 \cdot 10^{-2}$	$2.647 \cdot 10^{-2}$	$3.038 \cdot 10^{-2}$
	Fall	$9.071 \cdot 10^{-3}$	$1.112 \cdot 10^{-2}$	$1.343 \cdot 10^{-2}$	$1.599 \cdot 10^{-2}$	$1.882 \cdot 10^{-2}$	$2.193 \cdot 10^{-2}$	$2.532 \cdot 10^{-2}$
	Winter	$1.048 \cdot 10^{-2}$	$1.280 \cdot 10^{-2}$	$1.539 \cdot 10^{-3}$	$1.828 \cdot 10^{-2}$	$2.148 \cdot 10^{-2}$	$2.499 \cdot 10^{-2}$	$2.883 \cdot 10^{-2}$
23	Spring	$7.785 \cdot 10^{-3}$	$9.359 \cdot 10^{-3}$	$1.109 \cdot 10^{-2}$	$1.300 \cdot 10^{-2}$	$1.509 \cdot 10^{-2}$	$1.735 \cdot 10^{-2}$	$1.980 \cdot 10^{-2}$
	Summer	$8.546 \cdot 10^{-3}$	$1.061 \cdot 10^{-2}$	$1.295 \cdot 10^{-2}$	$1.557 \cdot 10^{-2}$	$1.847 \cdot 10^{-2}$	$2.168 \cdot 10^{-2}$	$2.519 \cdot 10^{-2}$
	Fall	$8.158 \cdot 10^{-3}$	$9.691 \cdot 10^{-3}$	$1.137 \cdot 10^{-2}$	$1.321 \cdot 10^{-2}$	$1.520 \cdot 10^{-2}$	$1.736 \cdot 10^{-2}$	$1.969 \cdot 10^{-2}$
	Winter	$6.448 \cdot 10^{-3}$	$7.775 \cdot 10^{-3}$	$9.241 \cdot 10^{-3}$	$1.085 \cdot 10^{-2}$	$1.260 \cdot 10^{-2}$	$1.451 \cdot 10^{-2}$	$1.657 \cdot 10^{-2}$
24	Spring	$5.798 \cdot 10^{-3}$	$7.038 \cdot 10^{-3}$	$8.412 \cdot 10^{-3}$	$9.925 \cdot 10^{-3}$	$1.157 \cdot 10^{-2}$	$1.337 \cdot 10^{-2}$	$1.532 \cdot 10^{-2}$
	Summer	$6.101 \cdot 10^{-3}$	$7.391 \cdot 10^{-3}$	$8.822 \cdot 10^{-3}$	$1.039 \cdot 10^{-2}$	$1.212 \cdot 10^{-2}$	$1.399 \cdot 10^{-2}$	$1.602 \cdot 10^{-2}$
	Fall	$6.160 \cdot 10^{-3}$	$7.363 \cdot 10^{-3}$	$8.686 \cdot 10^{-3}$	$1.013 \cdot 10^{-2}$	$1.170 \cdot 10^{-2}$	$1.340 \cdot 10^{-2}$	$1.524 \cdot 10^{-2}$
	Winter	$5.542 \cdot 10^{-3}$	$6.613 \cdot 10^{-3}$	$7.901 \cdot 10^{-3}$	$9.319 \cdot 10^{-3}$	$1.087 \cdot 10^{-2}$	$1.256 \cdot 10^{-2}$	$1.439 \cdot 10^{-2}$

Tab. 2: Probabilistic and deterministic daily losses for each season.

Season	P_{loss} (Probabilistic)	P_{loss} (Deterministic)
Spring	0.35542	0.35277
Summer	0.35777	0.35489
Fall	0.35465	0.35190
Winter	0.35859	0.35589

Tab. 3: Comparison of probabilistic and deterministic value of cumulative 24-hour voltage deviation of each in the summer.

Hour	1	2	3	4	5	6	7	8
Probabilistic	0.0523	0.0459	0.0422	0.0383	0.0395	0.0421	0.0518	0.075
Deterministic	0.0519	0.0456	0.0419	0.038	0.0392	0.0418	0.0515	0.0744
Hour	**9**	**10**	**11**	**12**	**13**	**14**	**15**	**16**
Probabilistic	0.0991	0.1175	0.133	0.1359	0.1319	0.136	0.1343	0.1237
Deterministic	0.0983	0.1166	0.1318	0.1346	0.131	0.1347	0.133	0.1227
Hour	**17**	**18**	**19**	**20**	**21**	**22**	**23**	**24**
Probabilistic	0.1248	0.1223	0.1154	0.1112	0.1132	0.1188	0.1013	0.0670
Deterministic	0.1239	0.1212	0.1144	0.1104	0.1122	0.1181	0.1006	0.0666

5.2.   Probabilistic Voltage Evaluation

Figure 11 to Fig. 13 illustrate voltage profile for all buses in summer and 24-hours for $(\mu_{PLj} - \sigma_{PLj}, \mu_{QLj} - \sigma_{QLj})$, (μ_{PLj}, μ_{QLj}), and $(\mu_{PLj} + \sigma_{PLj}, \mu_{QLj} + \sigma_{QLj})$. Voltage profile of the spring, fall and winter seasons are shown in Fig. 14 to Fig. 16 for all buses and 24-hour versus load average. Sum of voltage deviations squares in 24-hour for each bus in summer for the probabilistic and deterministic load flows are given in Tab. 3.

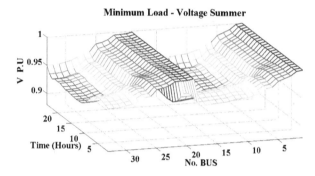

Fig. 11: Voltage profile of every hour in summer for $(\mu_{PLj} - \sigma_{PLj}, \mu_{QLj} - \sigma_{QLj})$.

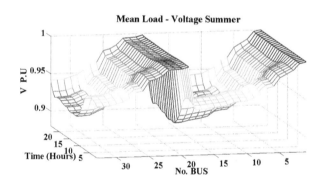

Fig. 12: Voltage profile of every hour in summer for (μ_{PLj}, μ_{QLj}).

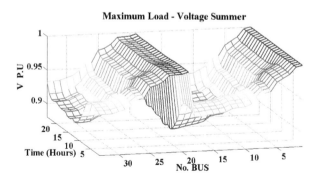

Fig. 13: Voltage profile of every hour in summer for $(\mu_{PLj} + \sigma_{PLj}, \mu_{QLj} + \sigma_{QLj})$.

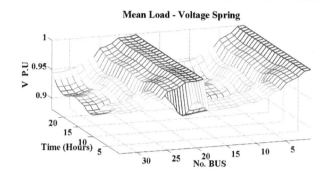

Fig. 14: Voltage profile for each hour in spring versus load average.

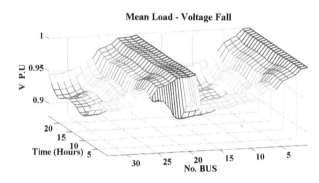

Fig. 15: Voltage profile for each hour in fall versus load average.

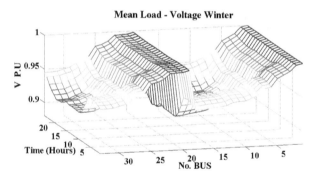

Fig. 16: Voltage profile for each hour in winter versus load average.

6.   Conclusion

In this paper, probabilistic power flow with normal distribution function of loads has been proposed to deliver a deeper insight into the system performance. This method relies on the statistical data obtained in different times in 24-hour of different seasons. The obtained data was computed using normal distribution function with seven standard deviations. The power losses variation during 24-hour and all seasons are illustrated. The proposed approach tested on the IEEE 33-bus system. Comparison of loss and total voltage deviation for each bus between conventional and proposed method shows accuracy and superiority of the suggested method.

References

[1] MORALES, J. M., L. BARINGO, A. J. CONEJO and R. MINGUEZ. Probabilistic power flow with correlated wind sources. *IET Generation, Transmission & Distribution*. 2010, vol. 4, iss. 5, pp. 641–651. ISSN 1751-8695. DOI: 10.1049/iet-gtd.2009.0639.

[2] BORKOWSKA, B. Probabilistic load flow. *IEEE Transactions on Power Apparatus and Systems*. 1974, vol. 93, iss. 3, pp. 752–759. ISSN 0018-9510. DOI: 10.1109/TPAS.1974.293973.

[3] DOPAZO, J. F., O. A. KLITIN and A. M. SASSON. Stochastic load flows. *IEEE Transactions on Power Apparatus and Systems*. 1975, vol. 94, iss. 2, pp. 299–309. ISSN 0018-9510. DOI: 10.1109/TPAS.1975.31855.

[4] ALLAN, R. N. and A. M. LEITE DA SILVA. Probabilistic load flow using multilinearisations. *IEE Proceedings C (Generation, Transmission and Distribution)*. 1981, vol. 128, iss. 5, pp. 280–287. ISSN 0143-7046. DOI: 10.1049/ip-c:19810047.

[5] LEITE DA SILVA, A. M., R. N. ALLAN, S. M. SOARES and V. L. ARIENTI. Probabilistic load flow considering network outages. *IEE Proceedings C (Generation, Transmission and Distribution)*. 1985, vol. 132, iss. 3, pp. 139–145. ISSN 0143-7046. DOI: 10.1049/ip-c:19850027.

[6] ZHANG, P. and S. T. LEE. Probabilistic load flow computation using the method of combined cumulants and Gram-Charlier expansion. *IEEE Transactions on Power Systems*. 2004, vol. 19, iss. 1, pp. 676–682. ISSN 0885-8950. DOI: 10.1109/TPWRS.2003.818743.

[7] SANABRIA, L. A. and T. S. DILON. Stochastic power flow using cumulants and Von Mises functions. *International Journal of Electrical Power and Energy Systems*. 1986, vol. 8, iss. 1, pp. 47–60. ISSN 0142-0615. DOI: 10.1016/0142-0615(86)90025-6.

[8] LEITE DA SILVA, A. M., V. L. ARIENTI and R. N. ALLAN. Probabilistic load flow considering dependence between input nodal powers. *IEEE Transactions on Power Apparatus and Systems*. 1984, vol. 103, iss. 6, pp. 1524–1530. ISSN 0018-9510. DOI: 10.1109/TPAS.1984.318493.

[9] TENG, J. A Network Topology-based Three Phase Load Flow for Distribution Systems. *Proceedings of the National Science Council*. 2000, vol. 24, no. 4, pp. 259–264. ISSN 0255-6596.

[10] BILLINTON, R. and W. LI. *Reliability Assessment of Electrical Power Systems Using Monte Carlo Methods*. New York: Plenum Press, 1994. ISBN 978-0306447815.

[11] ALLAN, R. N, A. M. LEITE DA SILVA and R. C. BURCHETT. Evaluation methods and accuracy in probabilistic load flow solutions. *IEEE Transactions on Power Apparatus and Systems*. 1981, vol. 100, no. 5, pp. 2539–2546. ISSN 0018-9510. DOI: 10.1109/TPAS.1981.316721.

[12] ZHANG, P. and S. T. LEE. Probabilistic Load Flow Computation Using the Method of Combined Cumulants and Gram-Charlier Expansion. *IEEE Transactions on Power Systems*. 2004, vol. 19, no. 1, pp. 676–682. ISSN 0885-8950. DOI: 10.1109/TPWRS.2003.818743.

[13] SUBCOMMITTEE, P. M. IEEE reliability test system. *IEEE Transactions on Power Apparatus and Systems*. 1979, vol. 98, no. 6, pp. 2047–2054. ISSN 0018-9510. DOI: 10.1109/TPAS.1979.319398.

[14] ACHARYA, N., P. MAHAT and N. MITHULANANTHAN. An analytical approach for DG allocation in primary distribution network. *International Journal of Electrical Power and Energy Systems*. 2006, vol. 28, iss. 10, pp. 669–678. ISSN 0142-0615.

[15] KASHEM, M. A., V. GANAPATHY, G. B. JASMON and M. I. BUHARI. A novel method for loss minimization in distribution networks. In: *International Conference on Electric Utility Deregulation and Restructuring and Power Technologies*. London: IEEE, 2000, pp. 251–256. ISBN 0-7803-5902-X. DOI: 10.1109/DRPT.2000.855672.

About Authors

Shahrokh SHOJAEIAN received his B.Sc. and M.Sc. degree from Isfahan University of Technology, Isfahan, Iran, in 1997 and 2000 respectively, and Ph.D. degree from Islamic Azad University, Science and Research Branch, Tehran, Iran, in 2012, all in electrical engineering. He is currently with the Faculty of Electrical Engineering, Islamic Azad University, Khomeinishahr Branch, Isfahan, Iran. His research interests are nonlinear control, power system control, stability, and reliability.

Ehsan SALLEALA-NAEENI received the B.Sc. and M.Sc. degree in electrical engineering from Islamic Azad University, Khomeinishahr Branch, Isfahan, Iran, in 2009 and 2010 respectively. His research topics include power system simulation, renewable energy resources, and reliability, and evolutionary algorithms.

Ehsan TASLIMI RENANI received the B.Sc. degree in electrical engineering from Islamic Azad University, Khomeinishahr Branch, Isfahan, Iran, in 2008 and M.Sc. degree in industrial electronic from University of Malaya (UM), Kuala Lumpur, Malaysia, in 2012. He is currently working as research assistance in the UM Power Energy Dedicated Advanced Center (UMPEDAC). His research topics include demand side management and power electronics.

2

THE ANALYSIS OF SUCCESS HPON NETWORKS USING THE HPON NETWORK CONFIGURATOR

Rastislav ROKA

Institute of Telecommunications, Faculty of Electrical Engineering and Information Technology, Slovak University of Technology in Bratislava, Ilkovicova 3, 812 19 Bratislava, Slovak Republic

rastislav.roka@stuba.sk

Abstract. *NG-PON systems present optical access infrastructures to support various applications of the many service providers. In the near future, we can expect NG-PON technologies with different motivations for developing of HPON networks. The HPON is a hybrid passive optical network in a way that utilizes on a physical layer both TDM and WDM multiplexing principles together. The HPON network utilizes similar or soft revised topologies as TDM-PON architectures. In this first paper, design requirements for SUCCESS HPON networks are introduced. A main part of the paper is dedicated to presentation of the HPON network configurator that allows configurating and analyzing the SUCCESS HPON characteristics from a viewpoint of various specific network parameters. Finally, a short introduction to the comparison of the SUCCESS and SARDANA HPON networks based on simulation results is presented.*

Keywords

HPON network configurator, hybrid passive optical networks, SUCCESS HPON.

1. Introduction

NG-PON systems present optical access infrastructures to support various applications of the many service providers. NG-PON technologies can be divided into two categories. The NG-PON1 presents an evolutionary growth with supporting the coexistence with the GPON on the same ODN. The coexistence feature enables seamless upgrade of individual customers on live optical fibers without disrupting services of other customers. The NG-PON2 presents a revolutionary change with no requirement in terms of coexistence with the GPON on the same ODN. In the near future, we can expect NG-PON technologies with different motivations for developing HPON networks. The

HPON is a hybrid passive optical network in a way that utilizes on a physical layer both TDM and WDM multiplexing principles together. The HPON network utilizes similar or soft revised topologies as TDM-PON architectures.

Hybrid passive optical networks can be divided into two possible groups. In the first one, a change of OLT and ONU equipment is executed and adding of both (WDM and TDM) ONU equipment into a common network architecture is allowed by using specialized remote nodes that utilize either passive optical power splitters or AWG elements. In the second one, preservation of TDM access networks combined with the DWDM multiplexing technique is predicted. For both approaches, various solutions were proposed.

The HPON presents a hybrid network as a necessary phase of the future transition from TDM to WDM passive optical networks [1]. Hybrid passive optical networks can be divided into two possible groups. In this paper, we focus on the first one where a change of OLT and ONU equipment is executed and adding of both (WDM and TDM) ONU equipment into a common network architecture is allowed by using specialized remote nodes that utilize either passive optical power splitters or AWG elements. By this way, a smooth transition from TDM to WDM networks is allowed. As an example, the SUCCESS (Stanford University aCCESS) HPON can be presented [2], [3]. The SUCCESS HPON network introduces a sequential transition to the pure WDM PON network in compliance with the TDM and WDM technology coexistence. The hybrid SUCCESS architecture comprises the ring topology for the WDM transmission. It contains two types of remote nodes RN for the WDM or TDM star connections. The WDM RN is created from AWG elements, the TDM RN from optical power splitters. The OLT terminal generates signals for both WDM and TDM ONU units by means of DWDM wavelengths; however the TDM ONU transmits signals on CWDM wavelengths. This architecture allows provisioning WDM services at preservation of the backward compatibility with initial/original TDM subscribers. The exchange of the TDM ONU is necessary. Information can be found in [4].

2. Simulation of HPON Networks

Our simulation model for comparing possibilities of various passive optical access networks is created by using the Microsoft Visual Studio 2008 software in the IDE development environment [5], [6], [7], [8]. There exist possibilities for the graphical interface created by using the MFC (Microsoft Foundation Class) library for the *C++* programming language. The simulation model has one main dialogue window for simulating a transition from TDM-PON to HPON networks. It allows comparing principal approaches for configuring of hybrid passive optical networks. A cut-out from the main window of the HPON configurator is shown on Fig. 1.

First, a selection of the optical fiber's type and the DWDM multiplexing density can be executed. A selected type of the optical fiber is presented by the specific attenuation values and by a number of transmission bands. These values correspond to various ITU-T recommendations – ITU-T G.652 A, G.652 B, G.652 C, G.652 D, G.656, G.657 – and, if available, measuring data can be inserted in the "Other values" option. Then, specific attenuation coefficients are used for calculating the optical fiber's attenuation in corresponding bands in specific network configurations. Also, a total number of CWDM and DWDM carrier wavelengths for particular bands is presented. The relationship between numbers of available wavelengths at various channel allocations is introduced in [7]. Then, a specification of parameters and features of the deployed TDM-PON network can be executed. More detailed information can be found in [9].

Three additional dialogue windows with a basic network scheme and short descriptions serve for the specific HPON configuration setup. The interactive window with the SUCCESS HPON description is presented on Fig. 2. For the SUCCESS HPON, a transition is expressed by interactive GIF animations. For their presentation, a free available CPictureEx class is used [10].

The HPON configurator allows simulating and analyzing a transition from TDM-PON networks to HPON networks and to compare three different approaches to hybrid networks. After inserting input parameters of TDM-PON networks, these parameters are evaluated and the total transmission capacity of the TDM network together with the average capacity per one subscriber, the total number of subscribers and the maximum attenuation of the TDM network are cal-

Tab. 1: The selection from specifications of HPON optical components.

Symbol	Description	Value
a_{FILTER}	the WDM filter	0, 4 dB
a_{AWG}	the AWG element	5 dB
$a_{50:50}$	the 50:50 power splitter	4, 4 dB
$a_{SPLIT1:N}$	the 1:16 splitter attenuation	14, 1 dB
	the 1:32 splitter attenuation	17, 4 dB
	the 1:64 splitter attenuation	21, 0 dB
a_{TDM-RN}	the TDM node attenuation (including connectors)	1, 5 dB
a_{WDM-RN}	the WDM node attenuation (including connectors)	1 dB

culated and presented. After configuration the SUCCESS HPON network, a number and type of used active and passive components with possibilities for future expanding are presented.

In the HPON network, power relationships are depending on specific network characteristics and applied optical components' parameters. We prefer real attenuation values of optical components utilized in passive optical networks. Some of them are presented in Tab. 1, further optical components together with corresponding attenuation values are presented in [7], [9]. In addition to a distance between the OLT and particular ONU, a number and type of used splitters are included for calculating of the total attenuation for specific network configurations.

3. Design of the SUCCESS HPON Network

The SUCCESS HPON network [2] allows a coexistence of TDM and WDM technologies within one network infrastructure and provides a possibility of the smooth transition TDM subscribers to the WDM. At its architecture, it is possible to utilize up to 17 CWDM wavelengths in all bands for upstream transmitting in TDM stars, the 18th wavelength is utilized for the downstream signal transmission to TDM ONU-s using DWDM multiplexing (a number of wavelengths can be found in Tab. 2).

A distribution of CWDM and DWDM wavelengths in particular transmission bands is introduced in Tab. 2. DWDM wavelengths can be distributed in S-, C- or L-bands. The CWDM channel spacing is fixed to the 20 nm [11], the DWDM channel spacing is variable from 0,2 to 0,8 nm depending on the multiplexing density [12]. After selecting a specific density, the total number of possible DWDM channels is calculated. By decreasing DWDM channel spacing, a negative influence of nonlinear effects presented in the optical transmission medium will be more expressive in real optical transmission networks.

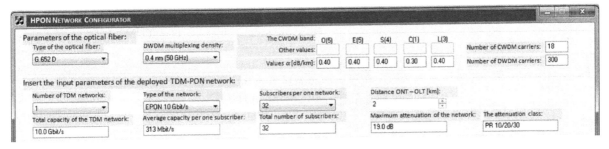

Fig. 1: The cut-out from the main window of the HPON network configurator.

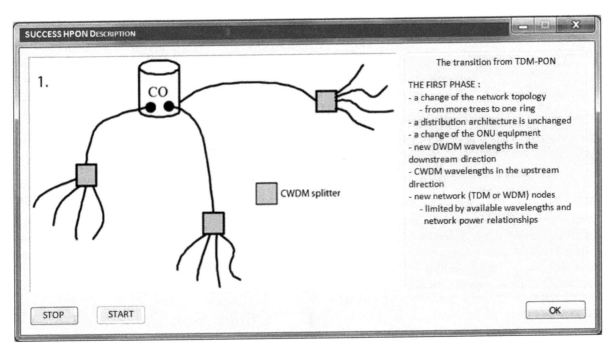

Fig. 2: The description window of the SUCCESS HPON network.

Tab. 2: Numbers of DWDM and CWDM wavelengths for particular transmission bands.

	O 1260–1360 nm	E 1360–1460 nm	S 1460–1530 nm	C 1530–1565 nm	L 1565–1625 nm	SUM Σ
DWDM (0,8 nm, 100 GHz)	-	-	50	25	75	150
DWDM (0,4 nm, 50 GHz)	-	-	100	50	150	300
DWDM (0,2 nm, 25 GHz)	-	-	200	100	300	600
CWDM (20 nm)	5	5	4	1	3	18

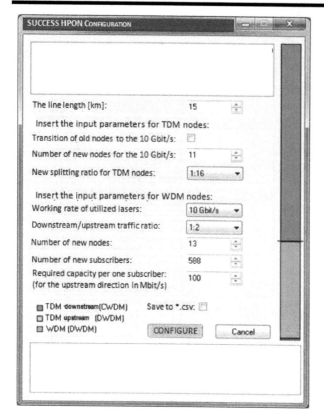

Fig. 3: The configuration window of the SUCCESS HPON network.

As a maximum, 17 TDM stars can be connected. The total number of DWDM wavelengths available for connecting WDM subscribers is decreased by a number of connected TDM nodes, one TDM node per one DWDM channel. In a case of the full DWDM bands availability, a maximum of possible joinable subscribers is acquiring. After connecting more than 11 TDM nodes, CWDM and DWDM bands are overlapping and a number of joinable WDM subscribers together with a total number of joinable subscribers are decreasing. The availability of DWDM and CWDM wavelengths is clearly and transparently displayed using graphical tools (Fig. 3).

For this presentation, following parameters were selected: the ITU-T G.652 D optical fiber, the 0,2 nm DWDM channel spacing, the ring length 15 km, the access fiber length 2 km. Characteristics of the SUCCESS HPON configuration with the 1:64 splitting ratio in TDM nodes and utilizing available wavelengths at 25 GHz DWDM channel spacing are presented on Fig. 4. The total number of subscribers (1356) can be reached for 11 TDM nodes. However, as we can see, their attenuation values are exceeded 40 dB. For comparison, attenuation values of WDM nodes are also presented. At the 1:32 splitting ratio in TDM nodes, the total number of subscribers (972) is decreased with lower attenuation values 37,2 dB. At the 1:16 splitting ratio in TDM nodes, the total number of subscribers

(780) is also decreased with still inconvenient lower attenuation values 33,9 dB (Fig. 5).

At this architecture, a number of subscribers is limited by high values of the TDM node attenuation. This high attenuation is caused by longer optical fibers in the ring topology and by inserted losses particular nodes. A solution can be found by placing of optical amplifiers in the RN, however, with limiting utilizable spectral bands and reducing a number of joinable TDM nodes. Moreover, this solution changes a character of passive optical networks to active.

At the SUCCESS network, it is necessary to take into account lower splitting ratios than 1:64 and a smaller number of TDM nodes due to their higher attenuation values. In the SUCCESS network, it is possible to utilize all transmission bands supported by selected optical fibers. However, an adding of optical amplifiers into TDM nodes brings band restrictions. In the SUCCESS HPON, the CWDM multiplexing is utilized at the TDM transmission and this restriction is too high. In the C-band suitable for EDFA amplifications, only 1 TDM node is possible for connecting. In the SUCCESS HPON, WDM nodes have very low values of the attenuation because using AWG elements instead of power optical splitters.

The ring topology allows a selection of the transmitting direction depending on network power arrangement and provides a traffic protection against fiber or node failures.

A comparison of two hybrid passive optical networks – SUCCESS and SARDANA - from various viewpoints will be presented in [9].

4.   Conclusion

The intermediate step between TDM and WDM-PON networks is presented by hybrid passive optical networks HPON. The HPON evolution allows using two different approaches. In the first approach, a network combining TDM and WDM-PON elements is created in order to increase a number of subscribers and a reach. In the second one, a smooth transition from TDM-PON to WDM networks is preferred without violation of service provisioning for original TDM subscribers.

In the HPON network configurator, some new features and upgrades for the SUCCESS HPON networks were prepared – the graphical presentation of available wavelength bands, more comfortable design and extension of utilized wavelengths.

Based on output values from this configuration program, it is possible to evaluate various different approaches for building hybrid passive optical networks

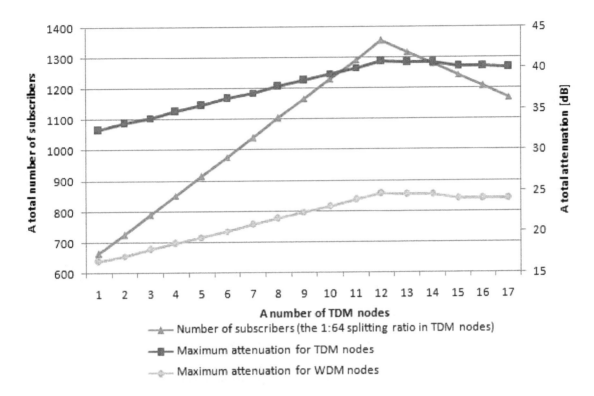

Fig. 4: Characteristics of the SUCCESS HPON network for the 1:64 splitting ratio.

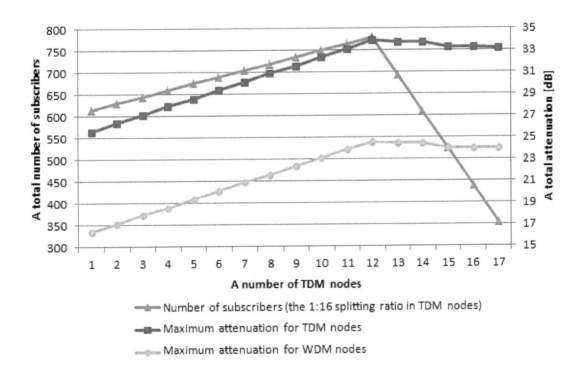

Fig. 5: Characteristics of the SUCCESS HPON network for the 1:16 splitting ratio.

and to compare them from many usable aspects – a number of subscribers, maximum reaches and transmission rates, optical components and technologies.

In these days, the HPON network configurator is not available to download for academic purposes (research). This possibility will be actual after solving the copyright and related rights.

Acknowledgment

This work is a part of research activities conducted at Slovak University of Technology Bratislava, Faculty of Electrical Engineering and Information Technology, Institute of Telecommunications, within the scope of the project VEGA No. 1/0106/11 "Analysis and proposal for advanced optical access networks in the NGN converged infrastructure utilizing fixed transmission media for supporting multimedia services".

References

[1] PETKO, Ladislav. G-PON Migration to New Technologies. In: *OK 2012 – 15th Conference and Exhibition on Optical Communications*. Praha: ActionM, 2012. ISBN 978-80-86742-36-6.

[2] FU-TAI AN, D. GUTIERREZ, KYEONG SOO KIM, JUNG WOO LEE and L.G. KAZOVSKY. SUCCESS-HPON: A next-generation optical access architecture for smooth migration from TDM-PON to WDM-PON. *IEEE Communications Magazine*. 2005, vol. 43, iss. 11, pp. S40–S47. ISSN 0163-6804. DOI: 10.1109/MCOM.2005.1541698.

[3] KAZOVSKY, Leonid G. *Broadband Optical Access Networks*. Hoboken: John Wiley, 2011. ISBN 978-0-470-18235-2.

[4] PETER, Juraj. *The Analysis of the Hybrid PON Utilization in the Optical Access Network*. Bratislava, 2012. Diploma Thesis. Faculty of Electrical Engineering and Information Technology, Slovak University of Technology in Bratislava.

[5] ROKA, Rastislav. The Designing of Passive Optical Networks using the HPON Network Configurator. *International Journal of Research and Reviews in Computer Science IJRRCS*. 2010, vol. 1, no. 3, pp. 38–43, ISSN 2079-2557.

[6] ROKA, Rastislav. The extension of the HPON network configurator at designing of NG-PON networks. In: *34th International Conference on Telecommunications and Signal Processing (TSP 2011)*. Budapest: IEEE, 2011, pp. 79–84. ISBN 978-1-4577-1410-8. DOI: 10.1109/TSP.2011.6043768.

[7] ROKA, Rastislav. The Designing of NG-PON Networks Using the HPON Network Configuration. *Journal of Communication and Computer JCC*. 2012, vol. 9, no. 6, pp. 669–678. ISSN 1548-7709.

[8] ROKA, R. and S. KHAN. The Modeling of Hybrid Passive Optical Networks using the Network Configurator. *International Journal of Research and Reviews in Computer Science IJRRCS*. 2011 - Special Issue, pp. 48–54, ISSN 2079-2557.

[9] ROKA, Rastislav. Analysis of Hybrid Passive Optical Networks using the HPON Network Configurator. In: *INTECH 2013 – International Conference on Innovative Technologies*. Budapest: INTECH, 2013, pp. 401–404, ISBN 978-953-6326-88-4.

[10] BYKOV, O. Code Project. *The CPictureEx Class* [online]. 2001. Available at: http://www.codeproject.com/Articles/1427/Add-GIF-animation-to-your-MFC-and-ATL-\projects-wit.

[11] ITU-T Recommendation G.694.2. *Spectral grids for WDM applications: CWDM frequency grid*. Switzerland: ITU-T, 2002.

[12] ITU-T Recommendation G.694.2. *Spectral grids for WDM applications: DWDM frequency grid*. Switzerland: ITU-T, 2002.

About Authors

Rastislav ROKA was born in Sala, Slovakia on January 27, 1972. He received his M.Sc. and Ph.D. degrees in Telecommunications from the Slovak University of Technology, Bratislava, in 1995 and 2002. Since 1997, he has been working as a senior lecturer at the Institute of Telecommunications, Faculty of Electrical Engineering and Information Technology, Slovak University of Technology in Bratislava. Since 2009, he is working as an associated professor at this institute. At present, his research activity is focused on the signal transmission through metallic access networks by means of xDSL/PLC technologies and through optical transport and access networks by means of WDM and TDM technologies using various techniques of the optical signal processing. A main effort is dedicated to effective utilization of the optical fiber's transmission capacity by using DBA/DWA algorithms.

3

The Data Extraction Using Distributed Crawler Inside the Multi-Agent System

Karel TOMALA[1], Jan PLUCAR[2], Patrik DUBEC[2], Lukas RAPANT[3], Miroslav VOZNAK[1]

[1]Department of Telecommunications, Faculty of Electrical Engineering and Computer Science, VSB–Technical University of Ostrava, 17. listopadu, 708 33 Ostrava-Poruba, Czech Republic
[2]Department of Computer Science, Faculty of Electrical Engineering and Computer Science, VSB–Technical University of Ostrava, 17. listopadu, 708 33 Ostrava-Poruba, Czech Republic
[3]Department of Applied Mathematics, Faculty of Electrical Engineering and Computer Science, VSB–Technical University of Ostrava, 17. listopadu, 708 33 Ostrava-Poruba, Czech Republic

karel.tomala@vsb.cz, jan.plucar@vsb.cz, patrik.dubec@vsb.cz, lukas.rapant@vsb.cz, miroslav.voznak@vsb.cz

Abstract. *The paper discusses the use of web crawler technology. We created an application based on standard web crawler. Our application is determined for data extraction. Primarily, the application was designed to extract data using keywords from a social network Twitter. First, we created a standard crawler, which went through a predefined list of URLs and gradually download page content of each of the URLs. Page content was then parsed and important text and metadata were stored in a database. Recently, the application was modified in to the form of the multi-agent system. The system was developed in the C# language, which is used to create web applications and sites etc. Obtained data was evaluated graphically. The system was created within Indect project at the VSB-Technical University of Ostrava.*

Keywords

Class diagram, multi-agent system, Twitter, web crawler.

1. Introduction

We have faced the problem of data mining from social networks, such as Twitter. Data mining is the methodology of obtaining non trivial hidden and potentially useful information from data. It is used in the commercial sector and scientific research, but also in other areas. In our case, we have used the data mining methods to extract keywords from content downloaded by web crawlers [1]. Social network has great potential for obtaining data and information about relationships between groups of people [2].

1.1. Web Crawler

A Web crawler (also known as a web spider or web robot) is a computer program or automated script which browses the World Wide Web in a methodical, automated manner or in an orderly fashion. This process is called Web crawling or spidering [3].

Users are browsing websites through a series of links from one page to another. This activity can be simulated and performed by robots. Browsing the code of web pages, gathering the information found in the code and search links to other websites is the most common task of robots. In principle, this type of robots are divided into two groups according to the size of the search area:

- Robots which browse websites on the pre-specified domain or a finite set of several domains.

- Robots browsing across large environment of WWW.

To start browsing website the robot needs the initial URL or a list of URLs (seed). Then it starts to browse the web pages from the given URLs and searches links leading to other sites (crawl frontier), which will crawler need to visit. This procedure is then repeated recursively. It also shows that the robot can visit only those web pages that can be accessed by following links leading from the initial web page. Some robots can simultaneously visit multiple web pages and browse them in parallel. Other robots move to the next web page after processing the current web page [4]. Architecture of crawler is shown in Fig. 1.

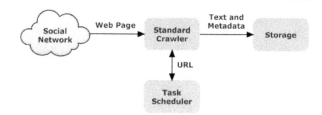

Fig. 1: Architecture of crawler.

1.2.   Multi-Agent System

Multi-agent system (MAS) is a simulated environment with the network character, in which there is interaction between certain types of actors (agents) to each other and / or with the environment in which they are located (Fig. 2). These agents collectively solve problems that go beyond the capabilities and skills of each of them [4].

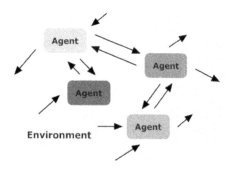

Fig. 2: Multi-agent system.

2.   Used Technology and Methodology

First, we have created a standard crawler, which browsed through a predefined list of URLs and gradually download page content of each of the URLs. Page content is then parsed and important text and metadata are stored in a database.

Crawler, demonstrated in Fig. 1 was working properly, but in terms of the volume of downloaded data was not sufficient. It was necessary to run the crawler on multiple machines and somehow coordinate these instances of crawler. We have decided to create a multi-agent system, which would provide support for the creation of agents and the organization of work between them. Figure 3 demonstrated the top level of the multi-agent system. This is a hierarchical structure in which two types of agents exist:

- Master agent: this agent creates new agents, maintains a database of addresses that are to be crawled, and distributes tasks to individual agents.

- Agent: this agent contains a module that is responsible for downloading the web page content.

2.1.   Distributed Web Crawling

Distributed web crawling is a distributed computing technology. Distributed web crawling is a basic element for any of the decentralized search applications. The web content collected by a distributed crawler can be indexed by decentralized search infrastructures, or archived using a permanent storage infrastructure. The distributed crawler uses the excess bandwidth and computing resources of clients to crawl the websites. Such systems may allow for users to offer their own computing and bandwidth resources for crawling web pages. Distributing the load of these tasks across many computers saves the cost that would otherwise be spent on maintaining large computing clusters [5].

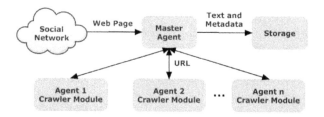

Fig. 3: Distributed web crawling.

The query is executed in a distributed manner as follows. Each crawler node starts the query engine and is responsible for crawling of different web pages. At first, the query is sent to all the crawler agents, and set to run according to exit criterion (crawling time, depth of crawl etc.). The crawl is started by publishing a set of URLs to each crawler, which is then responsible for downloading data from this given set. Once the crawler finishes crawling, it contacts manager crawler that provides more URLs to crawl [6].

2.2.   Twitter Search API

The Twitter Search API is used for running searches against the real-time index of recent Tweets. There are several important facts that you need to know before using the Twitter Search API [7]. Limitations:

- The Search API is not complete index of all Tweets, but is only an index of recent Tweets. Index includes between 6-9 days of Tweets.

- Complex queries can be limited and Search API will respond to such query with the error: "error":"Sorry, your query is too complex. Please reduce complexity and try again.".

- Search does not support authentication in which case all queries are anonymous.

- Search is focused in significance and not completeness. This means that some Tweets may be missing from search results. If you want to match for completeness you can use the Streaming API instead.

- The near operator cannot be used by the Search API. You need to use the geocode parameter.

- Queries are limited to 1000 characters in length.

- When performing geo-based searches with a radius, only one thousand distinct subregions will be considered when evaluating the query.

The Rate Limits for the Search API are other than for the REST API. Using the Search API you are not limited to a certain number of API requests per hour, but instead by the complexity and frequency. As requests to the Search API are anonymous, the rate limit is determined against the requesting client.

In order to prevent abuse the rate limit for Search API is not published. Should the rate limit is restricted. The Search API will respond with an HTTP 420 Error. "error":"You have been rate limited. Enhance your calm.". Sample result:

```
{
"created_at": "Tue, 15 Nov 2011 20:08:17
+0000",
"from_user": "fakekurrik",
"from_user_id": 370773112,
"from_user_id_str": "370773112",
"from_user_name": "fakekurrik",
"geo": null,
"id": 136536013832069120,
"id_str": "136536013832069120",
"iso_language_code": "en",
"metadata": {
"result_type": "recent"
},
"profile_image_url":
"http://a1.twimg.com/profile_images//
phatkicks_normal.jpg",
"source": "&lt;a href=&quot;http://
twitter.com/&quot;&gt;web&lt;/a&gt;",
"text": "@twitterapi, keep on keeping it
real",
"to_user": "twitterapi",
"to_user_id": 6253282,
"to_user_id_str": "6253282",
"to_user_name": "Twitter API"
}
```

3. Web Crawler Implementation

Web crawler itself is started within every agent instance. Multi-agent system is able to encapsulate any application that needs to be run inside the multi-agent system. This has been accomplished by following FIPA standards [8].

There are several types of the multi-agent system architectures. In our case, the most suitable architecture is the hierarchical one, in which the hierarchy of agent's roles is the most essential element. Central management element is also part of this architecture, but it does not perform all tasks itself. It may delegate part of communication and management tasks to the control elements in lower levels of the hierarchy. Such architecture can be represented in the form of a tree (Fig. 4). Leaves of the tree represent discrete and finite agents. The advantage of this architecture is scalability and robustness. Adding additional control elements supports load balancing management. New element can be simply added as a child of its parent agent and there is no need to change the implementation of the system.

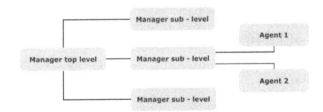

Fig. 4: Architecture of system.

Our MAS implementation offers two solutions: distributed implementation (agents distributed throughout network) or undistributed (MAS is started on one local work station).

In distributed version, every agent starts and runs both TCP client and TCP server in order to be able to receive and send messages. Both TCP server and TCP client of each agent are launched in their own thread so that running them does not oppress the main computational thread of the agent.

Message object is a communication element that uses XML format for the socket communication. The Message consists of Header and Content. The Header contains information about a sender and a receiver (IP address, port, etc.). The Content contains specific information which is the subject of the communication. A message can be encrypted before it is sent and decrypted when received. The MD5 algorithm is used for this encryption and it may as well be replaced by any other encryption algorithm. Finally, the message is converted into a binary form and sent.

Multi-agent system is running set of task simultaneously. Workflow of the system is depicted in the Fig. 5 and description below. The basic concept is to crawl URLs, download content of the URLs and analyze it using data mining processor. New set of URLs is created from this analysis. Example given from testing during Olympics in London 2012:

- Initial set of URLs contained search phrase: "Summer Olympics 2012".

- Suggested keywords for new search were: "London, Traffic jam, Accommodation, Tickets, etc.".

Fig. 5: System concept overview.

- Top level manager agent is started with the list of initial URLs. These URLs are divided as a task to sub level manager agents.

- Sub level manager agents create a number of agents to crawl Twitter social network.

- Every agent downloads target URL content and sends it to the manager.

- Manager saves content into the DB and informs top level manager about task completion.

- Content stored in DB is continuously passed and analyzed by data mining processor.

- Data mining processor creates a list of important keywords that shall be crawled for. This list is passed to top level manager.

- Top level manager agent divides task between sub level manager agents. New agents are created if necessary.

4.   Results

In order to test system efficiency, we have set up series of tests that have been executed during summer Olympics in London 2012. Please note that results are measured just for one sublevel segment: one sublevel manager agent and set of agents belonging under this

manager. To scale the system and balance the load, we can let the system create hundreds of these segments. Before we do so, we need to find out optimal size of the segment - meaning the number of agents working in one segment.

Figure 6 shows the dependence between the volume of downloaded data and the number of running crawler instances. It is natural to expect that higher number of agents will be able to process higher number of requests.

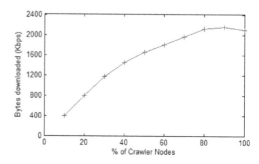

Fig. 6: Crawling load.

However, according to our experiments we have discovered that running about 30 – 40 crawlers is lowering the number of request that single crawler processes. This is caused by manager agent not being able to handle all requests. These requests are divided between inbound and outbound, inbound being data returned from crawler and outbound being URLs to be crawled. This phenomenon could be observed when running about 90 crawlers, where manager agent is overwhelmed with inbound requests and is not able to distribute new URLs to be crawled.

We were looking for a way to increase the number of agents which be fully served by manager. Critical point was communication with the database. Therefore, we focused on the performance of the database layer, which has been programmed using ADO.NET, Entity framework and LINQ to SQL. These three approaches were tested and compared mutually and results are described in Tab. 1.

Tab. 1: Non-transactional insertion - results.

	Time (ms)	CPU Time (ms)	Memory (B)
LINQ to SQL	52333	46819	2970942
Entity Framework	23091	12425	619352
ADO.NET	14333	7736	4418

Database layer using ADO.NET excelled in the means of completion time. When connecting to SQL Server, BULK INSERT method was added for quick data insertion. BULK INSERT method uses specific properties of the database [9]. Due to this implementation ADO.NET layer greatly exceeded the speed of Link to SQL and Entity Framework. Use of ADO.NET layer is suitable for applications with low requirements of abstraction and high requirements of performance. This could be for example a data pumps, import and export modules. The absence of a full conceptual layer is balanced by the speed of ADO.NET layer. LINQ to SQL returned worst results in terms of memory complexity and processing time. The results are caused by a complicated layering of LINQ to SQL. The LINQ to SQL seeks to provide a conceptual layer.

5. Conclusion

Contribution of this work lays in the creation of an open-source tool that will be usable in the scientific sphere. We have demonstrated the applicability of multi-agent approach enabling distributed crawling. Based on measurements at the laboratory of VSB we have tested and subsequently performed optimization of tool for downloading data. The obtained results show that the tool manages to download large amounts of data (we have to take into account that the data size depends on the size and number of tweets on Twitter). During the testing, we have found that the optimal number of concurrent crawlers varies between 30 and 40. Using more than 40 crawlers, relative performance per crawler is decreased. This is due to the fact that the manager can't handle processing requests for saving data into the database and simultaneous assignment of new tasks. This phenomenon is evident from Figure 5. When running 90 plus crawlers system loses total efficiency. Thanks to this test, we have set the maximum number of crawlers per segment to 65. If more than 65 crawlers are needed, another segment is automatically created and tasks are balanced between old and new segments.

Acknowledgment

The research leading to these results has received funding from the European Community's Seventh Framework Programme (FP7/2007-2013) under grant agreement no. 218086. This work was supported by the Grant Agency of the Czech Republic - GACR P103/13/08195S and project, reg. no. CZ.1.07/2.3.00/20.0072.

References

[1] LIU, B. *Web Data Mining: Exploring Hyperlinks, Contents, and Usage Data (Data-Centric Systems and Applications).* Springer, 2011. ISBN 978-3642194597.

[2] RUSSELL, M. A. *Mining the Social Web: Analyzing Data from Facebook, Twitter, LinkedIn, and Other Social Media Sites.* O'Reilly Media, 2011. ISBN 978-1449388348.

[3] MARMANIS, H. and D. BABENKO. *Algorithms of the Intelligent Web.* New York: Manning Publications, 2009. ISBN 978-1933988665.

[4] SCHRENK, Michael. *Webbots, Spiders, and Screen Scrapers: A Guide to Developing Internet Agents with PHP/CURL.* San Francisco: No Starch Press, 2012. ISBN 978-1449388348.

[5] BEER, M., M. FASLI and D. RICHARDS. *Multi-Agent Systems for Education and Interactive Entertainment: Design, Use and Experience.* Hershey: IGI Global, 2010. ISBN 978-1609600808.

[6] SHKAPENYUK, V. and T. SUEL. Design and implementation of a high-performance distributed Web crawler. In: *Proceedings 18th International Conference on Data Engineering.* New York: IEEE, 2002, pp. 357–368. ISBN 0-7695-1531-2. DOI: 10.1109/ICDE.2002.994750.

[7] MAKICE, K. *Twitter API: Up and Running: Learn How to Build Applications with the Twitter API.* Sebastopol: O'Reilly Media, 2009. ISBN 978-0596154615.

[8] GOMAA, H. *Software Modeling and Design: UML, Use Cases, Patterns, and Software Architectures.* Cambridge: Cambridge University Press, 2011. ISBN 978-0521764148.

[9] MEHTA, V. P. *Pro LINQ Object Relational Mapping in C# (Expert's Voice in .NET).* New York: Springer, 2008. ISBN 978-1-59059-965-9.

About Authors

Karel TOMALA was born in 1984. In 2007, received a Bachelor title in VSB–Technical University of Ostrava, Faculty of Electronics and Computer Science, Department of Telecommunications. Two years later he received the M.Sc. title focused on Telecommunications in the same workplace. Currently in the doctoral study he focuses on Voice over IP technology and Speech Quality in VoIP.

Jan PLUCAR was born in 1987. In 2011, received a Master title in VSB–Technical University of Ostrava, Faculty of Electronics and Computer Science, Department of Computer science. Jan Plucar is currently working on his Ph.D. in the field of computer security and bio inspired computations.

Patrik DUBEC was born in 1986. In 2011, received a Master title in VSB–Technical University of Ostrava, Faculty of Electronics and Computer Science, Department of Computer science. Patrik Dubec is currently working on his Ph.D. in the field of computer security and data mining methods.

Lukas RAPANT was born in 1986 in Ostrava. In 2009, he received the bachelor's degree in applied mathematics from VSB–Technical University of Ostrava, Faculty of Electronics and Computer Science, Department of Apllied Mathematics. In 2011, he received the master degree in the same field from the same university. Currently, he is undergoing his doctoral study on VSB–Technical University of Ostrava, where he focuses on applied staticstics and graph algorithms.

Miroslav VOZNAK is an associate professor with Department of Telecommunications, VSB–Technical University of Ostrava. He received his M.Sc. and Ph.D. degrees in telecommunications, dissertation thesis "Voice traffic optimization with regard to speech quality in network with VoIP technology" from the Technical University of Ostrava, in 1995 and 2002, respectively. Topics of his research interests are Next Generation Networks, IP telephony, speech quality and network security. He was involved in several FP EU projects. At present, he is also working for the Czech National Centre of Excellence IT4I.

4

Simple and Universal Current Modulator Circuit for Indoor Mobile Free-Space-Optical Communications Testing

Stanislav HEJDUK, Karel WITAS, Jan LATAL, Jan VITASEK, Jiri BOCHEZA, Vladimir VASINEK

Department of Telecommunications, Faculty of Electrical Engineering, VSB–Technical University of Ostrava, 17.listopadu 15/2172, 708 33 Ostrava-Poruba, Czech Republic

stanislav.hejduk@vsb.cz, karel.witas@vsb.cz, jan.latal@vsb.cz, jan.vitasek@vsb.cz, jiri.bocheza@vsb.cz, vladimir.vasinek@vsb.cz

Abstract. *The use of LEDs for illumination and simultaneous communication becomes more and more interesting and it goes hand in hand with the increasing deployment of LEDs to peoples homes and industrial buildings. Modulation of this kind of light sources is difficult because of high voltage and of current demands. Since the LED configurations and the values of current and voltage are different, the universal modulator suggested by the research team of the Department of Telecommunications should be able to operate even under various circumstances. The objective of this paper is to present a design of a simple and universal current modulator for LED lighting modulation for the frequencies of around 1 MHz. The modulator should allow the initial testing of different types of High Power LEDs and different photodetector configurations and circuits in diffusively based Free-Space-Optical networks. Also, in the experimental part, the results obtained in the testing were compared with some different types of LED light sources.*

Keywords

Current modulator, free space optics, FSO, LED, lighting, mobile, network, visible light communication, VLC.

1. Introduction

LED diodes have been a significant part of everyday life for many years. Thanks to the falling prices and the exceptional lifetime of LEDs as well as to their increasing optical power it can be expected that in a few years they will replace fluorescent and incandescent light bulbs.

Although the idea of contemporary lighting and communication is not new [1], utilization of LEDs is still mostly of the experimental nature. Anyway, the future development of this technology is very promising especially due to their coverage parameters. Although the idea of contemporary lighting and communication isn't new [1], deployment is still mostly experimental nature. But future development of this technology is still very promising, especially for its coverage parameters. Compared with the radio networks, there is virtually no interference between the two systems since light cannot penetrate walls and opaque obstacles. There is also a possibility of precise defining of the covered area as well as of using more identical systems in one area even without them being divided by any walls and obstacles [2], [3].

For this type of a Free-Space-Optical (FSO) network or, at present, for a more frequently used the term a Visible Light Communication (VLC) system, the covered area will be considered as a diffusive network. That means that the covered area is evenly flooded with high optical power and the signal can also be detected after its reflection from walls and other obstacles. Thanks to this phenomenon, communication is possible even behind the Line-Of-Sight (LOS). And, of course, the speed limitations have to be considered with regard to their multipath signal propagation, which causes expansion of the transmitted pulses and, as for higher frequencies, even their multiplication. As a result, the photodetector will receive the same data several times in succession [4]. To limit this phenomenon, either the reflections have to be avoided, or some suitable modulation has to be used [5].

The main point is that indoor LED lighting needs much more energy than the point-to-point communication. Lights usually consist of larger blocks with higher voltage for lower demands on operational current. In the end, there has to be some compromise made between the voltage and current suitable for the lighting applications. However, a new modulator with high power dissipation, high current capability and high output voltage has to be built at this stage. And due to higher parasitic capacity of these lights and their slower responses there is a loss of a valuable part of the modulation speed. At least, the response time of LEDs should not be a significant problem in the expected frequency range of around 1 MHz. The modulation fre-

Fig. 1: LED light with SMD LEDs matrix.

quency for white LEDs shown in Fig. 1 is limited to approximately 3 MHz due to the luminophore response. But this limit can be easily circumvented by using either the RGB LEDs (Fig. 2) instead of white LEDs, or a blue colour filter. This solution eliminates the long response component of luminophore and it theoretically increases the frequency response to 20 MHz [6].

Fig. 2: LED strips with SMD5050 RGB LEDs.

Another speed limitation is connected to the light propagation and photo detection. Light from LEDs

disperses conically and the photodetected power can be calculated at any cross section as [2]:

$$P_{det.} = \frac{SA_R}{SA_T + \frac{\pi}{4}(\theta R)^2}, \tag{1}$$

where SA_R is the surface area of receiver, SA_T is the surface area of transmitter, θ is the divergence angle and R is the range in meters [2]. It means that the optical power will drops to a quarter every time the distance between transmitter and receiver is doubled. It can be seen in Fig. 3 what a big difference there is between the received optical powers for the distances from 0.1 to 1 meter.

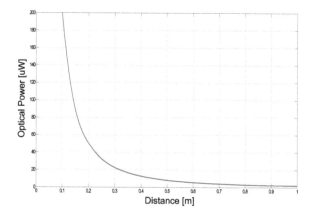

Fig. 3: Received power vs. transmitter distance.

The received power determines the required sensitivity of the photodetector. Higher sensitivity negatively affects the receiver speed [7]. The bandwidth of the photodetector has a high frequency cut-off given by:

$$B = \frac{1}{2\pi RC}, \tag{2}$$

where C is the parasitic capacitance of the photodetector and sensitivity is controlled by the value of the resistor R. The equivalent photodetector circuit is shown in Fig. 4.

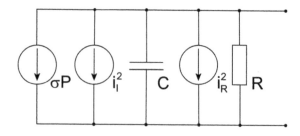

Fig. 4: Equivalent photodetector circuit.

Added to the signal, two noise contributions can also be found. The first one is the quantum noise associated with the discrete nature of the total current (the sum of the signal current and the dark current) and its value is given by:

$$i_I^2 = 2e\left(I_{ph} + I_d\right)B,\qquad(3)$$

where I_{ph} is the photodetected (signal) current, I_d is the dark current and B is the bandwidth.

The other one is the Johnson noise (or thermal noise) of resistance R:

$$i_R^2 = \frac{4kBT}{R},\qquad(4)$$

where k is the Boltzmann constant, T is the absolute temperature, B is the bandwidth and R is the value of the used load resistor.

With the background noise and all the above-mentioned assumptions the target frequencies are around 1 MHz, probably under or very close to the limit, and the usable bit rate is determined by the modulation used. Many modulation schemes have been tested under the Visible Light Communication (VLC) conditions so far. In addition to the basic OOK, the PWM (Pulse Width Modulation) [8] or the PPM (Pulse Position Modulation) [9], [10] can be mentioned as well. The main advantage of these modulations is the possibility of dimming the lights without any limitation of the transmitted power.

In the initial experiments worldwide the bitrates start at approximately 111 kbit·s^{-1} with the range of up to 1.5 meters [11]. On the other hand, in the laboratory conditions and with the appropriate modulation the commercial LEDs can reach the values of around 100 Mbit·s^{-1} [6], [12]. The increased interest in this type of communication has led to the introduction of the IEEE Standard for Local and Metropolitan Area Networks 802.15.7: Short-Range Wireless Optical Communication Using Visible Light [13], [15].

2. Requirements for the Modulator

Observability of communication is extremely important in contrast to the IR spectrum solutions. A person moving around in a room should not notice the difference between the normal and modulated lights. Due to the fact that communication is performed in the visible part of the spectrum, some special requirements have to be fulfilled. These requirements include the modulation scheme and the coding used for the data transmissions as well.

2.1. Modulation and Coding

The main requirement for the modulator is to keep a stable mean value of the transmitted signal. In that case no power fluctuations will occur during the communication. For the simple On-Off-Keying modulation (OOK), the light is turned ON for logical 1 and OFF for logical 0. It means that the logical levels at the input are simply transferred to the light intensity at the output. Thus, the long sequence of zeros causes the lights to go out. That is why it is necessary to use a specific coding scheme with the OOK modulation in order to keep the mean value of the signal stable.

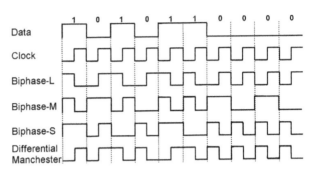

Fig. 5: Coding schemes suitable for the visible spectrum transmissions

All schemes mentioned in Fig. 5 keep the mean value stable for all possible data sequences. It makes the communication unobservable with the human eye. Of course, any modulation and configuration that keeps the mean value stable and that increases the bit rate to much more interesting values can be used e.g. MIMO (Multiple-Input Multiple-Output), [14].

2.2. Stability

Both the LEDs and the modulator have the tendency to change their parameters with the rising temperature and the frequency. The temperature problem is solved in the construction itself since the current source keeping the current values stable is used. But the frequency stability is much more complicated. The current gain of the transistors decreases with the increasing frequency. Thus, the integrated compensation is difficult to achieve, especially for different lights at the modulator output. As for the coding schemes shown in Fig. 5, the bounded range of frequencies is used. Then the modulator has to keep the light intensity stable for at least the used frequency range.

2.3. Energy Efficiency

In the above-mentioned application the power consumption of the used LEDs is higher. It is therefore necessary to minimize the system power consumption because the main advantage of the LEDs in terms of the energy consumption needs to be kept. The power dissipation of the modulator will also be associated with the required size of a cooler.

3. Construction

The block diagram of the proposed modulator is shown in the Fig. 6.

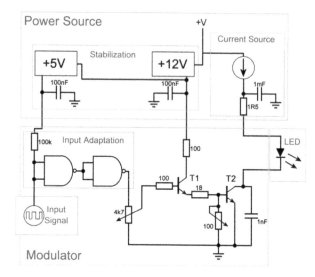

Fig. 6: Modulator block diagram.

The proposed modulator is described in the following part of the paper in accordance with the above-mentioned requirements and the block diagram.

3.1. Power Source

The energy is supplied by a single common power supply powering the LED and the modulator simultaneously. Thus, the whole modulator can be easily hidden inside any light without the need of any additional power source while maintaining the sufficiently high voltage level.

To ensure the stable output power, the LEDs are powered by an adjustable current source. The connection is extended by a capacitor keeping the current source under the load. This solution also conserves the useless energy when the light is OFF, and it releases it when the light is ON. It means that the light intensity is maintained despite the significant reduction of the LEDs activity time without increasing the current of the power source. This feature is also useful in the event of the input signal failure as the connected light cannot be overloaded with high current. However, this advantage may disappear if the LEDs lights have large additional internal resistors.

3.2. Control Circuit

The input circuit is adapted to the TTL logic to ensure stable reference for all performed measurements. And it can be easily replaced by a circuit with different parameters.

A key part of the modulator is a pair of bipolar transistors of high frequency and of high current capability. It is especially T2 that is very important and its type C2078 was chosen after several experiments. The operation points of both transistors are adjustable for maximum adaptability in the frequency and the current spectrum. This feature allows keeping both transistors right on the saturation limit. Otherwise, the transistors cannot open enough and due to this voltage drop limits the current flow.

Conversely, with too high saturation, the transistors are not able to close on time and the LEDs remain constantly lit. It is important for high frequencies to keep the switching times as short as possible, so the bases of both transistors are connected to the ground via resistors. The residual energy in the parasitic capacitances is immediately drained into the ground and the transistors can respond much faster.

The last part of the control circuit description deals with the LEDs parasitic capacity compensation. If the leading edge of the signal is too steep, some backswings in the transmitted signal can be experienced. It is caused by LEDs capacity and it can lead to significant signal degradation. Hence, the compensation capacitor is placed between the collector and the emitter of the T2 transistor. This capacitor effectively reduces the signal backswings, but, on the other hand, it, unfortunately, also limits the maximum operating frequency.

4. Measurement

The measurements were carried out on various types of LEDs used for illumination and on various ranges of frequencies. The first LED light was composed of a huge number of white SMD LEDs (shown in Fig. 1). Second light source was an RGB LED strip (Fig. 2). Thanks to the separation into different wavelengths, communication is possible on multiple wavelengths simultaneously. Then, the required communication wavelength can be easily chosen by an appropriate optical filter on the receiver side.

However, connection of the RGB LED strips was complemented by the series resistors of different values for the 12 V power source compensation. But these resistors are useful for the voltage control only. The last two lights are mainly designed for exterior lighting. The first outdoor fixture represents the streetlight with the total power of over 60 W. The other outdoor light is the 20 W LED replacement of a halogen reflector. Both lights are shown in Fig. 7.

Fig. 7: Outdoor light sources.

A closer look to the outdoor light sources (Fig. 8) shows the construction of the streetlight and of the 20 W LED chip. Due to the limited voltage range of the current source there was only one LED block used for the measurement of the streetlight.

Fig. 8: Outdoor light internals (street light-left, 20 W chip-right).

4.1. Capacitive Load Compensation

Fig. 9 shows the oscilloscope view screen for the T2 Collector-Emitter voltage (lower part) and the Photodetector output voltage (upper part) of the LED strip for the input frequency of 220 kHz without a compensation capacitor.

When the transistor is turned on, the voltage between the collector and the emitter (U_{CE}) drops nearly to zero and the LEDs begin to emit light and illuminate the surface of the photodetector (THORLABS PDA100A-EC). In the opposite case, when the transistor is turned off, voltage U_{CE} rises and stops the current flow. If this case is looked at more precisely (Fig. 10), a large distortion in the waveform can be seen. At this moment both the delayed turn-off time with the distortion of the light intensity as well as the U_{CE} waveform can be seen. This distortion is problematic at higher frequencies because it causes some visible changes in the light intensity. The compensation

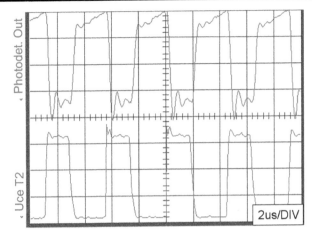

Fig. 9: Signal view on oscilloscope view screen.

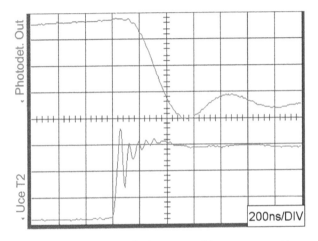

Fig. 10: Transistor turn OFF process without compensation.

for communication via the visible spectrum is necessary even at the cost of longer response times between switching off and on. In Fig. 11 there is a waveform with 3 nF compensation capacitor.

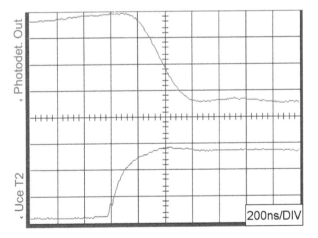

Fig. 11: Transistor turn OFF process with 3 nF compensation.

Fig. 11 shows the LED light mentioned in Fig. 1 (without serial resistances in its connection). It can be noticed that the distortions were much higher than in Fig. 9.

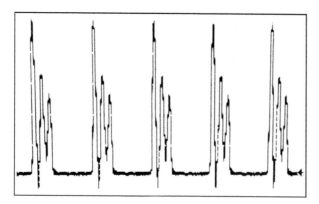

Fig. 12: U_{CE} waveform on T2 without serial resistors and compensation.

In this case the distortion of the transmitted signal is too high to ensure its clear detection. In the worst case the detected signal could be fragmented into several parts.

4.2. Frequency Response

Two parameters, the received signal amplitude at the photodetector output and the light intensity of the emitted light, were monitored during the frequency response measurement. The used photodetector has the bandwidth limitation at 2.4 MHz. Thus, the signal amplitude above this frequency is used for the detection of the optical signal presence in the emitted light only. Fig. 13 shows the results of LED light on the operating frequencies from 100 kHz to 3 MHz. In this case,

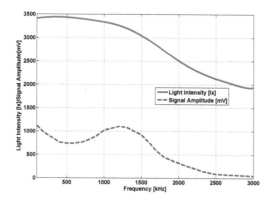

Fig. 13: LED light frequency characteristics ($I = 360$ mA $+V = 40$ V).

light intensity is stable at frequencies of up to 1 MHz. Then the light intensity starts to fade slowly. This is caused by the decreasing gain of the modulator. The communication signal is detectable even at frequencies

of around 3 MHz. With regard to the fact that the operating point is adjustable, the light intensity can even be kept in higher frequencies. This case is shown in Fig. 14 where two different operating points are set for the RGB LED strip. Communication can then con-

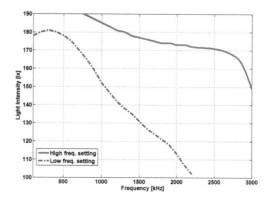

Fig. 14: LED strip frequency characteristics for two different setting.

tinue without the light fading even at frequencies of up to 2.8 MHz. However, this high frequency setting does not work at lower frequencies due to the higher saturation and the longer response times. Thus, for the practical use the working frequencies have to be considered and the operating point of the modulator has to be set. For the Differential Manchester, only a small part of the measured frequency spectrum is then needed. The above-mentioned lights were constructed from small LEDs. But at present much more powerful LEDs in streetlight have to be taken into account. As

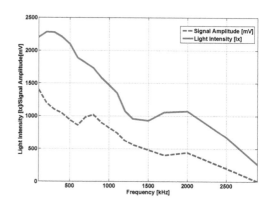

Fig. 15: Streetlight frequency characteristics

we can see in Fig. 15 the values are much more uneven in comparison with the low power LEDs (Fig. 13 and Fig. 14). To maintain the stable light intensity is much more difficult event with manual adjusting of the operating point. On the other hand, during the test the communication part of the signal worked even under these adverse circumstances at frequencies of around

2 MHz. Due to the loss of the light intensity and the distortion of the output signal the system limit at frequencies of around 1 MHz can be considered.

The results for the halogen lamp replacement with a 20 W LED chip are in Fig. 16. The light intensity for frequencies of up to 1.6 MHz is much more uniform compared to the streetlight. The significant increase in the light intensity at 2 MHz was very problematic to compensate and it could even be observable with the naked eye during the measurement. The usable communication frequencies are therefore limited to 1.6 MHz.

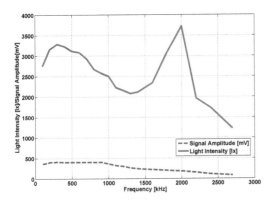

Fig. 16: 20 W LED chip frequency characteristics.

5. Conclusion

With respect to the measured values it can be confirmed that the applicable frequency decreases simultaneously with the increasing surface area of the used LEDs. The uniformity of the light intensity is also much better for smaller LEDs solutions.

Despite the communication functionality of the power LEDs at higher frequencies, the fluctuations of the light intensity can sometimes be observable and they therefore limit the usable frequency range. According to IEEE 802.15.7, the defined frequency for PHY1 [13], [15], (high power applications with OOK) is only 200 kHz, which is far below the achieved values.

The frequency limit for this modulator solution is 3 MHz, which is within the intended range. The main objectives of the construction were its low cost as well as its powering by a single power source. To properly evaluate this phenomenon as a whole, the parameters of the used LED lights as well as of the used photodetector have to be taken into account. The main limitation of this modulator is its output voltage, which is limited to 40 V, and it therefore does not allow connecting all the 3 blocks of the used streetlight.

If we take a look at some high-power LEDs datasheets, their rise-time and fall-time values can sometimes be seen. The normal values are around 100 nanoseconds and thus the current modulator is not limited by the LEDs response times.

The main problem with the mobile Free-Space-Optical communication is caused by the used photodetector. Because of the necessary sensitivity the photodetector bandwidth is limited. This phenomenon could also be observed during the measurement when the values measured by the photodetector declined despite the obvious presence of the output signal.

Acknowledgment

This article was created with the active support of the Ministry of Education of the Czech Republic within the projects no. SP2013/88, SP2013/69, SP2014/77 and SP2014/147 of VSB–Technical University of Ostrava. This article was supported by the projects no. VG20102015053 and TA03020439. The research has been partially supported by the project no. CZ.1.07/2.3.00/20.0217 "The development of Excellence of the Telecommunication Research Team in Relation to International Cooperation" within the frame of the operation programme "Education for Competitiveness" financed by the Structural Funds and from the state budget of the Czech Republic.

References

[1] LITTLE, T. D. C., P. DIB, K. SHAH, N. BARRAFORD and B. GALLAGHER. Using LED Lighting for Ubiquitous Indoor Wireless Networking. In: *4th IEEE International Conference on Wireless & Mobile Computing, Networking and Communication: WiMob 2008*. Avignon: IEEE, 2008, pp. 373–378. ISBN 978-0-7695-3393-3. DOI: 10.1109/WiMob.20008.57.

[2] AKELLA, J., Ch. LIU, D. PARTYKA, M. YUKSEL, S. KALYANARAMAN and Partha DUTTA. Building Blocks for Mobile Free-Space-Optical Networks. In: *Second IFIP International Conference on Wireless and Optical Communications Networks: WOCN 2005*. Dubai: IEEE, 2005, pp. 164–168. ISBN 0-7803-9019-9. DOI: 10.1109/WOCN.2005.1436011.

[3] DAYONG, Z., P. G. LOPRESTI and H. H. REFAI. Enlargement of Beam Coverage in FSO Mobile Network. *Journal of Lightwave Technology*. 2011, vol. 29, iss. 10, pp. 1583–1589. ISSN 0733-8724. DOI: 10.1109/JLT.2011.2134069.

[4] MIHAESCU, A. and P. BESNARD. Indoor wireless optical communications. In: *8th International Conference on Communications (COMM), 2010.* Bucharest: IEEE, 2010, pp. 359–362. ISBN 978-1-4244-6360-2. DOI: 10.1109/ICCOMM.2010.5509017.

[5] LUCACIU, R., A. MIHAESCU and C. VLADEANU. Dynamic OCDMA coding for indoor wireless optical communications. In: *8th International Conference on Communications (COMM), 2010.* Bucharest: IEEE, 2010, pp. 347–350. ISBN 978-1-4244-6360-2. DOI: 10.1109/ICCOMM.2010.5509009.

[6] GRUBOR, J., S. Ch. J. LEE, K.-D. LANGER, T. KOONEN and J. W. WALEWSKI. Wireless High-Speed Data Transmission with Phosphorescent White-Light LEDs. In: *Optical Communication, 2007 33rd European Conference and exhibition of: Post-Deadline Papers.* Berlin: IEEE, 2007, pp. 1–2. ISBN 978-3-8007-3059-9.

[7] DONATI, S. *Photodetectors: Devices, Circuits, and Applications.* Upper Saddle River, NJ: Prentice Hall, 2000. ISBN 01-302-0337-8.

[8] MIRVAKILI, A. and V. J. KOOMSON. High efficiency LED driver design for concurrent data transmission and PWM dimming control for indoor visible light communication. In: *Photonics Society Summer Topical Meeting Series, 2012 IEEE.* Seattle: IEEE, 2012, pp. 132–133. ISBN 978-1-4577-1526-6. DOI: 10.1109/PHOSST.2012.6280761.

[9] CHOI, S. New Type of White-light LED Lighting for Illumination and Optical Wireless Communication under Obstacles. *Journal of the Optical Society of Korea.* 2012, vol. 16, iss. 3, pp. 203–209. ISSN 1226-4776. DOI: 10.3807/JOSK.2012.16.3.203.

[10] XIAOXUE, M., Kyujin LEE and Kyesan LEE. Appropriate modulation scheme for visible light communication systems considering illumination. *Electronics Letters.* 2012, vol. 48, iss. 18. pp. 1137–1139. ISSN 0013-5194. DOI: 10.1049/el.2012.2195.

[11] WANG, J., N. ZOU, D. WANG, K. IRIE, Z. IHA and Y. NAMIHIRA. Experimental study on visible light communication based on LED. *The Journal of China Universities of Posts and Telecommunications.* 2012, vol. 19, supp. 2. pp. 197–200. ISSN 1005-8885. DOI: 10.1016/S1005-8885(11)60422-6.

[12] PISEK, E., S. RAJAGOPAL and S. ABU-SURRA. Gigabit rate mobile connectivity through visible light communication. In: *IEEE International Conference on Communications (ICC), 2012.* Ottawa: IEEE, 2012, pp. 3122–3127. ISBN 978-1-4577-2052-9, ISSN 1550-3607. DOI: 10.1109/ICC.2012.6363739.

[13] ITU-I. *802.15.7.: Short-Range Wireless Optical Communication Using Visible Light* [online]. 2011. Avaiable at: http://www.ieee802.org/15/pub/TG7.html.

[14] MESLEH, R., R. MEHMOOD, H. ELGALA and H. HAAS. Indoor MIMO Optical Wireless Communication Using Spatial Modulation. In: *IEEE International Conference on Communications (ICC), 2010.* Cape Town: IEEE, 2010, pp. 1–5. ISBN 978-1-4244-6402-9, ISSN 1550-3607. DOI: 10.1109/ICC.2010.5502062.

[15] ROBERTS, Richard D., Sridhar RAJAGOPAL and Sang-Kyu LIM. IEEE 802.15.7 physical layer summary. In: *GLOBECOM Workshops (GC Wkshps).* Houston: IEEE, 2011, pp.772–776. ISBN 978-1-4673-0039-1. DOI: 10.1109/GLOCOMW.2011.6162558.

About Authors

Stanislav HEJDUK was born in Ostrava, Czech Republic, in November 1985. He received his M.Sc. degree in telecommunication technologies from VSB–Technical University of Ostrava, in 2010. After that he became a postgradual student of Communication Technologies at the VSB–Technical University of Ostrava, department of Telecommunication. His research focuses on transmitters for Mobile Free-Space Optical Communications.

Karel WITAS was born in Frydek-Mistek, 1975. He received his M.Sc. degree in electrical engineering from VSB–Technical University of Ostrava, in 1998. He began his career in 2000 working on special test equipment for semiconductor devices evaluation at the SCG Czech Design Center, ON Semiconductor, Roznov p. Radhostem. In 2009, he joined the team of the Dept. of Telecommunication, VSB–Technical University of Ostrava, developing optical fiber sensors. His research interests include sub-nanoseconds pulse generators, noise free amplifiers and ultra-low current converters.

Jan LATAL was born in Prostejov. In 2006 he was awarded his B.Sc. degree at VSB–Technical University of Ostrava, Faculty of Electrical Engineering and Computer Science, Department of Electronics and Telecommunications. He was awarded his M.Sc.

degree at VSB–Technical University of Ostrava, Faculty of Electrical Engineering and Computer Science, Department of Telecommunications in 2008. He is currently Ph.D. student, and he works in the field of Wireless Optical Communications, Optical Communications and Distributed Temperature Sensing Systems. He is a member of SPIE and IEEE.

Jan VITASEK was born in Opava. In 2009 he finished M.Sc. study at Brno University of Technology, Faculty of Electrical Engineering and Communication. In present time he is Ph.D. student at Department of Telecommunications, VSB–Technical University of Ostrava. His interests are Free Space Optics and indoor Free Space Optics networks. He is a member of SPIE.

Jiri BOCHEZA was born in Zlin, Czech Republic, 27 July 1985. He received his M.Sc. degree in telecommunication technologies from VSB–Technical University of Ostrava, in 2010. After that he became a postgradual student of Communication Technologies at the VSB-TU Ostrava, Department of Telecommunications. His research focuses on optoelectronics and application of conductive polymers in fiber optics systems. In 2012 he started working at MESIT

with specialization on microprocessors and FPGAs programming.

Vladimir VASINEK was born in Ostrava. In 1980 - he graduated at the Science Faculty of the Palacky University, branch - Physics with specialization in Optoelectronics, RNDr. he obtained at the Science Faculty of the Palacky University at branch Applied Electronics, scientific degree Ph.D. he obtained in the year 1989 at branch Quantum Electronics and Optics, he became an associate professor in 1994 at branch Applied Physics, he is a professor of Electronics and Communication Science since 2007 and he works at this branch at the Department of Telecommunications of the Faculty of Electrical Engineering and Computer Science. His research work is dedicated to optical communications, optical fibers, optoelectronics, optical measurements, optical networks projecting, fiber optic sensors, MW access networks. He is a member of many societies – OSA, SPIE, EOS, IMEKO, Czech Photonics Society, he is a chairman of Ph.D. board at the VSB–Technical University of Ostrava, and he was a member of many boards for habilitation and professor appointment.

5

Small Cell Network Topology Comparison

Jan OPPOLZER, Robert BESTAK

Department of Telecommunication Engineering, Faculty of Electrical Engineering,
Czech Technical University in Prague, Technicka 2, 166 27 Prague, Czech Republic

oppoljan@fel.cvut.cz, robert.bestak@fel.cvut.cz

Abstract. *One of the essential problems in a mobile network with small cells is that there is only a limited number of Physical Cell Identifiers (PCIs) available. Due to this fact, operators face the inevitable need for reusing PCIs. In our contribution, we are dealing with a PCI assignment to Femtocell Access Points (FAPs) in three different topologies. The first model places FAPs randomly within the network while respecting overlapping defined. The second model places FAPs in a grid without other restrictions. The third model forms a grid as well, although buildings and roads are taken into account and FAPs are always inside buildings. The proposed models are compared and a conclusion is made based on simulation results.*

Keywords

Collision, confusion, femtocell, physical cell identifier, small cell, topology.

1. Introduction

Femtocells, also known as Femtocell Access Points (FAPs), are here for a few years yet. They are small, low-power and mainly low-cost personal or enterprise Base Stations (BSs) deployed by customers [1], not by operators as in case of macrocells, etc. Although FAPs are small, they are a big market worth $2,7 billion by 2017 [2].

Originally, FAPs were intended mainly for improving indoor coverage because poor coverage affects up to 30 % of businesses and 45 % of households [3]. Further reasons were enhancing Quality of Service (QoS) and network capacity as well as offering new services to customers and raise customer retention [1], [3].

Nowadays, FAPs and metrocells collectively called as "small cells", are used even to improve outdoor signal coverage in city centres and busy streets. For example, in Newcastle and Bristol, small cells are trail deployed and during the testing data transmission was three times faster compared to 3G network [4]. By 2016, small cells are expected to make up almost 90 % of all base stations [5]. Moreover, by 2016, small cells and Wi-Fi access points will carry up to 60 % of all mobile data traffic [6] which is a huge portion if we take into account the increase in mobile data usage.

Although small cells are a huge market, there are still some unresolved challenges. One of them is a Physical Cell Identifier (PCI) assignment mechanism. A PCI is composed of 168 unique groups each containing 3 identities which makes 504 identities in total [7]. Since every cell in the network need an identifier, this number is not sufficient and PCIs have to be reused which brings challenges, namely *i)* collision events and *ii)* confusion events.

A PCI collision means that neighbouring cells have identical identifier assigned. Such a problem produces interference which creates so-called coverage hole and none User Equipment (UE) is able to connect to any femtocell.

A PCI confusion arrives when a cell has more neighbours with the same identifier. In such a situation, when a handover should take place it will fail due to ambiguous destination where to transfer the connection [1], [3].

The aim of this paper is to develop and compare various topologies for small cell network simulations mainly dealing with PCI assignment techniques. Identifiers are assigned automatically, PCI collisions are completely avoided by scanning radio environment for neighbours' identifiers and PCI confusions are solved whenever occurred.

This paper is structured as follows. The second section briefly describes related works in this field of study which is not too wide yet. The third section is focused on three proposed topologies, their description, basic features and characteristics. The fourth section is devoted to simulations, comparing individual topologies and results. The fifth section summarizes the paper and outlines possible future work.

2.   Related Works

Nowadays, identifiers are usually assigned either manually by operators using network planning tools or automatically using random selection. However, neither method is efficient. The first method is costly, time-consuming and prone to human made errors. The second method is not reliable and might produce a confusion event or even worse a confusion event.

There is a number of articles focusing on PCI assignment techniques. For example, [8], [9], [10]. However, all those works are concerned about macrocell level only.

Authors in [8] are working with real 3G network from Vodafone Germany; however, 3G network with outdoor macrocells is far from 4G network with densely deployed small cells. In [9], handover measurements are utilized just to detect issues related to identifiers in macro and microcells. In another article [10], authors simulated very few BSs not representing future dense deployments.

In all honesty, we have really tried to find out any similar study trying to compare various topology models that deal with PCI assignment techniques, but we have not discovered any.

3.   Proposed Topologies

All the three proposed placements described later have a few common basic characteristics. There is always a single Macrocell Base Station (MBS) with circular coverage area under which all FAPs are deployed. For simplicity, all the FAPs have the same radius. To simulate various FAP densities (for example city centres on one hand and rural areas on the other hand), the number of FAPs generated within a topology is varying.

Although the Long Term Evolution (LTE) and LTE-Advanced (LTE-A) standards support up to 504 different PCIs, we have allowed only 480 of them at a maximum to be assigned in our simulation. The first reason behind this upper limit is that we would like to know whether a smaller portion of the identifiers is sufficient. The second reason is that other cells in a real network topology, such as macrocells, picocells, etc., require an identifier, too, so we have reserved at least a tiny PCI portion for those cells. And finally, the lower PCI range limit is required in order for the algorithm to converge and assign PCIs correctly.

FAPs need information about their neighbourhood (i.e. PCIs of neighbouring cells) whenever they are choosing an identifier in order to evade i) a PCI collision and ii) a PCI confusion.

Since FAPs have limited power, they can ask about neighbourhood only adjacent neighbours. However, this is not a sufficient amount of information when confusion events should be eliminated. To obtain data about unreachable neighbourhood in order to become aware of a greater part of the topology and evade a PCI confusion as mentioned, FAPs can employ neighbours as well simply by asking about their neighbourhood data. This is how a FAP can obtain information about neighbours multiple hops away. We term this as a hop count.

In all the three proposed topologies, a simulation works as follows. At first a MBS is generated. Then, depending on the topology selected, a defined number of FAPs is placed within the MBS area i) randomly, ii) in a precise grid, or iii) in a grid where FAPs are allowed to be placed only inside of buildings and forbidden outside.

Whenever a FAP is deployed, it scans radio environment for neighbouring cells. When the FAP has no neighbours we call it as a "standalone FAP" and such a FAP can select a PCI randomly. Alternatively, when neighbours are detected, the FAP selects such a PCI in order to avoid producing a PCI collision. After selecting a collision-free identifier, a bidirectional interface is established with detected neighbours for later usage. By establishing this interface a Neighbour Relation (NR) is set up and Neighbour Relation Tables (NRTs) containing lists of neighbouring PCIs are exchanged.

Now, a PCI confusion procedure check is launched. When a confusion event is discovered, a FAP that is confused by neighbours initiate a solving procedure. In our previous work, we have designed and implemented two techniques for solving confusion events, we call them "random method" and "smart method". Here, we deploy the mature one – smart method – which outperforms the other technique in terms of overhead introduced to the network.

Our "smart method" works as follows. When a FAP encounters a confusion event, it requests the involved FAPs (i.e. confusion producers) to report how many adjacent cells they have. After acquiring those numbers, the FAP with the fewest neighbours is chosen to reselect its PCI. Before a new PCI is chosen, the FAP scans radio environment (collision avoidance) and exchanges NRTs with neighbours up to 3 hops away (confusion avoidance). If the confusion event is still present, for example, when there are more than two confusion producers, this process is run again with remaining confusion producers.

Reselecting a PCI means that new NRs have to be established between neighbours and thus overhead is produced. Firstly, the FAP with a new PCI has to inform all its neighbours about this change. Secondly,

Tab. 1: Common simulation parameters.

Parameter	Value
MBS radius, r_{MBS}	564 m
MBS area, A_{MBS}	1 km^2
FAP radius, r_{FAP}	15 m
FAP count, N_{FAPs}	250–1500
PCI range	80–480
Hop count, N_h	3

Tab. 2: Random placement parameters.

Parameter	Value
FAP overlapping	$< 50\ \%$

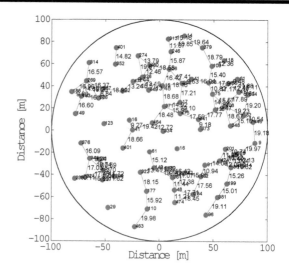

Fig. 1: Random placement demonstration.

the neighbours have to acknowledge this modification. When a FAP has n neighbours, this will eventually lead to $2n$ messages sent over the network.

Basic simulation parameters common to all topologies are stated in Tab. 1.

3.1. Random Placement

The first model is random placement which does not fully represent real conditions or a real topology even though it might be close enough by tweaking various parameters such as FAPs overlapping, etc.

In this model, FAPs are randomly placed within the MBS area using uniformly distributed pseudo-random numbers. Neighbouring FAPs can overlap each other; however, their mutual area is limited so scenarios where multiple FAPs are deployed at the same place (above each other) is eliminated. Overlapping and other parameters are stated in Tab. 2.

In Fig. 1, a demonstration of random placement is shown. Red dots represent individual FAPs. Blue lines between dots symbolise so-called NRs which means that those neighbours can communicate mutually and exchange information about neighbours including their PCIs stored in NRTs. Numbers next to red dots are PCIs assigned and numbers next to blue lines are euclidean distance between FAPs in metres.

3.2. Grid Placement #1

The second model in our comparison study is grid placement #1. It is the easiest topology where individual FAPs are deployed in a precise square grid under the area covered by a MBS. Although some spots might be left empty depending on the total number of FAPs deployed in the actual simulation. Grid placement #1 parameters are introduced in Tab. 3.

Tab. 3: Grid placement #1 parameters.

Parameter	Value
Vertical side of grid	10 m
Horizontal side of grid	10 m

Grid placement #1 demonstration is depicted in Fig. 2. The meaning of red dots, blue lines and numbers are the same as in the random placement demonstration. The figure is quite similar to random placement demonstration; however, it can be seen that FAPs are not placed randomly but in a precise grid. Also, it is obvious that in this demonstration there are more standalone FAPs than in random placement.

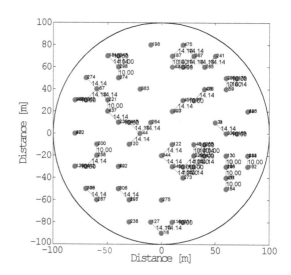

Fig. 2: Grid placement #1 demonstration.

Tab. 4: Grid placement #2 parameters.

Parameter	Value
Vertical side of grid	10 m
Horizontal side of grid	10 m
Flats in a building	10
Flat distribution	5×2 flats/building
Flat dimensions	10×10 m
Road width/height	10 m

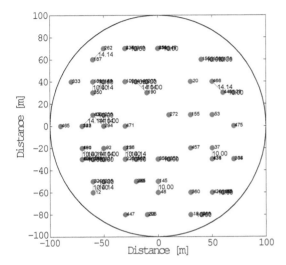

Fig. 3: Grid placement #2 demonstration.

3.3. Grid Placement #2

The third model, we have implemented for this comparison study, is grid placement #2 which is a variation on previous grid placement #1.

Area covered by a MBS is composed of single-floor rectangular buildings separated by roads. Every single building consists of flats arranged into a rectangular arrangement. Flats' and road dimensions as well as flats' distribution in buildings are the same throughout the whole topology. All the parameters are summarized in Tab. 4. And for simplicity, when a FAP is deployed, it might be placed only in the exact middle of a flat.

Figure 3 illustrates how this topology looks like. As this model is a variant of the previous one, it can be seen some similarities; however, separation of buildings by roads is very obvious at first sight. The meaning of dots, etc. is the same as in previous demonstrations.

4. Simulation Results

In Fig. 4, it can be seen that the absolute number of standalone FAPs (they have no neighbours) is not very varying in individual topologies. It is even more obvious in Fig. 5 where the number of standalone FAPs is expressed in percents of the whole topology. From these figures we can assume that all the proposed topologies are very similar eventually. The only difference seems to be in visual appearance of a particular model.

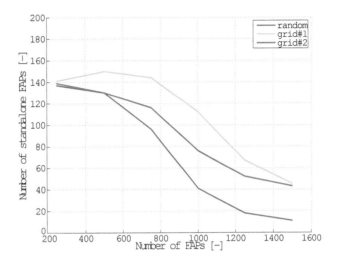

Fig. 4: Number of standalone FAPs (absolute values).

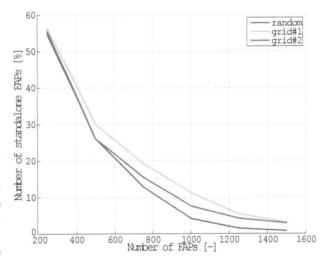

Fig. 5: Number of standalone FAPs (percents of the topology).

Figure 6 shows overhead introduced to the network while solving PCI confusion events. The overhead is counted in messages that have to be sent. This figure indicates that confusions are more common in random placement. Such a discovery is evident because FAPs in this model might be placed almost anywhere if they do not exceed allowed overlapping. However, in both grid topologies, there are more strict rules for placing FAPs. This means they can not be so close and it eventually leads to fewer confusion events.

Although grid #2 model topology experiences the fewest confusion events when only short PCI range is applied; however, with greater PCI range the differences are insignificant even when comparing to random placement as shown in Fig. 6.

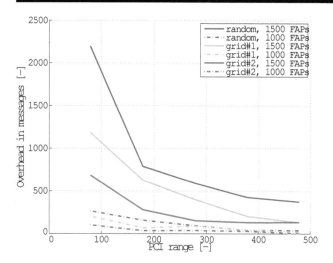

Fig. 6: Overhead caused by solving confusions events.

5.   Conclusion

In this paper, we have proposed three different topologies for small cell network simulations dealing mainly with PCI assignment techniques. It has been shown that there are no significant differences among those models, although the complexity of particular topologies are considerable.

From our simulation results, we can conclude that the easiest model to implement (random placement in this case) is the most suitable at the same time.

In the future, we are going to enhance our models further. For example, by enabling FAPs to have varying radius we get closer to a reality because this option could simulate different attenuation in separated buildings. Also, having more MBSs that partially cover the same area is another way how to get more real simulation results.

Acknowledgment

This research work has been supported by the Grant Agency of the Czech Technical University in Prague, grant no. SGS13/199/OHK3/3T/13.

References

[1] CHAMBERS, D. *Femtocell primer*. 2nd ed. United Kingdom: Lulu Com, 2010. ISBN 978-144-5744-346.

[2] TERAL, S. and R. WEBB. Small cell market forecast to hit \$2.7 billion by 2017. *Infonetics Research* [online]. 2013. Available at: http://www.infonetics.com/pr/2013/ 2H12-Small-Cell-Equipment-Market-Highlights. asp.

[3] ZHANG, J. and G. DE LA ROCHE. *Femtocells: Technologies and Deployment*. 2nd ed. Chichester: John Wiley, 2010. ISBN 978-0-470-74298-3.

[4] CURTIS, S. Virgin Media Business to offer "small cells as a service". *Techworld* [online]. 2012. Available at: http://news.techworld.com/networking/3400674/ virgin-media-business-to-offer-small\ -cells-as-a-service/.

[5] DUFFY, D. Small Cells to Make Up Almost 90% of All Base Stations by 2016. *Informa Telecoms & Media* [online]. 2012. Available at: http://www.smallcellforum.org/ newsstory-small-cells-to-make-up-almost\ -90-percent-of-all-base-stations-by-2016.

[6] CURTIS, S. Small cells and WiFi to carry 60% of mobile traffic by 2016. *Techworld* [online]. 2012. Available at: http://news.techworld.com/networking/3362145/ small-cells-and-wifi-to-carry-60-of\ -mobile-traffic-by-2016.

[7] 3GPP 36.211. *Evolved Universal Terrestrial Radio Access (E-UTRA); Physical channels and modulation*. 3GPP, 2013. Available at: http://www. 3gpp.org/ftp/Specs/html-info/36211.htm.

[8] BANDH, T., G. CARLE and H. SANNECK. Graph Coloring Based Physical-Cell-ID Assignment for LTE networks. In: *Proceedings of the 2009 ACM International Wireless Communications and Mobile Computing Conference, IWCMC*. New York: ACM Press, 2009, pp. 116–120. ISBN 978-160558569-7. DOI: 10.1145/1582379.1582406.

[9] AMIRIJOO, M., P. FRENGER, F. GUNNARSSON, H. KALLIN, J. MOE and K. ZETTERBERG. Neighbor Cell Relation List and Physical Cell Identity Self-Organization in LTE. In: *ICC Workshops '08. IEEE International Conference on Communications Workshops, 2008*. Beijing: IEEE, 2008, pp. 37–41. ISBN 978-1-4244-2052-0. DOI: 10.1109/ICCW.2008.12.

[10] JAESEUBG, S., M. TIEJUN and P. PETER. Towards Automated Verification of Autonomous Networks: A Case Study in Self-Configuration. In: *8th IEEE International Conference on Pervasive Computing and Communications Workshops: PERCOM Workshops 2010*. Mannheim: IEEE, 2010, pp. 582–587. ISBN 978-1-4244-6605-4. DOI: 10.1109/PERCOMW.2010.5470504.

About Authors

Jan OPPOLZER received his bachelor's (2009) and master's (2011) degrees from the Czech Technical University in Prague, Faculty of Electrical Engineering. In 2011, he has joined the Department of Telecommunication Engineering as a Ph.D. student. His research interests include future mobile networks with small cells, Physical Cell Identifier assignment methods, Self-Organizing Networks and related topics.

Robert BESTAK obtained a Ph.D. degree in Computer Science from ENST Paris, France (2003) and a MSc. degree in Telecommunications from Czech Technical University in Prague, CTU (1999). Since 2004, he has been an Assistant Professor at Department of Telecommunication Engineering, Faculty of Electrical Engineering (FEE). His research interests include radio resource management techniques in HSPA/LTE, cognitive networks and femtocells.

6

Adaptable System Increasing the Transmission Speed and Reliability in Packet Network by Optimizing Delay

Zbynek KOCUR, Peter MACEJKO, Petr CHLUMSKY, Jiri VODRAZKA, Ondrej VONDROUS

Department of Telecommunication Engineering, Faculty of Electrical Engineering, Czech Technical University in Prague, Technicka 2, 166 27, Prague, Czech Republic

zbynek.kocur@fel.cvut.cz, peter.macejko@fel.cvut.cz, chlumpet@fel.cvut.cz, vodrazka@fel.cvut.cz, vondrond@fel.cvut.cz

Abstract. *There is a great diversity in the transmission technologies in current data networks. Individual technologies are in most cases incompatible at physical and partially also at the link layer of the reference ISO/OSI model. Network compatibility, as the ability to transmit data, is realizable through the third layer, which is able to guarantee the operation of the different devices across their technological differences. The proposed inverse packet multiplexer addresses increase of the speed and reliability of packet transmission to the third layer, and at the same time it increases the stability of the data communication by the regulation of the delay value during the transmission. This article presents implementation of a communication system and its verification in real conditions. The conclusion compares the strengths and weaknesses of the proposed control system.*

Keywords

Delay regulator, inverse packet multiplex, multipath data transmission, packet network.

1. Introduction

The disadvantage of current solutions for the inverse multiplexing (an inverse multiplexer allows a fast data stream to be broken into multiple lower data rate communication links) is the uncoordinated sorting of packets to different transmission paths. Consequently, this can lead to uncontrolled growth of transmission delay [8] and/or a temporary increase of the packet loss and instability of communication with upper layer protocols, including congestion of network elements and connections collapse.

This problem is solved by the adaptable system for increasing the speed and reliability of data transmission in a packet network with the delay optimization using the packet regulator.

The advantage of the proposed solution is in the possibility to increase transfer speed and reliability by transmitting packets over multiple different paths which branches immediately after the placement queue [2]. The communication system is designed to allow the association of more transmission paths (typically from two to eight) with mutually different transmission speeds, even implemented on completely different physical channels. The system has the capability of intelligent handling of the transmitted data; according to the characteristics of transmission paths and the self-exclusion of one or more transmission paths in case of failure or increased packet loss over the allowable limit, system controls the sorting of packets in the transmission paths through the transmission delay regulator. With the aid of injection and detection of the control information in the transmission path the packet delay is examined. Based on this, the regulator controls the intensity of the packets sending to network interfaces.

Regulator sets the amount of transmitted data, optimal for the corresponding channel, according to the measured values of the delay. At the same time the regulator allocates appropriate contents of the input packet buffer. Number of packets in the input packet buffer is set to the amount of data that all network interfaces are currently able to transfer. Packets overflowing capacity of input packet buffer are not stored and not transmitted, thus, protects the interface, transmission channel and the packet network against overload. This behaviour results in optimizing delays in transmission.

The proposed system was implemented and tested in a cellular network using two independent channels through various operators. The results verified the correct function of the proposed algorithms and gave the basis for further optimization for different network scenarios.

The proposed solution is effective in solving communication infrastructure for mobile networks in disaster management [5].

2.   Transmission System

The basic idea of the system design is to create the most stable data channel in an environment with variable transmission parameters. Typically, the environment of mobile data networks or networks with high working load. The proposed system is adapted for the transmission of IP communication, especially TCP [7] and UDP [6] protocols.

Basic principle diagram is shown in Fig. 1. Packets entering the transmission system from the network **A** are, based on the current state of the communication lines between the inverse packet multiplexers, distributed into the communication lines in such a way to prevent the congestion and the deterioration of the transmission parameters. Once the packets are transmitted over the networks from one part of the system to the other, they are restored into its original form and sent to the network **B**. This process also works in reverse, so is made a fully transparent connection.

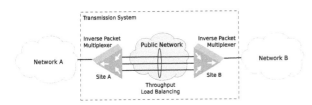

Fig. 1: The basic scheme.

Packet transmission between systems A and B is realized via our own communication protocol that uses UDP and which cares about establishing, termination and supervision of different communication channels over the assembled connection. The protocol is using the 4-byte header, which is located behind the UDP header. This header appears as a normal payload for common network devices. More detailed description of this protocol is beyond the scope of this article.

3.   Packet Regulator

The heart of the system is a packet (polyline) regulator, which is shown in Fig. 2 labeled as CU (Control Unit). CU controls packet splitter and filters on the inputs to each interfaces, and thus reduces the amount of packets that enter into them. Outgoing packets are supplemented by special information before leaving the system. This information is used on the receiver side to rebuild the original data stream.

Flow control can be implemented in several ways. This article will describe the regulation of passing packets using the control polyline curve. Appropriate additions of packet filter settings, depending on the change of delay per channel, are defined by this curve. An example of one possible polyline is shown in Fig. 3.

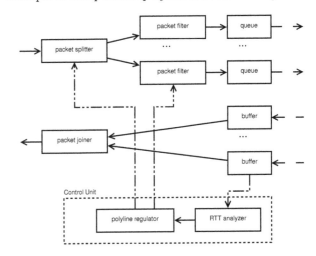

Fig. 2: Packet regulator diagram.

3.1.   Function of the Polyline Curve

The success of regulation is highly dependent on the choice of control polyline. This choice must be subordinated to the type of traffic (TCP, UDP), communication technology of the interface (GPRS, EDGE, UMTS, Ethernet, etc.) and also to the traffic load of the transmission network. Mobile technologies have delay parameter generally higher than Ethernet, so the overall response of the system is much less sensitive to regulation.

Definition of the polyline is based on the analysis of the transmission parameters of the communication channel [4]. In addition to the definition of limit values for transmission speed, delay, or packet loss at the time of measurement, it is necessary to know the progressions of these variables over time. Very important is the knowledge of the relative rate of change in throughput and delay, which are very important for maintaining optimal system dynamics. All these parameters can be obtained by using commonly available tools (ping, Iperf, etc.) [3] and thus formulate the polyline curve.

Typical appearance of the control polyline is shown in Fig. 3. On the Y-axis is plotted the gain control variable, in this case ΔTP, which is added to the current value of the size of the packet filter. The X-axis is indicative of the deviation of regulation from the desired value. In case of the mobile network (GPRS, EDGE, UMTS), where there is a strong dependence on the current RTT (Round-Trip Time) on the transmission speed, is suitable for controlling precisely the RTT. The periodical measurement shown that for wired networks, such as Ethernet or xDSL technology, is preferable to use the packet loss as controlling parameter.

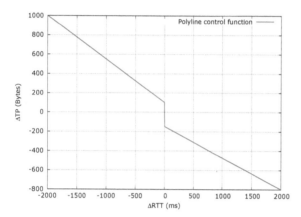

Fig. 3: Example of the polyline curve.

In practice has proven very effective to define a curve very conservatively for mobile networks, mainly due to high transport delays, which significantly reduces the response by regulatory intervention. Too drastic reduction transmission speeds result in significant fluctuations in the packet stream within a controlled channel. This phenomenon is particularly evident in the TCP protocol, which is due to own self-regulatory mechanism very sensitive for this type of control.

3.2. Round-Trip Time Measurement

Due to the significant variation of the delay parameter in mobile networks is necessary to perform straightening prior to its use for the regulation. If the regulation was implemented without smoothed delay, there would be a step changes in packet filter settings and thereby inadvertently increase of the error rate in regulated data channel. For smoothing can be used a variety of methods. One of these is the calculation of smooth TCP RTT taken from the TCP protocol [1].

The equation has the following form:

$$smtRTT_i = \alpha \times smtRTT_{i-1} + (1 - \alpha) \times actRTT_i. \quad (1)$$

The variables used in the pseudocode are defined as follows:

- $smtRTT$ - smoothed round trip time,

- $actRTT$ - actual round trip time,

- α - constant weighting factor ($0 \leq \alpha < 1$).

3.3. Link State Information Measurement

To effectively control the amount of transmitted packets by different interfaces is necessary to perform periodic collection of information about the current state of the interfaces. For this activity was designed the following algorithm, which is described as the Pseudocode 1 (Fig. 4). Shown pseudocode is aimed at monitoring the round trip time value. Loss rate is not taken into account.

Each side of the transmission system periodically sends monitoring packets through all available interfaces. These monitoring packets detect current round trip time and packet loss for the interface and the direction of communication (uplink, downlink). Based on the results of paths measurement, which is used in polyline control function, appropriate coefficients for regulatory interventions of packet filters are found.

For effective control, it is necessary maximize the rate of regulation packets sending. According to the practical measurement should be time between regulation packets at least 2 *times* smaller than the average RTT on the testing network. This requirement is easily achievable for fixed networks. Mobile networks are, due to lower throughput and higher delay, very sensitive to the amount and rate of monitoring packets.

Typical examples are GPRS/EDGE technologies, which can not transmit monitoring packets with such frequency as to be in UMTS or LTE. Too much monitoring packets could utilize the transmission channel so much that it would no longer be able to transfer any user data. Therefore, the time between monitoring packets is in mobile networks higher or equal than the average RTT of the channel. This situation must be taken into consideration when designing the control polyline function.

Monitoring and data packets are transmitted together. Monitoring packets are transmitted even if there is no request of data transfer from the user. In order to measure the individual communication routes as accurate as possible, monitoring packets has a higher priority than data packets. Packet filters actualization is performed with each received monitoring packet. The entire process including the packet filter setting is described in the Pseudocode 1 (Fig. 4).

1: **for** each received *monitoring* packet p on each interface i **do**
2:     $smtRTT_{p,i} \leftarrow f(actRTT_{p,i})$, $actRTT_{p,i} \in$ received monitoring packets;
3:     $\Delta RTT_{p,i} \leftarrow smtRTT_{p,i} - reqRTT_{p,i}$;
4:     $\Delta TP_{p,i} \leftarrow f(\Delta RTT_{p,i})$, $\Delta RTT_{p,i} \in$ polyline control function;
5:     $maxSize_{p,i} \leftarrow maxSize_{p,i} + \Delta TP_{p,i}$;
6: **end for**

Fig. 4: Pseudocode 1 - Link state algorithm.

The variables used in the pseudocode are defined as follows:

- $reqRTT$ - requested round trip time,

- $smtRTT$ - smoothed round trip time,

- $actRTT$ - actual round trip time,

- ΔRTT - increment of round trip time,

- ΔTP - increment of data in bytes,

- $maxSize$ - maximum amount of data in bytes which is allowed to send through interface.

3.4. Packet Handling

Classifying packets into individual interfaces according to the current state of the communication lines is going through the modified round-robin algorithm. The algorithm itself is described in the Pseudocode 2 (Fig. 5).

```
1:  for every incoming data packet do
2:      refresh the maxSize variable at all interfaces;
3:      load the packet;
4:      curIf ← ((lastIf + 1) mod maxIf)
5:      while curIf ≠ lastIf do
6:          if packetSize ≤ maxSize_curIf then
7:              maxSize_curIf ← maxSize_curIf − packetSize;
8:              lastIf ← curIf;
9:              return Send the packet;
10:         end if
11:         curIf ← ((curIf + 1) mod maxIf);
12:     end while
13:     return Discard the packet;
14: end for
```

Fig. 5: Pseudocode 2 - Packets distribution for each interface.

Variables used in pseudocode have the following meaning:

- $curIf$ - number of the current interface,

- $lastIf$ - number of the last used interface,

- $maxIf$ - the maximum number of interfaces,

- $packetSize$ - current amount of data in bytes for sending through the interface.

Subsequent packets composition received at the other end of the transmission route is going according to the algorithm, which is described in the Pseudocode 3 (Fig. 6).

The algorithm describes packets receiving on all available interfaces and their processing before sending it to the destination network.

The variables used in the pseudocode are defined as follows:

- $packetNum$ - number of the incoming packet (from the packet header),

- $lastNum$ - number of the last sent packet.

```
1:  for every incoming data packet do
2:      if packetNum ≤ lastNum then
3:          return Drop packet
4:      else if packetNum = lastNum + 1 then
5:          lastNum ← lastNum + 1;
6:          Send a packet to output;
7:      else
8:          Store packet in buffer;
9:      end if
10:     while (lastNum + 1) is in buffer do
11:         Pop packet from buffer
12:         lastNum ← lastNum + 1;
13:         Send a packet to output;
14:     end while
15: end for
```

Fig. 6: Pseudocode 3 - Incomings packets joining.

4. Real Measurement

The proposed transmission system was validated in mobile networks of operators Telefonica O2 CZ and T-Mobile CZ. Iperf application in TCP mode was used. Data were uploaded from the user to the server on the Internet. As data terminal we used embedded system based on Intel Atom (Z510, 512MB RAM) and with Linux OS (Voyage 0.8.0). Data terminals were at the same location during the entire test. The measurement lasted for one hour, the presented figures demonstrate the most interesting parts of the measurement. The transmission system used two UMTS modems Cinterion PH8, one of them was connected to O2 CZ and another in T-Mobile CZ. Before testing transmission speed of proposed system there were tests of each channel separately. Results of these initial tests are in Tab. 1.

Tab. 1: Results of the TCP uplink measurement at unloaded mobile network.

Parameter	Channel 0 Telefonica O2 CZ	Channel 1 T-Mobile CZ
Throughput	1.5 Mbps ± 230 kbps	1.8 Mbps ± 260 kbps
Round trip time	95 ms ± 40 ms	72 ms ± 20 ms
3G technology type	HSUPA	HSUPA
BCCH	-58 dBm	-67 dBm
CNR	-3.5	-4
Measurement location	Technicka 2, 166 27 Praha 6	

Tab. 2: Transmission system parameters.

Parameter	Value
Channel 0 information	UMTS, Telefonica O2 CZ
Channel 1 information	UMTS, T-Mobile CZ
Requested RTT	100 ms
RTT check interval	400 ms
RTT packet size	80 Bytes
Weighting factor α	0.8
Polyline ΔTP coefficients	[1000, 1000, 0, -1000, -1000] Bytes
Polyline ΔRTT coefficients	[-2000, -0.030, 0, 1, 2000] ms
Measurement location	Technicka 2, 166 27 Praha 6
Measurement time	27.08.2012 from 19:30:00 to 19:32:00

For measurement of the proposed transmission system configuration parameters listed in Tab. 2 were chosen. Parameters were chosen with regard to the demonstration of the positive and negative characteristics of the proposed system and the regulator.

Mobile networks parameters from the test time are listed in Tab. 3. Similarly as in the previous test, both data terminals were in the same place and they did not move.

Tab. 3: Mobile networks parameters.

Parameter	Telefonica O2 CZ	T-Mobile CZ
3G technology type	HSUPA	HSUPA
BCCH	-58 dBm	-67 dBm
CNR	-3.5	-4
Measurement location	Technicka 2, 166 27 Praha 6	

The control polyline function trend is shown in Fig. 7. Operation of the control polyline is the same for both channels as shown in Fig. 8.

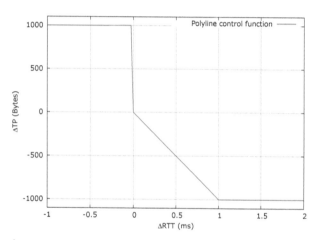

Fig. 7: The control polyline function definition for both channels.

Smoothed curve of the round trip time value $smtRTT$ is indicated by the dashed blue line. The course of the regulation deviation ΔRTT shows the red line. The green line then shows the increase of the action variable ΔTP.

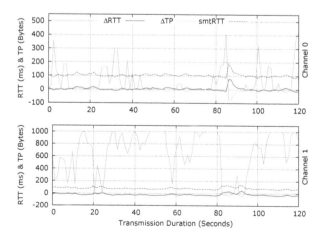

Fig. 8: Polyline function control mechanism.

The chart in Fig. 8 clearly shows that even with an identical set of control parameters for both channels are due to differences in $smtRTT$ differ also individual action interventions. The corresponding packet filter settings for both channels is shown in Fig. 9.

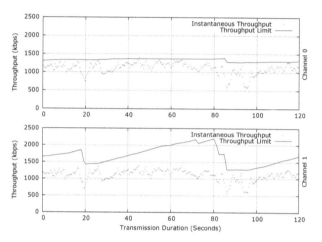

Fig. 9: Throughput control mechanism.

The graph in Fig. 9 shows changes in the course of packet filter settings based on the current state of the channel. This limit is marked by a red line. Blue crosses displays the measured throughput.

The graph in Fig. 9 also shows that the amount of transmitted data is regulated in channel 0. Instantaneous transfer rate exceeds the maximum limit defined by packet filter in some places. This limitation caused a decrease in overall transmission rate but kept RTT within the required limits. That is demonstrated on the graph for channel 0 in Fig. 10.

The fact that the desired RTT $reqRTT$ is set to 100 ms, which is 20 ms higher than the steady delay in channel 1 (about 80 ms), caused that courses of action variable are much greater than for channel 0. In this case is the current difference between the desired value of RTT and its steady size about 8 ms. Reaction of the action variable is also different due to the same control polyline but different RTT values. The packet filter settings in channel 1 is not optimal. Due to the large difference between the current RTT and the desired one is filter threshold set very high above the maximum physical limit of bandwidth of the channel. As a result, regulatory restrictions does not apply, this is demonstrated by the graph for channel 1 in Fig. 9. The maximum limit of the throughput defined by packet filter is much higher than the actual transmission rate generated by user data.

In addition to regulatory intervention of packet filter for each channel there was also regulation of the data stream through the internal mechanisms of TCP protocol. These interventions are evident in seconds 20 and 80. By detecting congestion, which will reflect as an

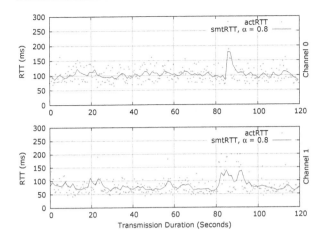

Fig. 10: Round trip time value during the transmission.

increase in the RTT, will be applied a mechanism that ultimately causes a reduction in the amount of sent data. This reduction in the amount of sent data will exhibit in a decrease of transmitted data in both channels. The situation is demonstrated in the decrease of the transmission speed in both channels in Fig. 9, as well as the progress of the limits of channel 1 packet filter.

The influence of the regulatory mechanism of TCP is evident on both channels, although there was an overflow primarily for channel 1. This phenomenon is caused by round-robin mechanism, see algorithm in the Pseudocode 2. This classifying packets method causes practically identical decrease of the transmitted data in all channels.

The course of the resulting transmission speed including displaying contributions of both channels is shown in Fig. 11.

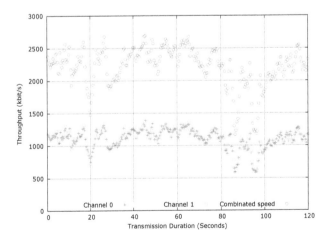

Fig. 11: The resulting transmission speed.

Red crosses and green squares represent the values of instantaneous transmission rate for channel 0, respectively channel 1. Blue circles displays trend of overall transmission speed which is the sum of the two contrib-

utory streams (channels). Results from the measurement of throughput per channel, also the total combined throughput, are given in Tab. 4.

Tab. 4: Results from the TCP uplink throughput measurement

Parameter	Telefonica O2 CZ	T-Mobile CZ
Throughput	1.1 Mbps ± 152 kbps	1.2 Mbps ± 154 kbps
Combined throughput	2.22 Mbps ± 301 kbps	

5. Conclusion

Results of measurement of the transmission system associating the two data channels UMTS HSUPA, created by two different mobile operators, confirmed the functionality of the proposed solution. Suitable design of the control polyline function managed to regulate the amount of data passing through the data channels. With this regulation it is possible to split the input high-speed data streams into two slower channels, and on the other side, make their reassembly. Due to the fact that control polyline function was not designed optimally for each of the channels, the regulation applied to only one of them.

Measurements also confirmed the weak points of the proposed regulator, which must be improved. It is mainly about worse dynamic properties of designed control polyline function which causes, especially at higher load of the data network, significant packet filter values fluctuation. This phenomenon is especially apparent in networks with high and fluctuating RTT. An effective solution to this problem should be to use a several control polyline functions, each will be responsible for a specific range of regulation deviation. An interesting variation might be some variant of the PID or the PSD regulator.

Acknowledgment

This work was supported by the Grant of the Technology Agency of the Czech Republic, No. TA02011015, "Research and development of a new communication system with multi-channel approach and multi-layer co-operation for industrial applications", and was researched in cooperation with CERTICON company and with the financial support by the Grant Agency of the Czech Technical University in Prague, grant no. SGS12/186/OHK3/3T/13.

References

[1] BRADEN, R. *Requirements for Internet Hosts - Communication Layers. RFC 1122 (Internet*

Standard), October 1989. Updated by RFCs 1349, 4379, 5884, 6093, 6298, 6633, 6864.

[2] CHLUMSKY, P., Z. KOCUR and J. VO-DRAZKA. Comparison of Different Scenarios for Path Diversity Packet Wireless Networks. *Advances in Electrical and Electronic Engineering.* 2012, vol. 10, no. 4, pp. 199–203. ISSN 1804-3119.

[3] CONSTANTINE, B., G. FORGET, R. GEIB and R. SCHRAGE. *Framework for TCP Throughput Testing. RFC 6349 (International)*, August 2011.

[4] KOCUR, Z., T. ZEMAN and J. HRAD. Prioritization of Data Communications in Wireless and Switched Networks. In: *International Workshop Research in Telecommunication Technologies 2009.* Prague: CVUT, 2009. pp. 61–68. ISBN 978-80-01-04411- 7.

[5] NERUDA, M., L. VOJTECH, J. HAJEK and D. MAGA. Control Procedure of Emergency Calls for Femtocells. In: *ICMT'13 - Proceedings of the International Conference on Military Technologies.* Brno: University of Defence, 2013. pp. 1331–1338. ISBN 978-80-7231-917-6.

[6] POSTEL, J. *User Datagram Protocol. RFC 768 (Internet Standard)*, August 1980.

[7] POSTEL, J. *Transmission Control Protocol. RFC 793 (Internet Standard)*, September 1981. Updated by RFCs 1122, 3168, 6093, 6528.

[8] VOZNAK, M. and M. HALAS. Delay Variation Model with RTP Flows Behavior in Accordance with M/D/1 Kendall's Notation. *Advances in Electrical and Electronic Engineering.* 2010, vol. 8, no. 5, pp. 124–129. ISSN 1804-3119.

About Authors

Zbynek KOCUR was born in 1982. He received his M.Sc. degree in electrical engineering from the Czech Technical University in Prague in 2008. Since 2008 he has been studying Ph.D. degree. He is teaching communication in data networks and networking technologies. His research is focused on wireless transmission and data flow analysis, simulation and optimization. He is currently actively involved in projects focused on high speed data transmission from fast moving objects and data optimization via satellite network.

Peter MACEJKO was born in Czech Republic in 1980. He received his M.Sc. degree in electrical engineering from the Czech Technical University in Prague in 2006. He is teaching networking technologies and distributed systems. His research is focused on scheduling in distributed systems and data flow and protocol analysis. He is currently actively involved in projects focused on high speed data transmission from fast moving objects.

Petr CHLUMSKY received his M.Sc. degree in electrical engineering from the Czech Technical University in Prague in 2010. Since 2010 he has been studying Ph.D. degree in telecommunication engineering. His research interests include wireless transmission, network coding and network simulation.

Jiri VODRAZKA was born in Prague, Czech Republic in 1966. He joined the Department of Telecommunication Engineering, Faculty of Electrical Engineering, Czech Technical University in Prague in 1996 as a research assistant and received his Ph.D. degree in electrical engineering in 2001. He has been the head of the Transmission Media and Systems scientific group since 2005 and became associate professor in 2008. He participates in numerous projects in cooperation with external bodies. Currently he also acts as vice-head of the Department.

Ondrej VONDROUS received his M.Sc. degree in electrical engineering from the Czech Technical University in Prague in 2011. Since 2011 he has been studying Ph.D. degree in telecommunication engineering. His research interests include network transmission control, data flow analysis and data flow optimization.

7

Anomaly-based Network Intrusion Detection Methods

Pavel NEVLUD, Miroslav BURES, Lukas KAPICAK, Jaroslav ZDRALEK

Department of Telecommunications, Faculty of Electrical Engineering and Computer Science,
VSB–Technical University of Ostrava, 17. listopadu 15, 708 33 Ostrava-Poruba, Czech Republic

pavel.nevlud@vsb.cz, miroslav.bures@vsb.cz, lukas.kapicak@vsb.cz, jaroslav.zdralek@vsb.cz

Abstract. *The article deals with detection of network anomalies. Network anomalies include everything that is quite different from the normal operation. For detection of anomalies were used machine learning systems. Machine learning can be considered as a support or a limited type of artificial intelligence. A machine learning system usually starts with some knowledge and a corresponding knowledge organization so that it can interpret, analyse, and test the knowledge acquired. There are several machine learning techniques available. We tested Decision tree learning and Bayesian networks. The open source data-mining framework WEKA was the tool we used for testing the classify, cluster, association algorithms and for visualization of our results. The WEKA is a collection of machine learning algorithms for data mining tasks.*

Keywords

Anomaly-based detection, attack, bayesian networks, WEKA.

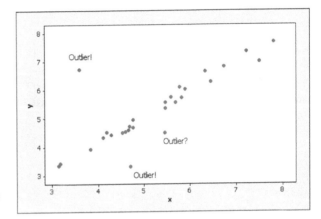

Fig. 1: A simple example of anomalies.

1. Introduction

Nowadays, computer network is a frequent target of attacks in order to obtain confidential data, or unavailability of network services. To detect and prevent these attacks, there are a large number of software or hardware solutions such as IDS (Intrusion Detection Systems), firewalls and monitoring systems.

These attacks increased normal network traffic that appears as something undesirable, what would not occur in the network. Such deviations from normal operation are called as network anomalies. Between network anomalies include everything that is quite different from the normal operation of the network [1].

Anomalies are values in a statistical sample which does not fit a pattern that describes most other data points. Figure 1 illustrates anomalies in a simple 2-dimensional data set. The data has one normal regions, since most observations lie in this region. Three points that are sufficiently far away from the regions are anomalies. One of these points is border point that can be detected as anomaly.

2. Detection of Network Anomalies

Network anomalies can be detected in several ways. Each method has its advantages and disadvantages, but in practice there are three commonly used methods. Them together they can develop systems such as IDS software.

2.1. Comparing Signatures

The principle of this method is the comparison of network data with a database of signatures. Signature database contains patterns of data anomalies. Data anomaly pattern is actually a description of a typical data sequence that characterizes the anomaly. The principle can be seen in Figure 2. It used the same principle as in the anti-virus programs.

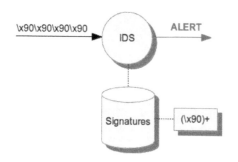

Fig. 2: Comparing signatures.

The effectiveness of anomaly detection using signature recognition is highly dependent on the quality of the database of signatures. The big disadvantage is almost no detection of new types of attacks called Zero day attack, because it is not in the database signature pattern for this type of anomaly [4].

2.2.   Stateful Protocol Analysis

Stateful protocol analysis assumes that each protocol used for network communication is specified, such as RFC. Thanks to precise specifications, all connections using protocols defined state. Each event must occur at the right moment, the state. This makes it possible to describe the protocol as a state machine. Figure 3 illustrates an example of stateful machine.

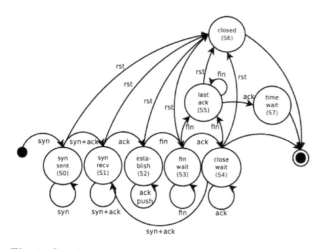

Fig. 3: Stateful protocol analysis.

The advantage of this method is less frequent updates. The stateful analysis needs update only after the change of protocol or the installation of a new one [3].

2.3.   Behavioral Analysis

The method of behavioral analysis is based on the assumption that the emergence of anomalies can be detected by the deviation from the normal or expected network behavior. Model of normally or anticipated behavior of the network is created based on network monitoring and collecting reference information.

The reference information is compiled model normal behavior and network traffic is subsequently compared with this model. Any deviation from such a learned model is automatically considered an anomaly. The principle can be seen in Fig. 4. For behavioral analysis and create network's model can be used MLS (Machine Learning Systems).

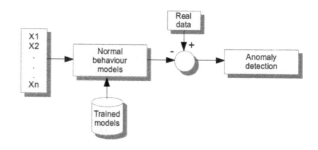

Fig. 4: Behavioral analysis.

The disadvantage of this method is precisely the fine detection. Any deviation from the normal model is detected even though it is not an attack or threat. It is due to the fact that the creation of the model can not capture all types of network traffic and user activity on the network. This model is created to some extent distorted.

On the other hand, behavioral analysis provides an advantage in terms of detection of completely new types of threats, for example, by comparing detection signatures did not react at all.

3.   Machine Learning Systems

If we want to be able to solve the computer problem, some intelligence is needed. Machine learning can be considered as a support or a limited type of artificial intelligence. Algorithms MLS can move on with the development of computers. This means that computers are no longer just a database comparing sets of data.

A machine learning system usually starts with some knowledge and a corresponding knowledge organization so that it can interpret, analyze, and test the knowledge acquired. The principle can be seen in Fig. 5.

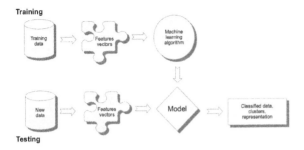

Fig. 5: Principle of machine learning system.

Training is the process of making the system able to learn. It may consist of randomly selected examples that include a variety of facts and details including irrelevant data. The learning techniques can be characterized as a search through a space of possible hypotheses or solutions. Background knowledge can be used to make learning more efficient by reducing the search space.

The success of machine learning system also depends on the algorithms. These algorithms control the search to find and build the knowledge structures. The algorithms should extract useful information from training examples. There are several machine learning techniques available [2].

Among the best-known machine learning algorithms include:

- Decision tree learning.
- Artificial neural networks.
- Genetic programming.
- Clustering.
- Bayesian networks.
- Representation learning.

4. Decision Tree Learning

Decision tree learning is 'a method for approximating discrete valued functions that is robust to noisy data and capable of learning disjunctive expressions' according to [5].

Ross Quinlan has produced several working decision tree induction methods that have been implemented in his programs, ID3, C4.5 and C5. Decision tree induction takes a set of known data and induces a decision tree from that data. The tree can then be used as a rule set for predicting the outcome from known attributes. The initial data set from which the tree is induced is known as the training set. The decision tree takes the top-down form. At the top is the first attribute and its values, from this next branch leads to either an attribute or an outcome. Every possible leaf of the tree eventually leads to an outcome.

4.1. Decision Trees – C4.5

C4.5 is an algorithm developed by Ross Quinlan that generates Decision Trees (DT), which can be used for classification problems. It improves (extends) the ID3 algorithm by dealing with both continuous and discrete attributes, missing values and pruning trees after construction. Its commercial successor is C5.0/See5, a lot faster that C4.5, more memory efficient and used for building smaller decision trees. J48 is an open source Java implementation of the C4.5 algorithm in the WEKA data mining tool.

Algorithm 1 C4.5(D)

Input: an attribute-valued dataset D
1: Tree = {}
2: **if** D is "pure" OR other stopping criteria met **then**
3:     terminate
4: **end if**
5: **for all** atribute a $\in D$ **do**
6:     Compute information-theoretic criteria if we split a
7: **end for**
8: a_{best} = Best attribute according to above computed criteria
9: Tree = Create a decision node that tests a_{best} in the root
10: D_v = Induced sub-datasets from D based on a_{best}
11: **for all** D_v **do**
12:     Tree$_v$ = C4.5(D_v)
13:     Attache Tree$_v$ to the corresponding branch of Tree
14: **end for**
15: **return** Tree

The generic description of how C4.5 works is shown in Algorithm 1. A decision tree is built top-down from a root node and involves partitioning the data into subsets that contain instances with similar values (homogenous). Decision tree algorithm uses entropy to calculate the homogeneity of a sample. If the sample is completely homogeneous the entropy is zero and if the sample is an equally divided it has entropy of one. The entropy of class random variable that takes on c values with probabilities $p_1, p_2, \ldots, p_c$ is given by:

$$Entropy(S) = \sum_{i=1}^{c} -p_i \log_2 p_i. \qquad (1)$$

Figure 6 shows the form of the entropy function relative to a binary classification.

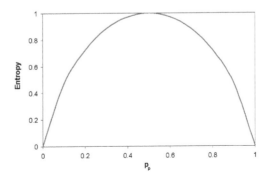

Fig. 6: Entropy function.

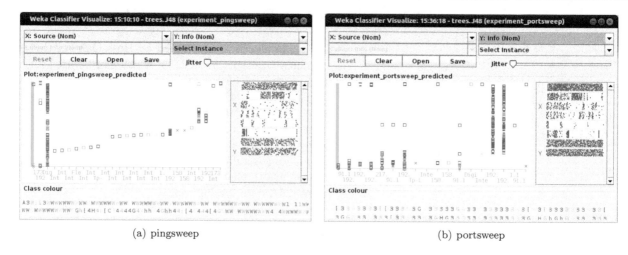

(a) pingsweep   (b) portsweep

Fig. 7: J48 classifier results.

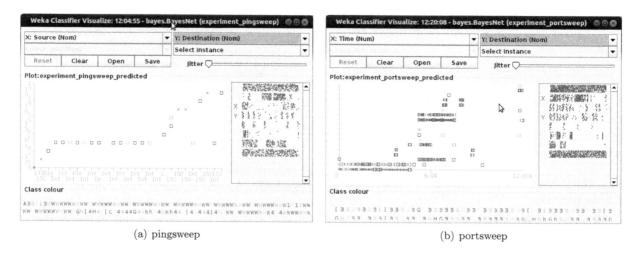

(a) pingsweep   (b) portsweep

Fig. 8: BayesNet classifier results.

The estimation criterion in the decision tree algorithm is the selection of an attribute to test at each decision node in the tree. The goal is to select the attribute that is most useful for classifying examples. A good quantitative measure of the worth of an attribute is a statistical property called information gain that measures how well a given attribute separates the training examples according to their target classification. This measure is used to select among the candidate attributes at each step while growing the tree. The information gain is based on the decrease in entropy after a dataset is split on an attribute. Constructing a decision tree is all about finding attribute that returns the highest information gain (i.e. the most homogeneous branches).

$$Gain(S, A) = Entropy(S) - \sum_{v \in Values(A)} \frac{|S_v|}{|S|} Entropy(S_v), \quad (2)$$

where $Values(A)$ is the set of all possible values for attribute A, and S_v is the subset of S for which attribute A has value v (i.e. $S_v = \{s\,\hat{I}\,S | A(s) = v\}$).

The first term in the equation for information gain is just the entropy of the original collection S and the second term is the expected value of the entropy after S is partitioned using attribute A. The expected entropy described by this second term is simply the sum of the entropies of each subset S_v, weighted by the fraction of examples $|S_v|/|S|$ that belong to S_v. $Gain(S, A)$ is therefore the expected reduction in entropy caused by knowing the value of attribute A. Put another way, $Gain(S, A)$ is the information provided about the target attribute value, given the value of some other attribute A. The value of $Gain(S, A)$ is the number of bits saved when encoding the target value of an arbitrary member of S, by knowing the value of attribute A.

5. Bayesian Networks

Bayesian networks are graphical representation of the relationship between variables. Graphical representation of Bayesian networks are directed acyclic graphs with nodes and edges. Nodes represent variables, parameters or hypotheses and edges represent conditional dependencies.

5.1. Algorithm of Naive Bayesian

The Naive Bayesian classifier is based on Bayes' theorem with independence assumptions between predictors. Bayes theorem provides a way of calculating the posterior probability, $P(c|x)$, from $P(c)$, $P(x)$, and $P(x|c)$. Naive Bayes classifier assumes that the effect of the value of a predictor (x) on a given class (c) is independent of the values of other predictors. This assumption is called class conditional independence.

$$P(c|x) = \frac{P(x|c)P(c)}{P(x)}, \quad (3)$$

$$P(c|x) = P(x_1|c) \times P(x_2|c) \times \cdots \times P(x_n|c) \times P(c), \quad (4)$$

where $P(c|x)$ is the posterior probability of class (target) given predictor (attribute), $P(c)$ is the prior probability of class, $P(x|c)$ is the likelihood which is the probability of predictor given class and $P(x)$ is the prior probability of predictor.

6. Experimental Results

For data mining platform was chosen open source project WEKA [6]. WEKA is a collection of machine

Fig. 9: Visualize results of pingsweep.

learning algorithms for data mining tasks. The algo-

rithms can either be applied directly to a dataset or called from your own Java code.

WEKA contains tools for data pre-processing, classification, regression, clustering, association rules, and visualization. It is also well-suited for developing new machine learning schemes.

Tested activities were captured by the network traffic collector and saved as pcap files. These pcap files are binary files and can't be read directly into most data mining applications.

These pcap files were converted into csv files with scripts using tshark [7]. WEKA accepts *.csv files, *.arff files or a connection to a database. For this research were used converted csv files that was opened in WEKA.

As part of the preprocessing step, information data were injected into the data which were useful for training of the data mining algorithm. Additionally insignificant data were eliminated if it were not serving the overall process. To begin running this data through the algorithms it was opened in WEKA explorer. For the purpose of these initial runs we selected all of the attributes.

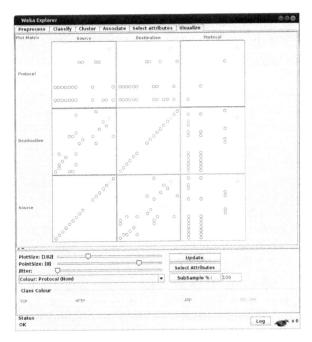

Fig. 10: Visualize results of portsweep.

Figure 7(a) shows the results in WEKA of a J48 Classifier training run on data acquired during ping sweep of the target network. The results described here were derived from single nmap target scan, where an attack computer scanned a victim network, probing for active IP addresses.

Also Fig. 7(b) shows the results in WEKA of a J48 Classifier training run on data acquired during port sweep of the target computer. The results described here were derived from single nmap target scan, where an attack computer scanned a victim computer, probing for open ports.

There were chosen only 3 attributes to visualize experimental results. These attributes were IP source address, IP destination address and Protocol. Figure 9 and Fig. 10 show relation between these attributes.

Figure 8(a) shows the results in WEKA of a Naive-Bayes Classifier training run on data acquired during ping sweep of the target network. Also Fig. 8(b) shows the results in WEKA of a NaiveBayes Classifier training run on data acquired during port sweep of the target computer.

7. Conclusion and Future Work

In this paper, we have presented detection of network anomalies by using machine learning systems. Machine learning system usually starts with some knowledge and during the rounds can improve its knowledge.

There were tested some attacks in regular network traffic. As the first attack was used ping sweep to sub network target to get information about active IP addresses. The port sweep was used as second attack to scanning open ports at the target victim computer.

First, we captured network traffic by the network collector and saved data as pcap format file. Next, we converted collected data from pcap file into csv format file. We used some scripts by means of tshark to convert data from pcap to csv file format. Next converted csv data was inserted in the WEKA software to use classification of data. Finally classified data was visualize by WEKA software.

Future work expects to use more attributes that will be get from pcap files. We also assume the use of other classification methods and other data mining algorithms.

Acknowledgment

The research leading to these results has received funding from the European Community's Seventh Framework Programme (FP7/2007-2013) under grant agreement no. 218086.

References

[1] FOWLER, Ch. A. and R. J. HAMMELL II. Building Baseline Preprocessed Common Data Sets for Multiple Follow-on Data Mining Algorithms. In: *Proceedings of the Conference on Information Systems Applied Research 2012*. New Orleans: EDSIG, 2012, pp. 1–17. ISSN 2167-1508.

[2] FARRAPOSO, F., P OWEZARSKI and E. MONTEIRO. NADA–Network Anomaly Detection Algorithm. In: *18th IFIP/IEEE International Workshop on Distributed Systems: Operations and Management, DSOM 2007*. San Jose: Springer Verlag, 2007, vol. 4785, pp 191—194, ISBN 978-3-540-75694-1.

[3] DAS, K. Protocol Anomaly Detection for Network-based Intrusion Detection. *The SANS Institute* [online]. 2002. Available at: `http://www.sans.org/reading_room/whitepapers/detection/protocol_anomaly_detection_for_networkbased_intrusion_detection_349?show=349.php&cat=detection`.

[4] RICHARD, M. Intrusion Detection FAQ: Are there limitations of Intrusion Signatures?. *The SANS Institute* [online]. 2001. Available at: `http://www.sans.org/resources/idfaq/limitations.php`.

[5] MITCHELL, Tom M. *Machine learning*. Boston: McGraw-Hill, 1997. ISBN 00-704-2807-7.

[6] WEKA 3. *Data Mining Software in Java* [online]. 2013. Available at: `http://www.cs.waikato.ac.nz/ml/weka/`

[7] TShark [online]. 2013. Available at: `http://www.wireshark.org/docs/man-pages/tshark.html`

About Authors

Pavel NEVLUD received his M.Sc. degree in telecommunication engineering from VSB–Technical University of Ostrava, Czech Republic in 1995. Since this year he has been holding position as an assistant professor at the Department of Telecommunications, VSB–Technical University of Ostrava. The topics of his research interests are communication technologies, networking and security.

Miroslav BURES received his M.Sc. degree in telecommunications from VSB–Technical University of Ostrava, Czech Republic in 2011. Since 2011 has been studying Ph.D. degree at the same university. His research is focused on networking, analysis of network's data and security.

Lukas KAPICAK received his M.Sc. degree in telecommunications from VSB–Technical University of Ostrava, Czech Republic in 2007. Since 2007 has been studying Ph.D. degree at the same university. His research is focused on wireless transmission and data flow analysis, simulation and optimization.

Jaroslav ZDRALEK holds position as an associate professor with Department of Telecommunications, VSB–Technical University of Ostrava, Czech Republic. He received his M.Sc. degree in Computer Science from Slovak Technical University of Bratislava, Slovakia in 1977. He received his Ph.D. degree from VSB–Technical University of Ostrava in 2002, dissertation thesis "Diagnostic system without dismantling of locomotive controller". His research is focused on fault tolerant system and communication technologies.

8

Modeling of Telecommunication Cables for Gigabit DSL Application

Marek NEVOSAD, Pavel LAFATA, Petr JARES

Department of Telecommunication Engineering, Faculty of Electrical Engineering, Czech Technical University in Prague, Technicka 2, 166 36 Prague, Czech Republic

marek.nevosad@fel.cvut.cz, pavel.lafata@fel.cvut.cz, petr.jares@fel.cvut.cz

Abstract. *The first part of our paper brings the description and analysis of method used for modeling of metallic cables' parameters according to the modified KPN model. Moreover we were able to perform measurements and estimations for real metallic cables with various transmission characteristics and constructional arrangement, for which we derived the necessary parameters of a new modeling method. Following part contains the comparison of measured characteristics with their models according to the modified KPN model. Finally, we discussed obtained results.*

Keywords

G-FAST, gigabit digital subscriber line, modeling, telecommunication cables, xDSL.

1. Introduction

Today, the existing metallic lines are still being widely used due to the slower development of passive optical networks in many countries. The continuously increasing demands for higher transmission speeds lead to exploit the potentials of metallic lines, which were not considered before. Until recently, the VDSL2 (Very High Speed Digital Subscriber Line) technology, which is standardized for frequencies up to 30 MHz and transfer speeds up to 100 Mbit·s^{-1}, has been considered as the fastest solution in data transmissions over metallic lines [1]. Many experiments tried to increase transmission performance of DSL (Digital Subscriber Line) technology; however, the main limitation is a crosstalk, especially far-end crosstalk (FEXT) [2]. The newly standardized G-fast system, which is currently being developed, will be based on vectored discrete multitone modulation (DMT) to eliminate FEXT and its frequency band will be extended up to 212 MHz.

These enhancements will enable reaching gigabit transmission speed. For that purpose, it is necessary to modify existing models and parameters of lines for such high frequencies or design completely new modeling methods. The current version of the G-FAST draft uses a new method of modeling that is not based on calculations of the primary parameters, but instead of it uses the modeling of longitudinal impedance Z_s and transverse admittance Y_p of a homogenous line. This type of modeling is conceptually based on the method specified in the recommendation ETSI TS 101 270-1, the number of parameters was reduced to 10 and additionally, several modifications were made. Furthermore, the draft also contains specific values of these parameters for four basic types of metallic lines frequently used in access networks.

The combined network architecture with the twisted pairs and the optical fibers, called FTTB or FTTC (Fiber to the Building, Fiber to the Curb), should be considered, because the broadband transmission can be used only for short lines. The designation "Fiber Distribution Point" (FTTdp) was introduced for these situations [6].

2. Theory

Instead of using standard primary parameters (R, L, C and G), the models presented within newly developed G-FAST draft are based on estimations of longitudinal impedance Z_s and transverse admittance Y_p of a homogenous line [4]. An empirical model, which is discussed below, can be used for modeling frequency characteristics up to 300 MHz. The model can be obtained by Eq. (1), Eq. (2), Eq. (3), Eq. (4), Eq. (5), Eq. (6) and Eq. (7) [4] and is conceptually based on the modified equations presented as KPN model [5]. Resistivity is considered as complex value in this model. It is a main difference from other reference models.

$$Z_s(j\omega) = j\omega \cdot L_{s\infty} + R_{s0} \cdot \left(1 - q_s \cdot q_x + \sqrt{q_s^2 \cdot q_x^2 + 2 \cdot \frac{j\omega}{\omega_s} \cdot \frac{q_s^2 + \frac{j\omega}{\omega_s} \cdot q_y}{\frac{q_s^2}{q_x} + \frac{j\omega}{\omega_s} \cdot q_y}}\right), \tag{1}$$

$$Y_p(j\omega) = j\omega \cdot C_{p0} \cdot (1 - q_c) \cdot \left(1 + \frac{j\omega}{\omega_d}\right)^{-2 \cdot \phi/\pi} + j\omega \cdot C_{p0} \cdot q + c, \tag{2}$$

$$L_{s\infty} = \frac{1}{\eta_{VF} \cdot c_0} \cdot Z_{0\infty}, \tag{3}$$

$$C_{p0} = \frac{1}{\eta_{VF} \cdot c_0} \cdot \frac{1}{Z_{0\infty}}, \tag{4}$$

$$q_s = \frac{1}{q_H^2 \cdot q_L}, \tag{5}$$

$$\omega_s = q_H^2 \cdot \omega_{s0} = q_H^2 \cdot \left(\frac{4\pi \cdot R_{s0}}{\mu_0}\right), \tag{6}$$

$$\omega_d = 2\pi \cdot f_d, \tag{7}$$

where $c_0 = 3{\cdot}10^8$ m·s^{-1} and $\mu_0 = 4\pi{\cdot}10^{-7}$ H·m^{-1}. This model can be usually simplify by $q_c = 0$ and $f_d = 1$. After this simplification, the transverse admittance Y_p is showed in Eq. (8).

$$Y_p = j2 \cdot \pi \cdot f \cdot C_{p0} \cdot (1 + j \cdot f)^{-2 \cdot \phi/\pi}. \tag{8}$$

The estimation of characteristic impedance $Z_{0\infty}$ of a line is also necessary for appropriate application of presented models, as well as the velocity of propagation η_{VF}, which can be obtained by using TDR (Time-Domain Reflectometer) method or direct calculations from the phase characteristics.

The formulas for the series impedance Z_s Eq. (11) and parallel admittance Y_p Eq. (12) can be derived from the equations for the secondary parameters Eq. (9), Eq. (10) of symmetrical lines.

$$\gamma = \sqrt{Z_s \cdot Y_p}, \tag{9}$$

$$Z_C = \sqrt{\frac{Z_s}{Y_p}}, \tag{10}$$

$$Z_s = \sqrt{\gamma \cdot Z_c}, \tag{11}$$

$$Y_p = \frac{\gamma}{Z_c}. \tag{12}$$

Parameters ϕ, q_H, q_L, q_x, q_y, R_{s0}, $Z_{0\infty}$, η_{VF} for reference model are obtained by measurements and approximation of characteristics.

Finally, attenuation factor α is a real part of γ as shown in Eq. (13).

$$\gamma = \alpha + j\beta. \tag{13}$$

2.1. The Method of Measuring the Transmission Parameters

The measurement workspace in the Department of Telecommunication Engineering, Faculty of Electrical Engineering, Czech Technical University in Prague had to be upgraded and optimized for measurement of gigabit digital subscriber lines. Figure 1 illustrates the basic schematic of measurements. The measurements were performed by network analyzer Rohde&Schwarz ZVRE (spectral analyzer with vector signal analyzer option) with balun transformers North Hills. The Automated Measuring Workplace (AMW) [3] was also used during our experiments.

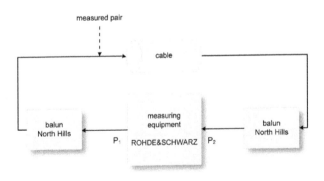

Fig. 1: The schematic illustration of measurements.

The measurements were performed for cable TCEP-KPFLE in the frequency band from 5 MHz up to 300 MHz due to the equipment limitations. The rest of the cables, measured by AMW, the frequency band was set from 100 kHz to 250 MHz.

3. The Results of Performed Measurements and Models

The measurements were performed for four typical communication cables:

- TCEPKPFLE $75 \times 4 \times 0, 4$ (one sub-group (8 randomly selected symmetrical pairs)),

- SYKFY $4 \times 2 \times 0, 5$,

- UTP CAT5e (Unshielded Twisted Pair),

- UTP CAT6.

3.1. The Results of Measurements

The results of measuring and modeling of attenuation factor and characteristic impedance are given in following figures.

1) TCEPKPFLE $75 \times 4 \times 0, 4$

The cable has star-quad construction with polyethylene insulation and is standard for use in telecommunication. The measuring and modeling of attenuation factor and characteristic impedance are shown in Fig. 2 and Fig. 3.

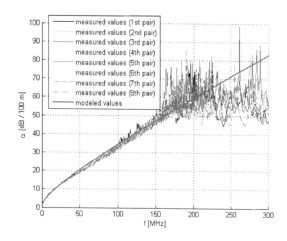

Fig. 2: Attenuation factor α TCEPKPFLE $75 \times 4 \times 0, 4$ and model.

2) SYKFY $4 \times 2 \times 0, 5$

This type of interior cable with four symmetrical pairs with PVC insulation corresponds to CAT3 (Category 3) for the frequency band up to a few MHz. Its frequency characteristics are presented in Fig. 4 and Fig. 5.

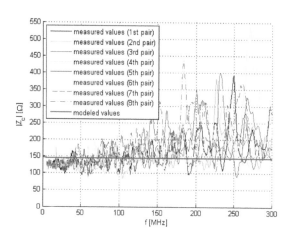

Fig. 3: Module of characteristic impedance Z_c TCEPKPFLE $75 \times 4 \times 0, 4$.

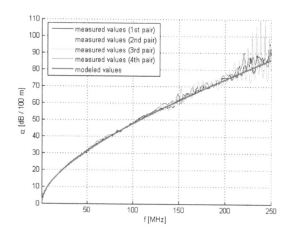

Fig. 4: Attenuation factor α SYKFY $4 \times 2 \times 0, 5$ and model.

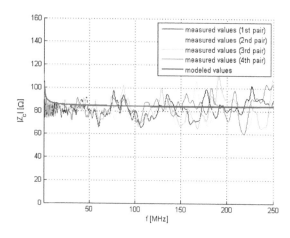

Fig. 5: Module of characteristic impedance Z_c SYKFY $4 \times 2 \times 0, 5$.

3) UTP CAT5e

The CAT5e is a category of cables primary used for local area networks with parameters guaranteed up to

100 MHz. The measuring and modeling of attenuation factor and characteristic impedance are shown in Fig. 6 and Fig. 7.

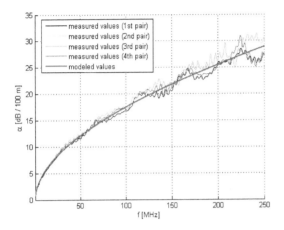

Fig. 6: Attenuation factor α UTP CAT5e and model.

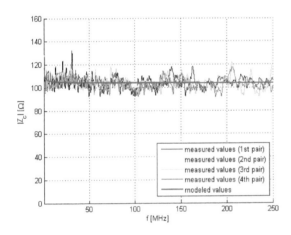

Fig. 7: Module of characteristic impedance Z_c UTP CAT5e.

4) UTP CAT6

The CAT6 is a category of cables with the same type of construction as CAT5e, furthermore, in this category the parameters are guaranteed up to 250 MHz. Its frequency characteristics are presented in Fig. 8 and Fig. 9.

3.2. Parameters of the Reference Model

The measured values were processed in program Matlab and optimized parameters were estimated. The parameters obtained for reference model (above) are presented in Tab. 1 and Tab. 2.

Output parameters of the reference model are presented in Tab. 3. The velocity of propagation η_{VF} was

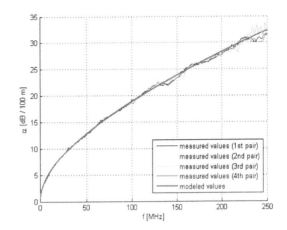

Fig. 8: Attenuation factor α UTP CAT6 and model.

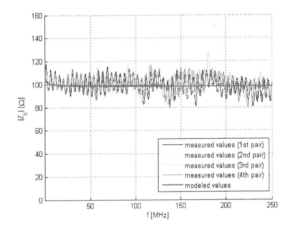

Fig. 9: Module of characteristic impedance Z_c UTP CAT6.

Tab. 1: q-parameters of the reference model.

Cable type	q_H	q_L	q_X	q_Y
TCEPKPFLE $75 \times 4 \times 0,4$	0,902	2,15	0,5	0,723
SYKFY $4 \times 2 \times 0,5$	0,501	2,75	0,2	1,492
UTP CAT5e	0,880	2,15	1,6	0,820
UTP CAT6	0,835	2,40	1,4	1,800

Tab. 2: Others parameters of the reference model.

Cable type	ϕ	$R_{S0}[\Omega \cdot \text{m}^{-1}]$	$Z_{0\infty}[\Omega]$
TCEPKPFLE $75 \times 4 \times 0,4$	1,530e-2	0,2800	131
SYKFY $4 \times 2 \times 0,5$	9,992e-3	0,1900	78
UTP CAT5e	1,100e-3	0,1659	97
UTP CAT6	2,200e-3	0,16100	102

Tab. 3: Output parameters of the reference model.

Cable type	$C_{p0}[\text{F} \cdot \text{m}^{-1}]$	$L_{S\infty}[\text{H} \cdot \text{m}^{-1}]$	η_{VF}
TCEPKPFLE $75 \times 4 \times 0,4$	3,877334e-11	6,653892e-07	0,6562575
SYKFY $4 \times 2 \times 0,5$	5,667929e-11	3,448368e-07	0,7539799
UTP CAT5e	4,405455e-11	4,145093e-07	0,7800388
UTP CAT6	4,655176e-11	4,843245e-07	0,7020087

calculated by using derivation of measured phase characteristic.

4. Conclusion

According to our results, the TCEPKPFLE cable can be used up to the frequency of 150 MHz (Fig. 2). The propagation of a signal at higher frequencies is performed by crosstalk and couplings between symmetrical pairs, which cannot be used for reliable transmissions. On the other hand, the frequency characteristics of SYKFY, UTP CAT5e and UTP CAT6 cables have the estimated shapes in the whole frequency band that is why the G-FAST models could be successfully applied. In conclusion, we can say that proposed reference model, which is presented in G-FAST draft of recommendation [4], can be used for modeling of metallic cables up to 300 MHz. The modeled parameters will be used for estimation of gigabit digital subscriber lines data rates in the on-line program "xDSL simulator" [7].

Acknowledgment

This work was supported by the Grant of the Technology Agency of the Czech Republic, No. TA02011015, Research and development of a new communication system with multi-channel approach and multi-layer co-operation for industrial applications, and was researched in cooperation with CERTICON.

References

[1] LAFATA, P., P. JARES and J. VODRAZKA. Increasing the Transmission Capacity of Digital Subscriber Lines. In: *35th International Conference on Telecommunications and Signal Processing*. Brno: IEEE, 2012, pp. 292–296. ISBN 978-1-4673-1118-2. DOI: 10.1109/TSP.2012.6256301.

[2] LAFATA, P. and J. VODRAZKA. Modeling of Transmission Functions and Crosstalk in Metallic Cables for Implementation of MIMO Concept. *Radioengineering*. 2009, vol. 18, no. 4, pp. 491–496. ISSN 1210-2512.

[3] CEPA, L., M. KOZAK and J. VODRAZKA. Innovation of Methods for Measurement and Modelling of Twisted Pair Parameters. *Advances in Electrical and Electronic Engineering*. 2011, vol. 9, no. 5, pp. 220–224. ISSN 1336-1376.

[4] ITU-T SG15. *Transport network structures*. Germany: International Telecommunication Union, 2012. Available at: `http://www.itu.int/md/T09-SG15-120910-TD-WP1-0759/en`.

[5] TS 101 270-1 V1.1.1. *Transmission and Multiplexing (TM); Access transmission systems on metallic access cables; Very high speed Digital Subscriber Line (VDSL); Part 1: Functional requirements*. France: European Telecommunications Standards Institute, 1998. Available at: `http://www.etsi.org/deliver/etsi_ts/101200_101299/10127001/01.02.01_60/ts_10127001v010201p.pdf`.

[6] VODRÁŽKA, J. Potential Use of Gigabit Digital Subscriber Lines in Hybrid Access Networks. In: *Proceedings of the Ninth International Conference on Digital Technologies*. Zilina: IEEE, 2013, pp. 71–74. ISBN 978-80-554-0682-4. DOI: 10.1109/DT.2013.6566290.

[7] *Simulator of xDSL lines* [online]. 2007. Matlab server. Available at: `http://matlab.feld.cvut.cz/view.php?cisloclanku=2005071801`.

About Authors

Marek NEVOSAD was born in Prague, Czech Republic. He received his M.Sc. degree in electrical engineering from Czech Technical University in Prague in 2004. His research interests include telecommunication transmission systems and software development. He also participates in numerous international projects focused on new methods in education as a software developer.

Pavel LAFATA was born in Ceske Budejovice, Czech Republic in 1982. He received his M.Sc. degree in 2007 and Ph.D. degree in 2011 at Faculty of Electrical Engineering, Czech Technical University in Prague, specializing in Telecommunication Engineering. Currently he works as an assistant professor and junior research assistant at the Department of Telecommunication Engineering of the CTU in Prague. He is a member of the Transmission Media and Systems scientific group at the Department. His research activities are focused mainly on fixed high-speed access networks, the problems related with disturbance and crosstalk in metallic cables for digital subscriber lines and optical access networks and their topologies.

Petr JARES is an assistant professor at the Department of Telecommunication Engineering, Faculty of Electrical Engineering, Czech Technical University in Prague. He received his Ph.D. degree in 2008 at Faculty of Electrical Engineering, Czech Technical University in Prague, specializing in

Telecommunication Engineering. For past few years he has worked on various projects in the transmission systems. His current focus of interest is on data transmission in metallic and optical access networks.

9

OpenFlow Deployment and Concept Analysis

Tomas HEGR, Leos BOHAC, Vojtech UHLIR, Petr CHLUMSKY

Department of Telecommunication Engineering, Faculty of Electrical Engineering, Czech Technical University in Prague, Technicka 2, 166 27 Prague, Czech Republic

tomas.hegr@fel.cvut.cz, bohac@fel.cvut.cz, uhlirvoj@fel.cvut.cz, petr.chlumsky@fel.cvut.cz

Abstract. *Terms such as SDN and OpenFlow (OF) are often used in the research and development of data networks. This paper deals with the analysis of the current state of OpenFlow protocol deployment options as it is the only real representative protocol that enables the implementation of Software Defined Networking outside an academic world. There is introduced an insight into the current state of the OpenFlow specification development at various levels is introduced. The possible limitations associated with this concept in conjunction with the latest version (1.3) of the specification published by ONF are also presented. In the conclusion there presented a demonstrative security application addressing the lack of IPv6 support in real network devices since most of today's switches and controllers support only OF v1.0.*

Keywords

Analysis, deployment, IPv6, OpenFlow, SDN, security.

1. Introduction

Software-Defined Networking (SDN) has recently become one of the most progressive sectors in terms of research and development in data networks. SDN concept comes up with the idea of breaking away the ties from a particular hardware platform and moving to the abstract model as it is done also in other sectors of information technologies. This shifts transmission and computing capabilities significantly to a higher level.

The original idea of SDN described in [1] was born at Stanford University around 2005. The SDN concept brings the separation of network device features to the control plane, and the data plane. While the control plane is programmatically accessible through well-defined API (Application Programming Interface), data plane ensures a data processing according to the rules uploaded to the device.

The key representative of the protocols enabling the creation and operation of the SDN is the OpenFlow (OF) protocol nowadays. It is also referred to as southbound protocol and it simply enables the transfer of control instructions driving individual data flows in network devices. More specifically it fills up their TCAM switching tables. Other potential future representatives of southbound protocols are XMPP (Extensible Messaging and Presence Protocol) or extended BGP (Border Gateway Protocol).

OpenFlow has been developed since 2007, and the first protocol specification was approved in 2009 [2]. Lately the development was adopted by the Open Networking Foundation (ONF) consortium. The protocol defines the structure of control messages and it describes the way how messages are exchanged. OF is based on the centralized approach with a controller as a main driving element. This controller runs a software platform with the API enabling the direct control of data flows in a network.

Although OF enables to control the data plane, it does not provide any management capabilities for individual network devices. For this reason ONF has published OpenFlow Management and Configuration Protocol shortly called OpenFlow Config [3]. It was designed to support all OF implementations and also the management of both physical and virtual switches. The protocol part running in the switch requires the support of NETCONF protocol that uses an XML-like configuration [4].

Among the presented SDN use cases there are these that enable dynamic creation of the topologically separated networks (scalability beyond VLAN), service management up to the application layer, intelligent load-balancing and even more [5]. It is obvious that the primary application is expected in data centers, mainly in conjunction with the virtualization of services to IaaS (Infrastructure as a Service).

Since the concept of the OF technology is centralized, its practical deployment may be difficult. We have identified and analyzed potential constraints and shortcomings. This is an important step in a possible use of OF outside the academic test beds in a real production environment.

The real deployment, dealing with shortcomings and security issues such as the attack against IPv6 Duplication Address Detection (DAD) was the reason for the creation of a demonstration admin tool built on currently the most widely spread OF version 1.0. It shows how to cope with constraints of the early OF versions.

2. OpenFlow Analysis

OpenFlow should not be considered only as a protocol, but as a concept built on the fundamental idea separating the control and the data plane. There is defined an unambiguous role of the central controller, which has a number of advantages and disadvantages examined below.

The specification proposes description of the control messages for filling Forwarding Information Base (FIB) realized as so-called FlowTables and at the hardware level utilizing either RAM or TCAM (Ternary Content-Addressable Memory). OF control messages are sent over TLS/SSL secured TCP connection.

Furthermore, the OF specification includes the matching fields definition called tuples. On their basis there are made decisions and taken actions (instructions) and counted statistics. Tuples in OF 1.0 are defined for header fields from the first to the fourth layer if we consider port number as physical layer. There are 12 of them. A switch component model summarizing all OF parts is shown in Fig. 1. The main protocol changes between versions will be discussed below.

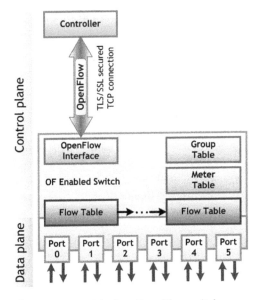

Fig. 1: Component model of an OpenFlow switch.

2.1. Concept Analysis

Regardless of the performance aspects it is necessary to draw attention to the potential risks and limitations associated with the concept of central control. It brings many benefits as collecting of statistical information and network devices status. The realization of the controller is independent of the third party applications creating the network control logic. On the other hand, the central control always raises issues relating primarily to the network reliability and its availability.

Controller as the software platform can be formed either central or distributed. Even though a distributed solution is apparently better in terms of the availability, it brings additional challenges such as consistency level throughout individual controller instances. Therefore we try to examine various restrictions associated with the OF networks control.

1) Hardware Failure

With the centralization of control functions in the controller there is a fundamental issue with the network reliability. While in networks with distributed protocols each switch always decides on the basis of its own view of the network, switches in OF networks are dependent on matching rules downloaded from the controller. In the case of connection failure the switch is not able to provide communication between end devices or it can behave like a standard switch. If we look at the test case in Fig. 2 we can get three failure probability formulas.

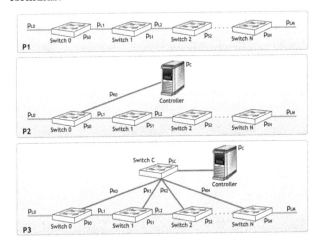

Fig. 2: Connection scheme of a classical non-OF network (P1) and an OF topology with one connection sharing payload means called the in-band control (P2) and full connection also called the out-band control (P3).

The first formula corresponds to the common topology of classical distributed control.

$$P_1 = \prod_{i=0}^{N} p_{Si} \cdot \prod_{j=0}^{M} p_{Lj}, \qquad (1)$$

where p_{Si} is the probability that the switch i will be available and p_{Lj} is the probability that the link j will be available.

The second formula assumes in-band control channel e.g. VLAN with single physical connection to the first switch in the chain.

$$P_2 = p_{K0} \cdot p_C \cdot P_1, \qquad (2)$$

where p_C is the probability that the controller will be available and p_{K0} is the probability that the link from the Switch 0 to the controller will be available.

The last scenario shows the full connected topology where every single switch has separated physical connection to the controller. The probability of availability can be described as in the third formula.

$$P_3 = \prod_{i=0}^{N} p_{Ki} \cdot p_{Ki} \cdot p_C \cdot p_{SC} \cdot P_1, \qquad (3)$$

where p_{SC} is the probability that the concentration switch will be available and p_{Ki} is the probability that the link from switch i to the controller will be available.

The original version of OF 1.0 specifies only one active TCP connection to the controller at the time. Later version 1.2 provides the ability to connect to more controllers at the same time and determine their role, including Master/Slave. The Master controller selection is out of scope the OF specification and it is a controller issue.

Loss detection of the switch-controller connection is not based on TCP features but must be made on the application layer by exchanging OF ECHO messages. There is no specification of the timer value in the specification for exchanging this type of messages. This means that the platform freedom does not need to meet QoS requirements of communicating applications because of late controller reconnection.

A second solution of such situations is a distributed controller, which can partially overcome the loss of the switch-controller connection. Currently, there are solutions such as HyperFlow or Onix by Nicira Company lately adopted by VMware as NVP [6], [7], [8].

Onix provides a higher level of abstraction than traditional controllers using Network Information Base (NBI) and it maintains a consistent state over controllers utilizing Distributed Hash Table (DHT). Onix leaves the level of reliability requirements on the user application.

HyperFlow is an extension for NOX controller and provides synchronization of controllers by propagating events affecting the controller state. Implementation is based on a Distributed File System (DFS) WheelFS [9].

The previous mentioned solutions imply that to ensure higher controller availability it must be always taken into account the time needed to identify the connection loss, the time for network reconfiguration and controller synchronization speed. The inter-plane synchronization is provided by east/westbound protocols. In 2012 there started works at IETF on the recommendation for exchanging messages in SDN networks, which should cover horizontal communication between controllers [10].

2)   Management Connectivity

For exchanging control messages between the OF controller and switches, the connectivity must be assured. It has two base types. The connectivity may be provided either on the same infrastructure, which operates payload flows, then it is so-called in-band or on the dedicated infrastructure which is called out-band.

When the in-band connectivity design is inappropriately utilized, there arises a danger of the control loss over the entire network in case of the single link failure. Therefore, it is important to think about appropriate diversification during designing of the controller location and its physical connection.

It is necessary to operate the management network on the basis of today's conventional technology using standard routing protocols such as IS-IS, OSPF, and more.

From this perspective, the switch still functions as a hybrid and that is the reason why there cannot be built the purely OF-based network. In addition, the separate infrastructure brings additional costs to build and operate any network. OF does not even reduce expenditures to the network administrator who has to take care of the initial implementation of the system setup and configuration.

3)   Software Failures

Since the matching rules are generated by a third party high level automated application, there can occur certain limitations for a network administrator. The administrator can have lower ability to intervene in the process of matching rules creating, understanding their granularity or capture a problem because of their timeout validity.

The possibility of bugs in the third party applications in comparison with distributed control of conventional networks may increase. Traditional, by standards described, behavior of distributed algorithms has been tested for years. Also a platform API provided to the third party applications may have higher bug rate than operating systems on network devices developed for decades due to the OF novelty.

It should be noted that unlike bugs occurring in the software of individual network devices, an incorrect central control may negatively affect the entire network. Nevertheless, compared to the traditional distributed approach OF definitely provides much higher degree of flexibility in eventual adjustment of these software bugs.

4) Security Vulnerabilities

As in the case of potential weaknesses in the form of hardware failure of the central controller is the central solution from the perspective of potential cyber-attack a great disadvantage. The secure channel between the switch and the controller is implemented to the transport layer using TLS, the standard protocol of which is derived the level of information security.

At the level of switch management the abilities of an attacker are basically the same as at today's traditional network devices. It depends on the attacker if he gets an access to the management network, consequently to a device CLI.

From the controller point of view, there primarily arises a threat of the third party application attack. This application generates matching rules and its vulnerability is vital for the whole network. This threat is also associated with the need of securing an operating system which runs an OF controller platform. It can be very difficult to detect such an attack or intrusion because of excluding the administrator from the rules generating process.

Neither the distribution controller nor the Master/Slave model provides the solution. Since that any of connected controllers can request Master role unidirectional, for the attacker it is enough to get control only over one instance of a controller. Then he just sets the Master parameter and he can act as a major decisive controller.

5) Scalability

At very large networks there comes the challenge of the sufficient performance on both switch and controller side. In extreme cases of huge flow numbers the controller should be able to manage hundreds of thousands of connections.

At the switch it is possible to move from realizing FlowTables using expensive TCAM that has a limited capacity to de facto software solution through the implementation in RAM. Typical count of entries in the FlowTables using TCAM is around 1500 entries [11]. It is therefore not appropriate to use OF in core switches. The only software implementation brings significant fall in processing time of the matching rules [12].

The scalability on the controller side can be solved in two ways. The first is a server-side scaling, thus utilizing multiple cores. There exist several platforms in this regard as NOX Destiny, Beacon or Maestro [13] [14]. The second approach uses additional controller instances for different areas as in the case with aforementioned HyperFlow or ONIX. Merging these approaches would cover both scalability and reliability issues.

2.2. Deployment Analysis

OF has been presented in the first usable version in 2009. Since then there is a high promoting activity of this specification in the incorporation into commercial equipment and deployment in real networks. The whole four years after its introduction the OF situation is getting clutter even because of rapid development under the ONF leadership.

We will discuss the current (June 2013) OF deployment status below, options in the production environment and the possibility of implementation of superstructure systems. Although the first OF version was perhaps academic matter there was an apparent target of transferring this technology to the commercial virtualization world. For testing reasons there were built several large academic networks such as GENI in the United States or Ofelia in Europe [15] [16].

1) OpenFlow 1.0 Features Development

In addition to the aforementioned limited number of tuples in OF v1.0 it does not include support of simultaneous connection to multiple controllers. This feature is supported up to the version 1.2. Moreover there is introduced replacement of actions by instructions and matching rules pipelining through more FlowTables.

Essential for the assumed application field, i.e. LAN in data centers, is the lack of IPv6 support. At the time of the OF first version development it was already obvious that it will be necessary to move to this type of addresses. The support came in version 1.2. Next was not a support for QoS. Solving QoS was left on the destination port queue. An aid in the form of the Meter Table comes in version 1.3.

2) Vendor Support

Even so, the protocol may be considered young; it is the only one southbound protocol suitable for implementing virtualized networks nowadays. Hence, it can be assumed that the effort of vendors will be a rapid development of both switches and controllers. However, the situation is different. From the outside view, most vendors after fast implementation of OF v1.0 enabled devices became petrified and the market stagnated. The OF support was often only part of the marketing strategy.

At the beginning of 2013 there was a few controllers often based on open solutions, but some of them are already commercial. One of the first was closed ONIX partly of which came open NOX [17]. Next one is BigSwitch controller based on Floodlight project, which was derived from Beacon controller. Another example is the IBM Programmable Network Controller and ProgramableFlow controller from NEC, which is based on open Helios later melted to Trema project [18], [19].

None of the aforementioned controllers does support OF version higher than 1.0 according to the available sources in June 2013.

Open solutions are based on different licenses as GPL and more. This may not be suitable for production environments because there is no support or warranty. Additionally OF is not standardized; it is just a specification developed by companies and its sustainability is disputable.

There is a reasonable supposition that during the next few years there will be progressive development in both software platforms and network devices over all big network vendors.

3)   Development and Simulations

It is important to keep in mind that the controller is only software platform not the application logic forming matching rules. Such applications are in their simple version a natural component of the controller, but they may be provided also as a third party product. This brings more demands on the reliability and the algorithms support. Since there is a responsibility transfer towards to algorithms, they have to be tested in details.

The testing can be divided into equipment conformance testing, control algorithms testing (network simulations) and performance testing such as throughput or latency.

One of the first conformity testing tools was OFtest, which is basically a controller comparing the received OF responses with the expected ones [20]. Currently, there are commercial solutions such as from Ixia [21]. ONF runs its own OpenFlow Conformance Testing Program.

For the development and testing of algorithms there was available Mininet at the first times of the OF release. Mininet creates a semi-virtual network topology built on OpenVSwitch [22]. It allows simulating various virtual network topologies. Its performance is dependable primarily on the test machine performance. Well-known NS-3 platform also supports OF, however it is limited to the internal controller [23]. Both platforms suffer by low degree of statistic gathering options.

There exists an implementation to the truly discrete simulation environment such as OMNeT++ [24]. It is also limited by only internal controller, but this solution can be better for collecting large statistical sets.

Another open solution for testing purposes is NICE project [25] focusing to the bug tracing. It forms an intermediate layer for NOX controller and helps to identify possible reasons of the third party application failure. Lastly there is a performance testing where for example sFlow can be used. Is able to monitor the number of active flows and it is described by RFC in [26].

For testing algorithms it would be appropriate to create a unified set of tests to ensure comparability of solutions supplied by third parties and by different device vendors.

3.   Monitoring Application

We have realized that OF is suitable for resolving security threats in a way known as First Hop Security. Focusing the known security threats we have picked up attack against Duplicate Address Detection (DAD) which is used by network hosts during the IPv6 address assignment.

As the first step we have created a security monitoring application. It should serve as a tool for network administrators for identification threats and solving security conflicts in a local network. It is based on Floodlight controller in version 0.9. This stable version supports OF v1.0, thus without the IPv6 address support at all. We have chosen this version because it was the only one accessible and spread version among both physical switches and controllers. Thanks to the OF features we have found the problem solution which has proved to be challenging.

3.1.   Problem Definition

Protocol DAD has a significant security issue in potential Deny of Service (DoS) attack as it is described in [27]. The situation when a potential host is unable to assign an address to itself is showed in Fig. 3.

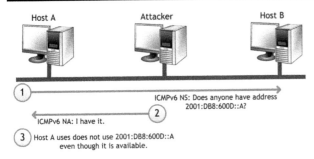

Fig. 3: Attack against IPv6 DAD.

There was an eminent need to extend the Floodlight module implementation for IPv6 address resolution.

3.2. Design and Implementation

Whole monitoring application is depicted in the deployment diagram in Fig. 4. The monitoring application is fundamentally based on the OpenFlow Security Engine (OFSE). OFSE accesses to Floodlight data via a REST API. Information about the network stored in the controller is transported to the OFSE in JSON format. A frontend graphical application Visualizing Console (VC) presents network topology with hosts by a graph using data obtained from OFSE.

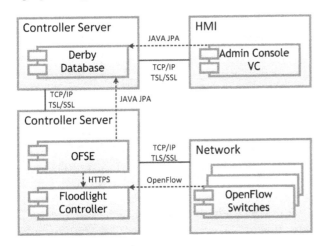

Fig. 4: Monitoring application deployment diagram.

Forwarding module in Floodlight handles every OpenFlow message for unknown data flow. It is sent from the OF switch to the controller. Floodlight has not implemented forwarding functionality for payload frames with Ethertype 0x08DD, thus IPv6. These frames fall into the default forwarding where the switch behaves as a usual learning switch. It was very essential to make modifications which add support to catch these types of frames.

Once a frame with IPv6 protocol is received by controller it is processed by the forwarding module. Then the IPv6 module receives frame thanks to listener; it

parses the IPv6 address and it stores the address internally in the controller logic. Further code implementation results that these IPv6 addresses are accessible via the REST API of the Floodlight to OFSE.

In case of DAD security issue, once the OFSE detects a higher rate of new source IPv6 addresses than a trigger level assigned to one particular network host in a given period of time, it supposes it is the attack against DAD. OFSE then marks up the attacker in the database for VC as a potential threat in the network. It is then possible to browse through history of a network topology but also to automatically identify and visualize attackers in a network.

This application is a first step for future improvement when it could be extended to a form of a proactive tool which would allow immediate autonomy action. This is not possible in this version because of a lack of IPv6 tuples and the action depends on the network administrator.

3.3. Evaluation

During the development phase the application was tested in Mininet software within Xubuntu Linux distribution. In the next phase a real network with OF switches was created. It included two switches HP E3800 and one HP 5406zl. Multiple client hosts were connected to these switches with enabled IPv4/IPv6 interfaces. The output for one moment of the testing is in Fig. 5. Red circles represent switches, green ones are for connected hosts and blue one represents the last database action.

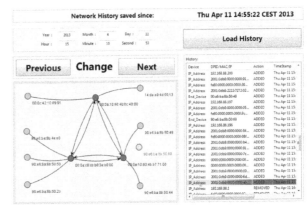

Fig. 5: Application screenshot from the real network testing.

There is a potential glitch in the functionality in case that matching rules within OF switch would be based only upon very low flow tuples e.g. MAC addresses. Since the general rules can cover the communication on higher levels, so it is not possible to catch an IPv6 address. Nonetheless, we found out during the testing on the real network that there was always additional information which distinguished any type of communication even with the default forwarding and all IPv6 addresses were successfully captured.

4.   Conclusion

The main goal of this paper is to present the current state of the OpenFlow protocol development. It seems that four years after the introduction of the first viable version the protocol still has a long way to the mass commercial deployment with the exception of specialized networks.

The analysis shows that the central control concentrated into a single controller brings a number of disadvantages that may be not suitable for certain deployments. Although the main expected deployment field is in data centers for optimizing communication within virtualized infrastructure, there exist use cases covering for example differentiated services on ISPs.

With the centralization there arise a number of questions, not only in a technical field such as ensuring greater availability of controllers but also how to share their control information between different operators. For this and other limitations we concluded that the appropriate OF deployment areas are primarily closed local area networks with a single administration without the critical infrastructure needs. We have also proposed the security demonstrational application solving OF 1.0 shortage in the lack of IPv6 support.

Acknowledgment

This work was supported by Grant Project SGS13/200/OHK3/3T/13.

References

[1] CASADO, M. and N. MCKEOWN. The virtual network system. In: *Proceedings of the 36th SIGCSE technical symposium on Computer science education - SIGCSE '05*. New York: ACM Press, 2005, pp. 76–80. ISBN 1-58113-997-7. DOI: 10.1145/1047344.1047383.

[2] OpenFlow Switch Specication: Version 1.0.0 (Wire Protocol 0x01). In: *OpenFlow* [online]. 2009. Available at: http://archive.openflow. org/documents/openflow-spec-v1.0.0.pdf.

[3] OpenFlow Management and Configuration Protocol: (OF-Config 1.1.1). In: *OpenFlow* [online]. 2013. Available at: https://www.opennetworking.org/images/ stories/downloads/sdn-resources/ onf-specifications/openflow-config/ of-config-1-1-1.pdf.

[4] ENNS, R., M. BJORKLUND, J. SCHOEN-WAELDER and A. BIERMAN. Network Configuration Protocol (NETCONF): RFC 6241. In: *RFC Editor* [online]. 2011. Available at: http: //www.rfc-editor.org/rfc/rfc6241.txt.

[5] SDN Use Cases. In: *SDN Central* [online]. 2012. Available at: http://www.sdncentral. com/sdn-use-cases/.

[6] TOOTOONCHIAN, A. and G. YASHAR. HyperFlow: A distributed control plane for OpenFlow. In: *INM/WREN '10: 2010 International Network Management Workshop/Workshop on Research on Enterprise Networking* [online]. 2010. Available at: https: //www.usenix.org/legacy/events/inmwren10/ tech/full_papers/Tootoonchian.pdf.

[7] KOPONEN, T., M. CASADO, N. GUDE, J. STRIBLING, L. POUTIEVSKI, M. ZHU, R. RA-MANATHAN, Y. IWATA, H. INOUE, T. HAMA and S. SHENKER. Onix: a distributed control platform for large-scale production networks. In: *Proceedings of the 9th USENIX conference on Operating systems design and implementation*. Berkeley: USENIX Association, 2010, pp. 37–40. ISBN 978-1-931971-79-9.

[8] Nicira Network Virtualization Platform. In: *Nicira* [online]. 2012. Available at: http://nicira.com/sites/default/files/ docs/NVPDatasheet.pdf.

[9] STRIBLING, J., Y. SOVRAN, I. ZHANG, X. PRETZER, J. LI, M. F. KAASHOEK and R. MORRIS. Flexible, wide-area storage for distributed systems with WheelFS. In: *NSDI '09: Proceedings of the 6th USENIX Symposium on Networked Systems Design and Implementation* [online]. 2009. Available at: https: //www.usenix.org/legacy/events/nsdi09/ tech/full_papers/stribling/stribling.pdf.

[10] YIN, H., H. XIE, T. TSOU, D. LOPEZ, P. ARANDA and R. SIDI. SDNi: A Message Exchange Protocol for Software Defined Networks (SDNS) across Multiple Domains. In: *The Internet Engineering Task Force (IETF)* [online]. 2012. Available at: http://tools.ietf.org/ html/draft-yin-sdn-sdni-00.

[11] ZAREK, A. OpenFlow Timeouts Demystified. In: *Computer Engineering Research Group: University of Toronto* [online]. Toronto, 2012. Avail-

able at: http://www.eecg.toronto.edu/~lie/papers/zarek_mscthesis.pdf.

[12] HEGR, T., L. BOHAC, Z. KOCUR, M. VOZNAK and P. CHLUMSKY. Methodology of the direct measurement of the switching latency. *Przeglad Elektrotechniczny*. 2013, vol. 89, iss. 7, pp. 59–63. ISSN 0033-2097.

[13] ERICKSON, D. The Beacon OpenFlow Controller. In: *HotSDN'13* [online]. 2013. Available at: http://yuba.stanford.edu/~derickso/docs/hotsdn15-erickson.pdf.

[14] CAI, Z. *Maestro: Achieving Scalability and Coordination in Centralized Network Control Plane*. Houston, 2011. Dissertation thesis. Rice University.

[15] Exploring networks of the future. *GENI: Global Environment for Network Innovations* [online]. 2013. Available at: http://www.geni.net.

[16] KOPSEL, A. and H. WOESNER. OFELIA-pan-european test facility for openflow experimentation. In: *4th European Conference – Towards a Service-Based Internet*. Berlin: Springer, 2011, pp. 311–312. ISBN 978-3-642-24755-2.

[17] GUDE, N., T. KOPONEN, J. PETTIT, B. PFAFF, M. CASADO, N. MCKEOWN and S. SHENKER. NOX: towards an operating system for networks. *ACM SIGCOMM Computer Communication Review*. 2008, vol. 38, iss. 3, pp. 105–110. ISSN 0146-4833.

[18] IBM Programmable Network Controller. In: *IBM* [online]. 2012. Available at: http://public.dhe.ibm.com/common/ssi/ecm/en/qcd03018usen/QCD03018USEN.PDF.

[19] ProgrammableFlow Controller. In: *NEC* [online]. 2012. Available at: http://www.necam.com/SDN/doc.cfm?t=PFlowController.

[20] OFTest framework. In: *Project Floodlight* [online]. 2013. Available at: http://www.projectfloodlight.org/oftest/.

[21] IXIA OpenFlow Validation Solutions. In: *IXIA* [online]. 2013. Available at: www.ixiacom.com/pdfs/library/quick_ref_sheets/OpenFlow-qrs.pdf.

[22] LANTZ, B., B. HELLER and N. MCKEOWN. A network in a laptop: rapid prototyping for software-defined networks. In: *Proceedings of the 9th ACM SIGCOMM Workshop on Hot Topics in Networks*. New York: ACM, 2010, pp. 1–6. ISBN 978-1-4503-0409-2. DOI: 10.1145/1868447.1868466.

[23] NS-3 OpenFlow switch support. In: *NS-3.13 documentation* [online]. 2013. Available at: http://www.nsnam.org/docs/release/3.13/models/html/openflow-switch.html.

[24] KLEIN, D. and M. JARSCHEL. An OpenFlow Extension for the OMNeT++ INET Framework. In: *Universitaet Wuerzburg* [online]. 2013. Available at: http://www3.informatik.uni-wuerzburg.de/research/ngn/ofomnet/paper-acm_with_font.pdf.

[25] CANINI, M., D. VENZANO, P. PERESINI, D. KOSTIC and J. REXFORD. A NICE way to test OpenFlow applications. In: *9th USENIX Symposium on Networked Systems Design and Implementation*. San Jose: UNISEX Association, 2012, pp. 127–140. ISBN 978-931971-92-8. Available at: https://www.usenix.org/system/files/tech-schedule/nsdi12_proceedings_full.pdf.

[26] PHAAL, P., S. PANCHEN and N. MCKEE. In-Mon Corporation's sFlow: A Method for Monitoring Traffic in Switched and Routed Networks: RFC 3176. In: *RFC Editor* [online]. 2001. Available at: http://www.rfc-editor.org/rfc/rfc3176.txt.

[27] NIKANDER, P., J. KEMOF and E. NORDMARK. IPv6 Neighbor Discovery (ND) Trust Models and Threats: RFC 3756. In: *RFC Editor* [online] 2004. Available at: http://www.rfc-editor.org/rfc/rfc3756.txt.

About Authors

Tomas HEGR was born in 1988. He received his M.Sc. in computer science at the Czech Technical University in Prague in 2012. His research interests include industrial networks based on Ethernet and SDN.

Leos BOHAC received the M.S. and Ph.D. degrees in electrical engineering from the Czech Technical University, Prague, in 1992 and 2001, respectively. Since 1992, he has been teaching optical communication systems and data networks with the Czech Technical University, Prague. His research interest is on the application of high-speed optical transmission systems in a data network.

Vojtech UHLIR was born in 1990. He received B.Sc. in Computer Systems in 2013 at FEE, CTU in Prague. His focus is in computer programming, embedded systems and networks.

Petr CHLUMSKY was born in 1985. He received his M.Sc. from the Czech Technical University in Prague in 2010. Since 2010 he has been studying Ph.D. degree. His research interests include wireless transmission, network coding and network simulation.

10

Implementation of Optical Meanders in the Temperature Measurement of the Extermination of Basidiomycete Serpula Lacrymans Using Microwave Heating

Andrej LINER[1], *Martin PAPES*[1], *Jakub JAROS*[1], *Jakub CUBIK*[1], *Stanislav KEPAK*[1], *Pavel SMIRA*[2], *Andrea NASSWETTROVA*[2], *Jiri GABRIEL*[3]

[1]Department of Telecommunications, Faculty of Electrical Engineering and Computer Science, VSB–Technical University of Ostrava, 17. listopadu 15/2172, 708 33 Ostrava-Poruba, Czech Republic
[2]Thermo Sanace s.r.o., Chamradova 475/23, 718 00 Ostrava-Kuncicky, Czech Republic
[3]Institute of Microbiology, Academy of Sciences of the Czech Republic, v.v.i., Videnska 1083, 142 20 Prague 4, Czech Republic

andrej.liner@vsb.cz, martin.papes@vsb.cz, jakub.jaros@vsb.cz, jakub.cubik@vsb.cz, stanislav.kepak@vsb.cz, andrea.nasswettrova@gmail.com, info@thermosanace.eu, gabriel@biomed.cas.cz

Abstract. *The dry rot basidiomycete Serpula lacrymans is the most common and destructive wood decay fungus, which attacks and damages houses and other wooden construction worldwide [1], [2]. Effective chemicals have been developed for remediation and treatment of dry rot outbreaks and for wood preservation against dry rot, but in most cases, control is most economically achieved by environmental management to avoid creating favourable growth conditions for the fungus [3]. Thermal treatment using microwaves represents one of possible approaches in fungal growth control and refurbishment of damaged wooden constructions. One of the possibilities, how to monitor this whole process seems to be the use of Optical fiber DTS (Distribution Temperature Systems). The Optical fiber DTS are unique distributed temperature systems using optical fiber as a sensor. Due to the electromagnetic resistance is this system suitable for the monitoring of these processes. This article deals with application of optical meanders in the temperature measurement during the extermination of basidiomycete Serpula lacrymans using microwave heating. Because of the adverse effect of microwave radiation on all other types of temperature sensors.*

Keywords

Microwave emitter, microwave heating, optical fiber DTS, optical meander, Serpula Lacrymans.

1. Introduction

The Optical Fiber DTS (Distributed Temperature System) are unique distributed temperature systems using optical fiber as a sensor. Temperature values are recorded along the optical fiber continuously in points. DTS system can be imagined as several thousand sensors providing information on the thermal state of the environment in which the optical fiber is located. These systems are mainly due to their advantages, utilized in many applications [4], [5]. The biggest advantages are:

- resistance to electromagnetic radiation,

- resistant to aggressive environments,

- the length of the measured section up to the 30 km.

As the name suggests, Optical Fiber DTS based on Stimulated Raman Scattering are using nonlinear Raman scattering. Lasers used in these systems operates at a wavelength of the 1064 nm. Raman spectra peaks are in this case shifted by ± 40 nm. That is equal to 1104 nm and 1024 nm. These two newly incurred components that arise from the reflections on the core and cladding boundary along the optical fiber are two parts of the spectrum and named as Stokes and Anti-Stokes component. Exactly the Anti-Stokes spectra component changes its intensity depending on the temperature along the fiber. The Stokes part of the spectrum is thermally independent. The DTS defines the location of temperature based on changes in the intensity of the

Anti-Stokes spectrum and final ratio between Stokes spectrum [6]. Spatial resolution of the DTS system is standardly about 1 m with accuracy of ±1 °C, at a resolution of 0,01 °C.

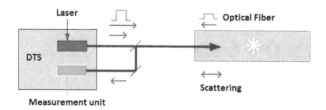

Fig. 1: Block diagram of the DTS system.

Spatial information about the temperature distribution along the optical fiber is achieved using a technique called Optical Time Domain Reflectometry (OTDR) which is nowadays mostly used for optical testing line [7] (seen in Fig. 1).

2. Optical Meanders in Point Mode

If it is necessary to ensure accurate localization in the measurement process, it is appropriate to apply optical meanders in the point mode. Point mode means that some point is created sensoric ring of optical fiber. In practice, it is often required the sensoric ring to have the smallest sizes (inner diameter and length of the optical fiber in the ring). It is obvious that the dimensions of the sensoric ring will vary with different parameters of optical fibers.

In the case of use multimode optical fiber with only primary protection (outer diameter 250 μm) decreases the critical inner diameter of sensoric ring to value 3 cm. The curve shows the different inner diameters of optical meander. If the inner diameter reduced below the 3 cm then created too large attenuation. This method will be inaccurate. Shown in Fig. 2.

According to another experimental measurement the length of multimode optical fiber in the sensoric ring has a critical value of 3 m [9].

3. Measurement of Microwave Emitter's Mean Power

This measurement was performed in the Department of Theoretical and Experimental Electrical Engineering laboratory. For measurements was used the microwave emitter with a magnetron type NL 10250. This emitter operates at the frequency of 2,45 GHz and at the wavelength of the EM wave 12,25 cm. The

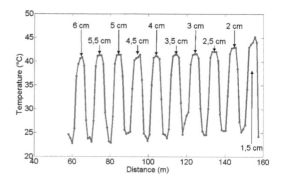

Fig. 2: Effect of the inner diameter of the sensoric ring on the measured temperature of the water bath (measured together, optical fiber with primary protection, inner diameter 250 μm), [8].

listed maximum power is 1,9 kW. Antenna for directing the flow of energy has a funnel shape with an aperture of 270 × 270 mm. A calorimetric method was chosen for the actual measurement of microwave emitter's mean power. Water was placed into the rectangular tank containing 10 litres. Time of microwave emitter radiation heating of the container with water was set to the 10 minutes. Temperature changes during the time of the experiment were measured by using DTS (Distributed Temperature System) and for larger precision of the measurement were used optical meanders. Scheme of measurement is shown in Fig. 3(a) and the process is shown in Fig. 3(b).

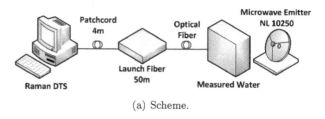

(a) Scheme.

(b) Process.

Fig. 3: Scheme and process of measurement microwave emitter's mean power.

Optical meander was immersed directly into the water in the container. Measurement was performed for two limit values of microwave emitters. At first the minimal power of microwave emitter P_{min} was set and then was set the maximal power P_{max}. From the default calorimetric equation:

$$Q = m \cdot c \cdot \Delta t = W = P \cdot t_c, \qquad (1)$$

was expressed the measured power of the microwave emitter and the value P_{min} was calculated, whose temperature process is shown in the Fig. 4. The starting water temperature was 15,6 °C and during the 10 min. heating was water warmed to 24,5 °C:

$$P_{min} = \frac{m \cdot c \cdot \Delta t}{t_c} = \frac{10 \cdot 4180 \cdot 15,4}{600} = 620 \ [W]. \quad (2)$$

After calculating the P_{min} value the power of microwave emitter was changed to the maximum value and then was the value P_{max} calculated, its temperature course is shown in Fig. 5. The starting water temperature was 22,5 °C and during the 10 minutes heating was water warmed to 37,9 °C:

$$P_{max} = \frac{m \cdot c \cdot \Delta t}{t_c} = \frac{10 \cdot 4180 \cdot 8,9}{600} = 1073 \ [W]. \quad (3)$$

Due to the easier calculation and better understanding of the temperature values were the values of the initial and final temperature of the water substituted in °C. The final values of the temperature differences are exactly the same as in the case of substituting values in Kelvin [10], [11].

4. Extermination of Serpula Lacrymans Using Microwave Heating

Oat flakes were mixed with water (6:4 W/W) and autoclaved. Bricks ($10 \times 10 \times 1,5$ cm) were prepared from the material in plastic bags in aluminium form and autoclaved again after 3 days. Bricks were then inoculated with agar plugs from ME agar on Petri dishes (malt extract 7 g/l, agar 20 g/l, pH 7,0) with S. lacrymans (CCBAS110) and cultivated at 25 °C in darkness for 14 days. After microwave heating, samples from all bags were taken and ME agars were re-inoculated. Mycelial growth was checked daily during the next 10 days.

Fig. 6: The temperature measurement for one optical meander.

Fig. 4: The temperature measurement for P_{min}. X-axis represents the total length of fiber, which is zooming in to the measured optical meander. Measured optical meander is located in the section between 60,5 m to 63,5 m.

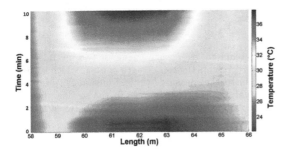

Fig. 5: The temperature measurement for P_{max}. X-axis represents the total length of fiber, which is zooming in to the measured optical meander. Measured optical meander is located in the section between 60 m to 63 m.

The measurement was carried out in the Department of Theoretical and Experimental Electrical Engineering laboratory again. In each measurement were used two samples and between these two samples was placed meander composed of measuring optical fiber (Fig. 6). The aim of this measurement was to determine the required time for the operation of the microwave emitter for the consumption of dry-rot fungus. The temperature of the sample had to be maintained over 90 °C, because this is the temperature limit for destruction of the tested Serpula Lacrymans. However, the temperature could not significantly exceed the value of 100 °C, because the measured sample could ignite. The microwave emitter was operating in the sample's temperature range between 90 to 100 °C so that was switched off at 100 °C and switched on if the sample's temperature dropped at 90 °C as can be seen in graphs.

The time intervals were chosen at 5, 15, 30, 120 and 240 minutes. This means that the sample had to be exposed to temperatures over 90 °C during this time intervals.

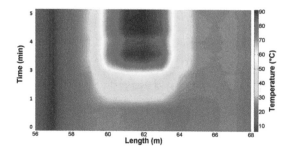

Fig. 7: The temperature measurement for one optical meander for a 5 min. X-axis represents the total length of fiber, which is zooming in to the measured optical meander. Measured optical meander is located in the section between 60 m to 63 m.

Measurements were divided into two parts. In the first part were first three time intervals (5, 15 and 30 min.) measured and in each time interval was used only one sample. The time course of the first measurement, 5 min. time interval is shown in Fig. 7.

After 5 minutes, the samples were changed and measurement in 15 min. time interval was initiated. The time course of this measurement is shown in Fig. 8.

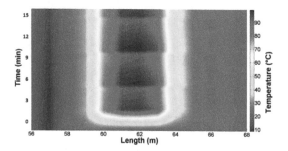

Fig. 8: The temperature measurement for one optical meander for a 15 min. X-axis represents the total length of fiber, which is zooming in to the measured optical meander. Measured optical meander is located in the section between 60 m to 63 m.

After 15 min. were the samples changed again the measurement in 30 min. was initiated. The time course of this measurement is shown in Fig. 9.

Due to the time demands were the last two measurements (120 and 240 min. time intervals) merged. In this measurement were used two optical meanders. Samples were placed one after another and heated together (Fig. 10). During measurement the first tested sample has been losing its original shape and was then less heated. Therefore, the operation of microwave emitter had to be longer. However, the second sample was heated much more. The temperature of the

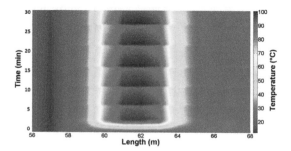

Fig. 9: The temperature measurement for one optical meander for a 30 min. X-axis represents the total length of fiber, which is zooming in to the measured optical meander. Measured optical meander is located in the section between 60 m to 63 m.

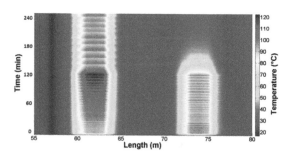

Fig. 10: The temperature measurement for two optical meanders.

second sample was reaching the values up to 115 °C and the sample had to be constantly monitored. After 120 min. was one sample taken and measurement continued with only the second sample (Fig. 11).

Fig. 11: The temperature measurement for two meanders. X-axis represents the total length of fiber, which is zooming in to the measured optical meanders. Measured optical meanders are located in the section: first between 71,5 m to 74,5 m and second between 60 m to 63 m.

After the measurement were the samples received by the researchers after from The Institute of Microbiology, on the Academy of Sciences of the Czech Republic (ASCR), v.v.i., for the next research and measurements, which had to confirm or contradict the extermination of the Serpula Lacrymans in the different time interval measurements.

The effect of high temperature on the fungal viability was tested by re-inoculation of treated samples on agar plates. No growth of the fungus was observed even after 5 min of microwave treatment. The experiments described here demonstrated the ability of microwaves to kill mycelial cultures of Serpula Lacrymans efficiently. However, the results obtained with oat flakes can not be generalized and applied to other materials such is wood or timber.

5. Conclusion

The aim of these measurements was to determine the functionality of using optical meanders to monitoring the temperature inside the tested samples during extermination of Serpula Lacrymans with microwave radiation. After successfully completing these experiments was ascertained the unique and reliable utilization of optical meanders and DTS in processes of extermination of Serpula Lacrymans by use of microwave radiation and that because of measured high accuracy of temperature and resistance to electromagnetic radiation. Given the current range of materials used in the sensors this method appears as the most reliable and most accurate.

Additional measurements and applications that we can use DTS resistance consisting in the application of optical meanders on a wooden beam. These beams will be heated up in two ways. In the first case it will be heated by hot air in the reconstruction process of old buildings. In the second case it will be heated by microwave emitter in the reconstruction process of old beams in laboratory. Our research team also done another measurements such as in terrain and the also at the research workplace in Zvolen.

Acknowledgment

The research described in this article could be carried out thanks to the active support of the Czech Science Foundation GAP108/11/1057 (Synthesis, structure and properties of nanocomposites conducting polymer/phyllosilicate) and the Ministry of Education of the Czech Republic within the project SP2013/69 of the VSB–Technical University of Ostrava. This article was also supported by project VG20102015053 (GUARDSENSE - The modern structure of photonic sensors and new innovative principles for intrusion detection systems, integrity and protection of critical infrastructure) and Technology Agency of the Czech Republic TA03020439. The research has been partially supported by the project No. CZ.1.07/2.3.00/20.0217 (The Development of Excellence of the Telecommunication Research Team in Relation to International Cooperation) within the frame of the operation programme "Education for competitiveness" financed by the European Structural Funds and from the state budget of the Czech Republic.

References

[1] MAURICE, S., L. COROLLER, S. DEBAETS, V. VASSEUR, G. LE FLOCH and G. BARBIER. Modelling the effect of temperature, water activity and pH on the growth of Serpula lacrymans. *Journal of Applied Microbiology*. 2011, vol. 111, iss. 6, pp. 1436–1446. ISSN: 1365-2672. DOI: 10.1111/j.1365-2672.2011.05161.x.

[2] SCHMIDT, O. Indoor wood-decay basidiomycetes: damage, causal fungi, physiology, identification and characterization, prevention and control. *Mycological Progress*. 2007, vol. 6, iss. 4, pp. 261–279. ISSN: 1617-416X. DOI: 10.1007/s11557-007-0534-0.

[3] WATKINSON S. C. and D. C. EASTWOOD. 2012. Serpula lacrymans, wood and buildings. *Advances in Applied Microbiology*. 1st ed. Boston: Academic Press, 2012, vol. 78, pp. 121–149. ISBN 978-0-12-394805-2.

[4] KOUDELKA P., B. PETRUJOVA, J. LATAL, F. HANACEK, P. SISKA, J. SKAPA and V. VASINEK. Optical fiber distributed sensing system applied in cement concrete commixture research. *Radioengineering*. 2010, vol. 19, no. 1, pp. 172–177. ISSN 1210-2512.

[5] LONG D. *The Raman Effect: A Unifield Treatment of the Theory Raman Scattering by Molecules*. New York: Wiley, 2002, pp. 598. ISBN 978-0-471-49028-9.

[6] BALL D.W. Theory of Raman Spectroscopy. *Spectroscopy*. 2001, vol. 16, iss. 11. ISSN 0887-6703. Available at: http://spectroscopyonline.findanalytichem.com/spectroscopy/data/articlestandard/spectroscopy/442001/836/article.pdf.

[7] RODERS A. Distributed optical-fibre sensing. *Measurement Science and Technology*. 1999, vol. 10, iss. 8. ISSN 1361-6501. DOI: 10.1088/0957-0233/10/8/201.

[8] KOUDELKA P., J. LATAL, J. VITASEK, J. HURTA, P. SISKA, A. LINER and M. PAPES. Implementation of Optical Meanders of the

Optical-fiber DTS System Based on Raman Stimulated Scattering into the Building Processes. *Advances in Electrical and Electronic Engineering*. 2012, vol. 10, no. 3, pp. 187–194. ISSN 1336-1376.

[9] KOUDELKA P., A. LINER, M. PAPES, J. LATAL, V. VASINEK, J. HURTA, T. VINKLER and P. SISKA. New Sophisticated Analisis Method of Crystallizer Temperature Profile Utilizing Optical Fiber DTS Based on the Stimulated Raman Scattering. *Advances in Electrical and Electronic Engineering*. 2012, vol. 10, no. 2, pp. 106–114. ISSN 1336-1376.

[10] DEDEK L. and J. DEDEKOVA. *Elektromagnetismus*. 2nd ed. Ed. Brno: VUTIUM, 2000. ISBN 80-214-1548-7.

[11] HALLIDAY D., R. RESNICK and J. WALKER. *Fyzika: Vysokoskolska ucebnice obecne fyziky*. 1st ed. Ed. Praha: Prometheus, 2000, xxiv. ISBN 80-214-1869-9.

About Authors

Andrej LINER was born in 1987 in Zlate Moravce. In 2009 received Bachelor's degree on University of Zilina, Faculty of Electrical Engineering, Department of Telecommunications and Multimedia. Two years later he received on the same workplace his Master's degree in the field of Telecommunications and Radio Communications Engineering. He is currently Ph.D. student, and he works in the field of wireless optical communications and fiber optic distributed systems.

Martin PAPES was born in 1987 in Nove Zamky. In 2009 received Bachelor's degree on University of Zilina, Faculty of Electrical Engineering, Department of Telecommunications and Multimedia. Two years later he received on the same workplace his Master's degree in the field of Telecommunications and Radio Communications Engineering. He is currently Ph.D. student, and he works in the field of wireless optical communications and fiber optic distributed systems.

Jakub JAROS was born in 1987 in Ostrava. In 2009 received Bachelor's degree on VSB-Technical University of Ostrava, Faculty of Electrical Engineering and Computer Science, Department of Telecommunications. Three years later he received on the same workplace his Master's degree in the field of Telecommunications. He is currently Ph.D. student, and he works in the field of optical communications and fiber optic sensor systems.

Jakub CUBIK was born in 1986 in Olomouc. In 2009 received Bachelor's degree on VSB-Technical University of Ostrava, Faculty of Electrical Engineering and Computer Science, Department of Telecommunications. Two years later he received on the same workplace his Master's degree in the field of Telecommunications. He is currently Ph.D. student, and he works in the field of optical communications and fiber optic sensor systems.

Stanislav KEPAK was born in 1987 in Ostrava. In 2009 received Bachelor's degree on VSB-Technical University of Ostrava, Faculty of Electrical Engineering and Computer Science, Department of Telecommunications. Two years later he received on the same workplace his Master's degree in the field of Telecommunications. He is currently Ph.D. student, and he works in the field of optical communications and fiber optic sensor systems.

Pavel SMIRA was born in Celadna, the district of Frydek-Mistek, the Czech Republic, in 1960. In 1983 he was awarded the Master degree in the field of civil engineering at the Faculty of Civil Engineering at the Brno University of Technology. In 1989 he founded Smira-Print, s.r.o. and in 2010 Thermo Sanace, s.r.o. which deals with the rehabilitation and reconstruction of historic structures of valued heritage. He develops the method of wood hot air sterilisation which efficiently kills active wood-destroying insects. In 2013 he completed the doctoral study programme in the theory of structures. At present he actively deals with the research in structural conservation and develops non-destructive methods for detecting damage to biological structures.

Andrea NASSWETTROVA was born in Olomouc, the Czech Republic in 1984. In 2008 she was awarded the Master degree in the field of wooden constructions and wooden structural members at the Mendel University in Brno, the Faculty of Forestry and Wood Technology. She gained the doctor's degree at the same Faculty three years later. She shortly worked as a researcher at the Institute of Wood Science, specializing in the properties of wood and wood-based materials. At present she is employed with Thermo Sanace, s.r.o. where she is responsible for professional and research activities. She works on innovations in the field of non-destructive methods of wood examination and the verification of efficiency of wood-destroying insect liquidation by means of hot air conservation method as well as the application of high frequency microwave heating.

Jiri GABRIEL was born in Liberec, the Czech Republic, in 1963. Graduated in analytical chemistry (Faculty of Science, Charles University, Prague, 1987), Ph.D. studies in the field of fungal physiology (Institute of Microbiology, Czechoslovak Academy of

Sciences, Prague, 1992). In general, he is interested in fungal physiology and metabolism. His main research interest is study of accumulation of toxic metals in mycelium of basidiomycetes, both under nature and laboratory conditions, and in effect of metals on fungal physiology and morphology. Also, he is interested in decay of wood and in biodegradation of xenobiotics by basidiomycetes. He participated in several projects dealing with biomonitoring of heavy metal pollution of environment in the Czech Republic. He is author and co-author of more than 50 papers in peer-reviewed journals. He is an external lecturer at Department of Microbiology and Genetics, Faculty of Science, Charles University, and Deputy Director of the Institute of Microbiology, Academy of Sciences of the Czech Republic. He is President of the Czechoslovak Society of Microbiology.

11

The Analysis of SARDANA HPON Networks Using the HPON Network Configurator

Rastislav ROKA

Institute of Telecommunications, Faculty of Electrical Engineering and Information Technology,
Slovak University of Technology in Bratislava, Ilkovicova 3, 812 19 Bratislava, Slovak Republic

rastislav.roka@stuba.sk

Abstract. *NG-PON systems present optical access infrastructures to support various applications of the many service providers. In the near future, we can expect NG-PON technologies with different motivations for developing of HPON networks. The HPON is a hybrid passive optical network in a way that utilizes on a physical layer both TDM and WDM multiplexing principles together. The HPON network utilizes similar or soft revised topologies as TDM-PON architectures. In this second paper, requirements for the SARDANA HPON networks are introduced. A main part of the paper is dedicated to presentation of the HPON network configurator that allows configurating and analyzing the SARDANA HPON characteristics from a viewpoint of various specific network parameters. Finally, a short introduction to the comparison of the SARDANA and SUCCESS HPON networks based on simulation results is presented.*

Keywords

HPON network configurator, hybrid passive optical networks, SARDANA HPON.

1. Introduction

NG-PON technologies can be divided into two categories. The NG-PON1 presents an evolutionary growth with supporting the coexistence with the GPON on the same ODN. The coexistence feature enables seamless upgrade of individual customers on live optical fibers without disrupting services of other customers. The NG-PON2 presents a revolutionary change with no requirement in terms of coexistence with the GPON on the same ODN.

The HPON presents a hybrid network as a necessary phase of the future transition from TDM to WDM passive optical networks [1]. It can be divided into two possible groups. In the first one, a change of OLT and ONU equipment is executed and adding of WDM and TDM ONU equipment into a common network architecture is allowed by using specialized remote nodes that utilize either power splitters or AWG elements. In the second one, preservation of TDM access networks combined with the DWDM technique is predicted. For both approaches, various solutions were proposed.

At the SARDANA (Scalable Advanced Ring-based passive Dense Access Network Architecture) design [2], [3], [4], a scope is to create a modular network and to enable service provisioning for more than 1000 subscribers at distances up to 100 km. It is considered a remote pumped amplification using EDFA principles and utilization of the colourless ONU units at subscriber side. Also, the backward compatibility with existing 1G-PON networks and a support for standardized 10G-PON networks are considered with 100–1000 Mbit/s transmission rates per one subscriber.

The PON fiber topology is creating by two main parts – the WDM ring with the central office and remote nodes, TDM trees connected to particular remote nodes. The WDM ring consists of two optical fibers – one per direction. A key element of the network is the RN. Used ONU units are colourless, they don't contain any optical source. Transmitting from the ONU is based on the RSOA by means of the re-modulation of received signals. The SARDANA network allows connecting a large number of subscribers either on smaller distances in populous urban areas or in larger geographical areas with a small population. Information can be found in [5].

2. Simulation of HPON Networks

Our simulation model for comparing possibilities of various passive optical access networks is created by using the Microsoft Visual Studio 2008 software in the

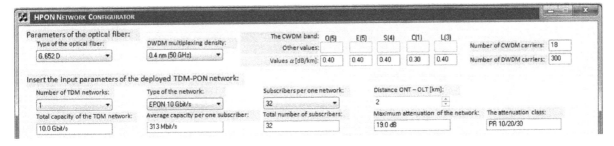

Fig. 1: The cut-out from the main window of the HPON network configurator.

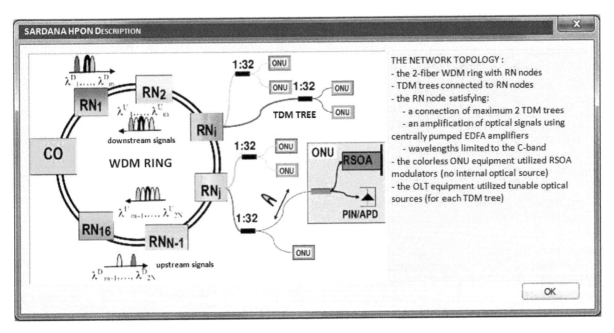

Fig. 2: The description window of the SARDANA HPON network.

IDE development environment [6], [7], [8], [9]. There exist possibilities for the graphical interface created by using the MFC (Microsoft Foundation Class) library for the $C++$ programming language. The simulation model has one main dialogue window for simulating a transition from TDM-PON to HPON networks. It allows comparing principal approaches for configuring of hybrid passive optical networks. A cut-out from the main window of the HPON configurator is shown on Fig. 1.

First, a selection of the optical fiber's type and the DWDM multiplexing density can be executed. A selected type of the optical fiber is presented by the specific attenuation values and by a number of transmission bands. These values correspond to various ITU-T recommendations - ITU-T G.652 A, G.652 B, G.652 C, G.652 D, G.656, G.657 – and, if available, measuring data can be inserted in the "Other values" option. Then, specific attenuation coefficients are used for calculating of the optical fiber's attenuation in corresponding bands in specific network configurations. Also, a total number of CWDM and DWDM carrier wavelengths for particular bands is presented. The relationship between numbers of available wavelengths at various channel allocations is introduced in [8]. Then, a specification of parameters and features of the deployed TDM-PON network can be executed. More detailed information can be found in [10].

Three additional dialogue windows with a basic network scheme and short descriptions serve for the specific HPON configuration setup. The description window with the SARDANA HPON network topology is presented on Fig. 2. For presentations of GIF animations related to the SARDANA HPON, a free available CPictureEx class is used [11].

The HPON Configurator allows to simulate and analyze a transition from TDM-PON networks to HPON networks and to compare three different approaches to hybrid networks. After inserting input parameters of TDM-PON networks, these parameters are evaluated and the total transmission capacity of the TDM network together with the average capacity per one subscriber, the total number of subscribers and the maximum attenuation of the TDM network are calculated and presented. After configuration the SARDANA HPON network, a number and type of used active and passive components with possibilities for future expanding are presented.

3. Design of the SARDANA HPON Network

The SARDANA network architecture is created by the two-fiber ring with connected remote nodes RN

that ensure bidirectional signal amplification and dropping/adding of DWDM wavelengths for particular TDM trees. There is a possibility for connection of 2 TDM trees to 1 RN, so a total number of utilized wavelengths (and thus also TDM trees) is double of a number of remote nodes. A transmission in both directions is limited to the C-band due to the operational bandwidth of used EDFA amplifiers. A number of joinable TDM trees is derived from the density of DWDM channel spacing and from a derivable number of wavelengths in the C-band. At the network deployment, a support for the 1G (EPON, GPON) and 10G (10G-EPON, XG-PON) recommendation is expected.

The interactive window with the SARDANA HPON configuration is presented on Fig. 3.

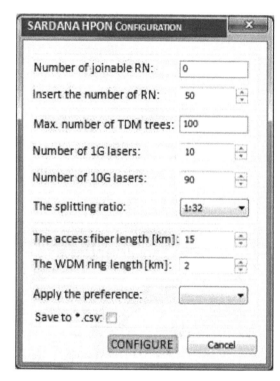

Fig. 3: The configuration window of the SARDANA HPON network.

At the configuration, it is possible to set network parameters manually or by using default values from the Tab. 1 [12]. Variables are expressing the ring length LRING, the access fiber length LACCESS, a number of remote nodes N and the splitting ratio of power optical splitters K. These default values present model cases from populous areas (Urban) up to geographically large areas (Rural).

The HPON configurator allows a calculation of the total number of subscribers U given by following relation:

$$U = 2.N.K \qquad (1)$$

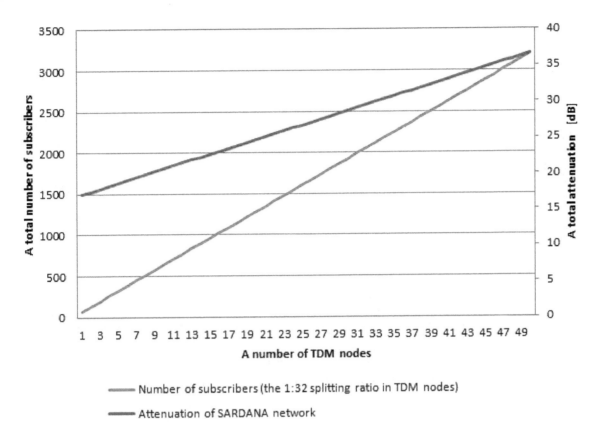

Fig. 4: Characteristics of the SARDANA HPON network for the 1:32 splitting ratio.

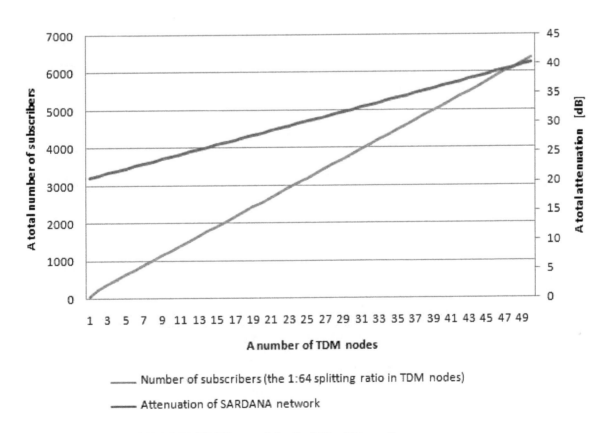

Fig. 5: Characteristics of the SARDANA HPON network for the 1:64 splitting ratio.

Tab. 1: Default values for model cases.

Model case	L_{RING*} [km]	L_{ACCES*} [km]	N	K
Urban 1	17	3	16	1 : 64
Urban 2	10	10	16	1 : 32
Metro	50	10	8	1 : 32
Rural	80	20	8	1 : 16

Tab. 2: Maximum values of network subscribers based on the DWDM spacing and the splitting ratio.

The splitting ratio K			1:16	1:32	1:64
DWDM spacing [nm]	N	TDM trees	U	U	U
0, 8	12	24	384	768	1536
0, 4	25	50	800	1600	3200
0, 2	50	100	1600	3200	6400

where K is the splitting ratio of power optical splitters and N is a number of remote nodes. A maximum number of joinable remote nodes N is depending on the DWDM multiplexing type (Tab. 2).

For this presentation, following parameters were selected: the ITU-T G.652 D optical fiber, the 0,2 nm DWDM channel spacing, the ring length 15 km, the access fiber length 2 km. A calculation of the total network attenuation comes out from features of components utilized in remote nodes, a number of remote nodes, a type of couplers and characteristics of the selected optical fiber. Following graphs (Fig. 4 and Fig. 5) represent dependencies of the total number of subscribers and the attenuation on the number of remote nodes in the connected network.

The SARDANA is a modular network with possibilities for connecting a large number of subscribers at acceptable attenuation values. These can be reached by placing of centrally pumped optical amplifiers into remote nodes. By this way, it is possible to increase a reach up to 30 km compared with common PON networks without utilization of the optical amplification. For a specific type of the EDFA amplifiers, the gain can be determined from minimum 10 dB to higher values in the simulation program. In a real network, gain values can be accommodated according to the length of optical fibers and to power characteristics of pumped lasers. The hybrid SARDANA network combines features of metropolitan and access networks to acquire maximum utilization of current technologies.

A comparison of two hybrid passive optical networks – SARDANA and SUCCESS - from various viewpoints will be presented in [10].

4.   Conclusion

Hybrid passive optical networks HPON presents the intermediate between TDM and WDM-PON networks with two different purposes/approaches. The first one is a creating of the network combining TDM and WDM-PON elements in order to increase a number of subscribers and a reach. The second one is an occasion for a smooth transition from TDM-PON to WDM networks without violation of service provisioning for original TDM subscribers.

In the HPON network configurator, some new features for the SARDANA HPON networks were prepared – the selection of transmission parameters utilized optical fibers, various wavelengths spacing at the DWDM multiplexing, a list of available transmission channels for DWDM and CWDM multiplexing, the presentation of available attenuation classes for the original TDM network. At the SARDANA configuration, it is not possible to select or insert incorrect values. For this case, a reason of actual limitation is presented.

Based on output values from this configuration program, it is possible to evaluate various different approaches for building hybrid passive optical networks and to compare them from many usable aspects – a number of subscribers, maximum reaches and transmission rates, optical components and technologies.

Acknowledgment

This work is a part of research activities conducted at Slovak University of Technology Bratislava, Faculty of Electrical Engineering and Information Technology, Institute of Telecommunications, within the scope of the project VEGA No. 1/0106/11 "Analysis and proposal for advanced optical access networks in the NGN converged infrastructure utilizing fixed transmission media for supporting multimedia services".

References

[1] PETKO, Ladislav. G-PON Migration to New Technologies. In: *OK 2012 – 15th Conference and Exhibition on Optical Communications*. Praha: ActionM, 2012. ISBN 978-80-86742-36-6.

[2] LAZARO, J. A., J. PRAT, P. CHANCLOU, G. M. Tosi BELEFFI, A. TEIXEIRA, I. TOMKOS, R. SOILA and V. KORATZINOS. Scalable Extended Reach PON. In: *OFC/NFOEC 2008 - 2008 Conference on Optical Fiber Communication/National Fiber Optic Engineers Conference*. San Diego: IEEE, 2008, pp. 1–3. ISBN 978-1-55752-856-8. DOI: 10.1109/OFC.2008.4528488.

[3] PRAT, J., J. A. LAZARO, P. CHANCLOU, R. SOILA, P. VELANAS, A. TEIXEIRA, G. TOSI

BELEFFI, I. TOMKOS, K. KANONAKIS. Passive Optical Network for Long-reach Scalable and Resilient Access. In: *ConTEL 2009. 10th International Conference on Telecommunications*. Zagreb: IEEE, 2009, pp. 271–275, ISBN 978-953-184-130-6 .

[4] KAZOVSKY, Leonid G. *Broadband Optical Access Networks*. Hoboken: John Wiley, 2011. ISBN 978-0-470-18235-2.

[5] PETER, Juraj. *The Analysis of the Hybrid PON Utilization in the Optical Access Network*. Bratislava, 2012. Diploma Thesis. Faculty of Electrical Engineering and Information Technology, Slovak University of Technology in Bratislava.

[6] ROKA, Rastislav. The Designing of Passive Optical Networks using the HPON Network Configurator. *International Journal of Research and Reviews in Computer Science IJRRCS*. 2010, vol. 1, no. 3, pp. 38–43, ISSN 2079-2557.

[7] ROKA, Rastislav. The extension of the HPON network configurator at designing of NG-PON networks. In: *34th International Conference on Telecommunications and Signal Processing (TSP 2011)*. Budapest: IEEE, 2011, pp. 79–84. ISBN 978-1-4577-1410-8. DOI: 10.1109/TSP.2011.6043768.

[8] ROKA, Rastislav. The Designing of NG-PON Networks Using the HPON Network Configuration. *Journal of Communication and Computer JCC*. 2012, vol. 9, no. 6, pp. 669–678. ISSN 1548-7709.

[9] ROKA, R. and S. KHAN. The Modeling of Hybrid Passive Optical Networks using the Network Configurator. *International Journal of Research and Reviews in Computer Science IJRRCS*. 2011 - Special Issue, pp. 48–54, ISSN 2079-2557.

[10] ROKA, Rastislav. Analysis of Hybrid Passive Optical Networks using the HPON Network Configurator. In: *INTECH 2013 – International Conference on Innovative Technologies*. Budapest: IN-TECH International Conference on Innovative Technologies, 2013, pp. 401–404, ISBN 978-953-6326-88-4.

[11] BYKOV, O. Code Project. *The CPictureEx Class* [online]. 2001. Available at: http://www.codeproject.com/Articles/1427/Add-GIF-animation-to-your-MFC-and-ATL-\projects-wit.

[12] JONG HOON LEE, KI-MAN CHOI, JUNG-HYUNG MOON and CHANG-HEE LEE. Seamless Upgrades From a TDM-PON With a Video Overlay to a WDM-PON. *Journal of Lightwave Technology*. 2009, vol. 27, iss. 15, pp. 3116–3123. ISSN 0733-8724. DOI: 10.1109/JLT.2008.2006861.

About Authors

Rastislav ROKA was born in Sala, Slovakia on January 27, 1972. He received his M.Sc. and Ph.D. degrees in Telecommunications from the Slovak University of Technology, Bratislava, in 1995 and 2002. Since 1997, he has been working as a senior lecturer at the Institute of Telecommunications, Faculty of Electrical Engineering and Information Technology, Slovak University of Technology in Bratislava. Since 2009, he is working as an associated professor at this institute. At present, his research activity is focused on the signal transmission through metallic access networks by means of xDSL/PLC technologies and through optical transport and access networks by means of WDM and TDM technologies using various techniques of the optical signal processing. A main effort is dedicated to effective utilization of the optical fiber's transmission capacity by using DBA/DWA algorithms.

12

Vehicular Networks and Road Safety: an Application for Emergency/Danger Situations Management Using the WAVE/802.11p Standard

Peppino FAZIO, Floriano DE RANGO, Andrea LUPIA

Department of Computer Science Engineering, Modeling, Electronics and Systems, University of Calabria, Via P. Bucci 42/C, 870 36 Arcavacata di Rende, Cosenza, Italy

pfazio@dimes.unical.it, derango@dimes.unical.it, andrea.lupia@gmail.com

Abstract. *Car-to-car communication makes possible offering many services for vehicular environment, mainly to improve the safety. The decentralized kind of these networks requires new protocols to distribute information. The advantages that it offers depend on the penetration rate, that will be enough only after years since the introduction, due to the longevity of the current cars. The V2X communication requires On-Board Units (OBUs) in the vehicles, and Road-Side Units (RSUs) on the roads. The proposed application uses the peculiarities of the VANETs to advise danger or emergency situations with V2V and V2I message exchange. IEEE 802.11p is standard on which the communication is based, that provides the physical and the MAC layers. The WAVE protocol uses this standard, implementing other protocols defined by the family of standards IEEE P1609 in the upper layers. They define security services, resource management, multichannel operations and the message exchange protocol in WAVE. The performance of the application will be evaluated through many simulations executed in different scenarios, to provide general data independent from them.*

Keywords

802.11p, car-to-car, communications, road safety, routing, VANET, vehicular, WAVE.

1. Introduction

More than 200 000 road accident happened in Italy in the 2010, causing more than 300 000 injuries, and 4 000 deaths [1]. If the cars involved in accidents can advise the event instantly to the emergency services, a timely intervention of rescue means would be possible. If also the near cars can receive this information, they would avoid danger situations, and reduce inconveniences. Car-to-car communication allows the development of many new applications in a vehicular environment, especially to the road safety. Current on sale applications that permits to manage some features tied to the reception of traffic information are based on GPS, users advise and institutional sources. The prevention and advising of accidents uses optical validation or connection with the car control unit. The advantages are just for the vehicles near the accident position. The research and development activity in the Intelligent Transport System (ITS) environment is due to the increasing diffusion of transport vehicles and, proportionally, to the number of accident that happens. The majority of them is caused by the violation of the traffic rules, so a solution that allows cooperation between vehicles, and with the infrastructures, will prevent danger situations. WAVE (Wireless Access in Vehicular Environment) technology was published in its final version in July 2010. The frequency that uses is situated around 5,9 GHz. It supports both communication typologies. The PHY and MAC layers are implemented by IEEE 802.11p standard, the upper layers by IEEE P1609.

2. State of the Art

Many applications developed to improve road safety use the GPS and users advisories. To prevent accidents, optical validation is used. To minimize the time necessary to the intervention of emergency vehicles, the detection of the accident is done by the connection with the car control unit, and the notification is done automatically by calling the emergency number or sending data to a dedicated server. Systems that allow the reception of information on traffic are usually integrated to navigation systems. They have a GPS receiver and a memory to store the maps. Through these systems, the Traffic Message Channel (TMC) transmits information of FM frequencies, using the protocol of the same name. It needs a dedicated hardware to receive messages. HD Traffic is another solution developed by TomTom, which allows receiving up-to-date information related to the path the vehicle is following, collecting data from other devices that use this service. A free navigation software that make use of advisories coming from other users about accidents, traffic jams, blocked roads and other dangers are Waze. To prevent accidents when driving, the current systems make use of vehicle detection through active (e.g. laser) or passive (e.g. camera) sensors. The laser allows calculating the distance from other cars that come across during the drive. Passive sensors permit to acquire data in a non-intrusive manner [2]. Accident detection allows reducing the time required to the notification, and makes possible a timely intervention by the emergency vehicles. Current systems use the OBD-II connection, available on all cars produced since 2003. European Union developed eCall to provide the warning of accidents, with the target of improving the road safety using intelligent safety systems based on advanced electronic technologies available on cars. The advisory happens by transmitting data to 112 service, available and free in all Europe.

3. WAVE/802.11p Protocol

WAVE (Wireless Access in Vehicular Environment) [3] consists in a set of a standard, that enable vehicles to V2X communication. Main components of architecture can be identified in Resource Manager, WAVE Short Message Protocol (defined by IEEE 1609.3 at the network layer), Multichannel Operation and IEEE 802.11p at underlying layers. WAVE is enabled to support IP and non-IP applications, the last ones using WSMP protocol, which let the applications control the physical properties of the transmission channel, like the transmission power and on which channel transmit. WAVE systems need two different device typologies: Road-Side Units (RSUs) and On-Board Units (OBUs). RSUs are placed statically on the roadside, whilst OBUs are situated on vehicles and can communicate with other OBUs and RSUs. Units can also organize themselves in small networks known as WAVE Basic Service Set (WBSS), in a way similar to BSS in IEEE 802.11 standard. A WBSS can be formed of just OBUs, or OBUs and RSUs. All its members communicate through a service channel. Furthermore, the whole set can connect to a WAN if the RSU is enabled to.

WAVE architecture is composed of two stacks, with common layers, as we can see in Fig. 1. One is for IP communication, whereas the other is for WSMP. The first one is used for TCP/UDP traffic, the last

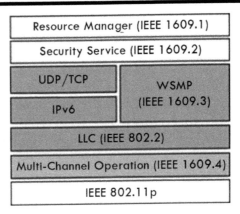

Fig. 1: WAVE stack.

one must support low latency and low error communications, like for example communications needed to road safety, when an accident needs to be advised. The basis of WAVE architecture is the IEEE 802.11 standard, modified by 802.11p to support the different properties of vehicular networks, offering many channels to use for communication, making possible also using schemes to reduce interferences in transmissions [4], with routing protocols that could maximize the signal-to-interference level [5]. It must be underlined that many routing protocols have been proposed for VANET environments, mainly aimed at multiobjective metric utilization [6] or user satisfaction [7].

4. Proposal

The application development is based on the use of WAVE protocol, which allows V2X communication. The target is to provide an application that permits reducing awkwardness and risk originated by an accident. Vehicles not involved in the accident will have benefits from the information they will receive, avoiding the road where the accident happened, so they will not come across in traffic jams or danger situations. Using this application, time of intervention of emergency vehicles will be reduced thanks to the immediate advisory; furthermore, the traffic near the accident will be lesser, because many vehicles will change their path to avoid the road subject to the event. The injured people will get assistance in a timely manner. Emergency vehicles will dynamically compute the fastest path to the destination, avoiding roads with traffic jams.

4.1. Message Typologies

Message exchange between vehicles using the application maintains traffic information always up-to-date. When an accident happens, the information is immediately transmitted to near vehicles, so they can take adequate countermeasures to avoid dangers and traffic jams. The proposed application uses two different message typologies: Cooperative Awareness Message (CAM) and Decentralized Environmental Notification Message (DENM). Each vehicle enabled to V2X communication sends CAM messages periodically. They contain information regarding the vehicle (actual speed, position, etc.). Using this information, vehicles can update traffic data in the surrounding area, so they can choose the best path to their destination. CAM messages are sent in a time interval within 0.1 and 1 seconds. Messages are broadcasted, but the application could use also more complex protocols, based on trajectory, map information or group motion [8], [9], [10]. To advise accidents and other danger situations, DENM are used. They are generated and sent immediately when a danger situation is detected. The dispatch is in broadcast, and it is repeated until the danger ceases, so the vehicles arriving later in the area will receive the information. The car subject to the accident sends the message, advising the seriousness of the happening, the position and the driving direction.

4.2.   Communication Sequent to the Accident

The application advises the accident happened to vehicles in a specific range from its position. An accident, depending from its seriousness, can require emergency means to give aid to injured people, and other means to clear out the road if it is blocked by the vehicles involved in the event. Vehicles nearby the area receive the communication in real-time.

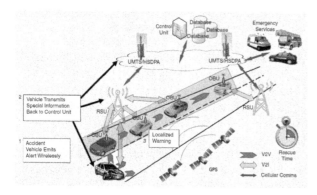

Fig. 2: Accident advisory.

A RSU sends the request to a server, which receives the DENM related to the accident and in its turn sends the request of assistance to another server enabled to manage this kind of data. The advisory is sent in real-time to authorities and/or to rescuer, so they can intervene in a timely manner to limit the effect of the accident, assisting injured people and/or restoring the viability (as in Fig. 2).

4.3.   Dynamic Choice of Path

Cars can change their path according to messages they receive. This operation can be done also when there is no accident, using the data contained in CAM messages about other vehicles. Storing and managing this information, the conditions of the road network around the vehicle are inferable. So, congested areas that require more time to be driven can be avoided.

4.4.   Optimal Path Planning

To plan the optimal path, Dijkstra algorithm is used. There are two nodes sets, S visited nodes and T nodes to visit. At each step, the node x_m successor of a node in S and contained in T, reachable at minimum cost, is chosen. It is moved in S, and for each of its successors x, the cost will be updated using the following formula:

$$c_x = minc_x, c_v + w_e, \qquad (1)$$

with c_x cost to reach node x, c_v cost to reach its predecessor, w_e weight of the connection edge. The algorithm ends when the destination is reached. Road network is represented as oriented graph, defined as:

$$G = \langle V, E \rangle, \qquad (2)$$

with V nodes set, E edges set. To each edge E is connected a weight with real values, as following:

$$w : E \longrightarrow R. \qquad (3)$$

Each node coincides with a crossroad. A road corresponds to an oriented edge for each driving direction. So, a one-way road will be represented as one edge, a two-way one as two edges oriented each one in a different direction. An example of conversion from the road network to graph is shown in Fig. 3.

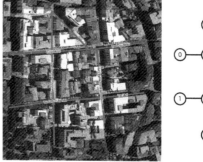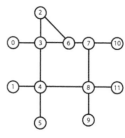

Fig. 3: Conversion from the road network to graph.

Each edge weight is given by the average travel time for its driving direction. This parameter is calculated using the following formula:

$$w(e) = l(e)/s(e), \qquad (4)$$

with e specifying the edge associated to the road, $l(e)$ its length, $s(e)$ the average speed on the road. If a vehicle did not receive any information about a road, the speed limit will be considered as its average speed.

4.5.   Algorithm Operations

Using the information about the position in CAM messages, the road that the message sender is going through can be established. Since the message contains also the speed, the average speed of the vehicles situated on the road can be calculated. From this, the average travel time can be determined. When an advisory of an accident is received by a DENM, the road on which the event happened is excluded from the new path computation, setting its average travel time to $+\infty$. Emergency means store the information received during their path to reach their destination, so they can calculate the fastest way. This is important especially when means arrive near the event position, since they have to change their path if they sense, from data collected, that there is a traffic jam on a road. Moreover, they can choose the way that leads as near as possible to the destination area.

4.6.   Requirements

To immediately advise the accident, a RSU is needed in the communication range of involved vehicle, because the request of assistance to emergency services is made through it. Missing this requirement, an alternative advisory system is needed (e.g. eCall). An adequate number of vehicles have to use the application: it is possible to collect data from a certain sample of vehicles.

5.   Results Analysis

The evaluation of the application performance is done using many simulations, changing various parameters to establish which ones influence its performance. Simulation is running using real maps, and it regarded many aspects implied by the application and the WAVE technology. The simulation framework used to simulate the V2X communication scenario is VSimRTI [11]. It permits to a couple different simulators, allowing to simulate various aspects of ITS. Simulators used combined to VSimRTI are SUMO [12], that simulate the traffic on the road network, and JiST/SWANS [13] for communication between nodes. The application was developed in two different versions: one

used by generic cars supplied by WAVE technology, another one used by emergency vehicle, because operations they carry out are different.

5.1.   Simulation

Various simulations were ran, to evaluate application performance and to denote differences when some conditions changes. Different sets of parameters were used to each simulation, keeping some fixed.

Parameters used in the simulation are the following:

- simulation duration: 30 minutes,

- transmission range: 250 meters,

- generated vehicles: 100, 200, 400,

- penetration rate of WAVE technology: 100 %, 75 %, 50 %, 25 %, 0 %.

One vehicle each 4, 8 and 16 seconds is generated during the simulation, respectively to a total number of 400, 200 and 100 vehicles. Each vehicle had random starting and ending point, with the only constraint that, between them, a distance of 500 meters in los must exist. Dijkstra algorithm is used to calculate the starting path offline, with no vehicles on the road network. During the simulation, path changes dynamically based on traffic conditions. The reaction time to the accident by emergency services was supposed as 2 minutes when WAVE technology is used, 10 minutes otherwise. Maps were chosen to offer a road network dense enough. During the simulations, every road was contemplated as two-way one. Two different types of map were considered, for a sum of 6 different maps. 3 of them regard urban areas, other 3 are suburban zones. The main difference between these categories is the number of roads available. Urban scenarios have more roads, so vehicles have more choices when computing a path. Furthermore, these scenarios allow more vehicles to pass through the road network at the same time, with respect to suburban scenarios. Using different kind of maps (from OpenStreetMap) is useful to evaluate the application on different scenario typologies. As urban areas, section of the cities of Cosenza, Paris and Valencia were chosen. Part of Barcelona, Munich and Rome were used to simulate suburbs. Each map area is about 1 km^2, without buildings and closed roads.

5.2.   Results

Main results generated by simulations, on which an evaluation will be made, are about emergency vehicle, and they are the final distance from the accident area, the time needed to reach it and the average speed during the trip. Average speed is calculated as following:

$$v_{avg} = travel_{length}/travel_{time}. \qquad (5)$$

1) Distance from the Accident

The application allows the emergency vehicle to drive through the fastest path, avoiding traffic jams. Regarding these last ones, they have a smaller probability to happen, because cars using the application change their path when they notice the event. From Fig. 4 it is possible to verify that highest distances from the accident are reached when 400 vehicles are generated, whereas the lower curve is about the least number of vehicles generated, that is 100. The curve representing simulation values with 200 vehicles is situated in the middle of them. The curves trend is decreasing when the penetration rate increases until 50 %, thereafter it stays almost stable, recording a light increment only with 400 vehicles. From data represented in this graph, it seems there is no difference in application performance when penetration rate is greater than or equal to 50 % of total vehicles.

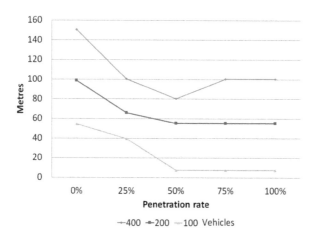

Fig. 4: Distance from the accident with different penetration rates.

A comparison between central and suburb scenarios about the distance of emergency vehicle from the position of the accident is shown in Fig. 5. Using the application, urban areas get a higher improvement than suburb ones, which coincides with distances lower than a half from what results when no application is used. This is due to denser road network in central areas, so emergency mean has more choices to reach the accident position. This opportunity does not occur sometimes in suburb zones, so the final position of emergency vehicle is farther.

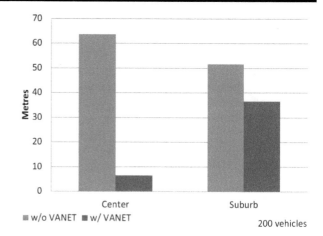

Fig. 5: Distance from the accident in the center and suburb scenarios.

2) Average Speed

Another outcome that allows evaluating the application and the benefits its use entails consists in the average speed achieved by emergency vehicle during the path to its destination. Therefore, it is possible to have an idea of the time it needs to reach the area also when the path length is different, like in this simulation, where the starting point and accident position are generated randomly. In Fig. 6, there is the graph concerning the average speed of emergency vehicle, with a comparison between the cases when vehicular network is used or not. In urban areas, average speed is higher, but improvement using the application is very little. Suburban zones allow reaching lower average speeds, but there is a notable improvement when the application is used. With reference to this parameter, the application provides a better improvement in suburb areas.

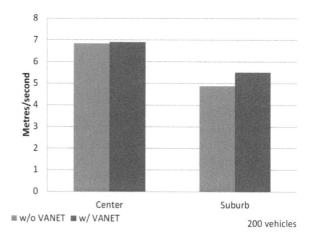

Fig. 6: Comparison between average speed in urban and suburb scenarios.

3)   Travel Time

To compare travel times between central and suburban zones, average values calculated using scenarios of the same type is taken in account. Furthermore, five runs were done on a particular scenario, keeping fixed the starting point of the emergency mean, and changing randomly, but in the same manner for the two cases, the point where the accident happens. Therefore, a more accurate evaluation of the advantage caused by the application is possible. Figure 7 shows how travel times of emergency vehicle are higher in urban scenarios. On average, a greater advantage is obtained in suburban zones. Examining this time saving in percentage, collected data points out that in central road networks the time required for intervention is lower of 7,3 % using the application. The percentage increases until 16,7 % in suburban zones.

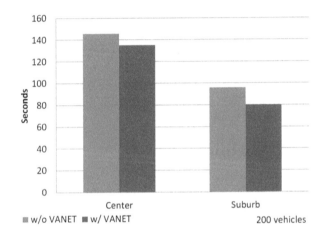

Fig. 7: Comparison between travel time in urban and suburban scenarios.

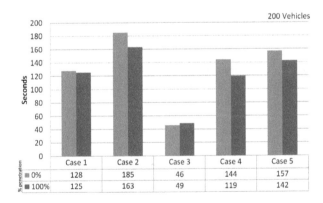

Fig. 8: Travel time with and without application.

Figure 8 shows a comparison between cases with the same starting and ending point for emergency mean. In percentage terms, the best saving is achieved in Case 4 (21 %). In other cases, there is a lower improvement. Case 3 needs more attention, because the travel time obtained using the application is higher than the one achieved without using it, with a worsening of 6 %.

Therefore, without the use of the application, emergency vehicle probably did not go through the fastest path, but the shortest, and the final distance from the accident is higher compared with the result obtained when the application is used, because in this last case the vehicle found a better path, resulting nearer to the accident position. Due to the low intervention time in this case, this approach caused a time travel higher, even though just 3 seconds. Computing average between cases, the advantage achieved using the application corresponds to travel times of 9,34 % lower needed to reach the event position by the emergency mean.

6.   Summary and Future Works

From the results obtained from simulations done, it is possible to establish that the proposed application to manage emergency and danger situations allows improving the reaction to those events, for general vehicles and emergency ones. The algorithm used by the application permits vehicle path updating, to avoid the generation of traffic jams near to the accident position, so they can save time and reach their destinations without incur into dangers originated by the event. Thanks to WAVE protocol, vehicles receive real-time communication about emergency generated by the accident, so they avoid the involved road, without causing other annoyance to traffic flow due to traffic jam that happens if they do not change their path. Based on collected data, intervention time of emergency means that use the application decreases. This is essential to intervene in a timely manner, to manage the danger situation in a better way. Also a little time saving can lead to benefits to injured people caused by the accident. Furthermore, in this way the normal traffic flow is restored in a lower time, minimizing inconvenience to vehicles near the event area. Distance reached by emergency means from the accident position decreases proportionally to the increasing of penetration rate. The advantage provided by the application is higher when there are more vehicles in the road network. Using an equal number of generated vehicles, the application allows achieving a greater advantage in suburbs, since their road networks are sparser than the central ones. Average speed of emergency vehicle is higher if it runs the application. As future developments of application, a better and more realistic vehicle generation model would be useful, using real data or based on a real car density in simulated area. Therefore, it is possible to get data that represent application performance in a more accurate way, compared to results using random generated data.

References

[1] ISTAT. *Incidenti stradali* [online]. 2011. Available at: http://www.istat.it/it/archivio/44757.

[2] SUN, Z., G. BEBIS and R. MILLER. On-road vehicle detection using optical sensors: A review. In: *The 7th International IEEE Conference on Intelligent Transportation Systems ,2004*. Washington: IEEE, 2004, pp. 585–590. ISBN 0-7803-8500-4. DOI: 10.1109/ITSC.2004.1398966.

[3] UZCATEGUI, R. and G. ACOSTA-MARUM. Wave: A tutorial. *IEEE Communications Magazine*. 2009, vol. 47, iss. 5, pp. 126–133. ISSN 0163-6804. DOI: 10.1109/MCOM.2009.4939288.

[4] FAZIO, P., F. DE RANGO, C. SOTTILE and C. CALAFATE. A New Channel Assignment Scheme for Interference-Aware Routing in Vehicular Networks. In: *73rd Vehicular Technology Conference (VTC Spring, 2011)*. Yokohama: IEEE, 2011, pp. 1–5. ISBN 978-1-4244-8332-7. DOI: 10.1109/VETECS.2011.5956777.

[5] FAZIO, P., F. DE RANGO and C. SOTTILE. A new interference aware on demand routing protocol for vehicular networks. In: *International Symposium on Performance Evaluation of Computer & Telecommunication Systems (SPECTS)*. The Hague: IEEE, 2011, pp. 98–103. ISBN 978-1-4577-0139-9.

[6] DE RANGO, F., F. GUERRIERO, S. MARANO and E. BRUNO. A multiobjective approach for energy consumption and link stability issues in ad hoc networks. *IEEE Communications Letters*. 2006, vol. 10, iss. 1, pp. 28–30. ISSN 1089-7798. DOI: 10.1109/LCOMM.2006.1576559.

[7] DE RANGO, F., P. FAZIO and S. MARANO. Utility-Based Predictive Services for Adaptive Wireless Networks With Mobile Hosts. *IEEE Transactions on Vehicular Technology*. 2009, vol. 58, iss. 3, pp. 1415–1428. ISSN 0018-9545. DOI: 10.1109/TVT.2008.924989.

[8] DE RANGO, F., F. VELTRI and S. MARANO. Hierarchical trajectory-based routing protocol for Vehicular Ad Hoc Networks. In: *International Symposium on Performance Evaluation of Computer and Telecommunication Systems (SPECTS 2008)*. Edinburgh: IEEE, 2008, pp. 189–196. ISBN 978-1-56555-320-0.

[9] DE RANGO, F., F. VELTRI, P. FAZIO and S. MARANO. Two-level trajectory-based routing protocol for vehicular ad hoc networks in freeway and Manhattan environments. *Journal of Networks*. 2009, vol. 4, iss. 9, pp. 866–880. ISSN 1796-2056. DOI: 10.4304/jnw.4.9.866-880.

[10] DE RANGO, F., M. GERLA and S. MARANO. A scalable routing scheme with group motion support in large and dense wireless ad hoc networks. *Computers & Electrical Engineering*. 2006, vol. 32, iss. 1–3, pp. 224–240. ISSN 0045-7906.

[11] SCHUNEMANN, B., K. MASSOW and I. RADUSCH. A Novel Approach for Realistic Emulation of Vehicle-2-X Communication Applications. In: *VTC Spring 2008 - IEEE Vehicular Technology Conference*. Singapore: IEEE, 2008, pp. 2709–2713. ISBN 978-1-4244-1644-8. DOI: 10.1109/VETECS.2008.593.

[12] BEHRISCH, M., L. BIEKER, J. ERDMANN and D. KRAJZEWICZ. SUMO - Simulation of Urban Mobility: An Overview. In: *The Third International Conference on Advances in System Simulation (SIMUL 2011)*. Barcelona: XPS(Xpert Publishing Services), 2011, pp. 55–60. ISBN 978-1-61208-169-4.

[13] BARR, R., Z. J. HAAS and R. VAN RENESSE. JiST: an efficient approach to simulation using virtual machines. *Software: Practice and Experience*. 2005, vol. 35, iss. 6, pp. 539–576. ISSN 1097-024X. DOI: 10.1002/spe.647.

About Authors

Peppino FAZIO was born in 1977. He received the degree in computer science engineering in May 2004. Since November 2004 he has been a Ph.D. student in Electronics and Communications Engineering at the University of Calabria and he has got the Ph.D. in January 2008; at the moment he is a research fellow at Department of Computer Science Engineering, Modeling, Electronics and Systems of University of Calabria. His research interests include mobile communication networks, QoS architectures and interworking wireless and wired networks, mobility modeling for WLAN environments and mobility analysis for prediction purposes.

Floriano DE RANGO received the degree in computer science engineering in October 2000, and a Ph.D. in electronics and communications engineering in January 2005, both at the University of Calabria, Italy. He served as reviewer and TPC member for many International Conferences such as IEEE VTC, ICC, WCNC, Globecom, Med Hoc Net, SPECTS, WirelessCOM, WinSys and reviewer for many journals such as IEEE Communication Letters, JSAC, IEEE Transactions on Vehicular Technology, etc. His interests include Satellite networks, IP QoS architectures, Adaptive Wireless Networks, Ad Hoc Networks and Pervasive Computing.

Andrea LUPIA was born in 1985. He received the degree in computer science engineering at the University of Calabria in May 2013. His thesis work regarded security measures for road safety using vehicular ad-hoc networks, which is the area for which he is actually collaborating with Department of Computer Science Engineering, Modeling, Electronics and Systems at University of Calabria.

13

Performance Analysis of IMS Network: the Proposal of new Algorithms for S-CSCF Assignment

Lubos NAGY[1], Vit NOVOTNY[1], Jana URAMOVA[2], Nermin MAKHLOUF[1]

[1]Department of Telecommunications, Faculty of Electrical Engineering and Communication, Brno University of Technology, Technicka 12, 616 00 Brno, Czech Republic

[2]Department of Information Networks, Faculty of Management Science and Informatics, University of Zilina, Univerzitna 8215/1, 010 26 Zilina, Slovak Republic

lubos.nagy@phd.feec.vutbr.cz, novotnyv@feec.vutbr.cz, jana.uramova@fri.uniza.sk, nermin.makhlouf@fri.uniza.sk

Abstract. *This article is focused on the proposal of three load balancing methods which can be used for a selection of S-CSCF (Serving-Call Session Control Server) server in IP Multimedia Subsystem (IMS) during the registration procedures of subscribers. All presented methods are implemented and evaluated for various inter-arrival and service times in the mathematical model based on queueing theory. In this article, two methods based on performance parameters (such as utilizations, etc.) and one method based on number of registered subscribers to each of available S-CSCF server are described. The main advantage of third method is that all related information is obtained from traffic analysis through I-CSCF (Interrogating-CSCF) node. Also, the designed methods are compared with other selection algorithms presented in previous research works by others researchers (Hwang et col., Cho et col. or Tirana et col.). The article shows that the implemented methods can optimize the service latency of whole IMS network.*

Keywords

File transfer, IP based Multimedia Subsystem, load balancer, S-CSCF selection, service latency, Video on Demand, Voice over IP.

1. Introduction

The current trends in telecommunication lead to the convergence of mobile, wireless and fixed network technologies and the integration of wide variety of services with particular quality of service requirements through common transport network and using a multifunction terminal. At present, the IP Multimedia Subsystem in role of the service control architecture represents a unifying solution for convergence of these technologies. One of the most important QoS-related network parameters whose values can be affected by unbalanced signalling traffic over core network is the service latency. In general, it is necessary to know the behaviour of whole unbalanced systems to perform optimization process. One of possible ways to determine the behaviour of a network is the performance benchmarking or various mathematical tools like a queueing theory.

The main motivation of this article is the proposal of new three algorithms for S-CSCF assignment [1] based on the analysis using queueing theory. One of causes of increased service latency over whole IMS network can be unbalanced signalling traffic over IMS core, mainly over the S-CSCF server as the central service provision node of whole IMS network. One possibility of load balancing is defined in technical specification [2]. The influence of unbalanced traffic on the service latency was written in [3], see second section of this article.

In this article, we will describe new selection algorithms of S-CSCF server to reduce the service latency causing by unbalancing traffic load of IMS core elements. These new algorithms do not use only the performance parameters like server utilization but also the parameter like the number of subscribers registered to S-CSCF servers.

2. Related Work

According to the recommendations defined in the technical specification by 3GPP, the I-CSCF performs the S-CSCF assignment only in three cases and using six main types of parameters (required capabilities for user services, operator preferences on a per-user basic, capabilities of individual S-CSCFs in the home network, topological information of where a subscriber is located and availability of S-CSCF servers). In the first case, the S-CSCF is selected during registration, then during execution services for unregistered subscribers or when the selected S-CSCF server is not responding. All needed information to S-CSCF assignment is transferred using Cx interface within grouped AVPs, and so within the DIAMETER Server-Capabilities AVP [1], [2], [4]. In the case that all transferred information from all available S-CSCF servers are equal, the I-CSCF server performs the selection using the best-fit function.

The proposals of effective algorithms or implementations of management system used to the S-CSCF selection are described in various research studies or papers ([5], [6], [7], [8], [9], [10], [11], [12], [13], [15]). In [5], Oh et at. proposed the data structure for S-CSCF selection (S-CSCF capability and load-balancing information) and three-step selection mechanism performed by I-CSCF. In document [6], the proposed method of S-CSCF assignment is based on periodical update mechanism of load related information of the S-CSCFs using SIP OPTIONS method. In [7], the SIP NOTIFY method is used to transfer the information (the number of registered subscribers, resources usage such as memory, CPU and queueing delays) in load-balancing mechanism designed by authors Abdalla et col. In [8], the authors proposed the re-associated schema of overloaded S-CSCFs based on the server utilization calculation for every $10,000$ request arrivals received by each of simulated S-CSCFs.

In next research works [9], [10], [11], [12], [13], a design of a dynamic routing algorithm for managing CSCF servers and its implementation is described by authors. The presented algorithm is based on five criteria with different priorities (system down or up with the highest priority, defined threshold of CPU and memory utilizations, throughput and response time with the lowest priority). However, the evaluation of described algorithm is not shown in [9], [10], [11], [12], [13]. Therefore, this algorithm is one of evaluated algorithms presented in this paper.

Four algorithms (based on uniform random allocation, round robin, lowest response time and shortest expected delay) used to distributed S-CSCF selection were proposed and evaluated for different grids in the next research studies published in [14], [15]. First two of them are well-known algorithms. In the case of *uniform random allocation*, the S-CSCF server was selected from the list of available servers randomly and in the case of *round robin algorithm*, the next available S-CSCF server was always chosen. Third method (*lowest response time*) was based on latency between the

P-CSCF and S-CSCF servers measured periodically by load balancer (located in the I-CSCF) using own updated protocol. In the case of the *shortest expected delay* algorithm ([15]), the selected node was chosen with the help of local information (such as queue size) without coordinating with other nodes. In [15], two scenarios were evaluated, in the first one the request message size was one unit and in the second case the message size was greater. The obtained results from first scenario showed that the method of *shortest expected delay* is the best selection algorithm. For second scenario, the results of *shortest expected delay* and *round robin* algorithms were very similar and both were better than *uniform random allocation* and *lowest response time* methods.

In the article [3] we presented the design of home IMS network model based on queueing theory. The IMS network (two Proxy-CSCF, five S-CSCFs, one I-CSCF, one Home Subscriber Server, one Application server and one Media Streaming Server) was described as a single queueing network with feedbacks. Also, we presented the support of three advanced telecommunication services (VoIP - Voice over Internet Protocol, Video on Demand and file transfer using SIP and Diameter for session control messages, and RTP/RTCP/RTSP and MSRP protocols for media transmission and its control) over designed mathematical model in more detail. All simulations presented in [3] were focused on the evaluation and influence of unbalanced signalling load over IMS core, mainly over five S-CSCF nodes (the effect of S-CSCFs on service latency was evaluated using the performance test-bed in [16]) during the registration procedures, on service latency of whole network. For purpose of load balancing, three algorithms of S-CSCF assignment were in more detail designed, described and evaluated. The obtained results of [3] showed that the algorithm based on the combination of two performance parameters, the server utilization of S-CSCF nodes and the number of waiting messages in the FIFO queue of S-CSCF nodes, is better than next two algorithms based on each of selected parameters separately. The algorithm with the best results is used in this article for comparison both with our new algorithms and with algorithms described in the papers of other scientists.

As has been written above, the influence of S-CSCF on service latency during various IMS procedures was evaluated in [16]. In the article, we have neglected the effects of lower signalling delays and the impact of delays outside IMS core elements. The derived service latency of successful registration procedures (D_{REG}) is showed in the Eq. (1)

$$D_{REG} \approx D_{(MAA \to 401)} + D_{(SAA \to 200)}, \qquad (1)$$

where $D_{(MAA \to 401)}$ is the delay of the DIAMETER MAA $\to$ SIP 401 processing during the first phases of registration procedure and $D_{(SAA\to200)}$ is the delay of the DIAMETER SAA $\to$ SIP 200 for SIP REGISTER processing during the second phases of registration procedure. The percentage ratio of derived D_{REG} is 94,4 % of measured D_{REG}. It can be seen (see the Eq. (1)) that the S-CSCF has the highest impact on delay of signalling within a home IMS network. We obtained the very similar results for session establishment procedures in [16].

Therefore, this article is focused on the problem how to optimize the latency of whole IMS network using load-balancing mechanism of S-CSCF servers.

3. Design of New Algorithms

The designed model of IMS network based on the GI/M/1 queueing systems (with a single server and FIFO queue with infinite capacity) is shown in the Fig. 1. The used queueing model (GI/M/1) is based on generally distributed inter-arrival times and exponentially distributed service times [17]. The most common queueing systems are M/M/1, M/GI/1 or GI/M/1. The designed network model can be defined as an open single class queueing network with feedbacks.

The IMS model (see the Fig. 1) can be divided from the point of view of horizontal layered architecture into four layers:

- *end-device layer* with load generator for support of VoD, VoIP and File transfer over IMS signalling,

- *transport layer* presents intermediate transport network technologies and routers,

- *control layer* presents the IMS core elements (an I-CSCF, an HSS, two P-CSCFs and three S-CSCFs),

- *application layer* presents the application (AS) and media streaming servers (MSS) for support of VoD service.

Each of services consists of three phases: *registration procedure with subscription, session establishment and termination procedures (only for registered subscribers),* and *de-registration procedure.* The *registration phase* consists of the registrar and subscription transactions. The generated signalling flows are created with the help of the standardized document [18]. The proposal of queueing network model using Matlab environment was described in more detail in our previous work [3].

3.1. Unbalanced S-CSCFs

The measured latencies of whole designed queueing network for different forms of random user request distributions among S-CSCF servers are shown in Fig. 2. In this case, the service times of all CSCFs, HSS, AS and MSS nodes are set to $0,075 - 0,055$ *time units* (the nodes have the same values for each simulation); others nodes are set to constant values of $0,000001$ *time units*.

Two following random distributions of load were used to simulations of conditions in IMS network during slightly and highly unbalanced distributions of requests among S-CSCF servers:

- defined load of S-CSCFs (no. 1, no. 2, no. 3): [33,33 %, 33,33 %, 33,33 %] (see Fig. 2(a)),

- defined load of S-CSCFs (no. 1, no. 2, no. 3): [95 %, 2,5 %, 2,5 %] (see Fig. 2(b)).

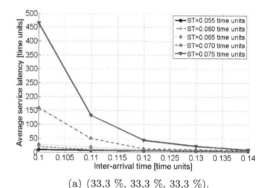

(a) (33,3 %, 33,3 %, 33,3 %).

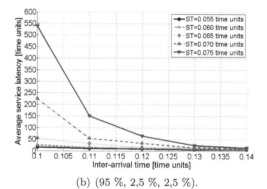

(b) (95 %, 2,5 %, 2,5 %).

Fig. 2: Service latencies vs. request inter-arrival times for various service times.

It can be seen that the influence of highly unbalanced distributions of requests among S-CSCF on latency of whole IMS subsystem is significantly large. In the case of first S-CSCF load ([33,33 %, 33,33 %, 33,33 %]), the latency of whole queueing system did not have steady state for shorter values of inter-arrival times than value of $0,1$ *time units* and for slow single servers (greater

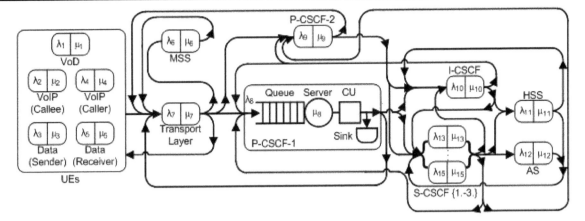

Fig. 1: Queueing network for simulation of latency in IMS network [3].

service times of request) of IMS nodes (CSCFs, HSS, AS and MSS) than 0,075 time units.

In second scenario ([95 %, 2,5 %, 2,5 %]), it can be seen that the obtained results of service latencies of whole network are higher than the values from the first scenario. The influence of unbalanced load of available S-CSCF servers is showed in Fig. 2. In the next subsections, we designed and described the algorithms for balancing of S-CSCF node to minimize latencies of whole IMS subsystem.

3.2. Algorithm I

First proposed method of S-CSCF selection (see Fig. 3) is based on combination of two performance parameters (see *Step 2*), *the number of waiting messages in FIFO queue* and *the server utilizations*. Firstly, the queue occupation is considered and if there is only one server with lowest queue occupation (see *Step 3*) then this server is selected (see *Step 4*). Provided there are more servers with the same lowest level of queue occupation then two of these servers with the lowest ID are chosen for the second round and the server with lower value of utilization is selected (see *Step 3b*).

This way of selection was designed after evaluation of methods based only on the number of waiting messages in queues and the server utilizations [3].

3.3. Algorithm II

The actual number of waiting messages in queues and *the service times* of S-CSCF servers are used as next performance parameters to S-CSCF assignment (see *Step 2* in Fig. 3). The I-CSCF node performs the selection of S-CSCF using waiting time calculation for incoming request (see PredictedTime - PT in Eq. (2), see *Step 3* and *Step 4*).

$$PT = ActNum * ServiceTime \ [time\ units]. \quad (2)$$

If there are more servers with the same results then the S-CSCF with the lowest priority ID is chosen (see *Step 3b* in Fig. 3).

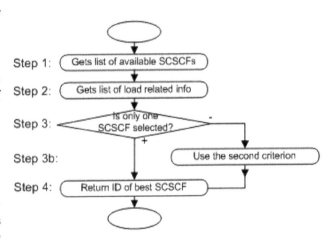

Fig. 3: The simplified idea of proposed algorithm I and II.

3.4. Algorithm III

The third algorithm is based on the balancing load of S-CSCF servers using the actual number of registered subscribers to each of simulated S-CSCF servers. This value is in I-CSCF record always incremented at the end of successful registration procedure and decremented at the end of de-registration procedure. If there are more servers with the same number of subscribers then the server with the lowest ID is selected. Moreover, unlike previous methods, this proposed algorithm is independent from the periodic update of the values of performance parameters (server utilization, etc.).

The main benefit of this method, in our designed model of home IMS subsystem, is that any interface for transferring information of S-CSCF is not required because all related information is obtained from traffic analysis through I-CSCF node.

4.   Simulation Results

The scenario with different performance conditions of S-CSCFs are simulated and each presented method for latency minimization of whole IMS network model are evaluated for various inter-arrival times $(0,095 - 0,14$ *time units*, the inter-arrival times of generated SIP signalling by generator to IMS core) and service times.   The service times of S-CSCF 1, S-CSCF 2, S-CSCF 3 are set to respectively as the following: $0,055$ *time units*, $0,065$ *time units* and $0,075$ *time units*. The P/I-CSCFs, HSS, AS and MSS nodes are set to $0,065$ *time units*; others nodes are set to values of $0,000001$ *time units*). The length of simulations is set on 5000 *time units*. Six algorithms of S-CSCF assignment are evaluated and compared with unbalanced scenario.   First three of evaluated algorithms (*Algorithm 1, Algorithm 2, Algorithm 3*, see subsections 3.2, 3.3 and 3.4) were in more detail described in the previous sections. Next three methods are the *Lowest response time* [14], [15], *Hwang's algorithm* [9], [10], [11], [12], [13] and also well-known selection method - the *Round robin* algorithm (see section 2) which is based on circular order (if the last selected S-CSCF of last registered subscriber was S-CSCF 1, then S-CSCF 2 will be selected for next subscriber during registration procedure).   Also, we can divided these algorithms into two main categories:

- the algorithms based on performance parameters (server utilizations, etc.),

- the algorithms based on analysis of signalling traffic through I-CSCF server (*Algorithm III* and *Round robin*).

In the first case, the best algorithms is Algorithm II and in the second one, the Algorithm III is better mainly for longer inter-arrival times (under value of $0,125$ *time units*) than round robin algorithm. The round robin algorithm is more effective to minimized of latency for shortly inter-arrival times. Also, the obtained results (see Fig. 4 and Fig. 5 or Tab. 1) show that the Algorithm II is most effective to minimize the service latency of whole network.

Table 1 show the overall improvement values compared with the method without load balancing for all simulated inter-arrival times.   As has been written

Tab. 1: The obtained overall improvement for service latency of whole IMS subsystem.

Implemented method	Improvement [%]
Round Robin	$26,067 \pm 6,151$
Hwang's algorithm [9], [10], [11], [12], [13]	$18,433 \pm 11,6$
LRT with feedbacks [14], [15]	$18,574 \pm 13,244$
Algorithm I (see section 3.2)	$20,761 \pm 13,19$
Algorithm II (see section 3.3)	$29,515 \pm 7,709$
Algorithm III (see section 3.4)	$25,274 \pm 3,487$

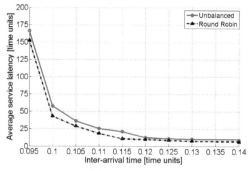

(a) Round robin.

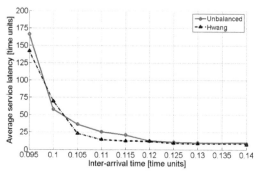

(b) Hwang's algorithm [9], [10], [11], [12], [13].

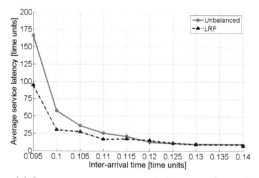

(c) Lowest response time with feedbacks [14, 15].

Fig. 4: Characteristics of latencies vs.   request inter-arrival times.

above (see section 2), in the case that all related information from available S-CSCFs are equal, the S-CSCF selection is based on the best-fit function. The most commonly best-fit function for S-CSCF assignment is just the Round robin algorithm. The average improvement value of algorithm II when compared with the round robin as best-fit function is $3,769$ %.

5.   Conclusion

Three types of S-CSCF selection algorithms were designed and then compared with algorithms presented in the papers of other researchers [9], [10], [11], [12], [13], [14], [15]. In the case of first two designed met-

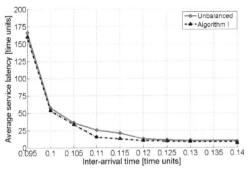

(a) Algorithm I.

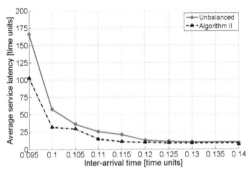

(b) Algorithm II.

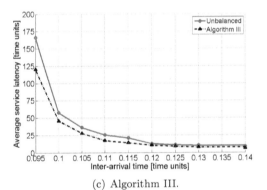

(c) Algorithm III.

Fig. 5: Characteristics of latencies vs. request inter-arrival times.

hods, the performance parameters (such as server utilizations, etc.) are used to choose the best of available S-CSCF servers. Third algorithm is based on analysis of signalling traffic through I-CSCF node.

In the graphs (see Fig. 4 and Fig. 5), the average values of service latencies within the inter-arrival rates (rate of generated messages by UEs within IMS network) are shown. It can be seen that the best load balancer methods for all values of inter-arrival and service times are the Algorithm II (based on prediction of waiting times for incoming requests) and Round Robin algorithms. The Algorithm II is the most effective to minimize service latency especially for shortly inter-arrival times. The service latency of whole designed network did not have steady state for shorter values of

inter-arrival times than value of $0,095$ *time units* for settings of service times defined in section *Simulation Results*. This value of inter-arrival time is affected by the relatively high influence of feedbacks in the presented IMS model.

The obtained results from simulation with different performance conditions of S-CSCFs show that designed algorithms are optimizing the service latency compared with the standardized solution and with algorithms presented by others researchers (Hwang et col., Cho et col. or Tirana et col.). The second algorithm is the most effective method to minimize the service latency especially for shortly inter-arrival times. The overall minimum improvement value when compared with the round robin method is under 5 %.

The possible weakness of presented model are the queue with infinite capacity or the service rate of all simulated IMS nodes are exponential distributed. Therefore, our future research work will be focusing on the modelling of the home IMS network with the help of GI/GI/1/k queueing systems. The service times for each of SIP or DIAMETER signalling over IMS core will be defined with the help of performance evaluation of the home IMS network. Thanks to this queueing system, the designed model will more correspond with the real IMS network and real network conditions.

Acknowledgment

This work was supported by Ministry of Education, Youth and Sports of the Czech Republic under projects SIX CZ.1.05/2.1.00/03.0072 and MPO FR-TI4/696.

References

[1] 3rd Generation Partnership Project. *Technical Specification Group Core Network and Terminals: IP Multimedia (IM) Subsystem Cx and Dx interfaces, Signaling flows and message contents (Release 11)*. TS 29.228 (v. 11.6.0), December 2012.

[2] 3rd Generation Partnership Project. *Technical Specification Group Services and System Aspects. IP Multimedia Subsystem (IMS) – Stage 2. Release 11*. 3GPP TS 23.228 (v11.7.0). December 2012.

[3] NAGY, L., J. TOMBAL and V. NOBOTNY. Proposal of a Queueing Model for Simulation of Advanced Telecommunication Services over IMS Architecture. In: *International Conference on Telecommunications and Signal Processing*. Rome: IEEE, 2013, pp. 326–330. ISBN 978-1-4799-0402-0. DOI: 10.1109/TSP.2013.6613945.

[4] 3rd Generation Partnership Project. *Technical Specification Group Core Network and Terminals: Cx and Dx interfaces based on the Diameter protocol, protocol details. Release 11*. 3GPP TS 29.229 (v11.2.0). December 2012.

[5] OH, S., Ch. LE and Y. SHIN. The Serving CSCF Assignment Algorithm in Wireless IP Multimedia Networks. In: *46th Midwest Symposium on Circuits and Systems*. Cairo: IEEE, 2003, pp. 440–445. ISBN 0-7803-8294-3. DOI: 10.1109/MWS-CAS.2003.1562313.

[6] CHATTOPADHAYAY, B. and M. A. MUNOZ DE LA TORRE. *S-CSCF load balancing*. Motorola, Inc. 2006.

[7] ABDALLA, I. and S. VENKATEASAN. Notification based S-CSCF load Balancing in IMS Networks. In: *Wireless Telecommunications Symposium (WTS)*. New York City: IEEE, 2011, pp. 1–5. ISBN 978-1-4577-0162-7. DOI: 10.1109/WTS.2011.5960852.

[8] XU, L., Ch. HUANG, J. YAN and T. DRWIEGA. De-Registration Based S-CSCF Load Balancing in IMS Core Network. In: *International Conference on Communications*. Dresden: IEEE, 2009, pp. 1–5. ISBN 978-1-4244-3435-0. DOI: 10.1109/ICC.2009.5198895.

[9] HWANG, J.-H., Y.-G. KOOK and J.-O. LEE. A Dynamic Routing Algorithm for Managing CSCF Agents in the IMS Network. In: *5th International Joint Conference on INC, IMS and IDC*. Seoul: IEEE, 2009, pp. 930–935. ISBN 978-1-4244-5209-5. DOI: 10.1109/NCM.2009.120.

[10] HWANG, J.-H. Routing Algorithm for Dynamic Management of CSCF Agent in the IMS Platform. In: *KNOM Review - Network Operations and Management*. 2008, vol. 11, iss. 2, pp. 14–27. ISSN 2287-1543.

[11] HWANG, J.-H., J.-H. CHO and J.-O. LEE. A Routing Management among CSCFs Using Management Technology. In: *12th Asia-Pacific Network Operations and Management Conference on Management enabling the future internet for changing business and new computing services*. Jeju: Springer Verlag, 2009, pp. 502–506. ISBN 978-3-642-04491-5. DOI: 10.1007/978-3-642-04492-2_63.

[12] HWANG, J.-H. and J.-O. LEE. An Implementation of Network Management System Using Dynamic Routing in IMS. *International Journal of Software Engineering and Its Applications*. 2012, vol. 6, iss. 4, pp. 201–206. ISSN 1738-9984.

[13] CHO, J.-H. and J.-O. LEE. A Management for the Deployment of Presence Service Using A Dynamic Routing Algorithm in the IMS nodes. In: *13th Asia-Pacific Network Operations and Management Symposium (APNOMS)*. Taipei: IEEE, 2011, pp. 1–4. ISBN 978-1-4577-1668-3. DOI: 10.1109/APNOMS.2011.6076957.

[14] TIRANA, P. and D. MEDHI. The effects of load distribution algorithms in application's response time in the IMS architecture. In: *Proceeding of 18th ITC Specialist Seminar on Quality of Experience*. Karlskrona: Blekinge Institute of Technology, 2008, pp. 173–181. ISSN 1103-1581.

[15] TIRANA, P. and D. MEDHI. Distributed Approaches to S-CSCF Selection in an IMS Network. In: *Network Operations and Management Symposium*. Osaka: IEEE, 2010. pp. 224–231. ISBN 978-1-4244-5366-5. DOI: 10.1109/NOMS.2010.5488465.

[16] NAGY, L., J. HOSEK, P. VAJSAR and V. NOVOTNY. Impact of Signalling Load on Response Times for Signalling over IMS Core. In: *Federated Conference on Computer Science and Information Systems*. Krakow: IEEE, 2013, pp. 663–666. ISBN 978-83-60810-53-8.

[17] KLEINROCK, L. *Queuing Systems, Vol. 1: Theory*. New York: Wiley Interscience, 1975. ISBN 0-471-49110-1.

[18] 3rd Generation Partnership Project. *Technical Specification Group Core Network and Terminals. Signalling flows for the IP multimedia call control based on Session Initiation Protocol (SIP) and Session Description Protocol (SDP); Stage 3. Release 5*. 3GPP TS 24.228 (v5.15.0). September 2006.

About Authors

Lubos NAGY was born in Ilava (Slovak Republic) in 1984. He received his M.Sc. in 2009 at the Department of Telecommunications at the Faculty and Communication at Brno University of Technology in Czech Republic. At the present, he is working toward the Ph.D. degree at the Brno University of Technology. The area of his professional interest is the IP Multimedia Subsystem, mainly the performance evaluation of IMS core entities. He is teaching the laboratory exercises: "Mobile Network Communication Systems", "Network Architecture", "Terminal Equipment" at the same department.

Vit NOVOTNY (born in 1969) received M.Sc.

in 1992 at the Faculty of Electrical Engineering and Computer Science in the Brno University of Technology, in 2001 he received the Ph.D. degree and in 2005 he received Associate Professor degree at the same university. He received or participated in anumber of projects focused on mobile networks or on telecommunication network technologies and services. His professional interests include: fixed, wireless and mobile networks, telecommunication services, integrated services networks and Internet technologies.

Jana URAMOVA was born in Zvolen, Slovakia, in 1980. She graduated at Grammar School of L. Stura in Zvolen and she studied at the University of P. J. Safarik in Kosice. She defended dissertation thesis in 2005 and she has been continuing her Ph.D. study and research of Information models of network throughput. She has been acting as a lecturer at the Department of information networks at University of Zilina from 2003. She is an instructor of Regional Cisco Network Academy in Zilina and she is lecturing the subjects exercises Communication Networks, Theory of Information, Introduction into Engineering and Computer Networks.

Nermin MAKHLOUF was born in Damascus (Syria Arab Republic). She received her Master's Degree at the department of Communication at Damascus University in 2009. At the present, she is studying the Ph.D. at the Brno University of Technology. Her research interests include Prediction of movement of wireless nodes in mobile ad-hoc networks MANETs and the Markov chains.

14

The Usability Analysis of Different Standard Single-Mode Optical Fibers and Its Installation Methods for the Interferometric Measurements

Jakub CUBIK, Stanislav KEPAK, Jan DORICAK, Vladimir VASINEK, Jakub JAROS, Andrej LINER, Martin PAPES, Marcel FAJKUS

Department of Telecommunications, Faculty of Electrical Engineering and Computer Science, VSB–Technical University of Ostrava, 17. listopadu 15/2172, 708 33 Ostrava-Poruba, Czech Republic

jakub.cubik@vsb.cz, stanislav.kepak@vsb.cz, jan.doricak@vsb.cz, vladimir.vasinek@vsb.cz, jakub.jaros@vsb.cz, andrej.liner@vsb.cz, martin.papes@vsb.cz, marcel.fajkus@vsb.cz

Abstract. *With optical fibers we are able to measure a variety of physical quantities. Optical fiber sensors sensitive to the change of the light phase, so-called interferometers referred in this article are one of the most sensitive sensors. Because we are able to detect phase changes with extreme precision, these sensors are thus suitable for demanding applications, where cost is not the main requirement. We have used the Mach-Zehnder configuration. The paper deals with the usage of different types of standard single-mode optical fibers in the civil engineering as an integrated acoustic sensor. Further experiments are focused on the different types of fiber installation methods, such as placement in the mounting foam, into the polystyrene or attachment onto the wooden surface and their effect on the measurements. Through the repeated measurements of harmonic frequencies were obtained information about the usable frequency range and sensitivity of the particular arrangement. Measurement was performed for both cases, where the specific type of fiber or specifically installed fiber was used as the measurement or as the reference. The final evaluation is based both on the experience gained during measurements and also using the statistical calculations.*

Keywords

Different singlemode optical fiber standards, fiber installation methods, fiber optic sensor, Mach–Zehnder interferometer.

1. Introduction

Development of fiber optics communication systems experiences slight stagnation at this time. In contrast, the use of optical components for sensor applications can be considered a region not yet fully explored. We can consider two basic groups of fiber-optic sensors based on the evaluation of light intensity or phase of the light. Sensors evaluating light intensity are generally used for measurement of displacement and other physical phenomena affecting the fiber. On the other hand phase sensors compare the phase of the light between the two beams. These sensors called interferometers are composed of measuring and reference arm. Ideally, the measured phenomenon should not affect the reference arm and should affect only the measuring arm. Phase sensors are more sensitive and more accurate than intensity sensors but their structure is more complicated, technically more demanding and expensive. Nowadays we find their use rather in special applications [1]. The basic types of interferometers are Mach-Zehnder, Fabry-Perot, Sagnac and Michelson. This paper uses the Mach-Zehnder configuration.

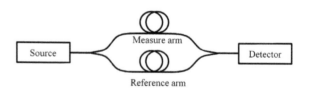

Fig. 1: Scheme of Mach-Zehnder interferometr.

In the case of Mach-Zehnder interferometer source light is split by coupler in two, representing the measuring and reference arm. Phase of the measured beam is affected by the measurand while the reference beam is experiencing a constant environment. These two beams then recombine at the second coupler and the resultant signal continues to a photodetector, which converts the optical power to electrical current. Visibility of interference depends on the relative intensity

$$I = I_0 \left[\alpha_r c_1 c_2 + \alpha_s \left(1 - c_1\right)\left(1 - c_2\right) + 2\sqrt{\alpha_r \alpha_s c_1 c_2 \left(1 - c_1\right)\left(1 - c_2\right)} \cos\left(\phi_r - \phi_s\right) \right]. \qquad (1)$$

of the measuring and reference beam, the relative state of polarization and their mutual coherence. Ideally, the relative intensity and polarization states are equal and the optical path length difference between the measured and the reference beam is much smaller than the coherence length of the light source [2].

Already published articles dealing with similar layout usable for measuring vibration, pressure, bending or temperature can be found [3], [4], [5], [6], [7], [8]. These articles are closely related to the issues addressed in this publication.

Results from previous experiments have already been published in papers [9], [10], [11], [12]. In case of [9] Mach-zehnder interferometer for movement monitoring is an early work on the configuration. Interferometric sensor based on the polarization-Maintaining Fibers discusses the use of polarization-maintaining fibers in interferometric fiber optic sensors due to increased sensitivity [10]. Fiber Bragg Grating vibration sensor with DFB laser diode uses the same measuring chain for measuring similar phenomena, but instead of interferometer bragg grating is used [11].

Unlike the above mentioned publications, this paper deals with an important aspect of practical use of optical fiber sensor namely the imposition of the interferometer arms. Therefore it is an analysis of different methods of imposing both the reference and measuring arm of the interferometer. Traditional materials used in both the construction and in everyday life were used.

2. Operating Principles

Following equations are inspired by Eric Udd and William B. Sppilman [13]. Optical phase delay of light passing through a fiber is given by:

$$\phi = n \cdot k \cdot L, \qquad (2)$$

where n is the refractive index of the fiber core, k is optical wavenumber in a vacuum and $k = 2\pi/\lambda$, where λ is a light source wavelength and L is the physical length of the fiber. Also $n \cdot L$ is often referred as an optical path length.

For variations in the phase delay (2) of interferometer, we can write:

$$\frac{\mathrm{d}\phi}{\phi} = \frac{\mathrm{d}L}{L} + \frac{\mathrm{d}n}{n} + \frac{\mathrm{d}k}{k}. \qquad (3)$$

With the stabilized light source k can be considered as a constant, because it depends only on the wavelength of the source. Phase change due to the measured

quantities is therefore proportional to the refractive index of fiber and fiber length. Usually, changes in the pressure, temperature or magnetic field results in different contributions to $\mathrm{d}\phi$ via the $\mathrm{d}L$ and $\mathrm{d}n$ terms. Low–frequency processes primarily produce $\mathrm{d}L$, while due changes of the coefficient of optical stress the refractive index changes.

Mach–Zehnder interferometer is compact of two couplers with coupling coefficients c_1 a c_2 and can be assumed a certain optical loss in measuring and reference arm, known as α_s and α_r. The output intensity of the interferometer can be expressed as Eq. 1, where ϕ_r is the phase shift in reference arm and ϕ_s is the phase shift in measuring arm. Definition of fringe visibility is given by standard definition which from Eq. 1 gives:

$$V = \frac{2\sqrt{\alpha_r \alpha_s c_1 c_2 \left(1 - c_1\right)\left(1 - c_2\right)}}{\alpha_r c_1 c_2 + \alpha_s \left(1 - c_1\right)\left(1 - c_2\right)}. \qquad (4)$$

It should be noted that two effects have been ignored in this calculation. One is the influence of polarization. The second effect is the coherence length of the source, which should be greater than the difference in length in the arms of the interferometer ΔL. Since we have used narrowband laser diode, these effects can be considered negligible.

Provided that $\alpha = \alpha_r = \alpha_s$, so that transmission losses in both arms of the interferometer are the same. And assuming that the coupling coefficients are $c_1 = c_2 = 0,5$. Resulting fringe visibility is then, substitution into Eq. 4, $V = 1$. And intensity at the output of the interferometer can be rewritten as:

$$I = \frac{I_0 \alpha}{2} \left(1 + cos\Delta\phi\right), \qquad (5)$$

where I_0 is light intensity on the input of first coupler and $\Delta\phi \left(\phi_r - \phi_s\right)$ is the phase difference between both arms of the interferometer. Intensity on the output of detector creates an electrical current of:

$$i = \epsilon I_0 \alpha cos\left(\phi_d + \phi_s sin\omega t\right), \qquad (6)$$

where ϵ is the responsivity of the photodetector and phase difference $\Delta\phi$ may be separated into signal term of amplitude ϕ_s, frequency ω and slowly varying phase shift ϕ_d. This resultant electric signal is further processed and converted into the frequency domain, as shown in Fig. 3.

3. Experimental Setup

3.1. Introducing of the Experimental Setup

As mentioned above in case of Mach-Zehnder interferometer the light is split between two arms (Fig. 2). The light is split using the coupler which has one input and two outputs. Coupling ratio between the arms is 50 % so the light is evenly distributed to both arms. The fiber of length 210 cm is then applied to each arm. The light from the two arms are then fed into the second coupler. It is then applied to the InGaAs photodetector using the short patchcord fiber. The detector converts the optical power into an electrical current, which is further processed. As a light source DFB laser at a wavelength of 1550 nm is used. Laser diode had a stabilized operating point using the current and temperature controller. Coupled power into the fiber was in this case 1,74 mW.

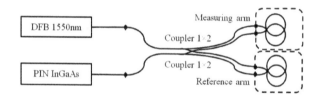

Fig. 2: Used configuration of Mach–Zehnder interferometer.

An electrical signal was fed to the LC high–pass filter with a cutoff frequency at 8 Hz via 50 Ω coaxial cable in order to suppress DC component (Fig. 3). After that was fed into a measuring card NI USB–6210 with sampling rate up to 250 kSps. The card was capturing voltage on analogue input using the application written in LabView development suite. The application also performs a discrete Fourier transform, so the voltage was transferred into the frequency domain. Hanning window function was used in our case. Peaks in calculated spectra were searched and their amplitudes written to a text file. Each measurement lasted one minute then spectrum with maximum amplitudes has been selected for further processing. The measured results were statistically processed, as will be described in the following chapter, based on ten of repeated measurements.

For excitation the rectangular signal with frequency of 160 Hz and voltage 10 V peak to peak, loudspeaker placed 1 m above fiber was used. Same signal was used for all measurement cases. Twelve different setups were measured. It was 24 measurements in total because of excitation both reference and measurement arm. Measuring and reference arms were placed on separate wooden boards. Wooden boards were placed on rubber pads to eliminate vibrations from floor.

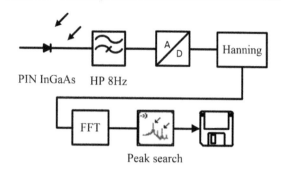

Fig. 3: Schematic diagram of electrical signal processing.

3.2. Measuring with Different Standard of Fibers and Polystyrene Boards

First two setups contained fibers of different standard in one of the interferometer arm, ITU-T G.652.D and ITU-T G.657.B, respectively. Another two measurements were with polystyrene boards. The first method was based on basic covering of the fiber with one polystyrene board, the second method was a little bit complicated, because fiber was placed between two polystyrene boards. These two boards were fixed together by double-sided adhesive tape. To achieve adequate fixation board were burdened for few minutes.

3.3. Measuring with Mounting Foam

Measuring with mounting foam was also little bit time consuming. According to the manufacturer's instructions the foam has to harden for at least 24 hours. Another obstacle was that it is very difficult or even impossible to extract fiber from fully hardened mounting foam. There were three measuring setups, which were utilizing mounting foam. First setup was foamed Tight buffered G.652.D (Fig. 4) fiber but without foamed lead fibers to the couplers. Second setup was containg the G.652.D fiber also but this time it was foamed with leads of the couplers. Finally third measuring setup was foamed Tight buffered G.657.B fiber but same as in the first case without foamed lead fibers to the couplers.

3.4. Measuring with Water and Temperature Shifts

For measuring in water was used jacketed fiber G.652.D. This arrangement was measured twice with two different temperatures of water. Firstly with warm water, temperature was from 41,8 °C at the beginning of measuring to 40,5 °C at the end of measuring. Then the measurement was repeated with cold water with

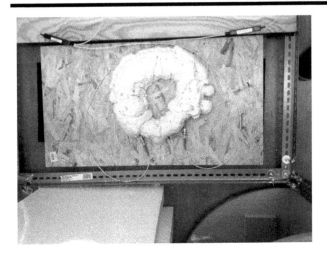

Fig. 4: Tight buffered fiber ITU-T G.652.D in mounting foam.

temperature from 24,5 °C at the beginning of measuring to 24,6 °C at the end of measuring. Total volume of water was 9 liters.

3.5. Measuring with Soil and Glue

One measuring was performed using soil. Optical cable was completely covered with two layers of soil. For completeness temperature of soil was 6,0 °C. Last measuring setup was consisted of glued jacketed fiber G.652.D glued to the wooden board by superglue.

4. Results and Discussion

For better clarity values were recalculated according to Eg. 7. Where V_1 is the voltage being measured, V_0 is a specified reference voltage for all cases and its values is 1 V, and G_{dB} is the power gain expressed in decibels:

$$G_{dB} = 20log\left(\frac{V_1}{V_0}\right). \qquad (7)$$

After applying Eg. 7 there are much more convenient values in dBV as can be seen in Tab. 1. In the measurement a variety of frequencies were recorded, but as mentioned above threshold was used for distinguishing distinct frequencies and frequencies drowned in noise. Logical groups of setups were chosen, for which statistical methods described below were used. The only setup located in each group is simple placing fibers on the wooden board. From this perspective, we can say that this is a reference measurement for other imposing possibilities. Statistical methods were used for the decision about the usability of imposing in practice.

The first group is the use of traditional materials used in construction. It is the case using polystyrene boards, mounting foam and soil (Tab. 2). These setups

represent a sample of possible imposing for reference arm of an interferometer. In practical terms a theoretical use of already stored fibers for interferometric measurements. Another group is the using Tight buffered fiber and bending insensitive fiber (G.657.B). Results are given in Tab. 3 and Tab. 4. Assumption of this experiments was increased sensitivity useful for special applications (single frequencies) or for general use (whole frequency band). ITU-T standard G.657.B for the possibility of a greater bending of fibers was used. This feature is particularly important in imposing of the fibers in construction and other rugged areas.

The last group is using mounting foam again for the reference branch of the interferometer. These cases are Tight buffered fiber in mounting foam, fiber in mounting foam with coupler arms (Tab. 4). The reason of this evaluation was the effect of mounting foam on a fiber. During hardening of the foam the increased pressure on the optical fiber is present. Especially Tight buffered fiber type is very sensitive to the mounting foam hardening. The suitability of the imposing of connectors and coupler arms to mounting foam were also evaluated. Table 1, Tab. 2, Tab. 3 and Tab. 4 shows the calculated medians of amplitudes in dBV for each frequency of the ten repeated measurements. For Tab. 1 and Tab. 4 statistical evaluation were performed using Kruskal–Wallis one–way analysis of variance, since there were not always fulfilled the conditions for parametric analysis of variance. Data was not distributed normally in all measurements and attempts to normalize data have failed.

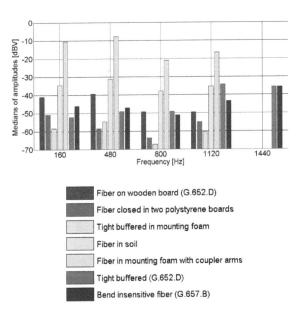

Fig. 5: Chart of statistically processed measurements.

For more clear comparison of important measured values was introduced chart of these results. Figure 5 shows a chart of calculated medians of amplitudes in dBV for significant frequencies. For Tab. 2

Tab. 1: Calculated medians of amplitudes in dBV for different setups based on ten repeated measurements (* denotes a statistically significant difference).

Frequency [Hz]	160	480	800	1120
Fiber on wooden board (G.652.D)	−28,963	−30,506	−20,698	−20,394
Fiber closed in two polystyrene boards	−19,165*	−11,488*	−6,3615*	−15,089
Tight buffered in mounting foam	−11,714*	−15,33*	−2,8265*	−9,544
Fiber in soil	−35,444	−38,765	−32,173	−34,573

Tab. 2: Calculated medians of amplitudes in dBV for different setups based on ten repeated measurements (* denotes a statistically significant difference).

Frequency [Hz]	160	480	800	1120	1440
Fiber on wooden board (G.652.D)	−21,401	−20,952	−27,619	−25,783*	−29,275*
Tight buffered (G.652.D)	−17,776*	−20,864	−20,959*	−35,663	−34,298

Tab. 3: Calculated medians of amplitudes in dBV for different setups based on ten repeated measurements (* denotes a statistically significant difference).

Frequency [Hz]	160	480	800	1120	1440
Bending insensitive fiber (G.657.B)	−23,895	−22,847	−18,774*	−26,501*	−34,298
Tight buffered (G.652.D)	−17,776*	−20,864*	−20,959	−35,663	−34,298

Tab. 4: Calculated medians of amplitudes in dBV for different setups based on ten repeated measurements (* denotes a statistically significant difference).

Frequency [Hz]	160	480	800	1120
Fiber on wooden board (G.652.D)	−28,963	−30,506	−20,698	−20,394
Tight buffered in mounting foam	−11,714*	−15,33	−2,827*	−9,5435*
Fiber in mounting foam with coupler arms	−59,447	−62,264	−49,095	−53,422

Tab. 5: Calculated arithmetic mean of amplitudes in dBV for different setups based on ten repeated measurements.

Frequency [Hz]		160	320	480	800	1120	1440	1760	2080
Fiber on wooden board (G.652.D)	Meas. [dBV]	−22,116	-	−21,251	−27,869	−26,018	−29,477	-	-
	Ref. [dBV]	−29,592	-	−30,221	−21,109	−20,777	-	-	-
Bending insensitive fiber (G.657.B)	Meas. [dBV]	−23,808	-	−23,125	−18,583	−26,311	−26,311	-	−31,448
	Ref. [dBV]	−17.201	−16,238	-	−22,431	−23,735	-	-	-
Fiber covered with polystyrene board	Meas. [dBV]	−30,250	-	−27,460	−21,645	−23,442	-	-	-
	Ref. [dBV]	−21,011	−31,210	−30,140	−19,792	−22,618	-	-	-
Fiber closed in two polystyrene boards	Meas. [dBV]	−13,096	-	−8,078	−8,078	−6,994	−14,504	−13,670	-
	Ref. [dBV]	−18,514	-	−11,530	−6,399	−16,695	−12,181	-	−11,707
Tight buffered (G.652.D)	Meas. [dBV]	−18,576	-	−21,078	−21,244	−36,374	−34,308	-	-
	Ref. [dBV]	−15,662	-	-	-	-	-	-	-
Tight buffered in mounting foam	Meas. [dBV]	−13,462	-	−13,194	−5,082	−16,538	-	−17,506	-
	Ref. [dBV]	−11,787	-	−15,264	−2,984	−9,680	-	-	-
Fiber in mounting foam with coup. arm.	Meas. [dBV]	−13,462	-	−13,194	−5,082	−16,538	-	−17,506	-
	Ref. [dBV]	−11,787	-	−15,264	−2,984	−9,680	-	-	-
Insensitive fiber in mounting foam	Meas. [dBV]	−72,571	-	−75,452	−73,416	−75,940	−74,135	-	−79,461
	Ref. [dBV]	−65,880	-	-	−68,940	−66,728	−68,046	−77,176	−76,978
Fiber in warm water	Meas. [dBV]	−31,524	-	-	−24,867	−26,770	−32,594	-	-
	Ref. [dBV]	-	-	-	−11,706	-	-	-	-
Fiber in cold water	Meas. [dBV]	-	-	−29,801	−18,182	−29,597	-	-	-
	Ref. [dBV]	−27,964	-	−32,635	−22,175	-	−24,567	−35,083	-
Fiber in soil	Meas. [dBV]	−27,964	-	−32,635	−22,175	-	−24,567	−35,083	-
	Ref. [dBV]	−34,079	-	−38,511	−32,178	−34,666	−28,057	−36,430	-
Fiber glued to wooden board	Meas. [dBV]	-	-	−56,591	−62,059	-	-	-	-
	Ref. [dBV]	-	-	−54,998	−53,841	−62,108	−63,479	-	-

and Tab. 3 statistical evaluation ware performed using Mann–Whitney–Wilcoxon non–parametric significance tests since there were not always fulfilled the conditions for parametric tests.

5. Conclusion

Measured results showed that the different installation of the reference and measuring arm of the interferometer gives the effect of changing the sensitivity of the measured. We were able to increase the sensitivity of interferometric sensor by installation of optical fibers to traditional materials used in construction. Polystyrene panel has proved the best results due to the easy handling and low cost. In the case of attempts to achieve the best sensitivity by modifying the configuration of the reference arm we would choose the installation with mounting foam. In contrast coupler arms and connectors installed in mounting foam proved wrong. This phenomenon was caused by hardening of the foam. For the measurements at lower frequencies is the absence of the jacket advantageous, but for higher frequencies it is advisable to have the measuring arm fully protected by the jacket. In practice the tight buffered fiber is not suitable for installation. Jacketed fibers are used for their solid and elasticity. These experiences exclude Tight buffered fibers in practical use.

Acknowledgment

This article was created with the active support by the Ministry of Education of the Czech Republic within the project no. SP2013/69 of the VSB–Technical University of Ostrava. This article was supported by project VG20102015053, TA03020439 and GACR (Czech Science Foundation) GAP108/11/1057 - Synthesis, structure and properties of nanocomposites conducting polymer/phyllosilicate. The research has been partially supported by the project No. CZ.1.07/2.3.00/20.0217 "The Development of Excellence of the Telecommunication Research Team in Relation to International Cooperation" within the frame of the operation programme "Education for competitiveness" financed by the Structural Funds and from the state budget of the Czech Republic.

References

[1] KROHN, D. *Fiber optic sensors: Fundamentals and apllications*. Research Triangle Park, NC: Instrument Society of America, 1988. ISBN 08-766-4997-5.

[2] LOPEZ-HIGUERA, J. M. *Handbook of optical fibre sensing technology: fundamentals and apllications*. New York: Wiley, 2002. ISBN 04-718-2053-9.

[3] SUN, M., B. XU, X. DONG and Y. LI. Optical fiber strain and temperature sensor based on an in-line Mach–Zehnder interferometer using thin-core fiber. *Optics Communications*. 2012, vol. 285, iss. 18, pp. 3721–3725. ISSN 0030-4018. DOI: 10.1016/j.optcom.2012.04.046.

[4] HERNANDEZ-SERRANO, A. I., G. SALCEDA-DELGADO, D. MORENO-HERNANDEZ, A. MARTINEZ-RIOS and D. MONZON-HERNANDEZ. Robust optical fiber bending sensor to measure frequency of vibration. *Optics and Lasers in Engineering*. 2013, vol. 51, iss. 9, pp. 1102–1105. ISSN 0143-8166. DOI: 10.1016/j.optlaseng.2013.03.011.

[5] SUN, Q., D. LIU, J. WANG, H. LIU and D. MONZON-HERNANDEZ. Distributed fiber-optic vibration sensor using a ring Mach-Zehnder interferometer. *Optics Communications*. 2008, vol. 281, iss. 6, pp. 1538–1544. ISSN 0030-4018. DOI: 10.1016/j.optcom.2007.11.055.

[6] ZHENG, J., P. YAN, Y. YU, Z. OU, J. WANG, X. CHEN and Ch. DU. Temperature and index insensitive strain sensor based on a photonic crystal fiber in line Mach–Zehnder interferometer. *Optics Communications*. 2013, vol. 297, iss. 6, pp. 7–11. ISSN 0030-4018. DOI: 10.1016/j.optcom.2013.01.063.

[7] KOUDELKA P., J. LATAL, J. VITASEK, J. HURTA, P. SISKA, A. LINER and M. PAPES. Implementation of Optical Meanders of the Optical-fiber DTS System Based on Raman Stimulated Scattering into the Building Processes. *Advances in Electrical and Electronic Engineering*. 2012, vol. 10, no. 3, pp. 187–194. ISSN 1336-1376.

[8] HARRIS, J., P. LU, H. LAROCQUE, Y. XU, L. CHEN, X. BAO and Ch. DU. Highly sensitive in-fiber interferometric refractometer with temperature and axial strain compensation. *Optics Express*. 2013, vol. 21, iss. 8, pp. 9996–10009. ISSN 1094-4087. DOI: 10.1364/OE.21.009996.

[9] VASINEK, V., J. CUBIK, S. KEPAK, J. DORICAK, J. LATAL and P. KOUDELKA. Mach-Zehnder interferometer for movement monitoring. In: *Proceedings of SPIE - Fiber Optic Sensors and Applications IX*. Baltimore, Maryland: SPIE, 2013, vol. 8370, pp. 1–7. ISBN 978-0-8194-9048-3. DOI: 10.1117/12.919349.

[10] CUBIK, J., S. KEPAK, J. DORICAK, V. VASINEK, A. LINER and M. PAPES. Interferometric sensor based on the polarization-maintaining fibers. In: *Proceedings of SPIE - 18th Czech-Polish-Slovak Optical Conference on Wave and Quantum Aspects of Contemporary Optics*. Ostravice: SPIE, 2012, vol. 8697, pp. 1–8. ISBN 978-0-8194-9048-3. DOI: 10.1117/12.2005893.

[11] SISKA, P., M. BROZOVIC, J. CUBIK, S. KEPAK, J. VITASEK, P. KOUDELKA, J. LATAL and V. VASINEK. Fiber Bragg Grating vibration sensor with DFB laser diode. In: *Proceedings of SPIE - 18th Czech-Polish-Slovak Optical Conference on Wave and Quantum Aspects of Contemporary Optics*. Ostravice: SPIE, 2012, vol. 8697, pp. 1–9. ISBN 978-0-8194-9048-3. DOI: 10.1117/12.2005893.

[12] KEPAK, S., J. CUBIK, J. DORICAK, V. VASINEK, P. SISKA, A. LINER and M. PAPES. The arms arrangement influence on the sensitivity of Mach–Zehnder fiber optic interferometer. In: *Proceedings of SPIE - Optical Sensors*. Prague: SPIE, 2013, vol. 8774, pp. 1–8. ISBN 978-0-8194-9576-1. DOI: 10.1117/12.2017305.

[13] UDD, E. and W. B. SPILLMAN. *Fiber optic sensors: An introduction for engineers and scientists*. Hoboken: Wiley, 2011. ISBN 978-0-470-12684-4.

About Authors

Jakub CUBIK was born in 1986 in Olomouc. In 2009 received Bachelor's degree on VSB–Technical University of Ostrava, Faculty of Electrical Engineering and Computer Science, Department of Telecommunications. Two years later he received on the same workplace his Master's degree in the field of Telecommunications. He is currently Ph.D. student, and he works in the field of optical communications and fiber optic sensor systems.

Stanislav KEPAK was born in 1987 in Ostrava. In 2009 received Bachelor's degree on VSB–Technical University of Ostrava, Faculty of Electrical Engineering and Computer Science, Department of Telecommunications. Two years later he received on the same workplace his Master's degree in the field of Telecommunications. He is currently Ph.D. student, and he works in the field of optical communications and fiber optic sensor systems.

Jan DORICAK was born in 1987 in Novy Jicin. In 2009 received Bachelor's degree on VSB–Technical University of Ostrava, Faculty of Electrical Engineering and Computer Science, Department of Telecommunications. Two years later he received on the same university Master's degree in the field of Telecommunications. He is currently Ph.D. student, he works in the field of optical communications and fiber optic sensor systems. He operate in Prague paralely with his study as project engineer in Safibra company which is focused on new types of optical and photonics sensors.

Vladimir VASINEK was born in Ostrava. In 1980 he graduated in Physics, specialization in Optoelectronics, from the Science Faculty of Palacky University. He was awarded the title of RNDr. At the Science Faculty of Palacky University in the field of Applied Electronics. The scientific degree of Ph.D. was conferred upon him in the branch of Quantum Electronics and Optics in 1989. He became an associate professor in 1994 in the branch of Applied Physics. He has been a professor of Electronics and Communication Science since 2007. He pursues this branch at the Department of Telecommunications at VSB–Technical University of Ostrava. His research work is dedicated to optical communications, optical fibers, optoelectronics, optical measurements, optical networks projecting, fiber optic sensors, MW access networks. He is a member of many societies - OSA, SPIE, EOS, Czech Photonics Society; he is a chairman of the Ph.D. board at the VSB–Technical University of Ostrava. He is also a member of habilitation boards and the boards appointing to professorship.

Jakub JAROS was born in 1987 in Ostrava. In 2009 received Bachelor's degree on VSB–Technical University of Ostrava, Faculty of Electrical Engineering and Computer Science, Department of Telecommunications. Three years later he received on the same workplace his Master's degree in the field of Telecommunications. He is currently Ph.D. student, and he works in the field of optical communications and fiber optic sensor systems.

Andrej LINER was born in 1987 in Zlate Moravce. In 2009 received Bachelor's degree on University of Zilina, Faculty of Electrical Engineering, Department of Telecommunications and Multimedia. Two years later he received on the same workplace his Master's degree in the field of Telecommunications and Radio Communications Engineering. He is currently Ph.D. student, and he works in the field of wireless optical communications and fiber optic distributed systems.

Martin PAPES was born in 1987 in Nove Zamky. In 2009 received Bachelor's degree on University of Zilina, Faculty of Electrical Engineering, Department of Telecommunications and Multimedia. Two years later he received on the same workplace his Master's degree in the field of Telecommunications and Radio Communications Engineering. He is currently Ph.D. student, and he works in the field of wireless optical communications and fiber optic distributed systems.

Marcel FAJKUS was born in 1987 in Ostrava.

In 2009 received Bachelor's degree on VSB–Technical University of Ostrava, Faculty of Electrical Engineering and Computer Science, Department of Telecommunications. Two years later he received on the same workplace his Master's degree in the field of Telecommunications. He is currently Ph.D. student, and he works in the field of optical communications.

15

Problem of Channel Utilization and Merging Flows in Buffered Optical Burst Switching Networks

Milos KOZAK[1], Brigitte JAUMARD[2], Leos BOHAC[1]

[1]Department of Telecommunications Engineering, Faculty of Electrical Engineering, Czech Technical University in Prague, Technicka 2, 160 00 Prague, Czech Republic

[2]Department of Computer Science and Software Engineering, Faculty of Engineering and Computer Science, Concordia University, 1515 St. Catherine St. West, Montreal (Quebec), Canada

milos.kozak@fel.cvut.cz, bjaumard@cse.concordia.ca, leos.bohac@fel.cvut.cz

Abstract. *In the paper authors verify two problems of methods of operational research in optical burst switching. The first problem is at edge node, related to the medium access delay. The second problem is at an intermediate node related to buffering delay. A correction coefficient K of transmission speed is obtained from the first analysis. It is used in to provide a full-featured link of nominal data rate. Simulations of the second problem reveal interesting results. It is not viable to prepare routing and wavelength assignment based on end-to-end delay, i.e. link's length or number of hops, as commonly used in other frameworks (OCS, Ethernet, IP, etc.) nowadays. Other parameters such as buffering probability must be taken into consideration as well. Based on the buffering probability an estimation of the number of optical/electrical converters can be made. This paper concentrates important traffic constraints of buffered optical burst switching. It allows authors to prepare optimization algorithms for regenerators placement in CAROBS networks using methods of operational research.*

Keywords

Analysis, hypothesis testing, optical burst switching, regenerator placement.

1. Introduction

While Optical burst switching (OBS) networks have been studied for more than 15 years now, there is still some controversy about their viability. Some authors study OBS networks as an alternative to Optical circuit switching (OCS) networks [8], other investigate OBS networks as best fit for some types of traffic (e.g., bursty traffic) or networks (e.g., access networks), see, e.g., [14]. OBS is very close to its deployment, some testbeds are operated and papers have been published. Currently authors focus on contention resolution which is the crucial problem of OBS and can occur even under low load. Authors have suggested various types of time slot mechanisms [13], deflection routing and metrics based on priorities. Also this issue was investigated by Coutelen et al. and let to the CAROBS framework. Therein, the authors consider burst concatenation. With the recourse to wavelength conversion throughout signal regeneration can resolve all burst contentions, offering a loss-free OBS framework. CAROBS uses electrical buffering for optical signal regeneration hence burst's end-to-end delay can increase significantly when a node is under high load. In order to reduce the load, it must be distributed among all nodes in network with proper routing. To distribute the load among nodes in a network a single node behaviour must be evaluated in the first place. There are two main obstacles of node performance in buffered OBS, it is buffering at an intermediate node and medium access delay at an edge node. Both must be verified under different node offered load.

In authors best knowledge there has not been papers on this topic dealing delays in buffered OBS networks. This paper tackles this problem under various link datarates (1, 10, 40 and 100 Gb·s^{-1}).

2. Problem Formulation

In OBS an optical burst is used in order to transmit data. Such a burst can contain a number of payload frames, that can be Ethernet, IP, etc [12]. Usually burst's length is around 10 Mb that is approximately 1 ms for 10 Gb·s^{-1} system and shorter for systems using more powerful modulation formats. Second very important parameter is Optical cross-connect (OXC) switching speed in the time domain of OBS. The OXC switching speed highly depends on technology. There are OXCs based on MEMS that have switched speed in order of μs, SOA based OXCs have switching speed in order of ns. SOA based OXCs are very often used nowadays. Using faster technology and longer bursts the link efficiency increases but the impact of contenting bursts on buffering delay as well. Therefore a reasonable tradeoff must be found. As was mentioned, the efficiency of OBS network highly depends on OXC switching speed. The reason is caused by the mandatory burst space between two consecutive bursts [3]. Such a space must be greater or equal to the switching speed of OXC. Unless this constraint is respected a piece of a burst might be switched to the same direction as the previously switched burst or might be lost at all [3].

This mandatory space limits maximum throughput (utilization) of a link. Using shorter bursts the delimiting space is used more often for the same offered load, then the link maximal throughput decreases significantly. In the following text we use two very similar terms "Offered load" and "load". The term "Offered load" is used for the first problem which is focused on edge node, i.e. a traffic of data packets offering certain level of load to a node. This term has its roots in traditional telecommunications. The term "load" is mostly used in the analysis of the second problem. It means an offered load to the egress port of a node:

$$load = \frac{1}{C} \sum_{\ell \in L_n} \alpha_\ell. \tag{1}$$

For example if node S_1 at Fig. 2, is offered by a load of nominal bandwidth of its egress link, ℓ_1, e.g. 10 Gb·s^{-1}. Then waiting time in access buffers at edge node can be endless. This problem is depicted on Fig. 1(a). Basically it means that link's bandwidth must be higher than the link's data rate.

The terms link's bandwidth and data rate are very similar. In systems derived from RM-OSI we speak about different speed at different layers. Since OBS is located at the 1st layer of RM-OSI, in the following text, we use term link's data rate (upper layer) in order to denote nominal, usable link's bandwidth at a certain wavelength. Term link's bandwidth (lower layer) in order to denote physical speed of a channel (combination of wavelengths and links). We will not use term modulation speed because we want to generalize problem [5].

The second problem, at this stage of research it is more or less observation, takes place on link data rate level. Needless to say there are some versions of OBS frameworks using timeslots where this problem does not exist. Currently when routing and wavelength assignment (RWA) is performed, all links are fully loaded with respect to Eq. (2). When merging of flows occurs

$\alpha < \mu$ constraint must be satisfied otherwise burst waiting in buffers will be eventually endless. Here α stands for total node's offered load and μ represents node's intensity of service, i.e. how much traffic a node can transmit. The main problem comes from the link usage maximization as a result of other optimizations. The maximal link usage is bounded by link capacity Eq. (2). When merging a number of flows offering load α_ℓ at a node, e.g. M, ($\sum_{\ell \in L_n} \alpha_\ell = \alpha$) only thing that can happen is $\alpha \geq \mu$, which eventually leads to behaviour depicted on Fig. 1(b). We consider capacity of all connected link to a node n have the same capacity. L_n is a set of links terminating at node n:

$$\sum_{i=0}^{N} \phi_i \leq C_\ell, \tag{2}$$

where ℓ stands for a link in the network, N is the number of flows that are supported by link ℓ, ϕ_i denotes required capacity by the flow i and C_ℓ represents maximal capacity of the link ℓ.

In order to avoid this situation, proper evaluation of a node's offered load must be carried out in the first place. The second aspect of buffering problem is the number of optical detectors (O/E), which are expensive thus their amount should be minimal. In other words minimizing the amount of O/E reduces CAPEX and OPEX and increases reliability of buffered OBS network.

3. Simulations

At this stage of the research, the aforementioned problems were tackled through simulations. The reason is that the OBS switches implementing buffering abilities do not exist nowadays. Simulations were performed using CAROBS models implemented in OMNeT++ [2], [3], [4]. Simulations were performed on the same basic network, that is depicted on Fig. 2. Both problems were not simulated at the same time but in the consecutive set of simulations. In the first place the analysis of the first problem was carried out. Results proved the claim from Section 2, that the link of nominal bandwidth does not support flow of the same data rate. Maximal flow data rate with stationary waiting in buffers was found. It lets to correction coefficient K, Tab. 1. Then the correction coefficient was implemented into the simulation models. In the second step simulations of buffering at an intermediate node were carried out.

The traffic was generated such that the payload packets of constant size (100 kb) making flow were supplied to edge nodes S_n according to Poisson distribution in order to generate bursts. Such that constant

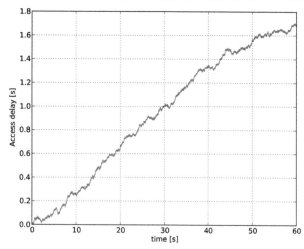

(a) Suboptimal link bandwidth results in endless waiting in an access buffer at edge node.

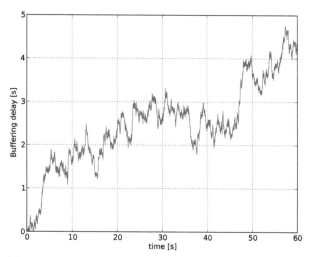

(b) If the sum of offered loads is equal to egress port intensity of service is equal, occurs endless waiting in contention resolution buffers at an intermediate node.

Fig. 1: When channel speed estimation is not optimal, data might persist in electrical buffers.

flow of a nominal required bandwidth was generated. In simulations we assumed that node M have unlimited electrical storage capacity. Duration of simulations was set to 60 s after a warm-up period. Only one wavelength was used.

3.1.   Access Delay

Link access delay is a value representing average waiting time of a burst before it is sent on the optical network. The value must be as small as possible. When it is not stationary, see Fig. 1, it means the system is overloaded and can not be used. It happens when the link's offered load is slightly higher than maximal link intensity of service, i.e. link capacity C_ℓ. Our approach was to gradually increase the offered load and evaluate egress link utilization as is depicted on

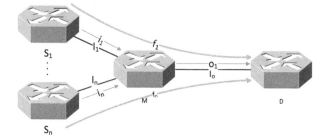

Fig. 2: Basic network topology used for simulations.

Fig. 3. The results of simulations were normalized in order to be comparable in one graph. One can read that egress link gets saturated before the offered load reaches value 1 erl, see Fig. 3(a). This is a sequel of problem visualized on Fig. 1(a). The original problem depicted on Fig. 1(a) is here extended on Fig. 3(b) with respect to the offered load. If the evaluation interval, 60 s, was longer the values of link access delay would be higher for the non-stationary simulations. Along that visualization, regression analysis was carried out to find the stationary simulations. Results of regression analysis were not depicted due to better readability of graphs. These results highly correlate with the trends on Fig. 3(b). When the value of link access delay increases with an increase of offered load the slope of link access delay is not zero, i.e. is not stationary anymore, i.e. egress link is already saturated. In order to keep the nominal datarate of the link, link's bandwidth must be increased.

In order to find the threshold when the link access delay is not stationary anymore we must formulate null hypothesis H_0 and alternate hypothesis H_a. Null hypothesis claims that H_0 is valid when N consecutive simulations meet requirement being stationary. Stationarity is verified by other testing based on linear regression analysis, which is out of scope of this article [6]. The H_0 is a criterion of a heuristic analysis. Every time the H_a is valid a new simulation is performed, in order to precise. The value of offered load of the new simulation is the average of offered load from last H_0 compliant simulation and the non compliant simulation. Doing so iteratively, correction coefficient K is found. We performed this analysis for OBS network with various nominal link data rates. Results of the analysis are captured in Tab. 1.

Applying these coefficients one can be sure, that further evaluations will not be affected by premature saturation of link caused by limited bandwidth.

3.2.   Buffering Delay

The evaluation of buffering delay relies on precise evaluation of link utilization of each ingress link. Therefore the previous analysis is necessary in order to achieve

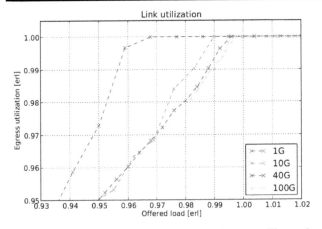

(a) The graphical representation of link utilization. The goal of link optimization is the reciprocity of offered load and egress link utilization, i.e. the offered load 1 erl causes link utilization 1. If otherwise the link properties must be optimized.

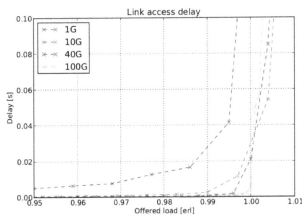

(b) The link access delay should be stationary and polynomially increase with an increase of offered load.

Fig. 3: Graphical representation of egress link utilization and link access delay at network ingress node.

meaningful results. All results from this analysis are gathered at node M, see Fig. 2. Simulations were performed such that the number of merging flows was changed as well as their data rate. The load was changed similarly to the previous study. Also various patterns of flows data rates were used, in order to obtain valid results. For better readability of graphs the confidence intervals are omitted. Egress port load was calculated using Eq. (1).

Offered load of each source was iteratively increased in order to achieve the egress link load vary from 0,5 to 1,05 erl. Based on this evaluation the values of buffering delay and buffering probability were captured, results are depicted on Fig. 4 and Fig. 5.

The average buffering time of a contenting burst depends on load, see Fig. 4. Particular details of buffering delay, Fig. 4(a), are provided in order to increase its readability. The average waiting time pertain to

Tab. 1: Values of bandwidth correction coefficient K.

Link data rate $[\text{B·s}^{-1}]$	Correction coefficient $[-]$	Extra bandwidth $[\text{b·s}^{-1}]$
100 M	1,00000125	125
200 M	1,0000025	500
1 G	1,0000126	12,6 k
2 G	1,0000125	25,0 k
10 G	1,000017856	178,5 k
40 G	1,00003846	1,53 M
100 G	1,00009616	9,6 M

50 km of fiber delay line (FDL) which is not negligible. When the buffered burst is sent back onto the optical network the burst is regenerated, as it was a new burst. This approach is very vital in wide area networks where the optical signal can be impaired. On the other hand looking at Fig. 5 one can read that the probability of buffering is very high, i.e. when load is higher than 0,6 erl, there is quite high probability that even not contenting burst is buffered. The reason is that, a contenting burst is buffered and scheduled to be withdrew later, but the later moment might overlap with a new coming burst. Then the new coming burst must be buffered even if is not contenting with other incoming burst. In the worst case two bursts are contenting, egress link is blocked by the withdrew burst, then both bursts must be buffered. It means two O/E conversions must be carried out at the same time. In other words two O/E units must be installed at the node. It increases its price, eventually price of whole buffered OBS network.

Additionally this study supports current trend of deploying faster systems over slower ones, see Fig. 4. There are almost negligible improvements of buffering probability but on the other hand there is a significant difference in buffering delay. Therefore it is vital to use higher datarate links for buffered OBS networks.

4. Conclusion

The OBS framework has been proved to be reliable for future access or metropolitan networks. Also some real implementations have been presented and are reaching to be commercially deployed by Internet service providers [1]. Still, there is a dark site off OBS networks. There are problems on the physical layer when the optical signal can be impaired. Generally this problem arises in geographically extensive installations. In order to avoid optical impairments the optical amplifiers [11], regenerators, etc. must be installed. The drawback of this approach is in increased CAPEX and OPEX of installation. Also there are no traffic models

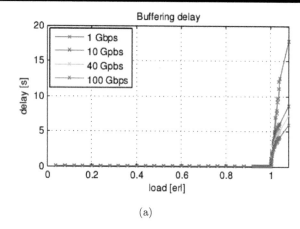

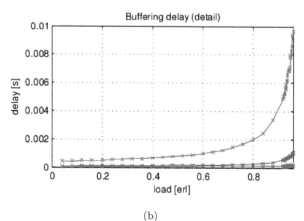

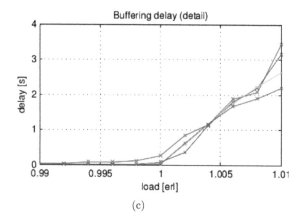

Fig. 4: Evaluation of buffering delay and buffering probability at merging node M. 4(b) and 4(c) are details of 4(a). It is interesting its proportion to the load, which is caused by non-dropping behaviour,i.e. everything is buffered ergo waiting time increases.

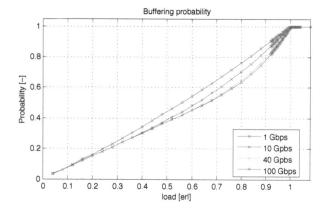

Fig. 5: Evaluation of buffering delay and buffering probability at merging node M. This Figure is bounded together with Fig. 4. Represents buffering probability, which almost linearly increases with the load.

imal required bandwidth margin in order not to saturate the link's bandwidth before it is necessary. Along that the models optimizations improve scheduling of egress port when a buffered burst is put back onto the optical network. This coefficient K is of importance, because it defines necessary link bandwidth even for real networks not only for simulations. On top of that the flow behaviour we observed in the analysis of buffering delay and its probability are of high importance for solving optimization algorithms. Since now we have gotten a new constraint representing bursty character of buffered OBS. This constraint allows us to use mature approaches know from OCS optimizations in OBS. Also this constraint allows us to estimate minimal number of O/E block that are needed.

Even though results seems to be optimistic a lot of work has to be done. This analysis was carried out for system using just one wavelength. On contrary using more wavelengths might relax the number of O/E blocks. Also there are not considered optical impairments that are the original motivation of our other analysis. The next logical steps are to carry out multiple wavelength system analysis [7], obtain buffering probabilities. Then construct optimization algorithm in order of minimizing amount of O/E blocks in network. Eventually consider optical impairments.

that could be used for regenerators placement [10] optimizations as is usually carried out in OCS. There has been some studies on regenerators placement problem [9] but authors focused on not-buffering OBS framework.

This article tried to tackle this lack of models by the edge and intermediate node observations. We bring a new correction coefficient which allows to define min-

Acknowledgment

The authors would like to thank to grants from Ministry of The Interior of Czech republic under the project name "Guardsence" and number VG20102015053, SGS13/200/OHK3/3T/13, SGS12/186/OHK3/3T/13 and TA02011015.

References

[1] Optical Packet Switch and Transport: Technical Introduction. In: *Intune Networks* [online]. 2012. Available at: `http://www.intunenetworks.com/home/shape-up/core_innovation/opst_technical_introduction/`.

[2] COUTELEN, T., B. JAUMARD and G. HEBUTERNE. An enhanced train assembly policy for lossless OBS with CAROBS. In: *Communication Networks and Services Research Conference (CNSR)*. Montreal: IEEE, 2010, pp. 61–68. ISBN 978-1-4244-6248-3. DOI: 10.1109/CNSR.2010.21.

[3] KOZAK, M. and L. BOHAC. The Labelled Optical Burst Switching OMNeT++ Model With Accurate Time Offset Evaluation. In: *Proceedings of the 11th International Conference Knowledge in Telecommunication Technologies and Optics*. Ostrava: VSB–TUO, 2011, pp. 75–77. ISBN 978-80-248-2399-7.

[4] KOZAK, M., B. JAUMARD, and L. BOHAC. On Regenerator Placement in Lossless Optical Burst Switching Networks. In: *36th International Conference on Telecommunications and Signal Processing*. Piscataway: IEEE, 2013, pp. 311–315. ISBN 978-1-4799-0404-4. DOI: 10.1109/TSP.2013.6613942.

[5] LATAL, J., J. VOGL, P. KOUDELKA, J. VITASEK, P. SISKA, A. LINER, M. PAPES, and V. VASINEK. Simulation and measurement of optical access network with different types of optical-fiber amplifiers. In: *18th Czech-Polish-Slovak Optical Conference on Wave and Quantum Aspects of Contemporary Optics*. Ostravice: SPIE, 2012, pp. 86971U–86971U–10. ISBN 9780819494818. DOI: 10.1117/12.2001263.

[6] LEHMANN, E. L. and J. P. ROMANO. *Testing Statistical Hypotheses*. New York: Springer, 2005. ISBN 978-0387988641.

[7] MUKHERJEE, B. *Optical WDM networks*. New York: Springer, 2006. ISBN 978-0-387-29055-3.

[8] PAVON-MARINO, P. and F. NERI. On the myths of optical burst switching. *IEEE Transactions on Communications*. 2011, vol. 59, iss. 9, pp. 2574–2584. ISSN 0090-6778. DOI: 10.1109/TCOMM.2011.063011.100192.

[9] PEDROLA, O., D. CAREGLIO, M. KLINKOWSKI, and J. SOLE-PARETA. Offline routing and regenerator placement and dimensioning for translucent OBS networks. *Journal of Optical Communications and Networking*. 2011, vol. 3, iss. 9, pp. 651–666. ISSN 1943-0620. DOI: 10.1364/JOCN.3.000651.

[10] PEDROLA, O., D. CAREGLIO, M. KLINKOWSKI, L. VELASCO, K. BERGMAN, and J. SOLE-PARETA. Metaheuristic hybridizations for the regenerator placement and dimensioning problem in subwavelength switching optical networks. *European Journal of Operational Research*. 2012, vol. 224, iss. 3, pp. 614-624. ISSN 0377-2217. DOI: 10.1016/j.ejor.2012.08.011.

[11] POBORIL, R., J. LATAL, P. KOUDELKA, J. VITASEK, P. SISKA, J. SKAPA, and V. VASINEK. A concept of a hybrid wdm/tdm topology using the fabry-perot laser in the optiwave simulation environment. *Advances in Electrical and Electronic Engineering*. 2011, vol. 9, iss. 4, pp. 167–178. ISSN 1336-1376.

[12] YOO M. and C. QIAO. Optical Burst Switching (OBS) - A New Paradigm for an Optical Internet. *Journal of High Speed Networks*. 1999, vol. 8, iss. 1, pp. 69–84. ISSN 0926-6801.

[13] XIANG Y., J. LI, X. CAO, Y. CHEN, and C. QIAO. Traffic statistics and performance evaluation in optical burst switched networks. *Journal of Lightwave Technology*, 2004, vol. 22, iss. 12, pp. 2722–2738. ISSN 0733-8724. DOI: 10.1109/JLT.2004.833527.

[14] ZOUGANELI, E., R. ANDREASSEN, B. FENG, A. SOLEM, N. STOL, H. KJØNSBERG, A. SUDBØ, B. HELVIK, and A. HAUGEN. Why bother with optical packets? An evaluation of the viability of optical packet/burst switching. *Telektronikk*. 2005, vol. 101, iss. 2, pp. 126–147. ISSN 0085-7130.

About Authors

Milos KOZAK received the M.Sc. degree in electrical engineering from the Czech Technical University, Prague, in 2009. Since 2009 until 2012, he had been teaching optical communication systems and data networks with the Czech Technical University in Prague. His research interest is on the application of high-speed optical transmission systems in a data network. Particularly regenerators placement in all optical networks.

Brigitte JAUMARD holds a Concordia University Research Chair, Tier 1, on the Optimization of Communication Networks in the Computer Science and

Software Engineering (CSE) Department at Concordia University. Her research focuses on mathematical modelling and algorithm design for large-scale optimization problems arising in communication networks, transportation networks and artificial intelligence. Recent studies include the design of the most efficient algorithms for p-cycle based protection schemes, under static and dynamic traffic, and their generalization to the so-called p-structures, which encompass all previously proposed pre-cross-connected pre-configured protection schemes. Other recent studies deal with dimensioning, provisioning and scheduling algorithms in optical grids or clouds, in broadband wireless networks and in passive optical networks. In Artificial Intelligence, contributions include the development of efficient optimization algorithms for probabilistic logic and for automated mechanical design in social networks. In transportation, her recent contributions include new algorithms for freight train scheduling and locomotive assignment. B. Jaumard has published over 300 papers in international journals in Operations Research and in Telecommunications.

Leos BOHAC received the M.S. and Ph.D. degrees in electrical engineering from the Czech Technical University, Prague, in 1992 and 2001, respectively. Since 1992, he has been teaching optical communication systems and data networks with the Czech Technical University, Prague. His research interest is on the application of high-speed optical transmission systems in a data network. He has also participated in the optical research project CESNET - the academic data network provider to help implement a long-haul high-speed optical research network. Currently, he has been actually involved in and led some of the projects on optimal protocol design, routing, high speed optical modulations and industrial network design.

16

FPGA Implementations of Feed Forward Neural Network by using Floating Point Hardware Accelerators

Gabriele-Maria LOZITO, Antonino LAUDANI, Francesco RIGANTI-FULGINEI,
Alessandro SALVINI

Department of Engineering, Roma Tre University, via Vito Volterra 62, 00146 Roma, Italy

gabrielemaria.lozito@uniroma3.it, alaudani@uniroma3.it, riganti@uniroma3.it,asalvini@uniroma3.it

Abstract. *This paper documents the research towards the analysis of different solutions to implement a Neural Network architecture on a FPGA design by using floating point accelerators. In particular, two different implementations are investigated: a high level solution to create a neural network on a soft processor design, with different strategies for enhancing the performance of the process; a low level solution, achieved by a cascade of floating point arithmetic elements. Comparisons of the achieved performance in terms of both time consumptions and FPGA resources employed for the architectures are presented.*

Keywords

Embedded floating point, FPGA, neural networks, soft-core processor, VHDL.

1. Introduction

Field Programmable Gate Arrays (FPGA) designs are very common in the field of computational electronics [1], [2], [3]. Digital Signal Processing (DSP) models, often analyzed in high level environments, show heavy restraints on performance once implemented on embedded systems whose bottleneck is, despite the ongoing advances in Floating Point Units (FPU) development, the low floating point operations per second (FLOPS), [4]. Compared to a microcontroller implementation (based on the sequential execution of instructions by the CPU) the nature of an FPGA design exploits the concepts of customization and parallelization to enhance the throughput of a computational system [5]. Customization allows the designer to create, through Hardware Description Language (HDL), the internal architecture of the system down to Register Transfer Level (RTL), defining as a matter of fact a flexible

Application Specific Integrated Circuit (ASIC). Parallelization spreads modular and sequential algorithms on a parallel interface, improving the throughput of complex algorithms by a multiplicative factor [6].

Neural Networks in embedded systems are frequently implemented on microcontroller units [7], [8]. A neural network implementation on a microcontroller, even when built with simple integer arithmetic, lacks the performance enhancement of a parallel design [9]. The choice of implementing a neural network architecture on FPGA benefits from customization and parallelization in different ways.

Very large Feed Forward Neural Networks (FFNN), especially if designed to work with floating point (FP) precision, performs a large number of elementary products and sums. Moreover, for each neuron of FFNN within the hidden layers, a non-linear function computation is required to determine the activation value of the neuron. Without dedicated FP hardware such computations can hinder the whole performance of the system, hence making the design difficult to be used in critical applications like real-time control systems [10].

In literature different approaches have been followed to reduce the computational cost of this particular activation function, using piecewise linear interpolation [11], polynomial fitting techniques [12], [13], [14], [15], enhanced computational algorithms [16], [17] and Look-Up Tables [18], [19], [20], [20], [21]. In this way, customization allows the designer to implement blocks inside the FPGA to speed up the calculus of FP operations.

The concept of parallelization is implicit in the high performance of the solutions explained above: a RTL-defined LUT can compute an arbitrarily complex operation in few clock cycles, assuming the memory of the system can contain the values. The same can be said for the arithmetic units, which can exploit powerful pipelines to speed up the calculus. The number of interconnection between the neurons, however, grows exponentially with the size (in terms of input and outputs) of the network. It's possible to reduce the complexity of the FFNN by splitting a Multiple Input Multiple Output (MIMO) FFNN into a smaller and simpler Single Input Single Output (SISO) FFNN that can be easily processed in parallel by means of multivariate function decomposition [22], [23].

2.   The Feed Forward Neural Network

The Feed Forward Neural Network implemented in this paper is a SISO Feed Forward Neural Network, composed by a single hidden layer of 10 neurons with a nonlinear activation function Logsig (Eq. 1) and\or Tansig (Eq. 2):

$$act = \frac{1}{1 + e^{-nst}}, \qquad (1)$$

$$act = \frac{2}{1 + e^{-2nst}} - 1. \qquad (2)$$

This architecture was chosen for the easiness of the training process and the modularity of the structure: indeed it is possible to face MIMO problems by using SISO FFNN as described in [22]. The FFNN was created and trained in Matlab® environment. The normalization of the inputs and outputs was disabled and the activation function of the output layer was a pure linear function.

3.   Implementation on Nios II/f Soft Processor

The first solution attempted to implement the network on FPGA makes usage of the soft core processor Nios II/f, released by Altera® as a crypted core. This core can be synthesized with as low as 1600 logic elements (LE) and supports a maximum frequency of 140 MHz [24], [25].

After synthesis and programming on the FPGA device, the soft core itself can be programmed and debugged in C using a JTAG tool chain running inside an Eclipse environment. This soft core processor supports hardware integer multiplication and division, and up to 255 custom instructions definable by the designer. These custom instructions can be defined at RTL level using Very High Speed Integrated Circuits (VHSIC) Hardware Description Language (VHDL) or Verilog® code, and are synthesized as parallel blocks of the internal Nios II Arithmetic Logic Unit (ALU) as shown in Fig. 1, when a custom instruction is called from the instruction memory of the Nios II, the operands are

transferred in the custom logic and, according to the type of custom instruction (combinatorial or sequential) the result is collected after a definite number of clock cycles [26].

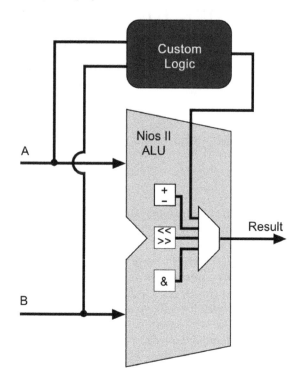

Fig. 1: Implementation of custom logic in the Nios II ALU.

3.1.   Overall System Description

The design proposed in this section is based on the Nios II/f core, modified to have a Floating Point ALU and two system works with a 100MHz clock, which is replicated by means of a PLL with a phase shift of -3 ns to control an external 8 Mb SDRAM [27]. As shown in Fig. 2, the processor was equipped with a standard JTAG interface for programming and a Performance Counter to determine the execution time of the implemented code. The Floating Point ALU was the standard block from the library released by Altera® as a part of the Quartus II® environment. Two Activation Function LUT(s) were created in VHDL (one for the Tansig and one for the Logsig) and imported into the design as user-made custom instructions.

3.2.   LUT(s) Use for Computing Activation Function

The main performance bottleneck for neural networks using floating point arithmetic lies in the activation function computation for the hidden layer. Computing

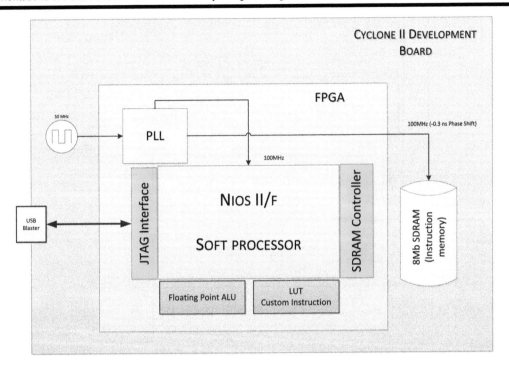

Fig. 2: Soft processor and Peripherals.

this function using "full precision" software functions is often too slow for time critical applications [28]. Instead of calculating the activation function, an alternative solution is to sample it, loading the obtained values in a LUT [18], [19], [20], [21]. In the present paper, the function was not sampled with a uniform and constant spacing between the sampling points. This is because the activation function assumes almost constant values near the saturation points, making it wasteful to choose a fine sampling in their proximity. On the other hand, near the origin, the slope of the function is very high, and a finer sampling may help in reducing quantization error. In [19] only two kinds of spacing are used: a fine one, near the origin, and a wide one, near the saturation branches. In this work, a different approach is proposed: the distance between a sample and the following one is inversely proportional to the slope of the function in the sampled point.

This yields a finer sampling near the origin, gradually getting wider near the saturation points. The Logsig function was sampled with 256 values between −16 and +16, while the Tansig, being an odd function, was sampled for positive arguments only, with 256 values between 0,2 and. Using these values, a VHDL combinatorial code was written and simulated in Altera ModelSim environment for RTL analysis.

The implemented block has a single floating point input, that is split in sign, exponent and mantissa. Through the use of a suitable IF-THEN-ELSE chain the input value addresses a specific entry in the LUT, that is propagated as output. If the input value magnitude is bigger than the saturation values, a suitable

constant value is propagated as output. Since the Tansig, near the origin, can be approximated to the bisector of the first quadrant, values smaller than 0,2 are directly propagated in output (thus approximating the function linearly). The synthesis result of this IF-THEN-ELSE structure is a very long chain of comparators. Propagation of the signal through this chain can be long, so a tunable delay of 4 clock cycles was introduced to ensure result stability (the delay is controlled by a simple counter that can be modified to suit the size of the LUT).

3.3.   Polynomial Fitting

The basic operations of floating point math are greatly fastened by the presence of a Floating Point ALU (about 10 times faster [29]). Thus, other than speeding up the Multiplier-Accumulation part of the FFNN, this hardware module can be used to compute a polynomial approximation of the activation function. A group of second-degree polynomials was chosen to fit the activation functions. The coefficients of the polynomials were determined in Matlab® environment through the use of the Curve Fitting Tool. Both the functions were fitted only for positive arguments.

For the Logsig polynomial fitting, a function (denoted as 5PY-L) composed by the superposition of 5 second-degree polynomials, has been implemented. Even if the Logsig function is not odd, a partial symmetry is present. This was exploited for its negative arguments: first, the value of the function is calculated

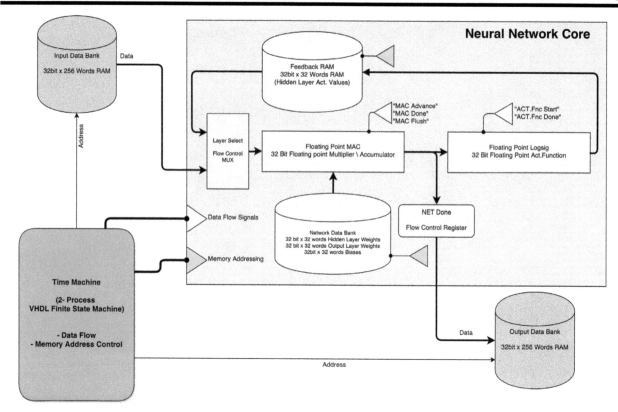

Fig. 3: NN Core schematic diagram.

Tab. 1: Nios II/f test results on FFNN with Logsig activation functions.

Function	MSE	Average time/sample
Floating Point	0.0000 (ref)	650 µs
LUT (Logsig)	0.1598	17.5 µs
5PY-L	0.0075	185 µs

Tab. 2: Nios II/f test results on FFNN with Tansig activation functions.

Function	MSE	Average time/sample
Floating Point	0.0000 (ref)	715 µs
LUT (Tansig)	0.0053	17.5 µs
4PY-L	0.0039	142 µs
5PY-L	0.0018	174 µs

considering the absolute value of the input; then, if the input is negative, the calculated value is subtracted by the value of 1. For the Tansig polynomial fitting, two functions, composed by 4 and 5 second-degree polynomials have been implemented, respectively denoted as 4PY-T and 5PY-T. This time, since the Tansig is an odd function, the argument is considered in absolute value, and the sign is directly propagated to the output.

3.4.   Test Results and Considerations

The design was used to simulate a FFNN trained on the function $y = x^2$, and was tested on a vector of 2048 linearly spaced inputs between −5 and +5. The results in Tab. 1 and Tab. 2 show the performance in terms of mean squared error (MSE) and execution time of the different solutions proposed above. As a reference for execution time, the performance of a FFNN featuring a

full precision software implementation of the activation function is shown in both tables.

4.   NN Core Implementation

In the following part of this paper a solution based on low level architecture is presented. The proposed design was used for the implementation of the same FFNN previously described.

4.1.   Overall System Description

The proposed design is an arithmetic core composed (see Fig. 3) by high performance floating point arithmetic blocks developed by Altera®, whose data flow is controlled by a Finite States Machine (FSM) written in VHDL. The arithmetic core is composed by 3 blocks: a multiplier-accumulator (MAC), an activation function,

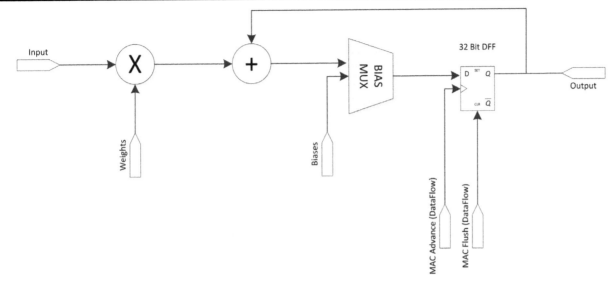

Fig. 4: MAC block diagram.

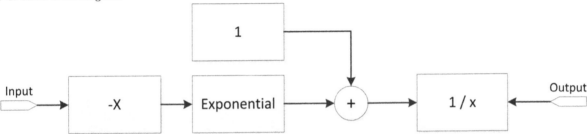

Fig. 5: Logsig block diagram.

and a feedback RAM. These three blocks constitute a suitable base to build a Neural Network [30]. The first block computes, for each neuron, the weighted sum of the inputs.

The second block has the results of the first block as inputs, and computes the activation values for the hidden layer. The third block, receiving the output from the activation function block, stores the values from the hidden layer. These values are then sent through a MUX back into the MAC block for the output layer computation. Both input and output data of the FFNN are stored in RAM blocks that are accessible through JTAG interface using the Quartus II® software. The whole Core and the data banks are controlled by a free running 2-Process Finite State Machine "Time Machine" using data flow control signals and address registers. Internal data flow of the core is regulated by a number of 32-bit wide MUXes and D-Type Flip Flops (DFFs). The design was implemented on a EP2C20F484C7 Cyclone II FPGA mounted on a DE2 – Development Board. After synthesis and fitting the full design occupied about 5000 logic elements (LE) and all the 52 hardware multipliers present on the FPGA.

4.2. Data Flow of the Arithmetic Core

The computation of the arithmetic core begins by loading the first sample from the Input Data Bank into the MAC block. The core contains into its internal memory the weights and biases of the FFNN. This memory is addressed directly by the Time Machine control block. Since the MAC is computing the hidden layer, each neuron will have a bias value that must be added to the weighted input. This bias value is preloaded into the 32-bit DFF accumulator using the Bias MUX. Inputs and weights are multiplied and the results are added to the preloaded bias (see Fig. 4). Since the hidden layer has only one input, the MAC is done for the first neuron, and the result is propagated to the next block, where the activation function is computed. In this section, a logical not is operated on the MSB of the input, changing its sign. The result is sent to an exponential arithmetic block whose output is connected to an adder that sums the result to the constant value of 1.

The result is then inverted and the activation value of the first neuron is finally written in the Feedback RAM. This operation is repeated for the 10 neurons, filling the RAM with the activation values of the hidden layer. Then, the Time Machine switches the Layer

Tab. 3: Best performance comparison.

Function	MSE	Average time/sample	Full Time (2048 Samples)
NN Core (50 MHz clock)	0.0000 (ref)	154 µs	315.4 ms
NN Core (100 MHz clock)	0.0000	78 µs	159.8 ms
5PY-L	0.0075	185 µs	378.8 ms
LUT (Tansig)	0.0054	17.5 µs	35.79 ms

Tab. 4: Nios II/f design main resources usage by entity.

Entity	LC Comb.	LC Reg.	DSP Elements
Nios II CPU	2382	1799	4
Floating Point Unit	5125	3783	7
LUT (Tansig)	1815	4	0
LUT (Logsig)	1617	4	0

Select MUX so that the MAC block is now connected to the Feedback RAM. The bias of the output neuron is preloaded in the accumulator, and the MAC computes the weighted sum of all the activation values from the hidden layer. This is the output result of the network, and is saved in the Output Data Bank.

4.3. Time Machine FSM

Data processing from input to output needs to be managed by some sort of control block, responsible for synchronizing the dataflow and, were needed, perform memory addressing. In a traditional programming language, like C, a popular approach to create such controller is to use a finite state machine (FSM). In its simplest form, a FSM is a set of code blocks, each identifying a particular function (e.g. "load data from RAM", "sum input A and input B", "transpose array C"), inside a switch/case structure. If the FSM is the sole controller of the system, the switch/case structure is confined in an endless loop. The variable controlling the switch is updated at the end of each code block, ensuring that every time the switch/case is evaluated the FSM will execute a specific code block (i.e. will be in a known and definite state). This rather simple approach is not as straightforward in HDL languages, since the code is not executed by a processor, thus not inherently sequential.

Hardware, emulating the processor sequential behaviour, must be created. A possible approach, proposed in [31], is to create an instruction counter whose value is increased at every clock edge. By using a net of comparators, when a particular value is assumed by the instruction counter, specific logic functions (states) are executed. Creating the FSM in this way grant an important advantage: since the instruction counter is updated on clock edge, the FSM can work synchronously with the other elements in the design. This is very important when some blocks in the design have definite input-output delays, since the FSM can be pro-grammed to remain in a "wait" state until the output is ready to be propagated to the next block. In VHDL this architecture can be defined by the use of two code blocks (processes), one sequential and one combinatorial.

The first one is responsible for the instruction counter increase at every clock edge, and is synthesized with a counter register. The second one is responsible for decoding the instruction counter into actual logic signals, and is synthesized with a network of comparators. The cycle of operations performed by the FSM is obviously limited, once the last operation is performed (i.e. the last output value has been loaded in the Output Data Bank), the FSM will reset and start over. With a 50 MHz clock, the computation of a single sample takes about 150 µs.

5. Solutions Comparison

In the Tab. 3, a comparison of the best performances among solutions is presented. At full precision, the NN Core design provides a quite lower computation time than the Nios II design. Moreover, by doubling the clock frequency through a PLL (thus using the same frequency used for the Nios II designs, 100 MHz) the computation time drops at 78 µs/sample. However, if full precision is not needed (and the choice of a particular activation function is not mandatory), implementing a FFNN based on a Tansig activation function yields the lowest computation time, using the Nios II design. In particular, implementing a LUT yields the best results in terms of precision over computation time.

In Tab. 4 and Tab. 5 the resources, in terms of dedicated Combinatorial and Register logics (LC Comb. and LC Reg.) are shown. The high level solution is expensive in terms of resources usage, peaking with 15 098 logic elements (LE) if both the LUT(s) are im-

Tab. 5: Best performance comparison.

Entity	LC Comb.	LC Reg.	DSP Elements
MAC Block	1015	620	7
Tansig Block	2784	1874	45
FSM Block	205	130	0

plemented as custom instructions. This is generally not necessary, since only one of the activation functions is used in the network. By excluding the Logsig LUT from the synthesis the LE usage drops to 12 699 LE. The low level solution, although completely saturating the DSP blocks of the FPGA, is contained in 5 037 LE.

6. Conclusions and Future Works

Two possible designs to implement a neural network in a FPGA environment were presented. The first design, taking advantage of the Nios II soft processor, used hardware accelerators to speed up both the calculus of the elementary products of neurons and the computation of the nonlinear activation functions for the hidden layer. By exploiting the soft processor hardware acceleration for floating point operations, an alternative polynomial approximation for the activation functions was implemented and tested for performance.

The second design proposed is composed by a chain of arithmetic units timed and coordinated by a VHDL state machine, which implemented a full precision floating point computation at a fraction of the execution time. The results acquired from this work can advance into a new form of neural network implementation on FPGA. The low level arithmetic chain implemented in the NN Core design could be split and included inside two custom instructions of a soft processor, hence combining the speed of the low level design with the flexibility of a C-programmable environment. This could benefit the design by allowing the inclusion of standard interfaces (like JTAG or I2C) to the system useful for many applications (see for example [32], [33]), while retaining RTL-wise control of the data flow.

In the hypothesis of using the network as a form of DSP for smart sensor or control systems, the floating point precision could be traded for a faster and smaller fixed-point or integer based system [34], [35]. Moreover, an improvement of the whole system can be always obtained if more complex and robust optimization algorithms [36], [37] are used in order to reduce the size of the implemented Neural Networks.

Acknowledgment

The research leading to these results has received funding from the European Community's Seventh Framework Programme (FP7/2007-2013) under grant agreement No. 218086.

References

[1] YAJUAN CH. and Q. WU. Design and implementation of PID controller based on FPGA and genetic algorithm. In: *Proceedings of 2011 International Conference on Electronics and Optoelectronics*. Dalian: IEEE, 2011, pp. 308–311. ISBN 978-1-61284-275-2. DOI: 10.1109/ICEOE.2011.6013491

[2] ZHENBIN G., X. ZENG, J. WANG and J. LIU. FPGA implementation of adaptive IIR filters with particle swarm optimization algorithm. In: *11th IEEE Singapore International Conference on Communication Systems*. Guangzhou: IEEE, 2008, pp. 1364–1367. ISBN 978-1-4244-2424-5. DOI: 10.1109/ICCS.2008.4737406.

[3] OTSUKA, T., T. AOKI, E. HOSOYA and A. ONOZAWA. An Image Recognition System for Multiple Video Inputs over a Multi-FPGA System. In: *IEEE 6th International Symposium on Embedded Multicore SoCs*. Aizu-Wakamatsu: IEEE, 2012, pp. 1–7. ISBN 978-0-7695-4800-5. DOI: 10.1109/MCSoC.2012.33.

[4] RAMAKRISHNAN, A. a J. M. CONRAD. Analysis of floating point operations in microcontrollers. In: *Proceedings of IEEE Southeastcon*. Nashville: IEEE, 2011, pp. 97–100. ISBN: 978-1-61284-739-9. DOI: 10.1109/SECON.2011.5752913.

[5] UNDERWOOD, K. FPGAs vs. CPUs. In: *Proceeding of the 2004 ACM/SIGDA 12th international symposium on Field programmable gate arrays*. New York: ACM Press, 2004, pp. 171–180. ISBN 1-58113-829-6. DOI: 10.1145/968280.968305.

[6] DELORIMIER, M. *Floating-point sparse matrix-vector multiply for FPGAs*. California, 2005. Master's thesis. California Institute of Technology. Research Advisor Andre DeHon.

[7] ELKATTAN, M., A. SALEM, F. SOLIMAN, A. KAMEL and H. EL-HENNAWY. Microcontroller based neural network for landmine detection using magnetic gradient data. In: *4th International Conference on Intelligent and Advanced Systems*. Kuala Lumpur: IEEE, 2012, pp. 46–50. ISBN 978-1-4577-1968-4. DOI: 10.1109/ICIAS.2012.6306156.

[8] BAYINDIR, R. and A. GORGUN. Hardware Implementation of a Real-Time Neural Network Controller Set for Reactive Power Compensation Systems. In: *Ninth International Conference on Machine Learning and Applications*. Washington: IEEE, 2010, pp. 699–703. ISBN 978-1-4244-9211-4. DOI: 10.1109/ICMLA.2010.107.

[9] PEDRONI, V. A. *Circuit design with VHDL*. Massachusetts: MIT Press, 2004. ISBN 02-621-6224-5.

[10] GHARIANI, M., M. W. KHARRAT, N. MASMOUDI and L. KAMOUN. Electronic implementation of a neural observer in FPGA technology application to the control of electric vehicle. In: *The 16th International Conference on Microelectronics*. Tunis: IEEE, 2004, pp. 450–455. ISBN 0-7803-8656-6. DOI: 10.1109/ICM.2004.1434611.

[11] AYALA, J. L., A. G. LOMENA, M. LOPEZ-VALLEJO and A. FERNANDEZ. Design of a pipelined hardware architecture for real-time neural network computations. In: *45th Midwest Symposium on Circuits and Systems*. MWSCAS-2002. Tulsa: IEEE, 2002. ISBN 0-7803-7523-8. DOI: 10.1109/MWSCAS.2002.1187247.

[12] ZURAIQI, E. A., M. JOLER and C. G. CHRISTODOULOU. Neural networks FPGA controller for reconfigurable antennas. In: *IEEE Antennas and Propagation Society International Symposium*. Toronto: IEEE, 2010, pp. 1–4. ISBN 978-1-4244-4967-5. DOI: 10.1109/APS.2010.5561011.

[13] BAPTISTA, D. a F. MORGADO-DIAS. Low-resource hardware implementation of the hyperbolic tangent for artificial neural networks. *Neural Computing and Applications*. 2013, vol. 23, iss. 3, pp. 601–607. ISSN 0941-0643. DOI: 10.1007/s00521-013-1407-x.

[14] NASCIMENTO, I., R. JARDIM a F. MORGADO-DIAS. A new solution to the hyperbolic tangent implementation in hardware: polynomial modeling of the fractional exponential part. *Neural Computing and Applications*. 2013, vol. 23, iss. 2, pp. 363–369. ISSN 1433-3058 DOI: 10.1007/s00521-012-0919-0.

[15] SOARES, A. M., L. C. LEITE, J. O. P. PINTO, L. E. B. DA SILVA, B. K. BOSE and M. E. ROMERO. Field Programmable Gate Array (FPGA) Based Neural Network Implementation of Stator Flux Oriented Vector Control of Induction Motor Drive. In: *IEEE International Conference on Industrial Technology*. Mumbai: IEEE, 2006, pp. 31–34. ISBN 1-4244-0726-5. DOI: 10.1109/ICIT.2006.372352.

[16] CHEN, X., G. WANG, W. ZHOU, S. CHANG and S. SUN. Efficient Sigmoid Function for Neural Networks Based FPGA Design. In: *International Conference on Intelligent Computing*. Kunming: Springer, 2006, pp. 672–677. ISBN 978-3-540-37271-4. DOI: 10.1007/11816157_80.

[17] FERREIRA, P., P. RIBEIRO, A. ANTUNES and F. M. DIAS. A high bit resolution FPGA implementation of a FNN with a new algorithm for the activation function. *Neurocomputing*. 2007, vol. 71, iss. 1-3, pp. 71–77. ISSN 0925-2312. DOI: 10.1016/j.neucom.2006.11.028.

[18] PRADO, R. N. A., J. D. MELO, J. A. N. OLIVEIRA and A. D. DORIA NETO. FPGA based implementation of a Fuzzy Neural Network modular architecture for embedded systems. In: *International Joint Conference on Neural Networks*. Brisbane: IEEE, 2012, pp. 1–7. ISBN 978-1-4673-1489-3. DOI: 10.1109/IJCNN.2012.6252447.

[19] SANTOS, P., D. OUELLET-POULIN, D. SHAPIRO and M. BOLIC. Artificial neural network acceleration on FPGA using custom instruction. In: *24th Canadian Conference on Electrical and Computer Engineering*. Niagara Falls: IEEE, 2011, pp. 000450–000455. ISBN 978-1-4244-9787-4. DOI: 10.1109/CCECE.2011.6030491.

[20] HIMAVATHI, S., D. ANITHA and A. MUTHURAMALINGAM. Feedforward Neural Network Implementation in FPGA Using Layer Multiplexing for Effective Resource Utilization. *Transactions on Neural Networks*. 2007, vol. 18, iss. 3, pp. 880-.888. ISSN 1045-9227. DOI: 10.1109/TNN.2007.891626.

[21] BAPTISTA, D. and F. MORGADO-DIAS. On the Implementation of Different Hyperbolic Tangent Solutions in FPGA. In: 10th *Portuguese Conference on Automatic Control*. Funchal: Controlo, 2012, pp. 204–209.

[22] RIGANTI-FULGINEI, F., A. SALVINI and M. PARODI. Learning optimization of neural networks used for MIMO applications based on multivariate functions decomposition. *Inverse Problems in Science and Engineering*. 2012,

vol. 20, iss. 1, pp. 29–39. ISSN 1741-5977. DOI: 10.1080/17415977.2011.629047.

[23] RIGANTI-FULGINEI, F., A. LAUDANI, A. SALVINI and M. PARODI. Automatic and Parallel Optimized Learning for Neural Networks performing MIMO Applications. *Advances in Electrical and Computer Engineering*. 2013, vol. 13, iss. 1, pp. 3–12. ISSN 1582-7445. DOI: 10.4316/aece.2013.01001.

[24] ALTERA. *Nios II Processor Reference: Handbook*. 11.0. San Jose, 2011. Availible at: http://www.altera.com/literature/hb/nios2/n2cpu_nii5v1.pdf.

[25] ALTERA. *Nios II Software Developer's: Handbook*. 11.0. San Jose, 2011. Availible at: http://www.altera.com/literature/hb/nios2/n2sw_nii5v2.pdf.

[26] ALTERA. *Nios II Custom Instruction: User Guide*. 11.0. San Jose, 2011. Availible at: http://www.altera.com/literature/ug/ug_nios2_custom_instruction.pdf.

[27] ALTERA. *Using the SDRAM Memory on Altera's DE2 Board with VHDL Design*. 8.0. San Jose, 2011. Availible at: http://www.cs.columbia.edu/~%20sedwards/classes/2013/4840/tut_DE2_sdram_vhdl.pdf.

[28] ORLOWSKA-KOWALSKA, T. and M. KAMINSKI. FPGA Implementation of the Multilayer Neural Network for the Speed Estimation of the Two-Mass Drive System. *IEEE Transactions on Industrial Informatics*. 2011, vol. 7, iss. 3, pp. 436–445. ISSN 1551-3203. DOI: 10.1109/TII.2011.2158843.

[29] ALTERA. *Using Nios II Floating-Point Custom Instructions: Tutorial*. 11.0. San Jose, 2011. Availible at: http://www.altera.com/literature/tt/tt_floating_point_custom_instructions.pdf.

[30] YOUSSEF, A., Karim. MOHAMMED a A. NASAR. A Reconfigurable, Generic and Programmable Feed Forward Neural Network Implementation in FPGA. In: *UKSim 14th International Conference on Computer Modelling and Simulation*. Cambridge: IEEE, 2012, pp. 9–13. ISBN 978-1-4673-1366-7. DOI: 10.1109/UKSim.2012.12.

[31] ZWOLINSKI, M. *Digital system design with VHDL*. Harlow: Prentice Hall, 2004. ISBN 01-303-9985-X.

[32] CARRASCO, M., F. MANCILLA-DAVID, F. RIGANTI-FULGINEI, A. LAUDANI and A. SALVINI. A neural networks-based maximum power point tracker with improved dynamics for variable dc-link grid-connected photovoltaic power plants. *Materials Science, Electromagnetics and Superconductors and Electromagnetics and Mechanics*. 2013, vol. 43, no. 1-2, pp. 127–135. ISSN 1383-5416. DOI: 10.3233/JAE-131716.

[33] MANCILLA-DAVID, F., F. RIGANTI-FULGINEI, A. LAUDANI and A. SALVINI. A Neural Network-Based Low-Cost Solar Irradiance Sensor. *IEEE Transactions on Instrumentation and Measurement*. 2014, vol. 63, iss. 3, pp. 583–591. ISSN 0018-9456. DOI: 10.1109/TIM.2013.2282005.

[34] PLAGIANAKOS, V. P. and M. N. VRAHATIS. Neural network training with constrained integer weights. In: *Proceedings of the 1999 Congress on Evolutionary Computation-CEC99*. Washington: IEEE, 1999, pp. 2007–2013. ISBN 0-7803-5536-9. DOI: 10.1109/CEC.1999.785521.

[35] CHEN, Y. and W. DU PLESSIS. Neural network implementation on a FPGA. In: *6th Africon Conference in Africa*. Nairobi: IEEE, 2002, pp. 337–342. ISBN 0-7803-7570-X. DOI: 10.1109/AFRCON.2002.1146859.

[36] LAUDANI, A., F. RIGANTI-FULGINEI, A. SALVINI, M. SCHMID and S. CONFORTO. CFSO3: A New Supervised Swarm-Based Optimization Algorithm. *Mathematical Problems in Engineering*. 2013, vol. 2013, pp. 1–13. ISSN 1563-5147. DOI: 10.1155/2013/560614.

[37] LAUDANI, A., F. RIGANTI-FULGINEI and A. SALVINI. Closed Forms for the Fully-Connected Continuous Flock of Starlings Optimization Algorithm. In: *UKSim 15th International Conference on Computer Modelling and Simulation*. Cambridge: IEEE, 2013, pp. 45–50. ISBN 978-1-4673-6421-8. DOI: 10.1109/UKSim.2013.25.

About Authors

Gabriele-Maria LOZITO is a Ph.D. student at the Roma Tre University, Department of Engineering, Rome, Italy. He received his master degree in Electronics Engineering in 2011 presenting a thesis on the characterization of an anechoic chamber for microwave equipment calibration. His research field involves the study of numerical computation applied to system modelling and non-linear optimization, with special interest for the implementation of soft computing techniques on embedded systems.

Antonino LAUDANI was born in Catania, Italy, in 1973. He received the Laurea degree Cum Laude from the University of Catania, Italy, in 1999 and the Ph.D. degree from the University of Reggio Calabria, Italy in 2003, both in Electronic Engineering. Currently, he is Assistant Professor of ElectricaL Engineering in the Department of Engineering at the University of Roma Tre. Dr. Laudani is the author of more than 70 international publications. His main research interests include finite element modeling of electromagnetic devices; particle-in-celland numerical methods; neural networks; optimization and inverse problem solutions; photovoltaic system; and the design of embedded systems.

Francesco RIGANTI-FULGINEI is an assistant professor at the University of Roma Tre, Department of Engineering, Rome, Italy, where he teaches and directs research in non–linear optimization and inverse problems as a faculty member of the Department of Applied Electronics. Prof. Riganti–Fulginei received the Ph.D. degree in biomedical electronics, electromagnetism and telecommunications engineering at the University of Roma Tre in 2007. He is the author of several international publications and has been a visiting professor at the University of Colorado Denver, Denver, Colorado, USA and Okayama University, Okayama, Japan. His research interests include non–linear optimization and inverse problems applied to complex systems, in particular power electronics and electromagnetic devices.

Alessandro SALVINI received the Laurea degree in Electrical Engineering Cum Laude from the University of Rome La Sapienza. He was Assistant Professor (1994), Associate Professor (2001) and, at the present, he is Full Professor at the University of Roma Tree, Department of Engineering where he is also the Scientific Coordinator of the Research Unit of Electrical Engineering. He is involved in tutoring Ph.D. students and is responsible for international agreements with foreign universities for the exchange of faculty and students. His research interests include magnetic material modeling, dynamic hysteresis, optimization and inverse problems, soft computing and evolutionary computation.

17

Design of Measurement System for Determining the Radioclimatology Effect on the Radio Signal Propagation Using Universal Software Radio

Martin TOMIS, Libor MICHALEK, Marek DVORSKY

Department of Telecommunications, Faculty of Electrical Engineering and Computer Science, VSB–Technical University of Ostrava, 17. listopadu 15, 708 33 Ostrava–Poruba, Czech Republic

martin.tomis@vsb.cz, libor.michalek@vsb.cz, marek.dvorsky@vsb.cz

Abstract. *In this paper, a developed point-to-point wireless link using Universal Software Radio Peripheral (USRP) is presented. The aim of the research is focused on the monitoring and analysing the transmission characteristics on the physical layer of such wireless communication link with the consideration that these parameters could be affected by atmospheric phenomenon and air pollution. For that reason, the wireless link is situated to heavily loaded environment of Ostrava agglomeration where it is assumed extreme atmospheric phenomena such as smog or inverse situation. In the next part, a developed application which perform a fully automatic long term measurement of the transmission characteristics using a wireless link is presented. Finally, the first experimental results based on mathematical regression are presented.*

Keywords

Interference, SDR, signal attenuation, radioclimatology, USRP.

1.   Introduction

The Universal Software Radio Peripheral (USRP) product by NI company has become a popular platform for a large number of complex measuring applications. These applications had been previously available only with professional tools such as RF Signal Generators and Analyzers.

Universal Software Radio Peripheral (USRP) [1] is a universal software-programmable radio transceiver controlled by a Personal Computer (PC). The device is designed as separated direct-conversion transmitter and receiver.

Frequency bandwidth for transmission and reception can be adjusted by changing the sampling frequency of transmitted data in the range of 0,2 to 50 MS·s^{-1}. However, sampling rates of AD and DA converters in the baseband are significantly higher, i.e. in the hundreds of mega-samples per second. The Field Programmable Gate Arrays (FPGA) converts high sample rate to lower sampling rate for the data transfer between USRP and PC.

Due to the extremely expensive hardware generators and analyzers, the common practice is to simulate real Radio Frequency (RF) signals using software simulators such as Matlab [2] or LabVIEW [3]. On the other hand, the USRP device is significantly cheaper, however, it does not reach such frequency accuracy as NI-RFSA (Radio Frequency Signal Analyzer) [4]. NI-RFSA is a measurement plug-in card made by National Instruments (NI) within a modular system PXI (PCI eXtensions for Instrumentation) [5].

The adverse weather causes microwave signal degradations mostly due to rain and suspended particles like fog and water vapor. Atmospheric gases cause signal attenuation through molecular absorption in certain characteristic frequency bands. In the case of Free Space Optical (FSO) connection, the most important impairment factor is the fog, which can be well characterized by its density. In [6], [7] some measurement results regarding the Free Space Optics (FSO) impacted by fog has been presented.

In [8], the aim was to find out the different types of losses to be incurred at the conventional window frequencies i.e., 30 and 94 GHz along with the losses at the first and weak water vapour resonance line i.e., around 22 GHz in the microwave/milimeter wave band.

In [9], [10], [11] some models have been proposed for satellite communication affected by rain attenuation. In [12] radio link have been adapted by radio channel state prediction method.

Up to present, it has not been comprehensively discussed the issue of measurement the attenuation and other transmission parameters for wireless data link in heavily loaded industrial areas such as the area of Ostrava agglomeration, Czech Republic. Ostrava's geomorphology and poor dispersion conditions both contribute to the air pollution and cause the pollution to concentrate here, especially in winter [13]. Therefore, significantly interesting and scientifically useful could be consider to follow the changes in states of extreme atmospheric phenomena such as smog or inverse situation. The smog and inverse situation are characterized by chemical or mechanical atmospheric pollution (e.g. increased content of suspended particulate matter PM10), which can affect the transmission characteristics of wireless links. In the concrete, atmospheric particulate matter (PM) can be classified as PM10, PM2.5 and PM1 by size with mass median aerodynamic diameter less than 10 μm, 2, 5 μm and 1 μm respectively.

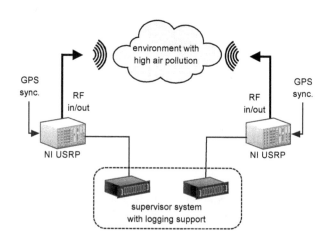

Fig. 1: General architecture of the measurement system.

2.   Experimental Wireless Link

Using the Software Defined Radio in the form of USRP device, a complex measurement system which monitors the influence of atmospheric phenomenon and air pollution on the physical layer of wireless communication link has been proposed. The system consists of two identical stations located in Ostrava-Poruba and Petrvald city respectively. Therefore, the wireless link itself is situated to the the Ostrava city environment. The general architecture of the proposed system is sketched in Fig. 1. It is based on two main classes of devices:

- RF units: designed using Software Defined Radio (SDR) device with external GPS synchronization.

- Supervisor system: consist of personal computers devoted to saving measured data into the database and remotely access to measured data.

RF units consist of SDR by National Instruments USRP 2920 with the directional antenna, which are directed against each other. For the synchronization between RF units, an external GPS module Meinberg GPS164 has been used.

The supervisor system is a workstation equipped with the software for retrieving, storing, and viewing measurement data collected by RF unit as well as for managing the data elaboration. Since the USRP is a product of NI, the LabView environment has been used for support the application (see next chapter).

If the time or frequency errors have to be measured, the exact time synchronization of RF units has to be

observed. The sync pulse ensures that the transmitter and the receiver start the measurement at the same time. Moreover, information about the current exact time is used to synchronize workstations. This is performed via serial line.

3.   Application

The measurement and control application have been developed in LabView [3] environment. The aim of the developed application is to control, manage and perform fully automatic long term measurement of transmission characteristics using the proposed wireless link. With regards to common practice, Amplitude Shift Keying (ASK), Frequency Shift Keying (FSK), Quadrature Phase-Shift Keying(QPSK) and 16-Quadrature Amplitude Modulation (16-QAM) have been chosen as the main representatives of modulation/ keying types. For this purpose, a testing sequence of bits, which is keyed and then transmitted by wireless link, have been proposed. The sequence consists of guard bits, synchronizing bits and data bits, see Tab. 1.

Tab. 1: Parameters for testing sequence.

	guard bits [−]	sync. bits [−]	data bits [−]	bit rate [kbit · s^{-1}]	symbol rate [kS · s^{-1}]
ASK	10	20	500	19,2	19,2
FSK	50	40	1000	100	100
QPSK	100	80	4000	200	100
16-QAM	200	160	5000	400	100

The sequence of bits is transmitted with the interval of 5 seconds while the type of keying is always changed. Figure 2 shows the general architecture of the application.

The following parameters are being determined and calculated.

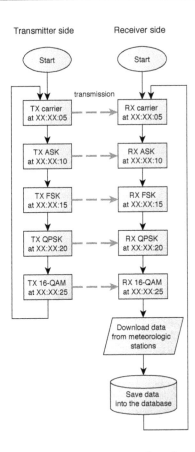

Fig. 2: The architecture of the developed application.

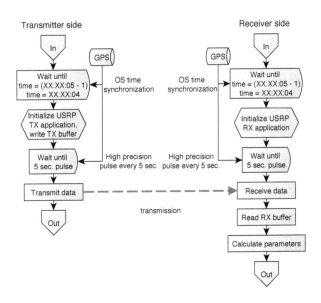

Fig. 3: The architecture of the carrier fluctuation measurement.

- **Carrier:** On the transmitter side, an amplitude modulated (AM) signal with modulation sine tone of 10 kHz is transmitted with constant radiated power. As the carrier frequency, the 869, 5 MHz sine has been used which belongs to ISM band according to [14]. At the receiver side, the carrier is demodulated, and the resulting tone is sampled by $200\ \mathrm{kS \cdot s^{-1}}$ sample rate. Both transmitter and receiver side have to be time synchronized with high precision. The second phase comprises calculation and determination of transmission parameters such as Carrier Fluctuation. Figure 3 depicts the architecture of amplitude fluctuation measurement.

- **ASK, FSK, QPSK, 16-QAM:** Here, the same carrier frequency (869,5 MHz) is used and then keyed by testing sequence. At the receiver side, the demodulation is being processed. In further analysis, we focus on parameters such as Modulation Error (MER), Carrier to Noise Ratio (CNR), Carrier Frequency Offset, Carrier Frequency Drift, Error Vector Magnitude (EVM), Magnitude Error, Phase Error, DC offset, Quadrature Skew or IQ Gain Imbalance. Figure 4 depicts the Labview block diagram for QAM transmission parameters determination.

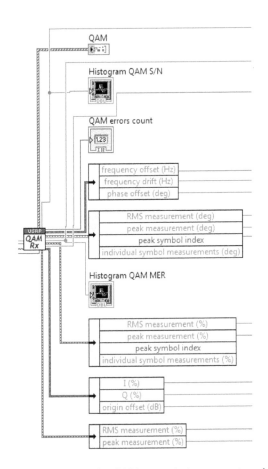

Fig. 4: Block diagram for QAM transmission parameters determination.

4.   Experimental Results

The purpose of all above mentioned measurements through the proposed wireless link is to find some mathematical relationship between transmission parameters and fluctuations in the properties of the atmospheric phenomenon or air pollution. For this purpose, the meteorological data from the automated weather stations (Czech Hydrometeorological Institute) located in the explored area are stored to the database together with the data containing the transmission parameters.

A simple regression [15] analysis has been used to assess the association between transmission parameters and properties of the atmospheric phenomenon or air pollution. A simple linear regression uses only one independent variable, and it describes the relationship between the independent variable and dependent variable as a straight line. A wide analysis has been done using the Statgraphic as the professional tool concerning statistical analysis. As the independent variables, the properties of the atmospheric phenomenon have been used. As the dependent variables, the transmission parameters, as mentioned in chapter 3., have been used.

The results of simple regression analysis show that some association between transmission parameters and properties of the atmospheric phenomenon or air pollution exists. Figure 5 shows a result of simple regression for Carrier Fluctuation parameter versus PM10 concentration. Since the P-value is less than 0,05 there is a statistically significant relationship between Carrier Fluctuation and PM10 concentration at the 95,0 % confidence level. The plot of the fitted model shows the original observations (blue dots), the fitted regression line (blue curve), the 95 % confidence limits (green curves) and the 95 % prediction limits (grey curves).

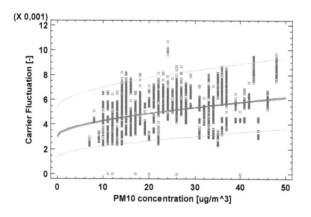

Fig. 5: Plot of Simple Regression - Carrier Fluctuation vs. PM10 concentration.

The output on the Fig. 6 shows the results of fitting an exponential model to describe the relationship between QAM Magnitude Error and PM10 Concentra-

tion. Since the P-value in is less than 0,05 there is a statistically significant relationship between QAM Magnitude Error and PM10 Concentration at the 95,0 % confidence level.

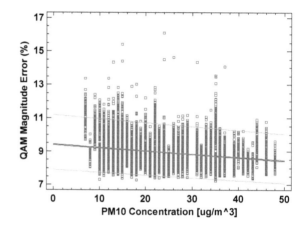

Fig. 6: Plot of Simple Regression - QAM Magnitude Error vs. PM10 concentration.

After the comprehensive analysis through the Statgraphic tool, the parameters of atmospheric phenomenon, which affected the transmission parameters at most, has been determined, see Tab. 2. It should be noted that, due to the lack measured data, the results show only direction on which parameters we have to focus in further analysis.

Tab. 2: Transmission parameters affected by atmospheric phenomenon.

	PM10	Temperature	Humidity
Carrier Fluctuation	+	++	
FSK Drift		-	
FSK Error	-		
QPSK Offset	-	++	-
QAM MER		+	
QAM Magn. Error	-		

Where:
+ Increases the level of parameter as $(x \cdot 0,001)$
++ Increases the level of parameter as $(x \cdot 0,01)$
− Decreases the level of parameter as $(x \cdot 0,001)$
−− Decreases the level of parameter as $(x \cdot 0,01)$

If the cell is empty, no affecting has been found.

5.   Conclusion

This paper describes a developed point-to-point wireless link that is situated to Ostrava agglomeration environment. The distance between the receiver and transmitter is about 14 km which allows to observe the changes in transmission parameters such as carrier fluctuation, MER, C/N, QAM magnitude error which can be affected by changes in states of atmospheric phenomenon. Even if the proposed wireless link using a very well known module USRP, the combination with the detecting if the transmission parameters are associated with concentration of PM10 as well as with other weather parameters is novel.

In the next part, a developed application for controlling and fully-automatic measurement using a wireless link is presented. Although the lack of the measured data does not allow us determine exactly whether the changes of atmospheric phenomenon affect the transmission parameters or not, some partial results have been presented. Using the statistical analysis, it was proved that the concentration of Particular Matter (PM10) affects the amplitude of carrier and QAM magnitude error. This confirms the fact that we should do the further research in this direction and examine the association of PM10 on these parameters in detail. The determination whether the PM1 or PM2,5 affects transmission parameters or not is not considered mainly because of these concentrations are not measured by automated weather stations.

The long-term measurements will continue for two years at least. We expect to expand the working frequency band to 433 MHz and 2,4 GHz in order to evaluate the influence of meteorological phenomena in these bands.

The aim of the presented research is, among others, to propose a mathematical model that describes the behavior of the communication channel and its transmission parameters depending on long-term changes of atmospheric phenomena, the concentration of PM10 primarily. The research of such type has not been published yet.

Acknowledgment

The research leading to these results has received funding from the Grant SGS SP2013/94 'Research on the influence of environment on the properties of the radio channel and the development of new approaches to the evaluation of quality of service (QoS) in 4G networks'.

References

[1] National Instruments. *NI USRP Lab: DQPSK Transceiver Design*, 2012.

[2] HUANG, Y. G. Z., Y. LI, J. SHAO and H. WEI. Processing digital signal using power spectral density function analysis in matlab toolkit. In: *International Conference on Computer Science and Network Technology (ICCSNT)*. Harbin: IEEE, 2011, vol. 1, pp. 553–556. ISBN 978-145771584-6. DOI: 10.1109/ICCSNT.2011.6182018.

[3] HIGA, M. L., D. M. TAWY and S. M. LORD. An introduction to labview exercise for an electronics class. In: *32nd Annual Frontiers in Education*. Boston: IEEE, 2002, vol. 1, pp. T1D/13–T1D/16. ISSN 0190-5848.

[4] FARES, A., A. KHACHAN, A. B. KASBAH, M. ZEIDAN and A. KAYSSI. GSM RF equipment testing and performance analysis. In: *International Symposium on Communications and Information Technology*. Sapporo: IEEE, 2004, vol. 2, pp. 807–811. ISBN 978-078038593-1. DOI: 10.1109/ISCIT.2004.1413828.

[5] GLADKOV, M. N. and G. S. RUDANOV. Programmable radio; platform on the basis of national instruments pxi-system. In: *18th International Crimean Conference Microwave and Telecommunication Technology*. Crimea: IEEE, 2008, pp. 10–11. ISBN 978-966335169-8. DOI: 10.1109/CRMICO.2008.4676677.

[6] CSURGAI-HORVATH, L., E. LEITGE, and J. TURAN. Measurement data for FSO and e-band radio propagation modeling. In: *Proceedings of the 5th European Conference on Antennas and Propagation (EUCAP)*. Prague: IEEE, 2011, pp. 2742–2745. ISBN 978-888202074-3.

[7] CSURGAI-HORVATH, L., J. BITO, P. PESICE and O. FISER. The impact of liquid water content on free space optical propagation. In: *6th European Conference on Antennas and Propagation (EUCAP)*. Prague: IEEE, 2012, pp. 323–325. ISBN 978-1-4577-0919-7. DOI: 10.1109/EuCAP.2012.6206177.

[8] KARMAKAR, P. K., L. SENGUPTA, M. MAIRI and C. F. ANGELIS. Some of the atmospheric influences on microwave propagation through atmosphere. *American Journal Of Scientific And Industrial Research*. 2010, vol. 1, iss. 2, pp. 350–358. ISSN 2153-649X. DOI: 10.5251/ajsir.2010.1.2.350.358.

[9] RAMACHANDRAN, V. and V. KUMAR. Modified rain attenuation model for tropical regions for ku-band signals. *International Journal of Satellite Communications and Networking*. 2007, vol. 25, iss. 1, pp. 53–67. ISSN 1542-0973.

[10] OJO, J. S., M. O. AJEWOLE and S. K. SARKAR. Rain rate and rain attenuation prediction for satellite communication in ku and ka bands over nigeria. *Progress In Electromagnetics*

Research B. 2008, vol. 5, pp. 207–223. ISSN 1937-6472. DOI: 10.2528/PIERB08021201.

[11] MANDEEP, J. S. and J. E. ALLNUTT. Rain attenuation predictions at ku-band in south east asia countries. *Progress In Electromagnetics Research.* 2007, vol. 76, pp. 65–74. ISSN 1070-4698.

[12] ZIACIK, P. and V. WIESER. Mobile radio link adaptation by radio channel state prediction. *Electronics and Electrical Engineering.* 2011, vol. 114, iss. 8, pp. 27–30. ISSN 1392-1215.

[13] KALICAKOVA, Z., V. MICKA, K. LACH and P. DANIHELKA. Urban air pollution by nanoparticles in ostrava region. *Journal of Physics: Conference Series.* 2013, vol. 429, iss. 1, 2013. ISSN 1742-6588. DOI: 10.1088/1742-6596/429/1/012005.

[14] Czech Telecommunications Institute. General license no. vor/10/04.2012-7. 2012.

[15] SEBER, G. A. F. and A. J. LEE. *Linear Regression Analysis.* Hoboken: Wiley, 2012. ISBN 978-1118274422.

About Authors

Martin TOMIS was born in 1987. He received his master degree from Department of Telecommunications, Faculty of Electrical Engineering and Computer Science, VSB–Technical University Ostrava in 2011. His research interests include virtual instrumentation.

Libor MICHALEK was born in 1979. He received his Ph.D. from Department of Telecommunications, Faculty of Electrical Engineering and Computer Science, VSB–Technical University Ostrava in 2008. His research interests include new digital telecommunication technologies.

Marek DVORSKY was born in 1981. He received his Ph.D. from Department of Telecommunications, Faculty of Electrical Engineering and Computer Science, VSB–Technical University Ostrava in 2009. His research interests include new digital radio-communication technologies and antennas engineering.

18

Automatic Classification of Attacks on IP Telephony

Jakub SAFARIK[1], Pavol PARTILA[1], Filip REZAC[1], Lukas MACURA[2], Miroslav VOZNAK[1]

[1]Department of Telecommunications, Faculty of Electrical Engineering and Computer Science, VSB–Technical University of Ostrava, 17. listopadu 15, 708 00 Ostrava-Poruba, Czech Republic
[2]Institute of Computer Science, Faculty of Philosophy and Science in Opava, Silesian University in Opava, Bezrucovo namesti 13, 746 01 Opava, Czech Republic

jakub.safarik@vsb.cz, pavol.partila@vsb.cz, filip.rezac@vsb.cz, macura@opf.slu.cz, miroslav.voznak@vsb.cz

Abstract. *This article proposes an algorithm for automatic analysis of attack data in IP telephony network with a neural network. Data for the analysis is gathered from variable monitoring application running in the network. These monitoring systems are a typical part of nowadays network. Information from them is usually used after attack. It is possible to use an automatic classification of IP telephony attacks for nearly real-time classification and counter attack or mitigation of potential attacks. The classification use proposed neural network, and the article covers design of a neural network and its practical implementation. It contains also methods for neural network learning and data gathering functions from honeypot application.*

Keywords

Attack classification, neural network, security, SIP attacks, VoIP attacks.

1. Introduction

The IP telephony environments based on Session Initiation Protocol (SIP) is a popular design for handling telecommunication services like calls, video calls and conferences. With the growing popularity of SIP protocol also raise a potential threat. The VoIP infrastructure based on SIP is very fragile to various kinds of attacks, which can lead to loss of money and other unpleasant consequences [1].

The partial solution of this situation is in properly set VoIP servers, encryptions and strict security policies. Nevertheless, the attacker can still corrupt whole IP telephony network and stole sensitive information, eavesdrop calls, stole caller identity or deny the service for legitimate users (DoS). Intrusion detection systems, network monitoring, and honeypot applications can detect these kinds of malicious activity in VoIP infrastructure. Some applications can also mitigate specific attacks. Even then, there is still a broad spectrum of attacks, which can impact VoIP servers. All information about these attacks is logged in some kind of detection mechanism. The automatic classification of this data can provide a tool for detection various types of attacks in the network and for the further successful mitigation.

The statistical analysis of attack data brings valuable information about attacks on VoIP but is not so suitable for attack classification. The solution of the attack classification is in evolutionary algorithms. This paper brings a proposal of a classification system for VoIP-based types of attacks. With properly classified regular and malicious traffic, it is possible to reduce the number of undetected attacks. Using this classification mechanism in a distributed monitoring network with a proactive reaction can lead to a diminishing impact of attacks on IP telephony networks.

2. Honeypot Network Concept

The classification engine based on neural network is only a part of solution for detecting malicious activity in an IP telephony infrastructure. A single honeypot application could bring valuable information. Combining different application at a different geographical location and network parts should provide more detailed data with other benefits.

But this exceeding numbers of running honeypots causes unwanted overhead in a data analysis and some kind of automatic mechanism must be used. Without this mechanism lead this situation only to decreasing profit from gathered data.

The concept of a honeypot network is shown in Fig. 1 and it's based on prepared nodes and a single server for data gathering and analysis. Neural network described in this paper is a module on the centralized server for classification of VoIP based attacks. More information about distributed honeypot network could be found in a previous article [2].

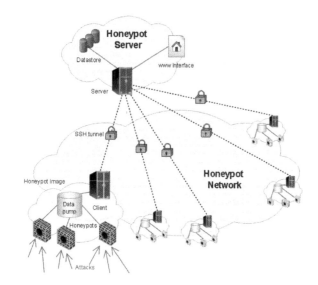

Fig. 1: The distributed honeypot network concept.

3.   Neural Network

Neural networks are an attempt, which try to model information processing capabilities of the nervous system. Animal nervous system is composed of millions of interconnected cells in a complex arrangement. The artificial neural networks use the lower number of cells called perceptron.

The function of a single animal neuron is well known and serves as a model for an artificial one. But the fundamental for consciousness and complex behaviour lies in interaction between neurons. The Massive and hierarchical networking of the brain with an incredible processing rate has not yet been completely elucidated. The artificial neural network tries to handle these complex and self-organizing networks handle with various topologies. Different versions of neural network topologies are known today, and each one has its pros and cons [3].

For a VoIP based attack classification was used a feed-forward MLP (Multilayer Perceptron) neural network. This type of neural network consists of multiple layers.

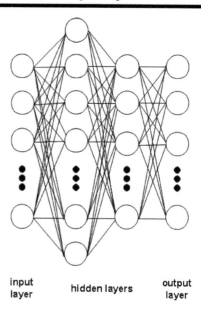

Fig. 2: MLP neural network topology.

In a MLP neural network topology, each neuron in one layer is connected to every perceptron in forward layer. This connection is so-called synapses and its purpose will be discussed later.

As shows the Fig. 2, 4 layer type of network was used. First layer serves as input layer. Each input neuron has a value of a single input parameter. All parameters for input neurons then form a single case for neural network analysis. Inner two hidden layers then solve the given problem. In this case, it is an attack classification. Each neuron itself solves a part of a solution. The last layer of the neural network is an output layer, and it represents the final set of solutions. Each output neuron is then a single class of learned attack.

3.1.   Perceptron

The perceptron itself is a more general computational model than McCulloch-Pitts units. The innovation is an introduction of numerical weights and a special interconnection pattern. The activation function of neuron impact the potential of the neuron and it is also then input information transmitted to other neurons in forward layer. Inputs for this activation function are real inputs $x_1, x_2, \ldots, x_n$ from previous layers with the associated weights $w_1, w_2, \ldots, w_n$.

The output is between 0 and 1, where 0 means inhibition and 1 excitation. The final value at output (y) depends on perceptron's activation function. The activation function used for attack recognition was sigmoid, a real function $S_c : \Re \longrightarrow (0,1)$.

$$y = S_c(z) = \frac{1}{1 + e^{-cz}}, \qquad (1)$$

$$z = \sum_{i=1}^{n} w_i x_i. \qquad (2)$$

As shows the Eq. (2), z parameter is a sum of output x from the previous layer multiplied by weight w of the connection. Parameter c represents a skewness of the sigmoid function (typically is 1, 0). Higher values of c bring the skewness of sigmoid closer to the step function [3], [4].

4. Backpropagation

Backpropagation represents a mechanism for neural network learning. In a feed-forward mode is information transferred from the input layer to the output layer. The backpropagation algorithm looks for the minimum error function in weight space. The combination of weights with a minimum error function is then considered as a solution of the learning problem. The solution of the learning problem is then saved in memory of neural network via weight adaptation process.

This weight adaptation is done on a training set of input with known correct outputs. With a specific learning rate is then corrected each connection weight to obtain a lower value of an error function. The backpropagation error is always counted backward as in feed-forward, so from higher layer to lower layer.

$$\delta_j = \sum_{k=1}^{n} \delta_k y_k (1 - y_k) c w_{jk}. \qquad (3)$$

As show Eq. (3), backpropagation error (δ) for connection in one layer (indexed as j) is count as a sum of connections to higher layer (indexed as k). Parameter y represents the output of neuron, x its inputs. Finally c is an expected output and w weight of the connection. Then is this backpropagation error used to count a change for weight update, as shows Eq. (4) and Eq. (5):

$$\Delta w_{ij} = \eta \delta_j y_i, \qquad (4)$$

$$w_{ij} = w_{ij} + \Delta w_{ij}. \qquad (5)$$

The parameter η serves as a learn rate parameter for selecting a proper step of correction in one backpropagation iteration [3], [4]. w_{ij} represents connection weight from the previous layer i to actual layer j (Fig. 3).

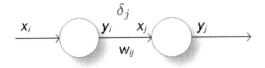

Fig. 3: Indexing between layers.

5. Practical Implementation

5.1. Neural Network Parameters

As was mentioned above a multilayer perceptron neural network was used for VoIP attack classification. The final neural network contains 10 input layer neurons which correspond to specific input parameters. The two hidden layers contain 16 and 12 neurons. The output layer, where each neuron specifies one class of attack type, contains 6 neurons.

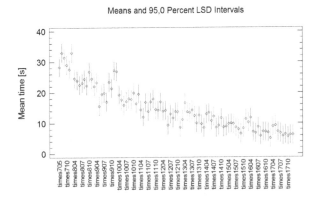

Fig. 4: 100 Backpropagation cycles mean time for different configurations of hidden layers.

The inner structure of neural network is based on tests of convergence for 100 backpropagation cycles. These tests prove different mean times of learning for different structures as shows Fig. 4. The impact of a structure is evident only for backpropagation learning. Because forward MLP classification use already learned neural network. This neural network then classifies the attack regardless of the inner structure of neural network. The test shows statistically significant difference between learning time of neural networks. Best results have a configuration with 16 neurons in first hidden layer and 10 neurons in second hidden layer.

The higher number of neurons in these layers is possible to decrease the mean time needed for neural network learning, but the memory requirement also raises. From a statistical point of view, there is not a statistically significant difference between learning mean times for neural network backpropagation learning with a confidence interval of 5 %. Final neural network configuration uses the following number of neurons 10 16 12 6 (from input to the output layer).

Other specific parameter for this neural network is a skewness of an activation function. This activation function is a sigmoid function with skewness set to 1, 0.

5.2.   Data Source for Classification

The data for classification with neural network is collected with an open-source honeypot application Dionaea. This multi-service oriented honeypot was used for its PBX emulation feature. It is possible to monitor and emulate typical behaviour of a SIP PBX with Dionaea.

The Dionaea attack log contains only information about malicious traffic. Because it is a honeypot application, no legitimate calls are connected with it, and even no regular end-point device tries to register to it and make calls. So it contains only information about malicious traffic.

All attack data store Dionaea in a sqlite database file. This database consists of several tables. Each table contains various information. This information is bind on traffic or protocol emulated by the honeypot. Most of this information is based on a request, response mechanism. So selecting a single line from the database for classification is valueless. All data about SIP attacks must be aggregated from different tables. Then is prepared a list of detected attacks. Each row in this list is a specific attack detected on an emulated SIP server. From all accessible attack features was created an array of 10 parameters. These individual 10 parameters serve as an input for a neural network classification and are following: used transport protocol (tcp – 0, udp – 1), connection count, REGISTER message count, INVITE message count, ACK message count, BYE message count, CANCEL message count, OPTIONS message count, SUBSCRIBE message count and connection rate. The connection count parameter is the number of connection made in one SIP session on the server. The connection rate is then a ratio of received SIP messages to connection count.

5.3.   Backpropagation Algorithm

For a neural network learning was used a backpropagation algorithm. Whole network is evaluated as learned, when the network correctly identify more than 95 % samples of the training set. So the confidence interval for neural network learning is always lower than 5 %.

On the beginning of backpropagation learning are weights of connections randomly selected from the interval (-1, 1). When all weights are randomly set, the backpropagation algorithm starts. After each 100 cycles of backpropagation learning is checked the successfulness of attack classification. When is successfulness higher than 0, 95, the neural network learning is done. Otherwise, continues more backpropagation learning cycles.

There is also a possibility that the learning algorithm is stuck in a local minimum, and final successfulness cannot reach desired 0, 95. If the neural network is not successfully learned after 2 500 000 backpropagation cycles, the learning starts again with a randomly selected connection weights.

5.4.   Training Set

The training set is one of most important parts of neural network learning. If the items in the training list are not a specific representative of an attack group, attack cannot be successfully classified.

As a source for the training set were used a real malicious traffic. Honeypot captured these attack data for a period of two months. All these attacks were aggregated and then one by one classified by human into six classes. These classes are call testing, client registration attempt, flood attacks, registration attempts, PBX scanning and the last unknown group.

When were all attacks classified, specific representatives of each class were chosen for the training set. The final training set contains 78 attacks, which means that each attack class has 13 subjects.

To increasing the impact of a SIP message counters are all parameters powered to four. After a successful backpropagation learning is possible to classify single attacks. As a final attack class is then chosen the output layer neuron with the highest potential.

6.   Conclusion

In typical nowadays IP networks are used some form VoIP services. The SIP protocol is an open-source standard for this purposes and also one of the most used protocols for handling VoIP services. This situation leads to higher exposition of this text based protocol to the various types of attacks. Previous researches in our lab prove a high vulnerability of a SIP server to different types of attacks [4], [5].

One way for improving security of whole IP telephony infrastructure lies in deployment of a monitoring mechanism. This monitoring mechanism based on distributed net of monitoring nodes can detect malicious activity in the network. With a possibility to change firewall rules or network routing even mitigate potential threats. The proposal is described above, and the main part of a monitoring node is a honeypot application. In case of a SIP protocol monitoring, this honeypot application is open-source Dionaea.

But to improve network security from data gathered at different honeypots, some kind of analysis must be made. Classification by humans is very precise, but also time consuming and expensive. An automatic classifying mechanism could bring a solution for the problem of VoIP attack classifying.

With a properly learned neural network, it is possible to classify various types of attacks. This article aims at describing a neural network design for VoIP attack classification.

One of the biggest disadvantages of this solution is that it cannot recognize a new type of attack. Whole neural network topology and learning set are prepared only for specific types of attacks. But even with this functionality is possible to use this neural network as a classifying module in distributed monitoring networks.

Future plans for this neural network attack classification lie in deploying other types of neural networks and testing its fitness for IP telephony attacks classification. One of the challenges is also in an implementation of self-learning mechanisms.

Acknowledgment

The research leading to these results has received funding from the Grant SGS no. SP2013/94 and has been partially supported by the project No. CZ.1.07/2.3.00/20.0217 "The Development of Excellence of the Telecommunication Research Team in Relation to International Cooperation" within the frame of the operation programme "Education for competitiveness" financed by the Structural Funds and from the state budget of the Czech Republic.

References

[1] SAFARIK, J., M. VOZNAK, F. REZAC and L. MACURA. Malicious Traffic Monitoring and its Evaluation in VoIP Infrastructure. In: *2012 35th International Conference on Telecommunications and Signal Processing (TSP)*. Prague: IEEE, 2012, pp. 259–262. ISBN 978-146731118-2. DOI: 10.1109/TSP.2012.6256294.

[2] VOZNAK, M., J. SAFARIK, L. MACURA and F. REZAC. Malicious Behavior in Voice over IP Infrastructure. In: *Recent researches in communications and computers proceedings of the 16th WSEAS International Conference on Communications*. Kos Island: WSEAS, 2012, pp. 178–182. ISBN 978-1-61804-109-8.

[3] ROJAS, R. *Neural Networks*. New York: Springer-Verlag, 1996. ISBN 35-406-0505-3.

[4] HEATON, J. *Introduction to Neural Networks for JAVA, 2nd Edition*. St. Louis: Heaton Research, 2008. ISBN 16-043-9008-5.

[5] REZAC, F., M. VOZNAK, K. TOMALA, J. ROZHON and J. VYCHODIL. Security Analysis System to Detect Threats on a SIP VoIP Infrastructure Elements. *Advances in Electrical and Electronic Engineering*. 2011, vol. 9, no. 5, pp. 225–232. ISSN 1336-1376.

[6] VOZNAK, M. and J. SAFARIK. SIP Proxy Robustness against DoS Attacks. In: *Proceedings of the Applied Computing Conference 2011, (ACC '11)*. Angers: Neuveden, 2011, pp. 223–227. ISBN 978-1-61804-051-0.

About Authors

Jakub SAFARIK received his M.Sc. degree in telecommunications from VSB–Technical University of Ostrava, Czech Republic, in 2011 and he continues in studying Ph.D. degree at the same university. His research is focused on IP telephony, computer networks and network security. He is with CESNET as a researcher since 2011.

Pavol PARTILA received the M.Sc. degree from University of Zilina, Faculty of Electrical Engineering in 2011. Currently, he is working toward the Ph.D. degree at the Dpt. of Telecommunications, VSB–Technical University of Ostrava. Topics of his research interests are Speech processing, speech quality and VoIP.

Filip REZAC was born in 1985. He received M.Sc. degree in telecommunications from VSB–Technical University of Ostrava, Czech Republic, in 2009 and he continues in studying Ph.D. degree at the same university. His research is focused on IP telephony, computer networks and network security. He is with CESNET since 2009 as a researcher.

Lukas MACURA is a Ph.D. student with Dpt. of Telecommunications at Faculty of Electrical Engineering and Computer Science, VSB-Technical University of Ostrava. He is also administrator of SIP infrastructure within CESNET where he is employed as a researcher with Dpt. of Multimedia, CESNET, Czech Republic.

Miroslav VOZNAK was born in 1971. He holds the position as an associate professor with Department of Telecommunications, VSB–Technical University of Ostrava, Czech Republic. Topics of his research interests are the Next Generation Network,

IP telephony, speech quality and network security. He is with CESNET since 1999, currently in R&D department.

19

Vehicular Networking Enhancement And Multi-Channel Routing Optimization, Based On Multi-Objective Metric And Minimum Spanning Tree

Peppino FAZIO, Cesare SOTTILE, Amilcare Francesco SANTAMARIA, Mauro TROPEA

Department of Computer Science, Modeling, Electronics and Systems Engineering (DIMES), Faculty of Engineering, Universita della Calabria, 870 36 Arcavacata di Rende (CS), Italy

pfazio@dimes.unical.it, sottile@dimes.unical.it, afsantamaria@dimes.unical.it, mtropea@dimes.unical.it

Abstract. *Vehicular Ad hoc NETworks (VANETs) represent a particular mobile technology that permits the communication among vehicles, offering security and comfort. Nowadays, distributed mobile wireless computing is becoming a very important communications paradigm, due to its flexibility to adapt to different mobile applications. VANETs are a practical example of data exchanging among real mobile nodes. To enable communications within an ad-hoc network, characterized by continuous node movements, routing protocols are needed to react to frequent changes in network topology. In this paper, the attention is focused mainly on the network layer of VANETs, proposing a novel approach to reduce the interference level during mobile transmission, based on the multi-channel nature of IEEE 802.11p (1609.4) standard. In this work a new routing protocol based on Distance Vector algorithm is presented to reduce the delay end to end and to increase packet delivery ratio (PDR) and throughput in VANETs. A new metric is also proposed, based on the maximization of the average Signal-to-Interference Ratio (SIR) level and the link duration probability between two VANET nodes. In order to relieve the effects of the co-channel interference perceived by mobile nodes, transmission channels are switched on a basis of a periodical SIR evaluation. A Network Simulator has been used for implementing and testing the proposed idea.*

Keywords

End-2-end delay, interference, link duration, multi-channel, routing, spanning tree, VANET, vehicular.

1. Introduction

In the last years, many efforts have been made in the mobile computing research field; in particular, the IEEE 802.11 standard completely dominates the market. In wireless networks, nodes are free to move randomly and organize themselves arbitrarily; thus, network topology may change rapidly and unpredictably. VANET is a fully mobile network whose nodes consist of vehicles equipped with a wireless router and a man/machine interface that acts as a heads-up display and monitoring for trade/infotainment services. Using vehicles to construct mobile networks can improve the quality of wireless communications and offer some kinds of entertainment during the trip. In fact, these networks aim to further improve road safety by providing real-time alerts to drivers about the risks of their planned journey and their immediate surroundings. This is possible through the interchange with other vehicles and units of transmission of road safety. VANETs provide wireless communication among vehicles and vehicle-to-road-side equipments. The roadside units can construct the infrastructure of the vehicular networks using wired and wireless communications among each other, as illustrated in Fig. 1. Communication performance strongly depends on how the routing takes place in the network: the existing routing protocols for VANETs are not so efficient to meet the needing of every traffic scenario, since the high degree of mobility and propagation phenomena have a high impact on VANET performance. In this paper, the multichannel characteristic of VANET devices is considered, in order to improve system performance in terms of routing optimization. In fact, in a distributed multi-hop architecture, a mobile node may potentially find multiple routes for a given destination and, when it evaluates the network topology through its routing table, the availability of different channels may enhance the quality of communication if properly exploited. The so called Quality of Service (QoS), for example in VoIP-based traffic applications as in [1], [2] and routing in multi-hop wireless networks are very challenging due to the high grade of mobility that causes interferences among different transmissions, but VANETs offer the chance to reduce them, since multiple simultaneous transmissions (on different channels) are possible. The main aim of this work is to introduce this feature when considering classical routing metrics. In detail, a new routing protocol for interference reduction and link-duration enhancement is proposed for VANET environments, taking advantage of a dynamic allocation of the Dedicated Short Range Communications (DSRC) spectrum, in order to reduce interference level among mobile nodes and to increase the overall link stability in the considered network. In this paper a new interference-aware routing protocol for VANET environments is proposed, the new metric take into account the best values of Signal-to-Interference Ratio (SIR), end-2-end (e2e) Delay and Link Duration Probability (LDP).

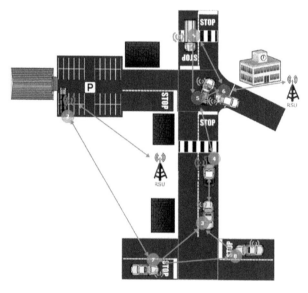

Fig. 1: Possible application scenario for VANET.

2.   Related Work

There are many studies in literature about routing over VANETs , investigating classical approaches, like AODV, DSR, GPSR, etc., and several routing protocols have been defined by many researchers. In [3] Distribution-Adaptive Distance with Channel Quality (DADCQ) protocol has been proposed and that utilizes the distance method to select forwarding nodes. In this work, authors created a decision threshold function that is simultaneously adaptive to the number of neighbors, the node clustering factor and the Rician fading parameter. In [4] a two-level trajectory based routing called TTBR has been proposed in order to face the

issue of protocol scalability and the reduction of routing overhead. Two joint geographic routing schemes for long range and short range forwarding have been adopted to improve the routing scheme under Manhattan and Freeway environment. Routing issues has been also considered in [5], [6], where DTN scenario has been studied, at the aim of minimizing energy consumption for the optimization of network layer operations. In [7] a novel multichannel TDMA MAC protocol (VeMAC) has been proposed for a Vanet Scenario. The VeMAC supports efficient one-hop and multi-hop broadcast services on the control channel by using implicit acknowledgments and eliminating the hidden terminal problem. The protocol reduces transmission collisions due to node mobility on the control channel by assigning disjoint sets of time slots to vehicles moving in opposite directions and to road side units. In [8] a contextual cooperative congestion control policy that exploits the traffic context information of each vehicle has been proposed to reduce the channel load and load on the communications channel, this is done satisfying the strict application's reliability requirements. In [9], [10], we propose a novel preliminary interference-aware algorithm for VANET environments able to optimize the paths from sources to destinations in terms of interference, by introducing a new routing protocol; however, time variations of SIR are not taken into account. This work represents an extension of [11] and [12] with the addition of parameters in the new metric of the proposed protocol.

3.   Vehicular Networks and Routing Decisions

There has been a lot of research to obtain the IEEE 802.11p standard, which specifies the technology suitable for vehicular communication networks.

3.1.   Standard Overview

The IEEE 802.11p standard specifies the technology suitable for vehicular communication networks. It is an amendment to the IEEE 802.11-2007 standard. Within this amendment, a new operational mode, called Wireless Access in Vehicular Environments (WAVE) [13], is defined to enable communication among high-speed vehicles or between a vehicle and a stationary roadside infrastructure network. The multi-channel operation in the WAVE mode is based on a combined FDMA/TDMA channel access scheme. It operates in the licensed ITS band of 5,9 GHz. WAVE aims at providing standard specifications to ensure the interoperability between wireless mobile nodes of a network with rapidly changing topology (that is to say, a set of vehicles in an urban or sub-urban environment). The DSRC spectrum is divided into 7 channels: one Control Channel (CCH) and six Service Channels (SCH), each of them occupying 10 MHz of bandwidth. A mobile/stationary station switches its channel between the control channel and one of the service channels each channel interval. VANET provides wireless communication among vehicles and vehicle-to-road-side equipments. The WAVE standard relies on a multi-channel concept which can be used for both safety-related and entertainment messages. The standard accounts for the priority of the packets using different Access Classes (ACs), having different channel access settings, as shown in Fig. 2. Each station continuously alternates between the Control Channel (CCH) and one of the Service Channels (SCHs). The MAC layer in WAVE is equivalent to the IEEE 802.11e Enhanced Distributed Channel Access (EDCA) Quality of Service (QoS) extension. Therefore, application messages are categorized into different ACs, where AC0 has the lowest and AC3 the highest priority. Within the MAC layer a packet queue exists for each AC.

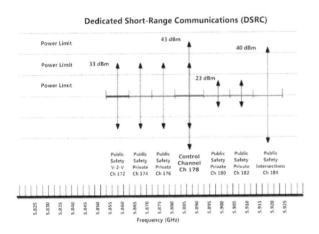

Fig. 2: Multi-channel EDCA extension for WAVE specifications.

3.2.   Routing Issues

The proposed solution works in a distributed manner and exploits protocol messages to perform routing decisions and to update the routing table entries. This approach needs more time than a centralized approach to reach a stable routing path, but it is possible initiate session faster. In fact, some paths could be change during sessions for several reasons. In the transitory period some paths can change because in the routing tables are not presenting the right or complete network configuration.

3.3.   Protocol Overview

VANET Adaptive Routing Optimization (VARO) is a distributed protocol and it works like the AODV protocol. In particular, a node of the network sends a neighbour discovery message to know its neighbours. The neighbour answers to this message sending its id and its routing table information. In this way, the node that sends neighbour discovery receives several messages from its neighbours, having the chance to build its own routing table. Once nodes change its routing table, it propagates changes to its neighbours. In order to maintain the presence of the node as neighbour, a node has to receive an alive message from its neighbours. If a node does not receive an alive message until 3-times the "alive period" then it erases the entry related to the neighbour from its routing table and propagates this information to its neighbour. When a new path is coming from a neighbour, the node checks if it has the entry related to the destination. If it is not present, then new path is inserted into the routing table, otherwise the node performs a routing decision algorithm, taking into account three different metrics, which will be faced in further sections of this work, to perform the update of the routing table. In order to maintain updated information about network topology, nodes exchange also messages about links information, such as end-to-end delay, LDP and SIR. This knowledge is used to perform the routing decision algorithm when multiple paths are available to reach a destination. Figure 3 resumes the main steps of the discovery process. The routing algorithm can be viewed as a linear optimization problem and its formulation is presented into the next section.

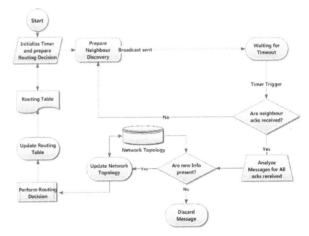

Fig. 3: Flow chart of neighbours discovery process.

3.4.   Linear Optimization

In order to present the linear optimization problems, it is convenient to recall some key concepts about the Graph Theory and its analytic representation. A generic graph can be presented as $G(V, E)$, where V is the set of nodes that compose the graph and E is the set of edges. Three terms are associated to each edge:

- $\delta_{i,j}$ is the term related to the delay along the link that connect a node (i) with a neighbor (j),

- $\gamma_{i,j}$ is the term related to the SIR among the node (i) and a neighbor node (j),

- $\varsigma_{i,j}$ is the term related to the Link Duration Probability (LDP) among the node (i) and a neighbor node (j).

Fig. 4: An example of a generic link and its related weights between two generic node (i, j).

Once a source node $s \in V$ is chosen, it is possible to define a set s and a set D, composed of all remaining nodes, which is defined as shown in Eq. (1):

$$D = V - S = \bigcup_{i=1}^{n} V_i \mid i \neq s. \tag{1}$$

V is the full set of nodes that composes the vehicular network therefore:

- $n = |V|$; $z = |D|$.

Given a source node s the related Tree (T_s) is defined as $T_s = G(V_T, E_T) \subset G(V, E)$ in particular:

- $V_T = V = S \cup D \mid S \cap D = \emptyset$,

- $E_T \subset E$.

Given a Tree (T) it is possible to define a Path between node s and other nodes. Therefore:

- $\forall_{j=1}^{Z} d_j \in D_T \; \exists \; \text{Path} \; (s, d_j)_T \subset V_T$,

- $m_j = | \; \text{Path}(s, d_j)_T \; |$.

Hence, m_j is the number of the nodes (HOPs) that a generic packet has to pass through to go from node s to node d_j.

1) Constraints Definition

Let us define the SIR contribute as:

$$\gamma_{i,j} = \frac{Ptx_{i,j}}{\sum_{k=1}^{Nch} Prx(i)_{j,k}}. \tag{2}$$

Where:

- Nch is number of the available channels to transmit the data packets between two neighbor nodes,

- $Ptx_{j,k}$ is the transmitted power between nodes (i) and node (j),

- $Prx(i)_{j,k}$ is the received measured power from neighbor node (j) to node (i) on the channel k.

The concept of End-to-End delay between two nodes can be described as in Eq. (3). Here the source node is the radix of the tree; instead, the destination node is one of the nodes that belong to the set D. However, the cumulative delay is carrying out considering each edge that belongs to the path between the source (s) and the considered destination (d).

The LDP on a generic path between tree source (s) and a generic destination (d) is presented in Eq. (4) for more details see at [14]:

2) Minimum Spanning Tree (MST)

Considering QoS constraints, it is possible to define the Minimum Spanning Tree (MST), modeling our issue as an optimization problem:

- $Min_{x \in X} \; F(x)$,

subject to:

- $Max_{j=1}^{z} \left\{ \sum_{k=1}^{m_j - 1} \Delta_{k,k+1} \mid k \in \text{Path}(s, d_j) \right\} \leq \Phi$,

- $Min_{j=1}^{z} \left\{ \forall_{k=1}^{m_j - 1} \gamma_{k,k+1} \mid k \in \text{Path}(s, d_j) \right\} \leq \Psi$,

- $Max_{j=1}^{z} \left\{ \forall_{k=1}^{m_j - 1} \zeta_{k,k+1} \mid k \in \text{Path}(s, d_j) \right\} \leq \Gamma$,

where the Φ, Ψ and Γ are the delay, SIR and LDP bounds respectively, $x \in X$ represent the Paths between the source node and destinations set along the tree T_x, while X is the set of all available Trees. Moreover, $f(x)$ is the objective function to minimize.

$$f(x) = C_\delta \cdot g(x) + C_\gamma \cdot h(x) + C_\zeta \cdot t(x). \tag{5}$$

$$\Delta_{s,d_j} = \sum_{k=1}^{m_j-1} \delta_{k,k+1} \mid s \in S, d_j \in D, k \in \text{Path}(s,d_j)_T. \tag{3}$$

$$\varsigma_{s,d_j} = \frac{1}{2} \cdot \prod_{k=1}^{m_j-1} \left[1 + erf\left(\frac{\beta_{th}(k,k+1) - \alpha\log\left(\frac{v_{k,k+1} \cdot \tau_{k,k+1}}{L}\right)}{\sqrt{2} \cdot \sigma} \right) \right]. \tag{4}$$

In Eq. (5) the $g(x)$ is the scalar evaluation of the delay along the path in Tx, $h(x)$ is the scalar evaluation of the SIR along the path in T_x and at last the $t(x)$ is the scalar evaluation of the LDP along the path in T_x. The C_δ, C_γ, C_ς is the set of the scalar weight costs related to delay, SIR and LDP function respectively. These weight costs have to be greater than zero, commonly, the above weight costs are set to one.

4. Performance Evaluation

The protocol proposed in Section 3.2 has been implemented in the NS2 simulator; first of all, the QoS MAC of IEEE 802.11e has been introduced and then it has been extended in order to include all the functionalities of the multi-channel IEEE 802.11p standard. The CityMob generator [15] has been used to create mobility log-files, with the following parameters: map dimensions 1800 m × 1800 m, maximum vehicle speed 13.9 m·s^{-1}. Transmission rate has been fixed to 3 Mbps and the number of mobile nodes from 40 to 100. The number of concurrent connections has been fixed to 15.

At this point, VARO metrics are completely defined and they can be used to evaluate the performance of the proposed protocol. VARO has been compared with AODV, GPSR and DSR. In this work some set-up campaigns have been carried out in order to find the right parameters. In particular, once a scenario is defined, it is important to well design the related bounds, otherwise it will be not possible to find admissible solutions. This step is made at simulation beginning and in future works it will be studied an automatic procedure to self-configure the bounds of the networks. From Fig. 5, it can be noticed how the VARO protocol outperforms other protocols in terms of PDR, Aggregated throughput (the sum of the throughputs of all connections) and delay end-to-end. Introducing a composite metric such as interference level and links durability more stable paths can be chosen by the routing decision algorithm achieving a reduction of packet loss probability, retransmissions number are reduced too following the packet loss trend.

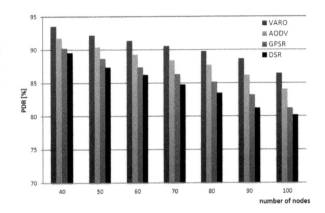

Fig. 5: Average PDR vs the number of mobile nodes.

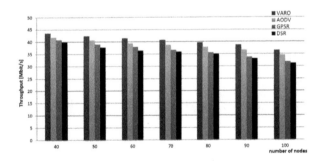

Fig. 6: Average aggregated throughput vs the number of mobile nodes.

So, this is evident when considering the percentage of correctly delivered packets and system throughput.

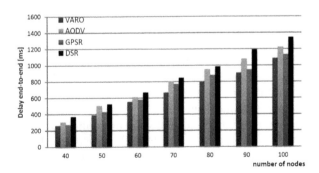

Fig. 7: Average E2E delay vs the number of vehicles.

Referring to the overhead performance, as illustrated in Fig. 8, the VARO protocol performs slightly worse than the other ones, because of the new signaling packets that are introduced into the network traffic for the construction of alternative paths.

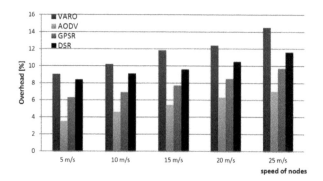

Fig. 8: System overhead for 60 mobile nodes and different average speeds.

The introduction of new protocol messages makes the overhead (evaluated as the ratio between the number of signaling packets and the number of total packets) of VARO higher than classical AODV protocol. Figure 9 shows the trend of the SIR level on selected channels to transmit data packets.

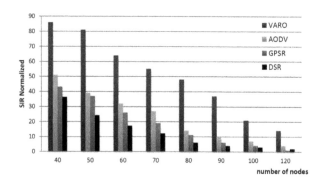

Fig. 9: SIR level normalized vs the number of vehicles.

5. Future Works and Conclusions

In the next works, we will provide some comparison campaigns in order to verify the goodness of the proposed routing algorithm and to find a better mechanism to self-adapt the parameters and the bounds of the metric in order to guarantee robustness and reliability for the found solutions. The main idea that will drive us is to search for the starting configuration considering an unloaded network and then change the optimization bounds following statistical data, which are achieved from historical sessions, and the current trend of the network load. In this work a new routing protocol for VANETs, dedicated to the optimization of path-length, interference level and link duration is proposed. It takes advantage of a dynamic al-

location of the DSRC spectrum, in order to reduce interference levels among nearby mobile nodes. A new composite metric, based on the evaluation of interference levels, end-to-end delay and link duration along the different links from sources towards destinations has been proposed. Through an NS2 implementation of the IEEE802.11p standard, with the simulation of vehicles mobility in a urban environment, it has been shown that the proposed idea enhances performance in terms of throughput, packet delivery ratio and e2e delay, despite of an increase in overhead.

References

[1] TOMALA, K. , L. MACURA, M. VOZNAK and J. VYCHODIL. Monitoring the quality of speech in the communication system BESIP. In: *Proceedings of 35th International Conference on Telecommunications and Signal Processing, TSP 2012.* Prague: IEEE, 2012, pp. 255–258. ISBN 978-146731118-2. DOI: 10.1109/TSP.2012.6256293.

[2] ROZHON, J. and M. VOZNAK. Development of a speech quality monitoring tool based on ITU-T P.862. In: *Proceedings of 34th International Conference on Telecommunications and Signal Processing (TSP), TSP 2011.* Budapest: IEEE, 2011, pp. 62–66. ISBN 978-145771411-5. DOI: 10.1109/TSP.2011.6043771.

[3] SLAVIK, M. and I. MAHGOUB. Spatial Distribution and Channel Quality Adaptive Protocol for Multihop Wireless Broadcast Routing in VANET. *IEEE Transaction on Mobile Computing*, 2013. vol. 12, iss. 4, pp. 722–734. ISSN 1536-1233. DOI: 10.1109/TMC.2012.42.

[4] DE RANGO, F., F. VELTRI, P. FAZIO and S. MARANO. Two-level Trajectory-based Routing Protocol fir Vehicular Ad Hoc Networks in Freeway and Manhattan Environments. *Journal of Networks*. 2009, vol. 4, no. 9, pp. 866–880. ISSN 1796-2056. DOI: 10.4304/jnw.4.9.866-880.

[5] SOCIEVOLE, A. and S. MARANO. Evaluating the impact of energy consumption on routing performance in delay tolerant networks. In: *Proceedings of the 8th International Wireless Communications and Mobile Computing Conference.* Limassol: IEEE, 2012, pp. 481–486. ISBN 978-145771378-1. DOI: 10.1109/IWCMC.2012.6314251.

[6] SOCIEVOLE, A. and F. DE RANGO. Evaluation of routing schemes in opportunistic networks considering energy consumption. In: *2012*

International Symposium on Performance Evaluation of Computer and Telecommunication Systems, SPECTS'12 - Part of SummerSim 2012 Multiconference. Genoa; IEEE, 2012, pp. 41–47. ISBN 978-161839982-3.

[7] OMAR, H. A., W. ZHUANG and L. LI. VeMAC: A TDMA-based MAC Protocol for Reliable Broadcast in VANETs. *IEEE Transaction on Mobile Computing.* 2012, vol. 12, iss. 9, pp. 1724–1736. ISSN 15361233. DOI: 10.1109/TMC.2012.142.

[8] SEPULCRE, M., J. GOZALYEZ, J. HARRI and H. HARTENSTEIN. Contextual Communications Congestion Control for Cooperative Vehicular Networks. *IEEE Transaction on Wireless Communications.* 2011, vol. 10, iss. 2, pp. 385–389. ISSN 1536-1276. DOI: 10.1109/TWC.2010.120610.100079.

[9] FAZIO, P., F. DE RANGO, C. SOTTILE, P. MANZONI and C. CALAFATE. A distance Vector Routing Protocol for VANET environemnt with Dynamic Frequency Assignment. In: *Wireless Communication and Network Symposium (WCNC 2011).* Cancun: IEEE, 2011, pp. 1016–1020. ISBN 978-1-61284-255-4. DOI: 10.1109/WCNC.2011.5779274.

[10] FAZIO, P., F. DE RANGO and C. SOTTILE. A new Interference aware on-demand routing protocol for Vechicular Networks. In: *Performance Evaluation of Computer and Telecommunication Systems (Spects 2011).* The Hague: IEEE, 2011, pp. 98–103. ISBN 978-1-4577-0139-9.

[11] FAZIO, P., F. DE RANGO and C. SOTTILE. An on demand interference aware routing protocol for VANETS. *Journal of Networks.* IEEE, 2012, vol. 7, iss. 11, pp. 1728–1738. ISSN 1796-2056. DOI: 10.4304/jnw.7.11.1728-1738.

[12] FAZIO, P., F. DE RANGO, C. SOTTILE and C. CALAFATE. A new channel assignment scheme for interference-aware routing. In: *2011 IEEE 73rd Vehicular Technology Conference (VTC Spring).* Budapest: IEEE, 2011, pp. 1–5. ISBN 978-1-4244-8332-7. DOI: 10.1109/VETECS.2011.5956777.

[13] IEEE 802.11p. *802.11p-2010: IEEE Standard for Information technology– Local and metropolitan area networks– Specific requirements– Part 11: Wireless LAN Medium Access Control (MAC) and Physical Layer (PHY) Specifications Amendment 6: Wireless Access in Vehicular Environments.* New Jersey: IEEE, 2010. ISBN 978-0-7381-6324-6. DOI: 10.1109/IEEESTD.2010.5514475.

[14] KHAYAM, S. A. and H. RADHA. Analyzing the Spread of Active Worms over VANET. In: *VANET - Proceedings of the First ACM International Workshop on Vehicular Ad Hoc Networks.* Philadelphia: Department of Electrical & Computer Engineering, 2004, pp. 86–87. ISBN 1581139225.

[15] MARTINEZ, F. J., J.-C. CANO, C. T. CALAFATE and P. MANZONI. CityMob: A Mobility Model Pattern Generator for VANETs. In: *ICC Workshops - 2008 IEEE International Conference on Communications Workshops.* Beijing: IEEE, 2008, pp. 370–374. ISBN 978-1-4244-2052-0. DOI: 10.1109/ICCW.2008.76.

About Authors

Peppino FAZIO was born in 1977. He received the degree in computer science engineering in May 2004. Since November 2004 he has been a Ph.D. student in Electronics and Communications Engineering at the University of Calabria and he has got the Ph.D. in January 2008; at the moment he is a research fellow at Department of Electronics, Computer Science and Systems (DEIS) of University of Calabria, after many collaborations with Department of "Universidad Politecnica de Valencia". His research interests include mobile communication networks, QoS architectures and interworking wireless and wired networks, mobility modeling for WLAN environments and mobility analysis for prediction purposes.

Cesare SOTTILE was born in 1983 and received the bachelor's degree in Computer Science Engineering in September 2007. Since December 2010 he received the master's degree in Telecommunications Engineeering at the University of Calabria. Nowadays, he is a Ph.D. student at University of Calabria, Department of Computer Science, Modeling, Electronics and Systems Engineering (DIMES). His research interests include mobile communication networks, satellites, vehicular networks and interworking wireless, energy efficient protocols for sensor networks.

Amilcare Francesco SANTAMARIA was born in 1978. He received the master's degree in computer science engineering in October 2005. Since November 2005 he was employed in the Department of Computer Science at the University of Calabria. Since January 2007 he was Ph.D. student at the University of Calabria and he has got the Ph.D. in Computer Science in the April 2012. Since April 2013 he is Research Fellow at University of Calabria, Department of Computer Science, Modeling, Electronics and Systems Engineering (DIMES). His research interests include Satellite and Broadband communications, multicast routing protocols and algorithms, wired and wireless architectures, VANET , QoS optimization and Evolutionary Algorithms.

Mauro TROPEA was born in 1975 and graduated in computer engineering at the University of Calabria, Italy, in 2003. Since 2003 he has been with the telecommunications research group of Department of Electronics, Computer Science and Systems (DEIS) of University of Calabria. In 2004 he won a regional scholarship on Satellite and Terrestrial broadband digital telecommunication systems. Since November 2005 he has a Ph.D. student in Electronics and Communications Engineering at University of Calabria. His research interests include satellite communication networks, QoS architectures and interworking wireless and wired networks, mobility model.

20

CATEGORIZATION OF UNORGANIZED TEXT CORPORA FOR BETTER DOMAIN-SPECIFIC LANGUAGE MODELING

Jan STAS, Daniel ZLACKY, Daniel HLADEK, Jozef JUHAR

Department of Electronics and Multimedia Communications,
Faculty of Electrical Engineering and Informatics, Technical University of Kosice,
Park Komenskeho 13, 042 00 Kosice, Slovak Republic

jan.stas@tuke.sk, daniel.zlacky@tuke.sk, daniel.hladek@tuke.sk, jozef.juhar@tuke.sk

Abstract. *This paper describes the process of categorization of unorganized text data gathered from the Internet to the in-domain and out-of-domain data for better domain-specific language modeling and speech recognition. An algorithm for text categorization and topic detection based on the most frequent key phrases is presented. In this scheme, each document entered into the process of text categorization is represented by a vector space model with term weighting based on computing the term frequency and inverse document frequency. Text documents are then classified to the in-domain and out-of-domain data automatically with predefined threshold using one of the selected distance/similarity measures comparing to the list of key phrases. The experimental results of the language modeling and adaptation to the judicial domain show significant improvement in the model perplexity about 19 % and decreasing of the word error rate of the Slovak transcription and dictation system about 5,54 %, relatively.*

Keywords

Language modeling, large vocabulary continuous speech recognition, similarity measure, term weighting, text categorization, topic detection.

1. Introduction

One of the key problems of the text data gathered from the Internet is their thematic heterogeneity. In the case of domain-specific speech recognition and statistical language modeling, these unorganized text data bring into the process of training language models many ambiguities caused by the overestimating such n-gram probabilities that are typically unrelated with the area, in which the speech recognition is performed. Therefore, it is necessary to divide the text data into the predefined domains in the best way as it is possible and adjust the parameters of language modeling for effective and robust task-oriented speech recognition.

With an increasing number of the text documents gathered from the Internet and growing need for more accurate and robust models of the Slovak language [1] for the transcription and dictation system from the judicial domain [2], a question how to categorize the text data according their content arises, considering the fact that one document may contain more than one theme within. This question is getting on importance especially with using unorganized text corpora without any knowledge about the document boundaries in the process of training domain-specific models. Therefore, we were looking for a way of categorizing the text data in unorganized text corpora to the in-domain and out-of-domain data for better language modeling.

Contemporary text categorization is usually based on topic detection with key word identification for categorization of text data into predefined domains [3] or text document clustering based on measuring similarity between two or more documents [4], [5] with using iterative or hierarchical clustering algorithms [6]. Based on this knowledge, we propose an algorithm for text categorization, which classifies short segments (blocks of texts or paragraphs) from unorganized text corpora to the in-domain and out-of-domain data. These data are then used in statistical language modeling for enhancing the quality and robustness of the large vocabulary continuous speech recognition (LVCSR) in Slovak. By combining of several principles, methods and algorithms widely used in text categorization, we propose an effective and unsupervised algorithm that brings a significant improvement of the quality the domain-specific modeling of the Slovak language.

This paper is organized as follows. In the Sec. 2, the text corpora used either for text categorization and statistical language modeling is mentioned. Our proposed approach for text categorization based on key phrases identification, term weighting, measuring similarity and automatic thresholding is presented in Sec. 3. Sec. 4 describes the speech recognition setup used in experiments that are discussed in the Sec. 5. Main contributions and future directions are summarized at the end of this paper in Sec. 6.

2. Text Corpora

The text data used in the process of text categorization and statistical language modeling was collected using an automatic system for text gathering and processing called webAgent [1], [7]. This system retrieves the text data from various web pages and electronic resources that are written in Slovak. The text data are then filtered from a large amount of grammatically incorrect words, symbols or numerals and normalized into their pronounced form. Finally, the processed text corpora were divided into smaller domain-specific subcorpora, ready for the training language models. Statistics of the number of tokens and sentences for particular text subcorpus is summarized in the Tab. 1.

It is important to say that the judicial corpus was obtained from the Ministry of Justice of the Slovak Republic, in order to develop the automatic transcription and dictation system for their internal purpose [2]. The corpus of fiction was created from a number of electronic books freely available on the Internet.

For morphological analysis we have used Dagger [8], the Slovak morphological classifier based on a hidden Markov model and suffix-based word clustering function. And as it was mentioned before, the preprocessed and morphologically annotated corpora were divided into five domain-specific subcorpora, oriented to the domain of fiction, justice, broadcast news, remaining web and other heterogeneous text.

3. Proposed Approach

We propose an approach for text categorization of unorganized text corpora (without knowledge about the document boundaries) to the in-domain and out-of-domain data, where the text corpora were segmented into blocks of at least 300 words. This value was determined empirically from statistical observation. In the process of text categorization, we have not considered removal of stop-words because we use key phrases that contain them in the step of key phrase identification (or topic detection). Also stemming or lemmatization would cause a high time and memory requirements, therefore it has not been introduced into the process of text categorization.

Tab. 1: Statistics on the text corpora.

Text corpus	# Tokens	# Sentences
corpus of fiction	101 234 475	8 039 739
judicial corpus	565 140 401	18 524 094
broadcast news	554 593 113	36 326 920
web corpus	748 854 697	50 694 708
other text	55 711 674	4 071 165
annotations	4 434 217	485 800
development set	55 163 941	1 782 333
Total	**2 085 132 518**	**119 924 759**

3.1. Key Phrases Identification

Based on morphologically annotated corpora, we also proposed a scheme for automatic extraction of multi-word units (key phrases) from judicial domain [9]. Using this approach, we created a list of 5 210 key phrases length from 1 to 4 words. These key phrases were later used in computing frequency of their occurrence in mentioned blocks of 300+ words – text documents. Documents that did not contain any key phrases were automatically classified as out-of-domain text data.

3.2. Vector Space Model

One of the simplest way how to represent the occurrence of words in text documents is to use a multidimensional vector space model, where each $i - th$ document $\vec{d_i}$ is represented by a vector of terms t_j (key words or key phrases) as follows [4]

$$\vec{d_i} = (t_{i,1}, t_{i,2}, \ldots, t_{i,N}). \quad (1)$$

In our case, each document was represented by a vector of 5 210 key phrases. Average number of words in one document after segmentation into blocks of 300+ words was 332. Then, the total number of text documents was 6 908 655. Main disadvantage of such representation is very high dimension and redundancy which result in high requirements on disc space.

3.3. Term Weighting

Key phrases in vector space model are represented by theirs occurrence in text documents. This value is often normalized considering its occurrence in the set of all examined text documents. Based on previous research [6], the term frequency and inverse document frequency (TF-IDF) are usually used for term weighting. TF-IDF weighting function is computed as [4]

$$w_{i,j} = tf_{i,j} \cdot idf_i = \frac{f_{i,j}}{\sum_k f_{k,j}} \cdot \log \frac{N}{|\{j : t; \in d_j\}|}, \quad (2)$$

where $f_{i,j}$ is the frequency of occurrence of term t_i in document d_j. The sum in the denominator of $tf_{i,j}$ component expresses the frequency of occurrence of all terms in document d_j, N is the total number of documents and denominator $|.|$ of idf_i component expresses the total number of documents that contain term t_i.

Beside standard TF-IDF, there are many other term weighting schemes such as TF-ICF, in which ICF component is computed on limited data set, or ATC, LTU and Okapi weighting schemes, which can use additional attributes giving information about the document, for example of its length [10].

3.4.   Measuring Similarity

The next step includes measuring distance between two documents. In our case, we measure similarity between reference text represented by a list of 5 210 key phrases and examined text document (hypothesis). Both text documents are transformed to the vector space model and weighted by TF-IDF scheme, so they could be compared. The weight of each key phrase in reference text was computed on development data set, which contain about 10 % of texts from the judicial corpus that were not used in training language model. By comparative study of distance/similarity metrics described in [11], we have chosen three measures, which satisfy a condition of: a. non-negativity; b. symmetricity; c. triangle inequality; and d. identity, when distance is equal to zero; namely the Bhattacharyya coefficient, Jaccard index and Jensen-Shannon divergence.

The Bhattacharyya coefficient is often used for clustering phonemes in the training acoustic models in LVCSR. This coefficient expresses the relative accuracy of the estimate the probability between two density functions and comes from the sum of the geometric mean of these probabilities. It specifies the separability of two classes x and y and is used as classification criterion as follows

$$d_{Bha} = -\ln \sum_{i=1}^{N} \sqrt{x_i y_i}, \qquad (3)$$

The Jaccard correlation index expresses scalar sum of two vectors and is usually used for measuring similarity between two probability density functions. It comes from harmonic mean and the equation for computing cosine similarity, normalized by absolute deviation of two probability distributions according formula

$$d_{Jac} = \frac{\sum_{i=1}^{N} (x_i + y_i)^2}{\sum_{i=1}^{N} x_i^2 + \sum_{i=1}^{N} y_i^2 - \sum_{i=1}^{N} x_i y_i}. \qquad (4)$$

And finally, the Jensen-Shannon divergence comes from the principle of uncertainty. This measure is a special case of averaged Kullback-Leibler divergence (also relative entropy), which satisfies the symmetry in the entire range of values. It is often used in information theory and natural language processing. Jensen-Shannon divergence is computed as

$$d_{JS} = \frac{1}{2} \left[\sum_{i=1}^{N} x_i \ln \left(\frac{2x_i}{x_i + y_i} \right) + \sum_{i=1}^{N} y_i \ln \left(\frac{2y_i}{x_i + y_i} \right) \right]. \qquad (5)$$

Note that each measure is represented as a distance for better implementation in our algorithm for text categorization. There exists a number of other distance/similarity measures used in text categorization, such as cosine similarity or Pearson correlation coefficient [5], which were omitted from observation because of similarity with Jaccard index or its asymmetricity.

3.5.   Automatic Thresholding

The last step in text categorization is appropriately setting the threshold, when text data appertain to the in-domain or out-of-domain area. This value is usually determined empirically from long-term observation or automatically from examined statistic values. We used automatic thresholding based on the calculation of median of a sequence of coefficients derived from computing one of the similarity measure described in the previous section. Threshold values were calculated on development set and used in the algorithm for text categorization to the in-domain and out-of-domain data.

4.   LVCSR Setup

Trigram language models were created using SRILM Toolkit [12] with vocabulary size of 325 555 of unique words. All models have been trained on the text corpora size of about 2 billion of tokens (see Sec. 2) and smoothed by the Witten-Bell back-off algorithm. Particular in-domain and out-of-domain language models were combined and adapted into the judicial domain using linear interpolation with computing interpolation weights based on minimization of perplexity on a development data set using our proposed algorithm [1].

The triphone context-dependent acoustic model (AM) based on hidden Markov models (HMMs) have been used. Each of 4 states of the AM had been modeled by 32 Gaussian probability density functions. The model has been generated from feature vectors containing 39 mel-frequency cepstral (MFC) coefficients using HTK Toolkit [13]. It has been trained on 120 h of readings of real adjudgments from the court, 130 h of read phonetically rich sentences, newspaper articles, and spelled items, recorded in offices and conference rooms and 100 h of spontaneous speech recorded at council hall. The acoustic database is characterized by gender-balanced speakers and contains read and spontaneous speech [2]. For modeling rare triphones the effective triphone mapping algorithm has been used [14].

For decoding, we have used the LVCSR engine Julius based on two-pass strategy, where input data are processed in the first pass with bigram LM and the final search for reverse n-gram is performed again using the result of the first pass to narrow the search space [15].

Test data were represented by 315 min. of recordings obtained from randomly selected speech segments from the acoustic database of judicial proceedings. These segments contain 41 820 words in 3 462 sentences that were not used in the training AM.

For evaluation, the word error rate (WER) and model perplexity (PPL) has beeen used. WER is the standard extrinsic measure of performance the LVCSR system, computed by comparing the reference text read by a speaker against the recognized results and it takes into account insertion, deletion and substitution errors. For intrinsic evaluation of the LMs the model perplexity has been used. PPL is defined as the reciprocal of the weighted (geometric) probability assigned by the LM to each word in the test set.

5. Experimental Results

Experiments have been oriented on the evaluation of model perplexity and word error rate of the LVCSR system after text categorization to the in-domain and out-of-domain data and statistical modeling of the Slovak language from the judicial domain.

Statistics of the number of text documents after term weighting, measuring the distance/similarity between examined documents and weighted list of key phrases and categorization of the text to the in-domain and out-of-domain data we can see in the Tab. 2.

We focused on two types of experiments. In the first experiment, proposed text categorization has been performed within particular text subcorpora apart, when the text data after categorization were merged to the two subcorpora: in-domain and out-of-domain corpora.

In the second experiment, particular text subcorpora described in the Sec. 2 were merged into one text corpus and text categorization has been performed on the entire corpus without any knowledge about the topic in every text document. The result of model perplexity after adaptation to the judicial domain and combination of in-domain and out-of-domain trigram models to the final domain-specific model of the Slovak language and word error rate of the Slovak transcription and dictation system is summarized in the Tab. 3.

As we can see from these results, the best class separation was achieved with Bhattacharyya coefficient as similarity measure. On the contrary, the worst class separation in both experiments was noticed for Jensen-Shannon divergence. Better class separation was observed when text categorization has been performed in particular text corpora that had a positive impact on the model PPL or WER of the LVCSR system. This fact is caused by using TF-IDF weighting, or its IDF component, computed for the entire set of documents, while the first experiment has been evaluated for not equal numbers of documents in particular subcorpora. Therefore, text categorization is more accurate when all text documents are concentrated in one corpus.

The results of model perplexity and WER of the LVCSR system for these two types of experiments are moderately different. However, the best distance/similarity measure in connection with TF-IDF weighting in proposed text categorization appears Jaccard index. This approach brought significant decrease of the model perplexity in modeling of the Slovak language approximately 19 % and WER of the Slovak transcription and dictation system about 5,54 %, relatively against language modeling on unorganized text corpora and approximately 11 % in model perplexity and 3,47 % in WER, relatively against previous categorization of text data based on rough categorization using the URL of downloaded text document or other additional information about it [1], [2].

6. Conclusion

This article was focused on design of the algorithm for categorization of unorganized text corpora to the in-domain and out-of-domain data with the aim of increasing the quality and robustness of language modeling in large vocabulary continuous speech recognition. By combining effective methods for topic detection based on most frequented key phrases, term weighting, measuring similarity between hypothesis and reference text and automatic thresholding, we have achieved significant improvement in modeling of the Slovak language, both in the model perplexity and in the word error rate values. Further research should be focused on application of more effective term weighting schemes such as ATC, LTU, Okapi, or TF-ICF that would not be evaluated through the entire text corpora to reduce the time and memory requirements of the algorithm for the text categorization.

Acknowledgment

The research presented in this paper was partially supported by the Ministry of Education, Science, Research and Sport of the Slovak Republic under the research project MS SR 3928/2010-11 (25 %) and Research and Development Operational Program funded by the ERDF under the projects ITMS-26220220155 (25 %) and ITMS-26220220141 (50 %).

Tab. 2: Statistics of the number of text blocks after text categorization.

Measure	Partially		Together	
	In-domain	Out-of-domain	In-domain	Out-of-domain
Bhattacharyya coefficient	684 598	6 224 057	1 166 805	5 741 850
Jaccard correlation index	969 853	5 938 802	1 258 169	5 650 486
Jensen-Shannon divergence	1 811 093	5 097 562	2 305 230	4 603 425

Tab. 3: Model perplexity and word error rate of the Slovak transcription and dictation system for the judicial domain.

Measure	Partially		Together	
	PPL	WER [%]	PPL	WER [%]
without text categorization	40,4302	5,48	44,3262	5,60
Bhattacharyya coefficient	42,0395	5,57	36,0428	5,32
Jaccard correlation index	41,2654	5,53	**35,9444**	**5,28**
Jensen-Shannon divergence	42,7054	5,66	38,1756	5,50

References

[1] JUHAR, J., J. STAS and D. HLADEK. Recent Progress in Development Language Model for Slovak Large Vocabulary Continuous Speech Recognition. In: *New Technologies – Trends, Innovations and Research*. Rijeka: InTech, 2012, pp. 261–276. ISBN 978-953-51-0480-3. DOI: 10.5772/32623.

[2] RUSKO, M., J. JUHAR, M. TRNKA, J. STAS, S. DARJAA, D. HLADEK, M. CERNAK, M. PAPCO, R. SABO, M. PLEVA, M. RITOMSKY and M. LOJKA. Slovak Automatic Transcription and Dictation System for the Judicial Domain. In: *Human Language Technologies as a Challenge for Computer Science and Linguistics: 5th Language & Technology Conference, 2011*. Poznan: Fundacja Uniwersytetu im A. Mickiewicza, 2011, pp. 365–369. ISBN 978-83-932640-1-8.

[3] YUE, L., S. XIAO, X. LV and T. WANG. Topic Detection based on Keyword. In: *Proc. of 2011 International Conference on Mechatronic Science, Electric Engineering and Computer*. Jilin: IEEE, 2011, pp. 464–467. ISBN 978-1-61284-719-1. DOI: 10.1109/MEC.2011.6025502.

[4] MANNING, Ch. D. and H. SCHUTZE. *Foundations of Statistical Natural Language Processing*. Cambridge: MIT Press, 1999. ISBN 02-621-3360-1.

[5] HUANG, A. Similarity Measures for Text Document Clustering. In: *Proc. of the 6th New Zealand Computer Science Research Student Conference*. Christchurch, New Zealand, 2008, pp. 49–56.

[6] ZLACKY, D., J. STAS, J. JUHAR and A. CIZMAR. Slovak Text Document Clustering. *Acta Electrotechnica et Informatica*. 2013, vol. 13, no. 2, will be published. ISSN 1338-3957.

[7] HLADEK, D. and J. STAS. Text Mining and Processing for Corpora Creation in Slovak Language.

Journal of Computer Science and Control Systems. 2010, vol. 6, iss. 1, pp. 65–68, ISSN 1844-6043.

[8] HLADEK, D., J. STAS and J. JUHAR. Dagger: The Slovak Morphological Classifier. In: *Proc. of the 54th International Symposium ELMAR 2012*. Zadar: IEEE, 2012, pp. 195–198. ISSN 1334-2630. ISBN 978-1-4673-1243-1.

[9] STAS, J., D. HLADEK, J. JUHAR and M. OLOSTIAK. Automatic Extraction of Multiword Units from Slovak Text Corpora. In: *Proc. of the 7th International Conference on NLP, Corpus Linguistics, SLOVKO 2013*. Bratislava: E/Learning, 2013, will be published.

[10] REED, J. W., Y. JIAO, T. E. POTOK, B. A. KLUMP, M. T. ELMORE and A. R. HURSON. TF-ICF: A New Term Weighting Scheme for Clustering Dynamic Data Streams. In: *Proc. of the 5th International Conference on Machine Learning and Applications*. Orlando: IEEE, 2006, pp. 258–263. ISBN 0-7695-2735-3. DOI: 10.1109/ICMLA.2006.50.

[11] CHA, S. Comprehensive Survey on Distance/Similarity Measures between Probability Density Functions. *International Journal of Mathematical Models and Methods in Applied Sciences*. 2007, vol. 1, no. 4, pp. 300–307. ISSN 1998-0140.

[12] STOLCKE, A. SRILM – An Extensible Language Modeling Toolkit. In: *Proc. of ICSLP*. Denver: ISCA, 2002, pp. 901–904. ISBN 1876346450.

[13] YOUNG, S., G. EVERMANN, M. GALES, T. HAIN, D. KERSHAW, X. LIU, G. MOORE, J. ODELL, D. OLLASON, D. POVEY, V. VALTCHEV and P. WOODLAND. *The HTK Book (for HTK Version 3.4)*. Massachusetts: Cambridge University Engineering Department, 2006. ISBN 978-1-4419-7712-0.

[14] DARJAA, S., M. CERNAK, M. TRNKA, M. RUSKO and R. SABO. Effective Triphone Mapping for Acoustic Modeling in Speech Recognition. In: *12th Annual Conference of the International Speech Communication Association, INTERSPEECH 2011*. Florence: DBLP, 2011, pp. 1717–1720. ISBN 9781618392701.

[15] LEE, A., T. KAWAHARA and K. SHIKANO. Julius - an Open Source Real-Time Large Vocabulary Recognition Engine. In: *7th European Conference on Speech Communication and Technology, EUROSPEECH 2001*. Aalborg: ISCA, 2001, pp. 1691–1694. ISBN 978-8-7908-3410-4.

About Authors

Jan STAS was born in Bardejov, Slovakia in 1984. In 2007 he graduated M.Sc. (Ing.) at the Department of Electronics and Multimedia Communications of the Faculty of Electrical Engineering and Informatics at the Technical University of Kosice. He received his Ph.D. degree at the same department in the field of Telecommunications in 2011. He is currently working as a post-doctoral researcher with focus on natural language processing and understanding, computational linguistics and statistical language modeling in speech recognition and is author of several conference and journal papers from this area.

Daniel ZLACKY was born in Poprad, Slovakia in 1988. He received his M.Sc. (Ing.) degree in the field of Telecommunications in 2012 at the Department of Electronics and Multimedia Communications of the Faculty of Electrical Engineering and Informatics at the Technical University of Kosice. He is currently Ph.D. student at the same department in the field of Telecommunications. His research interests include automatic word segmentation, text categorization, text document clustering and statistical language modeling in speech recognition and is author of several conference and journal papers from this area.

Daniel HLADEK was born in Kosice, Slovakia in 1982. In 2006 he graduated M.Sc. (Ing.) at the Department of Cybernetics and Artificial Intelligence of the Faculty of Electrical Engineering and Informatics at the Technical University of Kosice. He has obtained Ph.D. degree in 2009 at the same department in the field of Computational Intelligence. He is currently working as a post-doctoral researcher at the Department of Electronics and Multimedia Communications at the Technical University of Kosice with focus on natural language processing, speech and audio processing and intelligent decision methods. He is author of several conference and journal papers from this area.

Jozef JUHAR was born in Poproc, Slovakia in 1956. He graduated from the Technical University of Kosice in 1980. He received Ph.D. degree in Radioelectronics from Technical University of Kosice in 1991, where he works as a Full Professor at the Department of Electronics and Multimedia Communications. He is author and co-author of more than 200 scientific papers. His research interests include digital speech and audio processing, speech and speaker identification and verification, speech synthesis and development in spoken dialogue and speech recognition systems.

21

Structural Tolerances of Optical Characteristics in Various types of Photonic Lattices

Stanislav KRAUS, *Michal LUCKI*

Department of Telecommunications Engineering, Faculty of Electrical Engineering,
Czech Technical University in Prague, Technicka 2, 166 27 Prague, Czech Republic

stanislav.kraus@fel.cvut.cz, lucki@fel.cvut.cz

Abstract. *A systematic study of various photonic crystal lattices and their optical characteristics is carried out in this paper. Sensitivity of both dispersion and effective mode area characteristics to deviations of particular structural parameters of the lattices are the main studied topics. The presented results can be exploited during the design of fibers and new devices utilizing the studied lattices, when strict requirements on optical characteristics of the fabricated devices are imposed. Performance benefits for the implementation of particular lattices types in photonic designs are shown.*

Keywords

Dispersion, effective more area, FDFD, photonic lattice, tolerance.

1. Introduction

Photonic crystals fibers (PCFs) exhibit two-dimensional periodicity in a cross-section compared to traditional rotational symmetry. Dispersion profile of PCFs can be tailored for desired applications ranging from dispersion compensation [1] to non-linear optics [2]. Another distinctive advantage of a PCF over conventional fibers includes ability to achieve very small effective mode area for non-linear applications as well as large effective mode areas while maintaining unique single mode operation. A typical high-index guiding PCF structure consists of a solid core made of host material (typically silica glass), surrounded by cladding, and formed by the composition of multiple air holes along the fiber in the host material. These air holes are arranged in a periodic lattice and prevent light from escaping from the solid core. The high-index guiding mechanism is known as modified total internal reflection (M-TIR), [3]. Since lattice determines dimensions and shape of the core, it significantly influences the effective mode area and birefringence.

Geometry of a photonic lattice and the shape of holes affect dispersion, particularly its waveguide portion, since the lattice determines the field distribution of guided modes within the structure.

In this paper, the characteristics of photonic crystal lattices are discussed from the viewpoint of structural tolerances of dispersion and effective mode area. The outline of particular lattice types for their potential implementation in photonic designs is included.

2. State of the Art

The early designs of PCFs [4] utilized hexagonal lattice, still used in recent designs [5], [6], [7], although certain modifications of the hexagonal lattice for achieving desired properties, e.g. large mode area (larger than 80 μm^2) by insertion of core defects, are known [5]. The hexagonal lattice is attractive owing to its simplicity, since few design parameters is responsible for the lattice properties. Furthermore, the hexagonal layout of capillaries ensures that pressure among capillaries during the drawing process is applied omnidirectionally, thus preventing the transformation into different layout. The idea of stronger confinement of light within a core led to an increase in number of air holes within rings. This approach was utilized in [8], [9], where an octagonal lattice was proposed and also in [10], where the number of air holes within the first ring was even increased to ten, creating a decagonal lattice. The main benefits sourcing from the stronger confinement of light are the lower confinement loss and the wider range of wavelengths in the octagonal lattice compared to the hexagonal lattice [8]. The decagonal lattice can provide high negative dispersion slope for PCF designs with small lattice pitch (being about 1 μm) and may be promising for non-linear optics as well, since the effective mode area as low as 2 μm^2 has already been reported [10]. Designs of PCFs with a square lattice were also proposed in many papers [11], [12], [13]. The results presented in [12] show lower dispersion and lower dispersion slope for the square lattice than for the hexagonal lattice. This advantageous property was exploited to design a PCF for dispersion compensation from E to L wavelengths bands [12] or PCF for optical coherence tomography [13]. The achievement of the better control of effective mode area in PCFs was aimed in other proposals [14], [15], [16], which did not utilize the polygonal layout of air holes. On the other hand, in [15] and [16], the air holes form repeating equiangular spirals. The spiral is a geometrical arrangement that in many aspects resembles the form of a seashell. This allows controlling the optical characteristics by adjusting coefficients in exponential expressions of the spirals. In particular, very low effective mode area of 0.71 μm^2 [15] is obtained, if the spirals are tightly curled. Nevertheless, the repeatable fabrication of PCF deploying the equiangular spiral is still unresolved.

3.   Material and Methods

The studied photonic lattices are comprised of silica glass as a background material and circular cladding air holes. This shape of holes is the most common in the generally accepted PCF designs and the most suitable for fabrication, since a preform is formed by stacking capillaries with a circular inner hole. In order to simplify and without restricting generality, the refractive index of air is considered as being constant and equal to 1 in the simulated wavelength range, whereas the dependence of refractive index upon wavelength for silica glass whose properties accounts for material dispersion, is modeled using the Sellmeier dispersive formula 1, [17]:

$$n^2 - 1 = \frac{0.6961663\lambda^2}{\lambda^2-(0.0684043)^2} + \frac{0.4079426\lambda^2}{\lambda^2-(0.1162414)^2} +$$
$$+ \frac{0.8974794\lambda^2}{\lambda^2-(9.896161)^2}. \qquad (1)$$

Three different photonic lattices are considered in simulations presented in this paper:

- hexagonal,

- square,

- octagonal.

These lattices can be easily described by a few geometrical parameters mentioned below. The considered lattices are optimized to support the fundamental mode only. In all the studied lattices, omitting the central air hole of the lattice forms the core. The basic forming unit of the hexagonal lattice is an equilateral triangle of air holes with diameter d, which has pitch Λ between adjacent air holes. The air holes with

equidistance from the core center resemble hexagonal rings. The square lattice is obtained by repetition of the basic square unit with side length Λ. The octagonal lattice is formed by repeating an isosceles triangle of air holes with the vertex angle of 45° around the core center, which creates octagonal rings of air holes in the cladding, Fig. 1. The pitch between adjacent holes in the octagonal lattice is not uniform. The pitch between holes in adjacent rings is Λ, whereas the pitch between the adjacent holes in the same ring is $\Lambda_1 \cong 0.765\Lambda$. The diameter of the core is equal to $2\Lambda - d$ for all the studied lattices. The reference values of parameters are summarized in Tab. 1. The selection of reference values should ensure that trends in characteristics can be rescaled for other values of the parameters, if the ratio d/Λ is unchanged, and the optical characteristics fit within their linear region (i.e. results for a different set of parameters can be obtained by the shift of the reference characteristics).

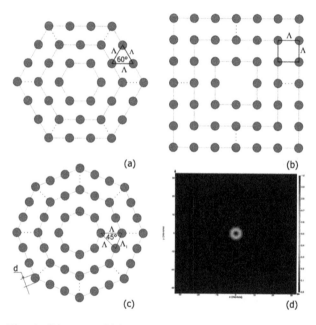

Fig. 1: Schematic of (a) hexagonal lattice, (b) square lattice, (c) octagonal lattice with denoted parameters, (d) optical mode profile within octagonal lattice.

Tab. 1: Reference design parameters of studied lattices.

pitch Λ [μm]	2
octagonal lattice - pitch Λ_1 [μm]	0.765Λ
air hole diameter d [μm]	2
number of rings N_r [$-$]	5
core diameter $2\Lambda - d$ [μm]	8

The results presented in this paper were obtained by using the full vectorial finite difference frequency domain method [18]. The meshing algorithm generates square mesh, which discretize the PCF structure, creating Yee computational cells. Alignment of field intensity vectors on edges and nodal positions within

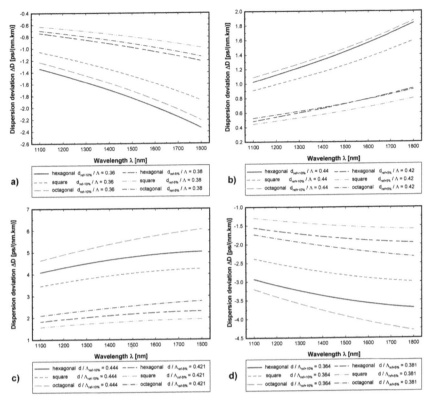

Fig. 2: Variation in chromatic dispersion with respect to wavelength for hexagonal, square and octagonal lattice for (a) −10 % decrease in diameter of air holes from the reference value, (b) +10 % increase in diameter of air holes from the reference value, (c) −10 % decrease in pitch from the reference value, (d) +10 % increase in pitch from the reference value.

each cell is chosen to satisfy continuity and boundary conditions between adjacent cells. Values of field intensity vectors are computed by employing approximation of Maxwell curl equations. Conformal mesh technique [19] is applied to the structure, where an interface between two materials is present within a computational cell. This improves the accuracy of the numerical solution, since Maxwell curl equations are computed along the material interface within the cell. Anisotropic perfectly matched layers (PMLs) [20] at the boundaries of the simulation region are utilized to model absorption of radiant energy from the simulation region. Utilization of PMLs at the edge of the simulation region satisfies the boundary conditions of Maxwell equations as well as reduces the necessary computational domain. Values of field intensity vectors are arranged in matrices, which enable to extract information about field profile and effective modal index n_{eff} of individual optical modes at different frequencies by solving these matrices.

The effective modal index is subsequently used to compute chromatic dispersion, which is the sum of material and waveguide dispersion. Dispersion is expressed using dispersion coefficient D [ps/(nm·km)], Eq. (2):

$$D = -\frac{1}{c} \frac{\partial^2 Re\{n_{eff}\}}{\partial \lambda^2} \frac{1}{L}, \tag{2}$$

where λ [nm] is wavelength, c [m·s^{-1}] is speed of light in vacuum, and L [km] is length of fiber. The quantitative assess of the transverse profile of the guided mode is expressed as an effective mode area A_{eff} [μm^2], Eq. (3), which is calculated based on the distribution of electric field intensity E [V·m^{-1}] within the structure:

$$A_{eff} = \frac{\left(\int\int |E|^2\, dxdy\right)^2}{\int\int |E|^4\, dxdy}. \tag{3}$$

The wavelength range considered in the simulations of lattice characteristics is 1100–1800 nm.

4. Results

Systematic study of wavelength-dependent variations in chromatic dispersion and in effective mode area of different photonic lattices with change in structural parameters is presented below. The absolute change in particular investigated parameter for 10 % and 5 % offset from the reference value of individual structural parameters is considered in the simulations. This corresponds to the independence of the considered geometrical parameters from the perspective of fabrication. The decision on the limit offset value would ensure that the

Tab. 2: Reference Values of Optical Characteristics.

Lattice	D [ps/(nm·km)] at 1550 nm	A_{eff} [μm^2] at 1550 nm	ZDW [nm]	DS [ps/(nm²·km)]
Hexagonal	39.08	38.9	1148	<0.144
Square	36.25	47.9	1146	<0.131
Octagonal	42.02	31.7	1166	<0.134

results are valid for various fabrication methods, regardless of attainable precision of each method. The reference values of effective mode area, dispersion as well as zero dispersion wavelength (ZDW) and dispersion slope (DS) for the studied lattices are listed in Tab. 2. Dispersion characteristics of the studied lattices are evaluated first. Subsequently, the wavelength evolution of the effective mode area is studied.

First, the diameter of air holes is varied and the resulting change in chromatic dispersion is observed, Fig. 1(a), Fig. 1(b). It can be seen from the simulation results in Fig. 2(a), Fig. 2(b), that chromatic dispersion in the square lattice is the most immune to diameter changes of the air holes, where dispersion deviation is less than 1 ps/(nm·km) at the wavelength of 1200 nm. This is considered for the 10 % offset from the reference diameter. The curves of dispersion deviation for a hexagonal lattice and an octagonal lattice evolve in such a way that the difference in the first order derivations with respect to wavelength is slowly decreasing. The intersection point of the curve is laid beyond the studied wavelength range. The reason for this is similar arrangement of the air holes in n sided polygons in these lattices compared to a square lattice. Nevertheless, the hexagonal lattice exhibits the highest change in dispersion for negative deviation of air holes, in contrast to the octagonal lattice, whose highest change in dispersion for positive air holes diameter deviation is a fact.

The variation in pitch upon chromatic dispersion is depicted in Fig. 2(c), Fig. 2(d). It can be concluded that the square lattice is the most immune to deviation in pitch from all the studied lattices. Therefore, the square lattice can be perceived as suitable for photonic applications with a strict requirement for dispersion, such as wavelength conversion or four-wave mixing. A potential problem of the square lattice for its deployment in PCF may be more complicated fabrication. Unlike in the square lattice, high variation in chromatic dispersion in the octagonal lattice with change in both studied structural parameters is reported. This can be explained as being the result of a smaller distance between adjacent air holes within particular rings of the octagonal lattice compared to the hexagonal lattice or the square lattice. Therefore, change in diameter of the air holes or change in pitch, results in more significant change in waveguide dispersion, as a consequence of the

change in field intensity in the vicinity of the boundary between the core and the cladding. Simulation results illustrated in Fig. 2(c) reveal that negative deviation of pitch alters dispersion characteristics for all the studied lattices more significantly. In addition, it can be concluded based on the comparison of Fig. 2(a) to Fig. 2(d) that the change in pitch affects chromatic dispersion of the studied lattices more than the change in diameter of the air holes. This property of lattices is related to change in core diameter, which is more prone to pitch deviation and less to the holes. Regardless of the lattice type, change in dispersion characteristics due to change in studied structural parameters is more of concern for long wavelength region.

The results on variation in effective mode area upon wavelength are depicted in Fig. 3. Proper design recommendations are provided based on the generalized characteristics of effective mode area of the studied lattices. For instance, negative deviation of air holes should be avoided during fabrication, since it alters the value of effective mode area (Fig. 3(a), Fig. 2(b)) more significantly, compared to enlargement of air holes. Deviation of pitch is more of concern for change in effective mode area than deviation of air holes, which can be inferred from Fig. 3. This can be attributed to higher sensitivity of the core size to variation in pitch rather than to variation in diameter of air holes. Moreover, the results reveal that the studied lattices are more prone to positive deviation in pitch. This finding demonstrates the octagonal lattice, for which the 10 % negative (resp. positive) deviation of pitch changes the effective mode area at 1500 nm by -7.4 μm^2 (resp. 8.7 μm^2). The effective mode area of octagonal lattice is the most insensitive to variation in both pitch and air hole diameter, which is caused by strong confinement (low value of A_{eff}) of the fundamental mode -98.5 % of power of the fundamental mode is located in the core, whereas only 94.3 % and 93.8 % of power is located in the same area for the hexagonal and the square lattice respectively. Changes in structural parameters affect the effective mode area mostly at long wavelengths (Fig. 3), since the electromagnetic field spreads more toward cladding with increase in wavelength. It is also noteworthy to mention that the wavelength dependence of variation in effective mode area is near-linear in the considered wavelength range, except for negative deviation of air holes in the hexagonal lat-

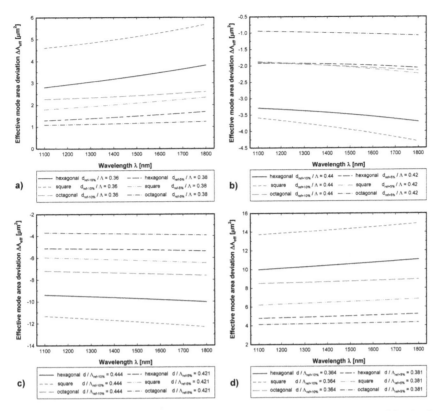

Fig. 3: Wavelength dependent variance in effective mode area for hexagonal, square and octagonal lattice for (a) −10 % decrease in diameter of air holes from the reference value, (b) +10 % increase in diameter of air holes from the reference value, (c) −10 % decrease in pitch from the reference value, (d) +10 % increase in pitch from the reference value.

tice Fig. 3(a). Hence, it is possible to predict a change in effective mode area of PCFs utilizing the studied lattices, if readjustment of the operating wavelength is required.

5. Conclusion

Different photonic lattices were investigated from the perspective of their structural parameters. Potential PCFs deploying the studied lattices should be designed to avoid variation in pitch, which predominantly influences characteristics of both chromatic dispersion and effective mode area. The highest insensitivity of chromatic dispersion to change in structural parameters is found for the square lattice. The utilization of the octagonal lattice is promising for applications requiring low variation in effective mode area, such as high power fiber lasers. For such applications one has to consider a lattice different from the hexagonal carefully. The main contribution of this paper is the presented sensitivity study of optical characteristics to structural deviations, which should be taken into account in future PCFs designs, especially those with non hexagonal lattice.

Acknowledgment

This work has been supported by the CTU grant under project SGS13/201/OHK3/3T/13.

References

[1] NAKAJIMA, K., T. MATSUI, K. KUROKAWA, K. TAJIMA and I. SANKAWA. High-Speed and Wideband Transmission Using Dispersion-Compensating/Managing Photonic Crystal Fiber and Dispersion-Shifted Fiber. *Journal of Lightwave Technology*. 2007, vol. 25, iss. 9, pp. 2719–2726. ISSN 0733-8724. DOI: 10.1109/JLT.2007.902754.

[2] SHASHIDHARAN, S., J. JOHNY, S. K. SUDHEER and K. S. KUMAR. Design and Simulation of Non Linear Photonic Crystal Fiber for Supercontinuum Generation and Its Application in Optical Coherence Tomography. In: *Symposium on Photonics and Optoelectronics*. Shanghai: IEEE, 2012, pp. 1–4. ISBN 978-1-4577-0909-8. DOI: 10.1109/SOPO.2012.6271023.

[3] BROENG, J., D. MOGILEVSTEV, S. E. BARKOU and A. BJARKLEV. Photonic Crystal Fibers: A New Class of Optical Waveguides. *Optical Fiber Technology*. 1999, vol. 5, iss. 3, pp. 305–330. ISSN 1068-5200. DOI: 10.1006/ofte.1998.0279.

[4] KNIGHT, J. C., T. A. BIRKS, P. St. J. RUSSELL and D. M. ATKIN. All-silica single-mode optical fiber with photonic crystal cladding. *Optics Letters*. 1996, vol. 21, iss. 19, pp. 1547–1549. ISSN 0146-9592. DOI: 10.1364/OL.21.001547.

[5] ROSTAMI, A. and H. SOOFI. Correspondence Between Effective Mode Area and Dispersion Variations in Defected Core Photonic Crystal Fibers. *Journal of Lightwave Technology*. 2011, vol. 29, iss. 2, pp. 234–241. ISSN 0733-8724. DOI: 10.1109/JLT.2010.2100808.

[6] LUCKI, M. Optimization of microstructured fiber for dispersion compensation purposes. In: *International Conference on Transparent Optical Networks*. Stockholm: IEEE, 2011, pp. 1–4. ISBN 978-1-4577-0881-7. DOI: 10.1109/ICTON.2011.5971024.

[7] LUCKI, M., R. ZELENY, K. KALLI, J. KANKA and A. MENDEZ. Broadband submicron flattened dispersion compensating fiber with asymmetrical fluoride doped core. In: *Micro-structured and Specialty Optical Fibres II*. Bellingham: SPIE, 2013, 87750M-1–87750M-8. ISBN 978-0-8194-9577-8. DOI: 10.1117/12.2017554.

[8] CHIANG, J.-S. and T.-L. WU. Analysis of propagation characteristics for an octagonal photonic crystal fiber (O-PCF). *Optics Communications*. 2006, vol. 258, iss. 2, pp. 170–176. ISSN 0030-4018. DOI: 10.1016/j.optcom.

[9] NEJAD, Sh. Mohammad, M. ALIRAMEZANI and M. POURMAHYABADI. Novel Design of an Octagonal Photonic Crystal Fiber with Ultra-Flattened Dispersion and Ultra-Low Loss. In: *International Conference on Broadband Communications, Information Technology*. Gauteng: IEEE, 2008, pp. 221–226. ISBN 978-1-4244-3281-3. DOI: 10.1109/BROADCOM.2008.12.

[10] RAZZAK, S. M. A., Y. NAMIHIRA, M. A. G. KHAN, F. BEGUM and S. KAIJAGE. Chromatic Dispersion Properties of A Decagonal Photonic Crystal Fiber. In: *International Conference on Information and Communication Technology*. Dhaka: IEEE, 2007, pp. 159–162. ISBN 984-32-3394-8. DOI: 10.1109/ICICT.2007.375365.

[11] ROJA, M. M. and R. K. SHEVGAONKAR. Geometrical Parameters Identification for Zero Dispersion in Square Lattice Photonic Crystal Fiber using Contour Plots. In: *International Conference on Signal Processing, Communications and Networking*. Chennai: IEEE, 2008, pp. 116–118. ISBN 978-1-4244-1924-1. DOI: 10.1109/ICSCN.2008.4447172.

[12] NEJAD, S. M. and N. EHTESHAMI. A novel design to compensate dispersion for square-lattice photonic crystal fiber over E to L wavelength bands. In: *International Symposium on Communication Systems Networks and Digital Signal Processing*. Newcastle: IEEE, 2010, pp. 654–658. ISBN 978-1-86135-369-6.

[13] NAMIHIRA, Y., M. A. HOSSAIN, J. LIU, T. KOGA, T. KINJO, Y. HIRAKO, F. BEGUM, S. F. KAIJAGE, S. M. A. RAZZAK and S. NOZAKI. Dispersion flattened nonlinear square photonic crystal fiber for dental OCT. In: *International Conference on Communication Technology and Application*. Beijing: IET, 2011, pp. 819–823. ISBN 978-1-61839-926-7. DOI: 10.1049/cp.2011.0783.

[14] RAZZAK, S. M. A., Y. NAMIHIRA, M. A. G KHAN, M. S. ANOWER and N. H. HAI. Transmission Characteristics of Circular Ring PCF and Octagonal PCF: A Comparison. In: *International Conference on Electrical and Computer Engineering*. Dhaka: IEEE, 2006, pp. 266–269. ISBN 98432-3814-1. DOI: 10.1109/ICECE.2006.355623.

[15] AGRAWAL, A., N. KEJALAKSHMY, B. M. A. RAHMAN and K. T. V. GRATTAN. Soft Glass Equiangular Spiral Photonic Crystal Fiber for Supercontinuum Generation. *Photonics Technology Letters*. 2009, vol. 21, iss. 22, pp. 1722–1724. ISSN 1041-1135. DOI: 10.1109/LPT.2009.2032523.

[16] HASAN, D. M. N., M. N. HOSSAIN, K. M. MOHSIN and M. S. ALAM. Optical characterization of a chalcogenide glass nanophotonic device. In: *International Technical Conference TENCON*. Fukuoka: IEEE, 2010, pp. 1915–1920. ISBN 978-1-4244-6889-8. DOI: 10.1109/TENCON.2010.5686431.

[17] BASS, M. *Handbook of Optics: Optical Properties of Materials, Nonlinear Optics, Quantum Optics*. New York: McGraw-Hill Education, 2009. ISBN 978-0-07-149892-0.

[18] ZHU, Z. and T. BROWN. Full-vectorial finite-difference analysis of microstructured optical fibers. *Optics Express*. 2002, vol. 10, iss. 17, pp. 853–864. ISSN 1094-4087. DOI: 10.1364/OE.10.000853.

[19] WENHUA Y. and R. MITTRA. A conformal finite difference time domain technique

for modeling curved dielectric surfaces. *Microwave and Wireless Components Letters*. 2001, vol. 11, iss. 1, pp. 25–27. ISSN 1531-1309. DOI: 10.1109/7260.905957.

[20] TAFLOVE, A. and S. C. HAGNESS. *Computational electrodynamics: the finite-difference time-domain method*. Boston: Artech House, 2005. ISBN 15-805-3832-0.

About Authors

Stanislav KRAUS was born in 1986. He received his M.Sc. in electrical engineering from the Czech Technical University in Prague in 2011. His research interests include design of optical photonic structures and optical communication systems.

Michal LUCKI received his Ph.D. from the Czech Technical University in Prague in 2007. His research interests include photonics, optoelectronics, material engineering and solid state physics. He is now a team leader and an investigator of a few grant projects focused on Photonic Crystal Fibers, among others.

22

Modelling and Control of Thermal System

Vratislav HLADKY, Radoslav BIELEK

Department of Cybernetics and Artificial Intelligence, Faculty of Electrical Engineering and Informatics,
Technical University of Kosice, Letna 9, 040 01 Kosice, Slovak Republic

vratislav.hladky@tuke.sk, radoslav.bielek@tuke.sk

Abstract. *Work presented here deals with the modelling of thermal processes in a thermal system consisting of direct and indirect heat exchangers. The overall thermal properties of the medium and the system itself such as liquid mixing or heat capacity are shortly analysed and their features required for modelling are reasoned and therefore simplified or neglected. Special attention is given to modelling heat losses radiated into the surroundings through the walls as they are the main issue of the effective work with the heat systems. Final part of the paper proposes several ways of controlling the individual parts' temperatures as well as the temperature of the system considering heating elements or flowage rate as actuators.*

Keywords

Automatic control, direct and indirect heat exchanger, thermal processes.

1. Introduction

Thermal processes are nowadays quite explored area, but the importance of their modelling is not decreasing as the present trends are focusing on the energy saving, therefore the more effective control is needed. One of the ways obtaining such kind of control is to derive the more precise model of the system.

This paper is divided into chapters reproducing the methodology of our work. It starts with the description of the whole system and its parts. The most important physical properties are considered in the following chapter together with the reasons for their simplifications. Using them the individual parts are modelled and the several ways of control are the most important outcome of our work.

Actual template for creating the model was the heat exchanger station located in the laboratory B513 of Faculty of Electrical Engineering and Informatics,

Technical University of Kosice (Fig. 1). Created model is planned to be used in lectures of Department of Cybernetics and Artificial Intelligence containing the principles of modelling, control, sensors and actuators.

2. Description of the Thermal System

The entire thermal system consists of several sensors (temperature, pressure, pressure difference), actuators (pump, regulating valve, heating element) and remaining components like indirect heat exchanger.

The goal of the system is to model the process of producing and supplying a dose of heat from the heat exchanger station to a household. Losses caused by transport and draw-off are simulated by the indirect heat exchanger.

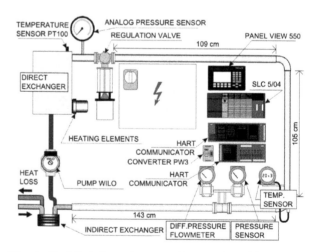

Fig. 1: Modelled thermal system, depicted from [1].

Working process of the system is as follows: water heated by the heating elements flows from the accumulation container into the indirect heat exchanger that has its other side connected to the cold water pipe. Hot water is thus cooled and then returned into the accumulation container. The goal of control is to compensate for these heat losses by controlling the heating elements and regulating the flow in the entire system.

2.1. Model Simplifications

Modelling thermal processes requires considering various simplifications as they are influenced by multiple physical properties of the material and flowing medium bringing nonlinearities into model. Together with its complexity the necessary computational power rises. From this reason, we decided to simplify or neglect few of the physical properties.

Walls of containers - during modelling we consider the walls to be without capacitance [2], i.e. we ignore the thickness of container walls. In reality, there is a slight temperature variation between the liquid and the container wall which we decided to ignore since the containers are made out of (metal) alloys that have high thermal conductivity, and will therefore quickly heat up to a temperature close to that of the liquid.

Other simplification, which is directly connected to the heat conduction, is the thermal inertia of the heating elements. Because of the high non-linear character of the heat elements' cooling process after their turn off we decided to neglect this feature.

Complete mixing - in reality mixed liquids don't have the same temperature in every point of their volume. During the simulation, however, we have to for simplicity consider complete mixing. In practice, this means that if the water is flowing into the exchanger then it has its temperature until the point of entry. Temperature of the water in the exchanger is then calculated from the total accumulated thermal energy [3].

Specific heat capacity - similarly to other properties of a medium its heat capacity also changes with temperature. It characterizes the amount of energy required to change a 1 kg substance temperature by 1 °C. During modelling and simulation, however, the mean value was used. This simplification does not visibly affect model's accuracy and lets us avoid highly increased computational requirements.

Thermal expansion - as the temperature of a medium changes so does its density and volume. This phenomenon is known as thermal expansion. Due to its negligible effect on the model we have decided to ignore it.

3. Modelling of Thermal Processes

For the physical model of thermal processes we have used an energy balance equation. This equation con-

sists of thermal flows, which enter and exit the system. Thus, we gain information about total accumulated energy, in this case heat. To create these equations we used physical formulae contained in [2] and [3].

3.1. Mathematical Model of Direct Heat Exchanger

Modelled direct heat exchanger consisted of accumulation container with inflow, outflow and three heating elements (merge into one with power of all three). From this, we can create an energy balance equation:

$$C_A \frac{\mathrm{d}T_A}{\mathrm{d}t} = Q_{Ain} - Q_{Aout} + Q_{AH} - Q_{AX}, \quad (1)$$

where Q_{Ain} is the heat flow entering the container (inflow of the container), Q_{Aout} is the heat flow exiting the container (outflow), Q_{AH} is the heat flow added by the heating elements and Q_{AX} is the heat flow as a consequence of thermal losses, while T_A is the current temperature in the exchanger and C_A is the medium's heat capacity. Index A represents the direct heat exchanger (useful in merging all equations later). The following equation applies [3]:

$$C_A = \rho_A \cdot V_A \cdot \overline{c_p}, \quad (2)$$

where ρ_A is the density of the medium, V_A is volume of the medium, $\overline{c_p}$ is the medium's mean value of specific heat capacity.

Individual heat flows can be expressed as:

$$Q_{Ain} = M_{Ain}\overline{c_p}T_{Ain}, \quad (3)$$

$$Q_{Aout} = M_{Aout}\overline{c_p}T_A, \quad (4)$$

$$Q_{AH} = P\eta, \quad (5)$$

$$Q_{AX} = k_{AX}F_{AX}(T_A - T_X), \quad (6)$$

where M_{Ain} and M_{Aout} are mass inflow and outflow of the container, T_{Ain} is the temperature of the inflowing medium, P is the actual power of the heating elements, η is the effectiveness of heating (with electric heating it is considered to be 98 %), k_{AX} is the heat transfer coefficient between the exchanger and its surroundings, F_{AX} is the contact area between the walls of the exchanger and its surroundings and T_X is the ambient temperature.

For heating in the real system three heating spirals were used each with the (theoretical) power of 1000 W.

In the model itself, the heat flows were integrated and to calculate the actual temperature they were divided by the heat capacity of the medium. The initial requirement was set as a conjunction of initial heat capacity C_{A0}, and the initial temperature T_{A0} (we therefore consider the accumulated energy received by the medium since the initial temperature of 0 °C during which the water can not circulate within the exchanger).

3.2. Mathematical Model of Indirect Heat Exchanger

This device, purposed to exchange heat between two mediums, consists of two chambers separated by a heat exchanging surface, which is constructed to have the largest surface area. Our model exchanger had a heat exchanging surface area of $F_N = 0.6$ m^2.

To differentiate the two chambers we denote them as primary and secondary. The primary chamber contains the hotter medium which then transfers heat to the medium in the secondary container. This way we get two balance equations, one for each side of the exchanger:

$$C_{BP}\frac{\mathrm{d}T_{BP}}{\mathrm{d}t} = Q_{BPin} - Q_{BPout} - Q_{BPS}, \qquad (7)$$

$$C_{BS}\frac{\mathrm{d}T_{BS}}{\mathrm{d}t} = Q_{BSin} - Q_{BSout} + Q_{BPS} - Q_{BX}, \quad (8)$$

where indexes next to the parameters represent B for the indirect exchanger, P primary side, S secondary side, X heat loss, in and out inflow and outflow respectively.

We consider the case in which the primary side has no thermal losses and all heat is transferred to the secondary side. It is only the secondary side from which some amount of heat is radiated into the surroundings. Individual heat flows are similar to those in the primary exchanger, specifically:

$$Q_{BPin} = M_{BPin}\overline{c_p}T_{BPin}, \qquad (9)$$

$$Q_{BPout} = M_{BPout}\overline{c_p}T_{BP}, \qquad (10)$$

$$Q_{BPS} = k_B F_B(T_{BP} - T_{BS}), \qquad (11)$$

$$Q_{BSin} = M_{BSin}\overline{c_p}T_{BSin}, \qquad (12)$$

$$Q_{BSout} = M_{BSout}\overline{c_p}T_{BS}, \qquad (13)$$

$$Q_{BX} = k_{BX}F_{BX}(T_{BS} - T_X), \qquad (14)$$

where M stands for mass flow, k stands for heat-transfer coefficient and F stands for contact area. Connecting the two sides of the indirect exchanger is Q_{BPS}

heat flow, which can be seen in both balance equations with a different plus/minus sign (minus on the primary side, which radiates heat and plus on the secondary side, which receives heat).

Such model's drawback is that we cannot determine whether the exchanger is counter-current or co-current. A certain solution could be provided by the space discretization of the two sides of the exchanger in space.

3.3. Mathematical Description of Heat Loss

Heat loss radiated into the surroundings is created as a result of the temperature difference between the surfaces of the exchangers or pipes and the outer temperature. These losses depend on (since we ignore thickness of the walls) the heat-transfer coefficient. To calculate it we need to ascertain the so-called Nusselt number for plate walls as described by this equation:

$$Nu_{Plate} = \left\{0.825 + 0.387\left[Ra \cdot f_1(Pr)\right]^{16/9}\right\}^2, \quad (15)$$

where:

$$f_1(Pr) = \left[1 + \left(\frac{0.492}{Pr}\right)^{9/16}\right]^{-16/9}. \qquad (16)$$

Pr stands for Prandtl number (according to tables of constants) and Ra stands for Rayleigh number, which we calculate by:

$$Ra = Gr \cdot Pr, \qquad (17)$$

where Gr-Grashof number determined thusly:

$$Gr = \frac{g \cdot \alpha_V \cdot \vartheta \cdot L^3}{v^2}, \qquad (18)$$

where g is gravity acceleration, α_V is coefficient of thermal expansion, ϑ is the temperature difference between the medium and ambient temperature, L is determining dimension (for flat walls it's height, for pipes it's diameter) and v is the kinematic viscosity of air.

The resulting heat transfer coefficient consists of two partial coefficients which consisted of part for dissipation and for conduction:

$$k_{BX} = \alpha_C + \alpha_D, \qquad (19)$$

where

$$\alpha_C = \frac{Nu \cdot \lambda}{l}, \qquad (20)$$

$$\alpha_D = \epsilon \cdot \sigma \cdot (T_1 + T_2)(T_1^2 + T_2^2), \qquad (21)$$

where λ is the thermal conductivity, l is the length of planar wall, $\epsilon = 0.7$, $\sigma = 5.67 \cdot 10^{-8}$, T_1 and T_2 are temperatures of water and air in Kelvin. All table values of parameters are searched for according to the characteristic temperature of air $T_m = 0.5 \cdot (T_S + T_t)$, where T_S is the water temperature and T_t is the temperature of the surrounding air.

To calculate the heat transfer coefficient in pipes we adjust the calculation of Nusselt number with a correcting element:

$$Nu_{Round} = Nu_{Plate} + 0.435 \frac{h}{D}, \qquad (22)$$

in which h stands for pipe length and D for its diameter. All equations listed above are used according to [4].

Individual properties of air were approximated with polynomials of varying degrees (according to sufficient accuracy of the approximation). Used data are summed up on Tab. 1, [4].

Tab. 1: Values for individual physical parameters of air used for the polynomial approximations.

t [°C]	ρ [kg·m^{-3}]	P_r [-]	$\nu \cdot 10^6$ [m^2·s^{-1}]	$\beta \cdot 10^{-3}$ [°C^{-1}]	$\lambda \cdot 10^3$ [W·m^{-1}·°C^{-1}]
0	1.2930	0.716	13.29	3.671	23.63
20	1.2048	0.717	15.10	3.419	25.11
40	1.1278	0.718	17.00	3.200	26.57
60	1.0601	0.719	18.97	3.007	27.99
80	1.0001	0.719	21.03	2.836	29.38
100	0.9465	0.720	23.17	2.684	30.75
120	0.8983	0.721	25.38	-	32.08
140	0.8549	0.722	27.66	-	33.39
160	0.8154	0.723	30.01	-	34.68
180	0.7794	0.724	32.43	-	35.94
200	0.7465	0.725	34.92	-	37.17

4. Control of the Thermal System

4.1. Control of the Heating Elements by Using PWM

Pulse Width Modulation (PWM) can create the impression of a continuous control of logical devices. During the control of heating elements, it has the advantage of a more accurate control and possible energy savings.

Due to computational requirements we have created two models of the accumulation container. The first one to truly simulate PWM control and to generate its signal with required duty cycle and the second one, which uses continuous values of power for its calculations. Comparison of the real experiment in accordance with [1] and these models is on Fig. 2. In this experiment, the water in the accumulation container

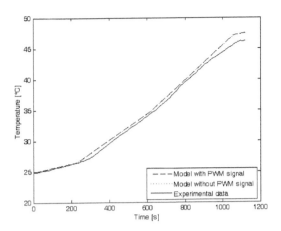

Fig. 2: Comparison model heating elements with the experimental results.

was heated without flow with gradual change of duty cycle.

On the Fig. 1, the difference between two models of PWM control can not be seen as they are almost equal.

4.2. Temperature Control of the Direct Exchanger by Heating Elements

In order to create a complex control of the entire system, control of the individual heat exchangers has to be designed first. During the synthesis of PI regulators, Naslin method was used with a maximum overshooting of 5 %.

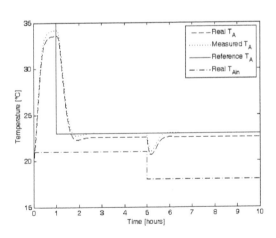

Fig. 3: Simulation of regulation of the temperature in the direct exchanger by using heating elements.

For the synthesis of the PI regulator we linearized the direct exchanger model near its equilibrium, in which equality between the temperatures of the medium and the surroundings occurs in the exchanger. The output of the system was the temperature in the exchanger and its input (and therefore actuating variable) was the required power of the heating elements. Results of the simulation can be seen on Fig. 3 and Fig. 4.

Main flaw of this type of control is in the impossibility to lower the temperature in the exchanger as we can only add heat to the system.

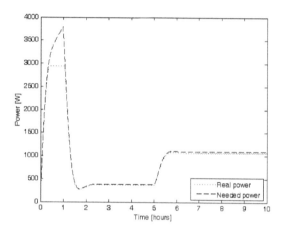

Fig. 4: Values of the real and required power during simulation of regulation of the direct exchanger by using heating elements.

4.3. Temperature Control of Direct Exchanger by Flowage

During linearization of the direct heat exchangers energy balance equation in its equilibrium in regard to flowage a problem has arisen in negating of the elements containing flowage (during equilibrium flowage is equal to inflow). For this reason change of thermal flow was chosen as the actuating variable, which was created by combining Q_{Ain} and Q_{Aout}.

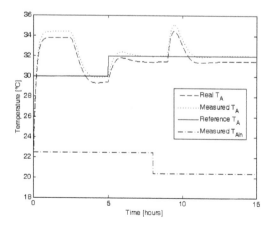

Fig. 5: Regulation of temperature of the direct exchanger by using flowage.

Regulator then calculates the required action as an energy variance in Joules, from which a specific value of flowage needs to be calculated. It has to be noted, that without full numeric communication and regulation this wouldn't be possible. Results of the simulation are on Fig. 5 and Fig. 6.

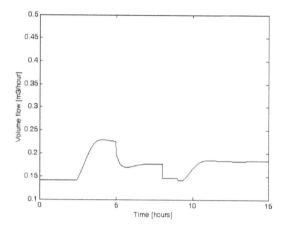

Fig. 6: Graph of mass flowage during regulation of the direct exchanger using flowage.

4.4. Temperature Control of Indirect Exchanger by Temperature of Input Medium

In regard to the impossibility of heat generation in the indirect exchanger we can, unlike the heating elements in the direct exchanger, affect its temperature by changing the temperature of the inflowing medium. Actuating variable is therefore the temperature in the primary side T_{BPin}. Graphs of the simulation with PI regulator control are on Fig. 7 and Fig. 8.

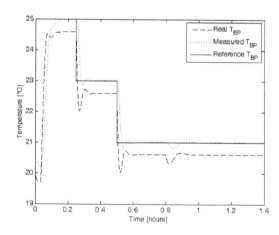

Fig. 7: Temperature regulation of the primary side of the indirect exchanger by controlling T_{BPin} with flowage malfunctions since $0.8h$.

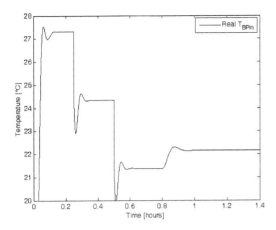

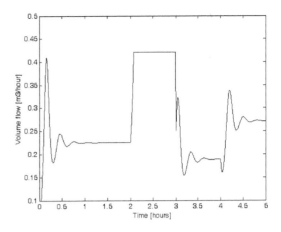

Fig. 8: Graph of the actuating variable - input temperature of the primary side during regulation of the indirect exchanger.

Fig. 10: Graph of the actuating variable - flowage during temperature control of the indirect heat exchanger.

4.5. Temperature Control of Indirect Exchanger by Flowage

As in the case of the direct exchanger, the temperature in the indirect exchanger can be affected by the flowage, however, during linearization of the system we again encounter the negating problem during equilibrium.

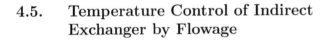

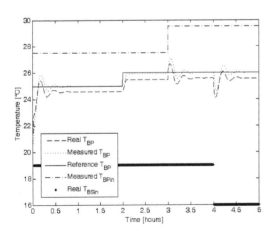

Fig. 9: Regulation of the primary side of the exchanger by controlling flowage.

We can, however, join the input and output thermal flows and consider the variation of this new flow to be the actuating variable, from which we need to calculate the value of flowage. Results of the simulations can be seen on Fig. 9 and Fig. 10.

4.6. Temperature Control of Indirect Exchanger in the Case of Serial Connection of Exchangers

Because we can not make new energy in the form of heat by controlling flowage (we can only affect the speed of thermal flows) we decided to create a complex control by using the heating elements.

We consider the temperature of the direct heat exchanger to be the input value of the primary side of the indirect exchanger. After a serial connection of linearized systems from chapters 4.2 and 4.4 we gained a transfer whose output is T_{BP} and whose input is power of the heating elements.

For the synthesis of a PI regulator we once again used Naslin method with a maximum overshooting of 5 %. Results of the simulation are on Fig. 11.

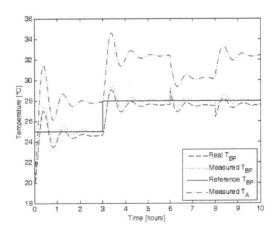

Fig. 11: Regulation of temperature of the indirect heat exchanger using heating elements during a serial connection of the two exchangers.

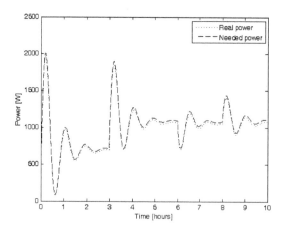

Fig. 12: Graph of the actuating variable - power of the heating elements during regulation of the entire thermal system.

5.   Practical Application

Proposed model can be used in the hot water distribution systems, for example in a flat-building with the number of flats 1 to 16, [6].

In the Fig. 13 is an example of hot water distribution system with the effect of the interrupted operations during the night in flat buildings. Heat losses in hot water pipes are negligible. A lost heat is indirectly used for the building heating in a winter season. However the heat from hot water transferred through the pipe walls into building flats is the unwanted heat energy loss in the summer season. Properly designed model can help to reduce the heat losses to the minimum [5].

Characterization of the distribution system:

- hot water is heated in the hot water storage tank installed in the house,

- supply water temperature is maintained by the hot water circulation,

- interrupted supply of the hot water is systems lasted for: 4, 5 and 6 hours a-day.

Assumed limit values of parameters:

- feed hot water temperature at the distribution system inlet is 55 °C,

- circulating hot water temperature at the end of distribution system is 50 °C,

- mean ambient temperature is 20 °C,

- thermal conductivity of thermal insulation is $\lambda = 0.04$ W·m^{-1}·°C^{-1},

- pipe material - steel (galvanized),

- volume of hot water delivered to flat at the specified temperature is 17.28 m^3/year.

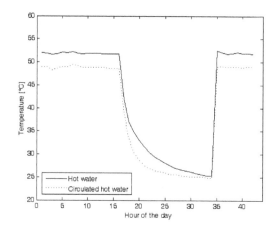

Fig. 13: Temperature trend in the distribution system.

6.   Conclusion

During the modelling of thermal systems we have to, due to their complexity, work with a number of simplifications. In practice, however, these simplifications have no profound effect on the model's accuracy. During the creation of regulation we have to account for the slow dynamic of the system, determine which parameters affect individual heat flows and adjust accordingly.

In the future work, we plan to use the implemented model for control in more complex structures on account of a better reference trajectory tracking using the predictive control. It would be suitable to have statistical data of heating water consumption at different time intervals. In that manner we could generate approximate trajectory of desired temperature for 24 hours a day and real data could help to specify the heat loss during the heat water consumption.

The important element of the system designed in such a way is a control by flow of heating water and also by heating spirals with the aim of electricity saving with respect to low energy consumption of control by the flow. It is necessary to emphasize that the use of the spirals is unavoidable (they, as the only actuator, are able to supply the heat energy to the system), however, control by the flow valve can save a significant amount of energy depending on temperature of the water returning from end user. Therefore, the more sophisticated control should prefer regulation by flow whenever possible. One of the options is using the controller in the form of neural networks, which allows the use of more outputs and it better reflects non-linearities of the system.

Acknowledgment

This work was supported by Scientific Grant Agency of Ministry of Education, Science, Research and Sport of Slovak Republic and Academy of Science of Slovak Republic under grant VEGA no. 1/0298/12.

References

[1] SUSTER, L. *Visualization and Monitoring of Electrical Characteristics within Control of Thermal System*. Kosice, 1999. Diploma thesis. Technical University of Kosice.

[2] JUHASZ, D. *System of Continuous Control of Laboratory Model of Thermal System*. Kosice, 2006. Diploma Thesis. Technical University of Kosice.

[3] NOSKIEVIC, P. *Modelling and Identification of Systems*. Ostrava: Montanex, 1999. ISBN 80-7225-030-2.

[4] SARNOVSKY, J., V. HLADKY and A. JADLOVSKA. *Control of Complex Systems*. Kosice: Elfa, 2005. ISBN 80-8086-011-4.

[5] LUKAC, P. and P. KAPALO. Analysis of Heat Exchange in the Hot Water Distribution Systems during Its Interrupted Operation. *Acta Metallurgica Slovaca*. 2011, vol. 2011, no. 4, pp. 253–262. ISSN 1338-1156.

[6] KAPALO, P. and P. LUKAC. Temperatute Changes of Hot Water Distribution System. *Journal of Applied Science in the Thermodynamics and Fluid Mechanics*. 2010, vol. 4, no. 1, pp. 1–5. ISSN 1802-9388.

[7] RAZNJEVIC, K. *Handbook of Thermodynamic Tables*. Bratislava: Alfa, 1984. ISBN 978-1-56700-046-7.

[8] HLADKY, V. and L. POPOVIC. Identification and Modelling of Object of Building of Kindergarten and Design of Temperature Control. *Automatizace*. 2008, vol. 51, no. 7–8, pp. 464–467. ISSN 0005-125X.

[9] SOKOLOWSKI, J. A. and C. M. BANKS. *Principles of Modeling and Simulation: A Multidisciplinary Approach*. New Jersey: John Wiley and Sons, 2009. ISBN 978-0-470-28943-3.

[10] BALATE, J. *Automatic Control*. Praha: BEN, 2004. ISBN 978-80-7300-148-3.

[11] DLASK, P. *Modelling at Control*. Praha: Wolters Kluwer, 2011. ISBN 978-80-7357-704-9.

About Authors

Vratislav HLADKY was born in 1968 in Bardejov, Slovak Republic. He received his M.Sc. degree in Control Systems and Robotics from Faculty of Electrical Engineering and Informatics Technical University of Kosice in 1991, finished his Ph.D. study at the same faculty in specialization Automation and Informatics in 1996. His research interests include control theory, theory of systems and sensors.

Radoslav BIELEK was born in Kosice, Slovakia. He graduated as bachelor of cybernetics on Technical Unversity of Kosice. He continued his master studies on the same university of field of cybernetics and Control Systems and he graduated with honors. Nowadays he works on his Ph.D. thesis under the supervision of associate professor Jan Jadlovsky.

23

Analysis and Comprehensive Analytical Modeling of Statistical Variations in Subthreshold MOSFET's High Frequency Characteristics

Rawid BANCHUIN

Department of Computer Engineering, Faculty of Engineering, Siam University,
38 Petkasem Road, Bangkok 10160, Thailand

rawid.ban@siam.edu

Abstract. *In this research, the analysis of statistical variations in subthreshold MOSFET's high frequency characteristics defined in terms of gate capacitance and transition frequency, have been shown and the resulting comprehensive analytical models of such variations in terms of their variances have been proposed. Major imperfection in the physical level properties including random dopant fluctuation and effects of variations in MOSFET's manufacturing process, have been taken into account in the proposed analysis and modeling. The up to dated comprehensive analytical model of statistical variation in MOSFET's parameter has been used as the basis of analysis and modeling. The resulting models have been found to be both analytic and comprehensive as they are the precise mathematical expressions in terms of physical level variables of MOSFET. Furthermore, they have been verified at the nanometer level by using 65 nm level BSIM4 based benchmarks and have been found to be very accurate with smaller than 5 % average percentages of errors. Hence, the performed analysis gives the resulting models which have been found to be the potential mathematical tool for the statistical and variability aware analysis and design of subthreshold MOSFET based VHF circuits, systems and applications.*

Keywords

Analysis, modeling, MOSFET, process variation effect, random dopant fluctuation, subthreshold, variation.

1. Introduction

Subthreshold region operated MOSFET has been adopted in various VHF circuits, systems and applications such as passive wireless Microsystems [1], low power receiver for wireless PAN [2], low power LNA [3], [4] and RF front-end for low power mobile TV applications [5] etc. Of course, the performances of these VHF apparatuses are mainly determined by two major high frequency characteristics of intrinsic subthreshold MOSFET entitled gate capacitance, C_g and transition frequency, f_T which is also known as unity gain frequency.

Obviously, imperfection in the physical level properties of MOSFET for example random dopant fluctuation along with those caused by variations in the manufacturing process of the device such as line edge roughness and gate length random fluctuation etc., cause the variations in MOSFET's electrical characteristics such as drain current and transconductance etc. These variations are crucial in the statistical and variability aware design of MOSFET based applications. So, there are many previous studies devoted to such variations in electrical characteristics such as [1], [6], [7], [8], [9], [10], [11], [12] which subthreshold region operated MOSFET has been focused in [1], [6], [10], [11], [12].

However, these studies did not mention anything about the variations in C_g and f_T even though they also exist and greatly affect the high frequency performances of the MOSFET based circuits and systems. By this motivation, analytical models of such variations in C_g and f_T have been performed [13], [14]. In [13], an analytical model of statistical variation in f_T as its variance expressed in term of the variance of C_g has been developed which strong inversion region operated MOSFET has been focused. Unfortunately, such model is incomprehensive as none of any related MOSFET's physical level variable has been involved. In [14], the comprehensive analytical models of random variations in C_g and f_T in term of their related MOSFET's physical level variables have been proposed where strong inversion region operated MOSFET has been focused as well. Since the subthreshold MOSFET has various applications which their performances can be strongly influenced by variations in C_g and f_T aforementioned, studies, analyses and analytical modeling of these variations with emphasis on subthreshold MOSFET have been found to be necessary.

According to this necessity, the statistical variations in C_g and f_T of subthreshold MOSFET's have been studied and analyzed in this research. As a result, the comprehensive analytical models of these variations in terms of their variances have been proposed. Unlike previous works on variations in subthreshold MOSFET such as [1], [6], [10], [11], [12] which focus to DC characteristics, this research is focused to variations in C_g and f_T which are high frequency ones. NMOS and PMOS technologies have been separately regarded in the analysis and modeling process according to some of their unique physical level variables. Major imperfection in the physical level properties including random dopant fluctuation and those effects of variations in MOSFET's manufacturing process which yield variations in MOSFET's electrical characteristics, have been taken into account. The up to dated comprehensive analytical model of statistical variation in MOSFET's parameter [15] has been adopted as the basis of this research. The resulting models have been found to be both analytic and comprehensive as they are the precise mathematical expressions in terms of MOSFET's physical level variables. Furthermore, they have been verified at the nanometer level by using 65 nm level BSIM4 based benchmarks and have been found to be very accurate with lower than 5 % average percentages of errors. Hence, the proposed analysis and modeling gives the results which have been found to be the potential mathematical tool for the statistical and variability aware analysis and design of subthreshold MOSFET based VHF circuits, systems and applications.

2. The Proposed Analysis and Modeling

Before proceeds further, it is worthy to give some foundation on the subthreshold region operated MOSFET. Firstly, the drain current, I_d of subthreshold MOSFET can be given by

$$I_d = \mu C_{dep}\frac{W}{L}\left(\frac{kT}{q}\right)^2\exp\left[\frac{V_{gs}-V_t}{nkT/q}\right]$$
$$\cdot\left[1-\exp\left[-\frac{V_{ds}}{kT/q}\right]\right], \quad (1)$$

where C_{dep} and n denote the capacitance of the depletion region under the gate area and the subthreshold parameter respectively. It should be mentioned here that the necessary condition for operating in the subthreshold region of any MOSFET is $V_{gs} < V_t$ which

can be simply given as follows [15]

$$V_t = V_{FB} + \phi_s + \epsilon_{ox}^{-1}qt_{inv}N_{sub}W_{dep}, \quad (2)$$

where N_{sub}, t_{inv}, W_{dep}, V_{FB} and ϕ_s stand for the substrate doping concentration, electrical gate dielectric thickness, depletion width, flat band voltage and surface potential respectively.

By using Eq. (1), the transconductance, g_m of subthreshold MOSFET can be given as

$$g_m = \frac{\mu}{n}C_{dep}\frac{W}{L}\left(\frac{kT}{q}\right)^2\exp\left[\frac{V_{gs}-V_t}{nkT/q}\right]$$
$$\left[1-\exp\left[-\frac{V_{ds}}{kT/q}\right]\right]. \quad (3)$$

At this point, it is ready to mention about the proposed analysis and modeling. Here, C_g can be mathematically defined as [16]

$$C_g \triangleq \frac{dQ_g}{dV_{gs}}, \quad (4)$$

where Q_g denotes the gate charge [16] which can be given by [17]

$$Q_g = \frac{\mu W^2 LC_{ox}^2}{I_d}\int_0^{V_{gs}-V_t}(V_{gs}-V_c-V_t)^2 dV_c$$
$$- Q_{B,\max}. \quad (5)$$

It should be mentioned here that $Q_{B,\max}$ denotes the maximum bulk charge [17]. By applying Eq. (1) for I_d in Eq. (5), Q_g of the subthreshold region operated MOSFET can be given by

$$Q_g = \frac{\left[\dfrac{WL^2C_{ox}^2}{C_{dep}(kT/q)^2}\right](V_{gs}-V_t)^3}{3\left[1-\exp\left[-\dfrac{V_{ds}}{kT/q}\right]\right]\exp\left[\dfrac{q}{nkT}(V_{gs}-V_t)\right]}$$
$$- Q_{B,\max}. \quad (6)$$

So, C_g of the subthreshold MOSFET can be given as follows

$$C_g = \frac{1}{3}\left[\frac{WL^2C_{ox}^2}{C_{dep}(kT/q)^2}\right]\left[3(V_{gs}-V_t)^2\right.$$
$$\left.-\frac{q}{nkT}(V_{gs}-V_t)^3\right]\exp\left[-\frac{q}{nkT}(V_{gs}-V_t)\right]. \quad (7)$$

Hence, the subthreshold MOSFET's f_T can be given by using the above equations as

$$f_T = \frac{3}{2}\left[\frac{\mu C_{dep}^2(kT/q)^3}{2n\pi L^3 C_{ox}^2}\right]\left[1-\exp\left[-\frac{V_{ds}}{kT/q}\right]\right]^2\cdot$$
$$\cdot\left[\frac{\exp\left[\dfrac{2q}{nkT}(V_{gs}-V_t)\right]}{3(V_{gs}-V_t)^2-\dfrac{q}{nkT}(V_{gs}-V_t)^3}\right]. \quad (8)$$

By taking random dopant fluctuation and effects of variations in MOSFET's manufacturing process into account, random variations in MOSFET's parameters such as V_t, W and L etc., existed. These variations can be mathematically modeled as random variables. As an example, variation in V_t can be modeled as a random variable denoted by ΔV_t with the following variance for uniformly doped channel MOSFET [15]

$$\sigma^2_{\Delta V_t} = \frac{N_{sub} W_{dep}}{3WL} \left(\frac{q t_{inv}}{\epsilon_{ox}} \right)^2. \tag{9}$$

Of course, ΔV_t and other variations which are also random variables e.g. ΔW, ΔL and so on, induce randomly varied C_g and f_T denoted by $C_g(\Delta V_t, \Delta W, \Delta L, \ldots)$ and $f_T(\Delta V_t, \Delta W, \Delta L, \ldots)$ respectively. So, variations in C_g and f_T which are denoted by ΔC_g and Δf_T respectively, can be mathematically defined as

$$\Delta C_g \triangleq C_g(\Delta V_t, \Delta W, \Delta L, \ldots) - C_g, \tag{10}$$

$$\Delta f_T \triangleq f_T(\Delta V_t, \Delta W, \Delta L, \ldots) - f_T. \tag{11}$$

By using Eq. (7) and Eq. (10), ΔC_g can be given based on NMOS and PMOS technology as ΔC_{gN} and ΔC_{gP} respectively. On the other hand, Δf_T can be respectively given based on NMOS and PMOS technology by using Eq. (8) and Eq. (11) as Δf_{TN} and Δf_{TP}. After performing the analysis by mathematical formulations and approximations of various random variations in MOSFET's parameters, ΔC_{gN}, ΔC_{gP}, Δf_{TN} and Δf_{TP} can be analytically given as in Eq. (12), Eq. (13), Eq. (14) and Eq. (15), where N_a, N_d and V_{sb} denote acceptor doping density, donor doping density and source to body voltage respectively.

$$\Delta C_{gN} = 2 \left[\sqrt{\frac{W}{C_{dep}}} \frac{LC_{ox}}{kT/q} \right]^2 \left[\exp\left[-\frac{V_{ds}}{kT/q} \right] - 1 \right]^{-1} \cdot \left[V_{gs} - V_{FB} - 2\phi_F - C_{ox}^{-1}\sqrt{2q\epsilon_{Si}N_a(2\phi_F + V_{sb})} \right]$$
$$\cdot \left[V_t - V_{FB} - 2\phi_F - C_{ox}^{-1}\sqrt{2q\epsilon_{Si}N_a(2\phi_F + V_{sb})} \right]. \tag{12}$$

$$\Delta C_{gP} = 2 \left[\sqrt{\frac{W}{C_{dep}}} \frac{LC_{ox}}{kT/q} \right]^2 \left[\exp\left[-\frac{V_{ds}}{kT/q} \right] - 1 \right]^{-1} \cdot \left[V_{gs} - V_{FB} + |2\phi_F| + C_{ox}^{-1}\sqrt{2q\epsilon_{Si}N_d(|2\phi_F| - V_{sb})} \right]$$
$$\cdot \left[V_t - V_{FB} + |2\phi_F| + C_{ox}^{-1}\sqrt{2q\epsilon_{Si}N_d(|2\phi_F| - V_{sb})} \right]. \tag{13}$$

$$\Delta f_{TN} = \frac{\mu C_{dep}^2 (kT/q)^3 \left[1 - \exp\left[-\frac{V_{ds}}{kT/q} \right] \right]^2}{\pi n L^3 C_{ox}^2 (V_{gs} - V_{FB} - 2\phi_F - C_{ox}^{-1}\sqrt{2q\epsilon_{Si}N_a(2\phi_F + V_{sb})})^3}$$
$$\cdot (V_{FB} + 2\phi_F + C_{ox}^{-1}\sqrt{2q\epsilon_{Si}N_a(2\phi_F + V_{sb})} - V_t)^{-1}. \tag{14}$$

$$\Delta f_{TP} = \frac{\mu C_{dep}^2 (kT/q)^3 \left[1 - \exp\left[-\frac{V_{ds}}{kT/q} \right] \right]^2}{\pi n L^3 C_{ox}^2 (V_{gs} - V_{FB} + |2\phi_F| + C_{ox}^{-1}\sqrt{2q\epsilon_{Si}N_d(|2\phi_F| + V_{sb})})^3}$$
$$\cdot (V_{FB} - |2\phi_F| + C_{ox}^{-1}\sqrt{2q\epsilon_{Si}N_d(|2\phi_F| + V_{sb})} - V_t)^{-1}. \tag{15}$$

Since these variations are random variables i.e. they are nondeterministic, it is reasonable to analyze their behaviors via their statistical parameters which variance has been chosen as it is a most convenience one. By using the up to dated comprehensive analytical model of statistical variation in MOSFET's parameter [15] as the basis without uniform channel doping profile assumption i.e. the MOSFET's channel doping profile can be non-uniform which is often in practice, the variances of these variations can be analytically formulated via statistical mathematic based analysis as

$$\sigma^2_{\Delta C_{gN}} = \frac{4q^2 N_{eff} W_{dep} L}{3C_{dep}(kT/q)^2} \left[\exp\left[-\frac{V_{ds}}{kT/q} \right] - 1 \right]^{-2} \cdot \frac{V_t \left[V_{gs} - V_{FB} - 2\phi_F - C_{ox}^{-1}\sqrt{2q\epsilon_{Si}N_a(2\phi_F + V_{sb})} \right]^2}{V_{FB} + 2\phi_F + C_{ox}^{-1}\sqrt{2q\epsilon_{Si}N_a(2\phi_F + V_{sb})}}, \tag{16}$$

$$\sigma^2_{\Delta C_{gP}} = \frac{4q^2 N_{eff} W_{dep} L}{3 C_{dep}(kT/q)^2} \left[\exp\left[-\frac{V_{ds}}{kT/q} \right] - 1 \right]^{-2}$$
$$\cdot \frac{V_t \left[V_{gs} - V_{FB} + |2\phi_F| + C_{ox}^{-1} \sqrt{2q\epsilon_{Si} N_d(2|\phi_F| - V_{sb})} \right]^2}{V_{FB} - 2|\phi_F| - C_{ox}^{-1} \sqrt{2q\epsilon_{Si} N_d(2|\phi_F| - V_{sb})}},$$
(17)

$$\sigma^2_{\Delta f_{TN}} = \frac{V_t q^2 \mu^2 N_{eff} W_{dep} C_{dep}^4 (kT/q)^6 \left[1 - \exp\left[-\frac{V_{ds}}{kT/q} \right] \right]^4}{3\pi^2 n^2 W L^7 C_{ox}^6 \left[V_{FB} + 2\phi_F + C_{ox}^{-1} \sqrt{2q\epsilon_{Si} N_a(2\phi_F + V_{sb})} \right]}$$
$$\cdot \frac{1}{(V_{gs} - V_{FB} - 2\phi_F - C_{ox}^{-1} \sqrt{2q\epsilon_{Si} N_a(2\phi_F + V_{sb})})^6},$$
(18)

$$\sigma^2_{\Delta f_{TP}} = \frac{V_t q^2 \mu^2 N_{eff} W_{dep} C_{dep}^4 (kT/q)^6 \left[1 - \exp\left[-\frac{V_{ds}}{kT/q} \right] \right]^4}{3\pi^2 n^2 W L^7 C_{ox}^6 \left[V_{FB} - |2\phi_F| - C_{ox}^{-1} \sqrt{2q\epsilon_{Si} N_d(2|\phi_F| - V_{sb})} \right]}$$
$$\cdot \frac{1}{(V_{gs} - V_{FB} + |2\phi_F| + C_{ox}^{-1} \sqrt{2q\epsilon_{Si} N_d(2|\phi_F| - V_{sb})})^6},$$
(19)

where N_{eff} denotes the effective value of the substrate doping concentration which is now depended on the channel region depth, x as the channel doping profile is non-uniform. Let such channel region depth dependent substrate doping concentration be denoted by $N_{sub}(x)$, N_{eff} can be obtained by weight averaging of $N_{sub}(x)$ as follows

$$N_{eff} = 3 \int_0^{W_{dep}} N_{sub}(x) \left(1 - \frac{x}{W_{dep}} \right)^2 \frac{dx}{W_{dep}}.$$
(20)

Here, it can be seen that Eq. (16), Eq. (17), Eq. (18) and Eq. (19) are analytical expressions in terms of many related physical level variables of MOSFET. At this point, the analysis and modeling of the random dopant fluctuation and effects of MOSFET's manufacturing process variation effects induced statistical variations in subthreshold MOSFET's C_g and f_T has been completed where as their comprehensive analytical models of have been obtained as shown in Eq. (16), Eq. (17), Eq. (18) and Eq. (19) as results. These resulting models can analytically and comprehensively describe such statistical variations as they are analytical expressions in terms of many related MOSFET's physical level variables. Unlike the previous models [13], [14] which dedicate to the strong inversion region operated transistor, these models are dedicated to the subthreshold region operated MOSFET.

By using the resulting models, the statistical relationship between ΔC_g and Δf_T of any transistor which is of either N-type or P-type, can be analyzed. In order to do so, their correlation coefficient must be determined. Let A and B be random variables, their correlation coefficient denoted by ρ_{AB} can be defined

as [18]

$$\rho_{AB} \triangleq \frac{E\left[(A - \overline{A})(B - \overline{B}) \right]}{\sqrt{\sigma_A^2} \sqrt{\sigma_B^2}}.$$
(21)

After applying the models, magnitude of the desired correlation coefficient has been found to be unity for both types of MOSFET. This means that there exists a very strong statistical relationship between ΔC_g and Δf_T of any certain device.

Furthermore, variation in any crucial parameter of any subthreshold MOSFET based VHF circuit/system can be analytically formulated by using the resulting models. As a case study, analytical formulation of variation in the resulting inductance of subthreshold MOSFET based Wu current-reuse active inductor proposed in [1] will be performed. This active inductor which its original strong inversion region operated MOSFET based version has been proposed in [19], can be depicted as follows.

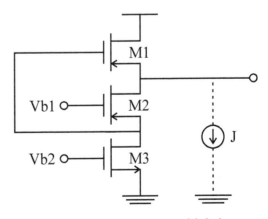

Fig. 1: Wu current-reuse active inductor [1], [19].

According to [1], the resulting inductance, L of this subthreshold MOSFET based active inductor is

$$L = \frac{C_{g1}}{g_{m1}g_{m2}}, \qquad (22)$$

where C_{g1}, g_{m1} and g_{m2} are gate capacitance of M1, transconductance of M1 and transconductance of M2 respectively.

As a result, variation in L and its variance i.e. ΔL and $\sigma^2_{\Delta L}$ can be immediately given by

$$\Delta L = \frac{\Delta C_{g1}}{g_{m1}g_{m2}}, \qquad (23)$$

$$\sigma^2_{\Delta L} = \frac{\sigma^2_{\Delta C_{g1}}}{g_{m1}g_{m2}}, \qquad (24)$$

where ΔC_{g1} and $\sigma^2_{\Delta C_{g1}}$ are a variation in C_{g1} and its variance respectively. It can be seen that $\sigma^2_{\Delta L}$ which is of our interested can be analytically formulated by using the resulting models. This is because $\sigma^2_{\Delta L}$ is a function of $\sigma^2_{\Delta C_{g1}}$ which can be determined by applying these models to M1. Moreover, it can be observed that

$$\sigma^2_{\Delta L} \; \alpha \; \sigma^2_{\Delta C_{g1}}, \qquad (25)$$

$$\sigma^2_{\Delta L} \; \alpha \; \frac{1}{g_{m1}g_{m2}}. \qquad (26)$$

This means that ΔL is related to ΔC_{g1} in a directly proportional manner, so, ΔC_{g1} should be eliminated in order to prevent the occurrence of ΔL which makes the active inductor under consideration become perfectly reliable. However, ΔC_{g1} cannot be avoided in practice. So, an alternative approach has been found to be the minimizations of g_{m1} and g_{m2}.

3.   Verification of the Results

In this section, the verification of these resulting models will be presented. The verifications of the resulting models obtained from the proposed analysis and modeling have been performed at the nanometer level based on 65 nm level CMOS process technology. The 65 nm level parameterized model based absolute standard deviations of ΔC_{gN}, ΔC_{gP}, Δf_{TN} and Δf_{TP} denoted by $|\sigma_{\Delta C_{gN}}|_M$, $|\sigma_{\Delta C_{gP}}|_M$, $|\sigma_{\Delta f_{TN}}|_M$ and $|\sigma_{\Delta f_{TP}}|_M$ respectively, have been graphically compared to their 65 nm level BSIM4 (SPICE LEVEL 54) based benchmarks which are respectively denoted by $|\sigma_{\Delta C_{gN}}|_B$, $|\sigma_{\Delta C_{gP}}|_B$, $|\sigma_{\Delta f_{TN}}|_B$ and $|\sigma_{\Delta f_{TP}}|_B$. It should be mentioned here that all necessary parameters have been provided by Predictive Technology Model (PTM) [20]. Furthermore, all absolute standard deviations are expressed in percentages of their corresponding nominal parameter values. Finally, W/L has been chosen to be 100/9.

The comparative plots of the resulting model based absolute standard deviations and their benchmarks against $|V_{GS}|$ are shown in Fig. 2, Fig. 3, Fig. 4 and Fig. 5 respectively where the minimum value of $|V_{GS}|$ is 0 V and the maximum value is 0.1 V which is well below

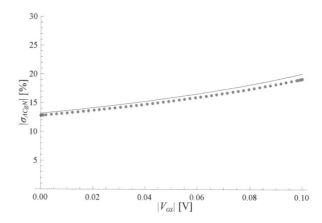

Fig. 2: NMOS based $|\sigma_{\Delta Cg}|_M$ (line) v.s. $|\sigma_{\Delta Cg}|_B$ (dot).

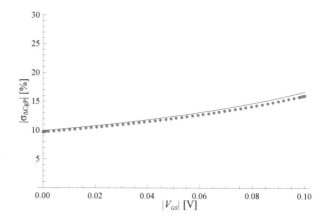

Fig. 3: PMOS based $|\sigma_{\Delta Cg}|_M$ (line) v.s. $|\sigma_{\Delta Cg}|_B$ (dot).

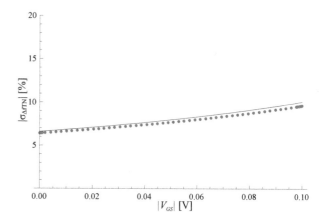

Fig. 4: NMOS based $|\sigma_{\Delta fT}|_M$ (line) v.s. $|\sigma_{\Delta fT}|_B$ (dot).

the nominal magnitude of V_t of both NMOS and PMOS transistors at 65 nm level for ensuring the subthreshold region operations. Obviously, strong agreements between the model based absolute standard deviations and their BSIM4 based benchmarks can be observed. Furthermore, it can also be seen that absolute standard deviations of ΔC_{gP} and Δf_{TP} are respectively smaller than those of ΔC_{gN} and Δf_{TN} for all values of $|V_{GS}|$. This means that C_g and f_T of P-type MOSFET is more robust to the random dopant fluctuation and effects of variations in the manufacturing process of MOSFET than those of N-type device.

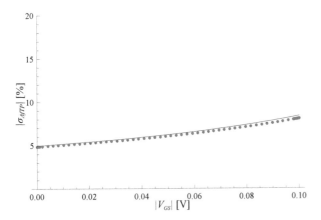

Fig. 5: PMOS based $|\sigma_{\Delta fT}|_M$ (line) v.s. $|\sigma_{\Delta fT}|_B$ (dot).

As the quantitative figure of merits of the resulting models, the average percentages of errors i.e. $\epsilon_{\Delta C_{gN},avr}$, $\epsilon_{\Delta C_{gP},avr}$, $\epsilon_{\Delta f_{TN},avr}$ and $\epsilon_{\Delta f_{TP},avr}$, have been evaluated from their corresponding comparative plots. These average percentages of errors can be generally denoted by $\epsilon_{\Delta\nu,avr}$ where $\{\Delta\nu\} = \{\Delta C_{gN}, \Delta f_{TN}, \Delta C_{gP}, \Delta f_{TP}\}$. Obviously, $\epsilon_{\Delta\nu,avr}$ can be given in terms of $|\sigma_{\Delta\nu}|_{M,i}$ and $|\sigma_{\Delta\nu}|_{B,i}$ which denote the value of $|\sigma_{\Delta\nu}|_M$ and $|\sigma_{\Delta\nu}|_B$ at any i^{th} data point respectively as follows

$$\epsilon_{\Delta\nu,avr} \triangleq \frac{1}{N_{\Delta\nu}} \sum_{i=1}^{N_{\Delta\nu}} \left[\left| \frac{|\sigma_{\Delta\nu}|_{M,i} - |\sigma_{\Delta\nu}|_{B,i}}{|\sigma_{\Delta\nu}|_{B,i}} \right| \cdot 100 \right], \quad (27)$$

where $N_{\Delta\nu}$ denotes the number of the uniformly distributed sampled data points of each of the comparative plots which is equal to each other.

With Eq. (27), it has been found that $\epsilon_{\Delta C_{gN},avr} = 3.82873$ %, $\epsilon_{\Delta C_{gP},avr} = 3.15939$ %, $\epsilon_{\Delta f_{TN},avr} = 3.7344$ % and $\epsilon_{\Delta f_{TP},avr} = 3.02822$ % which are considerably small as they are lower than 5 %. According to these pleasant quantitative figures of merits and the strong agreements seen in the comparative plots, it can be stated that the proposed analysis and modeling yield highly accurate results. Since the presented verification has been performed based on 65 nm level technology, the resulting models are obviously applicable to MOSFET in nanometer regime such as 65 nm etc.

In the subsequent section, interesting applications of these resulting models apart from those aforementioned will be shown.

4.   Applications of the Results

The results obtained from the proposed analysis and modeling have various interesting applications as follows.

4.1.   Motivation of the Effective Statistical and Variability Aware Designing Strategies

The effective statistical and variability aware designing strategies of the subthreshold MOSFET based VHF circuits, systems and applications can be obtained by using these resulting models. As a simple example, it can be seen from these models shown in Eq. (16), Eq. (17), Eq. (18) and Eq. (19) that

$$\sigma^2_{\Delta C_g} \, \alpha \, L, \qquad (28)$$

$$\sigma^2_{\Delta f_T} \, \alpha \, L^{-7}, \qquad (29)$$

where $\{\sigma^2_{\Delta C_g}, \sigma^2_{\Delta f_T}\}$ can be either $\{\sigma^2_{\Delta C_g N}, \sigma^2_{\Delta f_T N}\}$ or $\{\sigma^2_{\Delta C_g P}, \sigma^2_{\Delta f_T P}\}$ up to the type of MOSFET under consideration. So, it can be seen that even though the shrinking of gate length can reduce the ΔC_g, higher degree of increasing in Δf_T has been found to be a penalty. So, this trade-off issue must be taken into account in the designing of subthreshold region operated MOSFET based high frequency applications for any transistor type. For the statistical/variability aware design involving strong inversion region operated MOSFET, a similar trade-off can also be found since it can be seen from [14] which is dedicated to the MOSFET operated in this region that $\sigma^2_{\Delta C_g} \, \alpha \, L$ and $\sigma^2_{\Delta f_T} \, \alpha \, L^{-7}$. So, for the MOSFET of this region, shrinking of the gate length can reduce the ΔC_g with a higher degree of increasing in Δf_T as a penalty as well. However, it can be seen that such increasing in Δf_T is not as severe as that of the subthreshold MOSFET.

Let us turn our attention back to the subthreshold MOSFET which of our interested. It can also be seen from the resulting models that

$$\sigma^2_{\Delta C_g} \, \alpha \, T^{-2}, \qquad (30)$$

$$\sigma^2_{\Delta f_T} \, \alpha \, T^{-6}. \qquad (31)$$

It means that Δf_T is low and ΔC_g is high if the temperature is low and vice versa for high temperature. However, the rate of change in Δf_T to the temperature is greater than that of ΔC_g. Of course, this issue should be considered as well.

4.2. Bases of Subthreshold MOSFET's High Frequency Performances Optimization

The objective functions of subthreshold MOSFET's high frequency performances optimization scheme can be simply derived by using these models as bases. As an example, if such optimization scheme is of the multi objective type it may employ the following objective functions

$$\min[\sigma^2_{\Delta C_g}], \tag{32}$$

$$\min[\sigma^2_{\Delta f_T}], \tag{33}$$

where $\{\sigma^2_{\Delta C_g}, \sigma^2_{\Delta f_T}\}$ can be either $\{\sigma^2_{\Delta C_g N}, \sigma^2_{\Delta f_T N}\}$ or $\{\sigma^2_{\Delta C_g P}, \sigma^2_{\Delta f_T P}\}$ up to the type of MOSFET under consideration.

4.3. Bases of Analysis and Modeling of Variation in any High Frequency Parameter

The analysis and comprehensive analytical modeling of random dopant fluctuation and effects of manufacturing process variation induced statistical variation in any high frequency parameter of subthrehsold MOSFET, can be performed based on the resulting models where variance of such variation will be obtained as a result. In order to do so, let such high frequency parameter and its variation be denoted by X. Variation in X denoted by ΔX can be given in terms of ΔC_g and Δf_T as

$$\Delta X = \left(\frac{\partial X}{\partial C_g}\right)\Delta C_g + \left(\frac{\partial X}{\partial f_T}\right)\Delta f_T. \tag{34}$$

So, its variance i.e. $\sigma^2_{\Delta X}$ which is the desired result can be analytically given based on the already analyzed strong statistical relationship between ΔC_g and Δf_T as follows

$$\sigma^2_{\Delta X} = \left(\frac{\partial X}{\partial C_g}\right)^2 \sigma^2_{\Delta C_g} + \left(\frac{\partial X}{\partial f_T}\right)^2 \sigma^2_{\Delta f_T}$$
$$+ 2\left(\frac{\partial X}{\partial C_g}\right)\left(\frac{\partial X}{\partial f_T}\right)\sqrt{\sigma^2_{\Delta C_G} \sigma^2_{\Delta f_T}}. \tag{35}$$

Since $\{\sigma^2_{\Delta C_g}, \sigma^2_{\Delta f_T}\}$ can be either $\{\sigma^2_{\Delta C_g N}, \sigma^2_{\Delta f_T N}\}$ or $\{\sigma^2_{\Delta C_g P}, \sigma^2_{\Delta f_T P}\}$, and can be determined by using the resulting models. It should be mentioned here that both derivatives must be determined with regard to type of the transistor under consideration.

As an example, bandwidth, f_{BW} which is an often cited high frequency parameter will be considered. Obviously, f_{BW} can be given in term of gain, A and f_T by

$$f_{BW} = A^{-1}f_T. \tag{36}$$

By using the outlined principle, variation in f_{BW} and its variance i.e. Δf_{BW} and $\sigma^2_{\Delta f_{BW}}$ can be given as follows

$$\Delta f_{BW} = A^{-1}\Delta f_T, \tag{37}$$

$$\sigma^2_{\Delta f_{BW}} = A^{-2}\sigma^2_{\Delta f_T}, \tag{38}$$

where $\sigma^2_{\Delta f_T}$ can be determined by using the resulting models.

If a broader frequency spectrum must be considered i.e. a frequency parameter which is higher than f_T is of interested, the maximum oscillation frequency, $f_{\max}$ has been found to be a convenient one. According to [21], $f_{\max}$ can be given as a function of C_g and f_T under the assumption that C_g is equally divided between drain and source as

$$f_{\max} = \sqrt{\frac{f_T}{4\pi R_g C_g}}, \tag{39}$$

where R_g denotes the gate resistance of gate metallization [21] which belonged to the extrinsic part of MOSFET [22]. With the outlined principle, variation in $f_{\max}$ and its variance i.e. $\Delta f_{\max}$ and $\sigma^2_{\Delta f_{\max}}$ can be given by

$$\Delta f_{\max} = \frac{0.25}{\sqrt{\pi R_g}}\left[-\sqrt{\frac{f_T}{C_g^3}}\Delta C_g + \sqrt{\frac{1}{C_g f_T}}\Delta f_T\right], \tag{40}$$

$$\sigma^2_{\Delta f_{\max}} = \frac{0.0625 f_T}{\pi R_g C_g^3}\sigma^2_{\Delta C_g} + \frac{0.0625}{\pi R_g C_g f_T}\sigma^2_{\Delta f_T}$$
$$- \frac{0.125}{\pi R_g}\sqrt{\frac{\sigma^2_{\Delta C_g}\sigma^2_{\Delta f_T}}{C_g^3}}, \tag{41}$$

where C_g, f_T and R_g refer to their corresponding nominal values. Furthermore, $\sigma^2_{\Delta C_g}$ and $\sigma^2_{\Delta f_T}$ can be determined by the resulting models as usual.

4.4. Bases of Reduced Computational Effort Simulation of VHF Circuits, Systems and Applications

These resulting models can be mathematical bases of reduced computational effort simulation of the random dopant fluctuation and manufacturing process variation affected subthreshold MOSFET based VHF circuits, systems and applications because the standard deviation of the interested parameter of the simulated VHF circuit or system or application which is the desired outcome is a function of $\sigma^2_{\Delta C_g}$ and/or $\sigma^2_{\Delta f_T}$ which can be defined by the resulting models. If we let such interested parameter of the simulated circuit or system or application be denoted by Y, its standard deviation i.e. σ_Y can be given for any circuit or system or application with M MOSFETs as

$$\sigma_Y = \left[\sum_{i=1}^{M}\left[\left(S_{C_g}^Y|_i\right)^2\sigma_{\Delta C_g,i}^2 + \left(S_{f_T}^Y|_i\right)^2\sigma_{\Delta f_T,i}^2\right] + \sum_{\substack{i=1\\i\neq 1}}^{M}\sum_{i=1}^{M}\left[\left(S_{C_g}^Y|_i\right)\left(S_{C_g}^Y|_j\right)\rho_{\Delta C_g,i,\Delta C_g,j}\sqrt{\sigma_{\Delta C_g,i}^2}\sqrt{\sigma_{\Delta C_g,j}^2}\right.\right. \quad (42)$$

$$\left.\left. + \left(S_{f_T}^Y|_i\right)\left(S_{f_T}^Y|_j\right)\rho_{\Delta f_T,i,\Delta f_T,j}\sqrt{\sigma_{\Delta f_T,i}^2}\sqrt{\sigma_{\Delta f_T,j}^2}\right] + 2\sum_{i=1}^{M}\sum_{j=1}^{M}\left[\left(S_{C_g}^Y|_i\right)\left(S_{f_T}^Y|_j\right)\rho_{\Delta C_g,i,\Delta f_T,j}\sqrt{\sigma_{\Delta C_g,i}^2}\sqrt{\sigma_{\Delta f_T,j}^2}\right]\right]^{\frac{1}{2}},$$

where $\rho_{\Delta C_g,i,\Delta C_g,j}$, $\rho_{\Delta f_T,i,\Delta f_T,j}$ and $\rho_{\Delta C_g,i,\Delta f_T,j}$ denotes the correlation coefficient between ΔC_g of ith and j^{th} MOSFET, the similar quantity for Δf_T and the correlation coefficient between ΔC_g of ith MOSFET and Δf_T of jth MOSFET respectively. It should be mentioned here that the magnitude of $\rho_{\Delta C_g,i,\Delta f_T,j}$ can be approximated by unity when $i = j$. Furthermore, $\sigma_{\Delta C_g,i}^2$ and $\sigma_{\Delta f_T,i}^2$ denote $\sigma_{\Delta C_g}^2$ and $\sigma_{\Delta f_T}^2$ of ith MOSFET which can be either $\{\sigma_{\Delta C_{gN}}^2,\sigma_{\Delta f_{TN}}^2\}$ or $\{\sigma_{\Delta C_{gP}}^2,\sigma_{\Delta f_{TP}}^2\}$ where $\sigma_{\Delta C_g,j}^2$ and $\sigma_{\Delta f_T,j}^2$ stand for $\sigma_{\Delta C_g}^2$ and $\sigma_{\Delta f_T}^2$ of jth transistor which can be either $\{\sigma_{\Delta C_{gN}}^2,\sigma_{\Delta f_{TN}}^2\}$ or $\{\sigma_{\Delta C_{gP}}^2,\sigma_{\Delta f_{TP}}^2\}$ as well. Finally, $S_{C_g}^Y|_i$, $S_{C_g}^Y|_j$, $S_{f_T}^Y|_i$, and $S_{f_T}^Y|_j$ denote the sensitivity of Y to C_g of ith MOSFET, that to C_g of jth MOSFET, one to f_T of ith MOSFET and that to f_T of jth MOSFET respectively.

Obviously, $S_{C_g}^Y|_i$, $S_{C_g}^Y|_j$, $S_{f_T}^Y|_i$, and $S_{f_T}^Y|_j$ can be computationally determined via an efficient methodology entitled sensitivity analysis which has much lower computational effort than Monte-Carlo simulation based on the random variations of MOSFET's parameters such as V_t, W and L etc., since the simulated circuit is needed to be solved only once for obtaining these necessary sensitivities [20] then σ_Y can be immediately evaluated by using these sensitivities and the resulting models as shown in Eq. (42). On the other hand, Monte-Carlo simulation requires numerous runs in order to reach the similar outcome [23]. So, much of the computational effort can be significantly reduced by applying the resulting models and sensitivity analysis.

4.5. Bases of Analytical Modelling and Analysis of Mismatches in High Frequency Characteristics

The resulting model can be the mathematical bases of the analytical modeling and analysis of mismatches in high frequency characteristics of theoretically identical subthreshold MOSFETs even these models are dedicated to a single device. As simple illustrations, mismatches in C_g and f_T between theoretically identical MOSFETs indexed by i and j denoted by δC_{gij} and δf_{Tij} respectively will be considered.

As the analysis of any mismatch in MOSFET can be conveniently performed by using its variance [24], [25], the analysis of δC_{gij} and δf_{Tij} will be performed

in this manner. Let the variances of δC_{gij} and δf_{Tij} be denoted by $\sigma_{\delta C_{gij}}^2$ and $\sigma_{\delta f_{Tij}}^2$ respectively, the analytical model of can be given in terms of $\sigma_{\Delta C_{gi}}^2$ and $\sigma_{\Delta C_{gj}}^2$ as

$$\sigma_{\delta C_{gij}}^2 = \sigma_{\Delta C_g,i}^2 + \sigma_{\Delta C_g,j}^2 - 2\rho_{\Delta C_g,i,\Delta C_g,j}\sigma_{\Delta C_g,i}\sigma_{\Delta C_g,j}. \quad (43)$$

On the other hand, that of $\sigma_{\delta f_{Tij}}^2$ can be expressed in the similar manner in terms of $\sigma_{\Delta f_{Ti}}^2$ and $\sigma_{\Delta f_{Tj}}^2$ as follows

$$\sigma_{\delta f_{Tij}}^2 = \sigma_{\Delta f_T,i}^2 + \sigma_{\Delta f_T,j}^2 - 2\rho_{\Delta f_T,i,\Delta f_T,j}\sigma_{\Delta f_T,i}\sigma_{\Delta f_T,j}. \quad (44)$$

It can be immediately seen that the analytical modeling of $\sigma_{\delta C_{gij}}^2$ can be performed by using $\sigma_{\Delta C_{gi}}^2$ and $\sigma_{\Delta C_{gj}}^2$. On the other hand, that of $\sigma_{\delta f_{Tij}}^2$ can be done by using $\sigma_{\Delta f_{Ti}}^2$ and $\sigma_{\Delta f_{Tj}}^2$. By using the obtained models of $\sigma_{\delta C_{gij}}^2$ and $\sigma_{\delta f_{Tij}}^2$, δC_{gij} and δf_{Tij} can be conveniently analyzed. Since the resulting models of this research define $\sigma_{\Delta C_{gi}}^2$, $\sigma_{\Delta C_{gj}}^2$, $\sigma_{\Delta f_{Ti}}^2$ and $\sigma_{\Delta f_{Tj}}^2$ as aforementioned, they also define and serve as the mathematical bases of analytical modeling of $\sigma_{\delta C_{gij}}^2$ and $\sigma_{\delta f_{Tij}}^2$ which yields the convenient analysis of δC_{gij} and δf_{Tij}. The examples of such analysis can be given as follows. As the correlation between closely spaced MOSFETs is very strong [24], [25], $\sigma_{\delta C_{gij}}^2$ and $\sigma_{\delta f_{Tij}}^2$ for closely spaced and positively correlated devices can be given by

$$\sigma_{\delta C_{gij}}^2 = \sigma_{\Delta C_g,i}^2 + \sigma_{\Delta C_g,j}^2 - 2\sigma_{\Delta C_g,i}\sigma_{\Delta C_g,j}, \quad (45)$$

$$\sigma_{\delta f_{Tij}}^2 = \sigma_{\Delta f_T,i}^2 + \sigma_{\Delta f_T,j}^2 - 2\sigma_{\Delta f_T,i}\sigma_{\Delta f_T,j}. \quad (46)$$

For closely spaced devices with negative correlation hand, $\sigma_{\delta C_{gij}}^2$ and $\sigma_{\delta f_{Tij}}^2$ can be determined as

$$\sigma_{\delta C_{gij}}^2 = \sigma_{\Delta C_g,i}^2 + \sigma_{\Delta C_g,j}^2 + 2\sigma_{\Delta C_g,i}\sigma_{\Delta C_g,j}, \quad (47)$$

$$\sigma_{\delta f_{Tij}}^2 = \sigma_{\Delta f_T,i}^2 + \sigma_{\Delta f_T,j}^2 + 2\sigma_{\Delta f_T,i}\sigma_{\Delta f_T,j}. \quad (48)$$

Since δC_{gij} and δf_{Tij} are respectively directly proportional to $\sigma_{\delta C_{gij}}^2$ and $\sigma_{\delta f_{Tij}}^2$, it can be observed from Eq. (45), Eq. (46), Eq. (47) and Eq. (48) that δC_{gij} and δf_{Tij} are maximized when MOSFETs are closely spaced with negative correlation and minimized for those closely spaced and positively correlated devices.

Now, distanced MOSFETs will be considered. For such devices, $\sigma^2_{\delta C_{gij}}$ and $\sigma^2_{\delta f_{Tij}}$ become

$$\sigma^2_{\delta C_{gij}} = \sigma^2_{\Delta C_{g,i}} + \sigma^2_{\Delta C_{g,j}}, \qquad (49)$$

$$\sigma^2_{\delta f_{Tij}} = \sigma^2_{\Delta f_{T,i}} + \sigma^2_{\Delta f_{T,j}}. \qquad (50)$$

This is because the correlation between distanced devices can be neglected as it is very weak [24] so, it cannot affect δC_{gij} and δf_{Tij} as can be seen from Eq. (49) and Eq. (50) which have no correlation related terms.

If it is assumed that all transistors under consideration are statistically identical i.e. $\sigma^2_{\Delta C_{g,i}} = \sigma^2_{\Delta C_{g,j}} = \sigma^2_{\Delta C_g}$ and $\sigma^2_{\Delta f_{T,i}} = \sigma^2_{\Delta f_{T,j}} = \sigma^2_{\Delta f_T}$ where $\{\sigma^2_{\Delta C_g}, \sigma^2_{\Delta f_T}\}$ can be either $\{\sigma^2_{\Delta C_{gN}}, \sigma^2_{\Delta f_{TN}}\}$ or $\{\sigma^2_{\Delta C_{gP}}, \sigma^2_{\Delta f_{TP}}\}$ as usual, $\sigma^2_{\delta C_{gij}}$ and $\sigma^2_{\delta f_{Tij}}$ can be simplified as follows

$$\sigma^2_{\delta C_{gij}} = 2\sigma^2_{\Delta C_g}(1 - 2\rho_{\Delta C_{g,i}, \Delta C_{g,j}}), \qquad (51)$$

$$\sigma^2_{\delta f_{Tij}} = 2\sigma^2_{\Delta f_T}(1 - 2\rho_{\Delta f_{T,i}, \Delta f_{T,j}}). \qquad (52)$$

Obviously, $\sigma^2_{\delta C_{gij}}$ and $\sigma^2_{\delta f_{Tij}}$ for closely spaced and positively correlated devices can be approximated as $\sigma^2_{\delta C_{gij}} = 0$ and $\sigma^2_{\delta f_{Tij}} = 0$. This means that δC_{gij} and δf_{Tij} for statistically identical, closely spaced and positively correlated devices can be neglected.

5.   Conclusion

In this research, the analysis of statistical variations in subthreshold MOSFET's C_g and f_T, have been shown. As a result, the comprehensive analytical models of these variations in terms of their variances have been proposed. Both random dopant fluctuation and effects of variations in MOSFET's manufacturing process have been taken into account in the proposed analysis and modeling. The up to dated comprehensive analytical model of statistical variation in MOSFET's parameter [15] has been adopted as the basis. The resulting models have been found to be very accurate according to their pleasant verification results with less than 5 % average percentages of errors. They also have various applications for examples analytical study of random variation in crucial parameter of subthreshold MOSFET based VHF circuit/system e.g. variation in L of subthreshold MOSFET based Wu current-reuse active inductor [1] etc., and being the mathematical basis for various interesting tasks such as the optimization of subthreshold MOSFET's high frequency characteristic, analytical modeling of the mismatches in these characteristics and sensitivity analysis based simulation of any VHF circuit, system and application involving subthreshold MOSFET which is be more computationally efficient than the Monte-Carlo simulation

[23], etc. Hence, the analysis and modeling proposed in this research gives the results which have been found to be the convenient analytical tool for the statistical and variability aware analysis and design of various subthreshold MOSFET based VHF circuits, systems and applications.

Acknowledgment

The author would like to acknowledge Mahidol University, Thailand for online database service.

References

[1] YUSHI, Z. and F. YUAN. Subthreshold CMOS active inductor with applications to low-power injection-locked oscillators for passive wireless Microsystems. In: *53rd IEEE International Midwest Symposium on Circuits and System (MWSCAS), 2010.* Seattle: IEEE, 2010, pp. 885–888. ISBN 978-1-4244-7771-5. DOI: 10.1109/MWSCAS.2010.5548661.

[2] BEVIN, G., P., R. MUKHOPADHYAY, S. CHAKRABORTY, C.-H. LEE and J. LASKAR. A Low Power Fully Monolithic Subthreshold CMOS Receiver with Integrated LO Generation for 2.4 GHz Wireless PAN Application. *IEEE Journal of Solid-State Circuits.* 2008, vol. 43, iss. 10, pp. 2229–2238. ISSN 0018-9200. DOI: 10.1109/JSSC.2008.2004330.

[3] BEVIN G., P., S. CHAKRABORTY, C.-H. LEE and J. LASKAR. A Fully Monolithic 260-μW, 1-GHz Subthreshold Low Noise Amplifier. *IEEE Microwave and Wireless Components Letters.* 2005, vol. 15, iss. 6, pp. 428–430. ISSN 1531-1309. DOI: 10.1109/LMWC.2005.850563.

[4] HANIL, L. and S. MOHAMMADI. A 3GHz Subthreshold CMOS Low Noise Amplifier. In: *IEEE Radio Frequency Integrated Circuits (RFIC) Symposium, 2006.* San Francisco: IEEE, 2006, pp. 494–497. ISBN 0-7803-9572-7. DOI: 10.1109/RFIC.2006.1651199.

[5] SEONGDO, K., J. CHOI, J. LEE, B. KOO, C. KIM, N. EUM, H. YU and H. JUNG. A Subthreshold CMOS Front-End Design for Low-Power Band-III T-DMB/DAB Recievers. *ETRI Journal.* 2011, vol. 33, no. 6, pp. 969–972. ISSN 1225-6463. DOI: 10.4218/etrij.11.0211.0055.

[6] HIROO, M., T. KIDA and S.-I OHKAWA. Comprehensive Matching Characterization of Analog CMOS Circuits. *IEICE Transaction on Fundamentals of Electronics, Communications and*

Computer Sciences. 2009, vol. E92-A, no. 4, pp. 966–975. ISSN 0916-8508. DOI: 10.1587/transfun.E92.A.966.

[7] RAWID, B. Process Induced Random Variation models of Nanoscale MOS Performance: Efficient Tool for The Nanoscale Regime Analog/Mixed Signal CMOS Statistical/Variability Aware Design. In: *International Conference on Information and Electronics Engineering 2011.* Bangkok: IACSIT Press, 2011, pp. 6–12. ISBN 978-981-08-8637-0.

[8] RAWID, B. Complete Circuit Level Random Variation Models of Nanoscale MOS Performance. *International Journal of Information and Electronic Engineering.* 2011, vol. 1, iss. 1, pp. 9–15. ISSN 2010-3719. DOI: 10.7763/IJIEE.2011.V1.2.

[9] LU, W. and S. LING LING. Modeling of Current Mismatch Induced by Random Dopant Fluctuation. *Journal of Semiconductors.* 2011, vol. 32, iss. 8, pp. 1–6. ISSN 1674-4926. DOI: 10.1088/1674-4926/32/8/084003.

[10] KOSTAS, P. A Designer's Approach to Device Mismatch: Theory, Modeling, Simulation Techniques, Scripting, Applications and Examples. *Analog Integrated Circuits and Signal Processing.* 2006, vol. 48, iss. 2, pp. 95–106. ISSN 0925-1030. DOI: 10.1007/s10470-006-5367-2.

[11] RAJEEV, R., A. SRIVASTAVA, D. BLAAUW and D. SYLVESTER. Statistical Analysis of Subthreshold Leakage Current for VLSI Circuits. *IEEE Transactions on Very Large Scale Integration (VLSI) Systems.* 2004, vol. 12, iss. 2, pp. 131–139. ISSN 1063-8210. DOI: 10.1109/TVLSI.2003.821549.

[12] FRANCESCO, F. and M. E. WRIGHT. Measurement of MOS current mismatch in the weak inversion region. *IEEE Journal of Solid-State Circuits.* 1994, vol. 29, iss. 2, pp. 138–142. ISSN 0018-9200. DOI: 10.1109/4.272119.

[13] HAN-SU, K., C. CHUNG, J. LIM, K. PARK, H. OH and H.-K. KANG. Characterization and modeling of RF-performance (fT) fluctuation in MOSFETs. *IEEE Electron Device Letters.* 2009, vol. 30, iss. 8, pp. 855–857. ISSN 0741-3106. DOI: 10.1109/LED.2009.2023826.

[14] RAWID, B. Novel Complete Probabilistic Models of Random Variation in High Frequency Performance of Nanoscale MOSFET. *Journal of Electrical and Computer Engineering.* 2013, vol. 2013, iss. 189436, pp. 1–10. ISSN 2090-0147. DOI: 10.1155/2013/189436.

[15] KIYOSHI, T., A. NISHIDA and H. TOSHIRO. Random Fluctuations in Scaled MOS Devices. In: *International Conference on Simulation of Semiconductor Processes and Devices 2009.* San Diego: IEEE, 2009, pp. 1–7. ISBN 978-1-4244-3974-8. DOI: 10.1109/SISPAD.2009.5290243.

[16] ABEBE, H., H. MORRIS, E. CUMBERBATCH and V. TYREE. Compact Gate Capacitance Model with Polysilicon Depletion Effect for MOS Device. *Journal of Semiconductor Technology and Science.* 2007, vol. 7, no. 2, pp. 209–213. ISSN 1598-1657.

[17] HOWE, R. T. and C. G. SODINI. *Microelectronics: An Integrated Approach.* Upper Saddle River: Prentice Hall, 1996. ISBN 978-0-135-88518-5.

[18] HINES, W. W., D. C. MONTGOMERY, D. M. GOLDMAN and C. M. BORROR. *Probability and Statistics in Engineering.* 4th ed. Chichester: Wiley, 2003. ISBN 978-0-471-24087-7.

[19] YEU, W., X. DING, M. ISMAIL and H. K. OLSSON. RF bandpass filter design based on CMOS active inductors. *IEEE Transaction on Circuits and Systems II: Analog and Digital Signal Processing.* 2003, vol. 50, iss. 12, pp. 942–949. ISSN 1057-7130. DOI: 10.1109/TCSII.2003.820235.

[20] Predictive Technology Model. *Nanoscale Integration and Modeling (NIMO) Group* [online]. 2011. Available at: ptm.asu.edu.

[21] PULFREY, D. L. *Understanding Modern Transistors and Diodes.* 1st ed. Cambridge: Cambridge University press, 2010. ISBN 978-0-521-51460-6.

[22] CHENG, Y., M. J. DEEN and C.-H. CHEN. MOSFET modeling for RF IC design. *IEEE Transactions on Electron Devices.* 2005, vol. 52, iss. 7, pp. 1286–1303. ISSN 0018-9383. DOI: 10.1109/TED.2005.850656.

[23] CIJAN, G., T. TUMA and A. BURMEN. Modeling and Simulation of MOS Transistor Mismatch. In: *6th Eurosim Congress on Modeling and Simulation.* Ljubljana: ARGE Simulation News, 2007, pp. 1–8. ISBN 978-3-901608-32-2.

[24] CATHIGNOL, A., S. MENILLO, S. BORDEZ, L. VENDRAME and G. GHIBAUDO. Spacing Impact on MOSFET Mismatch. In: *IEEE International Conference on Microelectronic Test Structure 2008.* Edinburgh: IEEE, 2009, pp. 90–95. ISBN 978-1-4224-1800-8. DOI: 10.1109/ICMTS.2008.4509320.

[25] MEZZOMO, C. M., A. BAJOLET, A. CATHIGNOL, R. DI FRENZA and G. GHIBAUDO. Characterization and Modeling of Transistor

Variability in Advanced CMOS Technologies. *IEEE Transactions on Electron Devices*. 2011, vol. 58, iss. 8, pp. 2235–2248. ISSN 0018-9383. DOI: 10.1109/TED.2011.2141140.

About Authors

Rawid BANCHUIN was born in 1976. He received his Ph.D. Electrical and Computer Engineering from King Mongkut University of Technology Thonburi, Thailand in 2008. His research interests include application of fractional calculus in electrical and electronic engineering, fractional impedance, nanoscale CMOS circuits, systems and technologies, variability in CMOS circuits and systems, mathematical modeling of mixed signal circuits and systems, on-chip inductor and on-chip transformer.

24

AVAILABILITY MODEL FOR VIRTUALIZED PLATFORMS

Jiri HLAVACEK, Robert BESTAK

Department of Telecommunication Engineering, Faculty of Electrical Engineering, Czech Technical University in Prague, Technicka 2, 166 27 Prague, Czech Republic

hlavaji1@fel.cvut.cz, robert.bestak@fel.cvut.cz

Abstract. *Network virtualization is a method of providing virtual instances of physical networks. Virtualized networks are widely used with virtualized servers, forming a powerful dynamically reconfigurable platform. In this paper we discuss the impact of network virtualization on the overall system availability. We describe a system reflecting the network architecture usually deployed in today's data centres. The proposed system is modelled using Markov chains and fault trees. We compare the availability of virtualized system using standard physique network with the availability of virtualized system using virtualized network. Network virtualization introduces a new software layer to the network architecture. The proposed availability model integrates software failures in addition to the hardware failures. Based on the estimated numerical failure rates, we analyse system's availability.*

Keywords

Availability model, continuous-time Markov chains, network virtualization, server virtualization.

1. Introduction

Network virtualization [1] is a complementary technology to server virtualization. It is a software layer decoupling virtual logical networks from the network hardware. Main advantages of network virtualization are efficient use of network resources and simplification of configuration tasks by offering a unified user interface to heterogeneous network components. The hardware network infrastructure configuration and services are one of difficulties faced in today's data centres. Network virtualization significantly simplifies tasks such as network hardware configuration, dynamic adaptation of network configuration or deployment of new services.

In this paper we compare the availability of conventional non-virtualized network and a virtualized one.

Additionally, we evaluate the impact of network virtualization on the overall system availability. We use a two-level model using a fault tree for the system level modelling and a homogeneous continuous time Markov chain to model components' availability. Our model is proposed regarding network infrastructures deployed in nowadays data centres. We perform a numerical analysis allowing a comparison of the system availability values for the considered system.

The rest of this paper is organized as follows. In Section 2, we discuss related works. In Section 3, we detail the architecture of the considered system. Section 4 describes used modelling techniques. Results of numerical simulations are presented in Section 5. Finally, conclusions and future work are given in Section 6.

2. Related Work

In [2], D. S. Kim et al. compare the availability of highly available virtualized system with a non-virtualized one. The considered models are designed using a hierarchical model based on fault trees and homogeneous continuous time Markov chains. Authors show that as long as the availability of data storage system is high enough and the impact of the virtual machine monitor on the operating system's availability stays low, the steady-state availability of virtualized system is higher compared to the non-virtualized system. However, authors do not address the network virtualization process itself.

A typical enterprise server configuration is studied by L. H. S. Bomfim in [3]. The focus is on a server set hosting basic network services such as mail server and web server. A hierarchical model similar to the one proposed in [2] is considered. The impact of server virtualization on the availability is detailed. Authors show that the virtualization negatively impacts system's availability but the impact stays as low as 0,06 % of annual downtime.

A methodology to assess dependability attributes in virtualized networks is presented by S. Fernandes et al. in [4]. The result is intended as input for resource allocation techniques in virtual networks.

In [5], B. Silva et al. introduce a tool for dependability evaluation of data centre power infrastructures called ASTRO. This tool enables a hierarchical modelling of data centre systems by using reliability block diagrams and stochastic Petri nets.

Our work focuses on the impact of network virtualization on system availability. We evaluate the availability of standard network system and compare it with a system relying on a virtualized network.

3. Considered System

This section describes the analysed system. The network architecture is based on recent knowledge of data centre architecture. Considered servers are standard virtualized servers with integrated virtual network layer software.

3.1. Network Architecture

Following conclusions in [6], we take into account a switch-centric centre network architecture that is employed in majority today's data centres. Other architectures like server-centric or irregular network architecture are not considered as their practical application is marginal. The overall network architecture is depicted in Fig. 1. It is based on a recent survey of network virtualization in data centres that is presented in [7].

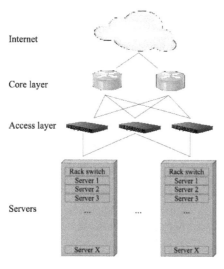

Fig. 1: Data centre network infrastructure.

The proposed architecture is composed of three parts: i) servers, ii) access layer, and iii) core layer.

Each server cabinet is equipped with a top-of-rack switch at the access level. The access level distributes data flows between different racks and the core layer. The core layer connects the data centre to the Internet and other external networks. The core level and the access level are fully redundant.

3.2. Network Virtualization

The network virtualization mechanism is based on a logical layer that is built on the top of hardware infrastructure. User data is separated by different tunnelling techniques (for more details see for example [8]). The network architecture shown in Fig. 1 doesn't address network virtualization. The virtualization layer has no impact on the physical network architecture. However, the network border equipments have to support network virtualization [9] that must be reflected in the availability model. In our configuration, the main impact is on the server's network connection and on the access router. A server connected to the virtual network runs a software component that enable connecting server's network interface to the virtual network. The access router providing outside network connectivity to the virtual network integrates an adaptation layer that ensure virtual network functions and has to run specialized software supporting virtual network capabilities. The impact of these components on the availability model is discussed in the next section. A virtual network is usually managed by an external management server. This server is not considered in our study as the server is not placed in the data flow path and its failure does not influence user's experience.

3.3. Server Configuration

There are two types of servers: i) servers hosting user's applications and ii) servers hosting virtual network access router functions.

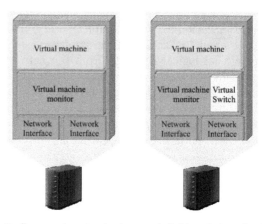

Fig. 2: Server using standard network (left) and virtualized network (right) modelling components.

Figure 2 illustrates models of two server's configurations that we design in our availability models. The first model represents a virtualized server without the network virtualization, whereas the second one includes the network virtualization layer. The network virtualization is ensured by the software package that is part of hypervisor [10]. Therefore, the virtual switch is positioned at the hypervisor level.

In our study we consider same server's architecture for both types of servers. The configuration consists of Quad-core CPU, 2 RAM modules, power supply, cooling system, motherboard, and network card. The access router server critical components (containing power supply, cooling and network cards) are redundant and therefore require specific component models.

4.   System Modelling

In this section we detail the investigated system. The general system model is represented by a fault tree in the upper level. In the lower level, we use homogeneous continuous time Markov chains to model each component.

4.1.   System Availability Model

The overall system model is adapted conforming to the objective of our work, i.e. to analyse the difference of system availability between non-virtualised and virtualised network.

The proposed fault tree is depicted in Fig. 3. Servers are composed of hardware (detailed in Fig. 4), virtual machine monitor and virtual machine operating system. A specific component called virtual switch is added when the server uses a virtualized network. This component is run by the virtual machine monitor as a kernel module [11]. Data storage is ensured by the Storage Area Network (SAN) component. As stated above, border network equipments host virtualized network components, which are included in the proposed model as well. Virtual network components are virtual switches depicted as Virtual Network Adaptors in Fig. 3. There's one on the server's side and one on the network access router's side. The access router is acting as access gateway for virtual networks. Network virtualization components are highlighted by a yellow background. These components are not considered for the non-virtualized network model. Figure 4 depicts server's hardware fault tree that we show in Fig. 3. All components in the considered system are repairable.

4.2.   Component Model

To model components, the Continuous Time Markov Models (CTMM) are used. As shown in [12] by A. Wood, these models are useful to model components availability once the burn-in period is over. Redundancy of critical components is taken into account by the component models. Used models are not presented for the sake of brevity.

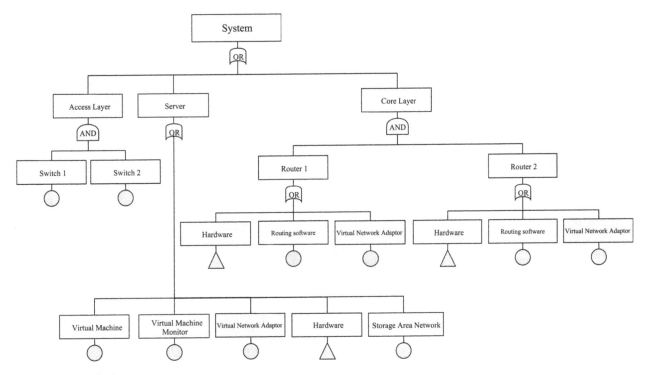

Fig. 3: System fault tree.

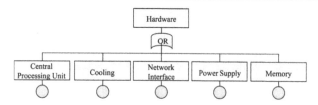

Fig. 4: System fault tree.

4.3. Numerical Results

We calculate numerical results by using a software tool called RAM Commander [13]. In the first step, we evaluate Markov chains in the steady-state to obtain the Mean Time To Failure (MTTF) and Mean Time To Repair (MTTR) values for each component model (e.g. memory component). Markov chains input data are MTTF and MTTR values of each model part (e.g. RAM module). These values are provided in manufacturer's technical documents for the given hardware components. The MTTF and MTTR of software components are much harder to obtain as there are many use scenarios and testing process would be too long. We used values found in [2] and [14]. To our best knowledge, we haven't found any values for the virtualization software layer. The MTTF and MTTR values of virtual network adaptor are estimated as follows. The estimation is based on the software's complexity, size and maturity. Virtual network adaptor is network processing software, therefore it's quite complex. It is small compared to the operating system and it's quite a new technology. Used values are described in Tab. 1.

Tab. 1: Used mean time to failure; mean time to repair values.

Component	Mean Time to Failure [hours]	Mean Time to Repair [hours]
Central Processing Unit	25 000 000	0,5
Memory	4 800 000	0,5
Network Interface Card	62 000 000	0,5
Power Supply	670 000	0,5
Cooling	3 100 000	1
Storage Area Network	20 000 000	2
Operating System	1 440	1
Linux Operating System	38 520	2
Virtual Network Adapter	2 160	0,5
Virtual Machine Monitor	2 880	1
Virtual Machine	2 880	1
Router	220 000	1
Switch	220 000	1

Outputs from Markov models serve as input values for the fault tree that is employed to calculate the overall system availability. The obtained values are given in Tab. 2. The simulations show a major impact of the network virtualization on the long-term steady-state average availability. The system built on standard network reaches four nines availability whereas the system with network virtualization only three nines availability. The network virtualization causes the system to be down almost 8 hours per year more than the standard network one.

Tab. 2: Avaliability values.

System Type	Avaliability
Standard Network Based System	0,9999104446
Virtualized Network Based System	0,999021907

The sensitivity analysis points out that the most critical components are software ones. These are not redundant and their mean time to failure is low. The impact of the network virtualization layer is reduced by redundant core network routers at the core network layer. The impact can be further reduced using a redundant server implementing the network virtualization adaptation at the access layer. However, this approach would degrade the network virtualization capabilities themselves.

5. Conclusion

In this paper we compare the availability of standard network based system with a virtual network based one. To evaluate the availability, we propose a fault tree models for these two systems. The fault tree model with continuous time Markov chain models are used to calculate the impact of network virtualization on the steady-state system availability. The results obtained via simulations show that the network virtualization based system availability is one nine lower than the system availability of standard network infrastructure. The network virtualization brings many advantages but also a perceptible impact on the system's availability. This drawback needs to be taken into account when deploying the network virtualization and defining the Service Level Agreement definition. In future work, we plan to investigate the redundant virtual network access layer in order to reduce the network virtualization's impact.

Acknowledgment

This research work was supported by the Grant Agency of the Czech Technical University in Prague, grant no. SGS13/199/OHK3/3T/13.

References

[1] WANG, A., M. IYER, R. DUTTA, G. N. ROUSKAS and I. BALDINE. Network Virtualization: Technologies, Perspectives, and Frontiers. *Journal of Lightwave Technology*. 2013,

vol. 31, no. 4, pp. 523–537. ISSN 0733-8724. DOI: 10.1109/JLT.2012.2213796.

[2] KIM, D.S., F. MACHIDA and K.S. TRIVEDI. Availability Modeling and Analysis of a Virtualized System. In: *Dependable Computing, 2009. PRDC '09. 15th IEEE Pacific Rim International Symposium*. Shanghai: IEEE, 2009. pp. 365–371. ISBN 978-0-7695-3849-5. DOI: 10.1109/PRDC.2009.64.

[3] BOMFIM, L.H.S., L.B. SILVA, R.J.P.B. SALGUEIRO and R.S. JACAUNA. Analysis of Availability of Virtualized Servers. *Scientia Plena*. 2012, vol. 8, no. 3, pp. 1–11. ISSN 1808-2793.

[4] FERNANDES, S., E. TAVARES, M. SANTOS, V. LIRA and P. MACIEL. Dependability Assessment of Virtualized Networks. In: *Communications (ICC), 2012 IEEE International Conference*. Ottawa: IEEE, 2012. pp. 2711–2716. ISSN 1550-3607. DOI: 10.1109/ICC.2012.6363992.

[5] SILVA, B., P. MACIEL, E. TAVARES, C. ARAUJO, G. CALLOU, E. SOUSA, N. ROSA, M. MARWAH, R. SHARMA, A. SHAH, T. CHRISTIAN and J.P. PIRES. ASTRO: A Tool for Dependability Evaluation of Data Center Infrastructures. In: *Systems Man and Cybernetics (SMC), 2010 IEEE International Conference*. Istanbul: IEEE, 2010. pp. 783–790. ISSN 1062-922X. DOI: 10.1109/ICSMC.2010.5641852.

[6] SUN, Y., J. CHENG, K. SHI and Q. LIU. Data Center Network Architecture. *ZTE Communications*. 2013, vol. 11, no. 1, pp. 54–61. ISSN 1673-5188.

[7] BARI, M.F., R. BOUTABA, R. ESTEVES, L.Z. GRANVILLE, M. PODLESNY, M.G. RABBANI, Q. ZHANG and M.F. ZHANI. Data Center Network Virtualization: A Survey. *IEEE Communications Surveys & Tutorials*. 2013, vol. 15, no. 2, pp. 909–928. ISSN 1553-877X. DOI: 10.1109/SURV.2012.090512.00043.

[8] WANG, A., M. IYER, R. DUTTA, G.N. ROUSKAS and I. BALDINE. Network Virtualization: Technologies, Perspectives, and Frontiers. *Journal of Lightwave Technology*. 2013, vol. 31, no. 4, pp. 523–537. ISSN 0733-8724. DOI: 10.1109/JLT.2012.2213796.

[9] NICIRA. *It is Time to Virtualize the Network (White Paper)*. Available at: http:////www.vmware.com/products/nsx/.

[10] PFAFF, B., J. PETTIT, T. KOPONEN, K. AMIDON, M. CASADO and S. SHENKER. Extending Networking into the Virtualization Layer. In: *Proceedings of workshop on Hot Topics in Networks (HotNets-VIII)*. 2009.

[11] PETTIT, J., J. GROSS, B. PFAFF and M. CASADO. Virtual Switching in an Era of Advanced Edges. In: *2nd Workshop on Data Center - Converged and Virtual Ethernet Switching (DC-CAVES)*. 2010.

[12] WOOD, A. Availability Modeling. *IEEE Circuits and Devices Magazine*. 1994, vol. 10, iss. 3, pp. 22–27. ISSN 8755-3996. DOI: 10.1109/101.283651.

[13] *Reliability, Availability, Maintainability and Safety Analysis Software - ALD Service*. Available at: http://www.aldservice.com/en/reliability-products/rams-software.html.

[14] KUMAR, S., A.K.D. DWIVEDI and A. TIWARI. Reliability Estimation and Analysis of Linux Kernel. *International Journal on Computer Science and Technology*. 2011. vol. 2, no. 2, pp. 45–51. ISSN 0976-8491.

About Authors

Jiri HLAVACEK was awarded his engineering degree after completing a double degree program at Czech Technical University (CTU) in Prague, Faculty of Electrical Engineering in the Czech Republic and at Telecom Bretagne in France in 2008. In 2007 he started a research work at the Department of telecommunication engineering, CTU in Prague. His research interests include availability of VoIP systems, software architectures of VoIP servers and system virtualization. He contributes to the development of an OpenSource VoIP solution XiVO.

Robert BESTAK received his engineering degree from the Czech Technical University in Prague, Faculty of Electrical Engineering, in 1999. Within 1999/2000, he did one-year engineering program in telecommunications and computer networks at the Institute EERIE de l'Ecole des Mines d'Ales, Nimes, France. In 2003, he received his Ph.D. degree in computer science from ENST Paris, France. Since 2004, he works as a researcher at the Department of telecommunication engineering, CTU in Prague. Since 2006, he heads wireless research group at the department. His research interests include RRM techniques in HSPA/LTE systems and multi-hop networks. He participated in EU FP projects ALLIPRO, FIREWORKS and he currently participates in EU FP7 project ROCKET. He has been involved in several R&D Centre projects.

25

JITTER ELIMINATION AT OPTICAL CONTROL OF SERVOMOTORS

Radek NOVAK, Karel WITAS

Department of Telecommunications, Faculty of Electrical Engineering and Computer Science,
VSB–Technical University of Ostrava, 17. Listopadu 15/2172, 708 33 Ostrava, Czech Republic

radek.novak@vsb.cz, karel.witas@vsb.cz

Abstract. *The article describes the application of microcontroller PIC18F25K22 to servomechanism electronics built – in the model of car. Model is controlled optically, in the infrared part of the spectrum. Used microcontroller is optimal for this application – it has timers with capture facilities, sufficient number of PWMs, powerfull instruction set. The main task for microcontroller is to process incoming PWM signals S1, S2 (having jitter) into output PWM signals P1, P2 (jitter free). The P1 controls the angle of wheels, and the P2 handles the speed. Values of incoming signals are continuously summarized and rounded. There was choiced method of hysterezis in sophisticated algorithm for setting output PWM signals P1, P2 using tables of duties.*

Keywords

Electronic, light control, microcontroller, PIC18F25K22, PWM, servomechanism.

1. Introduction

The main target of works with car model is to control it using light beams on maximal possible distance, in normal daylight conditions. Block schema is on the Fig. 1. Channel 1 serves for angle wheels control, channel 2 controls the speed. This paper describes one of solved tasks - processing of incoming two PWM signals S1, S2 (from standard electronics, with unwished jitter) and generating two output PWM signals P1, P2. To gain output signals P1, P2 jitter-free, it is the aim of all the application. The parameters of both incoming PWM processed signals - period 7 ms, duty 1.0–2.2 ms. Thanks these parameters the task for microcontroller isn't time-critical. Processor measures width of incoming PWM pulse, and in the rest of the period it is processing measured value. Then

rest of the period is in range 6.0–4.8 ms, it is sufficient time for processing. The PIC18(L)F2X/4XK22 Microchip family is powerfull set of 8-bit microcontrollers, that brings C-compiler optimized architecture, 16-bit wide instructions, 31-level software accesible hardware stack, 8×8 single-cycle hardware multiplier, 5 CCP (Capture/Compare/PWM) modules, 7 timers/counters, 33 sources of interrupt, SPI bus, I2C bus, operating frequency from DC to 64 MHz, [3].

2. General Description of Problem and its Solving

There are together two PWM signals in the system, P1 and P2. Together detector of light control signal is photodiode PD, Fig. 1. Existing electronic circuits unfortunately produce some parasit signals, those show themselves finally as some jitter (variation) of width pulse (signals of comparators S1, S2; Fig. 1). In the last time it led to sure mechanical vibration of servomechanism and its heating. Fundament of solution consists in created software, that exploates facilities of PIC18F25K22. The algorithm processing the signal passes over these parts:

- measuring of incoming pulse width,

- deciding whether actualization of duty for servomechanism is needed. If yes, then new value of duty is red from the table of duties, and is sent to PWM hardware of microcontroller. In channel 2 is only characteristic a few complicated, it has "V" shape (Fig. 3). Shape of characteristic has no influence on speed of application, because difference (compared with channel 1, see Fig. 2) is only in values of duties, that are held in the field of constant values duty2[ ]. Analogic the channel 1 has its values in field duty1[ ].

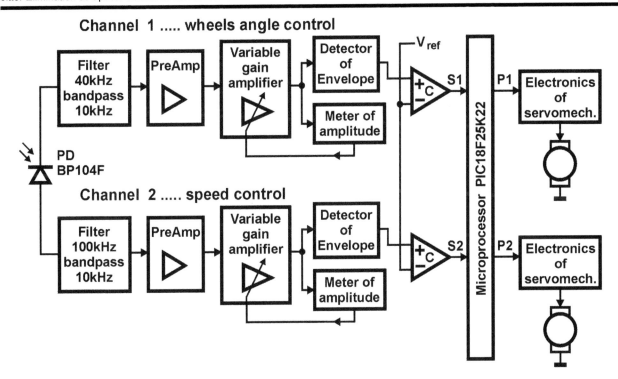

Fig. 1: Block schema of the system.

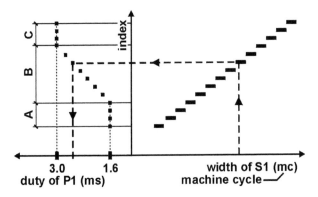

Fig. 2: Convert characteristic Channel_1.

Significant simplification, as to the creating table of duties, brings preprocessor of C language [1]. Classic (and lenghty) approach, how to create table values, is to calculate them handly using a calculator. Preprocessor of C enables assignment using arithmetic expression, even conditional arithmetic expression (that was used), [5]. Only a parameters "begin_duty", "end_duty", "index" must be specified by a man in the source file.

2.1. Incoming Pulse Width Measuring

There was used gated timers CT1 (for signal S1), CT3 (for signal S2) in the solution, in [3]. They are "gate controlled", this facility is used for pulse width measuring. Timer is increasing only if measured signal (pulse)

connected to gate control pin is H. If measured signal is L, then timer stays on reached value. Falling edge invokes an interrupt. In interrupt service routine the (reached) value of the timer is red and copied into variable. In final the timer is cleared by instruction.

2.2. Processing of Measured Widths

This algorithm is descripted in simplyfied flowchart Fig. 6. So transition to a new duty of PWM is performed only on label "lab_c" of flowchart. If the duty of PWM changes hardly, then servomechanism is susceptible to glimmering. So conclusion operations are necessary for a smooth transition to next duty. There was selected simple principe of arithmetic averaging, Fig. 4. Classic solution how to calculate arithmetic average is to summarize all values $v[i]$ using for cyclus ($i = 1$ to n), and then to divide the sum by the n. But in described system the task is little different. There is a clever solution, to use field $v[\ ]$ by a cyclic manner, and to establish variable "iom" i.e. index of the oldest member in the field $v[\ ]$. In showed example the "iom" has value 5.

At the moment of actualization all values will stay unchanged, from sum is substracted the oldest member $v[iom]$, then to sum is added actually measured value, $v[iom]$ is rewritten onto this actually measured value (it becomes by the most actual value), and "iom" is incremented on value 6 (increm. modulo 8, field $v[\ ]$ has 8 members). So by this elegant manner the sum is actualized. Described manner [9] is much faster than

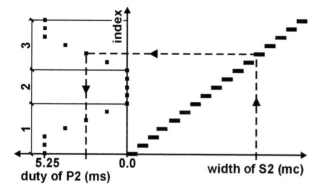

1 - backward movement
2 - stop
3 - forward movement

Fig. 3: Convert characteristic Channel_2.

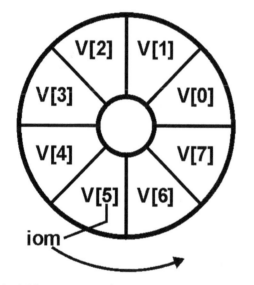

Fig. 4: Arithmetic average (iom is index of the oldest member).

sumarizing of all values $v[i]$ in cyclus for-type. Now calculating arithmetic average is executed, for this reason suitable size of field is power of 2, in the application was used size 8. Firstly sum is rounded by adding 1 in bit b2 position. Then value of the arithmetic average is simply calculated as sum shifted about 3 positions to right (operation is equal to dividing by 8), it is much faster manner than calculation of dividing "sum / n". Subsequent processing described in part 3 is working with this value of the arithmetic average.

3. Determining of Next Duty

There will be explained the situation in channel 1(in channel 2 it is analogous). Principe of the method is shown in Fig. 5, [6], [7]. Microprocessor must determine duty of the output signal P1 for next time. Principle will be explained on concrete values. Used symbols and variables:

- aw: actual width of the input signal S1, in shown example it has value 431mc,

- duty[]: field of fillings for output PWM signal P1,

- oi: old index, duty[oi] is just now ruling filling, in the example it has value 26,

- ni: new index, its value is calculated from "aw", in example it has value 27,

- AZ: attractive zone, it is the size of interval used for characteristic with hysteresis. Value of AZ is 2 in shown example,

- IDAZ: interval determined by attractive zone,

- IBD: interval of big difference in comparison with "oi", it is used for evaluating of "ni", it is equal to $(0, oi - 2\rangle \cup \langle oi + 2, 255\rangle$.

It is assumed, that momentarily signal P1 with duty[oi=26] is generated by PWM hardware of microprocessor. This momental duty[26] is the result of last evaluations. The "aw" serves as an argument for calculating the "ni" through rounded value. Rounded value is derived from "aw".

Rounding is made on the base of value bit b3 in "aw". So values 392–407 are rounded to 400, 408–423 rounded to 416, 424–439 rounded to 432. It is clear, that rounded values have bits b3—b0 equal to 0. Our "aw" = 431 is rounded to 432. Rest bits b15—b4 of rounded value will become by bits b11–b0 of "ni" (by shift about 4 positions to right). This implies that "ni" in our case is 27. Transition to new duty has next logic. If "ni" ∈ IBD that means "ni" is considerably different in comparison with "oi", then transition onto duty[ni] is carried in signal P1, and from this moment "ni" stays by "oi" (oi = ni).

Situation "ni" is as to the "oi" different only a few means (ni == (oi − 1)) OR ((oi + 1) == ni). Our case (oi = 26, ni = 27) is different only a few, therefore subsequently hysteresis principle is used. Hysteresis principle uses attractive zone "AZ". If "aw" lies in "IDAZ" then transition to new duty[ni = 27] is realized. It is our case, "aw = 431" lies in "IDAZ". It is clear, that the hysteresis depends on the size of "AZ", little size of "AZ" means big hysteresis and vice-versa. Our "AZ" has size 2, hysteresis is big. Using of hysteresis principle in a situation different only a few is necessary. It can be demonstrated on the situation, when exact width of incoming pulse is somewhere between values 423 and 424mc (width of incoming pulse is continuous quantity). Value of "aw" then is sometimes 423, sometimes 424. In solution without hysteresis principle sometimes duty would be of value duty[26], sometimes of value duty[27], and the jitter of length in output impulse P1 would not be eliminated.

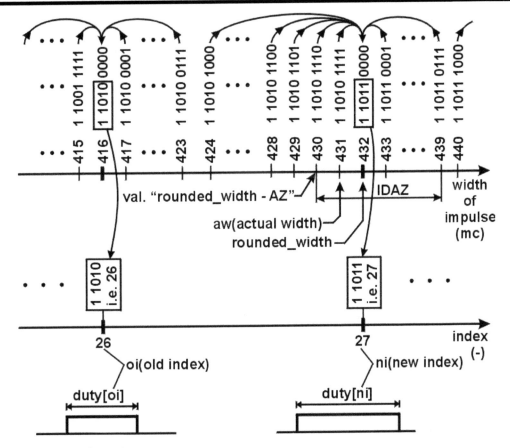

Fig. 5: Width to index transformation.

4. Experimental

Application for PIC18F25K22 removing the jitter is a matter of Radek Novak. Electronic circuits was made by K. Witas, total design and realisation electrooptic transmitter and receiver. There was used photodetector BP104F in optical receiver. The threshold optical power limit was found at 15 nW. There are considerably differences as to the indoor experiments and outdoor experiments. The worst case occurred on the roads inside nature, he built optical channel distance was no longer than 4.2 m. Vice-versa the best situation was within house hall and university corridor, The optical information transfer channel held stable up to 9.3 m distance. In all experiments was servomechanics working without jitter, thank to application of PIC18F25K22.

The jitter-free solution has a consequence, that angle-wheels positioning is divided on 17 levels (8 for left, 1 for direct, 8 for right); also speed is divided on 17 levels too (8 for forward, 1 for stop, 8 for backward). Optical transmitter can be divided into two parts: the first of them looks after two potentiometers giving information about the angle of wheels and speed. Their voltage levels are translated to the pulses widths and sent off to the power amplifier.

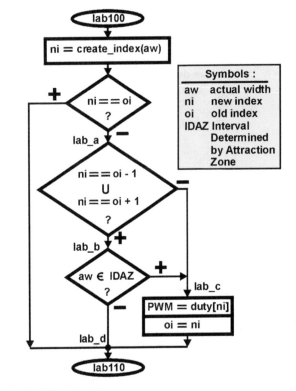

Fig. 6: Flowchart diagram.

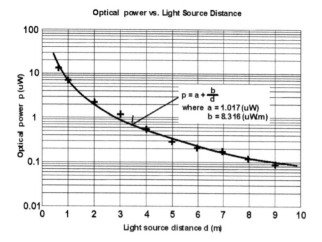

Fig. 7: Dependence power on distance.

The second part employs two powers LEDs H2W2-950 (Roithner Laser Technik) and their current booster. The 950 nm light wavelength has been used. To get square light coverage coming over the line of sight, the beam focused lenses are omitted. The light of LEDs runs to space without any modification. Figure 7 describes the dependence of optical power on the light source distance. Optimal regression curve in this dependence is hyperbolic [2], [4]. Then assumed dependence of power on distance is:

$$p = a + \frac{b}{d}, \tag{1}$$

where p is power [μW], a, b are coefficients [μW], [μW.m], and d is distance [m].

Now is for next derivation used a substitution. For constants a, b then was derived formulas [4]:

$$a = \frac{\sum p_i \sum t_i^2 - \sum t_i p_i \sum t_i}{n \sum t_i^2 - \left(\sum t_i\right)^2}, \tag{2}$$

$$b = \frac{n \sum t_i p_i - \sum t_i \sum p_i}{n \sum t_i^2 - \left(\sum t_i\right)^2}. \tag{3}$$

Concretely calculated values are a = 1.017 [μW], b = 8.316 [μW.m], they depend on measured values shown in Fig. 7.

5.   Conclusion

The described application is designed for controlling of two servomotors. It has meaning at combustion engines, because they need conversion of electric signals into mechanical. There is needing e.g. choke valve handling in combustion engine besides direction handling. As to the electromobil, for next time is intended solution with one servomotor only. Control signal then

must be modified and gained to be able to supply electromotor. Probably it will lead to conversion of one PWM signal into two signals; the first will contain direction information, and the second will be powerfull PWM having duty 0–90 %. So probably next works will deal with full bridge with the motor in diagonal. There must be defined idle duty of transmitter signal, whereat will be (default) defined straight direction with 0 % duty of powerfull PWM. If the duty from transmitter will increase, then forward movement will stay active with growth of duty towards 90 %. Vice-versa if the duty from transmitter will decrease, then a signal astern will be activated, in this situation powerfull signal will again increase towards 90 % respecting the duty fall.

In the current solution the processor PIC18F25K22 was succesfully applied for eliminating jitter of servos. The described application exploates facilities of processor only very little, and it opportunity to increase it about other needed functions in next time.

Acknowledgment

The research described in this article could be carried out thanks to the active support of the Ministry of Education of the Czech Republic within the project SP2014/147. This article was supported by project VG20102015053(GUARDSENSE-The modern structure of photonic sensors and new innovative principles for intrusion detection systems, integrity and protection of critical infrastructure) and Technology Agency of the Czech Republic TA03020439 and TA04021263. The research has been partially supported by the project no. CZ.1.07/2.3.00/20.0217 (The Development of Excellence of the Telecommunication Research Team in Relation to International Cooperation) within the frame of the operation programme Education for competitiveness financed by the European Structural Funds and from the state budget of the Czech Republic.

References

[1] Microchip Technology Inc. *MPLAB ® XC8 C Compiler: User's Guide* [online]. 2012. ISBN 978-162077-206-5. Available at: http://ww1.microchip.com/downloads/en/DeviceDoc/xc8-v1.21-manual.pdf.

[2] BACH, E. and J. O. SHALLIT. *Algorithmic number theory*. Cambridge, Mass.: MIT Press, 1996. ISBN 0-262-024055-1.

[3] Microchip Technology Inc. *PIC18(L)F2X/4XK22: Data Sheet* [online]. 2010. ISBN 978-1-60932-734-

7. Available at: `http://ww1.microchip.com/downloads/en/DeviceDoc/41412F.pdf`.

[4] REKTORYS, K. *Prehled uzite matematiky*. Praha: Prometheus, 2000. ISBN 978-80-7196-180-21.

[5] SALOUN, P. *Jazyk C*. Praha: Neokortex, 2003. ISBN 80-863-3008-7.

[6] ATALLAH, M. J. and M. BLANTON. *Algorithms and theory of computation handbook*. Boca Raton: CRC Press, 2010. ISBN 978-1-58488-820-8.

[7] BRTNIK, B. and D. MATOUSEK. *Algoritmy císlicoveho zpracovani signalu*. Praha: BEN - technická literatura, 2011. ISBN 978-80-7300-400-2.

[8] BRADLEY, A. R. *Programming for engineers: a foundational approach to learning C and Matlab*. New York: Springer, 2011. ISBN 978-364-2233-029.

[9] HLAVAC, V. and M. SEDLACEK. *Zpracovani signalu a obrazu*. Praha: CVUT, 2007. ISBN 978-80-01-03110-0.

About Authors

Radek NOVAK was born in 1961. He received his M.Sc. from VSB–Technical University of Ostrava in 1984. His research interests include single-chip microcontrollers, automation, real-time applications, industrial applications.

Karel WITAS was born in 1973. He received his M.Sc. from VSB–Technical University of Ostrava in 1997. His research interests high-tech electronics, fast signal electronics, electronics for very small signals.

26

Analyses and Modeling Impulse Noise Generated by Household Appliances

Jaroslav KREJCI, Tomas ZEMAN

Department of Telecommunication Engineering, Faculty of Electrical Engineering,
Czech Technical University in Prague, Technicka 2, 166 27 Prague, Czech Republic

krejcja1@fel.cvut.cz, zeman@fel.cvut.cz

Abstract. *This paper describes analysis of impulse noise generated by small household appliances. Furthermore we propose a new model of impulse noise based on the averaged power spectrum and the random phase generation with various phase distributions. The Gaussian, Weibull and Log-normal phase distributions were used to generate random phase. As a result of this approach, new impulses appear – they are different in the time domain but in the frequency domain new impulses have the desired power spectrum and the randomly generated phase.*

Keywords

Fourier transformation, Gaussian, Henkel–Kessler model, impulse noise, log-normal, probability density, Weibull.

1. Introduction

The digital subscriber lines (xDSL) technology is one of the most widely used technology for the Internet connection and the multimedia services to the household appliances in the Czech Republic. One of the most common DSL technology was Asymmetric Digital Subscriber Lines (ADSL2+) [4] which has been already replaced by Very-High Speed Digital Subscriber Lines (VDSL2) [5]. All the transmitted services are named as "Triple play" which is composed of Voice over IP (VoIP), Data and IPTV (TV over IP protocol).

The xDSL systems are carried on a metallic loop. Services transmitted in xDSL systems are influenced by different kinds of disturbances. The most common disturbance is mutual interference of signals from neighboring pairs within one cable – so-called far-end crosstalk (FEXT) and near-end crosstalk (NEXT). Other disturbances are the Radio-frequency interference (RFI), background noise and impulse noise. All of these types of disturbances have a negative impact on the quality of transmitted services. Especially IPTV and VoIP are very sensitive to the impulse noise, more in [11]. Therefore the aim of this paper is to analyse and model the impulse noise generated by household appliances.

2. Impulse Noise

Impulse noise is a specific noise which can originate in the electromagnetic radiation of power cables, power switching and control, and other installations and devices. Impulse noise has typical random amplitude with peak voltage and random arrival time.

Previously, there have been done several measurements and analyses by various telecommunication operators such as the British Telecom, France Telecom and others. It was proved that impulse noise is a random process and consequently PSD (power spectral density) is possible to make as a probability of estimations of so-called pseudo PSD [2].

2.1. Impulse Noise in Standardization

Special impulses are mentioned in the recommendation ITU-T G.996.1. There is described a method to testing DSL against to impulse noise. This method uses so called impulse No. 1 and No. 2 with specific amplitude (u_e) in milivolts at which impulses causes an error of estimated probability that a second will be errored [1].

2.2. Group of Electrical Impulse Noise

The group of electrical impulse noise consists of the REIN (Repetitive Electrical Impulse Noise), SHINE

(Single High Impulse Noise Event) and PEIN (Prolonged Electrical Impulse Noise) (e.g. [2], [3]).

- REIN is a typical repeating noise with a short length less than 1 ms and with constant frequency period (100 or 120 Hz) [2].

- SHINE is an impulse noise lasting more than 10 ms.

- PEIN is the disturbing signal composed of non-repeating interference pulses.

Table 1 compares all types of groups of electrical impulse noise.

Tab. 1: Comparison of groups of electrical impulse noise [3].

Noise type	Typical Burst length	Repetitive	Desired modem behavior
REIN	<1 ms	Yes	No bit errors
PEIN	1–10 ms	No	No bit errors
SHINE	>10 ms	No	No sync loss

2.3. Experimental Modeling of Impulse Noise

The measurements of impulse noise were carried out in networks of the Deutsche Telekom, British Telecom, KPN Netherland and others on the metallic line in the past time. The approach to the impulse noise by the Deutsche Telekom was based on a generator realizing the impulse-voltage density, see more in (e.g. [6], [7], [8], [9] and [10]). This is known as the:

$$f_i(u) = \frac{1}{240u_0} \cdot e^{-\left|\frac{u}{u_0}\right|^{\frac{1}{5}}},\qquad(1)$$

where u_0 is a parameter indicating the shape function.

The length density in the form of one or two lognormal densities

$$
\begin{aligned}
f_l(t) &= B\frac{1}{\sqrt{2\pi s_1 t}} \cdot e^{-\frac{1}{2s_1^2}ln^2\frac{t}{t_1}} + \\
&+ (1-B)\frac{1}{\sqrt{2\pi s_2 t}} \cdot e^{-\frac{1}{2s_2^2}ln^2\frac{t}{t_2}},
\end{aligned}
\qquad(2)
$$

where B is a parameter indicating xTU-R or xTU-C and t_1, t_2 are the median values and s_1, s_2 are the shape parameters of the lognormal densities.

The inter-arrival time density

$$f(t) = \lambda e^{-\lambda t},\qquad(3)$$

where λ is the average rate of arrivals.

3. Study of Impulses Noise by the Appliances

In our experimental measurement, we haven't observed the impulse noise on a real metallic line as the companies mentioned earlier but we have focused on the impulse noise from household appliances. The household appliances were connected to the power supply where a power supply cable was tightened in parallel with the telephone line of two meters length. The near-end of telephone line was terminated with an impedance terminator and the far-end of telephone line was terminated with a so called balun (balance-unbalance transformer). Signals from both the power cable and the telephone line were observed by the digital oscilloscope, more in (e.g. [11], [12]). The measuring workplace was proposed similarly according to the recommendation in ITU-T G.996.1 [1].

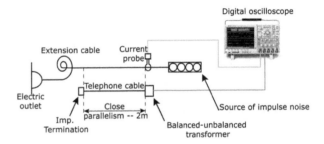

Fig. 1: Measuring workplace [12].

Devices used in this research: Drill (EXTOL), Blender (SOFTmix ETA), Battery charger (HAMA), Display, Fan, Dryer. In this paper, we only worked with results from the Drill, Blender and Dryer.

The time records of noise from household appliances have been recorded by a digital oscilloscope. The sample frequency was 50 MHz and the number of samples in the record was 10^7 of samples. The noise has been measured in different statuses as: e.g. startup, plugged in, shutoff, running, regulation and operation.

Figure 2 shows a record from running Blender in the time domain. Also Fig. 3 shows a record from running Drill and Fig. 4 shows a record from running Dryer. All records contain 200 ms of noise stream.

Each recorded noise has been studied from the viewpoint of the amplitude probability density, arrival time probability density and length of impulses.

3.1. Analysis of Amplitude of Impulse Noise

We focused on the analysis of probability density of amplitude in this subchapter. The modified exponential probability density has been selected as an approx-

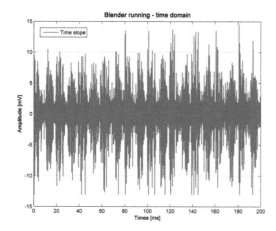

Fig. 2: Illustration of Blender running – time domain.

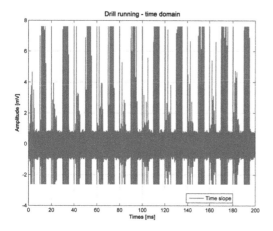

Fig. 3: Illustration of Drill running – time domain.

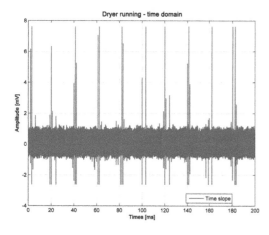

Fig. 4: Illustration of Dryer running – time domain.

imate model. The Henkel–Kessler model was selected as a reference model. The exponential probability density function (pdf) of amplitude is:

$$pdf_{ampl} = \lambda e^{-\lambda|u|}, \qquad (4)$$

where $|u|$ is a parameter of amplitude, λ is the reciprocal value of the mean amplitude.

The algorithm we proposed was created in the Matlab program and analyses the amplitude from noise record and compares the exponential probability density of amplitude with the Henkel-Kessler model (HK model).

We can see that the HK model tends to the probability from the histogram for the appropriate parameter u0 in Fig. 5, Fig. 6 and Fig. 7. The appropriate parameter u_0 is shown in the legend.

Figure 5 shows the histogram and probability density of amplitude for Drill running. Figure 6 shows the histogram and probability density of amplitude for Blender running. Figure 5 shows the histogram and probability density of amplitude for Dryer running.

In the end, in this subchapter we can note that the HK model is a better approximation of amplitude probability density but our results of the proposed model show that the model can be used for approximately the the exponential probability density as well.

3.2. Analyses of Inter-arrival Time of Impulse Noise

This subchapter deals with the analysis of inter-arrival time. The HK model uses the exponential probability density for the inter-arrival time.

During analyses of the inter-arrival time for the selected household appliances it has been observed that some groups of impulses occurred with the approximately same cycle.

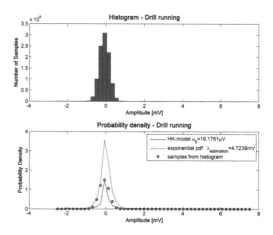

Fig. 5: Histogram and probability density of amplitude – Drill running.

This is the deterministic behaviour and the behaviour of impulses is typically the same as the REIN noise. The inter-arrival time between the impulses in

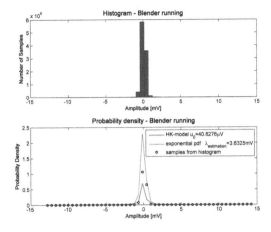

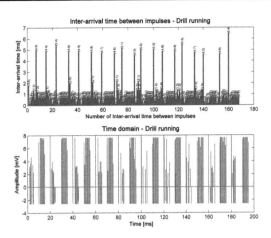

Fig. 6: Histogram and probability density of amplitude – Blender running.

Fig. 8: Inter-arrival time between impulses – Drill running.

The conclusion of this subchapter is that the inter-arrival time can have the deterministic behavior as the REIN noise or the exponential distribution which is used in the HK model.

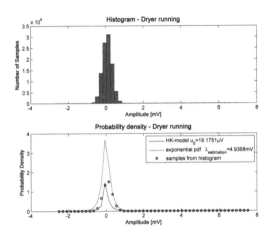

Fig. 7: Histogram and probability density of amplitude – Dryerr running.

the group is approximately the same or variety. Variety of the inter-arrival time tends to the approximation of the Poisson process with the cumulative function of exponential distribution.

The Drill has the mean inter-arrival time between groups of impulses $\tau_{iag} = 9.95$ ms and the mean inter-arrival time between impulses in groups $\tau_{iaing} = 0.67$ ms. The impulses have the typically behaviour like the REIN on the basis of τ_{iag} and the deterministic behaviour on the basis of τ_{iaing}. Figure 8 shows the inter-arrival of impulses.

The Blender has $\tau_{iag} = 10.86$ ms and $\tau_{iaing} = 0.17$ ms. The impulses have the typically behaviour as the REIN noise on the basis of τ_{iag} and the exponential distribution on the basis of τ_{iaing}.

The Dryer has similar a behaviour as the Drill; $\tau_{iag} = 18.21$ ms and $\tau_{iaing} = 1.47$ ms. The impulses have the typically behaviour as the REIN noise on the basis of τ_{iag} (the frequency period is 55 Hz) and the deterministic behaviour on the basis of τ_{iaing}.

4. Modeling of New Impulse Noise

In our experiment, we approached a model of impulse noise as follows: each recorded noise from household appliances has been studied separately. The model of impulse noise was divided into several steps:

- Firstly, we found impulses with the similar power spectrum.

- Then, we found out the averaged power spectrum from impulses of the first point.

- Next, we randomly modeled phase with various probability density.

- Next, by the help of IFFT (Inverse fast Fourier transform) we got time impulses.

- Finally, we compared the old average power spectrum (from the second point) with the average power spectrum obtained by the new time impulses.

It has been observed that the best of time length of impulse is $N = 512$ samples (i.e. 10.24 μs) in all records. The histogram length of impulse is shown in Fig. 9.

Estimation of the power spectrum has been calculated by Matlab from this formula:

$$
\begin{aligned}
C_{(s)}(n\omega_0) &\approx T_{Sa}\frac{1}{N}|DTF\{s_N[k]\}|^2 \\
&= \frac{T_{Sa}}{N}|DTF\{s_N T_{Sa}[kT_{Sa}]\}|^2, \quad (5)
\end{aligned}
$$

$$\Omega_0 = \frac{2\pi}{N} = \omega_0 T_{Sa} \Rightarrow \omega_0 \frac{2\pi}{T_{Sa}} \frac{1}{N} = \frac{\omega_{Sa}}{N}, \qquad (6)$$

where T_{Sa} is a sampling time, N is the number of samples from signal in the time domain, k is one of the samples, ω_0 is distance between samples in the spectrum and the DFT is the Discrete Fourier Transform. The matrix $\mathbf{C}$ presents the power spectral matrix type $N \times b$ where N represents 512 samples and b is the number of found impulses shown as column vectors.

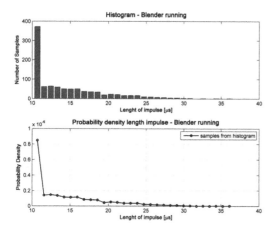

Fig. 9: Histogram and probability density length of impulse.

$$\mathbf{C} = \begin{pmatrix} c_{1,1} & c_{1,2} & \cdots, & c_{1,b} \\ c_{2,1} & c_{2,2} & \cdots, & c_{2,b} \\ \vdots & \vdots & \cdots, & \vdots \\ c_{N,1} & c_{N,2} & \cdots, & c_{N,b} \end{pmatrix}, \qquad (7)$$

where row $r \in \{1, 2, ..., N\}$ and column $s \in \{1, 2, ..., b\}$. The following technique has been used for location of similar impulses with the power spectrum. The extent dissimilarities in the power spectrum between two vectors are described in:

$$d_{i,j} = \sqrt{\frac{1}{N} \sum_{n=1}^{N} (C_i(n) - C_j(n))^2}, \qquad (8)$$

where i and j are indexes of vectors, C is the power spectrum and N is the number of samples. The matrix $\mathbf{D}$ is a type of matrix $b \times b$. This matrix contains the extent dissimilarities in the power spectral every by every column vectors, then $d_{i,j} = 0$ for $i = j$.

$$\mathbf{D}_{(b,b)} = \begin{pmatrix} d_{1,1} & d_{1,2} & \cdots, & d_{1,j} \\ d_{2,1} & d_{2,2} & \cdots, & d_{2,j} \\ \vdots & \vdots & \cdots, & \vdots \\ d_{i,1} & d_{i,2} & \cdots, & d_{i,j} \end{pmatrix}, \qquad (9)$$

where row $i \in \{1, 2, ..., b\}$ and the column $j \in \{1, 2, ..., b\}$. The vector $\mathbf{M}_{min}$ contains a minimal value from each column from the matrix $\mathbf{D}$. The matrix $\mathbf{M}$ is a type of matrix $b \times b$ and contains the vector $\mathbf{M}_{min}$ for each row.

$$\mathbf{M}_{min} = (min\{d_{*1}\} \cdots, min\{d_{*b}\}), \qquad (10)$$

$$\mathbf{M} = \begin{pmatrix} \mathbf{M}_{min,1} \\ \vdots \\ \mathbf{M}_{min,b} \end{pmatrix}. \qquad (11)$$

The matrix $\mathbf{W}$ is a type of matrix $b \times b$ and equals to the subtraction the matrix $\mathbf{D}$ and the matrix $\mathbf{M}$.

$$\mathbf{W} = \mathbf{D} - \mathbf{M}. \qquad (12)$$

The column vector $\mathbf{B}_{*j}$ is a vector which contains indexes of impulse with the similar power spectrum. The column vector $\mathbf{B}_{*j}$ is calculated in the Matlab program with the use of the function *find*. The function *find* finds out indexes from the column vector $\mathbf{W}_{*j}$ which are less than the maximal value in the column vector $\mathbf{D}_{*j}$ multiple by the parameter α. The parameter α ($\alpha = 0.1 = \frac{10\ \%}{100}$) is a value in percentage from the maximum of the column vector $\mathbf{D}_{*j}$.

$$\mathbf{B}_{*j} = find(\mathbf{W}_{*j} < max\{\mathbf{D}_{*j}\}\alpha). \qquad (13)$$

The matrix $\mathbf{Q}$ is a type of matrix $b \times b$ and contains indexes from impulses with the similar power spectrum.

$$\mathbf{Q} = (\mathbf{B}_{*j}, \cdots, \mathbf{B}_{*b}). \qquad (14)$$

The averaged power spectrum from the impulses with the similar power spectrum can be computed with the following formula:

$$C_{avg,N}(\omega) = \frac{1}{k} \sum_{i=1}^{k} C_{N,i}(\omega), \qquad (15)$$

where $C_{N,i}$ is the column vector of the power spectrum from matrix $\mathbf{C}$, k contains indexes of the column vector obtained by the column vector $\mathbf{Q}_{*j}$. These indexes correspond to the column indexes in the matrix $\mathbf{C}$.

4.1.   Generate Random Phase

Above it has been dealt with the average power spectral from impulse. If we want to create an impulse in the time domain with the average power spectrum we have to generate the random phase and then use the inverse Fourier transform. The impulses in the time domain have been transformed by the Fourier transformation.

$$S(\omega) = \int_{-\infty}^{\infty} s(t)e^{-j\omega t}dt, \qquad (16)$$

where $s(t)$ is a signal in the time domain, $S(\omega)$ is Fourier transform signal $s(t)$.

$$S(\omega) = |S(\omega)|e^{j\Phi(\omega)}, \qquad (17)$$

where $|S(\omega)|$ is an estimate of amplitude spectrum and $\Phi(\omega)$ is a phase function.

In our case, the phase function $\Phi(\omega)$ has been generated randomly with the relevant probability density. It has been used these probability densities – Weibull, Log-norm and Gaussian.

Figure 10, Fig. 13 and Fig. 17 show the power spectral density obtained from the time impulses with the similar power spectrum – gray line represents the average power spectral density (PSD) – black line is used for the appropriate household appliance. The sample frequency was $F_s = 50$ MHz and the impedance was $Z_C = 50\ \Omega$. The average power spectral density has been used to generate impulses with this power spectrum and random phase.

The PSDs in the Fig. 10 and Fig. 13 contain the peaks on the relevant frequencies. These peaks could cause the error in seconds as well as the block errors. This will affect adversely the quality of services for example the IPTV service. The current common VDSL modems are able to distinguish the white noise with PSD -140 dBm/Hz. The PSD in the Fig. 19 contains some peaks in bandwidth 5–10 MHz.

1) Drill

It was modeled 802 impulses with the random phase in this case, the Weibull distribution phase and the same of the average power spectrum from Fig. 10. Figure 11 shows a comparison of the required PSD (red line) and PSD from the modeled 802 impulses (blue line). It is visible that the PSD from the modeled impulses tends to the required PSD. Figure 12 shows one of the 802 modeled time impulses where the phase has the Weibull distribution.

2) Blender

There were modeled 803 impulses with random phase, the Gaussian distribution phase and the same of the average power spectrum from Fig. 13. The Figure 14

shows a comparison of the required PSD (red line) and PSD from the modeled 803 impulses (blue line). There is visible that the PSD from modeled impulses tends to the required PSD. The Figure 15 and Figure 16 show the modeled impulse in the time domain where the first one has the distribution phase – Gaussian and the second one has the distribution phase – Log-normal.

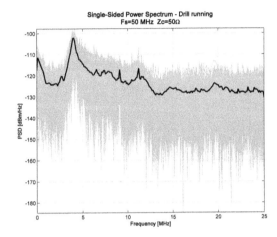

Fig. 10: Similar PSD obtained from 802 time impulses in Fig. 3 (Drill running).

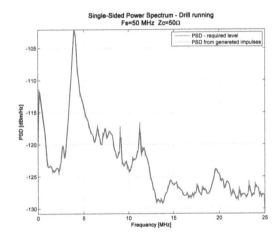

Fig. 11: The required PSD (red line) and PSD from modeled 802 impulses (Drill running).

3) Dryer

In this case it was modeled only 26 impulses with random phase; the Weibull distribution phase and the same of the average power spectrum from Fig. 17. Figure 18 shows a comparison of the required PSD (red line) and PSD from the modeled 26 impulses (blue line). It is visible that the PSD from the modeled impulses tends to the required PSD.

The conclusion of this subchapter is that it is possible to model the impulses with the similar power spectrum with the random density phase. The random den-

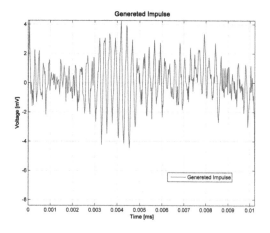

Fig. 12: Example one of the modeled time impulse with distribution phase – Weibull (Drill running).

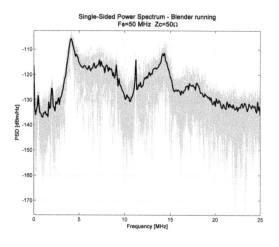

Fig. 13: Similar PSD obtained from 803 time impulses in Fig. 2 (Blender running).

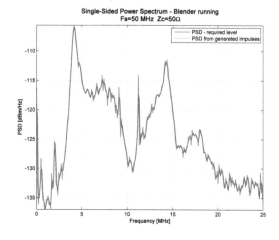

Fig. 14: The required PSD (red line) and PSD from modeled 803 impulses (Blender running).

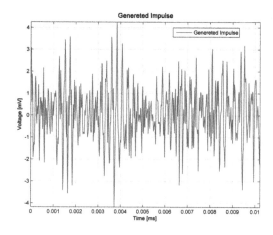

Fig. 15: Example one of the modeled time impulse with distribution phase – Gaussian (Blender running).

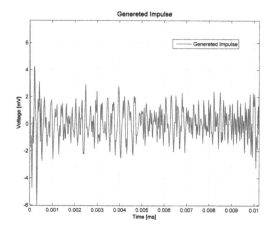

Fig. 16: Example one of the modeled time impulse with distribution phase – Log-normal (Blender running).

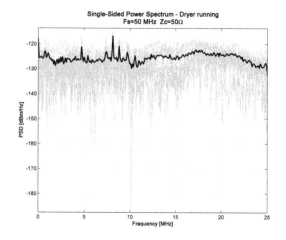

Fig. 17: Similar PSD obtained from 26 time impulses in Fig. 4 (Dryer running).

sity phase changes shape of the impulse in the time domain but the power spectrum tends to the required shape.

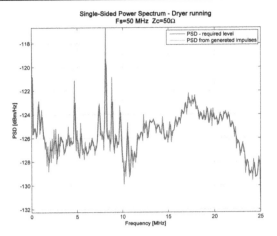

Fig. 18: The required PSD (red line) and PSD from modeled 26 impulses.

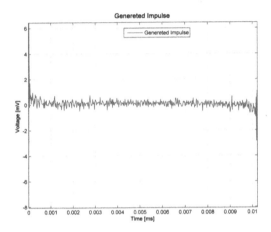

Fig. 19: Example one of the modeled time impulse with distribution phase – Weibull (Dryer running).

4.2. White Gaussian Noise

This subchapter deals with the modeling of the white Gaussian noise. A noise which is located between the impulses has been analysed e.g. in Fig. 3 or Fig. 4.

The white Gaussian noise has a PSD constant over the simulation bandwidth $|f| < \dfrac{f_s}{2}$. The variance is, by definition, the area under the power spectrum, more in [13].

$$\sigma^2 = \frac{1}{2} N_0 f_{Sa}, \qquad (18)$$

where N_0 is the random number (noise) generator variance, f_{Sa} is the sampling frequency.

Figure 20 represents the histogram of noise and the probability density of amplitude. It seems that the noise between the impulses tends to the white Gaussian noise. The PSD of noise is illustrated in Fig. 21; we can see some groups of peaks which can cause the block

errors. Nevertheless it is possible to approximate this noise by the white Gaussian noise as shown in Fig. 22.

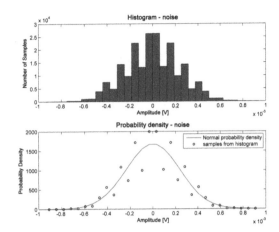

Fig. 20: Histogram and probability density of amplitude –noise.

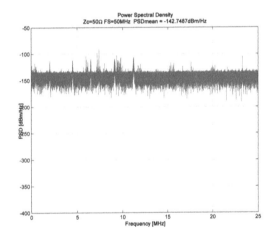

Fig. 21: Power spectral density – noise located between impulses e.g. at Fig. 4.

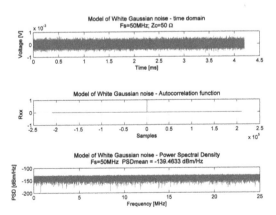

Fig. 22: Power spectral density – Model of White Gaussian noise.

5. Conclusion

Impulse noise negatively affects services provided on xDSL technology for example IPTV or VoIP. Therefore it is important to analyse this type of disturbance. Analyses of impulse noise in the telephone line were described in a model made by Mr. Henkel and Mr. Kessler [6], [7].

We mainly focused on impulse noise generated from the household appliances in our research. The home appliances are the most common source of interference penetrating into the telephone line in households. We obtained a conception of PSD of these impulses through the analysis of these impulses. We could obtain impulse noise models of household appliances using modeling of the new impulses. These models can be appropriate for correctness preserving configuration of xDSL (ADSL2+ and VDSL2) telephone lines against impulse noise.

Regarding our results shown in this paper, the probability density is very approximate to the HK model. The inter-arrival time seems to have deterministic behavior as the REIN noise or the exponential distribution which is used in the HK model.

Our modeling of impulse noise is based on the averaged power spectrum obtained from impulses with approximately similar power spectrum. The appropriate phase distribution in the frequency domain is created using random phase. New impulses were made with IFFT. New impulses had averaged power spectrum and random modeled phase. Furthermore new modeled impulses showed different shape in the time domain but the PSD was approximately the same. As we mentioned above, for this study we used the distribution phase with Gaussian, Weibull and Log-normal distribution. For the further research beta, exponential and uniform distribution will be tested. Noise between impulses tends to the best approximation by the use of the white Gaussian noise.

Practical application of this research can be used for the appropriate parameter settings for xDSL connections protection against impulsive interference. Impulse noise effects can be suppressed by the use of suitable combination of Reed-Solomon code and interleaving parameter e.g. [5] or [14] and newly retransmission (RTX) also known as ARQ (Automatic Repeat-reQuest) [14], but on the contrary, the maximum achievable transmission speed is reduced.

Acknowledgment

This paper has originated thanks to grant support obtained from the Technology Agency of the Czech Republic within the project TA03011192 "Research and Development of Next-generation Devices for Communication over High-voltage Power Lines".

References

[1] ITU-T G.996.1. *Test procedures for digital subscriber line (DSL) transceivers*. ITU-T, 2001.

[2] ETSI TD09 044t09. *REIN Test Methodology*. ETSI, 2004.

[3] ETSI STC TM6 TD 29 071t29. *VDSL2 should also withstand "PEIN" impulse noise*. ETSI, 2007.

[4] ITU-T G.992.5. *Asymmetric Digital Subscriber Line (ADSL) transceivers - Extended bandwidth ADSL2 (ADSL2plus)*. ITU-T, 2003.

[5] ITU-T G.993.2. *Very high speed digital subscriber line transceivers 2 (VDSL2)*. ITU-T, 2006.

[6] ETSI WG TM6 TD 29 994t29a0. *Comments to the latest impulse-noise modeling approach by BT and the University of Edinburgh*. ETSI, 1999.

[7] HENKEL, W. and T. KESSLER. A wideband impulsive noise survey in the German telephone network—Statistical description and modeling. *AEU. Archiv fur Elektronik und Ubertragungstechnik*. 1994, vol. 48, no. 6, pp. 277–288. ISSN 0001-1096.

[8] KESSLER, T. and W. HENKEL. Statistical description and modelling of impulsive noise on the German telephone network. *Electronics Letters*. 1994, vol. 30, iss. 12, pp. 935–936. ISSN 0013-5194. DOI: 10.1049/el:19940627.

[9] MANN, I., S. MCLAUGHLIN, W. HENKEL, R. KIRKBY and T. KESSLER. Impulse generation with appropriate amplitude, length, inter-arrival, and spectral characteristics. *IEEE Journal on Selected Areas in Communications*. 2002, vol. 20, iss. 5, pp. 901–912. ISSN 0733-8716. DOI: 10.1109/JSAC.2002.1007373.

[10] ETSI WG TM6 TD 55 002t55a0. Some Results of the Investigations of BT Impulse-Noise Data. ETSI, 2000.

[11] KREJCI, J. and T. ZEMAN. Diagnostics of Impulse Noise. In: *33th International Conference on Telecommunications and Signal Processing. TSP 2010*. Budapest: Asszisztencia Szervezo, 2010. pp. 411–416. ISBN 9789638898104.

[12] KREJCI, J., T. ZEMAN, J. HRAD and Z. KOCUR. Experimental Diagnostics of Impulse Noise. In: *17th International Conference on Systems, Signals and Image Processing, IWSSIP 2010*

proceedings. Rio de Janeiro: EdUFF - Editora da Universidade Federal Fluminense, 2010, pp. 268–271. ISBN 978-85-228-0565-5.

[13] TRANTER, William H. *Principles of communication systems simulation with wireless applications*. Upper Saddle River: Prentice Hall, 2003. ISBN 01-349-4790-8.

[14] ITU-T G.998.4. *Improved impulse noise protection for DSL transceivers*. ITU-T, 2010

About Authors

Jaroslav KREJCI was born in Strakonice in 1982. He received his Master (Ing.) degree in 2007 at the Faculty of Electrical Engineering, Czech Technical University in Prague, specializing in Telecommunication Engineering. Currently he is a combined Ph.D. student at the Department of Telecommunication Engineering of the Czech Technical University in Prague.

Tomas ZEMAN was born in Prague in 1965. He joined the Department of Telecommunication Engineering, Faculty of Electrical Engineering, Czech Technical University in Prague in 1989 as a research assistant and received his Ph.D. degree in electrical engineering in 2001. He has been the head of the caMEL scientific group since 2005. He participates in numerous projects in cooperation with external bodies.

27

Comparison among Models to Estimate the Shielding Effectiveness Applied to Conductive Textiles

Alberto LOPEZ, Lukas VOJTECH, Marek NERUDA

Department of Telecommunication Engineering, Faculty of Electrical Engineering, Czech Technical University in Prague, Technicka 2, 166 27 Prague, Czech Republic

alberto.lopez.caro@estudiant.upc.edu, vojtecl@fel.cvut.cz, nerudmar@fel.cvut.cz

Abstract. *The purpose of this paper is to present a comparison among two models and its measurement to calculate the shielding effectiveness of electromagnetic barriers, applying it to conductive textiles. Each one, models a conductive textile as either a (1) wire mesh screen or (2) compact material. Therefore, the objective is to perform an analysis of the models in order to determine which one is a better approximation for electromagnetic shielding fabrics. In order to provide results for the comparison, the shielding effectiveness of the sample has been measured by means of the standard ASTM D4935-99.*

Keywords

Compact barriers, conductive textiles, modelling, shielding effectiveness, wire mesh barriers.

1. Introduction

Textile-based shields are useful in areas such as in designing of EM barriers to shield devices' joints against external interferences [1], protective clothes for workers or patients in radiotherapy rooms or military applications.

The manufacture of conductive textiles has a significant cost, besides a waste of materials such as copper, nickel, iron or silver. The modelling of conductive textiles before their production in the industry [2] allows manufacturers to save money.

This paper presents two models to estimate the shielding effectiveness (SE) of different types of electromagnetic barriers: wire mesh screens and compact material. The models have been programmed in a Matlab environment performing an estimation of the shielding effectiveness between 30 MHz and 1,5 GHz of a real sample with characteristics as follows: $l = 220$ µm,

$s = 120$ µm, $\sigma = 2040$ S·m^{-1}, $t = 360$ µm and $d = 270$ µm, where l stands for length of apertures, width of apertures is defined by s, σ is the conductivity of the sample, t stands for thickness and d is the diameter of threads. The thickness of the sample was measured by using a micrometre, which is not an exact measurement method and can lead to errors. More exact techniques are used by the industry such as microscopic examination, resonance methods or laser diffraction [3]. The conductivity of the textile was obtained by placing two electrodes between the opposite boundaries of a square textile sample and bulk resistance was measured with an RLCG bridge ESCORT ELC-3133A.

The actual SE of the sample was measured with a network analyzer ZVRE Rohde&Schwarz by following the standard ASTM D4935-99 [4] in order to provide a point of reference to compare results. Although there is a new version of the standard and it is no longer supported, it is still used in many technical papers.

The rest of the paper is organized as follows: Section 2 describes modelling of wire mesh barriers. Section 3 presents modelling of compact material. Section 4 introduces measuring workplace and results are discussed in section 5. Finally, conclusions are presented in section 5.

2. Modelling of Wire Mesh Barriers

This section describes the method used to model the electromagnetic shielding behaviour of wire-mesh screens [5]. The main goal is to find out if a conductive textile can be modelled as a wire-mesh screen without a major error in the calculation.

Wire-mesh screens can be properly used in applications such as the screening of rooms or big scenarios because of saving material, compared to compact sheet screens. The advantage is lower cost and reduced weight per unit area. This method considers that the mesh dimensions are small compared to wavelength, the wire is circular and the mesh holes are square as Fig. 1 shows.

Wire mesh screens with bonded junctions can be described by their equivalent sheet impedance for a screen with square meshes of dimensions $a_s \times a_s$. Using Cartesian coordinates to represent its equivalent sheet impedance it is possible to obtain the parameters Z_{s1} and Z_{s2} [5]. Z_{s1} corresponds to the sheet impedance for perpendicularly polarized plane waves Eq. (1), while Z_{s2} corresponds to the effective sheet impedance for the parallel-polarized plane waves Eq. (2):

$$Z_{s1} = Z_w' a_s + j\omega L_s, \tag{1}$$

$$Z_{s2} = Z_{s1} - \frac{j\omega L_s}{2}\sin^2\theta, \tag{2}$$

where θ is the angle of incidence with respect to the normal direction to the mesh, L_s is the sheet inductance given by Eq. (3), r_w is the radius of the mesh wires and a_s the mesh aperture size. Z_w' is the internal impedance per unit length expressed as Eq. (4):

$$L_s = \frac{\mu_0 a_s}{2\pi}\ln\left(1 - e^{-2\pi r_w/a_s}\right)^{-1}, \tag{3}$$

$$Z_w' = R_w'\frac{\sqrt{j\omega\tau_w}I_0\left(\sqrt{j\omega\tau_w}\right)}{2I_1\sqrt{j\omega\tau_w}}, \tag{4}$$

where $k_0 = \omega\sqrt{\mu_0\epsilon_0}$ is the free-space wavenumber, $\tau_w = (\mu\sigma r_w^2)$ is the diffusion time constant, $R_w' = (\pi r_w^2\sigma)^{-1}$ is the dc resistance per unit length of the mesh wires and I_n denotes the modified Bessel function of the first kind of order n.

On the one hand, reflection and transmission coefficients for perpendicularly polarized plane waves are Eq. (5) and Eq. (6) respectively.

$$R_1 = \frac{-Z_0}{Z_0 + 2Z_{s1}\cos\theta}\sin^2\theta, \tag{5}$$

$$T_1 = \frac{2Z_{s1}\cos\theta}{Z_0 + 2Z_{s1}\cos\theta}. \tag{6}$$

On the other hand, reflection and transmission coefficients for parallel-polarized plane waves are Eq. (7) and Eq. (8) respectively. Figure 2 shows the difference between the incidence of parallel-polarized plane waves and perpendicularly polarized plane waves to a shield.

$$R_2 = \frac{Z_0\cos\theta}{2Z_{s2} + Z_0\cos\theta}, \tag{7}$$

$$T_2 = \frac{2Z_{s2}}{2Z_{s2} + Z_0\cos\theta}. \tag{8}$$

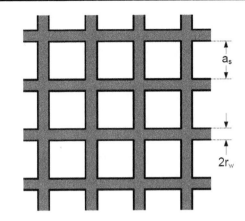

Fig. 1: Wire mesh with square apertures and bonded junctions.

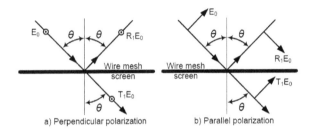

a) Perpendicular polarization   b) Parallel polarization

Fig. 2: Angle of incidence with respect to the normal incidence to a shielding barrier [5].

The shielding effectiveness for plane waves is defined as:

$$SE_{1,2}(\theta) = -20\log|T_{1,2}(\theta)|, \tag{9}$$

where in the case that the mesh wires are perfectly conducting, it is defined as Eq. (10) for perpendicularly polarized plane waves and as Eq. (11) for parallel-polarized plane waves:

$$SE_1(\theta) = -20\log\left|\frac{(2\omega L_s/Z_0)\cos\theta}{1 + (\omega L_s/Z_0)^2\cos\theta}\right|, \tag{10}$$

$$SE_2(\theta) = -20\log\left|\frac{(2\omega L_s/Z_0)\left(1 - \frac{1}{2}\sin^2\theta\right)}{(\omega L_s/Z_0)\left(1 - \frac{1}{2}\sin^2\theta\right)\cos^2\theta}\right|. \tag{11}$$

However, the polarization direction is likely unknown. Therefore, it must come into consideration a polarization-independent shielding effectiveness SE_0 given by:

$$SE_0(\theta) = -10\log\left\{\frac{1}{2}|T_1(\theta)|^2 + \frac{1}{2}|T_2(\theta)|^2\right\}. \tag{12}$$

3. Modelling of Compact Materials

This section describes the method used to model the electromagnetic shielding behaviour of compact sheet screens [6]. The main goal is to find out if a conductive textile can be modelled as a compact screen without a major error in the calculation. It can be possible since a mesh screen can be viewed as a compact screen for a range of frequencies.

This section presents a theoretical model for multi-layered structures to calculate its shielding effectiveness, which is based on the transmitted wave matrix in the far field area [6]. Figure 3 shows the transmission and reflection scheme of an N-layers structure.

Considering that all layers are isotropic and homogeneous, the intrinsic impedance of the ith layer Z_i is given by:

$$Z_i = \left[\frac{\mu_r}{\epsilon_i + \sigma_i/j\omega} \right]^2 \quad i = 1, 2, \ldots, N. \quad (13)$$

The characteristic matrix of the ith layer is given by:

$$\mathbf{M_1} = \begin{bmatrix} \cos(k_i d_i) & -jZ_i \sin(k_i d_i) \\ -j/Z_i \sin(k_i d_i) & \cos(k_i d_i) \end{bmatrix}, \quad (14)$$

where $\epsilon_i^{'}$ is the real part of the complex permittivity of the ith layer given by $\epsilon_i^* = \epsilon_i^{'} - \epsilon_i^{''}$ and k_i is the wavenumber, defined by:

$$k_i = \frac{2\pi}{\lambda_0} \left[\left(\epsilon_i^{'} + \sigma_i/(j\epsilon_0\omega) \right) \right]^2. \quad (15)$$

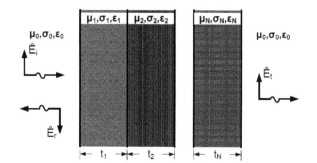

Fig. 3: Transmission and reflection of an EM wave with normal incidence [6].

The characteristic matrix of the whole structure is

$$[\mathbf{M}] = [\mathbf{M_1}] \cdot [\mathbf{M_2}] \ldots [\mathbf{M_N}] = \begin{bmatrix} M_{11} & M_{12} \\ M_{21} & M_{22} \end{bmatrix}, \quad (16)$$

and both reflection and transmission coefficient of the whole N-layered structure is given by Eq. (17) and Eq. (18) respectively:

$$R = \frac{(M_{11}Z_0 - M_{12}) - Z_1(M_{22} - M_{21}Z_0)}{(M_{11}Z_0 - M_{12}) + Z_1(M_{22} - M_{21}Z_0)}. \quad (17)$$

$$T = \frac{2\left[M_{22}(M_{11}Z_0 - M_{12}) + M_{12}(M_{22} - M_{21}Z_0)\right]}{(M_{11}Z_0 - M_{12}) + Z_1(M_{22} - M_{21}Z_0)}. \quad (18)$$

The shielding effectiveness takes into account the transmission parameter Eq. (18), which is therefore given by:

$$SE = -20 \log |T|. \quad (19)$$

4. Measuring Workplace

This section describes measuring principle and apparatus for shielding effectiveness measurement according to standard ASTM D4935-99 [4]. It was published in 1999 and in 2005 was removed from ASTM standards. However, it still remains the method used by professionals for measurement.

Measuring apparatus consists of a network analyser, we used ZVRE Rohde&Schwarz, RF connecting cables, measuring adapter, attenuators that prevent from unwanted reflections or signal interference and computer for data evaluation. Measuring adapter is formed by two symmetrical parts axially split coaxial line, Fig. 4.

The random error of this measurement method and used specimen is ±5 dB [4].

Measurement is the type of comparison measurement. At first, two circular calibration samples are inserted between two symmetrical parts of measuring adapter, i.e. not hatched part of the sample as shown in Fig. 4. Network analyzer is then calibrated, calibration samples are replaced by measuring samples (circular sample without any cut in Fig. 4 and the resulting values are stored in a computer.

The sample is conductive textile material which consists of 30 % SilveR.STAT®, 30 % SHIELDEX®and 40 % PES with 35,5 tex.

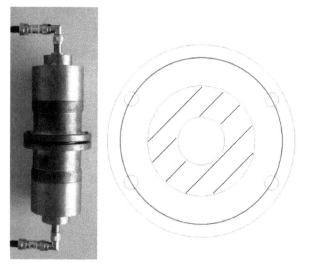

Fig. 4: Measuring adapter (left) and basis for sample preparation (right) according to standard ASTM D4935-99.

5.   Obtained Results

This section describes comparison of results obtained from modelling and measurement.

5.1.   Wire Mesh Barriers

In this section, the textile sample has been modelled as a wire mesh screen. Although, the real dimensions of apertures is 220 µm×120 µm, the equations described above requires of square apertures. Therefore, square apertures of dimensions 220 µm×220 µm were considered because the shielding effectiveness is mainly affected by the highest dimension of an aperture.

Figure 5 shows the calculation of the shielding effectiveness of the sample, modelled as an electromagnetic wire mesh barrier that is compared to its measured shielding effectiveness in the frequency range 30 MHz–1,5 GHz. Although both curves are flat and proportional, there is an offset about 3 dB between them at whole frequency range (3,2 dB at 1 GHz), which is less than ±5 dB (maximal random error of used measurement method).

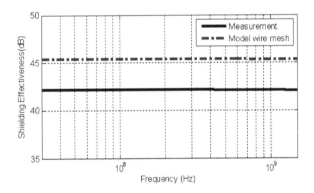

Fig. 5: Modelling of the sample as wire mesh.

5.2.   Compact Materials

This section shows the results obtained from modelling the textile sample as a compact electromagnetic barrier. A good approximation is expected because the higher dimension of apertures in the textile, 220 µm, is much lower than the wavelength at 1,5 GHz, $\lambda_{|f=1,5\ GHz} = 0,2$ m, so the textile barrier's behaviour as an EM shield is expected to follow the one of a compact electromagnetic barrier.

Figure 6 shows the calculation of the shielding effectiveness of the given sample, modelled as an electromagnetic compact barrier and compared to its measured shielding effectiveness also in the frequency range 30 MHz–1,5 GHz. The figure shows a good approximation to the actual values of shielding effectiveness. At

an example frequency of 1 GHz, the measured shielding efficiency is equal to $42,1 \pm 5$ dB, while the modelling of Sample A as a compact electromagnetic barrier gives shielding effectiveness of 43,5 dB. Therefore, it is inside the uncertainty margin of error given by the measurement method.

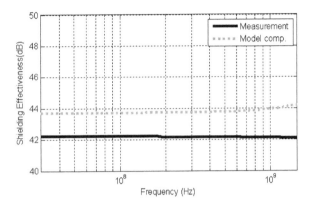

Fig. 6: Modelling of the sample as compact material.

6.   Conclusion

Two methods have been shown in order to model the shielding effectiveness of different type of materials and the results were compared to measurement of real sample. The first method is focused on modelling of wire mesh screens, and the second one on modelling of the shielding effectiveness of electromagnetic compact barriers.

In the case of the wire mesh model, an error of 3 dB at 1 GHz (and in the almost whole frequency range 30 MHz–1,5 GHz) with respect to measurements has been detected, i.e. about 45 dB for model and 42 dB for measurement. It is inside the uncertainty margin of ±5 dB due to the measurement method and it represents a good approximation.

Modelling of conductive textile as an electromagnetic compact barrier has achieved better results compared to measurements in the frequency band 30 MHz–1,5 GHz. Shielding effectiveness of about 44 dB has been achieved for the model in the frequency range 30 MHz–1,5 GHz (43,5 dB at 1 GHz) in comparison with measurement results, i.e. about 42 dB in the frequency range 30 MHz–1,5 GHz (42,1 dB at 1 GHz). Obtained values have been shown to be inside the uncertainty margin of the measurement method.

When comparing the results of modelling it is obvious there is a contradiction with theory. The shielding effectiveness of compact electromagnetic barrier must be in principle higher than the shielding effectiveness of wire mesh. This error is again smaller than the random error measurement method.

Acknowledgment

This work has been conducted in the Department of Telecommunication Engineering at the Czech Technical University in Prague in the scope of thesis called "Design and performance analysis of purely textile antenna for wireless applications" [7]. The work was supported by the project Kompozitex FR- TI4/202 - Composite textile materials for humans and technology protection from the effects of electromagnetic and electrostatic fields.

References

[1] VOJTECH, L. and M. NERUDA. Application of Shielding Textiles for Increasing Safety Airborne Systems - Limitation of GSM Interference. In: *Ninth International Conference on Networks 2010*. Los Alamitos: IEEE Computer Society, 2011, pp. 157–161. ISBN 978-0-7695-3979-9. DOI: 10.1109/ICN.2010.35.

[2] NERUDA, M. and L. VOJTECH. Verification of Surface Conductance Model of Textile Materials. *Journal of Applied Research and Technology*. 2012, vol. 10, iss. 4, pp. 579–585. ISSN 1665-6423.

[3] PERRY, A. J., B. INRICHEN and B. ELIASSON. Fibre diameter measurement by laser diffraction. *Journal of Materials Science*. 1974, vol. 9, iss. 8, pp. 1376–1378. ISSN 0022-2461. DOI: 10.1007/BF00551860.

[4] ASTM D4935 - 10: Standard Test Method for Measuring the Electromagnetic Shielding Effectiveness of Planar Materials. In: *ASTM International* [online]. 1999. DOI: 10.1520/D4935-10.

[5] CASEY, K. F. Electromagnetic Shielding Behaviour of Wire-Mesh Screens. *IEEE Transactions on Electromagnetic Compatibility*. 1988, vol. 30, iss. 3, pp. 298–306. ISSN 0018-9375. DOI: 10.1109/15.3309.

[6] HOANG, N. N., J. MIANE and J. WOJKIEWICZ. Modelling of Electromagnetic Shielding Effectiveness of Multilayer Conducting Composites in the Microwave Band. In: *First International Conference on Communications and Electronics, 2006*. Hanoi: IEEE, 2006, pp. 482–485. ISBN 1-4244-0568-8. DOI: 10.1109/CCE.2006.350874.

[7] LOPEZ, C., A. *Modelling of textile reinforced composite barriers against electromagnetic radiations*. Prague, 2011. Available at: http://upcommons.upc.edu/pfc/bitstream/2099.1/12719/1/memoria.pdf. Diploma thesis. Czech Technical Univesity in Prague.

About Authors

Alberto LOPEZ was born in Esplugues de Llobregat, Spain in 1986. He received his B.Sc. in Telecommunication Engineering from the Technical University of Catalonia, Castelldefels, Spain, in 2009 where he is currently pursuing his M.Sc in Telecommunication Engineering & Management. His main interests include signal processing, radiofrequency communications and electronics.

Lukas VOJTECH was born in 1977 in Nachod. He received the M.Sc. degree in electrical engineering from the Czech Technical University in Prague, Faculty of Electrical Engineering, in 2003. In 2005, he received the bachelor degree engineering pedagogy from the Masaryk Institute of Advanced Studies in Prague. In 2010, he received the Ph.D. degree from Czech Technical University in Prague, Faculty of Electrical Engineering. Currently, he works as an assistant professor at the Department of telecommunication engineering, CTU in Prague. His research interests include wireless technologies, technology RFID and mainly EMC in area of shielding materials.

Marek NERUDA was born in Hradec Kralove in Czech Republic in 1983. He received the M.Sc. degree in electrical engineering from the Czech Technical University in Prague, Faculty of Electrical Engineering, Czech Republic in 2007. In 2009, he received the bachelor degree engineering pedagogy from the Masaryk Institute of Advanced Studies in Prague, Czech Republic. In 2010, he received the M.Sc. degree in entrepreneurship and commercial engineering in industry from the Masaryk Institute of Advanced Studies in Prague, Czech Republic. Currently, he is a student of Ph.D. degree.

28

Financial Time Series Modelling with Hybrid Model Based on Customized RBF Neural Network Combined With Genetic Algorithm

Lukas FALAT[1], Dusan MARCEK[2]

[1]Department of Macro & Microeconomics, Faculty of Management Science and Informatics, University of Zilina, Univerzitna 8215/1, Zilina, Slovakia
[2]Department of Applied Informatics, Faculty of Economics, VSB–Technical University of Ostrava, Sokolska 33, 701 21 Ostrava, Czech Republic

lukas.falat@fri.uniza.sk, dusan.marcek@vsb.cz

Abstract. *In this paper, authors apply feed-forward artificial neural network (ANN) of RBF type into the process of modelling and forecasting the future value of USD/CAD time series. Authors test the customized version of the RBF and add the evolutionary approach into it. They also combine the standard algorithm for adapting weights in neural network with an unsupervised clustering algorithm called K-means. Finally, authors suggest the new hybrid model as a combination of a standard ANN and a moving average for error modeling that is used to enhance the outputs of the network using the error part of the original RBF. Using high-frequency data, they examine the ability to forecast exchange rate values for the horizon of one day. To determine the forecasting efficiency, authors perform the comparative out-of-sample analysis of the suggested hybrid model with statistical models and the standard neural network.*

Keywords

Artificial neural network, generic algorithm, hybrid model, RBF, time series, USD/CAD.

1. Introduction

Predicting time series using statistical analysis started in the 60s years of 20th century. First statistical models were based on the theory of exponential smoothing originally published in [1], [2] and [3]. Another breakthrough came with publishing a study from Box & Jenkins [4]. In this study, they integrated all the knowledge including autoregressive and moving average models into one book. From that time, the ARIMA models have been very popular in time series modelling for a long time as O'Donovan [5] showed that these models provide better results than other models used in that time. However, in 1982 Engle [6] showed that using ARIMA models in financial series modelling is not always correct as these series usually have conditional variance instead of constant. Therefore, he suggested ARCH (autoregressive conditional variance) models for financial modeling.

One of the reason computers started to apply in time series modeling was the study of Bollershev [7] where he proved the existence of nonlinearity in financial data. The first techniques of machine learning applied into time series forecasting were artificial neural networks (ANN). As ANN was a universal approximator, it was believed that these models could perform tasks like pattern recognition, classification or predictions [8], [9], [10]. Today, according to some studies [11] ANNs are the models having the biggest potential in predicting financial time series. The reason for the attractiveness of ANNs for financial prediction can be found in works of Hill et al. [12], where authors showed that ANNs works best in connection with high-frequential financial data.

While in the first application of ANNs into financial forecasting, perceptron network, the simplest feed-forward neural network, was used [13], nowadays it is mainly RBF network that is being used for this as they showed to be better approximators than the perceptron networks [14].

We decided to apply our neural networks models into the market of exchange rates. Forex, which is short for the foreign exchange market, is one of the world's largest and most liquid financial markets in the world. Therefore, it is no surprise that the exchange rates forecasting has attracted the attention of many financial researchers and analysts for a long time. Very common approach investors use for trading is technical analysis (TA). "Technical analysis can be seen as a collection of algorithms and mechanical rules which attempt to aid investors in forecasting future market movements, using only historic data" [15].

In this paper, forecasts of USD/CAD exchange rate through customized RBFGA neural network with Moving Average errors (RBFGA-SMA) was performed The standard RBF model will be extended by using Moving Average for modeling the errors of RBF network. Additionally, the hybridized version of ANN will be used; we will combine the standard ANN with EC technique called genetic algorithms that will be used in the process of finding optimal parameters of the neural network. According to some scientists [16], the use of technical analysis tools can lead to the efficient profitability on the market, we decided to combine our customized RBF network with a tool of the technical analysis. Investors use a large number of technical trading tools so as to make the decision-making process easier. In the process of searching an optimal tool of TA for hybridization with RBF, we were inspired by ARIMA models where the MA part is correcting the error of the AR model. Therefore, for our experiments one of the simplest tools of TA - Moving Averages was chosen. Just like many other tools of technical analysis, Moving Averages are also based on analyzing historical data using statistics. From a forecasting point of view, it is a type of finite impulse response filter used to predict the next value in the series by creating a series of averages of different subsets of the full data set. The simple moving average was used to model the error part of the RBF network as there was a suspicion it could enhance the prediction outputs of the model.

Our machine learning application to exchange rates forecasting is novel in two ways – we use the standard neural network hybridized with simple moving averages to form a whole new hybrid model for forecasting. Nowadays, there are lots of hybrid models of neural networks. Hassan et al. [17] tested a fusion model of Hidden Markov Models (HMM), ANN and GA for stock market forecasting. Thinyane and Millin [15] use the intelligent hybrid system composed of GA and ANN to enhance the decision-making process in the field of currency trading. Sterba and Hilovska [18] combine ANN and statistical ARIMA models to create a hybrid model. Other studies of hybrid models include, for example, those by Zhuang and Chan [19], Chikhi et al. [20], Choudhry and Garg [21] or Marcek and Falat [22]. However, none of the mentioned hybrid models does not focus on a combination of ANN with TA.

Moreover, we also use other than just the standard algorithm for training parameters of the neural network in order to achieve the maximal prediction accuracy of our suggested model.

2. Models and Methods

2.1. Box-Jenkins and GARCH Models

For more than 20 years Box-Jenkins ARMA models have been widely used for time series modelling. The models published in [4] are autoregressive models (AR) and moving average (MA) models. Let y_t be a stationary time series that is the realization of a stochastic process. General formula of ARMA(p,q) model is expressed as follows (for details, see [4]):

$$y_t = \xi + \sum_{i=1}^{p} \phi_i \, y_{t-i} + \varepsilon_t - \sum_{j=1}^{q} \theta_i \varepsilon_{t-j}. \qquad (1)$$

The weakness of ARMA models is the inability to model non-constant variance. As this type of variance is very common in currency pairs, constant volatility is not able to capture some of the basic properties of heteroscedastic volatility present in financial time series such as stochasticity of volatility, volatility clustering, mean reversion and existence of fat tails. In [6] Engle suggested the solution by creating so-called ARCH (Autoregressive Conditional Heteroscedastic) models which assume heteroscedastic variance of ε_t.

2.2. Feed-Forward Neural Network

The model of artificial neural network based on human neural system is an universal functional black-box approximator of non-linear type [23], [24], [25] which are especially helpful in modelling non-linear processes having a priori unknown functional relations or this system of relations is very complex to describe [26].

In [23] and [24] it has been showed that a neural network can approximate any continuous function into any demanded accuracy. Moreover, artificial neural network can generalize. After learning on a training set data, the network is very often able to produce good outputs on unknown inputs.

Let F be a function defined as:

$$F : x_t \in R^k \to y_t \in R^1, \qquad (2)$$

is a representation assigning one value y_t to k-dimensional input a given time period t. Let G be is a restriction of F defined as:

$$G(x_t, w_t) : x_t \in R_{train}^k \to y_t \in R_{train}^1, \qquad (3)$$

where R_{train} is a complement of R_{val} to R. Then, artificial neural network is a mathematical model defined by finding the values w_t so that the function in Eq. (1) would be minimal:

$$E(w_t) = \sum_{x_t y_t \in R_{train}^k} (G(x_t, w_t) - y_t). \qquad (4)$$

when E minimal, one can say $G(x_t, w_t)$ is adapted to approximate the function F.

Multilayer perceptron (MLP) is the type of feed-forward neural network usually having three layers. Input layer is composed of the input vector; the output layer is represented by just one neuron and contains the network output. Usually, there is also one or more hidden layers between inputs and output. In most cases, one hidden layer is sufficient since according to Cybenko theorem [27] the network with one hidden layer is able to approximate any continuous function. Layers are interconnected via synapses (also called weights), which represent parameters of the neural network model.

2.3. Radial Basis Neural Network

Radial Basis Function (RBF) ANN is the upgrade of MLP network. The name of this type of neural network comes from the name of its activation function. Generally, a radial basis function (RBF) is real-valued functions whose values depend only on the distance from the origin or from some other point c, called a center:

$$\varphi(x, c) = \varphi(\|x - c\|). \tag{5}$$

Any function ϕ that satisfies the property in Eq. (7) is a radial function. The norm is usually Euclidean distance.

Hence, the biggest difference between MLP and RBF is in using the different function for activating hidden neurons. RBF neural network uses radial basis function of Gaussian type instead of the sigmoid function for activating neurons in the hidden layer. This function is defined for j^{th} hidden neuron as:

$$\psi_1\left(u^j\right) = e^{\frac{-u^j}{2\sigma_j^2}} = e^{\frac{-\|x - w^j\|^2}{2\sigma_j^2}}, j = 1, 2, ...s, \tag{6}$$

where σ_j^2 is the variance of jth neuron. The network output for RBF neural network is then counted as follows:

$$y = \psi_2\left(\sum_j v_j * \psi_1(\|x - w\|)\right) = \sum_{j=1}^{s} v_j * e^{\frac{-\|x - w^j\|^2}{2\sigma_j^2}}. \tag{7}$$

2.4. Back-Propagation Algorithm

The most popular method for learning in multilayer networks is called back-propagation (BP). It was first invented in 1969 by Bryson and Ho [28], but was largely ignored until the mid-1980s. BP is a multi-stage dynamic system optimization method mainly used for adapting parameters of feed-forward neural networks. This algorithm, which is based on gradient descent

and is a generalization of the delta rule, is a supervised learning method. Hence, the training set of desired outputs, according to which the adaptation is performed, is required. The assumption of using back-propagation is that the activation function of the neurons is differentiable.

2.5. Genetic Algorithms

Genetic algorithms, which are algorithms for optimization, are stochastic search techniques that guide a population of solutions towards an optimum using the principles of evolution and natural genetics [29]. Their representation and operators characterize them. Basic genetic operators include reproduction, crossover and mutation [29].

A key concept for genetic algorithms is that of schemata, or building blocks . A schema is a subset of the fields of a chromosome set to particular values with the other fields left to vary. As originally observed in [30], the power of genetic algorithms lies in their ability to implicitly evaluate large numbers of schemata simultaneously and to combine smaller schemata into larger schemata [31].

Adopted from biological systems, genetic algorithms are based loosely on several features of biological evolution [23]. In order to work properly, they require five components (way of encoding solutions, evaluation function, way of initializing population, operators for reproduction and parameter settings). For details, see [31].

When the components of the GA are chosen appropriately, the reproduction process will continually generate better children from good parents, the algorithm can produce populations of better and better individuals, converging finally on results close to a global optimum. Additionally, GA can efficiently search large and complex (i.e., possessing many local optima) spaces to find nearly global optima [31]. In many cases, the standard operators, mutation and crossover, are sufficient for performing the optimization. Moreover, GAs are also capable of handling problems in which the objective function is discontinuous, non-differentiable, non-convex or noisy. Since the algorithms operate on a population instead of a single point in the search space, they climb many peaks in parallel and therefore reduce the probability of finding local minima [30].

3. Hypothesis

Scientists try to incorporate other methods into RBF network to better its outputs. For example, in [32] authors use genetic algorithms for creating "Evolving"

RBF – i.e. to automatically find the ideal number of hidden neurons. Montana in [31] uses genetic algorithms with multilayer perceptron neural network for weight adaptation.

First, RBF neural network will be combined with an unsupervised learning method for clustering called K-means. Since Kohonen [33] and Marcek [34] demonstrated that non-hierarchical clustering algorithms used with artificial neural networks could cause the better results of ANN, K-means will be used together with RBF in order to find out whether this combination can produce the effective improvement of this network in the domain of financial time series. The K-means will be used in the phase of non-random initialization of weight vector w performed before the phase of network learning. In many cases it is not necessary to interpolate the output value by radial functions, it is quite sufficient to use one function for a set of data (cluster), whose center is considered to be a center of activation function of a neuron. The values of centroids will be used as the initialization values of weight vector w. Weights should be located near the global minimum of the error function Eq. (4), and the lower number of epochs is supposed be used for network training. We will use adaptive version of K-means.

Also, the back-propagation itself is a weakness of RBF. The convergence is slow and in addition it generally converges to any local minimum on the error surface, since stochastic gradient descent exists on the surface, which is not flat. Therefore, the back-propagation will be substituted by the genetic algorithm (GA) as an alternative learning technique in the process of weights adaptation. GAs are generally not bothered by local minima. The mutation and crossover operators can step from a valley across a hill to an even lower valley with no more difficulty than descending directly into the valley.

Finally, in this paper we also suggest a hybrid model. The reason to use this hybridization is to create a model with better forecasting properties. There exist quite a lot hybrid models in time series forecasting; for example in [35] authors combine Hidden Markov Models (HMM) with GARCH models to forecast time series, authors in [36] and [37] use a combination of Support Vector Machines (SVM) and genetic algorithms and [38] constructed a hybrid model composed of SVM and self-organizing maps (SOM) in time series prediction process. Our suggested hybrid model combines RBF neural network and moving average used for error modeling. Hence, in the next part of this paper, hypothesis that a combination of ANN and statistical model can produce a model with better properties, will be tested.

4. Pre-Experimental Procedures

4.1. Data and Model Validation

For our experiments daily close price of the USD/CAD currency was chosen. The interval was from 10/31/2008 to 10/31/2012, i.e. 1044 daily observations. The data was downloaded from the website http://www.global-view.com/forex-trading-tools/forex-history. Due to va-

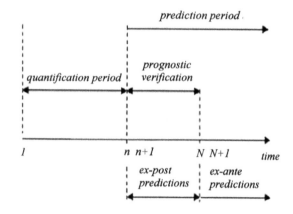

Fig. 1: Observations division of AUD/USD data.

lidation of the model, data were divided into two parts. The first part included 912 observations (from 10/31/2008 to 4/30/2012) and was used for training of the model. The second part of data (5/1/2012 to 10/31/2012) counting 132 observations, was used for model validation by making one-day-ahead ex-post forecast. These observations were not incorporated into model training (parameters of a model were not changing anymore) in order to find out the prediction power, as there is an assumption that if the model can handle to predict data from ex-post set, it will also be able to predict values of a currency pair in the future.

4.2. Box-Jenkins Analysis

Box-Jenkins analysis was performed to make a comparison between statistical models and our tested neural network models. For statistical modelling, Eviews software was used. The ADF unit root test confirmed the hypothesis that the series was non-stationary. To confirm stationarity, the series was differentiated which is a necessary condition in Box-Jenkins modeling.

By analyzing autocorrelation and partial autocorrelation functions of first differences of USD/CAD, there was no significant coefficient in the series. Therefore, we proceeded to model this series as a pure GARCH process. The suitability for using stochastic volatility model was also accepted by performed heteroscedasticity test. ARCH test confirmed the series was heteroscedastic since the null hypothesis of homoscedasticity was rejected at 5 % and so the residuals were characterized by the presence of ARCH effect which is quite a frequent phenomenon at financial time series. Several models of ARCH [6] and GARCH [7], were estimated. The estimation of different models was only based on 912 in-sample observations, in order to make ex-ante predictions with remaining 132 observations. Marquardt optimization procedure was used for finding the optimal values of GARCH parameters; initial values of parameters were counted using Ordinary Least Squares (OLS) method and these values were then by iterative process consisted of 500 iterations. Convergence rate was set to 0.0001. After GARCH model had completed, the standardized residuals of this series were tested with Ljung-Box Q test in order to confirm there are no significant coefficients in residuals of this model. Our assumption was confirmed, hence according to statistical tests the model was correct. The final definition of the model is:

$$\log(h_t) = -0.172109 + 0.117148\frac{\varepsilon_{t-1}}{\sqrt{h_t}} +$$

$$0.037398\frac{\varepsilon_{t-1}}{\sqrt{h_t}} + 0.992135\log(h_{t-1}). \tag{8}$$

5. Experiments

The estimation of all models was only based on 912 observations, in order to make further comparisons with the predictions of the 132 remaining observations. In this paper, only one-step-ahead forecast were used, i.e. horizon of predictions was equal to one day. MSE (Mean Square Error) numerical characteristic was used for assessing models. The result of a given model is from the best neuron configuration (in every model we tested number of hidden neuron from 3 to 10 to find the best output results of the network). Experiment for every model configuration was performed 12 times; the best and worst results were eliminated and from the rest the mean and standard deviation were counted. Our created models of neural networks were then compared to standard statistical models.

5.1. RBF Neural Network

Own application of RBF neural network (implemented in JAVA with one hidden layer where we tested from three to ten processing neurons to achieve best results of network) was used. For every model, just the result with the best configuration is stated. The identity function was used as an activation function for the input layer and the output layer too. For the hidden layer the radial basis function was used as an activation function as it has been showed that it provides

better accuracy than the perceptron network. In a normal case, the weights of neural network were initiated randomly – generated from the uniform distribution < 0.1). For the BP learning the learning rate was set to 0.001 to avoid the easy imprisonment in the local minimum. The number of epochs for each experiment with backpropagation was set to 5000 as this showed to be a good number for backpropagation convergence. The final results were taken from the best of 5000 epochs and not from the last epoch in order to avoid overfitting of the neural network. As raw (nonstandardized) data was used, we analyzed original nonstationary series for autocorrelation. As there was a strong dependence on the previous day (autocorrelation = 0.996), we used just one network input - the previous observation.

5.2. K-means Algorithm

K-means instead of random initialization of weights was used before they were adapted by BP. Coordinances of clusters were initiated as coordinances of randomly chosen input vector. After that, every input vector was assigned the nearest cluster. When this procedure has been done, the coordinates of clusters were recounted. This cycle was repeated 5000 times and the learning rate for the cluster adaptation was set to 0.001. The number of clusters was set to the number of hidden neurons.

In our experiments, the adaptive version of K-means will be used which is defined as follows:

- Random initialization of centroids in the dimension of the input vector.

- Introduction of the input vector x_i.

- Determination of the nearest from all centroids to a given input.

- Adaptation the coordinates of the centroid according to the rule: $c_{j'} = c_{j'}^* + \eta(x_i - c_{j'})$, where j' is the nearest cluster to the introduced input, η is a learning rate parameter.

- Termination of the algorithm if all inputs were processed or the coordinates of the cluster are not changing anymore.

5.3. Genetic Algorithm

Our own implementation of the genetic algorithm was used for weight adaptation. The chromosome length was set according to the formula: $D * s + s$, where s is the number of hidden neurons and D is the dimension of the input vector. A specific gene of the chromosome was a float value and represented a specific weight in the neural network. The whole chromosome represented weights of the whole neural network. The fitting function for evaluating the chromosomes was the mean square error function (MSE). The chromosome (individual) with the best MSE was automatically transferred into the next generation. The other individuals of the next generation were chosen as follows: By tournament selection (size of the tournament equaled to 100) 100 individuals were randomly chosen from the population. The fittest of them was then chosen as a parent. The second parent was chosen in the same way. The new individuals were then created by crossover operation. If the generated value from $\langle 0.1 \rangle$ was lower than 0.5 the weight of the first parent at the specific position was assigned to a new individual. Otherwise, a new individual received the weight of the second parent.

The mutation rate was set to 0.01. If performed, the specific gene (weight) of a chromosome was changed to a random value. The weight initialization for the first population of chromosomes was tested too. Testing intervals $\langle -1, 1 \rangle$, $\langle -10, 10 \rangle$ and $\langle -100, 100 \rangle$ it was found out that the best results are presented when using weights generation from -10 to 10.

The size of the population and the number of generation for the genetic algorithm were set accordingly to the settings of back-propagation. In back-propagation there were 5000 cycles of the forward signal propagation plus 5000 cycles of backward error propagation. In GA the size of the population equalled to 1000 and 10 was the number of generations. As the operators of mutation and crossover do little computation, the computational demand is relatively the same.

5.4. Hybrid Model

Hybrid model is a combination of more independent models integrated into one model to produce only one output in specific time t. The main point in constructing hybrid models is to find out how to combine independent models in order to produce the best possible results.

In this work the following hybrid model was tested - a combination of RBF neural network and the error moving average model. The inspiration for the moving average part came from Box-Jenkins statistical models. We try to eliminate the error of the neural network by modeling the residuals of RBF just like moving averages of random part in Box-Jenkins ARIMA models. The hybridized model which was suggested is defined as follows:

$$y = RBF(x, w, v, s) + MA^*(q), \qquad (9)$$

$$y = \psi_2(\sum_j v_j * \psi_1[\phi(\|x - w\|)]) + \sum_{i=1}^{q} \varepsilon_{t-i}, \qquad (10)$$

$$y = \sum_{j=1}^{s} v_j * exp^{\frac{-\|x-w^j\|^2}{2\sigma_j^2}} + \sum_{k=1}^{q} e_{k-i}^{RBF}, \quad j = 1..s, \qquad (11)$$

$$y_t = \sum_{j=1}^{s} v_j * exp^{\frac{-\sqrt{\sum_{i=1}^{k}(x_i^t - w_i^j)^2}^2}{2\sigma_j^2}} + \frac{1}{n}\sum_{n=1}^{q} e_{y_{t-n}}^{RBF}. \qquad (12)$$

6. Results and Discussion

The reason why the prediction qualities were applied on the validation set (ex-ante predictions) was the fact that an ANN can become so specialized for the training set that could lose accuracy in the test set. Therefore, it is obvious that even if the network provides acceptable results on the training set, it is not sure the results will not acceptable when they are applied to new data. Therefore, the estimation of all models was only based on 912 observations, in order to make further comparisons with the predictions of the 132 remaining observations. In this paper, only one-step-ahead forecast were used, i.e. horizon of predictions was equal to one day. We used MSE (Mean Square Error) numerical characteristic for assessing models. The result of a given model is from the best neuron configuration (in every model we tested number of hidden neuron from 3 to 10 to find the best output results of the network). Experiment for every model configuration was performed 12 times; the best and worst results were eliminated and from the rest the mean and standard deviation were counted.

First of all, from Tab. 1 it can be clearly seen (RBF network, one autoregressive input) that network with BP achieved the best results when there are 4 neurons in the hidden layer. On the other hand, the advanced methods for network learning (K-means + BP, GA) achieved the best results with 4 (GA), respectively 9 neurons (K-means + BP). However, when these advanced methods are used, the number of hidden neurons seem to not play an important role as the results where comparable . Following from that one can deduce that for remembering the relationships in this time series it is enough to use a smaller number of hidden neurons (three or four).

Secondly, the standard back-propagation algorithm for weights adaptation showed to be the great weakness of the neural network. The convergence was very slow and in addition, it generally converged to any local minimum on the error surface, since stochastic gradient descent existed on the surface which was not flat. It was due to the fact, that the gradient method does not guarantee to find optimal values of parameters and imprisonment in the local minimum is quite possible.

Bearing in mind the disadvantages of BP stated in the previous part of the paper, also other methods for network adaptation were tested– K-means, that was used in the phase of non-random initialization of weight vector w performed before the phase of network learning, and GA. It is no surprise that the RBF network combined with K-means or GA for weights adaptation provided significantly better results than the standard RBF (see Tab. 1). Moreover, besides lower MSE, another advantage of using a genetic algorithm or K-means upgrade is the consistency of predictions. The standard deviation of these methods is incomparably lower than the SD when the standard BP is used (see Tab. 1).

As for K-means, its biggest strength is in the speed of convergence of the network. Without K-means, it took considerably longer time to achieve the minimum. However, when the K-means was used to set the weights of the network before backpropagation, the time for reaching the minimum was much shorter. Therefore, the advantage of using K-means together with backpropagation is in the speed of adaptivity rather than in better predictions. Following from that one can say that in many cases it is not necessary to interpolate the output value by radial functions, it is quite sufficient to use one function for a set of data (cluster), whose center is considered to be a center of activation function of a neuron and the values of centroids can be used as an initialization values of weight vector w. The assumption used here was that weights should be located near the global minimum of the error function the (Eq. (4)). The advantage of this combination is that the lower number of epochs is supposed be used for network training. Moreover, Kmeans is quite simple to implement. However, one must bear in mind that Kmeans is a relatively efficient algorithm only in the domain of non-extreme values. Otherwise, other advanced non-hierarchical clustering algorithms must be used.

Having also tested GA in weights adaptation, it was found out the convergence was also considerably faster than at BP and therefore it was no surprise that sometimes the network converged only after 5 generations.

If we compare weights adaptation via GA and Kmeans plus backpropagation, the results are almost the same. Even though, K-means provided better results compared to GA, the differences are not very large. However, GA has a bigger potential to perform even better forecasts as there are more parameters needed to be optimized. Backpropagation, even though used with Kmeans, seemed to reach its global minimum as even with the higher number of epochs (we tested back-propagation up to 10000 cycles) the results were almost the same. The number of hidden neurons seemed to not play an important role as the results were comparable.

Also the number of inputs coming into the network in this paper was tested; the ANN with only one input provided better forecasts than the network with three autoregressive inputs (see Tab. 1).

For the RBF-SMA hybrid ANN model, the same strategy as for the standard ANN was used. With the given number of hidden neurons (step by step we tested the model with hidden neurons from three to ten) twelve testing procedures were performed. Just like for the standard model, we firstly trained the standard network, using either GA, BP or K-means plus BP, we then checked the predictive accuracy of the standard RBF using the last 133 observations which were not used for model training. Afterwards, the hybridization of the ex-ante predictions with moving averages of previous errors was performed. What for the value of parameter of the moving average, the values from one to one hundred were tested and we experimentally found out the best values for the tested data (for the majority of testing procedures the optimal value of moving average parameter was 44). Finally, just like for the standard RBF, from the best ten out of twelve experiments, the mean and standard deviation of the best results of RBF-SMA (having the optimal value of MA parameter) were counted. For every number of hidden neurons tested, the results are stated in the Tab. 1 which contains the results of out-of-sample predictions provided by the different models and optimization techniques, respectively.

To see the effectiveness or ineffectiveness of the suggested hybrid model, comparative analysis with individual model is usually performed. We provided the comparison with standard RBF network as well as the statistical ARIMA and GARCH model in order to show the prediction power of our suggested model. Table 2 states the final results of the numerical comparison of all tested and quantified models. Table 3 states the percentual comparison of our suggested model against the standard neural network.

Deducting from the Tab. 1 and Tab. 2, the network with only one input provided significantly better results in the validation set than the network with three inputs. The standard RBF provided the best outputs when it was combined with K-means and BP. The error of prediction at this network was a little bit lower compared to the statistical model; however these two models provided almost the same results.

Comparing the numerical (Tab. 2) as well as graphical results (Fig. 2 and Fig. 3), the suggested hybrid model improved the prediction power of the standard RBF considerably. Therefore, deducting from the performed experiments one can state that the application of our suggested new hybrid neural network model into the domain of exchange rates provides significantly bet-

Tab. 1: Prediction power of RBF-SMA model (back-propagation, one input).

Inputs	Neurons	Weights adaptation	RBF MSE	sd	RBF-SMA MSE	sd
Autoregressive(1)	3	BP	0.0000282628	1.29939E-05	1.69513E-05	0.0000039062
		KM + BP	0.0000175381	0.0000006224	0.0000137675	0.0000009931
		GA	0.0000180929	0.0000016469	0.0000136146	0.0000003816
	4	BP	0.0000183763	0.0000028765	0.0000136485	0.0000005710
		KM + BP	0.0000173006	0.0000004025	0.0000130549	0.0000003013
		GA	0.0000176860	0.0000006219	0.0000137306	0.0000010974
	5	BP	0.0000299369	0.0000812952	0.0000168334	0.0000069884
		KM + BP	0.0000174326	0.0000007575	0.0000133526	0.0000003885
		GA	0.0000176925	0.0000016246	0.0000141386	0.0000011016
	6	BP	0.0000248756	0.0000105719	0.0000140990	0.0000016518
		KM + BP	0.0000187115	0.0000024836	0.0000140002	0.0000011530
		GA	0.0000205995	0.0000073265	0.0000139753	0.0000010496
	7	BP	0.000029955	0.0000381995	0.0000152401	0.0000018918
		KM + BP	0.0000170959	0.0000002617	0.0000135883	0.0000004315
		GA	0.0000265817	0.0000100553	0.0000160908	0.0000033735
	8	BP	0.0000530843	0.0000462909	0.0000161911	0.0000018501
		KM + BP	0.0000169521	0.0000003200	0.0000133422	0.0000002243
		GA	0.0000181709	0.0000016133	0.0000152679	0.0000030365
	9	BP	0.0000594814	0.0000611668	0.0000156977	0.0000018874
		KM + BP	0.0000168649	0.0000002319	0.0000132936	0.0000003833
		GA	0.0000290958	0.0000136948	0.0000174571	0.0000049429
	10	BP	0.0000842809	0.0000580551	0.0000163252	0.0000019133
		KM + BP	0.0000179805	0.0000029834	0.0000139659	0.0000011918
		GA	0.0000236821	0.0000093964	0.0000193432	0.0000056131
Autoregressive(3)	3	BP	0.0000246627	0.0000009284	0.0000161939	0.0000006213
		KM + BP	0.0000294856	0.0000038188	0.0000206474	0.0000024092
		GA	0.0000211109	0.0000028368	0.0000145220	0.0000008942
	4	BP	0.0000272034	0.0000076035	0.0000167076	0.0000014736
		KM + BP	0.0000281149	0.0000049241	0.0000191500	0.0000028708
		GA	0.0000211384	0.0000022806	0.0000150333	0.0000009834
	5	BP	0.0000409725	0.0000299478	0.0000184556	0.0000017546
		KM + BP	0.0000256209	0.0000025080	0.0000173282	0.0000016944
		GA	0.0000208047	0.0000018349	0.0000147753	0.0000008241
	6	BP	0.0000864375	0.0001034218	0.0000170064	0.0000011602
		KM + BP	0.0000249070	0.0000011215	0.0000164002	0.0000004802
		GA	0.0000221589	0.0000039497	0.0000153159	0.0000029622
	7	BP	0.0001348482	0.0000953912	0.0000182209	0.0000007447
		KM + BP	0.0000271282	0.0000055004	0.0000165589	0.0000010142
		GA	0.0000208281	0.0000024914	0.0000148913	0.0000014674
	8	BP	0.0001732475	0.0000906953	0.0000178474	0.0000005939
		KM + BP	0.0000397440	0.0000458707	0.0000165625	0.0000007438
		GA	0.0000219612	0.0000041218	0.0000154261	0.0000019254
	9	BP	0.0001491386	0.0000806291	0.0000178850	0.0000010715
		KM + BP	0.0000323388	0.0000107404	0.0000182793	0.0000019037
		GA	0.0000227303	0.0000034871	0.0000156919	0.0000012017
	10	BP	0.0000965767	0.0000678169	0.0000182020	0.0000006811
		KM + BP	0.0000398751	0.0000456632	0.0000160730	0.0000011953
		GA	0.0000212117	0.0000042826	0.0000150181	0.0000027353

Tab. 2: Final comparison of predictive qualities – best configurations (out-of-sample predictions).

Model	Regressor(s)	Weights Adaptation	Mean MSE *1	sd*2
Standard ANN (RBF)	Autoregressive (1)	Back-propagation	$1.84 \cdot 10^{-5}$	$2.88 \cdot 10^{-6}$
		K-means + Back-propagation	$1.69 \cdot 10^{-5}$	$2.32 \cdot 10^{-7}$
		Genetic algorithm	$1.77 \cdot 10^{-5}$	$6.22 \cdot 10^{-7}$
	Autoregressive (3)	Back-propagation	$2.47 \cdot 10^{-5}$	$9.28 \cdot 10^{-7}$
		K-means + Back-propagation	$2.49 \cdot 10^{-5}$	$1.12 \cdot 10^{-6}$
		Genetic algorithm	$2.08 \cdot 10^{-5}$	$1.83 \cdot 10^{-6}$
Hybrid model	Autoregressive (1)	Back-Propagation	$1.36 \cdot 10^{-5}$	$5.71 \cdot 10^{-7}$
		K-means + Back-propagation	$1.31 \cdot 10^{-5}$	$3.01 \cdot 10^{-7}$
		Genetic Algorithm	$1.36 \cdot 10^{-5}$	$3.82 \cdot 10^{-7}$
	Autoregressive (3)	Back-propagation	$1.62 \cdot 10^{-5}$	$6.21 \cdot 10^{-7}$
		K-means + Back-propagation	$1.64 \cdot 10^{-5}$	$4.80 \cdot 10^{-7}$
		Genetic algorithm	$1.45 \cdot 10^{-5}$	$8.94 \cdot 10^{-7}$
AR(0)-EGARCH(1,1,1)	Conditional Variance (1)	Marquardt	$1.71 \cdot 10^{-5}$	-
		Berndt-Hall-Hall-Hausman	$1.71 \cdot 10^{-5}$	-

Tab. 3: Percentual improvement of the suggested hybrid model compared to the standard RBF.

Inputs	Neurons	Improvement of suggested hybrid compared to the standard RBF [%]		
		BP	K-means + BP	GA
Autoregressive(1)	3	40.022573	21.499478	24.751698
	4	25.727704	24.540767	22.364582
	5	43.770397	23.404426	20.087043
	6	43.32197	25.178633	32.157091
	7	49.123352	20.5172	39.466626
	8	69.499268	21.294707	15.976094
	9	73.609061	21.175933	40.001306
	10	80.630012	22.327521	18.321433
Autoregressive(3)	3	34.338495	29.974632	31.210891
	4	38.582677	31.886651	28.881562
	5	54.956129	32.366935	28.980951
	6	80.325206	34.154254	30.881497
	7	86.487843	38.960565	28.5038
	8	89.698322	58.327043	29.757481
	9	88.007799	43.475639	30.964835
	10	81.152804	59.691637	29.19898

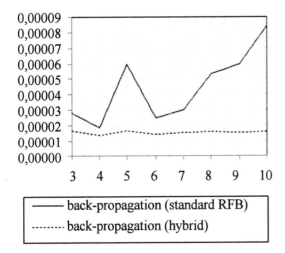

Fig. 2: Predictive accuracy of standard RBF model and RBF-SMA hybrid model (BP algorithm).

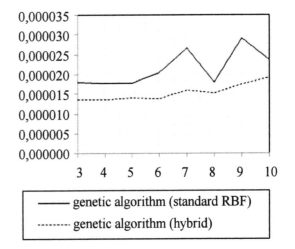

Fig. 3: Predictive accuracy of standard RBF model and RBF-SMA hybrid model (Kmeans + BP).

ter results than the standard RBF neural network as well as statistical ARIMA model.

7. Conclusion

In this paper we performed financial time series modeling with RBF neural networks as well as our suggested hybrid model. We used USD/CAD data that was divided into training set and validation due to model checking. Except for a standard ANN, we also combined an unsupervised learning method K-means and GA into the RBF in order to achieve better accuracy of the network. Both of the algorithms were used in the process of adapting weights of the network. The reason for incorporating other algorithms into the network was that the BP is considered a weakness of the RBF. Some of the drawbacks of BP include the scaling problem, the complexity problem, the slow convergence, the conver-

gence to a local minimum etc. K-means was used in the phase of non-random initialization of weight vector w before learning.

We also suggested the new hybrid neural network model in order to improve the prediction accuracy of the standard ANN. One can say we have used only the easiest and slow BP and not a more powerful version of BP. However, it is important to note that our main objective was to compare the standard neural network with our suggested hybrid model. Due to this we used only the standard BP in both models.

We performed experiments to find out that our suggested hybrid model based on RBF neural network had a significant predictive superiority over the statistical model as well as standard characteristics always overcame individual models (ANN, statistical model); the improvements were ranging from about 18 percent to more than 89 percent. Hence, the suggested hybrid showed to be a great improvement of the standard RBF neural network as we experimentally clearly proved that for the USD/CAD the hybrid model provided significantly better forecasts than the standard model of the RBF neural network and the statistical model and there was a clear benefit of better one-day-ahead forecasts. Following from these empirical findings for out-of-sample one-step-ahead forecasts, we believe that this model has a great potential in time series modeling.

Acknowledgment

This paper was supported by European Social Fund within the project CZ.1.07/2.3.00/20.0296.

References

[1] BROWN, R. G. *Smoothing Forecasting and Prediction of Discrete Time Series.* Englewood Cliffs, NJ: Prentice-Hall, 1963. ISBN 0-286-49592-2.

[2] HOLT, C. C. Forecasting seasonals and trends by exponentially weighted moving averages. *International Journal of Forecasting.* 2004, vol. 20, no. 1, pp. 5–10. ISSN 0169-2070. DOI: 10.1016/j.ijforecast.2003.09.015.

[3] WINTERS, P. R. Forecasting Sales by Exponentially Weighted Moving Averages. *Management Science.* 1960, vol. 6, no. 3, pp. 324–342. ISSN 1526-5501. DOI: 10.1287/mnsc.6.3.324.

[4] BOX, G., E. P. and G. M. JENKINS. *Time series analysis: forecasting and control.* San Fransisco, CA: Holden-Day, 2008. ISBN 978-0-470-27284-8.

[5] O'DONOVAN, T. M. *Short Term Forecasting: An Introduction to the Box-Jenkins Approach.* NY: New York, Wiley, 1983. ISBN 978-0-471-90013-9.

[6] ENGLE, R. F. Autoregressive Conditional Heteroskedasticity with Estimates of the Variance of United Kingdom Inflation. *Econometrica.* 1982, vol. 50, no. 4, pp. 987–1007. ISSN 1468-0262.

[7] BOLLERSHEV, T. Generalized Autoregressive Conditional Heteroskedasticity. *Journal of Econometrics.* 1986, vol. 31, no. 3, pp. 307–327. ISSN 0304-4076. DOI: 10.1016/0304-4076(86)90063-1.

[8] HECHT-NIELSEN, R. *Neurocomputing.* Indianapolis: Addison-Wesley, 1990. ISBN 978-0201093551.

[9] HERTZ, J. A., A. S. KROGH and R. G. PALMER. *Introduction To The Theory Of Neural Computation.* Boulder: Westview Press, 1991. ISBN 978-0-201-51560-2.

[10] HIEMSTRA, C. and J. D. JONES. Testing for linear and nonlinear Granger causality in the stock price-volume relation. *The Journal of Finance.* 1994, vol. 49, no. 5, pp. 1639–1664. ISSN 1540-6261. DOI: 10.1111/j.1540-6261.1994.tb04776.x.

[11] DE GOOIJER, J. G. and R. J. HYNDMAN. 25 years of time series forecasting. *International Journal of Forecasting.* 2006, vol. 22, no. 3, pp. 443–473. ISSN 0169-2070. DOI: 10.1016/j.ijforecast.2006.01.001.

[12] HILL, T., L. MARQUEZ, M. O'CONNOR and W. REMUS. Artificial neural network models for forecasting and decision making. *International Journal of Forecasting.* 1994, vol. 10, no. 1, pp. 5–15. ISSN 0169-2070. DOI: 10.1016/0169-2070(94)90045-0.

[13] HWITE, H. Economic prediction using neural networks: the case of IBM daily stock returns. In: *IEEE International Conference on Neural Networks.* San Diego: IEEE, 1988, pp. 451–458. DOI: 10.1109/ICNN.1988.23959.

[14] MARCEK, D. Some Intelligent Approaches to Stock Price Modelling and Forecasting. *Journal of Information, Control and Management Systems.* 2004, vol. 2, no. 1, pp. 1–6. ISSN 1336-1716.

[15] THINYANE, H. and J. MILLIN. An Investigation into the Use of Intelligent Systems for Currency Trading. *Computational Economics.* 2011, vol. 37, no. 4, pp. 363–374. ISSN 0927-7099. DOI: 10.1007/s10614-011-9260-4.

[16] PARK, C. H. and S. H. IRWIN. The profitability of technical analysis: A review. In: *Social Science Research Network* [online]. 2004. Available at: http://papers.ssrn.com/.

[17] HASSAN, R., B. NATH and M. KIRLEY. A fusion model of HMM, ANN and GA for stock market forecasting. *Expert Systems with Applications.* 2007, vol. 33, no. 1, pp. 171–180. ISSN 0957-4174. DOI: 10.1016/j.eswa.2006.04.007.

[18] STERBA, J. and K. HILOVSKA. The Implementation of Hybrid ARIMA-Neural Network Prediction Model for Agregate Water Consumption Prediction. *Aplimat–Journal of Applied Mathematics.* 2010, vol. 3, no. 3, pp. 377–384. ISBN 1337-6365.

[19] ZHUANG, X.-F. and L.-W. CHAN. Volatility Forecasts in Financial Time Series with HMM-GARCH Models. In: *Intelligent Data Engineering and Automated Learning–IDEAL 2004.* Exeter: Springer, 2004, pp. 807–812. ISBN 978-3-540-22881-3. DOI: 10.1007/978-3-540-28651-6_120.

[20] CHIKHI, M., A. PEGUIN-FEISSOLLE and M. TERRAZA. SEMIFARMA-HYGARCH Modeling of Dow Jones Return Persistence. *Computational Economics*. 2013, vol. 41, no. 2, pp. 249–265. ISSN 1572-9974. DOI: 10.1007/s10614-012-9328-9.

[21] CHOUDHRY, R. and K. GARG. A Hybrid Machine Learning System for Stock Market Forecasting. *World Academy of Science, Engineering and Technology*. 2008, vol. 39, no. 3, pp. 315–318. ISSN 1543-5962.

[22] FALAT, L. and D. MARCEK. Volatility Forecasting in Financial Risk Management with Statistical Models and ARCH-RBF Neural Networks. *Journal of Risk Analysis and Crisis Response*. 2014, vol. 4, no. 2, pp. 77–95. ISSN 2210-8505. DOI: 10.2991/jrarc.2014.4.2.4.

[23] HORNIK, K. Some new results on neural network approximation. *Neural Networks*. 1993, vol. 6, no. 8, pp. 1069–1072. ISSN 0893-6080. DOI: 10.1016/S0893-6080(09)80018-X.

[24] HORNIK, K., M. STINCHCOMBER and H. WHITE. Multilayer feedforward networks are universal approximations. *Neural Networks*. 1989, vol. 2, no. 5, pp. 359–366. ISSN 0893-6080. DOI: 10.1016/0893-6080(89)90020-8.

[25] MACIEL, L. S. and R. BALLINI. Design a Neural Network for Time Series Financial Forecasting: Accuracy and Robustness Analysis. In: *Computer Science & Engineering*. 2008. Available at: http://www.unr.edu/cse/.

[26] DARBELLAY, G. A. and M. SLAMA. Forecasting the short-term demand for electricity: Do neural networks stand a better chance? *International Journal of Forecasting*. 2000, vol. 16, no. 1, pp. 71–83. ISSN 0169-2070. DOI: 10.1016/S0169-2070(99)00045-X.

[27] CYBENKO, G. Approximation by superpositions of a sigmoidal function. *Mathematics of Control, Signals and Systems (MCSS)*. 1989, vol. 2, no. 4, pp. 303–314. ISSN 1435-568X. DOI: 10.1007/BF02551274.

[28] BRYSON, A., E. and Y.-Ch. HO. *Applied optimal control: optimization, estimation, and control*. London: Taylor & Francis, 1969. ISBN 978-0891162285.

[29] VISHWAKARMA, D. D. Genetic Algorithm based Weights Optimization of Artificial Neural Network. *Network International Journal of Advanced Research in Electrical, Electronics and Instrumentation Engineering*. 2012, vol. 1, no. 3, pp. 206–211. ISSN 2278-8875.

[30] HOLLAND, J. H. *Adaptation in Natural and Artificial Systems*. Michigan: University of Michigan Press. 1975. ISBN 9780262581110.

[31] MONTANA, D. J. and L. DAVIS. Training feedforward neural networks using genetics algorithms. In: *Proceedings of the 11th International Joint Conference on Artificial Intelligence*. San Francisco: Morgan Kaufmann Publishers Inc., 1989, pp. 762–767.

[32] RIVAS, V. M., J. J. MERELO, P. A. CASTILLO, M. G. ARENAS and J. G. CASTELLANO. Evolving RBF neural networks for time-series forecasting with EvRBF. *Information Sciences*. 2004, vol. 165, no. 3–4, pp. 207–220. ISSN 0020-0255. DOI: 10.1016/j.ins.2003.09.025.

[33] KOHONEN, T. *Self-organising maps*. Berlin: Springer, 1995. ISBN 3-540-58600-8.

[34] MARCEK, D. and M. MARCEK. *Neuronove siete a ich aplikacie*. Zilina: EDIS–Vydavatelstvo Z, 2006. ISBN 80-8070-497-X.

[35] ZHUANG, X.-F. and L.-W. CHAN. Volatility Forecasts in Financial Time Series with HMM-GARCH Models. In: *Intelligent Data Engineering and Automated Learning–IDEAL 2004*. Exeter: Springer, 2004, pp. 807–812. ISBN 978-3-540-22881-3. DOI: 10.1007/978-3-540-28651-6_120.

[36] CHOUDHRY, R. and K. GARG. A Hybrid Machine Learning System for Stock Market Forecasting. *World Academy of Science, Engineering and Technology*. 2008, vol. 2, no. 3, pp. 242–245. ISSN 1543-5962.

[37] HONG, W., P. PAI, S. YANG and R. THENG. Highway traffic forecasting by support vector regression model with tabu search algorithms. In: *Proceeding of Internationall Joint Conference on Neural Networks*. Vancouver: IEEE, 2006, pp. 1617–1621. ISBN 0-7803-9490-9. DOI: 10.1109/IJCNN.2006.246627.

[38] CAO, L. and E. H. F TAY. Modified support vector machines in financial time series forecasting. *Neurocomputing*. 2002, vol. 48, no. 1–4, pp. 847–861. ISSN 0925-2312. DOI: 10.1016/S0925-2312(01)00676-2.

About Authors

Lukas FALAT was born in 1986. He received his M.Sc. from University of Zilina in 2011. His research interests include feedforward neural networks, RBF networks, hybrid neural networks, time series modeling.

Dusan MARCEK is a Professor at VSB–Technical University of Ostrava. His research interests include RBF neural networks, fuzzy and soft neural networks. He has been invited to many world conferences in countries such as China, Singapore, Hong Kong, Turkey etc.

29

Segmentation of Mushroom and Cap Width Measurement Using Modified K-Means Clustering Algorithm

Eser SERT , Ibrahim Taner OKUMUS

Computer Engineering Department, Engineering and Architecture Faculty, Kahramanmaras Sutcu Imam University, Avsar Kampusu 46100 Kahramanmaras, Turkey

esersert@ksu.edu.tr, iokumus@ksu.edu.tr

Abstract. *Mushroom is one of the commonly consumed foods. Image processing is one of the effective way for examination of visual features and detecting the size of a mushroom. We developed software for segmentation of a mushroom in a picture and also to measure the cap width of the mushroom. K-Means clustering method is used for the process. K-Means is one of the most successful clustering methods. In our study we customized the algorithm to get the best result and tested the algorithm. In the system, at first mushroom picture is filtered, histograms are balanced and after that segmentation is performed. Results provided that customized algorithm performed better segmentation than classical K-Means algorithm. Tests performed on the designed software showed that segmentation on complex background pictures is performed with high accuracy, and 20 mushrooms caps are measured with 2.281 % average relative error.*

Keywords

K-Means clustering, mushroom cap measurement, mushroom image segmentation.

1. Introduction

Due to their high nutritive content, mushrooms are one of the commonly consumed foods. Image processing techniques can be used in classifying, quality control and determining the size of a mushroom.

In the system, at first image is preprocessed and after preprocessing segmentation is performed with k-means clustering algorithm. In image processing, it is important to correctly selecting these steps, and successful application is very important to achieve the appropriate result.

In Fig. 1, a comparison of classical color k-means algorithm and proposed color k-means algorithm is provided. Algorithms are tested on 3 different mushroom types and as can be seen from the figure, proposed algorithm resulted in more successful segmentation. Figure also shows that unpreprocessed image segmentation with classical color k-means algorithm causes some problems.

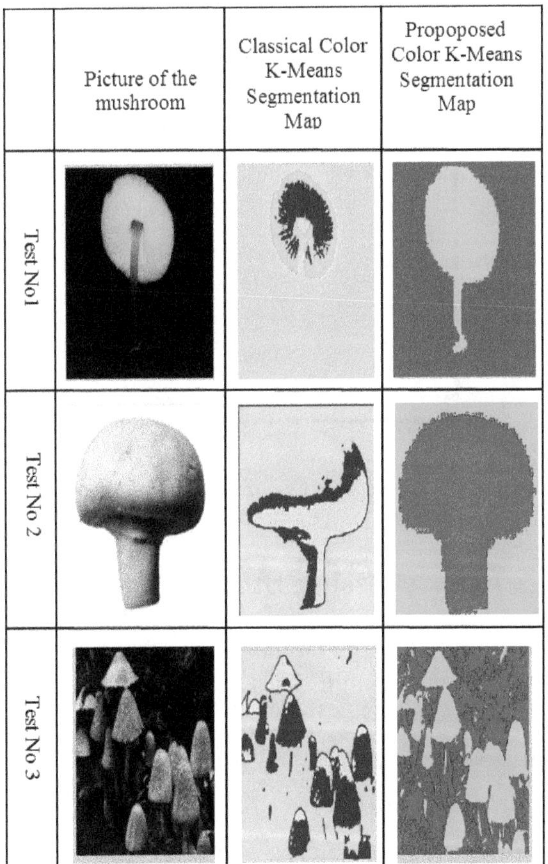

Fig. 1: Comparison of classical color K-Means and proposed color K-Means algorithms.

For the segmentation process methods such as neural networks, support vector machine, genetic algorithms can also be used. However, segmentation can be performed using k-means clustering in a simple and effective way. In the literature Hong Yao [1] successfully applied the segmentation on a fish picture. Yong Zhang [2] applied the segmentation using PSO and PCM. Zhiqiang Lao [3] segmented White matter lesions using support vector machine.

2. Working Principle of the System

System contains 3 steps as can be seen in Fig. 2. First step is preprocessing, second step is segmentation and last step is showing results.

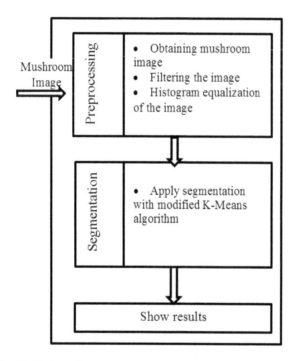

Fig. 2: System diagram.

2.1. Preprocessing Step

In the beginning of this step mushroom picture is obtained, then filtering and histogram equalization is applied to the image.

1) Filtering Process

In the beginning, the obtained mushroom picture is turned into greyscale format. After that 3×3 average filter is applied to the picture. The reason for applying average filter is providing a smooth transition among the pixels to prevent noise. Eq. (1) shows the application equation of average filter [4]:

$$f(x,y) = \frac{1}{m \times n} \sum_{(s,t) \in Sxy} \text{gray\_pixel}(s,t). \quad (1)$$

In the equation, m and n adjust the width of the region that the filtering will be applied. gray_pixel (s,t) is the intensity level at point (s,t). Since 3×3 filtering is used in the process, Eq. (2) shows the same equation for 3×3 filtering:

$$f(x,y) = \frac{1}{3 \times 3} \sum_{(s,t) \in Sxy} \text{gray\_pixel}(s,t). \quad (2)$$

Figure 3(a) show unprocessed mushroom picture and Fig. 3(b) shows filtered mushroom picture.

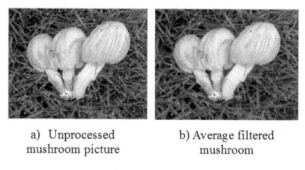

a) Unprocessed mushroom picture

b) Average filtered mushroom

Fig. 3: Applying average filtering to mushroom image.

2) Histogram Equalization

After filtering, histogram equalization is applied to the image. Histogram equalization ideally distributes the contrast of the image using the image's histogram. An image can be represented as a data array in the form of:

$$X = \{X(i,j) \mid X(i,j) \in \{X_0, X_1, \ldots, X_{L-1}\}\}. \quad (3)$$

In this data array, every component can be composed of L intensity level. In $X(i,j)$ image plane, (i,j) represents normalized intensity of a pixel. X_k is kth intensity level. Equation (4) is used to obtain probability distribution function (PDF) of the image [5]:

$$p(X_k) = \frac{n_k}{n}, 0 \leq X_k \leq 1, \quad (4)$$

where n is the total number of pixels in the input image and n_k is the number of X_k in the image X. To obtain a better contrast image Eq. (5) is used:

$$s_k = \sum_{j=0}^{L-1} p(X_j) = \sum_{j=0}^{L-1} \frac{n_j}{n} = 1, \quad (5)$$

where L is the total number of possible grey levels (such as 255 for 8 bit depth), s_k is the grey conversion value for a better contrast image. Figure 4(a) shows filtered image, Fig. 4(b) shows histogram image, Fig. 4(c) shows histogram equalized image and Fig. 4(d) shows the histogram of the image. As it can be seen from the figures after histogram equalization, intensities are equally distributed according to the pixels.

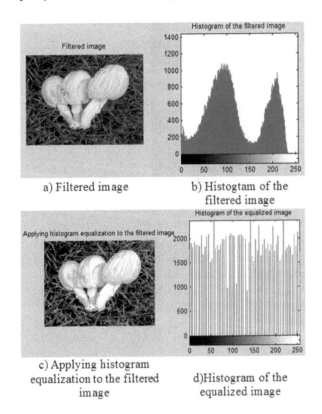

a) Filtered image

b) Histogtam of the filtered image

c) Applying histogram equalization to the filtered image

d)Histogram of the equalized image

Fig. 4: Histogram equalization process.

2.2.   Segmentation

In this step segmentation process will be explained.

1)   K-Means Method

K-Means is one of the most widely used uncontrolled learning processes. This method ensures that all data belong to a single cluster. This provides an efficient clustering mechanism. K-Means algorithm groups n data points into C number of clusters. Goal is at the end to have a high level of similarity in the clusters and low level of similarity among the clusters [1], [6].

Squared error criterion E is widely used to obtain the distance of cluster members to the cluster center. For the most successful clustering, E value is expected to be small. Equation (6) is used for obtaining the sum of the squares of the distances of members to the cluster center:

$$E = \sum_{i=1}^{C} \sum_{k=1}^{N} dist^2 (x_k, s_i). \qquad (6)$$

At the end of clustering N points are divided into C clusters. For the distance calculation Euclid equation given in Eq. (7) is commonly used [6]:

$$dist^2 (x_k, s_i) = \left\| x_k^{(i)} - s_i \right\|^2. \qquad (7)$$

2)   Color Segmentation with Modified K-Means Algorithm

Figure 5 shows the GUI structure used for mushroom segmentation and finding cap width. On the GUI shown in Fig. 5, mushroom image to be processed, grayscale k-means analysis results, color k-means analysis results, k-means clustering image is provided. Also from the GUI, edges of the interested segmentation are determined and cap width of the segmented mushroom is calculated.

Algorithm 1 provides software algorithm that is used for Gray K-Means segmentation. This stage is composed of 9 steps:

- **Preprocessing**: At this step previously described filtering and histogram equalization processes are performed. Lines 1–4 correspond to these processes in the algorithm.

- **Determination of the cluster center:** In the study, number of cluster is determined to be 3. Because of that 3 intensity levels chosen from HisteqMushroom image is set as cluster starting point. Line 5 of the algorithm shows this process, c_1, c_2 and c_3 keeps the center values.

- **Calculating distance from the cluster center:** At this step distance between each pixel in the image and the cluster centers c_1, c_2 and c_3 is calculated. Codes of the distance function are given in Algorithm-2. Function calculates the distances and keeps them in distance1, distance2, and distance3 variables.

- **Calculation of clustering data sums and producing K-Means cluster map:** Step 11 through 30 of Algorithm-1 reflects these steps. At the end of the process graykmeans variable holds the gray level k-means clustering map. `c1_sum` has cluster c_1, `c2_sum` has cluster c_2 and `c3_sum` has cluster c_3 data sum and `c1count`, `c2count`, `c3count` variables contain the respective cluster's number of members. Coordinates that lie inside cluster 1 are painted in black, coordinates that lie inside cluster 2 are painted in gray and coordinates that lie inside cluster 3 are painted in white.

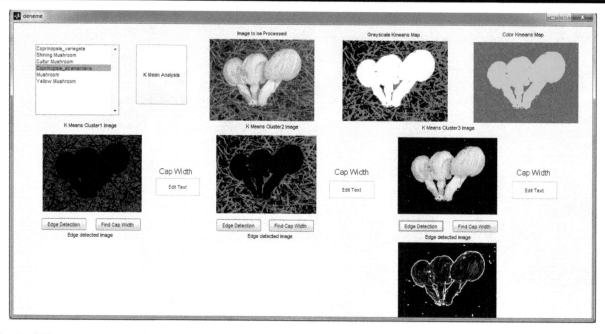

Fig. 5: GUI structure of the software that segments mushroom and calculates cap width.

- **Stopping Iteration:** `graykmean` variable and `comp_kmean` variable are equalized in line 10. If `comp_kmean` and `graykmean` are equal, iteration is stopped. Lines 31, 32 and 33 reflects this process.

- **Calculating the cluster centers:** Lines 35, 36, and 37 reflects this process. By dividing `c1_sum`, `c2_sum` and `c3_sum` into `c1count`, `c2count` and `c3count` respectively new cluster centers (c_1, c_2 and c_3) are obtained. Figure 6b) shows the grayscale segmentation map image that is stored in grayscale variable after running Algorithm-1.

- **Obtaining color segmentation map:** Grayscale segmentation map obtained in Algorithm-1 is converted into color segmentation map by Algorithm-3. Algorithm-3 turns black colored coordinates into red and corresponding data are moved to cluster 1. Similarly gray colored coordinates turned into blue and

corresponding data are moved to cluster 2 and white colored coordinates turned into green and corresponding data are moved to cluster 3. Figure 7 show Color Segmentation, Cluster1 Image, Cluster2 Image ve Cluster3 Images obtained after running algorithm 3. As it can be observed in Fig. 7f) mushroom image is successfully segmented.

- **Determining the cluster image boundaries:** At this stage sobel filter is applied to the user selected cluster image. Edge Detection button controls the boundary drawing action. After clicking

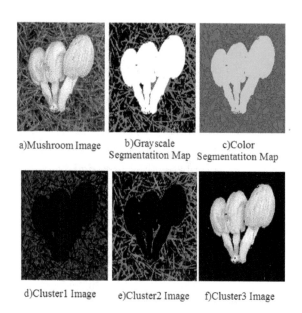

a)Mushroom Image   b)Grayscale   c)Color
Segmentatiton Map   Segmentatiton Map

d)Cluster1 Image   e)Cluster2 Image   f)Cluster3 Image

Fig. 7: Color segmentation map and cluster images.

a) Mushroom Image   b) Grayscale Segmentation
Map

Fig. 6: Grayscale Segmentation Map.

the button Edge Detected Image shows the filtered image.

- **Calculating cap width:** Find Hat Width button controls the action. `graykmean` variable is used in cap width finding algorithm. When the button is clicked by using `graykmean` value and gray level color information image is scanned from the top row to the bottom and cap width is calculated in pixels. Pixel value is then multiplied with preset calibration parameter (CP) to find the cap width in cm. In order for cap width to be measured by the software image must contain only one mushroom. On the test image cap width of the mushroom seen in cluster 3 image is calculated as 15.32 cm (Fig. 9).

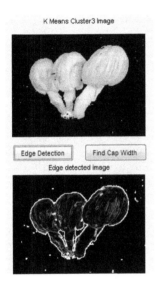

Fig. 8: Applying sobel filter to Cluster3 Image.

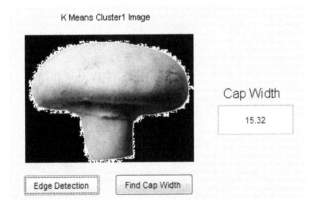

Fig. 9: Cap width calculation of cluster 1 image.

2.3. Showing the Results

Developed software shows the analysis results in separate image boxes. Calculated cap width value is provided in the textbox.

Algorithm 1 Gray K-Means segmentation algorithm.

```
1:  MushroomImage = imread('Mushroom.jpg')
2:  AverageMushroom  =  imfilter(MushroomImage,
    AverageFilter,'replicate');
3:  HisteqMushroom= histeq(AverageMushroom)
4:  [height width] = size(HisteqMushroom)
5:  c1,c2   and   c3   =   HisteqMushroom
    (randi(height,1,1), randi(width,1,1));
6:  continue = 1;
7:  while continue = 1 do
8:     c1_sum = 0; c2_sum = 0; c3_sum = 0;
9:     c1count = 0; c2count = 0; c3count = 0;
10:    comp_kmean == graykmean
11:    for i = 1:Height do
12:      for j = 1:Width do
13:        distance1 = distance(HisteqMushroom(i,j),
           c1);
14:        distance2 = distance(HisteqMushroom(i,j),
           c2);
15:        distance3 = distance(HisteqMushroom(i,j),
           c3);
16:        if distance1 < distance2 && distance1 <
           distance3 then
17:          graykmean(i,j) = 0;
18:          c1_sum  =  HisteqMushroom (i,j)  +
             c1_sum;
19:          c1count = c1count + 1;
20:        else if distance1 > distance2 & distance2 <
           distance3 then
21:          graykmean (i,j) = 0.5;
22:          c2_sum  =  HisteqMushroom (i,j )+
             c2_sum;
23:          c2count = c2count + 1;
24:        else if distance1 > distance3 && distance2
           > distance3 then
25:          graykmean (i,j) = 1;
26:          c3_sum  =  HisteqMushroom (i,j)  +
             c3_sum;
27:          c3count = c3count + 1;
28:        end if
29:      end for
30:    end for
31:    c1 = c1_sum/c1count;
32:    c2 = c2_sum/c2count;
33:    c3 = c3_sum/c3count;
34:  end while
```

Algorithm 2 Distance Calculation.

```
1:  function Euclid = distance (v1,v2)
2:  Euclid =((v1−v2)^2)^(1/2); (=ABS(v1−v2))
3:  end function
```

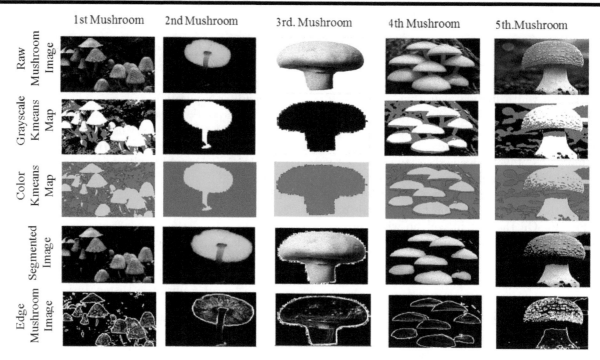

Fig. 10: Segmentation performance test images.

Algorithm 3

```
1: for i = 1:Height do
2:    for j = 1:Width do
3:       if graykmean(i,j) == 0 then
4:          cluster1(i,j,:) = MushroomImage(i,j,:);
5:          kcolormean(i,j,1) = 255;
6:          kcolormean(i,j,2) = 0;
7:          kcolormean(i,j,3) = 0;
8:       else if graykmean (i,j) == 0.5 then
9:          cluster3(i,j,:) = MushroomImage(i,j,:);
10:         kcolormean(i,j,1)=0;
11:         kcolormean(i,j,2)=255;
12:         kcolormean(i,j,3)=0;
13:      end if
14:   end for
15: end for
```

3.   Experimental Results

Several tests performed with the software whose GUI structure is shown in Fig. 5. In the first phase segmentation performance tests are carried out and in the second phase cap width measurement performance tests are carried out.

3.1.   Segmentation Performance Test

At this phase segmentation performance of the designed system is tested. Five different mushroom images are used for the tests. Test results are provided in Fig. 10. First row of Fig. 10 shows the images to be processed. Second row contains grayscale k-means maps, and third row contains color k-means maps of the corresponding images. In the fourth row segmented mushroom images can be observed. Fifth row contains edge determined segmented mushroom images. Results show that the designed system successfully segments the provided images. System performance does not change in complex background images.

3.2.   Mushroom Cap width Measurement Performance

In this step Cap Width Measurement is performed. Our software measured the cap width of the mushroom as 8.48 cm but the real cap width of the mushroom is 8.66 cm. To find the measurement error in this result, Absolute Error (Δae) and Relative Error ($re\%$) variables in Eq. (8) and Eq. (9) is used. Error analysis resulted in following error values: $\Delta ae = 0.18$ cm, $re\% = 2.12$:

$$\Delta ae = |m_{\text{measured}} - m_{\text{real value}}|, \qquad (8)$$

$$re\% = \frac{|\Delta m|}{m_{\text{real value}}} \cdot 100, \qquad (9)$$

$$\Delta ae = |8.48 - 8.66| = 0.18 \text{ cm}, \qquad (10)$$

$$re\% = \frac{0.18}{8.66} \cdot 100 = 2.12. \qquad (11)$$

During the test 19 different mushrooms with different size and type are used. Figure 11 provides the results ordered ascending according to $m_{\text{real value}}$.

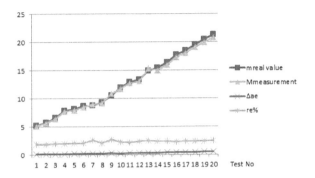

Fig. 11: Test result graphics.

Statistical analysis is performed on Δae and $re\%$ values found during tests and results are provided in Tab. 1. As results show Δae and $re\%$ are very low.

Tab. 1: Statistical results.

Statistical results of Δae [cm]		
Max	Arithmetic mean	Standard deviation
0.530	0.296	0.134
Statistical results of $re\%$ [cm]		
Max	Arithmetic mean	Standard deviation
2.756	2.286	0.231

4. Conclusion

In this study we developed a GUI based software for K-Means image segmentation. Raw input image is filtered and histogram equalized at the beginning of the process. On the processed image segmentation is performed with k-means method. To improve segmentation performance k-means algorithm is improved with modifications. Test results show that designed software successfully performs segmentation even on complex background images. The analysis also shows that histogram processes and noise reduction processes play an important role in a successful segmentation process. Software also has the capability to measure cap width of a mushroom to provide information about the size of the mushroom in the image.

References

[1] YAO, H., Q. DUAN, D. LI and J. WANG. An improved k-means clustering algorithm for fish image segmentation. *Mathematical and Computer Modelling*. 2013, vol. 58, iss. 3–4, pp. 790–798. ISSN 0895-7177. DOI: 10.1016/j.mcm.2012.12.025.

[2] ZHANG, Y., D. HUANG, M. JI and F. XIE. Image segmentation using PSO and PCM with Mahalanobis distance. *Expert Systems with Applications*. 2011, vol. 38, iss. 7, pp. 9036–9040. ISSN 0957-4174. DOI: 10.1016/j.eswa.2011.01.041.

[3] LAO, Z., D. SHEN, D. LIU, A. F. JAWAD, E. R. MELHEM, L. J. LAUNER, R. N. BRYAN and Ch. DAVATZIKOS. Computer-Assisted Segmentation of White Matter Lesions in 3D MR Images Using Support Vector Machine. *Academic Radiology*. 2008, vol. 15, iss. 3, pp. 300–313. ISSN 1076-6332. DOI: 10.1016/j.acra.2007.10.012.

[4] GONZALEZ, R. C. and R. E. WOODS. *Digital image processing*. Upper Saddle River: Prentice Hall, 2002. ISBN 978-02-011-8075-6.

[5] YOON, H., Y. HAN and H. HAHN. Image Contrast Enhancement based Sub-histogram Equalization Technique without Over-equalization Noise. *World Academy of Science, Engineering and Technology*. 2009, vol. 3, iss. 6, pp. 176–182. ISSN 2010-3778.

[6] HAN, J., M. KAMBER and A. K. H. TUNG. Spatial Clustering Methods in Data Mining: A Survey. In: *Geographic Data Mining and Knowledge Discovery*. New York: Taylor, 2001, pp. 1–29. ISBN 04-152-3369-0.

About Authors

Eser SERT received the M.Sc. degree in 2010 and the Ph.D. degree in 2013, all in Computer Engineering at Trakya University, Turkey. Currently he is Assistant Professor at Computer Engineering of Kahramanmaras Sutcu Imam University. His research interests include 3D modeling system, image processing, computer vision, field programmable gate arrays (FPGA) and artificial inteligence.

Ibrahim Taner OKUMUS was born in Kahramanmaras, Turkey. He received his M.Sc. and Ph.D. degrees from Sysracuse University, USA. He is currently working as an Associate Professor at Computer Engineering Department of Kahramanmaras Sutcu Imam University, Turkey. His research interests include wireless networks, software defined networks, wireless sensor networks and computer networks in general.

30

Benefits and Limits of Modulation Formats for Optical Communications

Rajdi AGALLIU, Michal LUCKI

Department of Telecommunications Engineering, Faculty of Electrical Engineering, Czech Technical University in Prague, Technicka 2, 166 27 Prague, Czech Republic

agallraj@fel.cvut.cz, lucki@fel.cvut.cz

Abstract. *This paper is focused on benefits and limits of intensity and phase modulation formats used in optical communications. The simulation results are obtained using OptSim software environment, employing Time Domain Split Step method. Non-Return to Zero, Return to Zero, Chirped Return to Zero and Carrier-Suppressed Return to Zero formats are compared in terms of Bit Error Rate and spectral efficiency to find the limits for selected transmission network topologies. It is shown that phase modulation formats offer many advantages compared to intensity formats. Differential Phase-Shift Keying and mainly Differential Quadrature Phase-Shift Keying improve the Bit Error Rate and transmission reach, among others. A promising solution is the application of Polarization Division Multiplexing Quadrature Phase-Shift Keying, which primarily benefits in spectral efficiency, estimated reach, optical signal to noise ratio and chromatic dispersion tolerances.*

Keywords

BER, CRZ, CSRZ, DPSK, DQPSK, Duobinary, eye diagram, modulation formats, NRZ, OptSim, PDM-QPSK, Q-factor, RZ.

1. Introduction

The upgrade of fiber optic telecommunication systems to higher bit rates very often requires solving the impact of polarization mode dispersion and nonlinear effects, such as Four Wave Mixing (FWM), that can significantly affect transmission at 10 $Gb \cdot s^{-1}$ speeds and higher. For transmission rates higher than 40 $Gb \cdot s^{-1}$ per channel, the use of more advanced formats is necessary and the design of new modulations is expected. This requires detailed knowledge on performance efficiency of modulation formats, as well as the clear spec-

ification of shortcomings to be solved while proposing new solutions.

This paper investigates modulation formats in OptSim software environment (version 5.2) from the perspective of the Bit Error Rate (BER), Q-factor and physical reach to find their main advantages, and the performance limits. The transmission schemes for high-density optical systems operating at 40 and 100 $Gb \cdot s^{-1}$ wavelength channels can use phase modulation combined with Polarization Division Multiplexing (PDM), coherent detection and digital signal processing [1], [2]. PDM halves the symbol rate, which enables usage of higher bit rates, cheaper components and fitting into a proper channel grid at the cost of an increased transceiver complexity [1], [3]. It has been shown that PDM Quadrature Phase-Shift Keying (PDM-QPSK) format is very promising for high fiber reaches and huge data flows. For this reason, the model of this modulation format has been developed.

2. State of the Art

2.1. Intensity Modulation Formats

This paper, among others, deals with binary intensity formats due to the significant back-to-back receiver sensitivity penalty of multilevel intensity formats [4], [5]. Although a certain combination of Amplitude Shift Keying (ASK) and phase modulations (e.g. RZ-DPSK-3ASK format) [1] have advantages, the limited extinction ratios of the ASK modulated levels limits the Optical Signal-to-Noise Ratio (OSNR) tolerance of the format.

The two most common intensity modulations are Non Return to Zero (NRZ) and Return to Zero (RZ). Conventional NRZ format has been widely implemented, mainly because of its signal bandwidth and its relatively easy generation. We compare and discuss features of these formats together with other binary intensity formats such as: Chirped Return to Zero (CRZ) and the most widespread pseudo-multilevel format: Carrier-Suppressed Return to Zero (CSRZ), which could be an optimal solution for high speed transmission systems [4].

Duobinary (DB) format represents correlative coding, a subclass of which is known as partial-response signaling. The main benefit of the DB format is its high tolerance to Chromatic Dispersion (CD) and narrowband optical filtering [4]. The main goal of using this format at 10 Gb·s^{-1} is to increase the dispersion tolerance, whereas at 40 Gb·s^{-1} it is to achieve high spectral efficiency in Wavelength Division Multiplexing (WDM) systems. Nevertheless, the immunity of DB to nonlinear effects at 40 Gb·s^{-1} does not differ much from similar duty cycle On/Off Keying (OOK). In section 3.3, we compare DB to OOK to find which of the formats performs better for a selected network topology. A further discussion and comparison of DB and Phase-Shaped Binary Transmission with respect to transmission impairments at 40 Gb·s^{-1} can be found in reference [6].

2.2. Phase Modulation Formats

Phase-based modulation formats provide higher spectral efficiency and better OSNR tolerances meanwhile increasing the complexity of a transceiver. The main advantage of Differential Binary Phase-Shift Keying (DBPSK or simply DPSK) over OOK is a 3 dB receiver sensitivity improvement [4]. Although the resistance of DPSK and CSRZ formats to fiber nonlinearities may be similar, the improved sensitivity of DPSK receivers generally results in a better overall system performance. Detectors for DPSK signals are also more complex as they must convert the phase difference into an intensity signal which can be converted into an electrical signal by photo detectors. In section 3.4, we compare the NRZ and RZ variants of DPSK to find which of them offers better results in terms of BER and Q-factor for a selected topology.

Knowing how to eliminate shortcomings of two-level formats, it is suitable to investigate models of multilevel formats. Differential Quadrature Phase-Shift Keying (DQPSK) is a multilevel format that has received appreciable attention. Leaving aside aspects of the transceiver design, DQPSK is an appropriate solution to achieve narrow signal spectra. At the same bit rate, DQPSK is more robust to Polarization Mode Dispersion due to its longer symbol duration, while comparing it with binary formats [4]. Its spectrum shape is similar to that of DPSK; however its compression in frequency enabled DQPSK to achieve higher spectral efficiency and increased tolerance to CD [4]. Similarly as for DPSK, we compare the NRZ and RZ variants of DQPSK, again in terms of BER and Q-factor.

2.3. Advanced Modulation Formats

PDM-QPSK has been widely differently denoted either by polarization division multiplexing, polarization multiplexing, dual polarization or orthogonal polarization [1]. Its transmitter is the same as in PDM-DQPSK. Innovation in PDM-QPSK stands for the employment of a coherent receiver. The use of digital signal processing simplifies the receiver design although a large number of components is required, as well as low-linewidth lasers [7]. Despite the fact that other formats have been designed and some of them are already commercially available, such as PM-OFDM-QPSK; PDM-QPSK proves to perform better at 100 Gb·s^{-1} and at greater reaches, with respect to estimated reach, spectral efficiency, OSNR, CD and differential group delay tolerances [1].

In PDM, two optical signals are coupled to two orthogonal polarizations being mutually delayed by a symbol period to improve OSNR. The two delayed lines: a coupled resonator and a photonic crystal waveguide are compared by using PDM transmission in the study by F. Morichetti et al [8]. PDM can also double transmission capacity of other modulation formats. The PDM has been applied experimentally by L. Cheng et al. to increase 8 DQPSK channels with 200 GHz DWDM grid from 100 Gb·s^{-1} to 200 Gb·s^{-1} [9]. Data were transmitted through a 1200 km long link with completely compensated chromatic dispersion. However, in their experiment, an automatic polarization control was not implemented and proper polarization should be set every ten minutes manually. In section 3.5, we investigate this modulation format at 100 Gb·s^{-1} in a 2400 km long transmission system.

3. Methods

Simulations are performed in OptSim environment using the Time Domain Split Step (TDSS) method. Simulation results are performed on the created models of modulation formats, incorporated into a model of an optical transmission system, with respect to the eye diagram, BER, OSNR and Q-factor.

3.1. Time Domain Split Step Method

OptSim employs the TDSS method to realize the signal distribution equation in a fiber. The method is based on the following formula [10]:

$$\frac{\partial A(t,z)}{\partial z} = (L + N) \cdot A(t,z), \qquad (1)$$

where A(t,z) is the complex envelope, L is the operator which describes linear effects and N describes the impact of non-linear phenomena on the signal propagation. The Split-Step algorithm applies L and N operators to calculate $A(t,z)$ over small fiber spans ∂z separately. The TDSS algorithm calculates L in the time domain by applying convolution in sampled time [10]:

$$TDSS \rightarrow AL\,[n] = A\,[n] * h\,[n] =$$
$$= \sum_{k=-\infty}^{\infty} A\,[k] \cdot h\,[n-k], \qquad (2)$$

where h is the impulse response of a linear operator L.

3.2. Monitors

1) Eye Diagram

The eye diagram is a graphical representation of signals, in which many cycles of the signal are superimposed on top of each other. The amount of noise, jitter and inter-symbol interference (ISI) of an optical signal can be judged from its appearance [11], as illustrated in Fig. 1. Less noise makes the eye diagram look "smoother", since there is less distortion of a signal. The larger the size of the eye opening is, the lower the error rate will be [12].

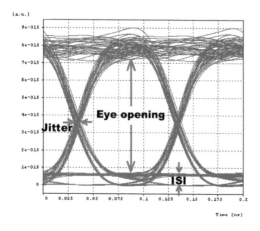

Fig. 1: Sample eye diagram showing jitter and representing error rate by its opening.

2) Bit Error Rate

BER specifies the ratio of bit errors to the total number of transmitted bits. Therefore, a lower BER indicates a better performance. BER is affected by attenuation, noise, dispersion, crosstalk between adjacent channels, nonlinear phenomena, jitter or by bit synchronization problems. Its performance may be improved by launching a strong signal into a transmission system unless this causes cross-talk and more errors; by choosing a robust modulation format, or finally by applying channel coding schemes, among others.

3) Optical Signal to Noise Ratio and Q Factor

OSNR is obtained as the ratio of the net signal power to the net noise power. The predominant source for its degradation is noise inserted by optical amplifiers. Q-factor is another important parameter, which is used in this paper for the evaluation of simulations. It can be expressed, as follows [12]:

$$Q\,[-] = \frac{\mu_1 - \mu_0}{\sigma_1 + \sigma_0}, \qquad (3)$$

where μ_0, μ_1 are the mean log.0, log.1 level values, and σ_0, σ_1 are the corresponding standard deviations. Q-factor specifies the minimum required OSNR to obtain a certain value of BER. The mathematical relation between Q-factor and BER is given by the following equation [12]:

$$BER\,[-] = \frac{1}{2}erfc\left(\frac{Q}{\sqrt{2}}\right). \qquad (4)$$

In general, the BER decreases as the Q-factor increases. For a Q-factor ranging from 6 to 7, the BER is obtained as of 10^{-9} up to 10^{-12}.

3.3. Intensity Modulation Formats Models

1) Non Return to Zero, Return to Zero, Chirped and Carrier-Suppressed Return to Zero

In the following simulation scheme, we compare NRZ, RZ, CRZ and CSRZ formats in a selected 10 Gb·s^{-1} transmission system. We assume a possible tree topology solution of a Passive Optical Network (PON), shown in Fig. 2.

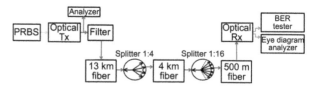

Fig. 2: Topology used for modeled modulation formats.

In the optical distribution network, we use three standard single-mode fibers (SSMF) with the lengths of 13 km, 4 km and 500 m respectively, each with 0.25 dB·km^{-1} loss. SSMFs are separated by two splitters with ratio 1:4 and 1:16. The output power level of the transmitters is set to 0 dBm. For filtering purposes, theraised cosine filter with a 2 dB loss and the center wavelength at the operating wavelength of this system (i.e. 1550 nm) is placed after the transmitter. In CRZ, a chirp is added to the RZ optical signal by applying a phase modulation. In the case of CSRZ, the RZ optical signal enters to a phase modulator, driven by a sine wave generator at frequency half of the bit rate. As a result, any two adjacent bits will have a π phase shift and the central peak at the carrier frequency is suppressed. The results from simulations are discussed in section 4.1.

2)   Duobinary Modulation Format

The aim of the next simulation scheme is to compare DB with OOK. For this purpose, a 10 Gb·s^{-1} passive optical network is implemented as illustrated in Fig. 3.

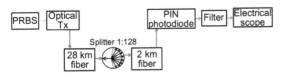

Fig. 3: Simulation scheme for DB modulation.

We consider another possible tree topology solution of a PON. The power level of lasers in each transmitter is set to -3 dBm. Modulated signals are launched over a 28 km long SSMF with 0.25 dB·km^{-1} loss, which is followed by a splitter with splitting ratio 1:128, and another SSMF with the length of 2 km. The receiver consists of a PIN photodiode, an electrical filter and electrical scope for measurement purposes. In this scenario, we compare DB's error performance with that of NRZ and CSRZ, which were chosen based on the results from the simulation described in the previous section. The DB transmitter is realized by driving an amplitude dual-arm Mach Zehnder (MZ) modulator with opposite phase signals [13]. The achieved simulation results are discussed in section 4.2.

3.4.   Phase Modulation Formats Models

1)   Non Return to Zero Differential Phase-Shift Keying and Return to Zero Differential Phase-Shift Keying modulation formats

Other investigated formats are NRZ-DPSK and RZ-DPSK, both evaluated in terms of BER and Q-factor for another 10 Gb·s^{-1} selected PON topology with physical reach 20 km and 32 subscribers, as illustrated in Fig. 4. The essential difference between DPSK and RZ-DPSK simulations stands in the transmitter's configuration. RZ-DPSK modulated pulses can also be created by using an MZ modulator instead of a phase modulator as done in our assumed scenario [4]. Modulated optical signals travel through a 19 km SSMF

with 0.25 dB·km^{-1} loss and optical splitter 1:32, followed by a second SSMF of length 1 km. Signals are demodulated by the Mach-Zehnder Delay Interferometer (MZDI) (block I in Fig. 4) [13] whose differential time delay is set to the bit duration, i.e. 100 ps. Both output interfaces of the MZDI, i.e. the "constructive", (in which there is no phase change between adjacent bits), and "destructive" port (phase change is π), are connected to a balanced receiver (block II in Fig. 4), which primarily consists of two receivers for these two signal parts. The electrical signal from one of the receivers is inverted and subsequently both electrical signals are added together as shown in Fig. 4. The results are presented in section 4.3.

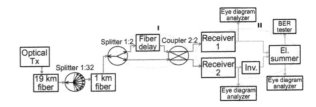

Fig. 4: Simulation scheme for the DPSK modulation format.

2)   Non Return to Zero Differential Quadrature Phase-Shift Keying and Return to Zero Differential Quadrature Phase-Shift Keying

Similarly as for DPSK (previous section), in the following simulation schemes we investigate the NRZ-DQPSK and RZ-DQPSK formats in terms of the error performance for a 10 Gb·s^{-1} transmission system. In orded to simplify, a 150 km long SSMF with 0.2 dB·km^{-1} loss is used. Two 5 Gb·s^{-1} data sources are encoded to generate appropriate in-phase (I) and quadrature (Q) modulation signals, as shown in Fig. 5.

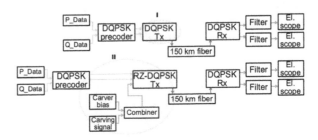

Fig. 5: NRZ-DQPSK and RZ-DPQSK simulation schemes.

The power level of lasers in each transmitter is set to -10 dBm. In RZ-DQPSK, the carving signal varies in the range $[V_{off} : V_{off} + V_\pi]$ (Fig. 5, block II). The receiver in both schemes is implemented in an explicit form by applying two 2DPSK receivers to obtain both I and Q components [13]. The results are given in section 4.4.

3.5. Polarization Division Multiplexing Quadrature Phase-Shift Keying

PDM-QPSK is a very promising modulation format especially in networks operating at 100 Gb·s^{-1} wavelength channels. For this purpose, we investigate the limit of the PDM-QPSK format in terms of error performance for a 100 Gb·s^{-1} transmission system operating at 193 THz, including a 7 % of Forward Error Correction (FEC) overhead. Four data sources are used to generating a single PDM-QPSK signal. The PDM-QPSK modulated signals travel through a 2400 km transmission system, composed of twenty-four non-zero dispersion shifted fibers (e.g. LEAF) with the loss of 0.2 dB·km^{-1} and chromatic dispersion being around 4 ps·nm^{-1}·km^{-1} at the considered band, as schematically shown in Fig. 6. Each of the fiber spans is 100 km long and is separated from one another by inline optical amplifiers (OA) with the fixed gain of 20 dB.

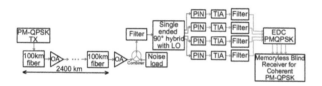

Fig. 6: PDM-QPSK simulation scheme.

Signals are noise loaded to extract the received BER as a function of OSNR [3]. At the receiver, a single ended 90 ° hybrid with the local oscillator and four PIN photodiodes in its four output interfaces enable the coherent detection. Signals further travel through trans-impedance amplifiers, electrical filters and subsequently through an ideal electronic dispersion compensator, which applies the same compensation on all signals. The final component in the PDM-QPSK receiver consists of a memoryless "blind" receiver, which separates orthogonal polarizations as well as in-phase and quadrature signals by applying the Constant Modulus and Viterbi & Viterbi algorithms [13]. The simulation results are given in section 4.5.

4. Results

4.1. Comparison of Non Return to Zero, Return to Zero, Chirped and Carrier-Suppressed Return to Zero

In this section, we discuss the simulation results referring to the scheme shown in Fig. 2 (section 3.3, part 1). The optical spectra of NRZ, RZ, CRZ and CSRZ formats are presented in Fig. 7.

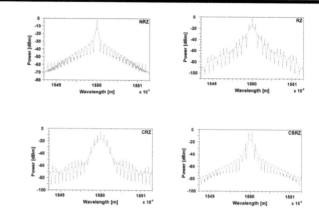

Fig. 7: Transmitter's optical spectra for the modulations: NRZ (top left), RZ (top right), CRZ (bottom left), and CSRZ (bottom right).

In NRZ, the local maxima of power can be observed at multiples of the bit rate [14]. The format exhibits a narrower main lobe than other investigated formats. However, this feature doesn't mean NRZ is more resistant to Cross-Phase Modulation (XPM) and FWM in Dense WDM systems, making it not the best choice for high-capacity optical systems [15]. In CRZ, phase varies within the time span of each pulse and its spectrum gets significantly broader (Fig. 7). Although the chirp can be used to suppress dispersion, it generally increases cross-talk penalty and deteriorate the overall performance. CSRZ's carrier suppression helps to reduce the interference between adjacent pulses and thus to improve the overall signal quality [14], resulting in a less distorted eye diagram (Fig. 8).

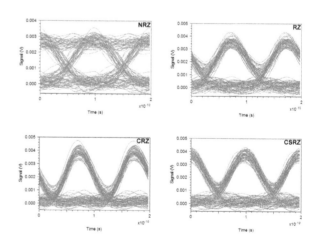

Fig. 8: Eye diagrams for NRZ, RZ, CRZ and CSRZ.

Table 1 summarizes the numerical results from this simulation. The obtained BER values and their corresponding Q-factors give a better performance characterization of these formats.

The results showed that CSRZ offers the lowest BER, mainly due to its carrier suppression. It can also

Tab. 1: Simulation results for NRZ, RZ, CRZ and CSRZ.

Modulation format	BER [-]	Q [-]
NRZ	$1.12 \cdot 10^{-6}$	4.73
RZ	$2.80 \cdot 10^{-9}$	5.83
CRZ	$6.10 \cdot 10^{-11}$	6.44
CSRZ	$4.02 \cdot 10^{-11}$	6.50

be concluded that conventional NRZ offers the worst BER and Q-factor.

4.2. Comparison of Non Return to Zero, Carrier-Suppressed Return to Zero and Duobinary modulation formats

The simulation results in section 4.1 show that CSRZ offers the lowest BER for the modeled PON topology, meanwhile NRZ the highest one. For such a reason, these two formats were chosen in the simulation scheme described in section 3.3 part 2 for comparison purpose with the DB format. The numerical results are presented in the following table.

Tab. 2: Simulation results for NRZ, CSRZ and DB.

Modulation format	BER [-]	Q [-]
NRZ	$1.29 \cdot 10^{-11}$	6.65
CSRZ	$3.27 \cdot 10^{-21}$	9.39
DB	$1.46 \cdot 10^{-16}$	8.37

The eye diagram of NRZ was found to be again the most distorted compared to CSRZ and DB. This results in a higher error rate in receiver's side as can be seen from BER and Q-factor values of NRZ, given in Tab. 2. According to these results, it can also be concluded that CSRZ offers the lowest BER value again.

4.3. Non Return to Zero Differential Phase-Shift Keying and Return to Zero Differential Phase-Shift Keying

The following results concern comparison of NRZ-DPSK and RZ-DPSK formats (section 3.4, part 1). The aim of the simulation is to figure out which of these two modulation formats performs better in terms of BER and Q-factor. Tab. 3 summarizes the obtained numerical results.

Tab. 3: Comparison of BER and Q-factor in NRZ-DPSK and RZ-DPSK.

Modulation format	BER [-]	Q [-]
NRZ-DPSK	$3.81 \cdot 10^{-7}$	4.95
RZ-DPSK	$9.65 \cdot 10^{-13}$	7.04

The eye diagram of RZ-DPSK was found to be less distorted than for NRZ-DPSK. The BER value we ob-

tained from NRZ-DPSK is high, making it not a proper solution for the assumed scenario. On the other hand, RZ-DPSK enables a transmission with a lower BER.

4.4. Non Return to Zero Differential Quadrature Phase-Shift Keying and Return to Zero Differential Quadrature Phase-Shift Keying

Simulation schemes for comparison of NRZ-DQPSK and RZ-DQPSK in terms of BER and Q-factor were described in section 3.4 part 2. Eye diagrams for both formats are measured at the receiver by using electrical scopes for both in-phase and quadrature components. The following table summarizes the obtained results.

Tab. 4: Comparison of BER and Q-factor in NRZ-DQPSK and RZ-DQPSK.

Modulation format		BER [-]	Q [-]
NRZ-DQPSK	In-phase	$3.12 \cdot 10^{-11}$	6.67
	Quadrature	$2.81 \cdot 10^{-11}$	6.65
RZ-DQPSK	In-phase	$2.09 \cdot 10^{-28}$	11.30
	Quadrature	$1.39 \cdot 10^{-31}$	11.74

It can be noticed from Tab. 4 that RZ-DQPSK offers a much lower BER, and higher Q-factor respectively. As a result, this format can enable a longer physical reach for a certain BER value compared to NRZ-DQPSK.

4.5. Polarization Division Multiplexing Quadrature Phase-Shift Keying

The following numerical results concern simulation of PDM-QPSK, described in section 3.5. Table 5 shows that the resulting pre-FEC BER value measured by the PDM-QPSK receiver is on the order of 10–5. This proves the suitability of this modulation format for such a long-distance transmission system.

Tab. 5: Simulation results for PDM-QPSK.

PDM-QPSK	Signal 1	Signal 2	Signal 3	Signal 4	Total
pre-FEC BER ($\cdot 10^{-5}$ [-])	3.05	3.05	1.53	15.26	5.72

The advantage of polarization formats has its source in slower accumulation of attenuation and dispersion influence because on the contrary to multilevel phase modulations, the performance is not increased by adding new states being closer and closer to each other, but by considering another polarization.

5. Conclusion

The CSRZ format proves to perform better than other investigated intensity modulation formats, mainly due to its carrier suppression that reduces the interference between adjacent pulses. On the other hand, it was shown that phase-based modulation formats, especially RZ-DQPSK due to its narrower optical spectrum, enable longer reaches among others. The most promising modulation is PDM-QPSK, which is developed for advanced transmission systems operating at 100 Gb·s^{-1} per channel. This format benefits from the combination of phase modulation with PDM, coherent detection and digital signal processing. PDM-QPSK was successfully simulated for a 2400 km long transmission system, operating at 100 Gb·s^{-1}. Significant improvements in terms of optical reach have been depicted, which was the main reason of gradually increasing the fiber length, or the splitting ratio respectively. The comparison is interesting especially when getting closer to the performance limits of the modulation formats. Frequency modulations show their benefits when increasing the bit rate per channel, as well as the overall transmission capacity, on the other hand, PDM-QPSK shows a huge progress when increasing the reach, while at short reaches it doesn't perform much better that the other formats. A future research would be focused on other advanced modulation formats and for higher transmission rates, since they open a large space for further improvements and proposals of new modulation formats.

Acknowledgment

This work has been supported by the CTU grant under project SGS13/201/OHK3/3T/13.

References

[1] LACH, E. and W. IDLER. Modulation formats for 100G and beyong. *Optical Fiber Technology.* 2011, vol. 17, iss. 5, pp. 377–386. ISSN 1068-5200. DOI: 10.1016/j.yofte.2011.07.012.

[2] ZIRNGIBL, M. 100Gbps for NexGen Content Distribution Networks. Bell Labs Research In: *NANOG45.* Santo Domingo, 2009.

[3] LAPERLE, CH., B. VILLENEUVE, Z. ZHANG, D. MCGHAN, H. SUN and M. O'SULLIVAN. WDM performance and PMD Tolerance of a Coherent 40-Gbit/s Dual-Polarization QPSK Transceiver. *Journal of Lightwave Technology.* 2008, vol. 26, iss. 1, pp. 1–3. ISSN 0733-8724. DOI: 10.1109/JLT.2007.913071.

[4] WINZER, P. and R.-J. ESSIAMBRE. Advanced Modulation Formats for High-Capacity Optical Transport Networks. *Journal of Lightwave Technology.* 2006, vol. 24, iss. 12, pp. 4711–4728. ISSN 0733-8724. DOI: 10.1109/JLT.2006.885260.

[5] BENEDIKOVIC, D., J. LITVIK and M. DADO. Modeling of Single-Channel Optical Transmission Systems with High-Order ASK and PSK Modulation formats. In: *ELEKTRO 2012.* Rajecke Teplice: IEEE, 2012. pp. 22–25. ISBN 978-1-4673-1180-9. DOI: 10.1109/ELEKTRO.2012.6225601.

[6] TAN, A. and E. PINCEMIN. Performance Comparison of Duobinary Formats for 40-Gb/s and Mixed 10/40-Gb/s Long-Haul WDM Transmission on SSMF and LEAF Fibers. *Journal of Lightwave Technology.* 2009, vol. 27, iss. 4, pp. 396–408. ISSN 0733-8724. DOI: 10.1109/JLT.2008.929117.

[7] SOTIROPOULIS, N., T. KOONEN and H. DE WAARDT. D8PSK/OOK Bidirectional Transmission over a TDM-PON. In: *14th International Conference on Transparent Optical Networks.* Coventry: IEEE, 2012, pp. 1325–1328. ISBN 2161-2056. DOI: 10.1109/ICTON.2012.6253937.

[8] MORICHETTI, F. Controlling the delay of 100 Gb/s polarization division multiplexed signals through silicon photonics delay lines. In: *Optical Communication (ECOC), 2010 36th European Conference and Exhibition on.* Torino: IEEE, 2010, pp. 1–3. ISBN 978-1-4244-8536-9. DOI: 10.1109/ECOC.2010.5621202.

[9] CHENG, L., Z. LI, Y. YANG, Ch. LU, Y. FANG, H. JIANG, X. XU, Q. XIONG, Sh. ZHONG, Z. CHEN, H. TAM and P. WAI. 8x200-Gbit/s polarization-division multiplexed CS-RZ-DQPSK transmission over 1200 km of SSMF. In: *Proceedings of OptoElectronics and Communications Conference (OECC).* Hong Kong: IEEE, 2009, pp. 13–17. ISBN 978-1-4244-4102-0.

[10] RSOFT DESIGN GROUP, INC. *OptSim User Guide,* 2010. Build OS0521010.

[11] SACKINGER, E. *Broadband circuits for optical fiber communication.* Hoboken: John Wiley & Sons Inc., 2005. ISBN 0-471-71233-7.

[12] FREUDE W., R. SCHMOGROW, B. NEBENDAHL, M. WINTER and A. JOSTEN. Quality metrics for optical signals: eye diagram, Q-factor, OSNR, EVM and BER. In: *14th International Conference on Transparent Optical Networks.* Coventry: IEEE, 2012, pp. 1–4. ISBN 2161-2056. DOI: 10.1109/ICTON.2012.6254380.

[13] RSOFT DESIGN GROUP, INC. *OptSim Application Notes and Examples,* 2010. Build OS0521010.

[14] YIP, S. and T. D. DE LA RUBIA. *Scientific Modeling and Simulations*. Lecture Notes in Computational Science and Engineering. Berlin: Springer, 2009. ISBN 9781402097416.

[15] XU Ch., X. LIU, L. F. MOLLENAUER and X. WEI. Comparison of Return-to-Zero Differential Phase-Shift Keying and ON–OFF Keying in Long-Haul Dispersion Managed Transmission. *IEEE Photonics Technology Letters*. 2003, vol. 15, iss. 4, pp. 617–619. ISSN 1041-1135. DOI: 10.1109/LPT.2003.809317.

About Authors

Rajdi AGALLIU was born in 1989. He received his Master's degree from the Czech Technical University in Prague FEE in 2013. He is now a Ph.D. student at the same faculty and his research interests include networking and optical communications.

Michal LUCKI was born in 1980. He received his M.Sc. from the Kielce University of Technology and Ph.D. from the Czech Technical University in Prague in 2004 and 2007, respectively. His research interests include photonics, fiber optics, material engineering and solid state physics.

31

ON-LINE MONITORING OF VoIP QUALITY USING IPFIX

Petr MATOUSEK , Martin KMET, Martin BASEL

Department of Information Systems, Faculty of Information Technology, Brno University of Technology,
Bozetechova 2, Brno, Czech Republic

matousp@fit.vutbr.cz, ikmet@fit.vutbr.cz, xbasel02@stud.fit.vutbr.cz

Abstract. *The main goal of VoIP services is to provide a reliable and high-quality voice transmission over packet networks. In order to prove the quality of VoIP transmission, several approaches were designed. In our approach, we are concerned about on-line monitoring of RTP and RTCP traffic. Based on these data, we are able to compute main VoIP quality metrics including jitter, delay, packet loss, and finally R-factor and MOS values. This technique of VoIP quality measuring can be directly incorporated into IPFIX monitoring framework where an IPFIX probe analyses RTP/RTCP packets, computes VoIP quality metrics, and adds these metrics into extended IPFIX flow records. Then, these extended data are stored in a central IPFIX monitoring system called collector where can be used for monitoring purposes. This paper presents a functional implementation of IPFIX plugin for VoIP quality measurement and compares the results with results obtained by other tools.*

Keywords

IPFIX, monitoring, R-factor, VoIP quality.

1. Introduction

Voice over IP (VoIP) is a technology used to transmit the real-time voice over the packet network built upon IP protocol. Today, VoIP is considered as a cheap alternative to the traditional Public Switched Telephone Network (PSTN) with a wide range of additional services including transmission of both audio and voice data, conferencing, voice mail, interconnection with Internet services like Web, directory services, IM, etc.

The most observed feature of VoIP technology is the quality of voice transmission. Since the VoIP traffic is transmitted over packet-based IP networks, the VoIP quality is influenced by a delay, jitter, or packet loss. There are also additional parameters with impact on the VoIP quality like selection of a voice codec, acoustic echo, quality of input signal, noise, etc.

There are two different approaches for the voice quality measuring: a subjective speech quality assessment and objective speech quality assessment [1]. *The subjective voice quality* tests are carried out by asking people to grade the quality of speech samples under controlled conditions. The methods and procedures for subjective evaluation are defined by ITU-T Rec. P.800 [2]. For listening-opinion tests, the recommended test method is Absolute Category Rating (ACR) in which the *mean opinion score* (MOS) value is obtained by averaging individual opinion scores for a given number of listeners. MOS uses the five-point opinion scale from 5 (for excellent) to 1 (for bad). A major drawback of subjective assessment methods is that these methods cannot be applied in the real-time monitoring.

The objective speech quality assessment includes intrusive and non-intrusive measurement. *The intrusive measurement* is an active method which needs an injection of a reference speech signal into the tested system where predicts speech quality by comparing the reference and the degraded speech signals. Intrusive objective test methods are sometimes called as "full-reference" or "double-ended" since they compare the original signal at sender's side with a signal measured at the output of the transmission network at receiver's side. Examples of such methods are Perceptual Speech Quality Measure (PSQM) [3], Perceptual Evaluation of Speech Quality (PESQ) [4], or Perceptual Objective Listening Quality Assessment (POLQA) [5].

The non-intrusive measurement is a passive method that computes speech quality by analyzing an IP packet header or by analyzing a degraded speech signal itself. It does not require the original signal. It is mainly used for quality monitoring for operational services. One of the non-intrusive measurement methods called *E-Model* is based on a parametric mathematical model. E-Model stands for European Telecommunication Standards Institute (ETSI)Computational Model that was originally described in [6]. The E-Model takes into account all possible impairments for an end-to-end speech transmission like a quantization noise, talker/listener echo, absolute delay, type of codec, packet loss, or jitter. Computation of E-Model is specified in ITU-T Rec. G.107 [7]. The result of computation is scalar R that describes quality of voice on scale from 100 to 0. Although non-intrusive methods are less accurate than intrusive methods, they are used for a voice quality assessment.

In our work, we focus on an application of a simplified E-Model for on-line voice quality assessment. The input data for E-Model are obtained from Real-Time Transport Protocol (RTP) packets [8]. VoIP systems are mostly based on two types of application protocols: signalization protocols like SIP, H.323, IAX, or SCCP, and transportation protocols like RTP or RTCP [8]. The signalization protocols provide a phone registration, negotiation of call parameters, call establishment, etc. The transport protocols transmit audio and video data between communicating end points. By monitoring RTP packets and observing RTP control protocol (RTCP) packets we are able to evaluate a speech quality of a given RTP stream.

However, there is an important issue related with RTP monitoring. RTP streams are transmitted over UDP transport using dynamic ports that can be different for each call. Information about dynamic RTP ports is usually transmitted via signalization protocols (SIP/SDP, H.225.0 CS) so that a receiver knows where audio data should be expected. If we are able to detect a signalization protocol, we can also find out RTP streams. There are situations when a signalization protocol uses a different path through the network than a RTP stream. It that case it is very difficult to detect RTP traffic and many monitoring tools are not able to identify VoIP streams and assess their quality. In order to make our monitoring robust, we developed a technique for on-line detection of RTP packets when signalization is missing [9]. This technique can be easily incorporated in our voice quality monitoring system.

Our work is focused on on-line monitoring of RTP flows on a network using IPFIX framework [10], [11]. IPFIX is a monitoring protocol based on Cisco Netflow [12] that collects statistical information about the traffic going through an observation point. Individual packets are grouped into *flows* that are identified by a source/destination IP address, a source/destination port, IP protocol number, ToS class, and an interface ID. An IPFIX probe checks packet headers and creates flow records for incoming packets. The flow record includes the number of packets and bytes of the flow and timestamps of the first and last packet of the flow.

Standard IPFIX records can be extended by user-defined information that are specified using IPFIX templates. In our case, we add information about the quality of VoIP traffic to every RTP or RTCP flow

record so that a network administrator can be informed about the presence of VoIP flows and their quality. This simple and effective solution does not require any additional monitoring devices and provides a single-ended speech quality assessment based on E-Model. Data monitoring can be used to detect and identify possible failures on the network that causes a packet delay, loss and degradation of VoIP transmission.

2.   Contribution

The main contribution of this paper is a design of the system for on-line monitoring of VoIP quality based on RTP detection and analysis. The system measures parameters of RTP packets passing through the monitoring system. It also monitors RTCP statistics that give additional information about RTP transmissions. Using RTP parameters and RTCP statistics we are able to compute an average jitter, packet delay and packet loss. Then a simplified E-Model is computed and R-factor with a corresponding MOS value added into an IPFIX flow record of a given voice stream.

When the flow cache expires, the flow is exported to a IPFIX collector. The paper describes how VoIP quality metrics are computed using RTP/RTCP traffic in a monitoring point only. The system was implemented in C as a plugin for the IPFIX probe. In our study, we show the comparison of our tool with Wireshark, PacketScan, and VoIPmonitor. The tests prove that our approach is viable and can be easily incorporated into common monitoring devices. We also propose an extension of this system that is able to detect RTP streams outside conversation. This enables to monitor VoIP data streams if signalization is missing.

2.1.   Structure of the Paper

The structure of the remainder of this paper is as follows. Section 2 describes current approaches in measuring VoIP quality and their possible deployment for on-line monitoring. Section 3 presents QoS metrics that are to be monitored using RTP and RTCP analysis and shows how R-factor is computed from these values. It also describes an extension of IPFIX flow records that is used for transmission of VoIP quality parameters. Section 4 shows comparison of our tool with three other tools for VoIP quality monitoring. The last section concludes the paper and proposes future work.

3.   Related Work

The area of VoIP quality measuring based on non-intrusive techniques has been researched for many years. One of the pioneering works was done by Cole and Rosenbluth in [13] where basic transport level parameters as a delay, packet loss and de-jitter buffer were discussed and a reduced E-Model was presented. They implemented their model in Perl as a part of SNMP monitoring [14]. Similar approaches can be found later, see [15], [16]. These approaches differ in a way how to compute E-Model parameters in order to get more accurate results. Jiang and Huang in [16] combine intrusive and non-intrusive methods to calculate average time using ICMP probes. It is an active approach in comparison to previous passive methods.

Many recent works combine E-Model with PESQ measuring in order to receive more accurate results. O'Sullivan et al. in [17] present an improvement of the simplified E-Model using correction coefficients for four common codecs (G.711, G.723, G.726, G.729) to better match PESQ scores. A different approach is presented in [18] where the author replaces the payload of the received RTP packets with the payloads that would these packets contained when they had been used to carry test voice signals according to P.50. However, all these methods need to work with an original and a distorted signal. This is not feasible for on-line monitoring. A new methodology for developing perceptually accurate models based on PESQ and E-Model is presented in [19] that computes predicted MOSc from RTP traffic based on measured MOSc from PESQ and E-Model.

There are also works based on ITU-T Rec. P.563 [20] that propose a single-ended method for objective speech quality assessment. Its computation is very complex and includes a reconstruction of a voice stream, signal pre-processing, etc. that cannot be done in a monitoring device. Works like [21] or [22] are mostly focused on a precise quality assessment using a received speech signal rather than on on-line quality measuring.

Monitoring tools like Wireshark observe IP, UDP, and RTP headers. Based on header values only, they compute VoIP statistical data like an end-to-end delay, inter-arrival jitter or cumulative packet loss [8]. This method gives interesting information about the quality of transmission. However, it does not take into account voice features like a codec type, one-way delay, etc.

Our method is also based on a simplified E-Model where its parameters are extracted from RTP headers. R-factor is computed on-the-fly during RTP stream processing. Computation of a simplified E-Model combines several published approaches in order to make it fast and accurate enough for an on-line monitoring using IPFIX architecture. Unlike of work [15], [23] our system includes automatic RTP identification using a set of features and it is fully incorporated into the standard IPFIX monitoring architecture.

4. Monitoring of VoIP Quality

This paper deals with VoIP quality measuring on the packet network using analysis of RTP streams that transmit encoded voice calls. An IPFIX monitoring probe can be connected in any place between communicating parties, see Fig. 1. The probe analyses incoming data, extracts and processes RTP packets, and finally computes R-factor value using the simplified E-Model. Voice quality metrics are added into IPFIX flow records of RTP or RTCP packets and exported via IPFIX protocol to an IPFIX collector.

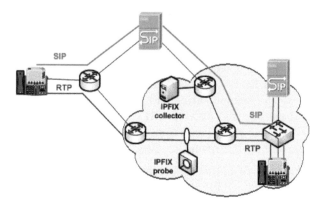

Fig. 1: Architecture of IPFIX monitoring.

Our system is able to monitor packets loss, cumulative jitter, and delay. R-factor is calculated using an Eq. 1 according to ITU-T Rec. G.107 [7]:

$$R = R_0 - I_S - I_d - I_{e-eff} + A, \qquad (1)$$

where R_0 is signal-to-noise ratio, I_S is simultaneous impairment factor, I_d is delay-related impairment, I_{e-eff} is equipment-related impairment, and A is advantage factor. The score obtained from E-Model can be converted to MOS-CQE (MOS conversational quality estimated) according to ITU-T Rec. G.107 [7, Ann. B].

4.1. On-line Computation of E-Model

In our approach, we are more focused on transmission quality of VoIP packets so we consider only wired connections ($A=0$), standard room or circuit noises and standard impairments on the voice signal (parameter I_S) in our computation. Thus, we use the simplified E-Model with default values recommended in [7, Sec. 7.7]. So, Eq. 1 can be simplified as follows [1]:

$$R = 93.2 - I_d - I_{e-eff}. \qquad (2)$$

In the following text, we show how I_d and I_{e-eff} can be computed on-the-fly.

1) Computing I_d

As the computational process to obtain I_d according to G.107 is too complicated, a simplified Eq. 3 was proposed in [13]. According to the authors, this function fits the values of I_d within the range of 0–400 ms:

$$I_d = 0.024d + 0.11\,(d - 117.3)\,H\,(d - 117.3),\quad (3)$$

where d is the one-way delay and $H(x)$ is the Heavyside (or step) function defined as $H(x) = 0$ for $x < 0$ or $H(x) = 1$ if $x \geq 0$. By application of linear regression [15], we get modified Eq. 4:

$$I_d = \begin{cases} 0.0267d & d \leq 175 \text{ ms} \\ 0.1194d - 15.876 & 175 \leq d \leq 400 \text{ ms} \end{cases}. \quad (4)$$

The computation of one-way delay d is not an easy task. A common approach is to send the probe packets like ICMP in [16]. Since we are focused on passive (non-intrusive) measurement, we can work with RTP/RTCP packets only. If we have RTCP, one-way delay can be computed from these packets that send periodic reports along with the RTP session. RTCP packets contain an NTP timestamp (TS) with the time at which this RTCP packet was sent, a timestamp of the last sender report received (LSR) and delay since the last sender report received (DLSR). By monitoring RTCP packets, we are able to compute the one-way delays as follows. First, we compute the round-trip delay (RTD) using two adjacent RTCP reports:

$$\begin{aligned} RTD_1 &= delay_1 + delay_2 = \\ &= TS_2 - DLSR_2 - DLSR_1 - TS_1, \end{aligned} \quad (5)$$

where TS_1 is an NTP timestamp when the first RTCP packet was sent, TS_2 is for the second RTCP packet, $DLSR_1$ and $DLSR_2$ is a delay from the last report received, see Fig. 2. In fact, Eq. 5 reflects computation of round-trip propagation delay in RFC 3550 [8] where recording time A corresponds to $(TS_2 - DLSR_2)$ and LSR to TS_1.

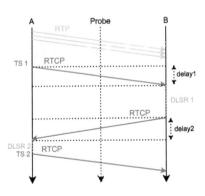

Fig. 2: Computing round-trip delay (RTD) from RTCP.

Since every packet can be routed using a different path, the average RTD delay over all RTCP packets

of the stream is considered. Thus, one-way delay d is given as follows:

$$d = \frac{\sum_{i=0}^{n} RTD_i}{2.n}. \quad (6)$$

In case of absent RTCP packets we have to use only RTP packets to determine one-way delay. Since the probe can be placed anywhere on the path between communicating parties, we are able to evaluate delay between the sender and the probe only. Precise measuring of the one-way delay of RTP packets is difficult because it requires NTP timestamps with synchronized clocks. However, RTP packets include only a sequence number and a relative timestamp that cannot be used for measurement. In our case, we use an approximated value based on assumption that the average delay relates to cumulative inter-arrival jitter. We use an algorithm implemented in VoIPmonitor, that computes delay d iteratively over subsequent packets, see Eq. 7. Similar approach can be found in [24]:

$$\begin{aligned} d_1 &= 0, \\ d_i &= \frac{(d_{i-1}.i-1)+J_i}{i}, \end{aligned} \quad (7)$$

where J_i is a cumulative interrarival jitter of packet i. Its value is calculated from the time difference D_{ij} between two adjacent packets i and j and the previous jitter as stated in RFC 3555 [8]:

$$\begin{aligned} J_1 &= 0, \\ J_i &= J_{i-1} + \frac{|D_{i-1,i}| - J_{i-1}}{16}. \end{aligned} \quad (8)$$

Delay $D_{i,j}$ between i and j is given as the difference between RTP timestamps and the times of arrival of these packets:

$$D_{i,j} = (TR_j - TR_i) - (TS_j - TS_i), \quad (9)$$

where TS_i is a RTP timestamp of packet i and TR_i is an arrival time of packet i. Since values TR_i in Eq. 9 represent actual arrival time and values TS_i represent RTP timestamp, these two values must be adjusted by dividing TS_i by sampling frequency for a given codec. Clock rates of RTP codecs are defined by IETF.

2) Computing I_{e-eff}

An effective equipment impairment factor I_{e-eff} is derived from the equipment impairment factor I_e, the packet-loss robustness factor B_{pl}, burst ratio $BurstR$ and the packet-loss probability P_{pl}. The value of I_{e-eff} can be calculated in Eq.10 according to ITU-T Rec. G.107 [7]:

$$I_{e-eff} = I_e + (95 - I_e).\frac{P_{pl}}{\frac{P_{pl}}{BurstR} + B_{pl}}, \quad (10)$$

where I_e is the equipment impairment factor at zero packet loss which reflects purely codec impairment. Its values depend on subjective mean opinion score test results as well as on network experience. Normally the lower the code bit rate is, the higher the I_e value for the codec is. Recommended values for common codecs are defined in ITU-T Rec. G.113 [25, Appendix I]. B_{pl} is defined as the packet-loss robustness factor which is also codec-specific. It reflects codec's built-in packet loss concealment ability to deal with packet loss. Its value is not only codec-dependent, but also packet-size dependent. B_{pl} values are also listed in ITU-T Rec. G.113. $BurstR$ is the the burst ratio. When a packet loss is independent, $BurstR = 1$, otherwise $BurstR > 1$. Its value is given using a 2-state Markov model with transition probabilities p from "No Loss" to "Loss" states, and q vice verse. Using these probabilities, $BurstR$ can be calculated as [7]:

$$BurstR = \frac{1}{p+q} = \frac{P_{pl}/100}{p} = \frac{1 - P_{pl}/100}{q}. \quad (11)$$

There is another way how to calculate I_{e-eff} based on Pareto/D/1/K modelling of the system proposed by [26]. In this approach, jitter buffer size, codec packetization and network jitter are included into E-Model by means of substitution of packet loss P_{pl} for effective packet loss P_{plef}. This parameter is calculated using Eq. 12 and Eq. 8:

$$P_{plef} = P_{pl} + P_{jitter} - P_{pl} \cdot P_{jitter}, \quad (12)$$

where P_{jitter} is calculated using jitter buffer size x and network jitter J as follows:

$$P_{jitter} = \frac{(1 + \frac{-0,1.x}{J})^{20}}{2}, \quad (13)$$

where x is an input parameter of the system and jitter J is a cumulative inter-arrival jitter computed using Eq. 8. Thus, the calculation of I_{e-eff} as shown in Eq. 10 can be modified using effective packet loss P_{pl} into Eq. 14:

$$I_{e-eff} = I_e + (95 - I_e).\frac{P_{plef}}{P_{plef} + B_{pl}}. \quad (14)$$

In our work, we calculate R-factor using Eq. 2. Delay impairment I_d is computed using Eq. 6 when RTCP packets are found or using Eq. 7 for RTP packets only. Effective impairment factor I_{e-eff} is calculated using effective packet loss P_{plef} as shown in Eq. 14.

4.2.   Packet Loss

A packet loss is a ratio between lost packets and expected packets. Number of lost packets is determined from the difference between the number of expected packets and received packets. When calculating the number of expected packets, sequence numbers are used. The number of packets expected can be computed as the difference between the highest sequence number and the first sequence number received. Since the sequence number is only 16 bits wide and will wrap around, it is necessary to extend the highest sequence number with the shifted count of sequence number wraparounds [8, Appendix A.3]. Also duplicated packets create another issue related with a packet loss computation. If we don't check duplicity, duplicated packets can be considered as correctly received and the number of received packets would be misinterpreted.

4.3.   Architecture of the IPFIX Probe

The goal of our work is to present a feasible solution for on-line monitoring of VoIP calls using IPFIX. In the previous part, we showed how quality parameters can be calculated with certain approximation from RTP or RTCP packets. Here, we introduce an operational architecture of our system within the IPFIX probe.

General architecture of the probe is shown in Fig. 3. At first, incoming packets are processed in the input plugin where the Call Table is stored. If an RTP packet is detected, it is forwarded into the process plugin where RTP flow records are stored in the flow cache. After the flow expires, it is moved into the export plugin and sent via IPFIX protocol to the collector. More details about the architecture can be found in [27].

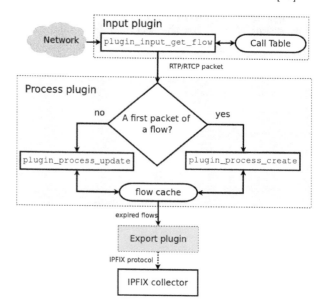

Fig. 3: Architecture of the probe.

Incoming packets are processed in the input plugin as shown in Fig. 4. There are two types of packets expected: signalization SIP packets and RTP/RTCP packets. If a SIP packet arrives, its header is analyzed and important values added into the Call Table in the input plugin. If an RTP or RTCP packet is received, it is moved into the process plugin, when VoIP metrics of a current call are computed. After finishing the call, VoIP metrics are inserted into extended IPFIX records and sent to the collector.

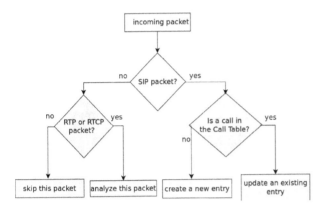

Fig. 4: VoIP packets processing.

Following VoIP metrics are added to RTP/RTCP flow records: type of the flow (RTP or RTCP), jitter, end-to-end delay, packet loss, R-factor, MOS value and the quality of the call based on MOS score, see Tab. 1. An example of IPFIX record extended by VoIP metrics is show in Fig. 5. You can see a newly defined entries with IDs 721 to 727 with entries from Tab. 1 in a hexadecimal format. In Fig. 6, there is an example of human readable output of IPFIX collector showing extended IPFIX records with voice quality metrics.

4.4. RTP Detection

In order to be able to process RTP packets even if signalization is missing we designed a new method for RTP detection [9]. It is a multi-stage filtering method that works with RTP packets first, and than with RTP streams. The method was implemented as an inde-

```
- Cisco NetFlow/IPFIX
    Version: 10
    Length: 380
  - Timestamp: Apr  2, 2014 12:35:26.000000000 CEST
    FlowSequence: 0
    Observation Domain Id: 0
  - Set 1
    FlowSet Id: (Data) (258)
    FlowSet Length: 364
  - Flow 1
    Octets: 178600
    Packets: 893
    - [Duration: 17.839000000 seconds]
    InputInt: 0
    OutputInt: 0
    IPVersion: 04
    SrcAddr: 91.221.212.167 (91.221.212.167)
    DstAddr: 192.168.1.4 (192.168.1.4)
    IP ToS: 0x00
    Protocol: 17
    SrcPort: 26456
    DstPort: 7078
    Enterprise Private entry: (VUT BRNO, faculty of EE and CS) Type 721: Value (hex bytes): 00
    Enterprise Private entry: (VUT BRNO, faculty of EE and CS) Type 722: Value (hex bytes): 3f 61 fb 9a
    Enterprise Private entry: (VUT BRNO, faculty of EE and CS) Type 723: Value (hex bytes): 00 00 00 10
    Enterprise Private entry: (VUT BRNO, faculty of EE and CS) Type 724: Value (hex bytes): 42 b9 03 00
    Enterprise Private entry: (VUT BRNO, faculty of EE and CS) Type 725: Value (hex bytes): 40 8c a7 83
    - [Enterprise Private entry: (VUT BRNO, faculty of EE and CS) Type 726: Value (hex bytes): 47 6f 6f 64
    - [Enterprise Private entry: (VUT BRNO, faculty of EE and CS) Type 727: Value (hex bytes): 52 54 50 00
    - Flow 2
    - Flow 3
    - Flow 4
```

Fig. 5: IPFIX protocol extended by VoIP metrics.

Tab. 1: Definition of IPFIX entries for VoIP quality metrics.

Entry	ID	Data type	Example
Packet Loss	721	Float	0
Jitter	722	Float	0.201
Delay	723	Uint32	0
R-Factor	724	Float	93.2
MOS	725	Float	4.409
Quality	726	Char	Excellent
FlowType	727	Char	RTP

pendent tool and successfully tested on RTP datasets. The first-stage of processing filters incoming packets by rules based on RTP validity checks [8, Appendix A] and our observations:

- Only IPv4/6 packets with UDP payload are permitted.

- The src/dst ports of UDP must be higher than 1023.

- The length of a packet header must be at least minimal RTP header length according to CSRC Count (CC), i.e., higher than $12 + 4 \times CC$ bytes.

- RTP version must be 2.

- RTP payload type must be within the range defined by RFC 3550. Packets with PT type containing *unassigned* or *reserved* values are filtered out.

- If padding bit P is set, the last byte of the padding is checked with the total length of the packet.

If a packet successfully passes all the above written filtering rules, it is marked as an RTP packet. Then, the second stage of detection using RTP flows observation is applied. This phase helps to decrease number of false negatives for short RTP streams. More details about the method can be found in [9].

5. Tests

This section presents the comparison of our implementation of on-line voice quality monitoring with three other tools: open-source packet analyzer Wireshark, a commercial tool PacketScan from GL Communication Inc. and VoIP analyzer VoIPmonitor. All these tools analyzed the same reference pcap file with G.711 codec. Generally, Wireshark monitors RTP jitter, skew time, delta time, and packet loss. PacketScan calculates conversational MOS, average gap, jitter and packet loss. VoIPmonitor is able to compute MOS for the fixed or adaptive size of jitter buffer and packet loss.

```
Src IPv4:sPort      ->  Dst IPv4:dPort     Flow_Type  Avg_Jitter[ms] Delay[ms] Packet_Loss[%]  R_Factor  MOS   Quality
192.168.2.106:7078  ->  213.168.165.12:13446  RTP       7.910          7         0.000          92.999   4.405 Excellent
192.168.2.106:7079  ->  213.168.165.12:13447  RTCP     76.062         15         0.000          90.091   4.341 Excellent
213.168.165.12:13447 ->  192.168.2.106:7079   RTCP      0.344         11         0.000          92.906   4.404 Excellent
213.168.165.12:13446 ->  192.168.2.106:7078   RTP       0.604          0         0.000          93.200   4.409 Excellent
```

Fig. 6: IPFIX protocol extended by VoIP metrics.

Our tests were done on-line using `tcpreplay` program to send test pcap files through the network. Table 2 shows the results obtained by analysis of RTP or RTCP packets.

Tab. 2: VoIP metrics by Wireshark (W), PacketScan (PS), VoIPmonitor (VPM) and IPFIX plugin (IPF).

Metric	W	PS	VPM	IPF
RTP Jitter (ms)	8.10	7.00	8.00	7.91
RTP Loss (%)	0.00	0.00	0.00	0.00
RTP Delay (ms)	–	0.00	–	0.00
R-factor	–	93.0	–	92.99
MOS	–	4.20	4.50	4.41
RTCP Jitter (ms)	–	7.60	7.61	7.60
RTCP Loss (%)	–	0.00	0.00	0.00
RTCP Delay (ms)	–	9.23	–	15.00
R-factor	–	–	–	90.09
MOS	–	–	–	4.34

In this table, we can see results computed using RTP packets only (the upper part of the table) and using RTCP packets (the lower part of the table). RTP delay is calculated using Eq. 6 for RTP and Eq. 5 using RTCP packets. You can see a great difference between RTP jitter and RTCP jitter. The reason is, that RTCP jitter is calculated by an end-point and sent to the sender while RTP jitter is calculated by an inter-mediated monitoring device. If a device is closer to the sender, jitter will be lower because of lower impact of intermediate network. In this case the probe was placed more likely very close to the sender. From the same reason, there is a difference between RTP and RTCP delay where RTP delay is a delay between the sender and the probe while RTCP delay corresponds to end-to-end delay between communicating end-points. We can also see that neither Wireshark nor PacketScan nor VoIPmonitor compute R-factor using RTCP values. In case of our IPFIX plugin, we can see that R-factor values based on RTP calculation and RTCP calculation are very similar. Due to end-to-end delay approximation in RTP, RTCP R-factor represents more accurate value than RTP R-factor.

There is also a significant difference between RTCP delay calculation in PacketScan and our tool. PacketScan documentation says that round-trip time is computed as $RTD = R_2 - R_1 - DLSR$ where R_2 is an arrival time of a RTCP SR recorded by PacketScan and R_1 is an arrival time of RTCP RR. This means that it is not an end-to-end delay but end-to-PacketScan delay. Thus its value is lower than our value measured between communicating end-points, see Eq. 5.

In the second test, we simulated packet loss by removing random packets from our pcap files using `editcap`. Since RTCP packets were not changed, only RTP calculation reflects packet loss, see Tab. 3.

Tab. 3: VoIP metrics by Wireshark (W), PacketScan (PS), VoIPmonitor (VPM) and IPFIX plugin (IPF).

Metric	W	PS	VPM	IPF
RTP Jitter (ms)	0.20	0.00	1.00	0.0202
RTP Loss (%)	1.50	1.50	–	1.48
RTP Delay (ms)	–	0.00	–	0.00
R-factor	–	93.0	–	80.96
MOS	–	4.20	4.10	4.06
RTCP Jitter (ms)	–	1	3.5	3.65
RTCP Loss(%)	1.5	1.5	1.48	1.48
RTCP Delay (ms)	–	2.65	–	41.00
R-factor	–	–	–	92.11
MOS	–	–	–	4.39

We can see that all tools were able to detect packet loss. R-factor and MOS values are worse for RTP where packet loss was detected in comparison to RTCP R-factor where packet loss was not simulated.

6. Conclusion

In this paper, we presented an improved technique for on-line monitoring of VoIP quality parameters using IPFIX frameworks. Our work includes a design of the monitoring system embedded into an IPFIX probe. The system detects RTP and RTCP packets, analyses their headers, and calculates a jitter, packet loss, delay, R-factor and MOS using the simplified E-Model abstraction on-the-fly. The simplified model uses provisional values for the equipment impairment factor I_e and packet-loss robustness factor B_{pl} as defined in ITU-T Rec. G.113 [25, Appendix I] for well-known codecs. For that reason, codecs detection was implemented as a part of RTP detection [9]. Even this approach is not as precise as PESQ methods, it can be useful for on-line monitoring.

In the future work, we will focus on improvements of end-to-end delay calculation based on [24] and comparison of our results with objective speech quality assessments.

Acknowledgment

Research presented in this paper is supported by project "Modern Tools for Detection and Mitigation of Cyber Criminality on the New Generation Internet", no. VG20102015022 granted by Ministry of the Interior of the Czech Republic and project "Research and application of advanced methods in ICT", no. FIT-S-14-2299 supported by Brno University of Technology.

References

[1] SUN, L., I.-H. Mkwawa, E. Jammeh and E. Ifeachor. *Guide to voice and video over IP for fixed and mobile networks.* London: Springer, 2013. ISBN 978-144-7149-057.

[2] ITU-T Recommendation P.800. *Methods for subjective determination of transmission quality.* 1996. Available at: http://www.itu.int/rec/T-REC-P.800.

[3] ITU-T Recommendation P.861. *Objective quality measurement of telephone-band (300–3400 Hz) speech codecs.* 1996. Available at: http://www.itu.int/rec/T-REC-P.861/en.

[4] ITU-T Recommendation P.862. *Perceptual evaluation of speech quality (PESQ): An objective method for end-to-end speech quality assessment of narrow-band telephone networks and speech codecs.* 2001. Available at: http://www.itu.int/rec/T-REC-P.862.

[5] ITU-T Recommendation P.863. *Perceptual objective listening quality assessment.* 2011. Available at: http://www.itu.int/rec/T-REC-P.863.

[6] ETR 250. *Transmission and Multiplexing (TM): Speech communication quality from mouth to ear for 3,1 kHz handset telephony across networks.* ETSI, 1996. Available at: http://www.etsi.org/deliver/etsi_etr/200_299/250/01_60/etr_250e01p.pdf.

[7] ITU-T Recommendation G.107. *The E-model: a computational model for use in transmission planning.* 2000. Available at: http://www.itu.int/rec/T-REC-G.107.

[8] RFC 3550. *RTP: A Transport Protocol for Real-Time Applications.* IETF, 2003. Available at: http://www.rfc-base.org/rfc-3550.html.

[9] KMET, M. *Analysis and Detection of Multimedia Types in RTP Traffic.* Brno, 2014. M.Sc. Thesis. Brno University of Technology. Supervisor Petr Matousek.

[10] RFC 7011. *Specification of the IP Flow Information Export (IPFIX) Protocol for the Exchange of Flow Information.* IETF, 2013. Available at: https://datatracker.ietf.org/doc/rfc7011.

[11] RFC 7012. *Information Model for IP Flow Information Export (IPFIX).* IETF, 2013. Available at: https://www.ietf.org/mail-archive/web/ietf-announce/current/msg11896.html.

[12] RFC 3954. *Cisco Systems NetFlow Services Export Version 9.* IETF, 2004. Available at: https://www.ietf.org/mail-archive/web/ietf-announce/current/msg11896.html.

[13] COLE, R. G. and J. H. ROSENBLUTH. Voice over IP performance monitoring. *ACM SIGCOMM Computer Communication Review.* 2001, vol. 31, iss. 2, pp. 9-24. ISSN 0146-4833. DOI: 10.1145/505666.505669.

[14] RFC 1155. *Structure and Identification of Management Information for TCP/IP-based Internets.* IETF, 2001. Available at: https://www.ietf.org/rfc/rfc1155.txt.

[15] VOZNAK, M. Recent Advances in Speech Quality Assessment and Their Implementation. In: *AETA 2013: Recent Advances in Electrical Engineering and Related Sciences.* Saigon: Springer, 2014, pp. 1–14. ISBN 978-3-642-41967-6. DOI: 10.1007/978-3-642-41968-3_1.

[16] JIANG, C. and P. HUANG. Research of Monitoring VoIP Voice QoS. In: *International Conference on Internet Computing & Information Services (ICICIS).* Hong Kong: IEEE, 2011, pp. 499–502. ISBN 978-1-4577-1561-7. DOI: 10.1109/ICICIS.2011.130.

[17] ASSEM, H., D. MALONE, J. DUNNE and P. O'SULLIVAN. Monitoring VoIP call quality using improved simplified E-model. In: *International Conference on Computing, Networking and Communications (ICNC).* San Diego: IEEE, 2013, pp. 927–931. ISBN 978-1-4673-5287-1. DOI: 10.1109/ICCNC.2013.6504214.

[18] CONWAY, A. E. A passive method for monitoring voice-over-IP call quality with ITU-T objective speech quality measurement methods. In: *International Conference on Communications.* New York: IEEE, 2002, pp. 2583–2586. ISBN 0-7803-7400-2. DOI: 10.1109/ICC.2002.997309.

[19] LINGFEN SUN and E.C. IFEACHOR. Voice quality prediction models and their application in VoIP networks. *IEEE Transactions on Multimedia*. 2006, vol. 8, iss. 4, pp. 809–820. ISSN 1520-9210. DOI: 10.1109/TMM.2006.876279.

[20] ITU-T Recommendation P.563. *Single-ended method for objective speech quality assessment in narrow-band telephony applications*. 2004. Available at: http://www.itu.int/rec/T-REC-P.563/en.

[21] MALFAIT, L., J. BERGER and M. KASTNER. P.563—The ITU-T Standard for Single-Ended Speech Quality Assessment. *IEEE Transactions on Audio, Speech and Language Processing*. 2006, vol. 14, iss. 6, pp. 1924–1934. ISSN 1558-7916. DOI: 10.1109/TASL.2006.883177.

[22] FALK, T. H. and W.-Y. CHAN. Single-Ended Speech Quality Measurement Using Machine Learning Methods. *IEEE Transactions on Audio, Speech and Language Processing*. 2006, vol. 14, iss. 6, pp. 1935–1947. ISSN 1558-7916. DOI: 10.1109/TASL.2006.883253.

[23] TOMALA, K., L. MACURA, M. VOZNAK and J. VYCHODIL. Monitoring the quality of speech in the communication system BESIP. In: *35th International Conference on Telecommunications and Signal Processing (TSP)*. Prague: IEEE, 2012, pp. 255–258. ISBN 978-1-4673-1117-5. DOI: 10.1109/TSP.2012.6256293.

[24] NGAMWONGWATTANA, B. and R. THOMPSON. Sync: VoIP Measurement Methodology for Assessing One-Way Delay Without Clock Synchronization. *IEEE Transactions on Instrumentation and Measurement*. 2010, vol. 59, iss. 5, pp. 1318–1326. ISSN 0018-9456. DOI: 10.1109/TIM.2010.2043978.

[25] ITU-T Recommendation G.113. *Transmission impairments due to speech processing*. 2002. Available at: https://www.itu.int/rec/T-REC-G.113.

[26] HALAS, M., A. KOVAC, M. ORGON and I. BESTAK. Computationally efficient E-model improvement of MOS estimate including jitter and buffer losses. In: *35th International Conference on Telecommunications and Signal Processing (TSP)*. Prague: IEEE, 2012, pp. 86–90. ISBN 978-1-4673-1117-5. DOI: 10.1109/TSP.2012.6256258.

[27] Basel, M. *Quality Analysis of VoIP Calls*. Brno, 2014. B.Sc. Thesis. Brno University of Technology. Supervisor Petr Matousek.

About Authors

Petr MATOUSEK was born in 1973 in Usti nad Labem. He received his M.Sc. in 1997 and Ph.D. in 2005 at Brno University of Technology where he is an assistant professor since 2003. His professional career includes interships at CERN, Geneva, and at LIAFA, Paris. His research interests include formal specification and verification, data analysis, network management and VoIP technologies.

Martin KMET was born in 1990 in Nove Mesto nad Vahom, Slovakia. He received his M.Sc. at Brno University of Technology, Faculty of Information Technology in specialization Computer Networks and Communication. Since 2014, he is a Ph.D. student there. His research is focused on VoIP technologies.

Martin BASEL was born in 1992 in Zlin. Currently, he studies his MSc. at Faculty of Information Technology, Brno University of Technology. In 2014, he successfully defended his bachelor project named Quality Analysis of VoIP calls.

32

A Methodology for Measuring Voice Quality Using PESQ and Interactive Voice Response in the GSM Channel Designed by OpenBTS

Pavol PARTILA , Marek KOHUT , Miroslav VOZNAK , Martin MIKULEC , Jakub SAFARIK , Karel TOMALA

Department of Telecommunications, Faculty of Electrical Engineering and Computer Science, VSB–Technical University of Ostrava, 17. listopadu 15/2172, 708 33 Ostrava-Poruba, Czech Republic

pavol.partila@vsb.cz, marek.kohut.st@vsb.cz, miroslav.voznak@vsb.cz, martin.mikulec@vsb.cz, jakub.safarik@vsb.cz, karel.tomala@vsb.cz

Abstract. *This article discusses a methodology for rating the quality of mobile calls. Majority telecommunications service from the perspective of the whole world is using mobile telephony networks. One of the problems affecting this service and its quality are landscape barriers, which prevent the spread signal. Price and complex construction of classic BTS does not allow their dense distribution. In such cases, one solution is to use OpenBTS technology. Design of OpenBTS is more available, so it can be applied to much more places and more complex points. Purpose of this measurement is a model for effective stations deployment, due to shape and distribution of local barriers that reduce signal power, and thus the quality of speech. GSM access point for our mobile terminals is OpenBTS USRP N210 station. The PESQ method for evaluating of speech quality is compared with the subjective evaluation, which provides Asterisk PBX with IVR call back. Measurement method was taken into account the call quality depending on terminal position. The measured results and its processing bring knowledge to use this technology for more complicated locations with degraded signal level and increases the quality of voice services in telecommunications.*

Keywords

Asterisk, openBTS, PESQ, SIP, speech quality.

1. Introduction

Testing QoS (Quality of Service) is one of the key challenges in modern telecommunications networks and the importance of these tests increases with increasing complexity of telecommunication networks, where the telecommunication chain involves more transmission technologies (called convergence networks).

To evaluate the quality of speech transmission over a telecommunications network, respectively after codecs processing. There are two basic evaluations, objective and subjective. This parameter is becoming one of the few measurable in general, to compare different transmission equipment, which is essentially the closest in terms of the end-users.

Speech coding becomes a key parameter in modern communication systems with limited bandwidth. The encoded data is sent via radio frequencies and are exposed to sensitive transmission lines which are susceptible to errors. Difficult, almost impossible is reconstruction of signal caused by these errors. One reason is the narrower bandwidth, which does not allow increasing redundancy.

Adaptive speech coding and transmission errors in mobile transmission systems may operate very distracting. Interference is quite different compared to traditional analog interference, and therefore this effect cannot be described by conventional measurement.

Typical errors encountered by mobile transfers are: impulse noise, short interruptions, trimming and nonlinear signal distortion using a loss-codecs. Another reason of distortion channel of communication in GSM networks are landscape barriers and constructions. This deficiency could be removed denser deployment of BTS, but it is financially and legislative demanding. Problem with barriers and complexity of land surface is handled by projects OpenBTS.

This project provides a smaller station, which are inexpensive and can be easier implemented [1], [2].

2.   OpenBTS

OpenBTS (Open Base Transceiver Station) is a term for software that will also allow the implementation of GSM access point. OpenBTS software itself is written in the programming language C++ and allows you to connect calls between registered stations to the created network and between networks of different providers too. For proper functioning of a mobile network is needed not only software for creating mobile network (OpenBTS), but also the hardware part - the transmitter. Figure 1 shows a product of Ettus ResearchTM, A National Instruments Company.

Fig. 1: OpenBTS USRP N210 from Ettus Research.

Asterisk PBX is necessary for making a call between registered endpoints. Asterisk PBX and OpenBTS software can be installed on the same workstation. This arises implementation of a fully functional mobile network operated by a single device. Mobile station that is successfully registered on the network created by the OpenBTS software is identified by "IMSIxxxxxxxxxxxxxx" shape in the VoIP network. Fourteen or fifteen digit unique identifier is the IMSI number of the SIM card present in the mobile station. For the IP address of the SIP user is using the same IP address, which has the BTS station. OpenBTS itself isn't visible in the VoIP network.

The OpenBTS system is utilized implementation Um radio interface, the same interface, which is used for communication with the normal BTS. Um provides radio interface for the GSM standard, which consists of three lowest layer of reference ISO/OSI model. Physical layer consists from three sublayers:

- The radio modem: radio transmitters support GMSK modulation with 13/48 MHz modulation rate and 200 kHz channel distance. Providing neighboring channels in the same cell isn't recommended because overlapping. OpenBTS supports four of the most commonly used GSM bands: GSM850, PGSM900, DCS1800 and PCS 1900.

- Multiplexing and coding: Each physical channel is divided into multiple logical channel using time division multiplex. GSM timing is controlled via the BTS with SCH and FCCH channels.

- FEC Encoding: Allows protection bits, thus provides error detection and correction of isolated bits.

The link layer uses the LAPDm protocol, which is a mobile version of the network communication protocols used in ISDN - LAPD. The protocol ensures that messages are sent without error and executed in the correct order. In this layer are also generated logical channels. Third layer of Um radio interface (network layer) provides:

- Management of network resources: This sublayer handles the assignment and release of the logical channels of the radio link.

- Mobility Management: sublayer provides authentication of the user and then monitors its movement between cells. The results are processed by OpenBTS using Asterisk SIP registry.

- Communication Management: Enables connecting telephone calls. Operations in OpenBTS are translated into the corresponding SIP operations and executed by Asterisk [3], [4], [10].

3.   Perceptual Evaluation of Speech Quality

PESQ is an algorithm for the measurement and evaluation of speech quality in telecommunication systems. The intrusive method is used to determine the quality of the speech, when the test system compares the original signal $x(t)$ with the degraded signal $y(t)$ taken at the other end of the transmission chain. Subsequently, reached values are evaluated in MOS-PESQ scale and then transferred using complementary recommendation P.862.1 on the values of the MOS-LQO scale, as shown in Fig. 2.

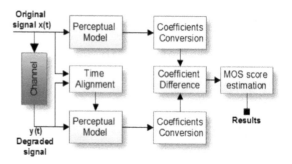

Fig. 2: MOS score estimated by PESQ algorithm.

The PESQ method first computes several series of delays between the original and degraded signal, where each of these series corresponds to one interval of signal. The delay for each interval is different due to ensure proper functioning of the PESQ algorithm. For each interval it is also determined start point and end point of time. Based on these series of delays, PESQ algorithm compares the original and degraded signal using the perceptual model.

The resulting PESQ-MOS score is expressed as a range of values from $-0,5$ to $4,5$. This score has to be converted to more accurate scope, more accurate for human subjective evaluation. Therefore, it is necessary to use complementary ITU-T P.862.1, which will provide scale transfer from MOS-PESQ to MOS-LQO. Scale MOS-LQO provides a range of values from 1 to 5. Conversion from PESQ MOS to MOS LQO is defined by Eg. (1), [5], [6]:

$$y = 0,999 + \frac{4,999 - 0,999}{1 + e^{-1,495x + 4,6607}}, \qquad (1)$$

where the variable x represents the value of the MOS-PESQ scale and the y represent MOS-LQO score. Inverse score (MOS-PESQ) from LQO is shown in Eg. (2):

$$x = \frac{4,6607 - ln\frac{4,999 - y}{y - 4,999}}{1,4945}. \qquad (2)$$

4. Interactive Voice Response

IVR service (Interactive Voice Response) allows us to use voice or DTMF tone dialing for operating with an automated system and choose from several options in the preset menu. IVR can be used for collecting data from the calling customer, such as account numbers, passwords or personal information, but also can make a call back or put the caller in queue. This service is expanding more and more, it helps to effectively solve problems instead of operators who may not always be available.

Figure 3 shows a hierarchy of IVR tree. IVR was used to compare the results of PESQ method in this case. CALL BACK service was activated after the call. The user was attended to evaluate the quality of call speech via DTMF feedback.

Questionnaire should contain as little as possible questions, because it might get bored caller. This follows from the statistical research about similar interviews. The end user evaluates various quality parameters with 1-5 values, via DTMF signaling. These data are logged in a database [7], [8].

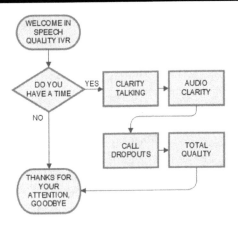

Fig. 3: IVR flowchart for speech quality measurements. Each question is evaluated from 1 to 5. One is the best quality.

5. Measurement

Measurement was performed in a laboratory at Department of Telecommunications, VŠB Technical University of Ostrava. Transmitting side of measuring workplace was compiled using PBX Asterisk and OpenBTS USRP N210 with antenna. Mobile phones with support for 2G serving the end users. Logic diagram is shown in Fig. 4.

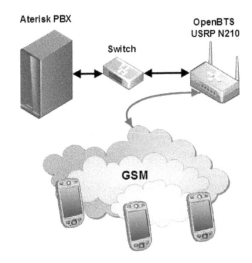

Fig. 4: Measurement schema for quality testing with components.

The N Building on the Department of Telecommunications, was measuring environment for testing voice quality transmitted through GSM created by OpenBTS.

Brick walls, doors and other building components formed barriers for propagation of the GSM network signal set up for this area. Each measuring point in the building has been strategically chosen to consider the barriers and the distance from the station. Measuring stations, five and their distribution show a plan of the ground floor of the building. The positions of the measuring points and station as shown Fig. 5.

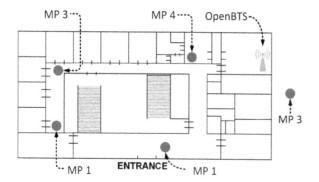

Fig. 5: First floor plan of the building N, where are marked measuring points (MB) and station (OpenBTS). Located in labN211.

6.   Results

Measurement was performed simultaneously on two points that BTS had to manage at least two calls. Nokia 5530 and Nokia E52 were used for terminal equipment. At these devices was recorded degraded part of the test call, the end user evaluates the quality via DTMF signaling too. After the call was established, the devices started with recording. Asterisk PBX provide a "Call Back" with IVR questions. Answers were interpreted by DTMF values from 1 to 5 as mentioned earlier.

6.1.   First Measurement Point – Entrance

First measurement place was selected into building near the entrance, as shown Fig. 5. The end user had not a direct view to the station, but all doors from station to point 1 were opened. Figure 6 represents results of PESQ and subjective IVR method.

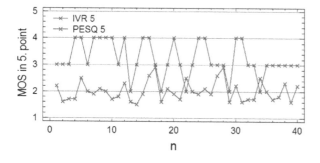

Fig. 6: Mean Opinion Score from PESQ and IVR methods for 1st measurement point.

6.2.   Second Measurement Point – Hallway

The end user with device provides calls from hallway. Distance was about 35 meters from OpenBTS station. Device antenna has a direct view to the station, because doors on view were opened. Results from this point are shown in Fig. 7.

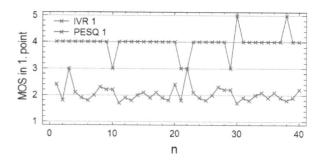

Fig. 7: Mean Opinion Score from PESQ and IVR methods for 2nd measurement point.

6.3.   Third Measurement Point - Outside

The aim of this measurement was to compare the results of signal quality when call is from outside the building. Antennas of devices have not a direct view with each other. Moreover, external windows of labN211 have the windows aluminum blinds. Quality of calls is shown in results in Fig. 8.

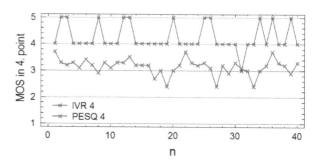

Fig. 8: Mean Opinion Score from PESQ and IVR methods for 3rd measurement point.

6.4.   Fourth Measurement Point – Office

This measurement point was selected in office near the station. Closed doors prevent direct view. Although, the results were the best of all measurement points. The end user submitted very well values through IVR method. Course of evaluation is shown in Fig. 9.

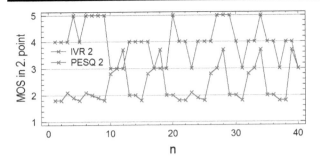

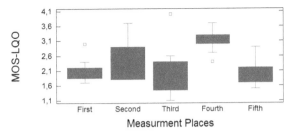

Fig. 11: PESQ method results for all measurements point. The Y axis explains mean opinion score from 1 to 5.

Fig. 9: Mean Opinion Score from PESQ and IVR methods for 4th measurement point.

6.5. Fifth Measurement Point – the End of Hallway

The fifth measurement point is located at the end of the hallway of the first floor. The end user is the largest distance from the transmitter overall. Therefore, the quality of signal has gone down, as shown in Fig. 10.

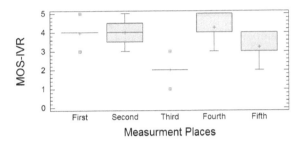

Fig. 12: The IVR method results for all five measure points. The Y axis explain a mean opinion score, same like previous picture.

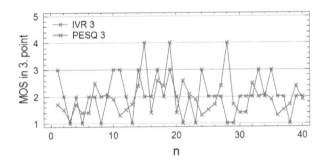

Fig. 10: Mean Opinion Score from PESQ and IVR methods for 5th measurement point.

7. Conclusion

This article shows how to use two methods to measure the quality of a call for GSM networks. It also evaluates the performance of the project OpenBTS in real operation. The idea that the OpenBTS used as an access point for complex areas is real.

To measure the quality of a call, that provided Asterisk and OpenBTS were two methods used. The first method which is used PESQ that using original and degraded, recording evaluate the quality of the connection. Subjective evaluation using IVR was chosen for the second method. Figure 11 shows a box-plot of all measuring points for the PESQ method.

Figure 12 shows results from DTMF signalling, which is results of IVR method.

Comparison Fig. 11 and Fig. 12 says that human evaluates the quality of the transmitted call differently than PESQ method. One reason is the imperfection of human hearing, which cannot detect small changes in

quality. This error will be decrease with numbers of measurements probably. End device record call from start of dialing, therefore it was necessary to cut off the top of degraded recordings to pick up. This can be a second reason of result differences [9].

On the other hand, the similarity in the results is due to the individual measuring points. Human evaluates various points as PESQ method if we do not take into account the scale. This means that a human value is about 2 MOS score higher than PESQ calculating in the majority of measurements. Finally also been measured signal level in the building on the ground floor, as shown in Fig. 13.

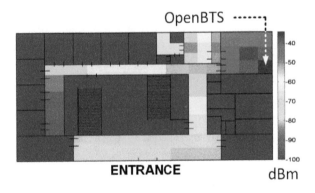

Fig. 13: Power of signal in the ground floor.

This graph shows a lack of performance when using one transmitting station. Logically, the strongest signal is close to the station. The signal level decreases with distance and buildings barriers.

This article presents a combination of two methods of evaluation the quality of voice services, and their possible implementation in practice. At the same time, it can be said that the project OpenBTS is an option for extending GSM networks in difficult areas, possibly to build a separate LAN GSM network.

Acknowledgment

The research leading to these results has received funding from the Grant SGS no. SP2013/94 and has been partially supported by the project of European Community's Seventh Framework Programme (FP7/2007-2013) under grant agreement no. 218086.

References

[1] WERNER, M., K. KAMPS, U. TUISEL, J. G. BEERENDS and P. VARY. Parameter-based speech quality measures for GSM. In: *14th IEEE Proceedings on Personal, Indoor and Mobile Radio Communications*. London: IEEE, 2003, pp. 2611–2615. ISBN 0-7803-7822-9. DOI: 10.1109/PIMRC.2003.1259200.

[2] MIKKONEN, J., M. TURUNEN, U. TUISEL, J. G. BEERENDS and P. VARY. An integrated QoS architecture for GSM networks. In: *IEEE 1998 International Conference on Universal Personal Communications*. Florence: IEEE, 1998, pp. 403–407. ISBN: 0-7803-5106-1. DOI: 10.1109/ICUPC.1998.733011.

[3] NATALIZIO, E., V. LOSCRI, G. ALOI, N. PAOLI and N. BARBARO. The practical experience of implementing a GSM BTS through open software/hardware. In: *3rd International Symposium on Applied Sciences in Biomedical and Communication Technologies (ISABEL 2010)*. Rome: IEEE, 2010, pp. 1–5. ISBN 978-1-4244-8131-6. DOI: 10.1109/ISABEL.2010.5702870.

[4] APVRILLE, Axelle. OpenBTS for dummies. In: *GNU Radio* [online]. 2013. Available at: http://gnuradio.org/redmine/attachments/420/fordummies.pdf.

[5] Recommendation P.862. *Perceptual evaluation of speech quality (PESQ): An objective method for end-to-end speech quality assessment of narrowband telephone networks and speech codecs*. International Telecommunication Union, 2001.

[6] ZHAO, J. Y., F. CAO, M. Y. LIANG a M. F. LIU. Very Low Bit Rate Speech Coding Algorithm and Its Implementation Based on DSP. *Computer Engineering*. 2011, vol. 37, iss. 21, pp. 261–263. ISSN 1000-3428. DOI: 10.3969/j.issn.1000-3428.2011.21.089.

[7] MADSEN, L. and MEGGELEN, J. V. *Asterisk: the definitive guide*. Sebastopol: O'Reilly Media, Inc. ISBN 978-059-6517-342.

[8] ATA, O. W., V. LOSCRI, G. ALOI, N. PAOLI and N. BARBARO. In Building Penetration Loss in Office and Residential Building Structures in Palestine at GSM 900 MHz Frequency. *Wireless Personal Communications*. 2013, vol. 70, iss. 1, pp. 1–14. ISSN 0929-6212. DOI: 10.1007/s11277-012-0675-6.

[9] Statgraphics® Mobile: User Guide. In: *Statgraphics* [online]. 2006. Available at: http://www.statgraphics.com/Statgraphics%20Mobile%20User%20Guide.pdf.

[10] DE RANGO, F., P. FAZIO, S. MARANO, N. PAOLI and N. BARBARO. Mobility independent and dependent predictive services management in wireless/mobile multimedia network. In: *60th Vehicular Technology Conference. VTC2004-Fall*. Los Angeles: IEEE, 2004, vol. 70, iss. 1, pp. 2596–2600. ISBN 0-7803-8521-7. DOI: 10.1109/VETECF.2004.1400526.

About Authors

Pavol PARTILA received the M.Sc. degree from University of Zilina, Faculty of Electrical Engineering in 2011. Currently, he is working toward the Ph.D. degree at the Department of Telecommunications, VSB–Technical University of Ostrava. Topics of his research interests are Speech processing, speech quality and VoIP.

Marek KOHUT received the Bc. degree from VSB–Technical University of Ostrava in 2013. His study field was Mobile technologies.

Miroslav VOZNAK is an Associate Professor with Department of Telecommunications, Technical University of Ostrava, Czech Republic. Topics of his research interests are Next Generation Networks, IP telephony, speech quality and network security.

Martin MIKULEC received the M.Sc. degree from Technical University of Ostrava in 2011. Currently, he is working toward the Ph.D. degree at the Deparment of Telecommunications, VSB–Technical University of Ostrava. His research is focused on advanced services in IP telephony and VoIP.

Jakub SAFARIK received his M.Sc. degree in telecommunications from VSB–Technical University of Ostrava, Czech Republic, in 2011 and he continues in studying Ph.D. degree at the same university. His research is focused on IP telephony, computer networks and network security. He is with CESNET as a researcher since 2011.

Karel TOMALA was born in 1984. In 2007, received a Bachelor title in VSB–Technical University of Ostrava, Faculty of Electronics and Computer Science, Department of Telecommunications. Two years later he received the M.Sc. title focused on Telecommunications in the same workplace. Currently in the doctoral study he focuses on Voice over IP technology and Call Quality in VoIP.

33

Dependence of Transfer Time of Bluetooth Payload Packets on the Surroundings and Distance

Premysl MER

Department of Telecommunications, Faculty of Electrical Engineering and Computer Science,
VSB–Technical University of Ostrava, 17. listopadu 15/2172, 708 33 Ostrava-Poruba, Czech Republic

premysl.mer@vsb.cz

Abstract. *This paper deals with the Bluetooth technology in telecommunication networks. The basis for the data transmission is a packet which has its own specifics in the wireless communication. The signal level is of higher importance, but other parameters like transfer time and a number of transferred packets are interesting too. The output of this paper is a proposed mathematical model, which describes dependencies of this output parameters on the distance between communicating devices and on the environment, in which these devices are placed. Some input criteria and conditions are defined for the functionality of the proposed design. The file transfer speed between the devices depends on the distance between them and on the surroundings, where the slave device is placed. For our purposes some possible surroundings that might be encountered were selected. It is free-space, paper with variable thickness, PVC or leather and wood with their respective density. Thanks to the application of the logarithmic regression on the output data the equation of mathematical model was found.*

Keywords

Bluetooth, environment, mathematical model, regression, transfer time.

1. Introduction

The basic parameters in information technologies are transmission parameters. Transmission parameters influence the ways of usage of this technology in specific applications. The Bluetooth technology belongs to PAN (Personal Area Network) networks. Their coverage and utilization are determined for applications as the data transmission among personal terminals or the configuration and control of various peripherals.

In the introduction are shortly presented the Bluetooth technology features. The basic for the data transmission is a packet which has its own specifics in the wireless communication. Some packets carry payload data, some packets synchronize and control the communication. This article is focused on data transmission features of the packets that carry useful data.

The possibilities and the utilization of the proposed model are tested in the next part of the paper by comparing results from a mathematical model and the experimental measurements.

Related works [6], [7], describes basic parameters of Bluetooth technology and presents measurement of file transfer delay with variable file size and variable distance with and without physical obstacle. This article is discovered specific parameter – transfer time of payload packets (it means packets with useful information no synchronize and service packets) – of Bluetooth technology in defined condition depend on surroundings and distance by transmitting the same file size data.

2. Feature of Bluetooth

The basic features of Bluetooth technology are frequency range, TX power and RX sensitivity. We overview some specific feature of Bluetooth technology in this chapter.

2.1. Indoor Propagation Mechanism

When radio waves strike a surface that is neither a perfect insulator nor a perfect conductor (in other words, all practical surfaces), part of the wave energy passes through, part is absorbed and part is reflected [8]. These characteristic give us the four paths by which a radio frequency signal can travel from a transmitter

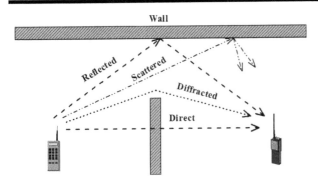

Fig. 1: Types of waves [1].

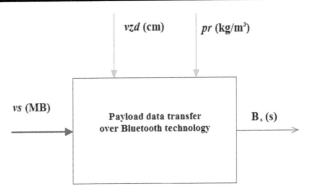

Fig. 2: Mathematical model.

to receiver. The paths are direct, reflected, diffracted and scattered (Fig. 1), [1], [5].

The classic free-space link budget equation is given by:

$$P_r = P_t \cdot G_t \cdot G_r \cdot \left(\frac{\lambda}{4\pi d}\right)^2, \qquad (1)$$

where P_r is received signal power, P_t is transmitted power, G_t is the gain of the transmit antenna in the direction of the received antenna and G_r is the gain of the receive antenna in the direction of the transmit antenna. The carrier wavelength λ is 0.122 m at 2.45 GHz and d is the distance (m) between transmitting and receiving antennas [1], [2].

2.2. System Parameters

The Bluetooth technology belongs to PAN (Personal Area Network) networks and their coverage and utilization are determined for applications as the data transmission among personal terminals or as a configuration and control of various peripherals. The Bluetooth devices are small and their range is usually up to 10 meters, for example mobile phones, PDA, mouse or keyboard are typical Bluetooth devices. Important factor of functionality is surroundings where these devices are placed [4].

For the mathematical model of data transmission by Bluetooth technology are distance and surrounding system parameters.

3. Mathematical Model

The mathematical model of data transmission describes communication between two devices. First master device sent data to second slave device. The file transfer between both devices depends on the distance between communicating devices and on the surroundings, where the slave device is placed. For our purposes were selected some possible surroundings that might be

encountered, it is free-space (density 1.204 kg/m^3), paper with variant thickness (density 700–1000 kg/m^3), PVC or leather (density 1200 kg/m^3), and wood (density 1000 kg/m^3).

The Bluetooth technology is packet oriented. During a transfer the several types of Bluetooth packets – payload packets, synchronizing packets, control packets or error packets are sent. This paper is oriented only on payload packets – packets with useful information. This idea originated during experiments with Bluetooth protocol analyzer.

With regard to complicated mathematics that describes signal propagation regressed form for creating the mathematical model is used [3]. Parameters of the mathematical model are distance between communicating devices and environment, where a slave device is placed. Used mathematical model of data transfer in Bluetooth technology is depicted in Fig. 2:

- input value: vs (MB),

- parameters: vzd (cm) and pr (kg/m^3),

- output function: B_s (cm).

3.1. Output Function

Data transfer was used in the experiment for compilation of the output function between master and slave devices. For all experiments was used the same file, the same master position and the same slave device. Measured data from Bluetooth protocol analyzer were sorted by direction and packets – only master-slave transfer and only payload packets.

3.2. Measuring Workplace

Measuring workplace illustrated in Fig. 3 shows the basic configuration of the experiment. Bluetooth device

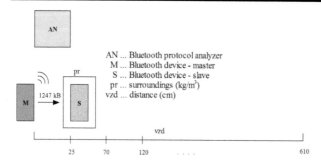

Fig. 3: Measuring workplace.

Tab. 1: Table of measurement data.

vzd (cm)	pr (kg/m³)				
	1.204	700	900	1200	1000
25	77.06	72.74	77.96	80.17	77.54
70	78.26	81.41	90.54	84.64	79.13
120	82.49	88.58	80.20	87.37	81.40
170	92.86	90.57	89.27	86.97	86.48
220	89.16	94.38	88.47	90.43	102.30
270	92.99	91.84	94.47	103.00	89.51
320	98.75	101.15	103.00	103.13	100.16
270	99.16	93.98	93.65	105.67	97.17
450	95.50	105.46	96.98	109.10	108.06
510	96.80	101.09	104.30	108.06	110.35
610	104.22	98.90	104.99	111.96	94.10

M sends data to device S in eleven distances, both devices master and slave are on class 3 (power 1 mW, 0 dB).

Transferred data was file (digital picture) with size of 1247 kB (1.217 MB). The experiment was implemented in real conditions for ordinary used Bluetooth applications. As a surroundings parameter were chosen air without obstruction, paper (thickness 2 and 4 mm), plastic obstruction (PVC) and wood. Every obstruction was in the box shape around slave device and experiment room was without special adjustment (obstruction, noise).

Input into the mathematical model was data file in MB, parameters were distance vzd (cm) and surroundings pr (kg/m³). The density of the air at 20 °C is 1.204 kg/m³, paper with a thickness of 2 mm have density of 700 kg/m³, paper with 4 mm have density of 900 kg/m³, wood have density of 1000 kg/m3 and plastic (PVC) have about 1200 kg/m³. Output of the mathematical model calculates average transfer time (s) in the dependence on the distance and obstruction surroundings.

4. Experiment

A table of measured data is needed to acquire a determination of dependencies (Tab. 1). First set of measurements was achieved with constant surroundings parameter – dependence of data transfer time on distance between Bluetooth devices. The second set of measurements was achieved with constant distance parameter – dependence of data transfer time on surroundings of slave Bluetooth device.

Measured data was used to create of partial mathematical equation by parametric regression analyse [3]. For graphical data output of time of transferred packets were established functions $B1$ and $B2$, where $B1$ (Fig. 4) is a function of distance with environment parameter (5 colour curves) and $B2$ (Fig. 5) is a function of sur-

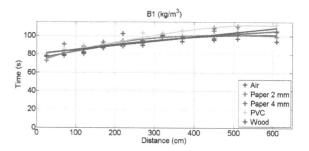

Fig. 4: Time of transferred packets depending on distance.

roundings with distance parameter (11 colour curves):

$$B1 = f\,(vzd)\,pr$$
$$B2 = f\,(pr)\,vzd. \qquad (2)$$

Equation of output function for data transfer time is:

$$B_s = \frac{vs}{1.217} \cdot k_s \cdot B1 \cdot B2, \qquad (3)$$

where B_s is output valuation of time of transferred packet from mathematical model and k_s is coefficient of the mathematical model.

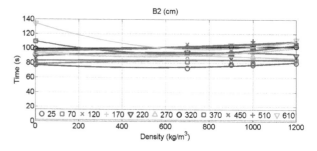

Fig. 5: Time of transferred packets depending on surroundings.

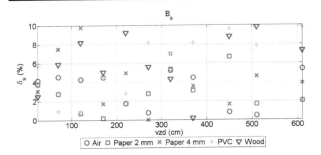

Fig. 6: Relative error.

4.1. Equation of Mathematical Model

Thanks to the application of logarithmic regression analysis on graphical output was found out the equation of a output function of the mathematical model. Because partial equations were multiplying, it is multiplicative (additive) regression model.

For a creation of equation it was needed to select referential point from graphical output from the middle of the graph – parameter vzd is 270 cm and parameter pr is 900 kg/m^3. Distance about 270 cm seemed as a typical distance for Bluetooth applications. It was the same in case of surroundings parameter, selected from the middle. Equation for $B1$ ($B2$) was created from referential point and function by logarithmic regression analysis:

$$B1 = 7.9938 \cdot ln\,(vzd) + 50.329, \qquad (4)$$

$$B2 = 0.3287 \cdot ln\,(pr) + 92.552. \qquad (5)$$

The constant k_s were needed to calculate from the mathematical model:

$$k_s = \frac{B_{(270.900)}}{B1 \cdot B2} = 0.010482, \qquad (6)$$

where $B_{(270.900)}$ is 94.47. In Fig. 6 is shown the final form of the mathematical model of Bluetooth technology data transmission. Final output equation:

$$B_s = \frac{vs}{1.217} \cdot 0.010482\,(7.9938 \cdot ln\,(vzd) + 50.329) \cdot$$
$$\cdot\,(0.3287 \cdot ln\,(pr) + 92.552). \qquad (7)$$

5. Conclusion

Created mathematical model describes dependencies of the output parameters – transfer time of payload packets – on the distance between communicating devices and on the surroundings, where these devices were placed. Some input criteria and requirements were necessary to define the functionality of the proposed model.

For verification of the mathematical model of Bluetooth technology data transmissions the output equation was applied to all measurements and values from experimental measurement were compared with values from the mathematical model. The relative error δ_s was also determined:

$$\delta_s = \left[\frac{\Delta x}{x}\right] = \left[\frac{B_m - B_s}{B_m}\right], \qquad (8)$$

where B_m is value from experiment measurement.

Total evaluation of issues of the mathematical model can be considered acceptable, because experiments and mathematical model were created for real conditions. The results of relative errors were about 5 %. It means that measurement data can be influenced by ordinary interferences and noises. The mathematical model does work the best for Bluetooth devices in class 3 in the range from 100 to 500 cm. Bluetooth functions and applications services were conformed to this range.

Acknowledgment

The research leading to these results has received funding from the European Community's Seventh Framework Programme (FP7/2007-2013) under grant agreement no. 218086.

References

[1] MORROW, Robert. *Bluetooth operation and use.* New York: McGrawHill, 2002. ISBN 00-713-8779-X.

[2] SIEP, Tom. *An IEEE guide: how to find what you need in the Bluetooth Spec.* New York: IEEE, 2001. ISBN 07-381-2636-5.

[3] BUDIKOVA, Marie, Tomas LERCH a Stepan MIKOLAS. *Zakladni statisticke metody.* Brno: Masarykova univerzita, 2005. ISBN 80-210-3886-1.

[4] BRAY, Jennifer and Charles F. STURMAN. *Bluetooth: connect without cables.* Upper Saddle River, N.J.: Prentice Hall, 2002. ISBN 01-306-6106-6.

[5] MORROW, Robert. *Wireless network coexistence.* New York: McGraw-Hill, 2004. ISBN 00-713-9915-1.

[6] HIPOLITO, Juan, Norma Candolfi ARBALLO, Jose Antonio MICHEL-MACARTY and Elitania Jimenez GARCIA. Bluetooth Performance Analysis in Wireless Personal Area Networks. *Electronics, Robotics and Automotive Mechanics Conference.* Cuernavaca, Mexico:

IEEE, 2009, pp. 38–43. ISBN 978-142-4453-412. DOI: 10.1109/CERMA.2009.48.

[7] RASHID, Rozeha A. and Rohaiza YUSOFF. Bluetooth Performance Analysis in Personal Area Network (PAN). *International RF and Microwave Conference*. Putrayaja, Malaysia: IEEE, 2006, pp. 393–397. ISBN 0-7803-9745-2. DOI: 10.1109/RFM.2006.331112.

[8] Bluetooth Specification Version 2.0 + EDR. *Specification of the Bluetooth System: Wireless connections made easy*. Bluetooth SIG, 2004. Available at: www.bluetoth.com.

About Authors

Premysl MER was born in Ostrava. He received his M.Sc. from University of Zilina in 1994. His research interests include access networks and multimedia. He received his Ph.D. from VSB–Technical University of Ostrava in 2010.

34

Smart Traffic Management Protocol Based on VANET architecture

Amilcare Francesco SANTAMARIA, Cesare SOTTILE

Department of Computer Science, Modeling, Electronics and Systems Engineering,
University of Calabria, Via Pietro Bucci, 870 36 Arcavacata di Rende CS, Italy

afsantamaria@dimes.unical.it, sottile@dimes.unical.it

Abstract. *Nowadays one of the hottest theme in wireless environments research is the application of the newest technologies to road safety problems and traffic management exploiting the Vehicular Ad-Hoc Network (VANET) architecture. In this work, a novel protocol that aims to achieve a better traffic management is proposed. The overal system is able to reduce traffic level inside the city exploiting inter-communication among vehicles and support infrastructures also known as Vehicle to Vehicle (V2V) and Vehicle to Infrastructure (V2I) communications. We design a network protocol called Smart Traffic Management Protocol (STMP) that takes advantages of IEEE 802.11p standard. On each road several sensors system are placed and they are responsible of monitoring. Gathered data are spread in the network exploiting ad-hoc protocol messages. The increasing knowledge about environment conditions make possible to take preventive actions. Moreover, having a realtime monitoring of the lanes it is possible to reveal roads and city blocks congestions in a shorter time. An external entity to the VANET is responsible to manage traffic and rearrange traffic along the lanes of the city avoiding huge traffic levels.*

Keywords

802.11p, CO_2 emissions reduction, geocasting, traffic management, VANET.

1. Introduction

Every year a high number of people lose their life in car accidents due to lack of a good traffic management. To overcome these troubles, in these last few years car manufactures and High Level Governance Institutions invested in IEEE 802.11p standard and road infrastructures to increase active and passive safety systems.

The major causes of collisions on our roads are the lack of information, limited sight and drivers distractions. Other accidents, instead, are caused by the irresponsible driving style of some drivers that unfortunately cannot be expected. With IEEE 802.11p, vehicles can exchange messages quite efficiently among themselves using ad-hoc connections with a multi-hop protocol to spread data in an efficient way in order to inform other vehicles about their conditions and about what they have recognized. These technologies can be also used to increase active and passive safety system informing vehicles and infrastructures about dangerous situations that can happen along the roads. Another important aspect of the traffic management can be also addressed in order to enhance the quality of the air around our cities. In fact, many researches surveys demonstrate that the higher is the traffic load, the higher will be the level of CO_2 emissions. Another cause that influences the CO_2 level is the vehicles speed and the average time spent by vehicles inside the city. With a better traffic management, the average time spent by the vehicles in the city will be considerably reduced while the average speed increases. In this way, the overall CO_2 produced by vehicles will be reduced thanks to the smaller number of congested roads. In order to obtain these results, we designed a full integration framework between car sensors and IEEE 802.11p.

The first issue that we faced is the dissemination of protocol messages because in IEEE 802.11p protocol there is a broadcast mechanism to reach all the vehicles with a On Board Unit (OBU). When a vehicle has to communicate some kind of warnings or accidents there is a protocol overhead increment caused by the exchange of warning and position messages. Considering also the general information messages there is a huge amount of packets travelling along the network that may cause a worsening of performances or even compromise network capabilities due to an excessive packet loss. Therefore, we have designed a protocol based on IEEE 802.11p paying attention also on protocol overhead issues. The work is organized as follow:

- A state of the art section in which we describe related works and address the differences and improvements between these works and the one here illustrated.

- The description of the reference architecture and the presentation of the network and system architecture we based on. We also present a brief analytic network model.

- How alerting system is implemented and how on board devices and core computation works.

- A simulation results section is introduced to present the results of several tests in different environments compared to current road system equipped with an IEEE 802.11p wave based protocol and STMP protocol. Our results will show many improvements in terms of average speed, traffic congestion and a notable reduction of CO_2 level inside urban environment.

- Conclusion and future works.

2.   Related Works

Recently, the studies related to vehicular networks focus on those solutions that improve the quality of life in the urban environments. Key aspects that are being considered are efficient traffic management and reduction of the CO_2 emissions and pollution. In the literature there are several works that aim to reach these goals. In [1], authors proposed a warning system composed of Intelligent Traffic Lights (ITLs) that provides information to drivers about traffic density and weather conditions. These ITLs reporting those statistics to the vehicles and also they will send warning messages to vehicles in the case of accidents to avoid further collisions. In [2], authors improved congestion control with heuristic techniques to reduce the traffic communication channels while considering reliability requirements of applications in VANETs. Heuristic techniques can be used to define heuristic rules and finding feasible and good enough solution to some problems in a reasonable time. In [3], authors considered the impacts of vehicular communications on efficiency of traffic in urban areas. They developed a Green Light Optimized Speed Advisory (GLOSA) application in a typical reference area and they presented the results of its performance analysis using an integrated cooperative ITS simulation platform. In [8], authors proposed an ITS-based system capable of guiding the driver's decisions, with the aim of reducing vehicle emissions. There is a direct relation between the car's emissions and its speed or acceleration. The goal of this system is to periodically guide the drivers through intersections equipped with ITLs, and recommend optimal speeds to

reduce the number of vain accelerations to catch green lights and the number of stop-starts due to red lights. In [5], the authors studied the performance of different warning message dissemination schemes for VANETs under situations classified as adverse due to the very low or very high density of vehicles in the scenario. The efficiency of warning message dissemination processes under these conditions is reduced as a result of frequent network partitioning under low densities, and high channel contention under high vehicle densities. Simulation results showed that these proposed schemes outperform the existing dissemination algorithms in terms of informed vehicles and messages received per vehicle. In [6],the authors designed and tested a primary-secondary resource-management controller on Vehicular Networks. They cast the resource-management problem into a suitable constrained stochastic Network Utility Maximization problem and derive the optimal cognitive resource management controller, which dynamically allocates the access time-windows at the primary users (the serving Roadside Units) and the access rates and traffic flows at the secondary users. They provided the optimal memoryless controllers under hard and soft primary-secondary collision constraints. In [7], authors defined and evaluated two traffic monitoring approaches that can be used leveraging the potentiality of VANETs. The protocols are based on a message exchange through a multi-hop path built on vehicles equipped with DSRC devices. No monitoring infrastructure is needed, except for a single Road Side Unit on a road span of almost 70 km. In [4], authors developed and implemented an instantaneous statistical model of emissions (CO_2, CO, HC, NO_x) and fuel consumption for light-duty vehicles, which is derived from the physical load-based approaches. The model is calibrated for a set of vehicles driven on standard as well as aggressive driving cycles. This model is implemented in Veins Framework that we used in our Simulations. In [9], [10], [11], [12], our previous studies, we focused on the reduction of the co-channel interference in VANETs due to the transmission of data packets between the nodes. Instead, in this paper we aim to find a whole system optimization able to reduce CO_2 emissions, to achieve a better management of urban traffic treating congestion and consequently to reduce the trip travel time of the vehicles.

3.   Reference Architecture

In this work, we use a heterogeneous architecture composed of a global city road manager that communicates with Road Side Unit (RSU) picking up information about the real condition of the roads in terms of traffic load. The RSU communicate with the Road Traffic Manager (RTM) in a periodic manner. In order to inform vehicles about roads condition the V2I commu-

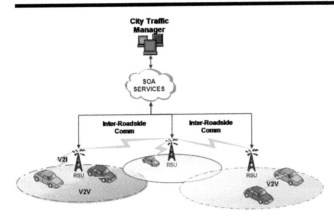

Fig. 1: Reference layered architecture.

nications are exploited. These messages exchanging allow vehicles to keep road information updated making possible a re-computation of the paths. The reference architecture is shown in Fig. 1. The RSU can communicate with the RTM every T_{update} seconds asking for network topology changes. In this message are also carried some important parameters related to covered lanes and roads that are served by the RSU. RTM can exploit these information to evaluate congestion levels updating lanes costs to reduce traffic loads. A dynamic cost is assigned in accordance with the formulas that will be presented in the further sections of this work.

3.1. Urban Environment Definitions

One of the main issues that this work tries to face is a better management of traffic and road congestion in urban and sub-urban areas. Commonly these blocks are recursive and the traffic congestion increase in an exponential way because the drivers cannot find feasible exit gates, and they may be involved into congestion as well as other vehicles that reach the congested areas before them. This represents a big issue for traffic management, in fact, as several surveys have already demonstrate that the higher is the traffic level the higher is the CO_2 level into the air. Using a protocol that allows communication among vehicles can help city traffic management in order to manage congestion in a faster way starting the treatments just at the beginning. This can be made acting a continuous monitoring of the traffic exploiting vehicles communications and fixed devices such as sensor devices along the roads. The whole system can be view as a hybrid network infrastructure composed of several devices with a given intelligence able to collect, store, send and elaborate grabbed information from the environment. Under this point of view, we have to describe some important entities that we are going to address. We refer to a generic Road (R) of the network, where each road is composed of one or more lanes. Each lane is indexed, so if we want to call 2-nd lane of the road

R_i we can recall it using the nomenclature $L_{2,i}$. Moreover, it is important to know the length of the j-th lane to perform further computations, these terms will be called $l_{j,i}$. In order to avoid congestion we have to define some critical constraints to model the queues. Thus, we assume that each lane related to a road R admits a certain maximum speed that we will define as $MaxSpeed_{j,i}$. Also, it is important to define an average vehicle length that we assume to be $v_{length} = 2.5$ m.

3.2. On Board Device Cooperation

Taking advantages of IEEE 802.11p based architecture and enhancing on-board device cooperation it is possible to collect a huge amount of data that can be used in order to better understand driver behaviors and predicting, where possible, if something is going wrong observing driver actions on the vehicles and monitoring distances among vehicles and known obstacles such as road borders. For example, it is possible to know information about distances exploiting related sensors, it is possible to have information about vehicle position exploiting the Global Position System (GPS). In this way, we can have the possibility to access all these information in a real-time manner. The OBU is smarter and a little bit more complex than a standard OBU, which is commonly used in an IEEE 802.11p environment. In our scheme, the OBU represents the core of the vehicle system able to communicate with an external world exploiting V2V and V2I communications.

3.3. Neighbor Clustering

A vehicle node can be considered as the neighbour if and only if the distance among nodes is lesser than a certain threshold. Therefore, a node is the neighbour of another one if following relations are satisfied:

$$r_{distance} = \sqrt{(x_1 - x_2)^2 + (y_1 - y_2)^2}, \qquad (1)$$

$$r_{distance} < \text{NeighThreshold}, \qquad (2)$$

where central node position into the Cartesian plane is $p_1 = (x_1, y_1)$, while the position of the second node is $p_2 = (x_2, y_2)$ and NeighThreshold is the threshold to identify if the second node is enough closer to be a neighbour. The neighbour lists are managed exploiting Position Updated (PosUpdate) protocol message. This message is periodic and it is sent by the vehicle in which the current position (achieved by GPS) are carried, this will be better explained in further sections. Of course, the Latitude and Longitude coordinates are converted into a Cartesian reference system, which has the origin in the upper left corner of the city map area. The propagation of this message PosUpdate is sent towards neighbours only limiting the dissemination on the basis of the vehicles position. This permits to avoid a drastic protocol overhead increasing.

4. Network Architecture

4.1. Entities

In this section, we describe the main entities we used. In particular, we considered three main entities that work in VANET layer and network layer. In the OBU, which is proposed in this work, we provide a core unit that can communicate with vehicles sensors, GPS unit and environmental sensors such as proximity, distance sensors and so on. All thus data are brief elaborated and filtered by the internal core application. Vehicles are equipped with this OBU and they can receive messages from the network layer exploiting multi-hop (V2V) and from the V2I communication that are established between RSU and OBU. The RSU is used to work as connector node between vehicles and Control and Management Center (CMC), in which the RTM takes place. It has also the task to spread messages along the network monitoring neighbour roads as well. When the OBUs reach a covered area they send messages regarding their location and become information suppliers for the RSU and the whole system, helping them to increase the real-time knowledge of the traffic, road and environment conditions. As it is possible to note the RSU is equipped with an internal STMP-Data Base (STMP-DB) that is used to collect protocol messages avoiding multiple sending of the same message and information about its own roads. The RTM that represents the entity that has the main task of managing the whole city traffic. The RTM takes information about roads and traffic level exploiting the VANET layer. In particular, the RSUs have the main task to collect information about vehicles, roads and sensors sending important data to RTM. Once the RTM recognizes a bad event it changes the weights of the related roads and sends messages towards the RSU to communicate weights changes. After that weights computation is made and these messages are sent to the vehicles following dissemination rules in order to avoid congestion and further blocks. Information are used by the vehicles in order to update their local map, a reroute is forced by inner functions.

4.2. Dedicated Protocol Messages

1) Position Update in Smart Traffic Management Protocol (STMP)

Position Updated (PosUpdate) is an inner function that give us the possibility to bring up informa-

tion about the neighbour vehicles. These information are picked up exploiting protocol messages called PosUpdate. In order to reduce protocol overhead, it is important to limit the total amount of protocol messages that will flood around the network. This is made sending some info-messages, which are related to local issues only to neighbours. In the PosUpdate messages are collected all information related to the position of a vehicle exploiting the on-board navigation systems such as GPS or the position system based on the inner elements of the OBU. Once this information are received they also elaborated and if and only if the distance among vehicles is lesser than a certain threshold the vehicle that has sent the messages becoming a new neighbour. If the distance is greater than the threshold, the vehicle is erased from the neighbour list and no messages are more sent towards it. In this way, messages flood only in a restricted area around the vehicle avoiding worst flooding effects on network performances. This message is generated in a periodic way by each vehicle.

2) Congestion Update

In this work, we try to increase the overall quality of the city traffic management. In order to design this activity we need to monitor the road condition in a real time way. This can be made exploiting several sensors around the city and exploiting also the RSU device that are involved into IEEE 802.11p communication. The working schema is shown in Fig. 2 where the protocol behaviour is shown. The RSU collects the messages coming from the OBU of the vehicles on the own Lanes and sends this information to the CMC. The CMC collects all the information sent by the RSU and sends back the elaboration through the Congestion Updated (CongUpdate) in order to advise if some traffic issues have been found. The RSU sends in broadcast way the messages into the network covering roads areas. In Fig. 2 the Car-A has found a better path going on Lane-A to reach its destination. When the CongUpdate message reaches the Car-A it recalculates the path choosing the Lane-B avoiding blocked road and avoiding wasting of time, saving fuel and reducing CO_2 emissions.

4.3. Traffic Block Detection and Management

Congestion as well as collisions often cannot be predicted or known in advantage due to dynamics of these events that can be directly connected with external factors. When congestion is raising the system can advice these events as traffic congestion to other vehicles that can change their paths avoiding critical traffic level in the involved areas and closer areas as well. But in case

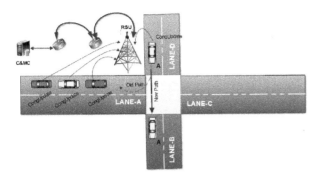

Fig. 2: Road congestion identification.

of high traffic level, this behaviour is not clever. In fact, could be better to find a relation that give us the possibility to identify a fair cost for those roads that momentary reach high traffic levels. Using a high cost, all vehicles can reroute their paths going towards the same area, this may determine another congestion area inside the city. This represents a big issue to address correctly and smarter weighting cost function has to be found in order to estimate the real impact of the collision. In this work, we try to find a relation among several parameters such as travelling time and number of vehicles on the roads, looking for the better trade-off that can allow us to manage in a finer way critical situations. Considering a generic i-th road R composed of one ore more lanes we can determine the travelling time as shown in Eq. (3). Where the $|n_{j,i}|$ represent the number of the vehicles on the considered lane. $l_{l,i}$ is the lane length and $S_{k,j,i}$ is the average speed of the k-th vehicle on that lane of the i-th road:

$$tt_{j,i} = \frac{|n_{j,i}| \cdot l_j}{\sum_{k=1}^{i=|n_{j,i}|} S_{k,j,i}} \; : \; j \in R_i. \tag{3}$$

In Eq. (4), the average space occupied by the k-th vehicle is presented, this space is directly connected with the speed of the vehicle. Commonly, it is $\frac{1}{3}$ of the current vehicle speed and it represent the stop space:

$$v_{space} = \frac{1}{n_j} \cdot \left(\sum_{k=1}^{n_{j,i}} length(vehicle_k) + \frac{\sum_{k=1}^{n_{j,i}} speed(vehicle_k)}{k_{speed}} \right). \tag{4}$$

Herein equation used to trigger congestion on a given lane are presented. In this equation, we take into account the current number of vehicles, lane length, the

average vehicle length, and the space occupied by the vehicle when their speed is close to 0. When the number of the vehicles is closer to the maximum admissible number of vehicles (see Eq. (5)) then the congestion trigger is raised, this means that the Th_{cong} threshold is reached:

$$maxV_{j,i} = \left[\gamma \cdot \frac{l_{j,i}}{v_{space}} + \left(\frac{\sum_{k=1}^{n_{j,i}} length(vehicle_{k,j,i})}{n_{j,i}} \cdot \delta \right) \right]. \tag{5}$$

The $maxV_{j,i}$ is given by the sum of two components: the first one is related to the number of the vehicles that can travel the lane respecting safety distances, the second one is related to the space taken by several vehicles that are waiting on the lane. It is possible, for example, to change the weight of the waiting queue time, such as a traffic light queue, acting on the δ parameter. Thus, in order to evaluate whether a lane is congested or not, we can use the equations herein shown:

$$h(n_{j,i}) = \{n_{j,i} - maxV_{j,i}\}, \tag{6}$$

$$K_{cong,j,i} = \begin{cases} \alpha & \text{if } h(n_{j,i}) \geq Th_{cong} \\ \beta & \text{otherwise} \end{cases}, \tag{7}$$

where $l_{j,i}$ is length of the j-th lane of the considered Road (R), $n_{j,i}$ is number of vehicles on the j-th lane of the road R, $tt_{j,i}$ is travelling time along the j-th lane of the considered Road (R), $S_{k,j,i}$ is the speed of the i-th vehicle on the j-th lane of the Road(R), $k_{cong,j,i}$ is the congestion factor related to j-th lane of the considered Road (R), k_{speed} is coefficient for safety distance computation, δ is coefficient to manage congestion level in terms of queue length, γ is coefficient to manage congestion level in terms of queue safety distance considering the average speed of the vehicles that are travelling the lane, α, β is congestion parameters that are configurable as system parameters. Th_{cong} is the congestion threshold configurable as system parameters, $h(n_{j,i})$ is function of the number of the vehicles that are on the j-th lane of the Road (R_i).

At the end the cost of the edge is given by Eq. (8):

$$w_{j,i} = tt_{j,i} + \left\{ K_{cong} \cdot \left(\frac{1}{UpBound_{j,i}} - \frac{1}{InRate_{j,i}} \right) \cdot [n_{j,i} \cdot v_{space}] \right\}. \tag{8}$$

$$Cost_{j,i} = \begin{cases} tt_{j,i} & \text{if } InRate_{j,i} = 0 \\ w_{j,i} & \text{otherwise} \end{cases}, \tag{9}$$

when K_{cong} is equal to α this means that is high probable that a certain level of congestion can be measured on the considered lane. Therefore, it is important to give a different weight on the lane advising other vehicles about this situation. This message is exchanged by protocol starting from RTM.

5. Simulation Results

In this section, we show the results achieved using the Smart Traffic Management Protocol (STMP), that we have already introduced in above sections comparing it with the Wave Short Message Protocol (WSMP) and the Cooperative Awareness Message (CAM). First of all we have to introduce the simulation environment and used constraints in order to better understand achieved results.

5.1.   Network Simulator

OMNet++ [13] Simulator with Veins [14] framework has been used to develop our proposal. It is a network simulator based on a modular implementation written in C++. To manage vehicles' mobility, the network simulator is connected with SUMO [15]. Our implementation, STMP has been written on the Veins framework introducing protocol rules and some important components of the system such as RSU and RTM. The aims of this section is to show the goodness of the proposal in terms of traffic management and the reduction of CO_2 emissions. Using the whole framework composed of on-board device collaboration and STMP it is possible to better spread traffic load along the city. It is also possible to view that the protocol help vehicles to reduce their travelling time around the city. The Simulation Parameters and the Congestion Parameters are the following (Tab. 1).

In order to evaluate the protocol performances we made a comparison among protocol proposal and the WSMP used for disseminate signalling message along the network, in particular when an accident is found or global information has to be spread along the network. It is important to recall that the WSMP is used to disseminate Wave Short Message (WSM) that are designed to carry signalling data and in further develops to also carry services and applications data ([16], [18]).

1)   Signalling Packets

In this simulation scenario, we focus on the protocol overhead reduction. In particular, we are going to show the flooding reduction of protocol messages in case of PosUpdate that will give us the possibility to save a

Tab. 1: Simulation table.

Parameter Name	Values
Map Size	1.5 [km^2]
Average road length	30 [km]
Average vehicle length	2.5 [m]
Maximum Speed of vehicles	15 [m·s^{-1}]
Vehicle In-Rate	$[2, 3, 4, 5] \cdot 10^2 \left[\frac{vehic.}{h}\right]$
K_{speed}	0.35
δ	0.35
Th_{cong}	3
α	1
β	2

lot of resources reserving them for data transmission. In this scenarios, we planned to use several vehicles that travel along the map roads and to demonstrate the goodness of the proposal we use a version of the protocol without neighbours management and the version equipped with neighbour management. In Fig. 3 is possible to see the total amount of packets in the network when the geocasting based rules are used to disseminate data along the network.

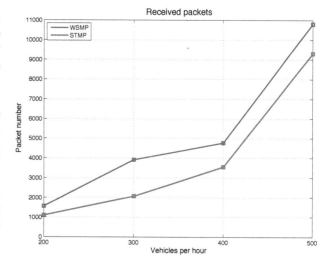

Fig. 3: Average number of received messages per node.

2)   Effects on Air Pollution

This simulation campaign aims to demonstrate that using communication and making an efficient cooperation among entities that share the same applicative context it is possible to reach important results for the communities. Thanks to this approach it has been possible to reduce the total amount of CO_2 emissions and the average travelling time and increasing the average speed of the vehicles into the urban area as well. As it is analysed in [3], it is possible to note that avoiding accelerations and decelerations a CO_2 emissions reduction is obtainable.

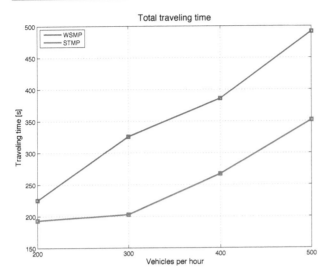

Fig. 4: Average traveling time.

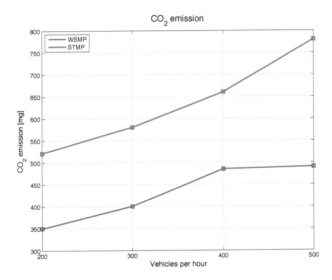

Fig. 5: Average CO$_2$ emission.

3)   Traffic and Congestion Management

In this simulation campaign, we show the benefits of the proposal in terms of traffic management, especially in the case of accidents or when something goes wrong on the lanes. In the first approach, we used the goodness of the idea has been evaluated. In particular, we added some accidents that involve several vehicles along the roads. The accidents we added in are spread along the urban area in order to distribute blocks on several districts of the city observing how the traffic moves around the city rearranging loads on the neighbour roads. We considered the impact of the traffic balancing when STMP protocol is used. Observing Fig. 6 it is possible to carry out some considerations. First of all we can state that the STMP protocol solves congestion issues finding several exit gates allowing vehicles to recalculate paths when the first signals of congestion are also triggered by the monitoring functions included

in the overall system. In the beginning the protocols behaviour are comparable but also in this first period the protocol carries out a better behaviour.

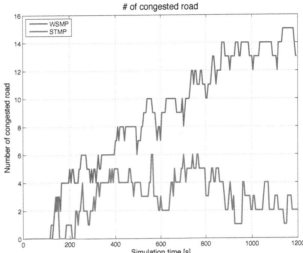

Fig. 6: STMP congestion avoidance behaviours.

In Fig. 6 the number of congested road is given by the sum of the overall city roads that results congested in the observing time. Therefore, as it is possible to note the STMP performs better than WSMP based protocol where only signalling messages such as collisions and warning messages are provided. Moreover, as already stated the congestion can be better managed if it is treated at the beginning of the first events that can cause blocks in the city areas. In Fig. 7 the performance of our proposal versus a CAM based protocol is made [16] and [17]; this protocol tries to manage congestion exploiting the warning and signalling messages to recognize events that may generate congestion in some area or blocks of the city. It is possible to note that our approach performs better reducing the number of congested roads. This is made because it acts previously than other one. In fact, using an efficient monitoring it can notice drivers about changing of the road status. This system helps us to reduce the incoming rate on the congested roads allowing road to keep a good ratio between the vehicles that are coming and those that exit from the road.

4)   Total Distance and Total Time Traveled

In this last campaign we have evaluated the performance of the protocols in the term of the total distance travelled by vehicles and total travel time of vehicles. As it is possible to note from Fig. 8 the total distance of the vehicles is higher with the proposal protocol because the STMP reduces congestion and blocks suggesting a route change to the vehicles that are closer to the involved area. Different performances are shown when the traffic loads increase. In Fig. 4 it is possi-

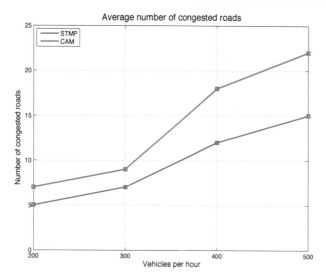

Fig. 7: CAM vs. STMP in term of average number of congested road.

ble to note that the total travel time decreases with the proposed protocol because the STMP avoids road blocks and reduces road congestion by use Traffic and Congestion Management.

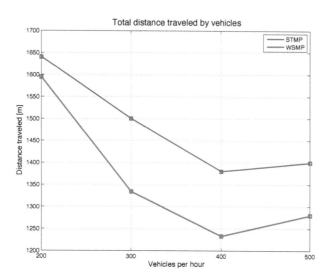

Fig. 8: Average distance per vehicle.

6. Conclusions

The IEEE 802.11p based protocol presented improves the management of the traffic and reduces the total number of the packets sent on the network using a more efficient dissemination technique based on geocasting distribution. In fact how demonstrated into simulation campaigns, some information are important only for those nodes closer to the interested area of the critical event. Integration of on-board devices such as the OBU with the external devices such as monitoring de-

vices, allows us to reach better performances. Spreading information collected by the on-board devices, the behaviour of behind and beyond vehicles is influenced. Finding new routes that allow drivers to reduce travelling time and to increase the average speed it is possible to reduce emissions. As depicted in the simulation results section, these advantages for the drivers bring up an indirect advantage for the air quality of the city reducing the total emissions of CO_2 gas. In this work, another subject of the simulation was the evaluation of the system in terms of protocol overhead, CO_2 level and congestion areas. Results of the simulations show that the proposed protocol enhances many quality indexes managing traffic in a better way addressing congestion before it reaches critical level.

References

[1] BARBA, C. T., M. A. MATEOS, P. R. SOTO, A. M. MEZHER and M. A. IGARTUA. Smart city for VANETs using warning messages, traffic statistics and intelligent traffic lights. In: *IEEE Intelligent Vehicles Symposium (IV)*. Alcala de Henares: IEEE, 2012, pp. 902–907. ISBN 978-1-4673-2119-8. DOI: 10.1109/IVS.2012.6232229.

[2] TAHERKHANI, N. and S. PIERRE. Congestion control in vehicular ad hoc networks using meta-heuristic techniques. In: *Proceedings of the second ACM international symposium on Design and analysis of intelligent vehicular networks and applications*. New York: ACM, 2012, pp. 47–54. ISBN 978-1-4503-1625-5. DOI: 10.1145/2386958.2386966.

[3] KATSAROS, K., R. KERNCHEN, M. DIANATI, D. RIECK and C. ZINOVIOU. Application of vehicular communications for improving the efficiency of traffic in urban areas. *Wireless Communications and Mobile Computing*. 2011, vol. 11, iss. 12, pp. 1657–1667. ISSN 1530-8677. DOI: 10.1002/wcm.1233.

[4] CAPPIELLO, A., I. CHABINI, E. K. NAM, A. LUE and M. A. Zeid. A statistical model of vehicle emissions and fuel consumption. In: *IEEE 5th International Conference on Intelligent Transportation Systems (IEEE ITSC)*. Singapore: IEEE, 2002, pp. 801–809. ISBN 0-7803-7389-8. DOI: 10.1109/ITSC.2002.1041322.

[5] SANGUESA, J., M. FOGUE, P. GARRIDO, F. J. MARTINEZ, J.-C. CANO and C. T. CALAFATE. Using topology and neighbor information to overcome adverse vehicle density conditions. *Transportation Research Part C: Emerging Technologies*. 2014, vol. 42, pp. 1–13. ISSN 0968-090X. DOI: 10.1016/j.trc.2014.02.010.

[6] CORDESCHI, N., D. AMENDOLA and E. BACCARELLI. Primary-secondary resource-management on vehicular networks under soft and hard collision constraints. In: *Proceedings of the fourth ACM international symposium on Development and analysis of intelligent vehicular networks and applications (DIVANet 2014).* New York: ACM, 2014, pp. 161–168. ISBN 978-1-4503-3028-2. DOI: 10.1145/2656346.2656362.

[7] DE FELICE, M., A. BAIOCCHI, F. CUOMO, G. FUSCO and C. COLOMBARONI. Traffic monitoring and incident detection through VANETs. In: *11th Annual Conference on Wireless On-demand Network Systems and Services.* Obergurgl: IEEE, 2014, pp. 122–129. ISBN 978-1-4799-4937-3. DOI: 10.1109/WONS.2014.6814732.

[8] DOBRE, C. Using Intelligent Traffic Lights to Reduce Vehicle Emissions. *International Journal of Innovative Computing, Information and Control.* 2012, vol. 8, no. 9, pp. 6283–6302. ISSN 1349-4198.

[9] FAZIO, P., F. DE RANGO, C. SOTTILE and A. F. SANTAMARIA. Routing Optimization in Vehicular Networks: A New Approach Based on Multi-objective Metricsand Minimum Spanning Tree. *International Journal of Distributed Sensor Networks.* 2013, vol. 2013, iss. ID598675, pp. 1–13. ISSN 1550-1477. DOI: 10.1155/2013/598675.

[10] FAZIO, P., F. DE RANGO and C. SOTTILE. A new interference aware on demand routing protocol for vehicular networks. In: *International Symposium on Performance Evaluation of Computer and Telecommunication Systems, SPECTS.* Hague: IEEE, 2011, pp. 98–103. ISBN 978-1-4577-0139-9.

[11] FAZIO, P., M. TROPEA, F. VELTRI and S. MARANO. A new routing protocol for interference and path-length minimization in vehicular networks. In: *IEEE 75th Vehicular Technology Conference, VTC Spring.* Yokohama: IEEE, 2012, pp. 1–5. ISBN 978-1-4673-0989-9. DOI: 10.1109/VETECS.2012.6240292.

[12] FAZIO, P., F. DE RANGO and C. SOTTILE. An on-demand interference aware routing protocol for VANETs. *Journal of Networks.* 2012, vol. 7, no. 11, pp. 1728–1738. ISSN 1796-2056. DOI: 10.4304/jnw.7.11.1728-1738.

[13] VARGA, A. and R. HORNIG. An overview of the OMNeT++ simulation environment. In: *Proceedings of the 1st international conference on Simulation tools and techniques for communications, networks and systems workshops.* Brussels: ICST, 2008, pp. 1–10. ISBN 978-963-9799-20-2.

[14] SOMMER, C., R. GERMAN and F. DRESSLER. Bidirectionally coupled network and road traffic simulation for improved ivc analysis. *IEEE Transactions on Mobile Computing.* 2011, vol. 10, no. 1, pp. 3–15. ISSN 1536-1233. DOI: 10.1109/TMC.2010.133.

[15] KRAJZEWICZ, D., J. ERDMANN, M. BEHRISCH and L. BIEKER. Recent development and applications of sumo - simulation of urban mobility. *International Journal On Advances in Systems and Measurements.* 2012, vol. 5, no. 3&4, pp. 128–138. ISSN 1942-261x.

[16] FAZIO, P., F. DE RANGO and A. LUPIA. Vehicular Networks and Road Safety: an Application for Emergency/Danger Situations Management Using the WAVE/802.11 p Standard. *Advances in Electrical and Electronic Engineering.* 2013, vol. 11, iss. 5, pp. 357–364. ISSN 1804-3119. DOI: 10.15598/aeee.v11i5.890.

[17] FAZIO, P., F. DE RANGO and A. LUPIA. A new application for enhancing VANET services in emergency situations using the WAVE/802.11p standard. In: *6th IFIP/IEEE Wireless Days Conference (WD).* Valencia: IEEE, 2013, pp. 1–3. ISBN 978-1-4799-0542-3. DOI: 10.1109/WD.2013.6686517.

[18] LI, Y. *An Overview of the DSRC/WAVE Technology.* Heidelberg: Springer, 2012, pp. 544–558. ISBN 978-3-642-29221-7.

About Authors

Amilcare Francesco SANTAMARIA was born in 1978. He received the master's degree in computer science engineering and Ph.D. in Computer Science in October 2005 and March 2012 respectively. Since November 2005 he was employed in the Department of Computer Science at the University of Calabria. Since November 2008 he was employed in the NEXT SpA Ingegneria dei Sistemi in Rome as senior Software Architect. He worked on several embedded systems for the defence field of application such as Electro-optical turret devices, core Radar Software Control and Naval applications. Since April 2013 he is Research Fellow at University of Calabria, Department of Computer Science, Modeling, Electronics and Systems Engineering (DIMES). His research interests include Satellite and Broadband communications, multicast routing protocols and algorithms, wired and wireless architectures, VANET , QoS optimization and Evolutionary and Bio-inspired Algorithms.

Cesare SOTTILE was born in 1983. He received the bachelor's degree in Computer Science Engineering in September 2007. Since December 2010 he received the master's degree in Telecommunications Engineeering at the University of Calabria. Nowadays, he is a Ph.D. student at Department of Computer Science, Modeling, Electronics and Systems Engineering (DIMES) at the University of Calabria. His research interests include mobile communication networks, satellites, vehicular networks and interworking wireless, energy efficient protocols for sensor networks.

35

Automatic Loss Adjustment for CDMA2000 and 1xEV-DO Standard for Downlink and Uplink

Jiri KOMINEK[1], Miroslav VOZNAK[2], Jan ZIDEK[1]

[1]Department of Cybernetics and Biomedical Engineering, Faculty of Electrical Engineering and Computer Science, VSB–Technical University of Ostrava, 17. listopadu 15/2172, 708 33 Ostrava, Czech Republic
[2]Department of Telecommunications, Faculty of Electrical Engineering and Computer Science, VSB–Technical University of Ostrava, 17. listopadu 15/2172, 708 33 Ostrava, Czech Republic

jiri.kominek@outlook.com, miroslav.voznak@vsb.cz, jan.zidek@vsb.cz

Abstract. *The functional and thermal testing of the mobile phone is always performed under various conditions that vary in terms of the connection between the DUT (Device Under Test) and the measuring instrument. To achieve repeatable measurements under such conditions, it is necessary to adjust uplink and downlink loss using the instrument's external attenuation. While for GSM, WCDMA and LTE this is a relatively easy task, CDMA2000 and 1×EV-DO make automation of the adjustment process somewhat challenging due to the nature of the CDMA standard. An especially forward link is more complicated as those tests are run in signaling mode and not all instruments provide an FER value measured by an MS. This paper describes the algorithm for forward link loss adjustment and its implementation using Rohde-Schwarz CMW500.*

Keywords

DUT, GSM, LTE, QoS, WCDMA.

1. Introduction

In CDMA2000 networks, control of the Mobile Station (MS) transmit power is essential to ensure stable transmission and an efficient radio resource management within the system. Generally speaking, the output power of the MS transmitter that is too low decreases the coverage area while an excess output power may cause interference to other channels or systems. Both effects decrease the system capacity [1], [2], [3].

CDMA2000 standard defines three methods for controlling the power of the MS, but when some power measurements need to be performed it is necessary to properly deal with the automatic power control to achieve repeatable and reliable measurement results under various conditions. This issue is described in the chapter entitled "CDMA2000 and Its Evolution" in [4].

During the initial connection setup, the open loop power control is active. It is crucial to estimate the output power from the measuring instrument so that a connection will be established. If the output power is too high, the DUT will lower its transmit signal because from a strong BS (Base Station) signal it assumes that the DUT is very close to the BS and thus it does not need to transmit with high power [5].

Thanks to the built-in functionality of some measuring instruments (Rohde & Schwarz CMW in this case, CMW is a wideband radio communication tester) it is possible to implement the automatic adjustment of the forward link signal with the help of FER (Frame Error Rate) measurement in signaling mode, which is sufficient for R&D tests. However, because the FER measurement is not particularly fast, the method depicted here is not suitable for EOL (End of Line) or production testing.

2. State of the Art

Three main methods of power control will be described in the following subchapters in order to give an overview of their built-in automatism. A description of the discovered solution will be presented via a concrete example based on the Rohde & Schwarz CMW500 instrument with the help of an attribute based instrument driver for the remote control of the instrument from LabVIEW [6], [7].

2.1.   Open Loop Power Control

In an open loop, the reverse link transmission power is set based upon the received power on the forward link. The transmitter attempts to minimize the transmit power using the average received signal strength as an indication of path loss. This mechanism inverses the slow fading effect (path loss, shadowing) and acts as a safety fuse when the fast power control fails [8].

When the forward link is lost, the closed loop reverse link power control freewheels and the terminal disruptively interferes with neighboring cells. In such case, the open loop reduces the terminal output power as it gets closer to any cell and therefore limits the impact to the system.

When a mobile first attempts to access the CDMA network, it uses Open Loop Power Control to assure that it achieves a good trade-off between the interference caused to the system and the access time. The interference caused to other users is inversely proportional to the mobile transmit power while the probability of network access for a given attempt is directly proportional to the transmit power.

In Open Loop Power Control, the mobile measures the pilot strength which is related to path loss. The transmit power is then set inversely to the measured pilot strength. If the pilot is weak, which means that there's a large path loss, the mobile station transmits on high power and vice versa.

2.2.   Fast Closed Loop Power Control

Unlike CDMA, where Fast Closed Loop Power Control was applied only to the reverse link, both CDMA2000 channels can be power controlled at up to 800 Hz in both reverse and forward directions. The main goal of fast closed loop power control is to dynamically adjust the allocated power for each user in a manner that meets the required quality of service (e.g. FER) of these users, and as a consequence maximizes system capacity.

Unlike open loop or slow closed loop power control, fast closed loop power control is sufficient for keeping track of multipath induced fading. The receiver measures the received signal's strength every 1.25 ms (800 Hz) and sends a power control command to the transmitter by means of power control bits. Power Control Bits (PCB) are used to request an increase or reduction in transmit power. A series of these power control bits is sent on the traffic channel instead of the scrambled data bits. The transmitter receives the PCB commands and adjusts its transmit power by a predetermined step size (e.g. 1 dB). One to four data bits (depending on the data rate) are replaced by the corresponding number of PCBs ("0...0" or "1...1").

The finer steps allow tighter power control for the low mobility or stationary phones. Tighter control (less power ripple) lowers the average power and thus raises the capacity of the system. If the statistical multiplexing of the forward link channels is sufficient, the gain in the link margin translates directly into an equivalent system capacity gain.

However, if statistical averaging is not sufficient - for example when the base station only transmits to one user with a very high data rate, the high dynamic range of the forward link signal may result in power amplifier inefficiencies and system instabilities due to the coupling with neighboring cells. In order to avoid any instability, the network may then limit the power dynamic range of the high rate channels by means of EIB (Erasure Indicator Bit) or QIB (Quality Indicator Bit) as described in patent [9].

2.3.   Outer Loop Power Control

This loop is slow compared to other power control loops (typically 50 Hz). Outer Loop Power Control is driven by QoS requirements and drives the closed loop power control to the desired set point based on the error statistics it collects from the supervised link (forward or reverse). Due to the expanded data rate range and various QoS requirements, different users will have different outer loop thresholds, i.e. different users will be received with different power at the base station. One difficulty associated with such a broad rate range appears in variable configurations when switching between rates. The required signal to the interference ratio value is not necessarily proportional to the data rate ratio, and changing rates may imply changing the QoS if the channel gain is not adapted accordingly. In the forward link, this issue is left for the manufacturer to solve. The remaining differences (depending on the radio environment) will be corrected by the outer loop itself. To deal with other differences the base station requires feedback about the QoS from the mobile station for a more accurate power control. The fastest feedback information is a frame error indication, which is transmitted once per frame. If the complete FER measurement is taken, outer loop power control is even slower.

Some measuring instruments, especially mobile station radio communication testers, do not implement forward link power control, yet such instruments are used for testing mobile stations. Power control can be simulated on the controlling PC using RX measurements to ensure repeatable measurements and to behave in a similar way as with outer loop power control. It is required by laboratories performing special measurements which are not conformant to the standard, such as temperature tests.

3. Frame and Bit Error Rate

The Bit Error Rate (BER) is the percentage of bits that have errors relative to the total number of bits received in a transmission, and its determination is quite simple. The radio communication tester sends a data stream to the mobile, which then sends it back to the tester (loop). The tester compares the sent and received data streams to determine the number of bit errors.

The Frame Error Rate (FER) measures the percentage of frame errors over the total number of frames received. The instrument Rhode&Schwarz CMW monitors the Fundamental Channel (FCH) and Supplemental Channel 0 (SCH0). The frame error rate is a variant of the bit error rate [10].

FER measurement has to be carried out over an active connection in the signaling mode. The CMW generates data that are transmitted to the DUT and back from the DUT to the measuring instrument. For this, a special service option with loopback functionality has to be selected during connection setup. As data, it is possible to use internally generated data, which are represented as a pseudo-random bit sequence, or real data using the instrument's special hardware option called DAU (Data Application Unit). As is usual when remote operation of measuring instruments, FER measurement was taken in single shot measurement mode.

4. Method

The selected method automatically sets the instrument's external attenuation in order to keep the signal power on the value set as a reference for the concrete type of DUT. Using the FER measurement during the established connection while lowering output power by means of external attenuation, the instrument can find a breaking point at which the connection drops, or the confidence level of the BER drops below 95 percent. By subtracting the last working output power value from the reference level an algorithm establishes the external attenuation (EA) value to provide the same output power level for various DUTs of the same type and various connections (conducted or wireless).

It is important to define the reference either by calculating the theoretical optimal value (as the middle of the interval of allowed power values for cellular connection type) or by conducting an experiment if the reference connection is less than perfect. In using experiment, it is important to have the best connection

available to ensure minimum loss (the conducted test with proper cabling should be sufficient).

We have found that with a proper connection the theoretically established reference is the same as the reference made by experiment. The CDMA power offset of the access probe for the cellular connection is -73 dBm and the allowed range of corrections is ± 32 dBm. If the CDMA output power was set on the instrument to a value -70 dBm and the external attenuation was left at 0 dB, the DUT showed a 50 percent signal strength and the established connection was stable over the whole testing period of circa 3 hours.

Initial power cannot be set to the maximum level just to avoid establishing a reference, because the initial connection is always done using open loop power control. Thus, if the DUT receives maximum power, it assumes that it is located a minimum distance from the base station according to the values in the preamble. Then it significantly lowers reverse link output power, and a connection cannot be established. Therefore, a reasonable initial reference power is important.

Algorithm 1 Individual steps of the algorithm.

1: FIND a reference using either calculation or experiment with the conducted test
2: CONNECT the DUT
3: CONFIGURE startup parameters. SET EA
4: ESTABLISH call
5: MEASURE BER
6: **while** confidence_level>0.95 BER **do**
7:     EA=EA$-$0.1
8: **end while**
9: SUBTRACT the last correct value from the reference and use the resulting value as the external attenuation value

---

To find the proper value of external attenuation, the following algorithm including 7 steps can be used. The individual steps are depicted in Alg. 1.

Tab. 1: CMW signal configuration.

Parameter	Value
CDMA Power	-70 dBm
Channel	200
Band Class	BC0:US Cellular
Service Option	SO2 (Loopback)
Radio configuration	1.I
Expected Power Mode	Open Loop
Number of measured frames	600
Sweep mode	Single
Confidence level	95 %
Power control bits	All Up

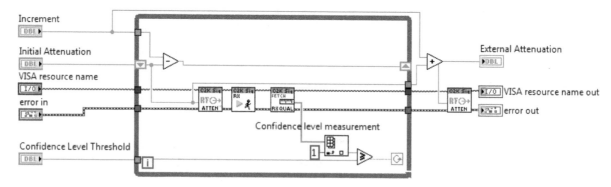

Fig. 1: Individual steps of the algorithm.

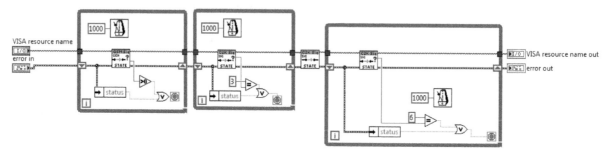

Fig. 2: Individual steps of the algorithm.

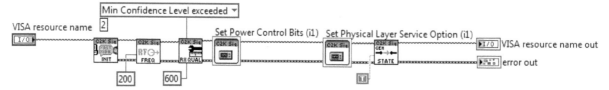

Fig. 3: Individual steps of the algorithm.

5.   Implementation

To prove the above-described algorithm, the radio communication tester CMW500 from Rohde & Schwarz and HTC EVO 4G was used as the DUT. The algorithm was implemented in LabVIEW using the downloaded attribute instrument driver.

The implementation of the experiment consists of three parts. First it is necessary to setup the instrument with the values listed in Tab. 1. The implementation of SubVI for instrument setup is in Fig. 1.

Establishing a call with previously set parameters is done in four steps, see Fig. 2. First it is necessary to turn on the signal generator and wait until it is settled.

The second step is simple while loop is waiting for the DUT to register in the network simulated by the instrument. Then it is possible to establish a call by sending the proper command to the instrument and performing a manual answer of the incoming call on the DUT. Waiting for the call establish is realized by the last while loop. The implementation of SubVI for establishing a call is shown in Fig. 2.

Measurement itself is a simple loop used to find the breaking point, which means the attenuation causing the connection drop or the confidence level falling under the threshold. The breaking point value can be added to the reference value, which is described in previous the chapter, to calculate the external attenuation needed to have a repeatable measurement. The implementation of measuring SubVI is shown in Fig. 3.

6.   Results

The setup described above was able to reliably detect the lowest power, below which the confidence level dropped under the acceptable 95 % threshold or the connection dropped completely. The value that was found, when used as external attenuation value, was suitable for compensation of the imperfections in the testing environment. When using standard production testing cables, the compensation was very small, with just 3.15 dB amplification of the signal. When a laboratory shielded chamber was used, the compensation was higher with a value of 11.5 dB. In both cases, the connection was stable for the duration of the testing period of 3 hours each.

7. Conclusion

CDMA2000 includes three methods for controlling the power of the MS, which are described in [4]. It brings serious problem in CDMA2000 during thermal testing when conditions change, and it is necessary to adjust uplink and downlink loss in order to achieve repeatable and reliable measurement results.

The contribution of this paper is a new approach for CDMA2000 which automatically sets the instrument's external attenuation under thermal testing in order to keep the signal power on the value set as reference for the concrete type of DUT. Speed of this is suitable for the purpose it was intended for and it is much better than manual periodic adjustment which presents current practice.

The solution, implemented using the standard commands in the .NET environment, is used for temperature testing in Nokia together with the Rohde & Schwarz CMW500 instrument. From the overall network perspective, it does not make much sense to compensate for downlink. The base station as part of the whole cellular network is set up to work with maximum efficiency of spectrum in mind and its cellular network operator task to do the setup. However, when testing new equipment, such as smartphones, it might be useful to have the comparison either between various types of DUT and also between different production batches of the same DUT type. The described method provides easy software-based compensation for the missing feature of the measuring instrument.

Acknowledgment

This work was supported by project of Moravian-Silesian Region No. 02540/2013/RRC and by internal grant of Faculty of electrical Engineering and Computer Science SGS No. SP2014/72. Partially was supported by the European Regional Development Fund in the IT4Innovations Centre of Excellence project (CZ.1.05/1.1.00/02.0070) and by the Development of human resources in research and development of latest soft computing methods and their application in practice project (CZ.1.07/2.3.00/20.0072) funded by the Operational Programme Education for Competitiveness.

References

[1] LI, X., C. LIU, K. TAM and F. LI. Statistical analysis of CDMA and 3G signal models. In: *11th International Conference on Signal Processing*. Beijing: IEEE, 2012, pp. 1269–1272. ISBN 978-1-4673-2196-9. DOI: 10.1109/ICoSP.2012.6491807.

[2] DE RANGO, F., F. VELTRI and S. MARANO. Channel modeling approach based on the concept of degradation level Discrete-Time Markov chain: UWB system case study. *IEEE Transactions on Wireless Communications*. 2011, vol. 10, iss. 4, pp. 1098–1107. ISSN 1536-1276. DOI: 10.1109/TWC.2011.012411.091590.

[3] FAZIO, P., M. TROPEA, F. VELTRI and S. MARANO. A novel rate adaptation scheme for dynamic bandwidth management in wireless networks. In: *75th Vehicular Technology Conference*. Yokohama: IEEE, 2012, pp. 1–5. ISBN 978-1-4673-0988-2. DOI: 10.1109/VETECS.2012.6240289.

[4] OVCHINNIKOV, A. *Modulation and Coding Techniques in Wireless Communications*. Hoboken: John Wiley and Sons, 2010. ISBN 978-0470976777. DOI: 10.1002/9780470976777.

[5] DABAK, A. G., S. HOSUR, T. SCHMIDL and C. SENGUPTA. A comparison of the open loop transmit diversity schemes for third generation wireless systems. In: *Wireless Communications and Networking Conference*. Chicago: IEEE, 2000, pp. 437–442. ISBN 0-7803-6596-8. DOI: 10.1109/WCNC.2000.904672.

[6] KOMINEK, J., J. STRAUB and J. ZIDEK. Attribute based instrument drivers. In: *International Conference on Intelligent Data Acquisition and Advanced Computing Systems: Technology and Applications*. Prague: IEEE, 2011, pp. 101–104. ISBN 978-1-4577-1426-9. DOI: 10.1109/IDAACS.2011.6072719.

[7] KOMINEK, J. and J. STRAUB. Quickly and simply programming testing systems: New architecture for VXIPlug&Play instrument drivers. *Mechatronik*. 2011, vol. 119, iss. 1-2, pp. 38–41. ISSN 1867-2590.

[8] CAMPOS-DELGADO, D. U. and J. M. LUNA-RIVERA. Power control in the uplink of a wireless multi-carrier CDMA system. In: *American Control Conference*. Washington: IEEE, 2013, pp. 2733–2738. ISBN 978-1-4799-0177-7. DOI: 10.1109/ACC.2013.6580248.

[9] BLESSENT, L. and Q. CHENG. Quality indicator bit (QIB) generation in wireless communications system. *Patent US7075905*. QUALCOMM, INCORPORATED, Publication date 11.6.2006.

[10] WERNER, M. *Advances in Digital Speech Transmission*. Hoboken: John Wiley and Sons, 2008. ISBN 978-0-470-51739-0.

About Authors

Jiri KOMINEK is a Ph.D. student with Dept. of Cybernetics and Biomedical Engineering, Faculty of Electrical Engineering and Computer Science, VSB–Technical University of Ostrava, Czech Republic and a developer with division of virtual instrumentation in Elcom, Czech Republic.

Miroslav VOZNAK is an Associate Professor with Deptartment of Telecommunications, Faculty of Electrical Engineering and Computer Science, VSB–Technical University of Ostrava, Czech Republic. Topics of his research interests are Next Generation Networks, IP telephony, speech quality and network security.

Jan ZIDEK is an Associate Professor with Deptartment of Cybernetics and Biomedical Engineering, Faculty of Electrical Engineering and Computer Science, VSB–Technical University of Ostrava, Czech Republic. Topics of his research interests are graphical programming, automated test and measurement systems design, measurement in communication systems and power quality measurement.

Permissions

All chapters in this book were first published in AEEE, by Technical University of Ostrava; hereby published with permission under the Creative Commons Attribution License or equivalent. Every chapter published in this book has been scrutinized by our experts. Their significance has been extensively debated. The topics covered herein carry significant findings which will fuel the growth of the discipline. They may even be implemented as practical applications or may be referred to as a beginning point for another development.

The contributors of this book come from diverse backgrounds, making this book a truly international effort. This book will bring forth new frontiers with its revolutionizing research information and detailed analysis of the nascent developments around the world.

We would like to thank all the contributing authors for lending their expertise to make the book truly unique. They have played a crucial role in the development of this book. Without their invaluable contributions this book wouldn't have been possible. They have made vital efforts to compile up to date information on the varied aspects of this subject to make this book a valuable addition to the collection of many professionals and students.

This book was conceptualized with the vision of imparting up-to-date information and advanced data in this field. To ensure the same, a matchless editorial board was set up. Every individual on the board went through rigorous rounds of assessment to prove their worth. After which they invested a large part of their time researching and compiling the most relevant data for our readers.

The editorial board has been involved in producing this book since its inception. They have spent rigorous hours researching and exploring the diverse topics which have resulted in the successful publishing of this book. They have passed on their knowledge of decades through this book. To expedite this challenging task, the publisher supported the team at every step. A small team of assistant editors was also appointed to further simplify the editing procedure and attain best results for the readers.

Apart from the editorial board, the designing team has also invested a significant amount of their time in understanding the subject and creating the most relevant covers. They scrutinized every image to scout for the most suitable representation of the subject and create an appropriate cover for the book.

The publishing team has been an ardent support to the editorial, designing and production team. Their endless efforts to recruit the best for this project, has resulted in the accomplishment of this book. They are a veteran in the field of academics and their pool of knowledge is as vast as their experience in printing. Their expertise and guidance has proved useful at every step. Their uncompromising quality standards have made this book an exceptional effort. Their encouragement from time to time has been an inspiration for everyone.

The publisher and the editorial board hope that this book will prove to be a valuable piece of knowledge for researchers, students, practitioners and scholars across the globe.

List of Contributors

Shahrokh SHOJAEIAN
Department of Electrical Engineerng, Faculty of Engineering, Khomeinishahr Branch, Islamic Azad University, No 159, 7th Boostan Street, Isfahan 84181-48499, Iran

Ehsan SALLEALA-NAEENI
Department of Electrical Engineerng, Faculty of Engineering, Khomeinishahr Branch, Islamic Azad University, No 159, 7th Boostan Street, Isfahan 84181-48499, Iran

Ehsan TASLIMI RENANI
Department of Electrical Engineering, Faculty of Engineering, University of Malaya, Lingkungan Budi, Kuala Lumpur 50603, Malaysia

Rastislav ROKA
Institute of Telecommunications, Faculty of Electrical Engineering and Information Technology, Slovak University of Technology in Bratislava, Ilkovicova 3, 812 19 Bratislava, Slovak Republic

Karel TOMALA
Department of Telecommunications, Faculty of Electrical Engineering and Computer Science, VSB Technical University of Ostrava, 17. listopadu, 708 33 Ostrava-Poruba, Czech Republic

Jan PLUCAR
Department of Computer Science, Faculty of Electrical Engineering and Computer Science, VSB Technical University of Ostrava, 17. listopadu, 708 33 Ostrava-Poruba, Czech Republic

Patrik DUBEC
Department of Computer Science, Faculty of Electrical Engineering and Computer Science, VSB Technical University of Ostrava, 17. listopadu, 708 33 Ostrava-Poruba, Czech Republic

Lukas RAPANT
Department of Applied Mathematics, Faculty of Electrical Engineering and Computer Science, VSB Technical University of Ostrava, 17. listopadu, 708 33 Ostrava-Poruba, Czech Republic

Miroslav VOZNAK
Department of Telecommunications, Faculty of Electrical Engineering and Computer Science, VSB Technical University of Ostrava, 17. listopadu, 708 33 Ostrava-Poruba, Czech Republic

Stanislav HEJDUK
Department of Telecommunications, Faculty of Electrical Engineering, VSB{Technical University of Ostrava, 17.listopadu 15/2172, 708 33 Ostrava-Poruba, Czech Republic

Karel WITAS
Department of Telecommunications, Faculty of Electrical Engineering, VSB{Technical University of Ostrava, 17.listopadu 15/2172, 708 33 Ostrava-Poruba, Czech Republic

Jan LATAL
Department of Telecommunications, Faculty of Electrical Engineering, VSB{Technical University of Ostrava, 17.listopadu 15/2172, 708 33 Ostrava-Poruba, Czech Republic

Jan VITASEK
Department of Telecommunications, Faculty of Electrical Engineering, VSB{Technical University of Ostrava, 17.listopadu 15/2172, 708 33 Ostrava-Poruba, Czech Republic

Jiri BOCHEZA
Department of Telecommunications, Faculty of Electrical Engineering, VSB{Technical University of Ostrava, 17.listopadu 15/2172, 708 33 Ostrava-Poruba, Czech Republic

Vladimir VASINEK
Department of Telecommunications, Faculty of Electrical Engineering, VSB{Technical University of Ostrava, 17.listopadu 15/2172, 708 33 Ostrava-Poruba, Czech Republic

Jan OPPOLZER
Department of Telecommunication Engineering, Faculty of Electrical Engineering,
Czech Technical University in Prague, Technicka 2, 166 27 Prague, Czech Republic

Robert BESTAK
Department of Telecommunication Engineering, Faculty of Electrical Engineering,
Czech Technical University in Prague, Technicka 2, 166 27 Prague, Czech Republic

Zbynek KOCUR
Department of Telecommunication Engineering, Faculty of Electrical Engineering, Czech Technical University in Prague, Technicka 2, 166 27, Prague, Czech Republic

Peter MACEJKO
Department of Telecommunication Engineering, Faculty of Electrical Engineering, Czech Technical University in Prague, Technicka 2, 166 27, Prague, Czech Republic

Petr CHLUMSKY
Department of Telecommunication Engineering, Faculty of Electrical Engineering, Czech Technical University in Prague, Technicka 2, 166 27, Prague, Czech Republic

Jiri VODRAZKA
Department of Telecommunication Engineering, Faculty of Electrical Engineering, Czech Technical University in Prague, Technicka 2, 166 27, Prague, Czech Republic

Ondrej VONDROUS
Department of Telecommunication Engineering, Faculty of Electrical Engineering, Czech Technical University in Prague, Technicka 2, 166 27, Prague, Czech Republic

Pavel NEVLUD
Department of Telecommunications, Faculty of Electrical Engineering and Computer Science, VSB Technical University of Ostrava, 17. listopadu 15, 708 33 Ostrava-Poruba, Czech Republic

Miroslav BURES
Department of Telecommunications, Faculty of Electrical Engineering and Computer Science, VSB Technical University of Ostrava, 17. listopadu 15, 708 33 Ostrava-Poruba, Czech Republic

Lukas KAPICAK
Department of Telecommunications, Faculty of Electrical Engineering and Computer Science, VSB{Technical University of Ostrava, 17. listopadu 15, 708 33 Ostrava-Poruba, Czech Republic

Jaroslav ZDRALEK
Department of Telecommunications, Faculty of Electrical Engineering and Computer Science, VSB Technical University of Ostrava, 17. listopadu 15, 708 33 Ostrava-Poruba, Czech Republic

Marek NEVOSAD
Department of Telecommunication Engineering, Faculty of Electrical Engineering, Czech Technical University in Prague, Technicka 2, 166 36 Prague, Czech Republic

Pavel LAFATA
Department of Telecommunication Engineering, Faculty of Electrical Engineering, Czech Technical University in Prague, Technicka 2, 166 36 Prague, Czech Republic

Petr JARES
Department of Telecommunication Engineering, Faculty of Electrical Engineering, Czech Technical University in Prague, Technicka 2, 166 36 Prague, Czech Republic

Tomas HEGR
Department of Telecommunication Engineering, Faculty of Electrical Engineering, Czech Technical University in Prague, Technicka 2, 166 27 Prague, Czech Republic

Leos BOHAC
Department of Telecommunication Engineering, Faculty of Electrical Engineering, Czech Technical University in Prague, Technicka 2, 166 27 Prague, Czech Republic

Vojtech UHLIR
Department of Telecommunication Engineering, Faculty of Electrical Engineering, Czech Technical University in Prague, Technicka 2, 166 27 Prague, Czech Republic

Petr CHLUMSKY
Department of Telecommunication Engineering, Faculty of Electrical Engineering, Czech Technical University in Prague, Technicka 2, 166 27 Prague, Czech Republic

Andrej LINER
Department of Telecommunications, Faculty of Electrical Engineering and Computer Science, VSB Technical University of Ostrava, 17. listopadu 15/2172, 708 33 Ostrava-Poruba, Czech Republic

Martin PAPES
Department of Telecommunications, Faculty of Electrical Engineering and Computer Science, VSB Technical University of Ostrava, 17. listopadu 15/2172, 708 33 Ostrava-Poruba, Czech Republic

Jakub JAROS
Department of Telecommunications, Faculty of Electrical Engineering and Computer Science, VSB Technical University of Ostrava, 17. listopadu 15/2172, 708 33 Ostrava-Poruba, Czech Republic

Jakub CUBIK
Department of Telecommunications, Faculty of Electrical Engineering and Computer Science, VSB Technical University of Ostrava, 17. listopadu 15/2172, 708 33 Ostrava Poruba, Czech Republic

Stanislav KEPAK
Department of Telecommunications, Faculty of Electrical Engineering and Computer Science, VSB Technical University of Ostrava, 17. listopadu 15/2172, 708 33 Ostrava Poruba, Czech Republic

Pavel SMIRA
Thermo Sanace s.r.o., Chamradova 475/23, 718 00 Ostrava-Kuncicky, Czech Republic

Andrea NASSWETTROVA
Thermo Sanace s.r.o., Chamradova 475/23, 718 00 Ostrava-Kuncicky, Czech Republic

Jiri GABRIEL
Institute of Microbiology, Academy of Sciences of the Czech Republic, v.v.i., Videnska 1083,142 20 Prague 4, Czech Republic

Rastislav ROKA
Institute of Telecommunications, Faculty of Electrical Engineering and Information Technology, Slovak University of Technology in Bratislava, Ilkovicova 3, 812 19 Bratislava, Slovak Republic

Peppino FAZIO
Department of Computer Science Engineering, Modeling, Electronics and Systems, University of Calabria, Via P. Bucci 42/C, 870 36 Arcavacata di Rende, Cosenza, Italy

Floriano DE RANGO
Department of Computer Science Engineering, Modeling, Electronics and Systems, University of Calabria, Via P. Bucci 42/C, 870 36 Arcavacata di Rende, Cosenza, Italy

Andrea LUPIA
Department of Computer Science Engineering, Modeling, Electronics and Systems, University of Calabria, Via P. Bucci 42/C, 870 36 Arcavacata di Rende, Cosenza, Italy

Lubos NAGY
Department of Telecommunications, Faculty of Electrical Engineering and Communication, Brno University of Technology, Technicka 12, 616 00 Brno, Czech Republic

Vit NOVOTNY
Department of Telecommunications, Faculty of Electrical Engineering and Communication, Brno University of Technology, Technicka 12, 616 00 Brno, Czech Republic

Jana URAMOVA
Department of Information Networks, Faculty of Management Science and Informatics, University of Zilina, Univerzitna 8215/1, 010 26 Zilina, Slovak Republic

Nermin MAKHLOUF
Department of Telecommunications, Faculty of Electrical Engineering and Communication, Brno University of Technology, Technicka 12, 616 00 Brno, Czech Republic

Jakub CUBIK
Department of Telecommunications, Faculty of Electrical Engineering and Computer Science, VSB Technical University of Ostrava, 17. listopadu 15/2172, 708 33 Ostrava Poruba, Czech Republic

Stanislav KEPAK
Department of Telecommunications, Faculty of Electrical Engineering and Computer Science, VSB Technical University of Ostrava, 17. listopadu 15/2172, 708 33 Ostrava Poruba, Czech Republic

Jan DORICAK
Department of Telecommunications, Faculty of Electrical Engineering and Computer Science, VSB Technical University of Ostrava, 17. listopadu 15/2172, 708 33 Ostrava Poruba, Czech Republic

Vladimir VASINEK
Department of Telecommunications, Faculty of Electrical Engineering and Computer Science, VSB Technical University of Ostrava, 17. listopadu 15/2172, 708 33 Ostrava Poruba, Czech Republic

Jakub JAROS
Department of Telecommunications, Faculty of Electrical Engineering and Computer Science, VSB Technical University of Ostrava, 17. listopadu 15/2172, 708 33 Ostrava Poruba, Czech Republic

Andrej LINER
Department of Telecommunications, Faculty of Electrical Engineering and Computer Science, VSB Technical University of Ostrava, 17. listopadu 15/2172, 708 33 Ostrava Poruba, Czech Republic

Martin PAPES
Department of Telecommunications, Faculty of Electrical Engineering and Computer Science, VSB Technical University of Ostrava, 17. listopadu 15/2172, 708 33 Ostrava Poruba, Czech Republic

Marcel FAJKUS
Department of Telecommunications, Faculty of Electrical Engineering and Computer Science, VSB Technical University of Ostrava, 17. listopadu 15/2172, 708 33 Ostrava Poruba, Czech Republic

Milos KOZAK
Department of Telecommunications Engineering, Faculty of Electrical Engineering, Czech Technical University in Prague, Technicka 2, 160 00 Prague, Czech Republic

Brigitte JAUMARD
Department of Computer Science and Software Engineering, Faculty of Engineering and Computer Science, Concordia University, 1515 St. Catherine St. West, Montreal (Quebec), Canada

Leos BOHAC
Department of Telecommunications Engineering, Faculty of Electrical Engineering, Czech Technical University in Prague, Technicka 2, 160 00 Prague, Czech Republic

Gabriele-Maria LOZITO
Department of Engineering, Roma Tre University, via Vito Volterra 62, 00146 Roma, Italy

Antonino LAUDANI
Department of Engineering, Roma Tre University, via Vito Volterra 62, 00146 Roma, Italy

Francesco RIGANTI-FULGINEI
Department of Engineering, Roma Tre University, via Vito Volterra 62, 00146 Roma, Italy

Alessandro SALVINI
Department of Engineering, Roma Tre University, via Vito Volterra 62, 00146 Roma, Italy

Martin TOMIS
Department of Telecommunications, Faculty of Electrical Engineering and Computer Science, VSB Technical University of Ostrava, 17. listopadu 15, 708 33 Ostrava{Poruba, Czech Republic

Libor MICHALEK
Department of Telecommunications, Faculty of Electrical Engineering and Computer Science, VSB Technical University of Ostrava, 17. listopadu 15, 708 33 Ostrava{Poruba, Czech Republic

Marek DVORSKY
Department of Telecommunications, Faculty of Electrical Engineering and Computer Science, VSB Technical University of Ostrava, 17. listopadu 15, 708 33 Ostrava{Poruba, Czech Republic

Jakub SAFARIK
Department of Telecommunications, Faculty of Electrical Engineering and Computer Science, VSB Technical University of Ostrava, 17. listopadu 15, 708 00 Ostrava-Poruba, Czech Republic

Pavol PARTILA
Department of Telecommunications, Faculty of Electrical Engineering and Computer Science, VSB{Technical University of Ostrava, 17. listopadu 15, 708 00 Ostrava-Poruba, Czech Republic

Filip REZAC
Department of Telecommunications, Faculty of Electrical Engineering and Computer Science, VSB Technical University of Ostrava, 17. listopadu 15, 708 00 Ostrava-Poruba, Czech Republic

Lukas MACURA
Institute of Computer Science, Faculty of Philosophy and Science in Opava, Silesian University in Opava, Bezrucovo namesti 13, 746 01 Opava, Czech Republic

Miroslav VOZNAK
Department of Telecommunications, Faculty of Electrical Engineering and Computer Science, VSB Technical University of Ostrava, 17. listopadu 15, 708 00 Ostrava-Poruba, Czech Republic

Peppino FAZIO
Department of Computer Science, Modeling, Electronics and Systems Engineering (DIMES), Faculty of Engineering, Universita della Calabria, 870 36 Arcavacata di Rende (CS), Italy

Cesare SOTTILE
Department of Computer Science, Modeling, Electronics and Systems Engineering (DIMES), Faculty of Engineering, Universita della Calabria, 870 36 Arcavacata di Rende (CS), Italy

Amilcare Francesco SANTAMARIA
Department of Computer Science, Modeling, Electronics and Systems Engineering (DIMES), Faculty of Engineering, Universita della Calabria, 870 36 Arcavacata di Rende (CS), Italy

Mauro TROPEA
Department of Computer Science, Modeling, Electronics and Systems Engineering (DIMES), Faculty of Engineering, Universita della Calabria, 870 36 Arcavacata di Rende (CS), Italy

Jan STAS
Department of Electronics and Multimedia Communications, Faculty of Electrical Engineering and Informatics, Technical University of Kosice, Park Komenskeho 13, 042 00 Kosice, Slovak Republic

Daniel ZLACKY
Department of Electronics and Multimedia Communications, Faculty of Electrical Engineering and Informatics, Technical University of Kosice, Park Komenskeho 13, 042 00 Kosice, Slovak Republic

Daniel HLADEK
Department of Electronics and Multimedia Communications, Faculty of Electrical Engineering and Informatics, Technical University of Kosice, Park Komenskeho 13, 042 00 Kosice, Slovak Republic

Jozef JUHAR
Department of Electronics and Multimedia Communications, Faculty of Electrical Engineering and Informatics, Technical University of Kosice, Park Komenskeho 13, 042 00 Kosice, Slovak Republic

Stanislav KRAUS
Department of Telecommunications Engineering, Faculty of Electrical Engineering, Czech Technical University in Prague, Technicka 2, 166 27 Prague, Czech Republic

Michal LUCKI
Department of Telecommunications Engineering, Faculty of Electrical Engineering, Czech Technical University in Prague, Technicka 2, 166 27 Prague, Czech Republic

Vratislav HLADKY
Department of Cybernetics and Artificial Intelligence, Faculty of Electrical Engineering and Informatics, Technical University of Kosice, Letna 9, 040 01 Kosice, Slovak Republic

Radoslav BIELEK
Department of Cybernetics and Artificial Intelligence, Faculty of Electrical Engineering and Informatics, Technical University of Kosice, Letna 9, 040 01 Kosice, Slovak Republic

Rawid BANCHUIN
Department of Computer Engineering, Faculty of Engineering, Siam University, 38 Petkasem Road, Bangkok 10160, Thailand

Jiri HLAVACEK
Department of Telecommunication Engineering, Faculty of Electrical Engineering, Czech Technical University in Prague, Technicka 2, 166 27 Prague, Czech Republic

Robert BESTAK
Department of Telecommunication Engineering, Faculty of Electrical Engineering, Czech Technical University in Prague, Technicka 2, 166 27 Prague, Czech Republic

Radek NOVAK
Department of Telecommunications, Faculty of Electrical Engineering and Computer Science, VSB–Technical University of Ostrava, 17. Listopadu 15/2172, 708 33 Ostrava, Czech Republic

Karel WITAS
Department of Telecommunications, Faculty of Electrical Engineering and Computer Science, VSB–Technical University of Ostrava, 17. Listopadu 15/2172, 708 33 Ostrava, Czech Republic

Jaroslav KREJCI
Department of Telecommunication Engineering, Faculty of Electrical Engineering,
Czech Technical University in Prague, Technicka 2, 166 27 Prague, Czech Republic

Tomas ZEMAN
Department of Telecommunication Engineering, Faculty of Electrical Engineering,
Czech Technical University in Prague, Technicka 2, 166 27 Prague, Czech Republic

Alberto LOPEZ
Department of Telecommunication Engineering, Faculty of Electrical Engineering, Czech Technical University in Prague, Technicka 2, 166 27 Prague, Czech Republic

Lukas VOJTECH
Department of Telecommunication Engineering, Faculty of Electrical Engineering, Czech Technical University in Prague, Technicka 2, 166 27 Prague, Czech Republic

Marek NERUDA
Department of Telecommunication Engineering, Faculty of Electrical Engineering, Czech Technical University in Prague, Technicka 2, 166 27 Prague, Czech Republic

Lukas FALAT
Department of Macro & Microeconomics, Faculty of Management Science and Informatics, University of Zilina, Univerzitna 8215/1, Zilina, Slovakia

Dusan MARCEK
Department of Applied Informatics, Faculty of Economics, VSB–Technical University of Ostrava, Sokolska 33, 701 21 Ostrava, Czech Republic

Eser SERT
Computer Engineering Department, Engineering and Architecture Faculty, Kahramanmaras Sutcu Imam University, Avsar Kampusu 46100 Kahramanmaras, Turkey

Ibrahim Taner OKUMUS
Computer Engineering Department, Engineering and Architecture Faculty, Kahramanmaras Sutcu Imam University, Avsar Kampusu 46100 Kahramanmaras, Turkey

Rajdi AGALLIU
Department of Telecommunications Engineering, Faculty of Electrical Engineering, Czech Technical University in Prague, Technicka 2, 166 27 Prague, Czech Republic

Michal LUCKI
Department of Telecommunications Engineering, Faculty of Electrical Engineering, Czech Technical University in Prague, Technicka 2, 166 27 Prague, Czech Republic

Petr MATOUSEK
Department of Information Systems, Faculty of Information Technology, Brno University of Technology, Bozetechova 2, Brno, Czech Republic

Martin KMET
Department of Information Systems, Faculty of Information Technology, Brno University of Technology, Bozetechova 2, Brno, Czech Republic

Martin BASEL
Department of Information Systems, Faculty of Information Technology, Brno University of Technology, Bozetechova 2, Brno, Czech Republic

Pavol PARTILA
Department of Telecommunications, Faculty of Electrical Engineering and Computer Science, VSB Technical University of Ostrava, 17. listopadu 15/2172, 708 33 Ostrava Poruba, Czech Republic

Marek KOHUT
Department of Telecommunications, Faculty of Electrical Engineering and Computer Science, VSB Technical University of Ostrava, 17. listopadu 15/2172, 708 33 Ostrava Poruba, Czech Republic

Miroslav VOZNAK
Department of Telecommunications, Faculty of Electrical Engineering and Computer Science, VSB Technical University of Ostrava, 17. listopadu 15/2172, 708 33 Ostrava Poruba, Czech Republic

Martin MIKULEC
Department of Telecommunications, Faculty of Electrical Engineering and Computer Science, VSB Technical University of Ostrava, 17. listopadu 15/2172, 708 33 Ostrava Poruba, Czech Republic

Jakub SAFARIK
Department of Telecommunications, Faculty of Electrical Engineering and Computer Science, VSB Technical University of Ostrava, 17. listopadu 15/2172, 708 33 Ostrava Poruba, Czech Republic

Karel TOMALA
Department of Telecommunications, Faculty of Electrical Engineering and Computer Science, VSB Technical University of Ostrava, 17. listopadu 15/2172, 708 33 Ostrava Poruba, Czech Republic

Premysl MER
Department of Telecommunications, Faculty of Electrical Engineering and Computer Science, VSB–Technical University of Ostrava, 17. listopadu 15/2172, 708 33 Ostrava-Poruba, Czech Republic

Amilcare Francesco SANTAMARIA
Department of Computer Science, Modeling, Electronics and Systems Engineering, University of Calabria, Via Pietro Bucci, 870 36 Arcavacata di Rende CS, Italy

Cesare SOTTILE
Department of Computer Science, Modeling, Electronics and Systems Engineering, University of Calabria, Via Pietro Bucci, 870 36 Arcavacata di Rende CS, Italy

Jiri KOMINEK
Department of Cybernetics and Biomedical Engineering, Faculty of Electrical Engineering and Computer Science, VSB–Technical University of Ostrava, 17. listopadu 15/2172, 708 33 Ostrava, Czech Republic

Miroslav VOZNAK
Department of Telecommunications, Faculty of Electrical Engineering and Computer Science, VSB–Technical University of Ostrava, 17. listopadu 15/2172, 708 33 Ostrava, Czech Republic

Jan ZIDEK
Department of Cybernetics and Biomedical Engineering, Faculty of Electrical Engineering and Computer Science, VSB–Technical University of Ostrava, 17. listopadu 15/2172, 708 33 Ostrava, Czech Republi

Printed in the USA
CPSIA information can be obtained
at www.ICGtesting.com
JSHW051429221024
72173JS00006B/1411